Developmental Influences
on Adult Intelligence

Developmental Influences
on Adult Intelligence

The Seattle Longitudinal Study

K. Warner Schaie

OXFORD

UNIVERSITY PRESS

2005

OXFORD
UNIVERSITY PRESS

Oxford   New York

Auckland   Bangkok   Buenos Aires   Cape Town   Chennai
Dar es Salaam   Delhi   Hong Kong   Istanbul   Karachi   Kolkata
Kuala Lumpur   Madrid   Melbourne   Mexico City   Mumbai   Nairobi
São Paulo   Shanghai   Taipei   Tokyo   Toronto

Copyright © 2005 by Oxford University Press, Inc.

Published by Oxford University Press, Inc.
198 Madison Avenue, New York, New York 10016

www.oup.com

Library of Congress Cataloging-in-Publication Data
Schaie, K. Warner (Klaus Warner), 1928–
Developmental influences on adult intelligence: the Seattle longitudinal study
K. Warner Shaie.—[Update].
p.   cm.
Rev. ed. of: Intellectual development in adulthood.
Includes bibliographical references (p.   ) and indexes.
ISBN 0-19-515673-0
1. Cognition—Age factors—Longitudinal studies.   2. Adulthood—Psychological
aspects—Longitudinal studies.   3. Aging—Psychological aspects—Longitudinal studies.   I.
Schaie, K. Warner (Klaus Warner), 1928– Intellectual development in adulthood.   II. Title.
BF724.55.C63S32 2005
155.6—dc22   2003065465

1 3 5 7 9 8 6 4 2

Printed in the United States of America
on acid-free paper

Acknowledgments

MANY COLLEAGUES, STUDENTS, AND SUPPORT STAFF made extensive contributions to the collection, analysis, and interpretation of data from the study. Much credit for the many aspects of the work that went well goes to these contributors; the responsibility for what went awry is, of course, mine. A very special acknowledgment, however, is due Sherry L. Willis, my wife and colleague, who has co-directed the Seattle Longitudinal Study efforts since 1982 and without whose patient support and many helpful suggestions this volume would not exist. Recognition is also owed for the enthusiastic support provided by the staff and membership of the Group Health Cooperative of Puget Sound throughout our long period of collaboration.

The following colleagues, students, and support staff (in alphabetical order) participated in one or more of the various data collections and analyses and/or contributed to the resultant scholarly products: Christopher Adams, David Adams, Diane Backschies, Margret Baltes, Paul Baltes, Thomas Barrett, Ute Bayen, Timothy Benner, Gisela Bertulis, Julie Blaskevicz Boron, Joy Bodnar, Hayden Bosworth, Barbara Buech, Michael Cady, Heather Chipuer, Soyeon Cho, Theresa Cooney, Jean Day, Cindy DeFrias, Robin Dunlap, Ranjana Dutta, Walter Eden, Charles Fick, Carrie Frech, Michael Gilewski, Judith Gonda, Kathy Gribbin, Ann Gruber-Baldini, Cheryl Guyer, Brian Hallett, Elaine Hardin, Gene Hardin, Sarah Haessler, Charlene Herold, Christopher Hertzog, Judy Higgins, Jenifer Hoffman, Robert Intrieri, Gina Jay, Christine Johnson, Heather Johnson, John Just, Alfred Kaszniak, Iseli Krauss, Eric Labouvie, Gisela Labouvie-Vief, Tamra Lair, Karen Lala, Karen Laughlin, Thomas Lederman, Christine Lehl, Helen Leisowitz, Jackie Levine, Holly Mack, Heiner Maier, Scott Maitland, Hiroko Makiyama, Renee Marquardt, Dean Melang, Sherry Murr, Ann Nardi, John Nesselroade, Ha Nguyen, Shirley Paton Norleen, Ann O'Hanlon, Phyllis Olson, Holly Overman, Sara Paneck, Iris Parham, Julie Parmentier, Cherill Perera, Robert Peterson, Robert

Plomin, Samuel Popkin, Alan Posthumer, Margaret Quayhagen, Andrew Revell, Sarah Rosen, Amy Roth, Christine Roy, Pat Sand, Coloma Harrison Schaie, Carolyn Seszniak, John Schulenberg, Anna Shuey, Michael Singer, Anita Stolov, Vicki Stone, Charles Strother, Alejandra Suarez, Linda Teri, Richard Vigesaa, Nathaniel Wagner, Faika Zanjani, and Elizabeth Zelinski.

The Seattle Longitudinal Study has previously been funded by grants from the National Institute of Child Health and Human Development (HD00367, 1963–1965; HD04476, 1970–1973) and by the National Institute on Aging (AG00480, 1973–1979; AG03544, 1982–1986; AG04770, 1984–1989). Current support from the latter institute (R037 AG08055, 1989–2005) is funding the collection of data for the family studies, the follow-up cognitive training studies, the seventh wave of the Seattle Longitudinal Study, the neuropsychology studies, and the data analyses still in progress. Parts of this volume were written while I was a visiting scientist in the Faculty of Psychology and Education, the Interfaculty Center of Gerontology, and the Lemanic Center for Lifespan Research, all at the University of Geneva, Switzerland.

Contents

Developmental Influences
on Adult Intelligence

CHAPTER ONE

Introduction and Preview

THE PURPOSE OF THIS VOLUME is to update my monograph *Intellectual Development in Adulthood: The Seattle Longitudinal Study* (Schaie, 1996b), which was written to present in one place the program of studies conducted by me, my associates, and my students that has come to be known as the Seattle Longitudinal Study (SLS). I want to make clear from the outset that this volume is not simply an update, but has the major purpose of showing more explicitly how environmental, health-related, and familial influences affect intellectual development across adulthood.

This study originally began as my doctoral dissertation at the University of Washington (Seattle) in 1956. The earlier monograph covered data and findings through the 1991 data collection and included materials that previously had been reported only at scientific meetings but were not available in archival form. The present volume updates data and findings to include the 1998 longitudinal cycle and our efforts to take advantage of our long-term data by linking psychometric and neuropsychological assessments with the hope of contributing to the early assessment of risk for dementia in late life. We have also revisited the impact of personality on cognition. In addition, we provide correlation matrices and information on obtaining Web access to selected data sets from our study that other scientists might wish to use for secondary analysis or as example data sets for exercises in methods classes.

Origin of the Seattle Longitudinal Study

At an early stage of my career, I was confronted with addressing the discrepancies between cross-sectional and longitudinal findings in the study of adult intellectual development. I soon became convinced that this issue needed to be addressed by following over time a structured cross-sectional sample such as the one I had collected for my doctoral dissertation. As a consequence, I designed a follow-up study, put into the field in 1963, that provided some answers, but also raised enough methodological and substantive questions to demand a continuing program of studies that is still in progress and has included seven major and several collateral data collections as well as three cognitive training studies.

The SLS has charted the course of selected cognitive abilities from young adulthood through advanced old age. It has investigated individual differences and differential patterns of change. In so doing, it has focused not only on demonstrating the presence or absence of age-related changes and differences, but also has attended to the magnitude and relative importance of the observed phenomena. An important aspect of the study has been the investigation of cohort differences and their implications for the study of adult cognition. In the more recent phases of the study, a number of contextual, health, and personality variables have been identified that offer explanations for differential change and that provide a basis for possible intervention. Within the context of our monitoring of individual change, it has therefore been possible to design cognitive interventions that have been successful in remediating carefully documented declines and in improving the cognitive functions of older persons who have remained stable.

Keeping pace with changes in scientific practice, we progressed from the study of individual markers of ability domains to the study of age changes and differences in cognitive ability structures at the latent construct level. We have conducted analyses of the relative effect of speed and accuracy in age decline and training gain, and we have investigated the relevance of cognitive training to real-life tasks. In this volume, data are reported that link knowledge of normal cognitive aging to issues of early diagnosis of dementia. Finally, parent-offspring and sibling similarity were studied, as was the influence of original and current family environments on adult cognitive performance.

Some Caveats

This volume is not designed to provide an extensive overview of theories of intelligence or of the vast literature on adult intellectual development or other longitudinal inquiries in the study of human aging (see Schaie & Hofer, 2001, for a review). References to the work of other major authors in the field of intelligence or of adult intellectual development are therefore limited to those instances for which such references provide context or are directly relevant to the issues raised and data collected in the course of the SLS. For example, it is quite apparent that the Genevan approach to intelligence has not had a significant impact on our empirical work. At the time our studies began, Piagetians were simply not interested in adulthood, even though I would readily wish to acknowledge the influence of Piaget's (1972) late-life concerns and the important contributions of recent authors interested in postformal operations (e.g., Commons, Sinnott, Richards, & Armon, 1989) on some of my own theoretical writing (see Schaie, 1977–1978; Schaie & Willis, 2000b). Neither does our work lean to a great extent on the information processing literature and the exciting work on the basic components of psychometric abilities (see Baltes, Staudinger, & Lindenberger, 1999; Sternberg, 1977) nor does it attend to alternate models of structures of intellect (e.g., Gardner, 1993; Guilford, 1967).

I have always subscribed intuitively to a hierarchical model of intelligence that considers information processing components as a basic process level, combinations and permutations of skills that result in the products represented by the traditional work on psychometric intelligence. Combinations and permutations of mental abilities in turn represent the basic components underlying practical intelligence as expressed in specific everyday tasks. This model has only recently been explicated more formally (cf. Schaie & Willis, 1999; Willis & Schaie, 1993). Because of the more general nature of psychometric abilities and their strong relationship to everyday performance, I elected to concentrate my efforts at a middle level of exploration (see Schaie, 1987). I apologize in advance to my many friends and colleagues whose work I may have inadvertently slighted by these limiting decisions.

Why Study Intelligence in Adulthood?

For all practical purposes, applied psychology began with the investigation of intellectual competence. Early objectives of this interest may be found in efforts to design procedures for the orderly removal of mentally retarded children from the public school classroom (Binet & Simon, 1905) or in the study of the distribution of individual differences in the interest of demonstrating their Darwinian characteristics (Galton, 1869). What are the mental functions that early investigators sought to describe that we are still pursuing today? Binet and Simon's (1905) definition remains a classic guide: "To judge well, to comprehend well, to reason well, these are the essentials of intelligence. A person may be a moron or an imbecile if he lacks judgment; but with judgment he could not be either" (p. 106).

In the beginning, empirical studies of intelligence investigated primarily how complex mental functions were acquired early in life (Brooks & Weintraub, 1976). But, a concern with following the complexities of intellectual development beyond childhood soon arose, beginning with the theoretical expositions of classical developmental psychologists such as G. Stanley Hall (1922), H. L. Hollingsworth (1927), and Sidney Pressey (Pressey, Janney, & Kuhlen, 1939). Questions raised by these authors concerned matters involving the age of attaining peak performance levels, the maintenance or transformation of intellectual structures, and the decremental changes thought to occur from late midlife into old age.

Empirical work relevant to these questions was not long in following. In his original standardization of the Binet tests for American use, Terman (1916) had reason to assume that intellectual development reached a peak at 16 years of age and then remained level throughout adulthood. Large-scale studies with the Army Alpha Intelligence Test (Yerkes, 1921) suggested that the peak level of intellectual functioning for young adults might already be reached, on average, by the even earlier age of 13 years. However, other empirical studies questioned these inferences.

One of the most influential cross-sectional studies, that by Jones and Conrad (1933), collected data on most of the inhabitants of a New England community who were between the ages of 10 and 60 years. Interestingly, age differences found in this study were quite substantial on some of the subtests of the Army Alpha, but not on others. In a similar fashion, Wechsler's standardization studies that led to the development of the Wechsler-Bellevue Adult Intelligence scales found that growth of intelligence does not cease in adolescence. In fact, peak ages were found to differ for various aspects of intellectual functioning, and decrements at older ages were clearly not uniform across the different measures used to define intelligence (Wechsler, 1939).

The practice of intelligence testing peaked following World War II with the spread of clinical psychology and the widespread introduction into clinical practice of the Wechsler Adult Intelligence Scale (WAIS) and its derivatives (Matarazzo, 1972). Also important was the almost universal introduction of intelligence and aptitude testing in the public schools and the development of widely accepted aptitude/ability batteries such as the Differential Aptitude Test (DAT) and the General Aptitude Test Battery (GATB; see Anastasi, 1976; Cronbach, 1970).

L. L. Thurstone's (1938) monumental work in creating a taxonomy of mental abilities for children and adolescents was soon followed by even more extensive taxonomies based on work with college students (Guilford, 1967) and work by Cattell and Horn (e.g., Cattell, 1963; Horn, 1970) using male prison inmates ranging in age from young adulthood to early old age. The work by Cattell and Horn is of particular interest because it posited differential developmental trajectories for fluid abilities (Gf), which were thought to be biologically based and thus subject to early decline, and crystallized abilities (Gc), which were culturally acquired and thus likely to show growth into old age. A broad compendium of factor-referenced tests also became available, allowing investigators to select multiple markers for specific mental abilities (Ekstrom, French, Harman, & Derman, 1976; French, Ekstrom, & Price, 1963).

Disenchantment with ability measurement began to set in following widespread criticism of the misapplication of intelligence tests in education (e.g., Kamin, 1974). Clinicians began to realize that profile analyses of intelligence tests were less useful than had originally been thought, and that the information gained on intellectual status often seemed to contribute little to guide therapeutic interventions.

Despite these criticisms, it remains obvious that omnibus measures of intelligence have been rather useful in predicting persons' competence in dealing with the standard educational systems of our country. They have also been useful in predicting success in vocational pursuits whenever job requirements depend on educationally based knowledge or skills or involve high levels of analytic or basic problem-solving skills. Measures of specific abilities, although somewhat more controversial, have nevertheless had utility in predicting competence in those specific situations when special abilities can be expected to be important.

Many reasonable arguments have been made for the proposition that motivational and other personality variables might have greater potency in predicting adjustment and competence in midlife than does intelligence, but the empirical evidence for this proposition is less than convincing. Certainly, when dealing with the elderly it becomes readily apparent that the assessment of intellectual competence, whether or not it may have been irrelevant during midlife, again reaches paramount importance. Questions such as who should be retired for cause (read incompetence) in the absence of mandatory retirement at relatively early ages; whether there is sufficient remaining competence for independent living; or whether persons can continue to conserve and dispose of their property all involve the assessment of intellectual functioning (see also Schaie, 1988a, 1988b; Willis, 1995; Willis & Schaie, 1994a).

If the reader agrees with me that the issues mentioned above are important to our society, it then becomes necessary to examine in detail the factual issues involved in the development of adult intelligence. We must begin to differentiate intraindividual decremental changes from intcrindividual differences that result in behavior of older cohorts that appears to be obsolete when compared with the behavior of their younger peers. We need to examine at what age developmental peaks do occur and assess generational differences as well as within-generation age changes. Most important, we must determine the reasons why some individuals show intellectual decline in early adulthood, while others maintain or increase their level of intellectual functioning well into advanced old age.

A Theoretical Framework for Understanding Adult Intellectual Development

To understand intellectual development from early adulthood to old age, we must embed what we know about development within the context of changing environmental influences and changes in individuals' physiological infrastructure. Figure 1.1 displays a schematic that indicates how these influences are likely to operate over the adult life course. The schematic contains two end points: First, we are concerned with those lifelong influences that affect the level of late-life cognitive functioning. But a secondary end point of interest is represented by the status of the cortex at life's end that would describe the physiological infrastructure required for the maintenance of cognitive functioning, generally only determinable at postmortem. In this conceptual path model, rectangles are used to identify those individual indicators observed directly; ovals are used to indicate the latent constructs inferred from measurement models for sets of observed variables.

It can, of course, be readily argued that the arrows in figure 1.1 that represent the interplay of various causal influences may be too simplistic. Indeed, it would have been plausible to posit several reciprocal relationships. However, I have tried to keep the model as simple as possible because I intend to use it here primarily for its heuristic value, rather than fitting the model to specific data sets. However, all of the causal paths specified in the model have been suggested by the results

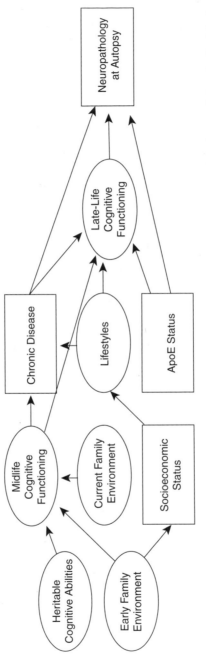

FIGURE 1.1 *Heuristic Model Summarizing the Developmental Influences and Their Interrelations Studied in the Seattle Longitudinal Study.*

of empirical investigations conducted in my own laboratory or by the work of other cognitive developmentalists.

Let me now try to explicate some of the attributes of the heuristic model. The initial bases for the development of adult intelligence must, of course, be attributed to both heritable (genetic) influences and early environmental influences, typically experienced within the home of the biological parents. Although some of the behavior genetic literature suggests that much of the early environmental variance is nonshared (e.g., Plomin & Daniels, 1987), there is recent retrospective evidence that there may indeed be some early shared environmental influences on later cognitive performance (Schaie & Zuo, 2001).

Both genetic and early environmental factors are thought to influence midlife cognitive functioning. The early environmental influences will, of course, also exert influences on midlife social status (Nguyen, 2000). By contrast, virtually no correlations have been found between retrospective accounts of family environment in the family of origin and that in the current family (Schaie & Willis, 1995). However, the current family environment does seem to influence midlife cognitive performance. Genetic factors are also likely to be implicated in the rate of cognitive decline in adulthood. Thus far, the best-studied gene in this context is the *ApoE* gene, which has an allele thought to be a risk factor for Alzheimer's disease. *ApoE* status is therefore added as a factor; the expression of the gene is probably not at issue prior to midlife.

We are now ready to specify the causal influences that determine the level of intellectual functioning in late life as well as cortical status at autopsy. The direct influences to be implicated, in addition to genes with expression that is turned on in late life, most likely originate in midlife. They include level of cognitive functioning in midlife, midlife lifestyles, and the incidence and severity of chronic disease. But there are indirect influences attributable to the effects of midlife cognitive function and lifestyles on chronic disease, as well as shared family influences on midlife cognition and of social status on midlife life styles.

It will immediately be noted that some of these paths represent concurrent observations that would allow alternative (respectively reciprocal) causal paths. However, most of the paths specified by the model represent antecedent–consequent relationships that require longitudinal data for their estimation and understanding. Over the course of the SLS, most of the influences specified in this model either have already been systematically investigated or are currently under investigation (also see Schaie, 2000b).

History of the Seattle Longitudinal Study

The origins of the SLS can be traced to work I did as an undergraduate at the University of California at Berkeley while doing directed studies under the supervision of Professor Read D. Tuddenham. He had introduced me, in an inspiring tests-and-measurements course, to the basic concepts of factor analysis and the writings of L. L. Thurstone (1938). (A more extensive account of my scientific autobiography can be found in Schaie [1996c, 2000c]). I soon inferred that, although the work of Wechsler (1939) on adult intelligence might be of great concern to clinical psychologists, the Wechsler-Bellevue test and its derivatives, because of their factorial complexity, did not have the most desirable attributes for the exploration of developmental issues. I also learned that the more explicitly defined Primary Mental Abilities (PMA; L. L. Thurstone, 1938) had not been studied beyond adolescence, and I concluded that such an exploration might possibly be a fruitful topic for systematic research.

Pilot Studies

In an initial study, I explored whether the factorial independence of the five abilities measured in the most advanced form of the PMA test (PMA 11–14; L. L. Thurstone & Thurstone, 1949) would be retained in adulthood. I then proceeded to ask whether adults would function at the same level as did adolescents. I also raised the question whether there might be ability-related differentials in adult PMA performance, and whether such differences in pattern would remain if the PMA test were administered under nonspeeded conditions (Schaie, Rosenthal, & Perlman, 1953).

My appetite having been whetted by some provocative results from the early pilot study, I continued to explore a variety of corollaries of intelligence in adulthood during my graduate work at the University of Washington (Schaie, Baltes, & Strother, 1964; Schaie & Strother, 1968a, 1968d; Strother, Schaie, & Horst, 1957). As part of this work, I also developed a new factored Test of Behavioral Rigidity (TBR; Schaie, 1955, 1960; Schaie & Parham, 1975). These activities culminated in a doctoral dissertation designed to replicate the earlier work on differential ability patterns across a wider portion of the adult life span as well as to look at the effect of rigidity-flexibility on the maintenance or decline of intellectual functioning (Schaie, 1958a, 1958b, 1958c, 1959a, 1959b, 1962). This dissertation, of course, became the base for the subsequent longitudinal-sequential studies described in this volume.

Finding a Sampling Frame

The search for an appropriate population frame for the base study was guided by the consideration that what was needed was a subject pool with reasonably well-known demographic characteristics, one that had been established for reasons other than research on cognitive behavior. That is, if possible, the initial selection of volunteer participants for the study should be designed to minimize selection in terms of the potential participants' interest in, concern with, or performance level on the dependent variables of interest.

When plans for the study matured, my mentor, Professor Charles R. Strother, was by fortunate coincidence president of the lay board of the Group Health Cooperative of Puget Sound, one of the first broadly based health maintenance organizations (HMOs) in the United States. An arrangement was worked out with the administration of the health plan that permitted me to recruit potential research participants selected by a random draw from the age/sex stratification of plan members aged 22 years or older. The appeal for participation was made by the plan's medical director as part of a membership satisfaction survey, the administration and analysis of which was my quid pro quo for gaining access to this population.

The Cross-Sectional Base Study

Results of the 1956 cross-sectional base study did not support a causal model involving differential patterns of intellectual performance across age for flexible and rigid individuals. The study did demonstrate significant relationships between flexibility-rigidity and intelligence at all ages. More important, however, it provided a sound demonstration of differential patterns of intellectual functioning across age and, by virtue of its design, serendipitously provided the basis for the following longitudinal-sequential studies.

My interest in aging issues continued during a postdoctoral fellowship in medical psychology at Washington University, St. Louis, under the mentorship of Ivan Mensh. There I was able to apply psychological scaling techniques to the assessment of psychiatric complaints in elderly outpatients (e.g., Schaie, Chatham, & Weiss, 1961; Schaie, Rommel, & Weiss, 1959). However, when I entered the job market in the late 1950s, there were not yet any positions for someone interested in the psychology of aging, and I therefore accepted a position at the University of Nebraska in Lincoln that involved teaching psychological assessment to students in clinical psychology. My research interest during that period turned to the unobtrusive assessment of personality characteristics by investigating the use of color preference and its relation to moods (see Schaie, 1963; Schaie & Heiss, 1964), but soon my concern returned to the issue of intellectual development in adulthood.

The Longitudinal Study

Beginnings of the Study   Perhaps the most immediate stimulation leading to the conversion of a one-time cross-sectional study into a series of longitudinal studies was my reading of reports on longitudinal studies of individuals reaching middle adulthood, such as the articles by Bayley and Oden (1955); Jarvik, Kallman, and Falek (1962); and Owens (1953, 1959). Taken together, findings from these studies suggested to me that there was strong evidence that most intellectual abilities were maintained at least into midlife, and that some abilities remained stable beyond that period. These findings clearly contrasted with the results of the earlier cross-sectional literature, including my own dissertation data. What seemed to be called for was the follow-up of a broad cross-sectional panel, such as the one I had been able to examine, by means of a short-term longitudinal inquiry. Intensive discussions of such a project with Charles Strother were followed by a grant application to the National Institutes of Health, which funded the study in time to collect the first set of follow-up data in the summer of 1963.

In addition to tracking down and retesting as many of the individuals studied in 1956 as possible, we decided to draw a new random sample from the original population frame to provide the necessary controls for examining retest effects and to begin addressing the possibility that sociocultural change affects intellectual performance. The latter concern was stimulated by the thoughtful admonitions previously voiced by Raymond Kuhlen (1940, 1963). Our new sample extended over the original age range (22–70 years) plus an additional 7-year interval to match the age range now reached by the original sample.

The second cross-sectional study essentially replicated the findings of the base study. The short-term longitudinal study, however, disclosed substantially different information about peak levels and rate of decline. Publication of findings was therefore delayed until a theoretical model could be built that accounted for the discrepancy between the longitudinal and cross-sectional data (Schaie, 1965, 1967, 1996b). These analyses suggested that comparisons of age group means needed to be conducted for the repeatedly measured samples as well as for successive independent samples drawn from the same cohort. Results were reported that called attention to substantial cohort differences and that questioned the universality and significance of intellectual decrement with advancing age in community-dwelling persons (Nesselroade, Baltes, & Schaie, 1972; Schaie, 1970; Schaie & Strother, 1968b, 1968c).

The Second Longitudinal Follow-up Study   It soon became evident that the conclusions based on data covering a single 7-year interval required further replication, if only because two occasions of measurement permit the examination of cross-sectional sequences, but not of longitudinal sequences (see chapter 2; see also Baltes, Reese, & Nesselroade, 1977), the latter requiring a minimum of three measurement occasions. Only longitudinal sequences allow designs that permit contrasting age and cohort effects. Hence, plans were made for a third data collection, which was conducted in 1970. In that cycle, as many persons as possible examined on the first two test occasions were retested, and a third random sample was drawn from the residual members of the base population (Schaie, 1979; Schaie, Labouvie, & Buech, 1973; Schaie & Labouvie-Vief, 1974; Schaie & Parham, 1977).

The Third Longitudinal Follow-up Study   The results from the third data collection seemed rather definitive in replicating the short-term longitudinal findings, but a number of questions remained. Discrepancies between findings in the repeated-measurement and independent-sampling studies suggested the need for a replication of the 14-year longitudinal sequences, and it further seemed useful to follow the original sample for as long as 21 years. A fourth data collection was therefore conducted in 1977, again retesting the previous samples and adding a new random sample, this time from an expanded population frame (Schaie & Hertzog, 1983, 1986). Continuous funding also made it possible to address a number of bothersome collateral questions. These included analyses of the consequences of shifting from a sampling-without-replacement to a sampling-with-replacement paradigm (Gribbin, Schaie, & Stone, 1976); an analysis of the effects of monetary incentives on participant characteristics (Gribbin & Schaie, 1976); an examination of the aging of tests (Gribbin & Schaie, 1977); and the beginning of causal analyses of health and environmental factors on change or maintenance of adult intellectual performance (Gribbin, Schaie, & Parham, 1980; Hertzog, Schaie, & Gribbin, 1978).

Influences From Neighboring Sciences   My early introduction to the issues of cohort differences and secular trends led to serious questions as to what the meaning of these effects might be beyond their role as control variables or as bothersome design confounds. I therefore began to pay increased attention to the impact of social structures and microenvironments on cognitive change (see Schaie, 1974; Schaie & Gribbin, 1975; Schaie & O'Hanlon, 1990). This work was influenced early by the writing of Matilda Riley (Riley, 1985; Riley, Johnson, & Foner, 1972) and later by the work of Carmi Schooler (1972, 1987), as well as many other sociologists, anthropologists, and epidemiologists who have contributed to the Penn State social structure conference series (see Bengtson, Schaie, & Burton, 1995; Charness & Schaie, 2003; Kertzer & Schaie, 1989; Rodin, Schooler, & Schaie, 1990; Schaie & Achenbaum, 1993; Schaie, Blazer, & House, 1992; Schaie & Hendricks, 2000; Schaie, Leventhal, & Willis, 2002; Schaie & Pietrucha, 2000; Schaie & Schooler, 1989, 1998; Smyer, Schaie, & Kapp, 1996; Willis, Schaie, & Hayward, 1997; Zarit, Pearlin, & Schaie, 1993, 2002).

The Study of Latent Constructs   Until the fourth (1977) cycle of the SLS, we followed the then-conventional wisdom of assessing each primary ability with the observable marker variable deemed to be the most reliable and valid measure of the latent construct to be estimated. With the widespread introduction of modern methods of confirmatory (restricted) factor analysis, it became obvious that we needed to extend our concern with changes in level of intellectual functioning in adulthood to the assessment of structural relationships within the ability domain. This concern argued for collecting further data with a much expanded battery in which each ability would be multiply marked (Schaie, Dutta, & Willis, 1991; Schaie, Maitland, Willis, & Intrieri, 1998; Schaie, Willis, Hertzog, & Schulenberg, 1987; Schaie, Willis, Jay, & Chipuer, 1989).

Introducing Cognitive Interventions   The fifth (1984) SLS cycle also marked the assumption of a major role in this project by Sherry L. Willis, who brought to this project her skills in designing and implementing cognitive training paradigms. Thus, a major part of the fifth cycle was the implementation of a cognitive training study with our long-term participants aged 64 years or older, designed to assess whether cognitive training in the elderly serves to remediate cognitive decrement or increase levels of skill beyond those attained at earlier ages (Schaie & Willis, 1986b; Willis & Schaie, 1986b, 1986c, 1988, 1994b).

The database available through the fifth cycle also made it possible to update the normative data on age changes and cohort differences (Schaie, 1990a, 1990b,

1990c; Schaie & Willis, 1993) and to apply sequential analysis designs controlled for the effects of experimental mortality and practice (Cooney, Schaie, & Willis, 1988; Schaie, 1988d). Finally, this cycle saw the introduction of measures of practical intelligence (Willis & Schaie, 1986b), analyses of marital assortativity using data on married couples followed over as long as 21 years (Gruber & Schaie, 1986; Gruber-Baldini, Schaie, & Willis, 1995), and the application of event history methods to hazard analysis of cognitive change with age (Schaie, 1989a).

Excursions Into Behavior Genetics and Chronic Diseases   The sixth (1989–1991) SLS cycle included a set of four related studies. First, with the collaboration of Robert Plomin, a noted developmental behavior geneticist, we took advantage of the longitudinal database to collect data to implement a study of cognitive family resemblance in adulthood. We did this by recruiting the participation of a large number of adult offspring and siblings of our longitudinal panel members (Schaie, Plomin, Willis, Gruber-Baldini, & Dutta, 1992; Schaie et al., 1993; Schaie & Willis, 1995; Schaie & Zuo, 2001). Second, we abstracted the health histories on our panel members and conducted more detailed investigations of the relationship between health and maintenance of intellectual functioning (Bosworth & Schaie, 1997, 1999; Gruber-Baldini, 1991a; Gruber-Baldini & Schaie, 1990; Gruber-Baldini, Willis, & Schaie, 1989). Third, we conducted a 7-year follow-up of the cognitive training study and have replicated the study with a more recent cohort of older persons (Willis & Schaie, 1992, 1994b). Fourth, we were able to conduct longitudinal analyses of cognitive ability structures and further update our normative database with the collection of a sixth (1991) wave using the standard approach of retesting and drawing a sixth new independent sample (Schaie, 1993, 1994a).

Explorations of Neuropsychology, the ApoE *Gene, and the NEO*   From 1997 to 1999, we conducted a follow-up of all previous participants who could be retrieved as well as a new seventh (1998) wave. In addition, we began to collect blood for genotyping on the *ApoE* gene and administered a neuropsychological test battery to participants aged 60 years or older. This battery continues to be administered in a 3-year follow-up cycle. We also conducted a 14-year follow-up for members of the family study and recruited additional eligible participants.

Between study waves, in 1993, we conducted a mail survey of health behaviors for those persons who had been in the 1989 family study and the 1991 longitudinal and sixth-wave studies. This survey was used to develop a set of latent dimensions for the study of health behaviors (Maier, 1995; see chapter 10). Another mail survey, collecting data on the NEO scales (Costa & McCrae, 1992) was conducted in 2001. Finally, we recruited several hundred third-generation members (those with at least one parent and one grandparent in the study) to expand the family analyses.

Results from many of these studies are presented in this volume. Some represent de novo studies; other reanalyses help increase the stability of normative data or allow comparison of data for additional cohorts.

Objectives of the Seattle Longitudinal Study

Throughout the history of the SLS, an effort now extending over 48 years, our focus has been on five major questions, which we have attempted to ask with greater clarity and increasingly more sophisticated methodologies at each successive stage of the study. These are elaborated next.

Does Intelligence Change Uniformly Through Adulthood, or Are There Different Life Course Ability Patterns?

Our studies have shown that there is no uniform pattern of age-related changes across all intellectual abilities, and that studies of an overall Index of Intellectual Ability (IQ) therefore do not suffice to monitor age changes and age differences in intellectual functioning for either individuals or groups. Our data do lend some support to the notion that fluid abilities tend to decline earlier than crystallized abilities. There are, however, important ability-by-age, ability-by-gender, and ability-by-cohort interactions that complicate matters. Moreover, whereas fluid abilities begin to decline earlier, crystallized abilities appear to show steeper decrement once the late 70s are reached.

Although cohort-related differences in the rate and magnitude of age changes in intelligence remained fairly linear for cohorts who entered old age during the first three cycles of our study, they have since shown substantial shifts. For example, rates of decremental age change have abated somewhat, and at the same time modestly negative cohort trends are beginning to appear as we begin to study members of the baby boom generation. Also, patterns of socialization unique to a given gender role in a specific historical period may be a major determinant of the pattern of change in abilities. More fine-grained analyses suggested, moreover, that there may be substantial gender differences as well as differential changes for those who decline and those who remain sturdy when age changes are decomposed into accuracy and speed.

With multiple markers of abilities, we have conducted both cross-sectional and longitudinal analyses of the invariance of ability structure over a wide age range. In cross-sectional analyses, it is possible to demonstrate configural but not metric factor invariance across wide age/cohort ranges. In longitudinal analyses, metric invariance obtains within cohorts over most of adulthood, except for the youngest and oldest cohorts. Finally, we examined the relationship of everyday tasks to the framework of practical intelligence and perceptions of competence in everyday situations facing older persons.

At What Age Is There a Reliably Detectable Decrement in Ability, and What Is Its Magnitude?

We have generally shown that reliably replicable average age decrements in psychometric abilities do not occur prior to 60 years of age, but that such reliable decrement can be found for all abilities by 74 years of age. Analyses from the most recent phases of the SLS, however, suggested that small but statistically significant average decrement can be found for some, but not all, cohorts beginning in the sixth decade. However, more detailed analyses of individual differences in intellectual change demonstrated that even at the age of 81 years fewer than half of all observed individuals have shown reliable decremental change over the preceding 7 years. In addition, average decrement below 60 years of age amounts to less than 0.2 of a standard deviation; but by 81 years of age, average decrement rises to approximately 1 population standard deviation for most variables.

As data from the SLS cover more cohorts and wider age ranges within individuals, they attain increasing importance in providing a normative base to determine at what ages declines reach practically significant levels of importance for public policy issues. Thus, our data have become relevant to issues such as mandatory retirement, age discrimination in employment, and prediction of proportions of the population that can be expected to live independently in the community. These bases will shift over time because we have demonstrated in the SLS that both level of performance and rate of decline show significant age-by-cohort interactions.

What Are the Patterns of Generational Differences, and What Is Their Magnitude?

Results from the SLS have conclusively demonstrated the prevalence of substantial generational (cohort) differences in psychometric abilities. These cohort trends differ in magnitude and direction by ability and therefore cannot be determined from composite IQ indices. As a consequence of these findings, it was concluded that cross-sectional studies used to model age change will overestimate age changes prior to the 60s for those variables that show negative cohort gradients and underestimate age changes for those variables with positive cohort gradients.

Our studies of generational shifts in abilities have in the past been conducted with random samples from arbitrarily defined birth cohorts. As a supplement and an even more powerful demonstration, we have also conducted family studies that compared performance levels for individuals and their adult children. By following the family members longitudinally, we are also able to provide data on differential rates of aging across generations. In addition, we have also recruited siblings of our longitudinal participants to obtain data that allow extending the knowledge base in the developmental behavior genetics of cognition to the adult level by providing data on parent-offspring and sibling correlations in adulthood.

What Accounts for Individual Differences in Age-Related Change in Adulthood?

The most powerful and unique contribution of a longitudinal study of adult development arises from the fact that only longitudinal data permit the investigation of individual differences in antecedent variables that lead to early decrement for some persons and maintenance of high levels of functioning for others into very advanced age. A number of factors that account for these individual differences have been implicated; of these, some have been amenable to experimental intervention. The variables that have been implicated in reducing risk of cognitive decline in old age have included (a) absence of cardiovascular and other chronic diseases; (b) a favorable environment mediated by high socioeconomic status; (c) involvement in a complex and intellectually stimulating environment; (d) flexible personality style at midlife; (e) high cognitive status of spouse; and (f) maintenance of high levels of perceptual processing speed.

Can Intellectual Decline With Increasing Age Be Reversed by Educational Intervention?

Because longitudinal studies permit tracking stability or decline on an individual level, it has also been feasible to carry out interventions designed to remediate known intellectual decline as well as to reduce cohort differences in individuals who have remained stable in their own performance over time but who have become disadvantaged when compared with younger peers. Findings from the cognitive training studies conducted with our longitudinal subjects (under the primary direction of Sherry L. Willis) suggested that observed decline in many community-dwelling older people might well be a function of disuse and is clearly reversible for many. Indeed, cognitive training resulted in approximately two thirds of the experimental subjects showing significant improvement; and about 40% of those who had declined significantly over 14 years were returned to their predecline level. In addition, we were able to show that we did not simply "train to the test" but rather trained at the ability (latent construct) level, and that the training did not disturb the ability structure. We have now extended these studies to include both a 7-year and a 14-year follow-up that suggest the long-term advantage of cognitive interventions.

The dialectical process between data collection and model building that has been part of the SLS has made possible substantial methodological advances in the design and analysis of studies of human development and aging. In addition, the study has provided baselines for clinical assessment and has made contributions relevant to education, basic instruction in psychological aging, and a variety of public policy issues.

Plan for the Volume

Much of the progress made in the study of adult intellectual development has occurred as the consequence of paradigm shifts and improved research methodology. I therefore begin with a brief discussion of the methodological issues that have informed our program of research (chapter 2). This discussion involves a review of the age-period-cohort model to examine the relationship among cross-sectional, longitudinal, and sequential data collections. I then deal with the fact that our study is a quasi experiment and describe the associated internal validity threats and the manner in which we have dealt with these validity threats. Finally, in chapter 2, I consider the problem of structural equivalence of observed measures across comparison groups and time and describe the approaches taken to deal with these thorny issues.

Chapter 3 contains a detailed presentation of our database. This includes a description of our study participants and of the measurement battery. The latter, in addition to the cognitive ability measures, includes a neuropsychological assessment battery; measures of cognitive style; everyday problem solving; self-reported cognitive change; descriptions of lifestyles, health status, health behaviors, and the subjective environment; as well as measures of personality traits and attitudes.

The basic substantive findings of the SLS on cognitive aging are organized into three sections: cross-sectional studies (chapter 4), longitudinal studies (chapter 5), and studies of cohort and period differences (chapter 6). These presentations are followed by the results of the cognitive intervention studies, including their long-term follow-up and replication with new cohorts (chapter 7).

A number of methodological studies were required in the course of this project (chapter 8). These included a sampling study designed to assess whether it was feasible to move from a sampling-without-replacement to a sampling-with-replacement strategy, a study on the aging of tests, as well as assessments of the effects of experimental mortality (subject attrition), of repeated testing, of offering monetary rewards, and of the structural equivalence of our data across samples differing in age and gender, across experimental interventions, and within cohorts across time.

The next three chapters explore interrelationships between the cognitive variables and their context: the relationship between cognitive styles and intellectual functioning (chapter 9); the effects of health on the maintenance of intellectual functioning, the role of health behaviors, the effects of cognitive abilities as predictors of physical health, mortality, and medication use, as well as the role of perceptions of social support on health (chapter 10); and a discussion of lifestyle variables that affect intellectual functioning (chapter 11).

Throughout the study, some limited data have been collected on a number of personality traits and attitudes. Comprehensive analyses of these variables as well as new data on age differences in NEO personality traits and in self-reported depression are presented in chapter 12, followed by a new chapter describing studies on the relation between personality and cognition (chapter 13). This is followed by a chapter giving an account of our family studies of intellectual abilities in adulthood designed to consider similarities in adult parent-offspring and sibling pairs as well as similarity in married couples. Of particular interest is new material on changes in the rate of cognitive change across biologically related generations (chapter 14).

Our study participants' perceptions of change in their cognitive functioning over time and their perceptions of the effects of the cognitive training are treated in chapter 15, including new material on the stability of the relationship between perceived and objective changes in cognitive performance. Two new chapters are devoted to studies of the influence of family environments on cognition (chapter 16) and of the role of longitudinal studies in the early detection of risk for dementia (chapter 17). The latter chapter also describes analyses of the effects of apolipoprotein E alleles on cognition in a normal population and describes the results of an extension analysis that projects neuropsychological diagnostic measures into the primary mental ability space. Finally, there is a brief summary and a listing of those conclusions I believe are firmly supported by the data presented in this volume (chapter 18).

Most of the material presented in this volume was originally reported in book chapters and scientific journals. An extensive summary of the cognitive abilities part of the study through the fourth (1977) data collection can be found in Schaie (1983a), with updates through the fifth (1984) data collection in Schaie (1988e, 1990a, 1993, 1994a; Schaie & Hertzog, 1986) and a monograph that covers all data collections through 1991 (Schaie, 1996b). Other original sources are cited where the relevant material is presented. However, a portion of the content of this volume was previously available only in the form of convention papers, theses, or other manuscripts of limited circulation. Much of that material was first reported in archival form in the previous volume (Schaie, 1996b). Other materials represent summary previews of yet-unpublished analyses from the most recent, seventh (1998) cycle of the study.

Chapter Summary

This chapter describes the scientific odyssey that began with my emerging interest in the complex phenomena of adult cognitive development. It lays out the reasons why intelligence in adulthood should be studied by giving a brief history of the field of adult intelligence and by pointing out that intellectual competence attains increasing importance from middle adulthood on, when level of intellectual competence may determine job retention, whether independent living within the community remains possible, and maintenance of control over financial decision making.

A conceptual model is then given to represent my view on the developmental influences that have an impact on the life course of cognition. These influences include genetic factors, the family environment, the experience of chronic diseases, and various personality attributes. The model provides the rationale for the various influences related to cognitive development as part of this study.

An account is then given of the history of the SLS, which began as my doctoral dissertation. The objectives of the SLS are then described. These involve the questions (a) whether intelligence changes uniformly through adulthood or whether there are different life course ability patterns; (b) at what age decrement in ability can reliably be detected and what the magnitude of that decrement is; (c) what the patterns of generational differences are and what their magnitude is; (d) what accounts for individual differences in age-related change in adulthood; and (e) whether intellectual decline with increasing age can be reversed by educational intervention. Finally, there is a preview of the organization and content of this volume.

CHAPTER TWO

Methodological Issues

THE PURPOSE OF THIS CHAPTER is to summarize several methodological issues, including certain research design and analysis paradigms, familiarity with which is essential to understand the design of the studies reported in this volume and to interpret their findings correctly. I begin with a brief exposition of the relationship between cross-sectional and longitudinal data within the context of what I have called the *general developmental model* (Schaie, 1965). I then present the rationale for a variety of simple and sequential schemes for data acquisition and analysis. Next, I deal with the problems of internal validity of developmental studies and sketch designs for the measurement and control of the most obvious internal validity problems that plague developmental studies. Finally, I deal with the relationship between observed measures and latent (unobserved) variables and describe how confirmatory (restricted) factor analysis can be applied to assess construct equivalence across cohorts, age, and time in the study of developmental problems.

Cross-Sectional and Longitudinal Data

One of the major contributions of the Seattle Longitudinal Study (SLS) has been the didactic interplay between data acquisition and the formulation and testing of analytic models of interest to developmental scientists. Once the original cross-sectional study had been converted (in the first follow-up) to a mixed cross-sectional–longitudinal design, it became necessary for me to try to understand the relationship of the two forms of data acquisition to interpret the differing cross-sectional and longitudinal findings occurring in a particular data set. This need led me to explore what I termed a general developmental model (Schaie, 1965, 1967), which would help organize and clarify the relationships among these data. Interestingly, the model parallels the age-period-cohort model introduced into sociology by Ryder (1965).

The general developmental model characterizes the developmental status of a given behavior B as a function of three components, such that $B = f(A, C, T)$. In this context, age (A) refers to the number of years from birth to the chronological point at which the organism is observed or measured. Cohort (C) denotes a group of individuals who enter the environment at the same point in time (usually, but not necessarily, at birth), and time of measurement or period (T) indicates the temporal occasion (calendar date) on which a given individual or group of individuals is observed or measured. (Each of these components can be defined also independent of calendar time; see Schaie, 1984a, 1986, 1994b.)

The three components are confounded in the sense that once any two are specified, then the third is known—similar to the confounding of temperature, pressure, and volume in the physical sciences. Nevertheless, each of the three components may be of primary interest for some scientific questions in the developmental sciences, and it is therefore useful to be able to estimate the specific contribution attributable to each component.

The general developmental model allows us to specify how the above-described components are confounded in the research designs traditionally used by developmentalists. In addition, novel designs can be derived from the model that allow estimation of the components confounded in different combinations, even though their unconfounded estimation still eludes us except under specific circumstances and with certain collateral assumptions (Schaie, 1986, 1994b). In turn, these designs can lead to new departures in theory building (Schaie, 1988c, 1992).

Simple Data Collection Designs

Most empirical studies in the developmental sciences involve age comparisons either at one point in time or at successive time intervals (see also Nesselroade & Labouvie, 1985). The cross sectional, longitudinal, and time-lag designs represent the traditional strategies used for this purpose.

Cross-Sectional Strategy   The hypothesis to be investigated simply asks whether there are differences in a given characteristic for samples drawn from different cohorts but measured at the same point in time. This is an important question for the study of interindividual differences. Age differences in behavior at a particular point in historical time may require different societal responses regardless of the antecedent conditions that may be responsible for the age differences. It must be recognized, however, that age differences detected in a cross-sectional data set are inextricably confounded with cohort differences. Because cross-sectional subsamples are measured only once, no information is available on intraindividual change. Unless there is independent evidence to suggest that older cohorts performed at the same level as younger cohorts at equivalent ages, it would be most parsimonious to assume, at least in comparisons of adult samples, that cross-sectional age differences represent estimates of cohort differences that may be either inflated or reduced by maturational changes occurring over a specified age range.

Longitudinal Strategy   For longitudinal strategy, the hypothesis to be investigated is whether there are age-related changes within the same population cohort measured on two or more occasions. This is the question that must be asked whenever there is interest in predicting age differentiation in behavior occurring over time. However, longitudinal data do not provide unambiguous estimates of intraindividual change. Unless the behavior to be studied is impervious to environmental influences, it must be concluded that a single-cohort longitudinal study will confound age-related (maturational) change with time-of-measurement (period) effects that are specific to the particular historical period over which the behavior is monitored (Schaie, 1972). The time-of-measurement effects could either mask or grossly inflate maturational changes. In addition, longitudinal studies are subject to additional threats to their internal validity that would be controlled for in cross-sectional designs (see discussion of internal validity).

Time-Lag Strategy   In the time-lag design, two samples of individuals drawn from successive cohorts are compared at successive points in time at the same chronological age. The hypothesis to be tested is whether there are differences in a given behavior for samples of equal age that are drawn at different points in time. This strategy is of particular interest to social and educational psychologists. It is particularly appropriate when one wishes to study performance of individuals of similar age in successive cohorts (e.g., comparing baby boomers with the preceding generation). The simple time-lag design, however, also confounds the cohort effect with time-of-measurement effects and therefore may provide cohort estimates that are inflated or reduced depending on whether the temporal interval between the cohorts represents a period of favorable or adverse environmental influences.

Sequential Data Collection Designs

To reduce the limitations inherent in the simple data collection schemes, several alternative sequential strategies have been suggested (see Baltes, 1968; Schaie, 1965, 1973b, 1977, 1986; Schaie & Caskie, 2005). The term *sequential* implies that the required sampling strategy includes acquisition of a sequence of samples taken across several measurement occasions. To understand the application of sequential strategies, we must first distinguish between their roles as sampling designs and as data analysis strategies (see Schaie, 1983b; Schaie & Baltes, 1975). Sampling design refers to the particular cells of a Cohort × Age (time) matrix that are to be sampled in a developmental study. Analysis strategies refer to the manner in which the cells that have been sampled can be organized to disaggregate the effects of A, C, and T. Figure 2.1 presents a typical Cohort × Age matrix identifying the several possible sequential designs. This figure also illustrates the confounding of the three developmental parameters of interest. A and C appear as the rows and columns of the matrix; T is the parameter listed inside the matrix

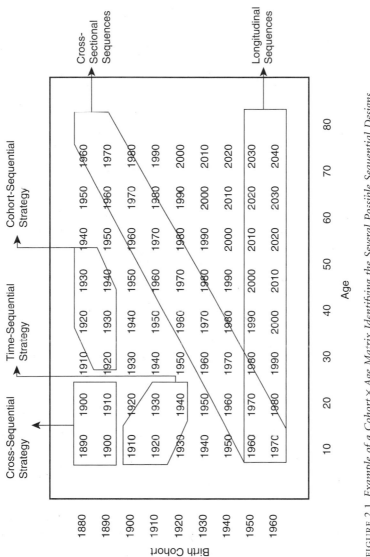

FIGURE 2.1 *Example of a Cohort × Age Matrix Identifying the Several Possible Sequential Designs.*

cells. There has been an extended debate on how these effects might be unconfounded. Those interested in this debate are referred to the work of Adam (1978); Buss (1979–1980); George, Siegler, and Okun (1981); Glenn (1976, 1981); Horn and McArdle (1980); Mason, Mason, Winsborough, and Poole (1973); Schaie (1965, 1967, 1973b, 1977, 1984a, 1986a, 1994b); and Schaie and Hertzog (1982).

Sampling Designs   It is possible to distinguish two types of sequential sampling designs: those using the same panel of individuals repeatedly to fill the cells of the matrix and those using independent random samples of individuals (each observed only once) from the same cohorts. The matrix shown in figure 2.1 could be filled by either approach. Using Baltes's (1968) terminology, the two approaches can be called longitudinal and cross-sectional sequences, respectively. A cross-sectional sequence will usually involve the replication of a cross-sectional study so that the same age range of interest is assessed for at least two time periods, obtaining the estimate for each age level across multiple cohorts, with each sample measured only once. By contrast, the longitudinal sequence represents the measurement of at least two cohorts over the same age range. Here also, estimates from each cohort are obtained at two or more points in time. The critical difference between the two approaches is that the longitudinal sequence permits the evaluation of intraindividual age change and interindividual differences in rate of change, information about which cannot be obtained from cross-sectional sequences. Figure 2.1 has equal intervals for the age ranges and cohort ranges investigated. However, intervals do not have to be equal, although unequal intervals introduce special problems in analysis and should be avoided if possible (see Botwinick & Arenberg, 1976).

Analysis Strategies   Data matrices of the type shown in figure 2.1 permit a variety of alternative analytic strategies (see Schaie, 1965, 1977, 1992; Schaie & Caskie, 2004). Specifically, each row of the matrix can be treated as a single-cohort longitudinal study, each diagonal as a cross-sectional study, and each column as a time-lag study. The sequential designs (except under the special circumstance when one of the components is reconceptualized [see Schaie, 1986]) do not permit complete disentanglement of all components of the $B = f(A, C, T)$ function owing to the obvious linear dependency of the three factors. Despite this problem, I have suggested that, given the model, there exist three distinct analytic designs, created by considering the distinct effects of any two of the components while assuming the constancy or irrelevance of the third component on theoretical or empirical grounds.

The minimum designs indicated in figure 2.1 provide examples of three analytic approaches. The first, which I have called the *cohort-sequential* strategy, permits separation of age changes from cohort differences under the assumption of trivial time-of-measurement (period) effects. The second or *time-sequential* strategy further permits the separation of age differences from period differences, assuming only trivial cohort effects. Finally, the *cross-sequential* strategy permits the separation of cohort differences from period differences.

Longitudinal Sequences

When data are collected in the form of longitudinal sequences, as in the SLS, to examine intraindividual age changes it is possible to apply both the cohort-sequential and the cross-sequential strategies for data analysis. Developmental psychologists often find the cohort-sequential design of greatest interest because it explicitly differentiates intraindividual age changes within cohorts from interindividual differences between cohorts (see Baltes & Nesselroade, 1979; Schaie & Baltes, 1975; but see Schaie, 1986). This design also permits a check of the consistency of age functions over successive cohorts, thereby offering greater external validity than would be provided by a single-cohort longitudinal design.

As noted, a critical assumption for the application of the cohort-sequential analysis strategy is the absence of time-of-measurement effects in the data under consideration. This assumption may be parsimonious for many psychological variables, but others may still be affected by "true" period effects or other internal validity threats, such as differences in instrumentation or experimenter behavior across test occasions (see section on internal and external validity). The question arises, then, how violations of the assumption of no T effects would be reflected in the results of the cohort-sequential analysis. Logical analysis suggests that all estimated effects will be perturbed, although the most direct evidence of the violation would be shown in a significant $C \times A$ interaction (see Schaie, 1973b). However, lack of such an interaction does not necessarily guarantee the absence of T effects; in extensive studies such as ours, they might well be localized in a small subset of test occasions, thus biasing all estimates.

The essential consequence of the interpretational determinacy in sequential analysis is that, if design assumptions are violated, then all effect estimates will be biased to some degree. The problem of interpretation may be lessened, however, by estimating the relative likelihood of confounded T effects given a strong theory about the nature and direction of estimated and confounded effects. We have found that the practical application of a strong theory to sequential designs may require the specification of confounds in an "invalid" design to obtain direct estimates of the confounded effects (see Schaie, 1994b).

An example of the planned violation of design assumptions is use of the cross-sequential strategy under the assumption of the absence of A effects, an assumption that most developmental psychologists might find hard to swallow. Such an approach may be quite reasonable, however, when longitudinal data are available for only a limited number of measurement occasions but extend over a wide range of cohort groupings. The cross-sequential design can then be implemented after only two measurement occasions, whereas a cohort-sequential design would require at least three such occasions. Moreover, the number of measurement occasions required to estimate cohort-sequential designs that span a wide age and/or cohort range would be prohibitive if we insist that no data analyses be performed until the data for the entire cohort-sequential design appropriate for the research question of interest have been acquired. Given a strong developmental theory about the nature of the confounded A effects, a misspecified cross-sequential design can provide useful information about the significance of the A effects represented in both the C and T components. As will be seen, the early work in the SLS (analysis of the data from the first two cycles) began with such misspecification in a cross-sequential design to permit preliminary inferences regarding the relative importance of C and A effects prior to the availability of data that permitted direct simultaneous assessment of these effects (see Schaie & Labouvie-Vief, 1974; Schaie & Strother, 1968b).

Although it is always preferable to estimate parameter effects from the most appropriate design—one that incorporates the correct limiting assumptions—one must often settle for something less than the optimal, whether this is a temporary expedient or one dictated by the phenomenon studied.

Threats to the Internal and External Validity of Developmental Studies

Although the longitudinal approach has advantages over studies based on one-time observations, it is also beset with many methodological problems, some of which have necessitated a variety of design refinements, which may be noted in following the account of the SLS from its earlier to its later phases. In this section, I wish to alert the reader to some of these issues by discussing threats to the internal and external validity of our study, and I suggest approaches to possible solutions of the remaining problems, which will again be encountered as they are applied to various analyses described in this volume.

Longitudinal Studies as Quasi Experiments

Longitudinal studies cannot meet all of the rules for designing true experiments because age is a fixed personal attribute that cannot be experimentally assigned. Consequently, longitudinal studies are subject to all the problems inherent in the type of study that Campbell and Stanley (1963) have denoted "quasi experiments." These problems may result in threats to the internal validity of the study. That is, factors analyzed in a given design that are thought to assess the hypothesized construct may in fact be confounded by other factors not explicitly included in the design. Alternatively, design problems may threaten the external validity of a study, that is, the extent to which valid generalizations from the sample can be applied to other populations.

Internal Validity

Eight threats to the internal validity of quasi experiments such as longitudinal studies have been described by Campbell and Stanley (1963): maturation, effects of history, testing, instrumentation, statistical regression, mortality, selection, and the selection-maturation interaction. The first two, history and maturation, have special meaning for the developmental psychologist beyond their threat to the internal validity of any pretest-posttest type of study design. They may be topics of investigation in their own right. *Maturation*, quite obviously, is not a threat to the validity of developmental studies, but rather is the specific effect of primary interest to the developmentally oriented investigator. Nevertheless, the measurement of maturation is not always unambiguous because, given a specific developmental model, it may be necessary to go beyond a test of the null hypothesis negating maturational effects to test instead some quite explicit alternative hypotheses that specify direction and magnitude of the expected maturational effect.

By contrast, *historical* effects are indeed the primary internal validity problem for the developmental scientist. History is directly involved in both cohort and time-of-measurement (period) effects. However, cohort effects represent the impact of historical effects on a group of individuals who share similar environmental circumstances at equivalent points in their maturation sequence. On the other hand, time-of-measurement effects represent those events that have an impact on all members of the population experiencing a common historical exposure, regardless of cohort membership. The specific threat to longitudinal studies is that historical effects may threaten the internal validity of designs that attempt to measure the effect of maturation (aging effects).

The traditional single-cohort longitudinal design is a special case of the pretest-posttest design in that it repeatedly measures the same individuals over time. Hence, such studies are affected also by the other six threats to internal validity described by Campbell and Stanley (1963). There are actually two different aspects of *testing:* reactivity and practice. Reactivity involves the possible effect on subsequently observed behavior of exposure to certain procedures that are part of the experimental protocol. Longitudinal study participants might respond to a second test in a very different manner than would be the case if they had not been tested previously, a behavior change that could be confused with the effects of maturation. Practice effects, on the other hand, may simply mean that, on subsequent tests, study participants will spend less time in figuring out items previously solved and thus can improve their overall performance by attempting a greater range of problems in the time allowed.

The internal validity threat of *instrumentation* refers to differences in measurement techniques that covary with measurement occasions. In long-term longitudinal studies, such differences may occur when study personnel change or when records regarding the study protocol on previous occasions have been lost and slight variations in protocol are introduced inadvertently. Such effects, again, may either lead to the erroneous inference of having demonstrated maturational trends or may obscure reliable, but small, developmental changes actually occurring.

Statistical regression involves the tendency of variables containing measurement error to regress toward the population mean from one occasion to the next. This problem is of particular importance in two-occasion longitudinal studies (see Baltes, Nesselroade, Schaie, & Labouvie, 1972; Schaie & Willis, 1986b, for examples of applications of the time-reversal method, which tests for the effect of regression in such studies). It has been shown, however, that regression effects do not necessarily cumulate over extended longitudinal series (Nesselroade, Stigler, & Baltes, 1980).

Members of longitudinal panels obviously cannot be forced to continue their participation. Consequently, another serious threat to the internal validity of longitudinal studies is *experimental mortality*. This term describes the attrition of participants from a sample between measurement occasions, whether such attrition occurs because of biological mortality, morbidity, or simply experimenter ineptness in maintaining good relations with panel members. Most empirical studies of experimental mortality suggest that attrition is nonrandom at least between the first and second measurement occasions (Cooney et al., 1988; Gribbin & Schaie, 1979; Riegel & Riegel, 1972; Schaie, 1988d, 1996b; Schaie, Labouvie, & Barrett, 1973; also see chapter 8).

Selection refers to the process of obtaining a sample from the population such that the observed effect arises from the specific sample characteristics rather than from the maturational effect we wish to estimate. For example, a change over time that occurs in a subset of the population regardless of age. The *selection-maturation interaction* refers, of course, to the case where maturational effects may be found in some samples of one age, but not in samples of other ages.

It is not possible to control or measure the effects of any of the above internal validity threats in single-cohort longitudinal studies. When multiple data sets such as ours are available, however, the magnitude of some of these effects can be estimated and appropriate corrections applied to obtain less-biased estimates in the substantive studies. Specific designs for the appropriate analyses have been provided (Schaie, 1977, 1988d) and are applied to some of the data sets presented in chapter 8.

External Validity

As quasi experiments, longitudinal-sequential studies also share certain limitations with respect to the generalizability of their findings (see Cook & Campbell, 1979; Schaie, 1978). Four major issues can be identified. The first concerns *experimental units*, that is, the extent to which longitudinal data collected on one sample can be generalized to other populations (see Gribbin et al., 1976; chapter 8). The second involves *experimental settings,* or the extent to which findings have cross-situational validity (see Scheidt & Schaie, 1978; Willis & Schaie, 1986a). The third is concerned with *treatment variables*, that is, the limitations imposed by specific settings or measurement-implicit reinforcement schedules (see Birkhill & Schaie, 1975; Schaie & Goulet, 1977). Finally, external validity may be threatened by certain aspects intrinsic to the measurement variables to the extent to which task characteristics remain appropriate at different developmental stages as a longitudinal study progresses (see Schaie, 1977–1978; Schaie et al., 1989, 1998; Sinnott, 1989).

Schaie's "Most Efficient Design"

Given the considerations above, I have collected data in the SLS using an approach that allows some useful analyses early on in the course of a longitudinal study, but that over time generates data that can be used eventually to address most of the methodological questions I have raised here. I include a description of this design here (see also Schaie & Willis, 2002, pp. 116–120) to provide some guidance to those who would start a longitudinal study de novo as well as to describe the design rationale of the SLS.

Features of the Design   As should be obvious from the preceding discussion, the "most efficient design" is a combination of cross-sectional and longitudinal sequences created in a systematic way. In brief, the researchers begin with a cross-sectional study that includes multiple age groups. Then, after a period of years, all of those participants who can be retrieved are retested, providing longitudinal data on several cohorts (a longitudinal sequence). At the same time, a new group of participants over the same age range as the original sample is tested. The new sample together with the first cross-sectional study forms a cross-sectional sequence. This whole process can be repeated over and over (ideally, with age groups and time intervals identical), retesting the previously tested participants (adding to the longitudinal data) and initially testing new participants (adding to the cross-sectional data).

In the SLS, we first tested seven groups of people ranging in age from 22 to 70 years in 1956 (see chapter 3). This was a straightforward cross-sectional study. In 1963, those participants who could be found were retested. Hence, we were able to examine, for each of seven cohorts, what happened to average ability scores as the participants aged 7 years. At the same time, we recruited new participants in the same age groups as the original participants (plus an additional group at the age now attained by the oldest original group) and tested them for the first time. The second cross-sectional study represents a replication of the first study. A discrepancy between the two replications suggests the presence of either cohort or time-of-measurement effects. In 1970, we retested the original sample for the third time, adding more data to the longitudinal sequence. Participants who were added at T_2 in 1963 were also retested, adding a new longitudinal sequence. Again, new participants were recruited to form a third replication of the cross-sectional study. A similar approach was taken on subsequent test occasions, which in our case occurred in 1977, 1984, 1991, and 1998.

Analytical Approaches   Data from the most efficient design or comparable designs can be analyzed in several ways. The approach of greatest interest to developmental psychologists is to contrast age changes and cohort effects (Schaie & Baltes, 1975), termed a *cohort-sequential* analysis. Such a comparison permits a strong test of an irreversible age decrement model (Schaie, 1973b). At least two cohorts are required, and each cohort must be observed at least at two different ages. In a traditional longitudinal study, data would be available only for a single cohort, and it would not be known, therefore, whether the observed change holds true beyond the specific cohort studied. For example, one cohort may show an increase and the other a decrease, or one cohort may increase at a slower rate than the other. One cohort may have a higher average IQ than the other at both 60 and 70 years of age, although the increase or decrease may be similar for the two cohorts.

In *cross-sequential* analyses, cohort effects are contrasted with time of measurement. At least two cohorts are compared at two or more times of measurement. This strategy may be particularly appropriate for data sets that cover age ranges for which, on average, stability is likely to obtain (such as in midlife). No age changes are expected, and the primary interest turns to identifying the presence and magnitude of cohort and time-of-measurement effects. The cross-sequential analysis is helpful when the researcher is interested in, say, the effects of some event or sociocultural change that occurs between the two times of measurement and suspects that different cohorts might react differently to such change. In addition, if there is reason to suppose that time-of-measurement effects are slight or nonexistent, then cross-sequential analysis can be used to estimate age changes because participants are obviously older at the second time of measurement.

If the cohort-sequential analysis contrasts cohort and age and the cross-sequential analysis contrasts cohort and time of measurement, there is one logical possibility left: the *time-sequential* strategy, which contrasts age and time of measurement. We might find that the difference between age groups narrows over a given period, or perhaps both age groups change in the same manner, but the gap between them remains sizable. The time-sequential approach would be appropriate also for a test of a decrement-with-compensation model. When a new compensatory method is introduced (say, a computerized memory prosthesis or a drug affecting declining memory), the time-sequential method could show that age differences over the same age range would be smaller at Time 1 than at Time 2.

Repeated Measures Versus Independent Samples   In a typical longitudinal study, *repeated measures* are taken of the same participants at different times. Another possibility is to use the same research design but with *independent samples* at each point on the longitudinal timescale. A longitudinal study usually begins by testing participants at an initial time point, with plans to retest the same individuals at intervals. The alternative strategy would be to draw a new (independent) sample from the same cohort at each test occasion. The independent sampling approach works well when large samples are drawn from a large population. If small samples are used, it is of course necessary to make sure that successive samples are matched on factors such as gender, income, and education to avoid possible differences because of selection biases.

The independent samples procedure, used conjointly with the repeated-measurement procedure, permits estimation of the effects of experimental mortality and of instrumentation (practice) effects. The independent samples are initially drawn at each occasion; hence, they reflect the likely composition of the single sample the repeated-measurement study would have had if no participants had been lost between testing—and of course if the participants would not have had any practice on the test instruments.

Which Analyses Can Be Conducted on Successive Measurement Occasions?
Time 1. The first occasion of any multiple-cohort longitudinal study will simply represent an *n*-group cross-sectional comparison.

Time 2. The second occasion provides a replication of the original cross-sectional study. There are as many two-point longitudinal studies as there are different age groups in the T_1 design. Both time-sequential and cross-sequential analysis schemes can be applied. A simple cross-sectional experimental mortality by age/cohort analysis can be done by contrasting T_1 scores for those participants who return and those who do not. Simple cross-sectional practice analyses can be made by contrasting T_1 means for Sample 1 participants with the T_2 scores of Sample 2 participants at equivalent ages.

Time 3. A third cross-sectional replication is now available, as well as a second replication of the two-point longitudinal study. Three-point longitudinal studies are now available from the initial sample. It is now possible to conduct 2×2 cohort sequential analyses. Time-sequential and cross-sequential analyses can be extended to $n \times 3$ designs, allowing estimation of quadratic trends. Alternatively, it is also possible to estimate either experimental mortality or practice effects in the time- or cross-sequential analyses.

Time 4. The data collection at Time 4 adds a fourth cross-sectional replication, a third two-point longitudinal replication, a second replication of the three-point longitudinal study, and an initial four-point longitudinal study. It is now possible to conduct $n \times 3$ cohort sequential analyses, allowing quadratic estimates, as well as $n \times 4$ time-sequential and cross-sequential analyses that allow estimation of cubic trends. It is also possible to estimate the joint effects of experimental mortality and practice effects in the time- or cross-sequential analyses and to estimate either of these effects in the cohort-sequential analysis.

Time 5. In addition to adding one further layer to all of the above analyses, these additional data will allow estimation of joint effects of experimental mortality and practice in the cohort-sequential schema.

Structural Equivalence

Except for a limited number of demographic attributes and gross anthropometric indices, there are very few observable characteristics that directly contribute to our understanding of human behavior. Behavioral scientists who investigate phenomena in areas such as intellectual abilities, motivation, and personality are rarely interested in their participants' response to specific items or even the summary scores obtained on a particular measurement scale. Instead, such responses are treated as one of many possible indicators of the respondents' location on an unobservable construct that has either been theoretically defined or has been abstracted from empirically observed data. By the same token, scientists studying psychopathology are rarely interested in the occurrence of specific clinically observed symptoms, other than that such symptoms serve as indicators of diagnostic syndromes associated with broader import and consequences (cf. Schaie, 2000d).

Observed Variables and Latent Constructs

Although we can measure directly only the observable phenotype or surface trait, it is usually the unobserved (latent) genotype or source trait that is the object of inquiry for the definition of developmental change. In fact, directly observable variables in the developmental sciences are typically used to define independent variables. Most dependent variables, by contrast, usually represent latent constructs that must be measured indirectly by means of multiple observations or indicators. This is perhaps fortunate because the equivalence of single measures of a particular construct over wide age ranges and time periods is often questionable.

Testing the Invariance Hypothesis

Horn, McArdle, and Mason (1983) drew attention to an important distinction between two levels of invariance in factor loadings, a distinction first introduced by L. L. Thurstone (1947, pp. 360–369), that may have different implications for age change and age difference research: configural invariance and metric invariance. Meredith (1993) spelled out in greater detail what he considered necessary conditions to satisfy this factorial invariance at different levels of stringency.

To demonstrate factorial invariance, it is necessary to show at least that factor patterns across groups or time would display *configural invariance.* In this case, all measures marking the factors (latent constructs) have their primary nonzero loading on the *same* ability construct across test occasions or groups. They must also have zero loadings on the same measures for all factor dimensions.

A second (more desirable) level of factorial invariance (termed *weak factorial invariance* by Meredith) requires that the unstandardized factor pattern weights (factor loadings) can be constrained equal across groups or time. The technical and substantive considerations for this level of factorial invariance have found extensive discussion in the literature (cf. Horn, 1991; Horn & McArdle, 1992; Jöreskog & Sörbom, 1977; Meredith, 1993; Schaie & Hertzog, 1985; Sörbom, 1975; L. L. Thurstone, 1947). If this level of invariance can be accepted, then it becomes possible to test hypotheses about the equivalence of factor means. One can then also test further hypotheses about the latent factor variances and covariances.

However, it should be stressed that it is probably questionable whether even the assumptions of weak factorial invariance can be met in complex empirical data sets such as is found in many aging studies. In fact, Horn et al. (1983) early on argued that configural invariance is likely to be the best solution that can be obtained. Nevertheless, it should be possible to demonstrate more stringent levels of invariance for subsystems across some ages and cohorts. Byrne, Shavelson, and Muthén (1989) have proposed, therefore, that one should test for partial measurement invariance. This proposition has been received with much controversy in the factor-analytic literature. Because of the undue sensitivity of most fit estimates in structural equation models to local disturbances of model fit, it seems that testing for partial invariance is quite reasonable as seen from the point of view of the substantively oriented scientist.

In any event, it is evident that, for both cross-sectional and longitudinal studies, configural invariance remains a minimal requirement and demonstration of some form of metric invariance is essential before valid comparisons of factor scores can be created. Tests of factorial invariance would proceed as follows:

1. Test the least restricted acceptable model, configural invariance:
   a. Constrain all nonsalient factor loading to zero.
   b. Estimate all other loadings for each group/time.
   c. Estimate factor variances/covariances for each group/time.
2. Test the weak invariance model:
   a. Constrain all factor loading to be equal across groups/time.
   b. Estimate factor variances/covariances for each group/time.
3. If necessary, test partial invariance model:
   a. Examine modification indices and/or standard errors of measurement (SEMs) for factor loadings to determine the partial invariance model.
   b. Constrain all factor loading to be equal across groups/time, except those determined to be freed up in Step a.
   c. Estimate all other loadings for each group/time.
   d. Estimate factor variances/covariances for each group/time.

Improvement of fit would generally be examined in terms of delta chi square, but other fit indices can obviously be used as well, although their distributional characteristics are not as well established for the purpose of model comparison (cf. Browne & Cudeck, 1993).

Structural Equivalence Across Comparison Groups

Equivalence of groups must be considered whenever (a) cross-sectional data have been collected and age differences in score level are to be interpreted under the assumption that factor structure is equivalent across the different age groups; (b) when we wish to demonstrate equivalence of factor structure across multiple cohort groups; (c) when the same population is followed by means of drawing successive random samples across time; and (d) when subpopulations are to be compared on multiple dependent variables of interest.

Contradictory findings in the literature on age group differences in factor structure can often be attributed to problems associated with conducting separate exploratory factor analyses of correlations specific to a particular group (see Cunningham, 1978, 1991; Jöreskog, 1971; Reinert, 1970). However, as has been shown by Meredith (1964, 1993), when level of performance differs across groups, it is only the unstandardized factor loadings that can remain invariant across groups. These difficulties can readily be overcome by the joint SEM analysis of multiple covariance matrices in which equality constraints are imposed across groups. Likelihood ratio tests are then available that can test the hypothesis that the unstandardized regression coefficients mapping variables on their latent constructs are indeed equivalent across groups (see also Alwin & Jackson, 1981).

Alternatively, if large enough population samples are available, a population factor structure can be determined and then tested as to how well a subpopulation structure can be fitted by the factor structure obtained for the total population (e.g., Schaie et al., 1989, 1998; chapter 8).

Structural Equivalence Across Time

The demonstration of factorial invariance is also important in showing that the relations between observations and latent constructs remain stable across time or that the introduction of an intervention might affect such relationships. When multiple measures of a set of latent constructs are available for two or more occasions across time, the highest covariances among observed variables will often be the covariances of the variables with themselves across measurement occasions. Exploratory factor analyses of such matrices would result in test-specific factors that would be less than optimal in representing change processes over time.

The longitudinal factor analysis procedures developed by Jöreskog and Sörbom (1977; also see Meredith, 1993) represent a particularly appropriate method for the study of factorial equivalence across time. First, they allow testing of the hypothesis that the regressions of variables on latent constructs can be constrained to be equal across the successive longitudinal testing occasions. Second, they permit assessment of interindividual differences in intraindividual change by testing longitudinal changes in factor variance (change in factor variance over time could occur only if there were individual differences in magnitude of change over time). Third, they allow estimation of the stability of intraindividual differences (high factor covariances across time represent stability of individuals about their own factor means). Finally, they allow the simultaneous test of stability of means on the latent factor scores. Extensions of these models suitable for the cohort-sequential designs used in the SLS have been discussed by Jöreskog and Sörbom (1980) and Hertzog (1985) and in the SLS have been applied to longitudinal data (Hertzog & Schaie, 1986, 1988; Maitland, Intrieri, Schaie, & Willis, 2000; Schaie et al., 1998) and to the evaluation of intervention effects on factorial invariance (Schaie et al., 1987; see also chapter 8).

For completeness, it should be noted that all the design recommendations provided for the comparison of repeated or independent estimates of performance level can also be applied to the analyses of structural invariance described in this section.

The Differentiation-Dedifferentiation Hypothesis

One of the major controversies in the literature on adult development concerns the question whether evidence is available from longitudinal studies of adults that would offer support for the concept of dedifferentiation in cognitive abilities structures from young adulthood to old age.

The conceptual basis for this controversy comes from the theorizing of Kurt Lewin (1935; also see Schaie, 1962) and particularly Heinz Werner (1948), who argued that the cognitive structures of young children were amorphous and undifferentiated, but that the process of development would lead to a greater differentiation of distinct mental processes. The reason for the original lack of differentiation was attributed to the fact that, during early development, all psychological processes are heavily dependent on their physiological infrastructures and hence would need to develop in an undifferentiated tandem with the physiological development. As adulthood is reached, however, environmental and experiential phenomena tend to dominate the psychological processes, with far less dependence on their physiological bases.

Once late midlife is reached, however, the declines of sensory, motor, and central nervous system functions tend to lead to a renewed dependence of individual differences on physiological infrastructures. Hence, a reversal of the earlier differentiation is to be expected as psychological processes increasingly depend on the physiological infrastructure (cf. Baltes & Lindenberger, 1997). This dedifferentiation can be expressed in more modern terms as the progressive decrease of individual differences variance and the corresponding increase of individual differences covariance.

Evidence for the dedifferentiation phenomenon has been reported for individual variables since the 1940s (e.g., Balinsky, 1941; Cornelius, Willis, Nesselroade, & Baltes, 1983; Garrett, 1946; Reinert, 1970). More recent work has also demonstrated increases in correlations between cognitive and sensory functions (e.g., Lindenberger & Baltes, 1994; Salthouse, Hancock, Meinz, & Hambrick, 1996). Much of this work, however, either has been at the level of individual marker variables or has relied heavily on cross-sectional data (e.g., Schaie et al., 1989). However, there is now work, particularly in the SLS (Maitland et al., 2000; Schaie et al., 1998) as well as the Victoria Longitudinal Study, which suggests that dedifferentiation can also be demonstrated at the latent construct level. These studies also permit direct comparison of longitudinal and cross-sectional dedifferentiation patterns by contrasting covariation of change trajectories across different abilities to dedifferentiation in age/cohort differences. Our own findings with respect to this controversy are reported in chapter 8, but here I provide the methodological requirements for testing relevant paradigms.

If factorial invariance within cohorts can be demonstrated, it is then possible to conduct a substantive test of the proposition that factor variances decrease and factor covariance increases with age during adulthood. This is essentially an operationalization of the differentiation-dedifferentiation hypothesis. These tests proceed essentially as indicated above for the tests of factorial invariance except that they involve placing additional constraints on the factor variance-covariance matrix across groups or time (also see Schaie, 2000d; Schaie, Maitland, & Willis, 2000).

The Role of Postdiction in Longitudinal Studies

One of the common limitations ascribed to longitudinal studies is the problem that, as new questions arise and new measurement instruments are added at advanced stages of the study, such information is difficult to relate back to other information obtained at earlier points in time. One possible solution of this problem is to study the concurrent relationship between the new instruments and measures of related variables for which earlier (longitudinal) data are available.

Such studies can attempt to project the new measures into the latent variable space for the variables in the longitudinal data set. The analytic procedure used for this purpose is the method of extension analysis, originally proposed by Dwyer (1937). If sufficiently strong projections of the new measures on the longitudinal measures are found, it is then possible to "postdict" estimated scores for the new measures for earlier data points.

Extension Analysis in Longitudinal Studies

An important application of confirmatory factor analysis is to use this procedure to implement the Dwyer (1937) extension method. As Tucker (1971) demonstrated, it is not appropriate to use factor scores on a latent variable to estimate their regression on an observed variable. However, confirmatory factor analysis permits the estimation of the location of some new observed variable or variables of interest within a previously known factor (latent construct) space. This is a situation that frequently arises in aging studies as samples are followed over long time periods.

To conduct an optimal extension analysis, it is necessary to have a sample for whom data are concurrently available both on a set of measures whose dimensionality (i.e., latent constructs) has been well established as well as the other measures whose relation to these constructs is to be studied. We have thus far used this approach in two studies to postdict longitudinal data for measures for which only concurrent observations are available. The first of these studies postdicted NEO score from our 13 Personality Factor measure (Schaie, Willis, & Caskie, 2004), and the second postdicted scores for our neuropsychological test battery from the longitudinal psychometric factors (Schaie et al., 2004).

In the extension analyses, factor loadings were constrained to the unstandardized values from the confirmatory factor analysis solution for the respective personality or cognitive variables for the concurrent sample. Factor loadings for the new measures were then freely estimated, providing information on the projection of these measures into the previously established factor space. The factor loadings were then orthonormalized to provide weights for the estimation of the postdicted factor scores. Descriptions of the results of these analyses can be found in chapters 12 and 17, respectively.

Chapter Summary

This chapter discusses the methodological issues that have arisen from the SLS data collections and in a dialectic process have led to subsequent empirical study components. I summarize the general developmental model and specify the relationship between cross-sectional and longitudinal data in the context of that model. A rationale is presented for the simple and sequential schemes of data acquisition and analysis employed in the study. Consideration is then given to the problems of internal and external validity of developmental studies, and designs are presented that are used in the SLS to control for internal validity problems. I include a description of what has been called Schaie's most efficient design for multiple-cohort longitudinal studies and describe the analysis modes available at each of the first five test occasions in a longitudinal study thus designed.

The data presented in the following chapters concern both observed variables and latent constructs inferred from them. Therefore I also discuss the relationship between observed measures and latent variables and describe the applicability of confirmatory (restricted) factor analysis to the assessment of construct equivalence across cohorts, age, and time in the study of developmental problems. Also explained is the differentiation-dedifferentiation hypothesis, one of the major theoretical propositions in adult development, and I indicate how this hypothesis can be tested by means of SEM modeling. Finally, I preview the application of extension analysis to the postdiction of nonobserved data for more recently added measurement variables.

CHAPTER THREE

The Database

THE DATABASE FOR THE Seattle Longitudinal Study (SLS) consists of the assessments conducted during seven major testing cycles (1956, 1963, 1970, 1977, 1984, 1991, and 1998). As part of the 1984, 1991, and 1998 cycles, cognitive intervention studies were conducted with a number of participants who were in their 60s or older. In addition, three pilot studies were conducted that were concerned with the characteristics of the Primary Mental Abilities (PMA) test and the Test of Behavioral Rigidity (TBR) when used with adults (1952, 1953, 1954).

Two collateral studies were undertaken to determine the consequences of shifting to an expanded sampling frame and providing monetary incentives (1974) and to investigate the aging of our test battery (1975). Beginning in 1997, continuous neuropsychological assessment (in 3-year intervals) was conducted with study participants over age 60. The basic test battery was administered to the adult offspring and siblings of our longitudinal panel members (1989–1990 and 1996–1997). In 1993, a health behavior mail survey (the health behavior questionnaire, HBQ) was conducted. This instrument was also included in all later test administration sessions.

In 2001, the NEO Personality Inventory was administered by mail, and will be added to future data collections. Finally, a third-generation study (persons with both a parent and a grandparent in the study) was begun in 2001.

The Participant Population

All of our study participants (with the exception of those involved in the pilot and family studies) were members of the Group Health Cooperative of Puget Sound in Washington State at the time they entered the study. Our original 1956 population frame consisted of approximately 18,000 potential participants 22 years of age or older. These individuals were stratified by age and sex, and 25 men and 25 women were randomly selected for each year of birth from 1882 to 1934. After removing individuals who were not in the area, 2,818 persons were actually contacted; of these, 910 agreed to participate. Testing then proceeded in groups of 10 to 30 persons until 25 men and 25 women had been tested in each 5-year birth interval over the age range from 22 to 70 years (see Schaie, 1958c, 1959a).

For the second (1963) cycle, in addition to the longitudinal follow-up, approximately 3,000 names were again drawn randomly from the 1956 population after deleting names of all individuals tested in 1956. Of these, 997 persons ranging in age from 22 to 77 years were successfully tested. A similar procedure was followed in 1970: survivors of the 1956 and 1963 panels were retested, and a new randomly selected panel (aged 22 to 84), consisting of 705 individuals, was established.

Because our population frame was virtually exhausted, we determined by means of a collateral study (Gribbin, Schaie, & Stone, 1976; chapter 8) that it would be feasible to shift to a sampling-with-replacement basis. For the 1977 cycle, we therefore again sampled approximately 3,000 persons from what had now become a 210,000-member health plan. Of these, 609 new participants were tested. A similar scheme was used in 1984, when 629 new participants were assessed; in 1991, when we added 693 new participants; and in 1998, when 719 new participants were added from what by now had become a 420,000-member health maintenance organization (HMO).

Because of the 7-year intervals between waves, all data were organized into 7-year age and cohort groupings. Tables 3.1 to 3.7 show that, for purposes of analysis, the main study now consists of 28 data sets. These consist of cross-sectional and longitudinal sequences (see Baltes, 1968) as discussed next.

The Cross-Sectional Sequence

The cross-sectional sequence consists of seven independent data sets with a total of 4,850 participants (see table 3.1 for detailed breakdown):

Aa ($n = 500$): seven cohorts tested in 1956 (mean ages 25 to 67; mean birth years 1889 to 1931)

Bb ($n = 998$): eight cohorts tested in 1963 (mean ages 25 to 74; mean birth years 1889 to 1938)

Cc ($n = 705$): nine cohorts tested in 1970 (mean ages 25 to 81; mean birth years 1889 to 1945)

Dd ($n = 609$): nine cohorts tested in 1977 (mean ages 25 to 81; mean birth years 1897 to 1952)

Ee ($n = 628$): nine cohorts tested in 1984 (mean ages 25 to 81; mean birth years 1903 to 1959)

Ff ($n = 691$): nine cohorts tested in 1991 (mean ages 25 to 81; mean birth years 1910 to 1966)

Gg ($n = 719$): nine cohorts tested in 1998 (mean ages 25 to 81; mean birth years 1917 to 1973)

TABLE 3.1 Frequency Distribution of Subjects at First Test by Cohort, Sex, and Year of Entry Into the Study

	Mean Year of Birth (Cohort)													
	1889	1896	1903	1910	1917	1924	1931	1938	1945	1952	1959	1966	1973	Total
1956 sample														
mean age	(67)	(60)	(53)	(46)	(39)	(32)	(25)							
Male	38	35	35	35	36	33	38							250
Female	38	37	35	30	35	37	38							250
Total	76	72	70	65	71	70	76							500
1963 sample														
mean age	(74)	(67)	(60)	(53)	(46)	(39)	(32)	(25)						
Male	38	64	68	62	70	71	52	42						467
Female	39	63	64	81	76	79	70	58						530
Total	77	127	132	143	146	150	122	100						997
1970 sample														
mean age	(81)	(74)	(67)	(60)	(53)	(46)	(39)	(32)	(25)					
Male	26	46	42	38	40	44	34	28	31					329
Female	24	42	49	42	49	43	50	37	40					376
Total	50	88	91	80	89	87	84	65	71					705
1974–1975 sample														
mean age	(85)	(78)	(71)	(64)	(57)	(50)	(43)	(36)	(29)	(25)				
Male	23	47	55	63	58	61	37	15	11	12				392
Female	31	69	59	69	58	55	52	13	16	10				432
Total	54	116	114	132	116	116	89	28	27	22				824
1977 sample														
mean age		(81)	(74)	(67)	(60)	(53)	(46)	(39)	(32)	(25)				
Male		27	37	35	35	40	32	37	29	28				300
Female		31	33	38	37	37	37	36	33	27				309
Total		58	70	73	72	77	69	73	62	55				609
1984 sample														
mean age			(81)	(74)	(67)	(60)	(53)	(46)	(39)	(32)	(25)			
Male			24	39	40	36	33	26	30	27	27			282
Female			28	38	42	43	33	39	40	28	56			347
Total			52	77	82	79	66	65	70	55	83			629
1991 sample														
mean age				(81)	(74)	(67)	(60)	(53)	(46)	(39)	(32)	(25)		
Male				33	41	41	32	38	34	39	31	27		316
Female				34	43	56	41	40	49	40	40	34		377
Total				67	84	97	73	78	83	79	71	61		693
1998 sample														
mean age					(81)	(74)	(67)	(60)	(53)	(46)	(39)	(32)	(25)	
Male					29	26	60	40	43	63	49	37	16	363
Female					30	31	34	33	50	62	59	32	25	356
Total					59	57	94	73	93	125	108	69	41	719
Grand total (by cohort)														
Male	125	219	261	305	349	352	318	226	178	169	107	64	16	2,699
Female	132	242	268	332	370	381	355	256	228	167	155	66	25	2,977
Total	257	461	529	637	719	733	673	482	406	336	262	130	41	5,676

TABLE 3.2 Frequency Distribution of Longitudinal Subjects Tested in 1963 by Cohort and Sex

	Mean Year of Birth (Cohort)							
	1889	1896	1903	1910	1917	1924	1931	Total
Mean age in 1963	(74)	(67)	(60)	(53)	(46)	(39)	(32)	
Male	25	13	21	22	23	19	18	141
Female	23	27	23	18	24	25	21	161
Total	48	40	44	40	47	44	39	302

The Longitudinal Sequences

Longitudinal sequences involve 21 data sets comprising six 7-year, five 14-year, four 21-year, three 28-year, two 35-year, and one 42-year follow-up groups (see tables 3.2 to 3.7 for details).

Seven-Year Longitudinal Data

Ab ($n = 303$): seven cohorts followed from 1956 to 1963
Bc ($n = 420$): eight cohorts followed from 1963 to 1970
Cd ($n = 340$): nine cohorts followed from 1970 to 1977
De ($n = 294$): nine cohorts followed from 1977 to 1984
Ef ($n = 428$): nine cohorts followed from 1984 to 1991
Fg ($n = 408$): nine cohorts followed from 1991 to 1998

TABLE 3.3 Frequency Distribution of Longitudinal Subjects Tested in 1970 by Cohort, Sex, and Year of Entry Into the Study

	Mean Year of Birth (Cohort)								
	1889	1896	1903	1910	1917	1924	1931	1938	Total
Mean age in 1970	(81)	(74)	(67)	(60)	(53)	(46)	(39)	(32)	
1956 sample									
Male	8	3	13	18	12	10	10		74
Female	6	12	15	15	15	15	11		89
Total	14	15	28	33	27	25	21		163
1963 sample									
Male	8	20	19	29	36	36	21	9	178
Female	6	24	22	45	37	43	38	26	241
Total	14	44	41	74	73	79	59	35	419
Grand total									
Male	16	23	32	47	48	46	31	9	252
Female	12	36	37	60	52	58	49	26	330
Total	28	59	69	107	100	104	80	35	582

TABLE 3.4 Frequency Distribution of Longitudinal Subjects Tested in 1977 by Cohort, Sex, and Year of Entry Into the Study

	Mean Year of Birth (Cohort)									
	1889	1896	1903	1910	1917	1924	1931	1938	1945	Total
Mean age in 1977	(88)	(81)	(74)	(67)	(60)	(53)	(46)	(39)	(32)	
1956 sample										
Male	3	2	10	15	11	7	10			58
Female	2	7	14	16	13	11	9			72
Total	5	9	24	31	24	18	19			130
1963 sample										
Male	1	11	11	27	30	31	19	10		140
Female	3	14	12	40	38	35	36	15		193
Total	4	25	23	67	68	66	55	25		333
1970 sample										
Male	3	12	18	21	24	28	17	14	10	147
Female	3	17	16	25	29	25	29	22	24	190
Total	6	29	34	46	53	53	46	36	34	337
Grand total										
Male	7	25	39	63	65	66	46	24	10	345
Female	8	38	42	81	80	71	74	37	24	455
Total	15	63	81	144	145	137	120	61	34	800

Fourteen-Year Longitudinal Data

Ac ($n = 162$): seven cohorts followed from 1956 to 1970
Bd ($n = 337$): eight cohorts followed from 1963 to 1977
Ce ($n = 224$): nine cohorts followed from 1970 to 1984
Df ($n = 201$): nine cohorts followed from 1977 to 1991
Eg ($n = 265$): nine cohorts followed from 1984 to 1998

Twenty-One-Year Longitudinal Data

Ad ($n = 130$): seven cohorts followed from 1956 to 1977
Be ($n = 225$): eight cohorts followed from 1963 to 1984
Cf ($n = 175$): eight cohorts followed from 1970 to 1991
Dg ($n = 132$): seven cohorts followed from 1977 to 1998

Twenty-Eight-Year Longitudinal Data

Ae ($n = 97$): seven cohorts followed from 1956 to 1984
Bf ($n = 161$): seven cohorts followed from 1963 to 1991
Cf ($n = 123$): seven cohorts followed from 1970 to 1998

TABLE 3.5 Frequency Distribution of Longitudinal Subjects Tested in 1984 by Cohort, Sex, and Year of Entry Into the Study

| | *Mean Year of Birth (Cohort)* | | | | | | | | | | |
	1889	1896	1903	1910	1917	1924	1931	1938	1945	1952	Total
Mean age in 1984	(95)	(88)	(81)	(74)	(67)	(60)	(53)	(46)	(39)	(32)	
1956 sample											
Male	1	1	7	10	9	8	8				44
Female	0	2	9	14	9	12	7				53
Total	1	3	16	24	18	20	15				97
1963 sample											
Male	0	1	6	16	24	21	17	6			91
Female	1	4	8	26	29	26	28	12			134
Total	1	5	14	42	53	47	45	18			225
1970 sample											
Male	1	1	10	14	19	23	14	12	8		102
Female	1	3	5	19	22	20	17	17	18		122
Total	2	4	15	33	41	43	31	29	26		224
1974–1975 sample											
Male		8	10	20	24	10					72
Female		7	15	28	31	10					91
Total		15	25	48	55	20					163
1977 sample											
Male		5	5	22	21	29	19	19	15	16	151
Female		5	10	16	23	25	16	24	13	10	142
Total		10	15	38	44	54	35	43	28	26	293
Grand total											
Male	2	16	38	82	97	91	58	37	23	16	460
Female	2	21	47	105	114	93	68	53	31	10	542
Total	4	37	85	185	211	184	126	90	54	26	1,002

Thirty-Five-Year Longitudinal Data

Af ($n = 71$): six cohorts followed from 1956 to 1991
Bf ($n = 87$): six cohorts followed from 1963 to 1998

Forty-Two-Year Longitudinal Data

Ag ($n = 38$): five cohorts followed from 1956 to 1998

Successively longer studies, of course, involve subsets of those examined earlier. The main SLS database consequently consists of the 9,476 complete records on 4,857 participants, of whom 36 were tested seven times, 122 were tested six times, 223 were tested five times, 281 were tested four times, 527 were tested three times, 1,004 were tested twice, and 2,664 participants tested only once. Cumulatively, this results in a total of 2,193 participants followed over 7 years, 1,189 over 14 years, 662 over 21 years, 381 over 28 years, 158 over 35 years, and 36 over 42 years.

TABLE 3.6 Frequency Distribution of Longitudinal Subjects Tested in 1991 by Cohort, Sex, and Year of Entry Into the Study

Sample (No. of Tests)	Mean Year of Birth (Cohort)										Total
	1896	1903	1910	1917	1924	1931	1938	1945	1952	1959	
Mean age in 1991	(95)	(88)	(81)	(74)	(67)	(60)	(53)	(46)	(39)	(32)	
1956 sample (6)											
Male	1	2	8	9	7	7					34
Female	0	2	11	11	9	8					41
Total	1	4	19	20	16	15					75
1963 sample (5)											
Male	0	1	7	12	22	13	5				60
Female	1	5	16	24	21	25	11				103
Total	1	6	23	36	43	38	16				163
1970 sample (4)											
Male	1	0	9	14	20	12	12	8			76
Female	0	1	12	19	16	17	16	18			99
Total	1	1	21	33	36	29	28	26			175
1974–1975 sample (3)											
Male	0	3	10	14	7						34
Female	1	6	14	21	6						48
Total	1	9	24	35	13						82
1977 sample (3)											
Male	1	1	15	14	21	9	19	13	13		106
Female	0	3	9	11	18	15	20	11	10		97
Total	1	4	24	25	39	24	39	24	23		203
1984 sample (2)											
Male	—	8	18	30	27	24	25	24	20	17	193
Female	—	8	18	30	32	29	34	30	18	35	234
Total	—	16	36	60	59	53	59	54	38	52	427
Grand total											
Male	3	15	67	93	104	65	61	45	33	17	503
Female	2	25	80	116	102	94	81	59	28	35	622
Total	5	40	147	209	206	159	142	104	61	52	1,125

Characteristics of the Base Population

Our source of study participants provides a population frame that is reasonably close to the demographic pattern of the community from which it was drawn, although somewhat sparse at the lowest socioeconomic levels. In this section, I provide data on educational and occupational levels for the seven successive cycles and discuss shifts caused by nonrandom participant attrition (for further details on the substantive consequences of attrition, see chapter 8). Data on income were also collected, but because of inflationary factors, they are not directly comparable across occasions.

Table 3.8 provides proportions for our 28 data sets by educational level (grade school, high school, college, and graduate training), and table 3.9 lists similar data for occupational level (unskilled = cleaning services, maintenance services,

TABLE 3.7 Frequency Distribution of Longitudinal Subjects Tested in 1998 by Cohort, Sex, and Year of Entry Into the Study

Sample (No. of Tests)	Mean Year of Birth (Cohort)										Total
	1903	1910	1917	1924	1931	1938	1945	1952	1959	1966	
Mean age in 1998	(95)	(88)	(81)	(74)	(67)	(60)	(53)	(46)	(39)	(32)	
1956 sample (7)											
Male	0	2	6	4	3						15
Female	1	4	5	7	6						23
Total	1	6	11	11	9						38
1963 sample (6)											
Male	0	1	7	16	11	5					40
Female	1	7	16	17	20	10					71
Total	1	8	23	33	31	15					111
1970 sample (5)											
Male	0	1	10	16	9	11	6				53
Female	1	5	14	13	15	13	13				74
Total	1	6	24	29	24	24	19				127
1974–1975 sample (4)											
Male	0	4	6	4							14
Female	2	6	16	3							27
Total	2	10	22	7							41
1977 sample (4)											
Male	0	6	10	14	7	14	11	9			71
Female	0	4	5	13	12	14	10	7			65
Total	0	10	15	27	19	28	21	16			136
1984 sample (3)											
Male	1	7	15	20	17	18	16	11	11		116
Female	1	8	18	23	23	24	21	12	20		150
Total	2	15	33	43	40	42	37	23	31		266
1991 sample (2)											
Male	—	11	21	25	22	22	25	28	12	10	176
Female	—	14	24	43	31	22	30	28	19	19	230
Total	—	25	45	68	53	44	55	56	31	29	406
Grand total											
Male	1	32	75	99	69	70	58	48	23	10	485
Female	6	48	98	119	107	83	70	47	39	19	640
Total	7	80	159	206	165	151	121	95	62	29	1,125

laborers, factory workers, fishermen; semiskilled = protective services, bartenders, personal services, custodians; skilled = mechanical-technical and clerical occupations; semiprofessional = managers, proprietors, professions requiring less than a master's degree; professional = professions requiring a master's degree or more advanced education). For the more recent samples, we also separately identify the proportion of homemakers who have worked, those retired, and those still in the educational process. Inspection of these tables indicates that, as suggested, we do experience an upwardly skewed socioeconomic distribution on completion of the acquisition of our volunteer participants.

TABLE 3.8 Educational Levels for Data Sets in the Main Study as Proportions of Each Sample

	First Test	Second Test	Third Test	Fourth Test	Fifth Test	Sixth Test	Seventh Test
1956 Sample							
0–8 years (grade school)	11.0	9.2	4.3	4.2	3.3	2.5	0.0
9–12 years (high school)	42.4	38.2	41.0	38.7	27.9	21.3	13.9
13–16 years (college)	32.6	35.6	36.6	38.7	38.9	45.0	44.4
17 years plus (graduate)	14.0	16.8	18.0	18.5	30.0	31.2	41.7
1963 Sample							
0–8 years (grade school)	12.9	7.4	4.2	1.6	0.6	0.0	
9–12 years (high school)	46.1	43.8	42.3	41.6	38.1	26.4	
13–16 years (college)	30.9	37.4	40.6	39.8	43.4	50.6	
17 years plus (graduate)	10.0	11.4	12.9	17.1	17.9	23.0	
1970 Sample							
0–8 years (grade school)	10.1	4.4	3.8	1.1	2.4		
9–12 years (high school)	40.4	37.4	29.7	31.9	26.8		
13–16 years (college)	35.5	40.6	42.9	44.8	51.2		
17 years plus (graduate)	14.0	17.6	23.6	22.2	19.5		
1977 Sample							
0–8 years (grade school)	9.7	5.9	2.0	0.8			
9–12 years (high school)	32.8	27.3	19.9	13.7			
13–16 years (college)	38.0	40.2	47.8	49.6			
17 years plus (graduate)	19.5	26.6	22.2	35.9			
1984 Sample							
0–8 years (grade school)	3.6	3.3	1.1				
9–12 years (high school)	27.9	23.8	17.7				
13–16 years (college)	41.2	43.9	42.3				
17 years plus (graduate)	27.3	29.0	38.9				
1991 Sample							
0–8 years (grade school)	0.9	1.2					
9–12 years (high school)	20.2	13.2					
13–16 years (college)	49.3	49.3					
17 years plus (graduate)	29.6	36.3					
1998 Sample							
0–8 years (grade school)	0.1						
9–12 years (high school)	17.0						
13–16 years (college)	50.9						
17 years plus (graduate)	32.0						

TABLE 3.9 Occupational Levels for Data Sets in the Main Study as Proportions of Each Sample

	First Test	Second Test	Third Test	Fourth Test	Fifth Test	Sixth Test	Seventh Test
1956 Sample							
Unskilled	4.5	4.0	2.5	3.3	7.6	1.3	2.8
Semiskilled	10.9	8.6	3.7	4.2	3.7	2.6	0.0
Skilled	47.2	45.5	48.1	47.5	26.6	16.1	2.8
Semiprofessional	32.2	36.0	40.1	38.3	32.4	6.7	2.8
Professional	5.3	5.9	5.6	6.7	5.4	5.3	0.0
Retired	NA	NA	NA	NA	24.3	68.0	77.8
Homemaker[a]	NA	NA	NA	NA	NA	NA	13.9
1963 Sample							
Unskilled	5.1	2.9	2.0	5.1	1.9	2.3	
Semiskilled	11.3	7.2	7.1	5.1	0.6	1.1	
Skilled	56.5	57.7	56.0	34.8	24.4	5.8	
Semiprofessional	23.4	29.0	31.7	32.3	8.4	5.8	
Professional	3.8	3.1	3.2	6.2	5.1	2.3	
Retired	NA	NA	NA	15.5	59.6	71.2	
Homemaker	NA	NA	NA	NA	NA	11.5	
1970 Sample							
Unskilled	0.6	0.9	4.7	4.0	3.3		
Semiskilled	5.0	5.0	5.1	2.9	1.6		
Skilled	48.7	44.1	29.8	28.6	5.7		
Semiprofessional	38.0	39.7	31.3	12.0	3.3		
Professional	7.7	7.3	12.6	9.1	13.1		
Retired	NA	NA	16.5	43.4	57.4		
Homemaker	NA	NA	NA	NA	15.6		
1977 Sample							
Unskilled	6.6	5.2	2.5	5.4			
Semiskilled	8.0	3.7	1.0	6.2			
Skilled	30.6	31.3	16.7	5.4			
Semiprofessional	32.8	40.1	23.7	6.1			
Professional	22.0	11.7	15.2	23.1			
Retired	NA	8.0	40.9	40.8			
Homemaker	NA	NA	NA	13.1			
1984 Sample							
Unskilled	4.2	5.4	3.9				
Semiskilled	5.2	2.9	3.5				
Skilled	29.1	20.4	7.4				
Semiprofessional	34.1	22.1	5.1				
Professional	15.2	12.3	25.0				
Retired	12.2	35.9	44.5				
Homemaker	NA	NA	10.6				

(*continued*)

TABLE 3.9 Continued

	First Test	Second Test	Third Test	Fourth Test	Fifth Test	Sixth Test	Seventh Test
1991 Sample							
Unskilled	3.5	8.1					
Semiskilled	4.2	4.1					
Skilled	20.6	9.6					
Semiprofessional	25.4	11.6					
Professional	16.6	32.5					
Retired	29.7	23.5					
Homemaker	NA	9.3					
1998 Sample							
Unskilled	0.7						
Semiskilled	11.5						
Skilled	8.5						
Semiprofessional	38.0						
Professional	9.1						
Retired	25.5						
Homemaker	5.2						
Student	1.6						

Note. NA, not applicable.
[a]Never in the workforce.

Further complications arise through nonrandom retest attrition and nonrandom outflow from the population frame, which occurs at a lower rate for the economically advantaged. Nevertheless, our sample structure does represent as reasonable an approximation of the urban population as can be achieved with volunteer study participants, and shifts across samples, although worthy of further investigation, would not seem to interfere seriously with the comparisons reported in this volume.

The Measurement Battery

The test battery includes the psychometric ability and rigidity-flexibility measures that have been collected since the inception of the SLS as well as additional markers for the ability factors included in the basic battery. The additional measures included markers of the abilities of perceptual speed and verbal memory, as well as multiple choice items sampling real-life tasks, used as an ecological validity measure. In addition, for some test occasions, measures of certain personality traits, family environment, lifestyles (including health behaviors), neuropsychological measures, and health history variables were added. Raw score means, standard deviations, and ranges for the psychometric measurement battery are provided in table 3.10.

TABLE 3.10 Raw Score Means, Standard Deviations, and Ranges for the Psychometric Measurement Battery[a]

Variable	N	Mean	SD	Range
Inductive Reasoning				
PMA Reasoning	4,847	14.60	7.40	0–30
ADEPT Letter Series	2,405	10.78	4.39	0–20
Word Series	2,408	18.30	5.85	0–30
Number Series	2,452	6.37	3.11	0–15
Spatial Orientation				
PMA Space	4,852	18.85	11.46	−15–54
Object Rotation	2,476	35.25	13.78	−13–54
Alphanumeric Rotation	2,410	40.15	11.99	−1–54
Cube Comparison	2,407	19.78	7.48	0–42
Numeric Facility				
PMA Number	4,851	23.24	10.71	−15–70
Addition	2,474	43.01	12.81	2–92
Subtraction and Multiplication	2,408	55.69	18.58	0–96
Verbal Comprehension				
PMA Verbal Meaning	4,853	35.21	11.37	1–50
ETS Vocabulary	2,409	28.99	4.78	7–36
ETS Advanced Vocabulary	2,409	24.74	6.59	4–36
Perceptual Speed				
Identical Pictures	2,501	35.09	8.37	3–48
Finding A's	2,436	27.71	8.32	4–75
Number Comparison	2,475	22.95	5.97	5–47
Verbal Memory				
Immediate Memory	2,406	14.02	4.03	0–20
Delayed Memory	2,403	12.03	4.88	0–20
PMA Word Fluency	4,851	40.96	13.21	1–98
Composite Measures				
Index of Intellectual Ability	4,846	170.86	54.84	4–364
Index of Educational Aptitude	4,849	85.08	28.41	2–140
Rigidity-Flexibility				
Motor-Cognitive Flexibility	4,837	51.22	7.81	17–75
Attitudinal Flexibility	4,778	51.45	8.59	24–77
Psychomotor Speed	4,699	50.88	9.96	23–77

Note. ADEPT, Adult Development and Enrichment Project; ETS, Educational Testing Service; PMA, Primary Mental Abilities.
[a]Means and standard deviations at first test across the entire database.

The Cognitive Ability Battery

The psychometric ability battery was expanded in 1984 to permit structural analyses that require multiple measures to mark each ability factor. In addition, it introduces alternate forms that may have differential validity by age (see Gonda, Quayhagen, & Schaie, 1981; Schaie, 1978). The longitudinal markers included in this battery of necessity (i.e., for consistency across administration) employ the test booklet and answer sheet format used since the beginning of the SLS. All other forms use disposable booklets on which answers are marked directly (see Schaie, 1985). Brief descriptions of the ability factors, the longitudinal marker of each ability (contained in the basic test battery), and the additional measures are given next.

Inductive Reasoning   Inductive reasoning is the ability to recognize and understand novel concepts or relationships; it involves the solution of logical problems—to foresee and plan. L. L. and T. G. Thurstone (1949) proposed that persons with good reasoning ability could solve problems, foresee consequences, analyze situations on the basis of past experience, and make and carry out plans according to recognized facts.

> *PMA Reasoning* (R; longitudinal marker). The study participant is shown
> a series of letters (e.g., *a b x c d x e f x g h x*). The letters in the row
> form a series based on one or more rules. The study participant is
> asked to discover the rule(s) and mark the letter that should come next
> in the series. In this case, the rule is that the normal alphabetical pro-
> gression is interrupted with an *x* after every second letter. The solution
> would therefore be the letter *i*. There are 30 test items, with a time
> limit of 6 minutes.
> *ADEPT (Adult Development and Enrichment Project) Letter Series* (LS;
> Blieszner, Willis, & Baltes, 1981). This is a parallel form to the PMA
> Reasoning test. It has 20 test items, with a time limit of 4.5 minutes.
> *Word Series* (WS; Schaie, 1985). The study participant is shown a series of
> words (e.g., January, March, May) and is asked to identify the next
> word in the series. Positional patterns used in this test are identical to
> the PMA Reasoning test. There are 30 test items, with a time limit of 6
> minutes.
> *Number Series* (NS; T. G. Thurstone, 1962). The study participant is
> shown a series of numbers (e.g., 6, 11, 15, 18, 20) and is asked to iden-
> tify the number that would continue the series. There are 20 items,
> with a time limit of 4.5 minutes.

Spatial Orientation   Spatial orientation is the ability to visualize and mentally manipulate spatial configurations in two or three dimensions, to maintain orientation with respect to spatial objects, and to perceive relationships among objects in space. This ability is important in tasks that require deducing one's physical orientation from a map or visualizing what objects would look like when assembled from pieces.

PMA Space (S; longitudinal marker). The study participant is shown an abstract figure and is asked to identify which of six other drawings represents the model in two-dimensional space. There are 20 test items, with a time limit of 5 minutes.

Object Rotation (OR; Quayhagen, 1979; Schaie, 1985). The study participant is shown a line drawing of a meaningful object (e.g., an umbrella) and is asked to identify which of six other drawings represents the model rotated in two-dimensional space. There are 20 test items, with a time limit of 5 minutes.

Alphanumeric Rotation (AR; Willis & Schaie, 1983). The study participant is shown a letter or number and is asked to identify which of six other drawings represents the model rotated in two-dimensional space. There are 20 test items, with a time limit of 5 minutes.

Test stimuli in the Object and Alphanumeric Rotation tests have the same angle of rotation as the abstract figure in the PMA Space test.

Cube Comparison (CC; Ekstrom et al., 1976). In each item, two drawings of a cube are presented; the study participant is asked to indicate whether the two drawings are of the same cube rotated in three-dimensional space. The Cube Comparison test has two parts, each with 15 items, and a time limit of 3 minutes.

Numeric Facility   Numeric facility is the ability to understand numerical relationships, to work with figures, and to solve simple quantitative problems rapidly and accurately.

PMA Number (N; longitudinal marker). The study participant checks whether additions of simple sums shown are correct or incorrect. The test contains 60 items, with a time limit of 6 minutes.

Addition (AD; Ekstrom et al., 1976). This is a test of speed and accuracy in adding three single or two-digit numbers. The test has two parts, each with 20 items, and a time limit of 3 minutes.

Subtraction and Multiplication (SM; Ekstrom et al., 1976). This is a test of speed and accuracy with alternate rows of simple subtraction and multiplication problems. The test has two parts, each with 20 items, and a time limit of 3 minutes.

Verbal Comprehension   Verbal comprehension is the ability to understand ideas expressed in words. It indicates the range of a person's passive vocabulary used in activities in which information is obtained by reading or listening.

PMA Verbal Meaning (V; longitudinal marker). A four-choice synonym test, this is a highly speeded test with significant loading on Perceptual Speed (Hertzog, 1989; Schaie et al., 1989). The test has 50 items, with a time limit of 4 minutes.

ETS (Educational Testing Service) Vocabulary V-2 (VC; Ekstrom et al.,
1976). A five-choice synonym test, the test has two parts, each with 18
items, and a time limit of 4 minutes.

ETS Vocabulary V-4 (AVC; Ekstrom et al., 1976). A more advanced five-
choice synonym test consisting mainly of difficult items, this test also
has two parts, each with 18 items, and a time limit of 4 minutes. Both
ETS vocabulary tests are virtually unspeeded.

Word Fluency   The word fluency ability is concerned with the verbal recall involved in writing and talking easily. It differs from verbal ability in that it focuses
on the speed and ease with which words are used rather than on the degree of
understanding of verbal concepts.

PMA Word Fluency (W; longitudinal marker). The study participant
recalls as many words as possible according to a lexical rule in a
5-minute period. No additional markers were included for this ability
because it appears to be factorially more complex than suggested by
Thurstone's original work. The test is retained, however, because of the
availability of extensive longitudinal data for this variable. In factor analytic work, it has been shown to load on Verbal Memory and Verbal
Ability (Schaie et al., 1991).

Perceptual Speed   Perceptual speed is the ability to find figures, make comparisons, and carry out other simple tasks involving visual perception with speed and
accuracy.

Identical Pictures (IP; Ekstrom et al., 1976; longitudinal marker beginning
in 1975). The study participant identifies which of five numbered
shapes or pictures in a row is identical to the model at the left of the
row. There are 50 items, with a time limit of 1.5 minutes.

Finding A's (FA; Ekstrom et al., 1976; longitudinal marker beginning in
1975). In each column of 40 words, the study participant must identify
the 5 words containing the letter *a*. There are 50 columns of numbers
and a time limit of 1.5 minutes.

Number Comparison (NC; Ekstrom et al., 1976). The study participant in-
spects pairs of multidigit numbers and indicates whether the two numbers in each pair are the same or different. There are 40 items, with a
time limit of 1.5 minutes.

Verbal Memory   The verbal memory ability involves the memorization and recall
of meaningful language units (Zelinski, Gilewski, & Schaie, 1993).

Immediate Recall (IR). Participants study a list of 20 words for 3.5 minutes. They are then given an equal period of time to recall the words
in any order.

Delayed Recall (DR). Participants are asked to recall the same list of words as in Immediate Recall after an hour of other activities (other psychometric tests).

Composite Indexes   From the original five longitudinal markers, we have consistently derived and reported data on five linear composites. Both indexes were originally suggested by L. L. and T. G. Thurstone (1949). The first is an index of intellectual ability (IQ), a composite measure likely to approximate a conventional deviation IQ, obtained by summing subtest scores weighted approximately inversely to their standard deviation of each test:

$$IQ = V + S + 2R + 2N + W$$

The second composite score is an index of educational aptitude (EQ) suggested by T. G. Thurstone (1958) as the best predictor from the PMA test battery of performance in educational settings:

$$EQ = 2V + R$$

Latent Variables   Following the factor analyses reported in chapter 8, we also report data, beginning with the sixth wave (1984), on six latent variables. These are Inductive Reasoning (PMA Reasoning, ADEPT Letter Series, Word Series, Number Series); Spatial Orientation (PMA Space, Object Rotation, Alphanumeric Rotation, Cube Comparison); Verbal Ability (PMA Verbal Meaning, ETS Vocabulary, ETS Advanced Vocabulary, PMA Word Fluency); Numeric Ability (PMA Number, ETS Addition, ETS Subtraction and Multiplication; ETS Number Comparison); Perceptual Speed (ETS Identical Pictures, ETS Finding A's, ETS Number Comparison, PMA Verbal Meaning); and Verbal Memory (Immediate Recall, Delayed Recall, PMA Word Fluency).

The Neuropsychology Battery

During the 1997–1998 cycle, we also added a 2.5-hour neuropsychology battery that includes the measures recommended by CERAD (Consortium to Establish a Registry for Alzheimer's Disease) as well as several other assessment procedures commonly used by neuropsychologists, as described next.

Mini Mental State Examination (MMSE). This measure is widely used as a screening technique for identifying individuals with possible mental impairment (Crum, Anthony, Bassett, & Folstein, 1993; Folstein, Folstein, & McHugh, 1975; Tombaugh & McIntyre, 1992). This test was included to link with existent literature and to obtain a better understanding of how this screening instrument projects into the domains commonly measured in the assessment of older, normal, community-dwelling populations.

Verbal Fluency Test "Animal Category." The test measures impairment in verbal production, semantic memory, and language (Isaacs & Kennis, 1973).

Modified Boston Naming Test. This measure involves the verbal identification of two-dimensional objects within 20 seconds. If the name is not produced in that time, a semantic cue is given, and after another 20 seconds, a phonemic cue is provided with cueing if the subject has difficulty. It is used clinically to measure impairment of language functions (Kaplan, Goodglass, & Weintraub, 1984; Van Gorp, Satz, Kiersch, & Henry, 1986).

Word List Recall. A free-recall task of newly learned information involving a 10-word list with multiple trials. The test contains a delayed trial. Differences between immediate and delayed trials are thought to be particularly sensitive to early cognitive impairment (Atkinson & Shiffrin, 1971; Cahn et al., 1995).

Constructional Praxis. The test involves four line drawings in increasing complexity. This test measures recognition of the words from the Word List Memory task when presented among 10 distractor words (Rosen, Mohs, & Davis, 1984).

Wechsler Adult Intelligence Scale–Revised (WAIS-R) *short form.* The short form consists of the two most commonly used tests from both Verbal and Performance scales, tests that show early as well as late decline in old age (Ryan, Paolo, & Brugardt, 1990, 1992; Wechsler, 1981):

1. *Vocabulary test.* This vocabulary test is the most commonly used measure of maintained verbal functions in clinical practice and clinically oriented research.
2. *Comprehension test.* A measure of common knowledge that may reflect intactness of logical thought and that should map into the crystallized intelligence space.
3. *Digit symbol substitution test.* Numbers are substituted for abstract symbols. This test is expected to map into the perceptual speed domain.
4. *Block design test.* This is the classical clinical test of spatial visualization and has sometimes been used by neuropsychologists to identify problems in the visuomotor pathways. method.
5. In addition to the short form, we also give the *Digit Span* test. This test requires the reproduction of forward and backward number series of increasing length.

Wechsler Memory Scale–Revised (WMS-R; Cahn et al., 1995; Wechsler, 1981). This one of the oldest clinical instruments for assessing memory impairment. However, we only use Logical memory with immediate and delayed recall because other parts of the WMS overlap with other measures in our battery.

Trail Making Test. This is one of the earliest measures used by neuropsychologists to detect difficulty in attention and cognitive inflexibility (Reitan & Wolfson, 1985). Part A requires tracing a path among a set of numbers. Part B involves tracing a path that requires shifting between numbers and letters.

Fuld Object Memory Test. This is a free-recall measure of objects (Fuld, 1977). Five trials are given and scored for retrieval and rapid verbal retrieval.

Mattis Dementia Rating Scale (MDRS). This is a sensitive index of cognitive functioning in patients with Alzheimer's disease (Mattis, 1989). It yields a total score and five subscale scores (attention, initiation and perseveration, construction, conceptualization, and memory). It provides good discrimination between normal and cognitively impaired groups (Vitaliano, Russo, Breen, Vitello, & Prinz, 1986). The MDRS has also been found sensitive to change as dementia progresses (Kiyak, Teri, & Borson, 1994).

McMaster Problem-Solving Scale. This is a five-item scale that assesses the ability to resolve problems effectively (Epstein, Baldwin, & Bishop, 1983; Epstein, Bishop, Ryan, Miller, & Keitner, 1993). The scale is used to assess how problem-solving strategies change over time in relation to physical, cognitive, and interpersonal changes.

Quality-of-Life Scale (QOL-AD). This scale was developed to assess subjectively perceived quality of life of adults (Logsdon, Gibbons, McCurry, & Teri, 1999). It includes assessments of the individual's relationships with friends and family, concerns about finances, physical condition, mood, and an overall assessment of life quality.

Activities of Daily Living. Self-reported measures of performance capability on activities of daily living (ADLs) and instrumental activities of daily living (IADLs; Lawton & Brody, 1969) are also given. These measures are conventionally given to have subjects rate their ability to engage in common daily activities without help, with different levels of help, or not at all (cf. description of the Everyday Problems Test, an objective test of IADL performance).

Memory Function Questionnaire (MFQ). This is a measure of metamemory that permits subjective report of perceived memory problems in different content areas (Gilewski & Zelinski, 1988).

Measures of Self-Reported Cognitive Change

The *PMA Retrospective Questionnaire* (PMARQ; first used in 1984) is given immediately after the five basic longitudinal marker tests have been administered. Participants are asked to rate whether they think their performance at the current testing session was the same, better, or worse than when they took the tests 7 years earlier. Data collected with this questionnaire showed only a modest correlation between participants' estimate of change and magnitude of actual change in 1984 and in 1991 (Roth, 2001; Schaie, Willis, & O'Hanlon, 1994). The major function of this questionnaire, therefore, is to provide semiprojective data on the participants' perception of changes in their abilities over time. The PMARQ is also used in the posttest phase of our training studies to obtain the participants' rating of experienced training gain.

Measures of Everyday Problem Solving

The *Basic Skills Assessment* test developed at the Educational Testing Service (1977) contains 65 items that simulate real-life tasks. Examples of such tasks included in the test involve reading a bus schedule, identifying locations on a road map, interpreting a medicine bottle label, finding information in the yellow pages of the telephone book, and so on. In addition to a total score, this test can also be scored for four factor scales identified in an item factor analysis. This test was administered during the 1984 and 1991 testing waves. The factor scales have been named (a) inferences from text, (b) facts from text, (c) commercial information, and (d) directions and charts.

The *Everyday Problems Test* (Willis, 1992b) is a more structured test that was developed to map on the IADLs. It includes 21 sets of stimuli that involve printed materials obtained from real-life documents, charts, and labels presented without a time limit. Two multiple-choice questions are asked with respect to each stimulus. In addition to the total score, there are 7 six-item subscales assessing everyday competence on the dimensions of medication use, shopping, telephone use, financial matters, household activities, meal preparation, and transportation.

Measures of Cognitive Style

The *Test of Behavioral Rigidity* (TBR; Schaie, 1955, 1960; Schaie & Parham, 1975) contains the following three subtests:

> *Capitals Test*. This test was adapted from Bernstein's (1924) study of quickness and intelligence and represents the Spearmanian or "functional" approach to the study of perseveration and rigidity. Participants copy a printed paragraph that contains some words starting with capital letters, others spelled entirely in capitals, and some starting with lowercase letters and with the remaining letters in capitals. In the second half of the test, participants recopy the paragraph, substituting capitals for lowercase letters and lowercase letters for capitals. The time allowed for each half of the test is 2.5 minutes. This test yields two scores: *copying speed* (Cap), the number of words correctly copied in the first half of the test, and *instructional set flexibility* (Cap-R). The latter score represents the ratio (rounded to integers) of the number of correctly copied words in the second series to those in the first series.
>
> *Opposites Test*. In this newly constructed test, following the work of Scheier and Ferguson (1952), three lists of simple words must be responded to by first giving antonyms, then synonyms, and finally antonyms or synonyms, depending on whether the stimulus word is printed in upper- or lowercase letters. Each list has 40 stimulus words and a time limit of 2 minutes. The test yields three scores: an *associational speed* (Opp) score, which is the sum of correct responses in the first two lists, and two *associational flexibility* scores. For this purpose, List 3 is examined for responses that are incorrect, responses started incorrectly, and erasures. The first score (Opp-R1) is obtained by the formula

$$100 - \frac{\text{Series 3 Errors}}{\text{Series 3 Total}} \times 100$$

The second score (Opp-R2) involves the formula

$$\frac{\text{Series 3 Correct}}{(1/2\ [\text{Series 1 Correct} + \text{Series 2 Correct}])} \times 100$$

TBR Questionnaire. The 75 true-or-false items include 22 modified flexibil-ity-rigidity items (R scale) and 44 masking Social Responsibility items from the California Psychological Inventory (Gough, 1957; Gough, Mc-Closkey, & Meehl, 1952; Schaie, 1959b). Also included are 9 items (P scale) constructed by Guttman scaling of a perseverative behavior scale first used by Lankes (1915). The TBR yields factor scores for the latent dimensions of Psychomotor Speed, Motor-Cognitive Flexibility, and At-titudinal Flexibility. It also yields several personality trait scores (dis-cussed in a separate section). The three factor scores are obtained by multiplying the standardized factor scores for the eight observed scores from the TBR subtests as follows:

$$\text{MCF} = .25 \text{ Cap-R} + .35 \text{ Opp-R1} + .40 \text{ Opp-R2}$$

$$\text{AF} = .50 \text{ R scale} + .50 \text{ P scale}$$

$$\text{PS} = .60 \text{ Cap} + .40 \text{ Opp}$$

For comparison across measures, all psychometric tests were standardized to *T* scores with a mean of 50 and a standard deviation of 10 based on all data col-lected at first test.

Descriptions of Lifestyles and Demographic Characteristics

The *Life Complexity Inventory* (LCI; Gribbin et al., 1980) provides information on participants' demographic characteristics, activity patterns, work characteristics, continuing educational pursuits, and living arrangements. The LCI was initially administered by interviewers and then converted into a mail survey in 1974 and has been administered routinely (as a take-home task) since the fourth SLS cycle. Early analyses were based on the identification of eight item clusters in early work for use in relating the LCI to the cognitive variables. These are:

1. Subjective dissatisfaction with life status
2. Social status
3. Noisy environment
4. Family dissolution
5. Disengagement from interaction with the environment
6. Semipassive engagement with the environment
7. Maintenance of acculturation
8. Female homemaker characteristics

Current scoring approaches are guided by results of a more recent factor anal-ysis (O'Hanlon, 1993). The factors used in the more recent analyses represent the following eight constructs:

1. Social prestige
2. Demographic status
3. Leisure activities

4. Physical environment
5. Mobility characteristics
6. Intellectual environment
7. Social network
8. Work environment

The leisure activities have also been factored and are scored as proportion of activity devoted to the following six types of activities:

1. Fitness activities
2. Educational activities
3. Social activities
4. Communicative activities
5. Solitary activities
6. Household chores

Descriptions of Health Status

Health History Abstracts   Health history data for the longitudinal study participants were obtained from time of entry into the study through 1998 for all participants remaining in the study and for those who dropped out for the 7 years following their last assessment or until their death if the latter occurred earlier.

Health history data consist of the number of annual physician visits or hospital days by diagnosis (coded according to the *International Classification of Diseases*, ICDA, eighth edition, until 1984 and the ninth edition thereafter). In addition, the number of continuous illness episodes per year are also coded. Health histories were physically abstracted by medical librarians until 1991. Data thereafter come from the computerized HMO records.

Medication Reports   Beginning with the sixth (1991) cycle, medication data have been collected by a brown bag procedure in which participants bring their current medications to the testing site, where the medication identifiers are recorded. Diseases for the treatment of which these medications are prescribed are identified using the procedure advocated by the American Society of Hospital Pharmacists (1985). In addition, we were able to obtain complete computerized pharmacy records for the 4-month window preceding the actual testing date for all participants in the seventh (1998) cycle.

Identification of Relatives With Dementia   Beginning with the sixth cycle, we asked all participants to list blood relatives who they thought had been diagnosed as suffering from disease of the Alzheimer's type. Information was also sought on whether such relatives were still living and, if dead, their age at death.

Blood Samples   Since 1998, we have been able to obtain blood samples from most participants over age 60 within a 1-month window of the psychological assessment. Data obtained from the blood samples consist of Apolipoprotein E genotypes and a lipid profile. Blood cells have been cryopreserved for potential future genetic analyses. Beginning with the current family study cycles, genotyping will be extended over all study participants.

Health Behavior Questionnaire   An 85-item HBQ covering preventive health behaviors and health practices was developed and first administered to participants in the sixth cycle and the first family study in 1993. The questionnaire continues to be administered in all subsequent data collections. The HBQ has been factored and represents the following eight clusters of health behavior:

1. Not smoking
2. Alcohol abstention
3. Avoiding unhealthy food
4. Healthy food preparation
5. Exercise
6. Wearing seat belts
7. Dental care
8. Medical checkups

There is also a two-factor measure of subjectively reported health status: Self-Reported Objective Health Status and Positive Health Perception.

Descriptions of the Subjective Environment

The descriptions of the subjective environment data have been collected in the longitudinal study since the sixth (1991) cycle as well as in all family studies.

Family Environment   The eight scales of the *Family Environment Scale* (Moos & Moos, 1986) were abbreviated to five items for each scale, and the individual items were converted into 5-point Likert scales. Items were edited to be suitable for inclusion in two versions of the instrument: (a) a form suitable for describing the perceived environment in the family of origin; (b) a form suitable for describing the perceived environment in the current family. For the latter, two versions were prepared, one suitable for individuals living in multimember family settings and one for individuals currently living by themselves. For purposes of the latter form, *family* was defined as those individuals who the respondent felt were close to him or her and with whom a personal interaction occurred at least once every week.

The eight family environment scales are thought to assess the following dimensions:

Cohesion (relationship). Example: "Family members really help one another."
Expressivity (relationship). Example: "We tell each other about our personal problems."

Conflict (relationship). Example: "Family members hardly ever lose their temper."

Achievement Orientation (personal growth). Example: "We feel it is important to be the best at whatever we do."

Intellectual-Cultural Orientation (personal growth). Example: "We often talk about political and social problems."

Active-Recreational Orientation (personal growth). Example: "Friends often come over for dinner or to visit."

Organization (system maintenance). Example: "We are generally very neat and orderly."

Control (system maintenance). Example: "There are set ways of doing things at home."

Work Environment   In a manner similar to the family environment scales, three scales of the Work Environment Inventory (Moos, 1981) were also abbreviated to five items and converted to 5-point Likert scales. The content attributed to these dimensions is as follows:

Autonomy. The extent to which employees are encouraged to be self-sufficient and make their own decisions. Example: "You have a great deal of freedom to do as you like in your workplace."

Control. The extent to which management uses rules and pressure to keep employees under control. Example: "You are expected to follow set rules in doing your work."

Innovation. The degree of emphasis on variety, change, and new approaches. Example: "You are encouraged to do your work in different ways."

Family Contact   A seven-item (6-point Likert scale) form assesses the degree of actual contact between family members. Items inquire about the number of years family members have lived in the same household and the frequency of current personal contact, telephone contact, written contact, and contact through other informants.

Personality Traits and Attitudes

Social Responsibility   The TBR questionnaire was designed to include 44 masking items derived from the Social Responsibility scale of the California Psychological Inventory (CPI; Gough, 1957; Gough et al., 1952; Schaie, 1959b). The scale is of interest because it has allowed us to chronicle attitudinal shifts toward society over time (Schaie & Parham, 1974) as well as attitudinal differences within families (Schaie et al., 1992).

Derived Traits   A factor analysis of the 75 items contained in the TBR questionnaires collected during the first three study cycles resulted in the identification of 19 personality factors, several of which could be matched in content to at least one of the poles of Cattell et al.'s 16-PF scale (Schaie & Parham, 1976). More recently, we have replicated 13 of these factors for the entire database through the fifth SLS cycle (Maitland, Dutta, Schaie, & Willis, 1992; Willis, Schaie, & Maitland, 1992; see also chapter 12).

The Center for Epidemologic Studies–Depression Scale   The Center for Epidemologic Studies–Depression Scale (CES-D) is a brief 20-item scale originally designed for epidemiological studies (Radloff, 1977; Radloff & Teri, 1986). The scale has been useful in work with older persons. Since 1997, we have used this scale as part of the neuropsychological battery administered to participants older than 60 years. Inclusion of a clinical interview such as the Hamilton Depression Scale did not seem logistically feasible, hence selection of a brief self-report scale such as the CES-D.

The NEO Personality Questionnaire (Form PI-R)   The 240-item NEO Personality Questionnaire (Form PI-R), representing the big five personality factors (Costa & McCrae, 1992), was administered by mail to individuals participating in the 1996–1997 family study and in the 1998 longitudinal cycle. The questionnaire measures the personality factors of neuroticism (N), extroversion (E), openness to experience (O), agreeableness (A), and conscientiousness (C). Each of these factors is defined by a number of more specific traits or facets.

Chapter Summary

This chapter describes the database for the SLS. The participant population for this study consists of random samples drawn at seven 7-year intervals over a 42-year period from a large HMO, as well as adult children, siblings, and grandchildren of many of the panel participants. The sociodemographic characteristics of these samples are quite representative of the upper 75% of the Seattle metropolitan area, although underrepresenting minorities during the early phases of the study.

The central measures included in the study are theoretically based on Thurstone's primary mental abilities, sampling the ability domains of Inductive Reasoning, Spatial Orientation, Perceptual Speed, Verbal Ability, Numeric Ability, and Verbal Memory. Since 1997, we have also administered an extensive neuropsychological test battery to study participants over 60 years of age. The cognitive assessment battery is supplemented by measures of cognitive style, lifestyle characteristics, measures of everyday cognition (practical intelligence), personality questionnaires, and rating scales measuring perceptions of health behaviors, family and work environments, and cognitive change. Abstracts of health and medication histories as well as blood samples used for Apolipoprotein E genotyping and the determination of lipid profiles have also been collected.

CHAPTER FOUR

Cross-Sectional Studies

T HIS CHAPTER BEGINS WITH A DESCRIPTION of the pilot studies that led to the selection and validation of the measures used in our research program. I then present the 1956 baseline study and compare its findings with the six cross-sectional replications. For purposes of an orderly presentation, I begin with the analyses of the basic cognitive battery that is common to all study cycles. I then present data for the fifth, sixth, and seventh cycles for the extended cognitive battery and the practical intelligence measures. Finally, I consider the cross-sectional findings for the measures of cognitive style (Test of Behavioral Rigidity, TBR).

The Pilot Studies

Our inquiry began by questioning whether factorially defined measures of intellectual abilities would show differential age patterns. Before this question could be examined parametrically, it was necessary to examine the applicability of the Primary Mental Abilities (PMA) test to an older population, with respect to both its level of difficulty and whether the low correlations among abilities observed in childhood would continue to prevail for adults. Two pilot studies concerned with these questions are described in this section. In addition, our interest in cognitive style as a concomitant of intellectual aging required the development of a set of psychometrically sound measurement instruments for the multiple dimensions of rigidity-flexibility. A third pilot study was concerned with demonstrating the construct validity of the resultant measure (the TBR).

Study 1: Suitability of the Primary Mental Abilities Tests for Adults

Sixty-one study participants, gathered from the geriatric practice of a family physician and from the membership of the small first cohort of the San Francisco

Senior Citizen Center, were given the PMA tests under standard conditions. For purposes of analysis, participants were arbitrarily divided into four approximately equal groups: ages 53 to 58, 59 to 64, 65 to 70, and 71 to 78. In the absence of adult norms and to permit comparison across the five abilities measured by the test, raw scores were converted into percentiles employing norms for 17-year-old adolescents (L. L. Thurstone & Thurstone, 1949). Thus, for example, if our participants, on average, were at the 50th percentile, this would imply that their level of functioning would be similar to that of 17-year-olds.

The results of this study are shown in figure 4.1. For the group in their 50s, stability is suggested for Verbal Meaning and Number (performance is slightly above the adolescents' 50th percentile), but performance appears to be substantially lower for the other three tests. Indeed, it was lowest for Spatial Orientation and Inductive Reasoning, measures of the kind of ability later to be termed *fluid* by Cattell (1963). The differential pattern was observed for all age groups, with some further lowering of scores into the 60s and apparent maintenance of the lower level for the group in their 70s (Schaie et al., 1953).

On the off chance that the differential pattern might be caused by unequal effects of the slightly speeded instructions for the performance of older individuals, four of the tests were administered to 31 participants without a time limit. Results shown in figure 4.2 indicate that, if anything, differential performance levels were greater and in the same order as under the standard conditions of instruction.

The first pilot study also investigated the construct validity of the PMA 11–17 when used with older individuals. Intercorrelations between the tests were computed and were quite low, ranging from .07 for the correlation between Spatial Orientation and Number to .31 for the correlation between Spatial Orientation

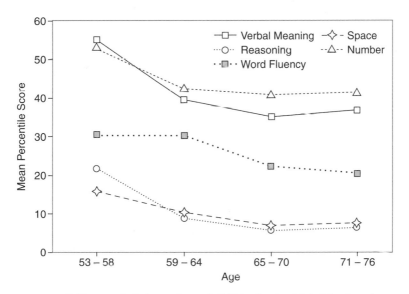

FIGURE 4.1 *Age Differences in Primary Mental Abilities for the Adult Pilot Sample.*

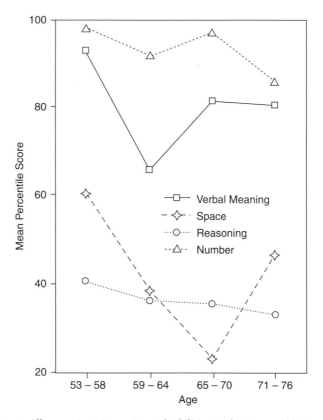

FIGURE 4.2 *Age Differences in Primary Mental Abilities Under Unspeeded Conditions of Test Administration.*

and Inductive Reasoning. These correlations did not differ significantly from those obtained for an adolescent comparison group (Schaie, 1958d). Split-half reliabilities computed under the power test condition were also quite satisfactory, with all above .92 after Spearman-Brown correction.

Study 2: Suitability of the Primary Mental Abilities Tests for Older Adults

A second pilot study was conducted in 1954 as part of an investigation of community-dwelling older persons (more completely described in Schaie & Strother, 1968a, 1968d). A campus and community appeal resulted in the selection of 25 men and 25 women, all college graduates with professional careers, ranging in age from 70 to 88 years (mean age 76.5 years). These study participants were all in fair-to-superior health and free of diagnosable psychiatric symptoms. The differential ability pattern shown in the first pilot study was replicated, with performance on Number, Word Fluency, and Verbal Meaning substantially above that observed for Spatial Orientation and Inductive Reasoning. Also noteworthy was the finding that some of the octogenarians in this study still equaled or exceeded the adolescent mean on some of the verbal tests, even though it was most likely that this performance represented a decrement from previously higher levels, suggested by the unusually advantaged demographic characteristics of this sample. In this study, findings also indicated sex differences in favor of the males for the Spatial Orientation and Number abilities and in favor of the females for Verbal Meaning, Inductive Reasoning, and Word Fluency (Strother et al., 1957).

Study 3: Construct Validity of the Test
of Behavioral Rigidity

The third pilot study was concerned with demonstrating the construct validity of a set of measures defining the multiple dimensions of rigidity-flexibility. This study began as my master's thesis (Schaie, 1953), in which I factor-analyzed a number of tests representing the functional, structural, and attitudinal approaches to the study of rigidity-flexibility (see Chown, 1959). Although use of an unorthodox method of rotation (Horst, 1956b) made the result of the initial analysis somewhat tenuous, it provided the basis for selecting the variables to be included in the more definitive construct validation study (Schaie, 1955). Because I intended to use the final battery for studies of aging, only those tests were included that could be adapted for use with both adult and elderly populations. For practical reasons, only tests suitable for group administration were retained, and those tests were selected that were minimally influenced by social status and education in the initial study.

The measures included in the construct validity study, for what eventually became the TBR (Schaie & Parham, 1975), are described in the section that discusses measures of cognitive style in chapter 3. Not described there are the *Jar test* (Luchins, 1942) and the *Alphabet test* (Bernstein, 1924), which were subsequently dropped from the final battery. The Jar test involves participants correctly identifying the use of jars of different sizes in measuring a given quantity of water, with different methods of solution appropriate at various times. The so-called Einstellung effect is tested by first conditioning the participant to employ a complex method of solution. Critical problems are then presented for which a more direct solution is available. The rigidity measure then becomes the number of problems unnecessarily solved in the more complex manner. The Alphabet test involves the letter combinations *abcde* and *lmnopq* first written forward and then backward.

The validation sample consisted of 216 participants who were drawn from day and evening classes at the University of Washington (Seattle), from a social club for older people, from the membership of a liberal church, from a Rotary club, and from a group of YMCA members. The sample ranged in age from 17 to 79 years, with a mean age of 38 years. Educational level ranged from 4 to 20 years, with a mean of 14.2 years. The participants' occupational levels averaged 6.3 on a 10-point scale from unskilled to professional. For purposes of cross-validation, a second sample of 200 participants was drawn from a restricted population of college students between the ages of 19 and 26 years, with a mean age of 21.4 years.

The correlation matrix for the first sample was factored using a simplification of Thurstone's multiple group method (Horst, 1956a; L. L. Thurstone, 1947, pp. 170 ff.). Note that this approach is an early forerunner of modern confirmatory factor analysis. The first hypothesis specified the existence of a single rigidity factor and a motor speed factor. This hypothesis had to be rejected, and instead a three-factor combination emerged that, on appropriate oblique rotation (Horst & Schaie, 1956), yielded an acceptable simple structure solution (see table 4.1).

Factor I was originally named Motor-Cognitive Speed (the current term is Psychomotor Speed [PS]), Factor II was identified as Personality-Perceptual Rigidity (now called Attitudinal Flexibility [AF]), and Factor III was thought to be a representation of Motor-Cognitive Rigidity (now called Motor-Cognitive Flexibility [MCF]). These factors were next cross-validated by factoring the correlation matrix for the second sample and rotating it to the same factor pattern. As indicated by table 4.1, the resulting pattern replicates that obtained for the original sample. The major difference between results from the two samples can be seen in the factor intercorrelations. All three factors are moderately correlated in the heterogeneous sample, whereas the factor correlations are quite small in the homogeneous sample of college students.

TABLE 4.1 Factor Loadings and Factor Intercorrelations After Oblique Rotation

| | Factor Pattern | | | | | |
| | PS | | AF | | MCF | |
Tests	S1	S2	S1	S2	S1	S2
Capitals–NR	.66	.74	−.02	.03	−.12	−.06
Alphabet–NR	.66	.68	−.03	−.02	−.03	−.06
Opposites–NR	.46	.49	.09	−.01	.14	.09
Water Jar test	.00	.00	.31	.28	−.05	.05
P Scale	.00	−.09	.50	.57	.07	.01
R Scale	.05	.09	.56	.58	−.01	.04
Opposites–R1	.05	.04	.00	−.02	.55	.69
Opposites–R2	.05	.03	−.10	−.02	.64	.64
Capitals–R	−.04	−.09	.07	.02	.39	.25
Alphabet–R	−.07	−.01	.03	.10	.25	.30

Factor Intercorrelations

I. Motor-Cognitive Speed			.427	−.049	.508	.075
II. Attitudinal Flexibility					.422	.148
III. Motor-Cognitive Flexibility						

Note. AF, Attitudinal Flexibility; MCF, Motor-Cognitive Flexibility; PS, Psychomotor Speed; S1, Sample 1; S2, Sample 2.

As a result of this study, we decided to retain the four subtests (Capitals, Opposites, R scale, P scale) that provided the best factor definition for inclusion in the final version of the TBR used throughout the SLS.

The 1956 Baseline Study

In our effort to determine the pattern of age differences, we sampled 500 individuals from our health maintenance organization population frame distributed evenly by gender and 5-year age interval from 21 to 70. For ease of comparison, we standardized all variables across the entire sample to T-score format ($M = 50$, $SD = 10$). We have followed this procedure throughout, always restandardizing on the basis of the largest total sample of individuals' scores at first test (entry into the study). Age difference findings from the baseline study are shown in figure 4.3.

What is most noteworthy about the baseline study is that, although negative age differences are found on all five abilities, peak ability ages occur generally later than had been observed in the previous literature (see Jones & Conrad, 1933; Wechsler, 1939), and that the differential ability patterns noted in our first pilot study could be confirmed in this reasonably representative and age-continuous investigation.

More specifically, we noted that peak levels of the abilities were reached for Reasoning by the 21- to 28-year-old group, for Space, Verbal Meaning, and Word Fluency by the 29- to 33-year-olds, but for Number only at ages 43–49. Similarly,

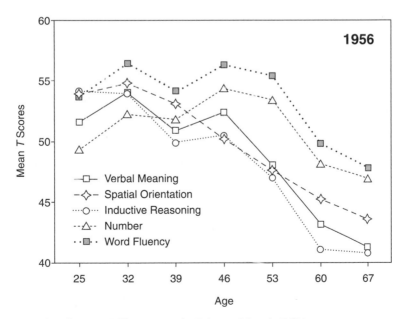

FIGURE 4.3 *Baseline Age Differences on the Primary Mental Abilities.*

there are differences among abilities for the first occurrence of a significant age difference from performance at the peak age. Such significantly lower average performance levels were observed for Verbal Meaning, Space, Reasoning, and Word Fluency with respect to the 36- to 42-year-olds, but for Number only for the 50- to 56-year-olds. Differences were found also in the absolute magnitude of the age difference between the group at peak age and the oldest observed group (ages 66–70). This difference amounted to 1.5 SD for Verbal Meaning, Space, and Reasoning, but slightly less than 1 SD for Number and Word Fluency. The absolute differences between the youngest and oldest age groups was greatest for Reasoning (1.5 SD), next largest for Space and Verbal Meaning (1.2 and 1 SD, respectively), and smallest for Word Fluency and Number (0.6 and 0.2 SD, respectively). These differences could be interpreted as of substantial magnitude for Reasoning, Space, and Verbal Meaning; moderate for Word Fluency; and near trivial for Number.

Cross-Sectional Replications

This section begins with the basic cognitive data collected throughout the study. I then turn to the expanded battery and consider the age difference patterns within ability domains as well as the age difference patterns in the factor scores for the latent ability constructs. Finally, cross-sectional results are provided for the measure of practical intelligence and the measures of cognitive style.

Basic Cognitive Data

Given the 7-year interval between our data cycles, all data were reorganized into 7-year age intervals. Thus, the baseline study for purposes of comparison with the subsequent replications contains seven age groups, with mean ages from 25 to 67 years. In the second cross-sectional sample (1963, $N = 998$), we included eight age groups, with mean ages from 25 to 74 years. The third sample (1970, $N = 705$) and the remaining three cross-sectional samples (1977, $N = 609$; 1984, $N = 629$; 1991, $N = 691$; and 1998, $N = 719$) include nine age groups, with mean ages from 25 to 81 years.

Again, for ease of comparison, all raw scores were converted to T scores with means of 50 and standard deviations of 10 based on the entire set of 4,851 observations at first test.

Differential Ability Patterns   Mean scores by age and gender for the five PMA subtests and the two composite measures of Intellectual Ability and Educational Aptitude are presented in table 4.2. For a more dramatic presentation of differences across abilities in age difference pattern, we graphed mean values by gender for the first (1956) and last (1998) cross-sectional comparisons (see figure 4.4).

Age difference patterns for males have remained relatively constant over the course of the study, with the exception that peak ages for Verbal Meaning and Number shift to age 60 and Word Fluency shifts to the late 30s. For the female

TABLE 4.2 Means and Standard Deviations for the Basic Ability Battery by Sample and Gender

	Age								
	25	32	39	46	53	60	67	74	81
Verbal Meaning									
1956									
Male	50.68	52.55	51.28	49.54	48.29	41.11	41.89	—	—
	(9.46)	(9.50)	(10.23)	(10.11)	(10.01)	(9.74)	(8.46)	—	—
Female	52.50	55.27	50.43	55.73	47.71	45.16	40.68	—	—
	(7.35)	(7.15)	(10.87)	(7.45)	(9.01)	(8.74)	(87.31)	—	—
Total	51.59	53.99	50.86	52.40	48.00	43.19	41.29	—	—
	(8.47)	(8.39)	(10.48)	(9.44)	(9.46)	(9.40)	(8.36)	—	—
1963									
Male	51.43	52.29	53.92	49.65	46.05	43.74	39.92	38.03	—
	(8.63)	(8.64)	(8.03)	(9.30)	(10.25)	(9.54)	(9.37)	(9.53)	—
Female	52.98	53.63	52.58	51.79	48.12	47.45	42.75	38.60	—
	(8.48)	(7.79)	(7.68)	(8.56)	(9.51)	(10.44)	(8.86)	(9.14)	—
Total	52.33	53.06	53.21	50.70	47.22	45.69	41.32	38.32	—
	(8.54)	(8.16)	(7.85)	(8.98)	(9.86)	(10.16)	(9.19)	(9.28)	—
1970									
Male	51.81	51.39	53.15	53.51	54.48	53.18	42.86	37.04	35.73
	(8.27)	(9.15)	(7.64)	(8.14)	(7.41)	(9.68)	(7.67)	(7.57)	(8.67)
Female	53.72	53.93	52.90	54.33	52.67	49.57	45.10	40.27	36.96
	(7.84)	(8.31)	(7.76)	(8.21)	(7.54)	(8.45)	(8.73)	(5.87)	(7.88)
Total	52.89	52.83	53.00	53.92	53.48	51.29	44.07	38.55	36.32
	(8.03)	(8.71)	(7.66)	(8.14)	(7.49)	(9.18)	(8.29)	(6.98)	(8.24)
1977									
Male	53.07	54.31	53.11	52.59	52.90	49.91	43.91	38.22	34.32
	(7.73)	(7.17)	(10.01)	(9.33)	(9.79)	(10.20)	(8.98)	(9.17)	(7.05)
Female	54.21	56.12	54.97	50.49	40.78	49.37	46.55	41.00	34.19
	(9.84)	(7.02)	(8.06)	(10.40)	(9.97)	(9.17)	(8.95)	(10.33)	(6.99)
Total	53.64	55.27	54.03	51.46	51.88	49.63	45.29	39.53	34.25
	(8.78)	(7.09)	(9.08)	(9.90)	(9.87)	(9.61)	(9.00)	(9.76)	(6.96)
1984									
Male	53.29	55.37	56.13	55.50	52.27	51.08	46.55	41.72	39.92
	(8.25)	(6.14)	(6.52)	(6.37)	(8.17)	(8.33)	(8.81)	(6.80)	(9.39)
Female	55.11	52.61	55.82	57.15	55.43	51.86	48.43	44.69	38.78
	(7.40)	(8.59)	(6.57)	(6.17)	(6.69)	(7.88)	(8.38)	(8.35)	(7.91)
Total	54.50	53.96	53.96	56.49	53.85	51.51	47.51	43.15	39.33
	(7.70)	(7.56)	(6.50)	(6.26)	(7.58)	(8.05)	(8.59)	(7.68)	(8.59)
1991									
Male	51.89	55.32	56.97	56.03	54.05	53.16	49.40	47.15	39.17
	(8.14)	(6.72)	(6.41)	(6.27)	(7.46)	(8.69)	(9.07)	(8.58)	(7.59)
Female	54.27	52.78	57.10	56.49	57.08	51.83	52.60	47.77	41.94
	(6.87)	(8.62)	(6.06)	(6.66)	(6.68)	(8.26)	(8.51)	(9.35)	(10.02)
Total	53.20	53.88	57.04	56.30	55.60	52.41	51.22	47.46	40.54
	(7.50)	(7.91)	(6.19)	(6.47)	(7.19)	(8.49)	(8.85)	(8.93)	(8.91)

(*continued*)

TABLE 4.2 Continued

					Age				
	25	32	39	46	53	60	67	74	81
1998									
Male	53.56	54.26	55.23	54.19	54.74	55.43	51.67	47.88	45.47
	(6.29)	(6.90)	(6.66)	(8.03)	(8.85)	(7.09)	(8.21)	(8.47)	(7.48)
Female	52.92	53.56	52.79	55.81	55.36	52.73	51.54	49.29	44.33
	(6.93)	(7.65)	(8.01)	(7.33)	(6.86)	(8.44)	(6.95)	(8.71)	(8.31)
Total	53.17	53.94	53.89	55.01	55.08	54.21	51.62	48.66	44.90
	(6.61)	(7.21)	(7.50)	(7.70)	(7.81)	(7.79)	(7.73)	(8.56)	(8.03)
Spatial Orientation									
1956									
Male	56.87	56.18	54.39	52.37	49.63	47.97	45.92	—	—
	(9.54)	(10.29)	(6.84)	(8.12)	(9.50)	(9.82)	(7.78)	—	—
Female	50.97	53.49	49.74	47.67	45.60	42.49	41.34	—	—
	(9.65)	(7.84)	(7.91)	(10.48)	(7.02)	(8.21)	(6.15)	—	—
Total	53.92	54.76	52.10	50.20	47.61	45.15	43.63	—	—
	(9.99)	(9.11)	(7.70)	(9.51)	(8.54)	(9.38)	(7.34)	—	—
1963									
Male	58.95	56.48	56.39	54.01	50.87	49.05	45.16	42.97	—
	(8.41)	(7.90)	(7.84)	(8.50)	(7.21)	(8.55)	(7.85)	(6.46)	—
Female	56.19	52.50	50.06	48.58	46.84	45.19	41.51	39.85	—
	(9.12)	(8.11)	(7.78)	(8.26)	(8.66)	(7.68)	(6.34)	(5.38)	—
Total	57.35	54.20	53.06	51.35	48.59	47.02	43.35	41.37	—
	(8.89)	(8.23)	(8.40)	(8.79)	(8.28)	(8.30)	(7.34)	(6.10)	—
1970									
Male	60.97	59.75	57.21	56.19	52.98	51.79	46.74	42.47	42.62
	(10.87)	(6.66)	(9.38)	(8.25)	(8.29)	(8.68)	(5.96)	(7.98)	(6.34)
Female	55.38	55.27	50.76	51.67	48.76	46.95	41.00	39.80	37.42
	(10.30)	(9.68)	(8.99)	(8.96)	(8.12)	(6.43)	(7.12)	(5.93)	(5.95)
Total	57.82	57.20	53.37	53.93	50.65	49.25	43.65	41.23	40.12
	(10.84)	(8.74)	(9.64)	(8.86)	(8.42)	(7.91)	(7.18)	(7.18)	(6.63)
1977									
Male	58.36	56.17	57.35	54.31	53.68	49.37	47.89	43.46	41.57
	(8.39)	(6.40)	(7.95)	(7.25)	(8.19)	(10.13)	(8.02)	(7.38)	(6.80)
Female	51.75	55.94	52.50	50.84	48.11	45.63	46.89	40.70	36.94
	(7.91)	(7.64)	(7.60)	(8.70)	(8.23)	(8.32)	(8.81)	(7.13)	(6.64)
Total	55.05	56.05	54.96	52.45	51.00	47.42	47.37	42.16	39.14
	(8.74)	(7.03)	(8.10)	(8.19)	(8.62)	(9.36)	(8.40)	(7.34)	(7.06)
1984									
Male	58.57	54.52	56.43	54.00	51.52	51.47	46.02	43.79	41.88
	(11.07)	(8.64)	(9.51)	(10.42)	(8.79)	(8.51)	(8.53)	(7.88)	(6.84)
Female	53.95	53.86	50.45	53.95	48.42	45.58	42.95	40.61	39.30
	(10.04)	(7.33)	(11.59)	(7.83)	(8.06)	(9.84)	(8.89)	(8.72)	(6.90)
Total	55.49	54.18	53.01	53.97	49.97	48.27	44.45	42.24	40.54
	(10.56)	(7.93)	(11.09)	(8.88)	(8.51)	(9.66)	(8.80)	(8.39)	(6.93)

TABLE 4.2 Continued

	Age								
	25	32	39	46	53	60	67	74	81
1991									
Male	60.26	57.26	59.92	56.88	54.84	51.50	49.14	45.95	40.62
	(8.10)	(8.29)	(8.26)	(7.51)	(8.99)	(7.12)	(7.38)	(8.38)	(7.21)
Female	59.45	54.02	53.38	52.10	50.35	47.24	43.76	41.00	38.42
	(8.05)	(8.49)	(8.15)	(9.10)	(9.73)	(6.81)	(8.57)	(7.63)	(8.33)
Total	59.82	55.42	56.61	54.06	52.54	49.11	46.09	43.42	39.54
	(8.01)	(8.50)	(8.79)	(8.76)	(9.59)	(7.22)	(8.47)	(8.34)	(7.80)
1998									
Male	63.50	58.97	57.83	54.06	52.91	53.05	50.20	45.08	44.10
	(8.34)	(7.89)	(7.06)	(8.50)	(8.46)	(7.68)	(8.15)	(8.50)	(6.88)
Female	58.52	54.06	53.78	50.71	50.58	48.88	45.91	42.68	39.53
	(6.56)	(7.80)	(10.88)	(10.24)	(8.98)	(7.33)	(7.68)	(7.25)	(6.39)
Total	60.46	56.73	55.61	52.38	51.66	51.06	48.62	43.75	41.82
	(7.62)	(8.17)	(9.52)	(9.53)	(8.77)	(7.76)	(8.20)	(7.85)	(6.98)

Inductive Reasoning

	25	32	39	46	53	60	67	74	81
1956									
Male	52.79	52.70	48.89	49.74	46.63	39.46	40.84	—	—
	(8.38)	(9.31)	(8.64)	(9.19)	(8.77)	(6.89)	(7.32)	—	—
Female	55.42	55.05	50.97	51.43	47.43	42.68	40.66	—	—
	(9.04)	(8.28)	(9.41)	(8.16)	(10.04)	(7.01)	(7.07)	—	—
Total	54.10	53.94	49.92	50.52	47.03	41.11	40.75	—	—
	(8.76)	(8.79)	(9.03)	(8.70)	(9.37)	(7.09)	(7.15)	—	—
1963									
Male	56.83	53.17	53.18	47.75	44.81	42.17	38.94	40.03	—
	(7.31)	(8.32)	(8.45)	(7.92)	(8.38)	(7.58)	(6.71)	(6.83)	—
Female	58.12	56.27	52.39	50.20	45.64	44.49	39.81	37.00	—
	(7.91)	(6.92)	(7.46)	(9.18)	(8.23)	(9.35)	(6.78)	(4.77)	—
Total	57.58	54.95	52.77	48.95	45.28	43.44	39.37	38.47	—
	(7.65)	(7.68)	(7.93)	(8.62)	(8.27)	(8.61)	(6.73)	(6.02)	—
1970									
Male	59.00	56.61	53.62	52.30	49.20	49.76	40.55	37.68	37.12
	(7.51)	(8.63)	(7.72)	(9.18)	(8.08)	(8.88)	(7.36)	(5.39)	(6.91)
Female	58.58	57.46	52.70	52.70	50.27	47.19	41.53	38.66	37.08
	(7.12)	(7.70)	(7.42)	(8.42)	(8.31)	(7.82)	(7.54)	(5.38)	(4.62)
Total	58.76	57.09	53.07	52.50	49.79	48.41	41.08	38.14	37.10
	(7.24)	(8.06)	(7.51)	(8.76)	(8.18)	(8.39)	(7.43)	(5.38)	(5.86)
1977									
Male	56.00	55.97	55.08	50.72	51.42	47.74	42.77	39.38	36.48
	(8.09)	(6.69)	(8.97)	(8.29)	(8.73)	(8.70)	(6.84)	(5.75)	(4.44)
Female	59.93	57.21	55.97	52.05	49.38	46.66	44.87	39.67	38.32
	(7.73)	(7.42)	(7.07)	(8.41)	(8.39)	(7.74)	(8.68)	(6.57)	(8.08)
Total	57.96	56.63	55.52	51.43	50.44	47.18	43.86	39.51	37.47
	(8.09)	(7.06)	(8.05)	(8.32)	(8.57)	(8.17)	(7.87)	(6.10)	(6.65)

(*continued*)

TABLE 4.2 Continued

					Age				
	25	32	39	46	53	60	67	74	81
1984									
Male	58.64	57.78	56.50	52.81	49.18	49.83	43.59	42.34	38.20
	(6.86)	(7.07)	(7.15)	(6.58)	(8.34)	(7.67)	(7.12)	(6.70)	(6.18)
Female	59.14	57.75	56.98	56.64	54.79	49.93	48.02	44.82	37.22
	(7.60)	(8.13)	(6.01)	(7.58)	(6.69)	(8.48)	(7.51)	(7.96)	(4.84)
Total	58.98	57.76	56.77	55.11	51.98	49.89	45.89	43.51	37.69
	(7.33)	(7.56)	(6.48)	(7.39)	(8.02)	(8.07)	(7.61)	(7.38)	(5.49)
1991									
Male	58.81	58.06	57.69	56.00	52.82	49.53	47.14	44.41	39.55
	(7.47)	(5.70)	(7.56)	(7.89)	(8.11)	(4.82)	(7.40)	(8.46)	(4.88)
Female	61.55	58.46	58.50	58.02	55.28	50.20	50.15	46.44	39.42
	(5.78)	(7.05)	(5.13)	(7.18)	(7.91)	(7.16)	(7.98)	(7.48)	(5.63)
Total	60.32	58.29	58.10	57.19	54.08	49.90	48.85	45.45	39.48
	(6.68)	(6.47)	(6.42)	(7.50)	(8.05)	(6.21)	(7.84)	(7.99)	(5.23)
1998									
Male	63.12	58.74	58.06	54.55	53.81	54.20	48.28	44.60	43.77
	(5.75)	(6.85)	(6.00)	(6.38)	(8.08)	(7.46)	(7.09)	(6.91)	(6.20)
Female	61.36	59.78	57.93	56.78	54.94	51.97	49.11	45.77	42.97
	(4.39)	(6.54)	(6.95)	(7.32)	(7.27)	(6.79)	(6.79)	(6.71)	(5.69)
Total	62.05	59.21	57.99	55.67	54.42	53.19	48.59	45.25	43.37
	(4.97)	(6.68)	(6.51)	(6.93)	(7.63)	(7.21)	(6.96)	(6.76)	(5.91)
Number									
1956									
Male	48.00	53.88	53.17	56.80	53.86	48.34	47.61	—	—
	(8.30)	(10.24)	(10.53)	(8.76)	(9.91)	(8.64)	(9.66)	—	—
Female	50.61	50.78	50.46	51.30	52.97	47.84	46.18	—	—
	(10.27)	(8.67)	(10.46)	(8.48)	(11.65)	(7.51)	(9.46)	—	—
Total	49.30	52.24	51.83	54.26	53.41	48.08	46.89	—	—
	(9.37)	(9.50)	(10.51)	(9.00)	(10.75)	(8.03)	(9.52)	—	—
1963									
Male	51.12	55.88	57.25	53.57	51.60	49.84	47.28	46.82	—
	(8.03)	(12.42)	(10.44)	(10.66)	(10.96)	(13.53)	(10.40)	(9.15)	—
Female	51.48	53.33	52.94	53.70	49.25	49.05	44.51	42.32	—
	(8.38)	(9.46)	(10.21)	(10.38)	(10.87)	(11.09)	(9.73)	(9.62)	—
Total	51.33	54.42	54.98	53.63	50.27	49.43	45.91	44.51	—
	(8.20)	(10.85)	(10.51)	(10.49)	(10.93)	(12.26)	(10.13)	(9.60)	—
1970									
Male	52.97	58.82	54.59	56.47	55.42	56.84	49.14	44.32	43.88
	(9.65)	(14.00)	(10.76)	(9.21)	(12.61)	(10.97)	(8.95)	(8.95)	(9.63)
Female	51.10	50.57	51.88	54.58	54.69	55.07	47.51	44.73	38.12
	(8.63)	(9.28)	(8.59)	(9.93)	(10.90)	(11.81)	(8.01)	(7.92)	(6.17)
Total	51.92	54.12	52.98	55.52	55.02	55.91	48.26	44.51	41.12
	(9.07)	(12.17)	(9.56)	(9.57)	(11.63)	(11.38)	(8.45)	(8.44)	(8.58)

TABLE 4.2 Continued

	Age								
	25	32	39	46	53	60	67	74	81
1977									
Male	49.36	49.69	51.84	49.12	55.02	51.77	50.71	44.89	42.21
	(9.79)	(8.86)	(10.11)	(9.81)	(13.18)	(10.90)	(10.93)	(9.41)	(9.10)
Female	50.14	52.67	51.61	48.14	48.86	50.13	49.95	44.88	42.03
	(9.95)	(8.29)	(8.88)	(9.08)	(8.04)	(10.79)	(10.51)	(10.50)	(8.39)
Total	49.75	51.27	51.72	48.59	52.06	50.92	50.32	44.89	42.12
	(9.79)	(8.62)	(9.46)	(9.37)	(11.38)	(10.80)	(10.64)	(9.87)	(8.66)
1984									
Male	50.50	53.63	48.60	51.92	48.79	52.69	48.42	48.44	44.71
	(9.32)	(10.59)	(7.71)	(6.72)	(11.23)	(9.99)	(9.73)	(8.36)	(6.46)
Female	47.77	48.71	49.95	52.26	50.21	47.77	49.69	46.28	39.11
	(7.84)	(8.06)	(8.47)	(7.86)	(8.95)	(9.43)	(9.48)	(7.70)	(9.09)
Total	48.68	51.13	49.37	52.12	49.50	50.01	49.07	47.40	41.75
	(8.41)	(9.62)	(8.12)	(7.37)	(10.10)	(9.94)	(9.56)	(8.07)	(8.38)
1991									
Male	47.89	49.26	51.44	53.56	52.03	49.22	51.21	48.61	45.06
	(6.77)	(7.91)	(9.72)	(9.50)	(10.01)	(8.11)	(8.03)	(11.58)	(10.76)
Female	48.18	47.39	50.20	50.80	50.28	49.56	49.04	50.07	48.18
	(7.35)	(7.20)	(7.71)	(10.05)	(8.61)	(9.26)	(8.42)	(8.16)	(8.67)
Total	48.05	48.19	50.81	51.93	51.13	49.41	49.98	49.36	46.62
	(7.04)	(7.52)	(8.73)	(9.87)	(9.30)	(8.72)	(8.28)	(9.94)	(9.82)
1998									
Male	52.31	48.18	50.50	49.58	50.35	51.92	48.83	48.24	47.73
	(10.27)	(8.81)	(9.31)	(10.23)	(10.86)	(8.76)	(8.55)	(8.61)	(7.86)
Female	47.96	48.59	48.28	48.03	49.24	47.58	47.80	48.55	44.67
	(7.74)	(6.12)	(6.85)	(8.87)	(6.59)	(8.03)	(6.53)	(8.64)	(9.49)
Total	49.66	48.37	49.28	48.80	49.75	49.96	48.45	48.41	46.20
	(8.95)	(7.65)	(8.09)	(9.56)	(8.79)	(8.66)	(7.84)	(8.55)	(8.77)
Word Fluency									
1956									
Male	53.87	53.76	53.36	54.14	53.57	48.77	48.50	—	—
	(9.57)	(9.92)	(9.04)	(10.63)	(11.30)	(10.96)	(11.18)	—	—
Female	53.53	58.78	54.83	58.87	57.14	50.78	47.03	—	—
	(10.57)	(10.91)	(10.27)	(9.47)	(10.12)	(8.97)	(10.43)	—	—
Total	53.70	56.41	54.08	56.32	55.36	49.81	47.76	—	—
	(10.02)	(10.69)	(9.62)	(10.31)	(10.80)	(9.97)	(10.76)	—	—
1963									
Male	50.86	49.15	52.30	49.42	45.69	46.83	43.94	44.74	—
	(8.32)	(9.11)	(9.00)	(9.65)	(9.50)	(7.59)	(9.42)	(8.17)	—
Female	53.00	54.66	51.10	51.80	48.81	50.80	44.92	44.18	—
	(8.04)	(8.88)	(7.57)	(9.41)	(8.37)	(10.53)	(9.11)	(8.15)	—
Total	52.10	52.31	51.67	50.59	47.46	48.91	44.43	44.45	—
	(8.19)	(9.35)	(8.27)	(9.58)	(8.98)	(9.43)	(9.24)	(8.11)	—

(*continued*)

TABLE 4.2 Continued

	Age								
	25	32	39	46	53	60	67	74	81
1970									
Male	52.36	47.64	48.88	51.40	52.00	50.32	42.38	39.74	41.19
	(8.07)	(9.05)	(8.08)	(8.78)	(10.40)	(10.04)	(8.49)	(8.12)	(9.73)
Female	53.78	52.73	51.00	53.51	53.23	50.10	45.20	43.15	43.54
	(8.18)	(9.26)	(9.06)	(7.14)	(6.86)	(6.50)	(9.00)	(8.17)	(7.08)
Total	53.11	50.54	50.14	52.45	52.62	50.20	43.90	41.33	42.32
	(8.11)	(9.45)	(8.69)	(8.03)	(8.59)	(8.32)	(8.84)	(8.28)	(8.56)
1977									
Male	53.21	53.03	50.03	48.84	51.55	48.83	46.37	40.43	38.46
	(8.36)	(8.26)	(8.55)	(9.85)	(11.48)	(8.01)	(8.60)	(7.98)	(6.86)
Female	53.32	55.88	53.61	49.84	49.70	50.84	48.47	45.64	44.45
	(10.99)	(6.97)	(8.02)	(8.38)	(8.70)	(9.28)	(7.34)	(9.87)	(8.66)
Total	53.27	54.55	51.79	49.38	50.66	49.88	47.47	42.89	41.61
	(9.68)	(7.67)	(8.43)	(9.04)	(10.22)	(8.70)	(7.99)	(9.23)	(8.35)
1984									
Male	56.00	56.07	55.00	51.27	51.21	46.80	44.78	44.08	39.50
	(13.79)	(6.93)	(10.26)	(9.92)	(10.05)	(7.05)	(9.22)	(8.43)	(7.35)
Female	54.33	53.29	54.08	54.59	52.42	48.60	48.67	45.11	42.41
	(9.41)	(10.39)	(9.24)	(10.29)	(8.83)	(10.91)	(8.93)	(8.79)	(7.13)
Total	54.89	54.65	54.47	53.26	51.82	47.79	46.78	44.57	41.04
	(11.01)	(8.89)	(9.63)	(10.20)	(9.41)	(9.37)	(9.23)	(8.56)	(7.31)
1991									
Male	55.41	53.81	55.03	51.03	49.76	50.44	47.07	45.71	42.15
	(9.43)	(9.03)	(9.99)	(8.67)	(8.91)	(9.30)	(9.06)	(10.64)	(8.80)
Female	57.33	53.88	53.42	52.78	50.72	50.54	48.76	48.35	43.55
	(9.98)	(10.13)	(8.74)	(10.42)	(9.13)	(9.09)	(7.37)	(8.99)	(8.21)
Total	56.47	53.85	54.22	52.06	50.26	50.49	48.03	47.06	42.84
	(9.70)	(9.61)	(9.35)	(9.72)	(8.98)	(9.12)	(8.14)	(9.86)	(8.48)
1998									
Male	58.94	53.84	54.77	52.58	49.47	47.68	46.55	44.00	40.80
	(10.55)	(8.68)	(8.83)	(8.99)	(9.22)	(8.94)	(9.42)	(8.42)	(6.48)
Female	56.24	56.12	54.64	53.03	52.48	49.82	47.29	47.71	41.50
	(9.77)	(10.08)	(9.55)	(0.57)	(9.78)	(10.21)	(9.53)	(10.55)	(9.90)
Total	57.29	54.89	54.70	52.81	51.09	48.64	46.82	46.05	41.15
	(10.04)	(9.35)	(9.19)	(9.25)	(9.59)	(9.53)	(9.42)	(9.75)	(8.30)

Index of Intellectual Ability

	25	32	39	46	53	60	67	74	81
1956									
Male	52.47	55.03	52.97	53.97	51.00	43.94	43.66	—	—
	(8.86)	(10.48)	(9.55)	(8.54)	(9.72)	(8.56)	(8.73)	—	—
Female	53.24	55.62	51.60	53.70	50.80	44.81	41.50	—	—
	(10.19)	(9.14)	(9.21)	(8.88)	(10.80)	(7.70)	(8.77)	—	—
Total	52.86	55.34	52.30	53.85	50.90	44.39	42.58	—	—
	(9.49)	(9.73)	(9.34)	(8.63)	(10.20)	(8.09)	(8.76)	—	—

TABLE 4.2 Continued

					Age				
	25	32	39	46	53	60	67	74	81
1963									
Male	54.60	54.75	56.37	51.39	47.52	45.57	41.30	40.84	—
	(7.53)	(8.51)	(7.71)	(9.29)	(9.11)	(10.04)	(9.54)	(7.40)	—
Female	55.36	55.44	52.59	52.00	47.20	46.77	40.57	37.52	—
	(8.29)	(8.08)	(7.04)	(8.89)	(9.87)	(10.49)	(8.90)	(7.48)	—
Total	55.04	55.15	54.38	51.69	47.34	46.20	40.94	39.14	—
	(7.95)	(8.23)	(7.58)	(9.07)	(9.51)	(10.25)	(9.20)	(7.58)	—
1970									
Male	56.71	57.00	54.71	55.40	54.00	53.74	43.07	37.79	37.46
	(8.23)	(9.08)	(8.55)	(8.01)	(9.33)	(9.74)	(7.77)	(7.79)	(8.85)
Female	55.50	54.76	52.46	54.53	53.02	50.43	42.73	39.07	35.04
	(8.02)	(7.95)	(8.11)	(8.04)	(8.15)	(8.24)	(7.80)	(6.15)	(6.05)
Total	56.03	55.72	53.37	54.97	53.46	52.00	42.89	38.39	36.30
	(8.07)	(8.46)	(8.32)	(7.99)	(8.67)	(9.08)	(7.74)	(7.06)	(7.66)
1977									
Male	54.50	54.44	54.27	51.00	53.97	49.66	45.77	39.00	35.78
	(7.89)	(6.70)	(9.04)	(7.88)	(11.13)	(9.38)	(8.01)	(8.42)	(6.70)
Female	54.75	56.82	54.64	50.00	49.08	48.26	46.84	40.27	36.42
	(10.48)	(5.70)	(7.14)	(8.84)	(8.40)	(9.84)	(9.02)	(9.21)	(7.59)
Total	54.62	55.71	54.45	50.46	51.62	48.93	46.33	39.60	36.12
	(9.19)	(6.25)	(8.10)	(8.36)	(10.15)	(9.58)	(8.51)	(8.76)	(7.14)
1984									
Male	56.43	57.11	55.07	53.77	50.24	50.77	45.65	43.21	38.58
	(9.72)	(7.43)	(6.84)	(6.71)	(9.00)	(8.11)	(9.71)	(6.95)	(6.96)
Female	54.61	53.71	54.05	56.08	52.64	48.23	47.12	43.83	35.89
	(7.98)	(8.10)	(7.11)	(7.07)	(7.54)	(8.53)	(8.62)	(8.89)	(6.39)
Total	55.21	55.38	54.49	55.15	51.44	48.37	46.40	43.51	37.16
	(8.59)	(7.89)	(6.97)	(6.96)	(8.33)	(8.39)	(9.14)	(7.89)	(6.74)
1991									
Male	55.30	55.48	57.41	56.03	53.32	50.62	48.67	45.49	39.62
	(7.41)	(6.62)	(8.72)	(7.89)	(9.06)	(6.81)	(7.53)	(9.36)	(7.31)
Female	57.09	53.63	55.35	54.90	53.15	49.73	48.58	46.30	40.82
	(6.91)	(8.28)	(6.49)	(9.07)	(8.25)	(8.03)	(8.03)	(8.19)	(7.80)
Total	56.28	54.43	56.37	55.36	53.23	50.12	48.62	45.90	40.23
	(7.14)	(7.61)	(7.69)	(8.57)	(8.60)	(7.49)	(7.77)	(8.74)	(7.53)
1998									
Male	60.06	55.32	56.21	53.34	52.58	53.02	48.60	44.88	43.03
	(8.54)	(7.15)	(7.00)	(6.98)	(8.88)	(7.55)	(7.90)	(7.76)	(6.38)
Female	56.08	55.03	54.00	53.03	52.90	49.79	47.71	46.03	40.60
	(5.68)	(6.36)	(7.87)	(8.53)	(6.85)	(7.14)	(6.51)	(7.37)	(8.41)
Total	57.63	55.19	55.00	53.18	52.75	51.56	48.27	45.52	41.82
	(7.11)	(6.75)	(7.53)	(7.77)	(7.81)	(7.50)	(7.39)	(7.50)	(7.50)

(*continued*)

TABLE 4.2 Continued

					Age				
	25	32	39	46	53	60	67	74	81
Index of Educational Aptitude									
1956									
Male	51.26	52.70	50.72	49.57	47.66	40.23	41.03	—	—
	(8.77)	(9.59)	(9.39)	(9.68)	(10.09)	(9.01)	(7.92)	—	—
Female	53.50	55.49	50.69	55.03	47.46	44.24	40.08	—	—
	(7.65)	(7.51)	(10.45)	(7.32)	(9.28)	(8.29)	(7.84)	—	—
Total	52.38	54.17	50.70	52.09	47.56	42.29	40.55	—	—
	(8.25)	(8.61)	(9.86)	(9.04)	(9.62)	(8.82)	(7.84)	—	—
1963									
Male	52.88	52.77	54.00	49.11	45.55	42.90	38.92	37.66	—
	(8.25)	(8.37)	(7.78)	(9.12)	(9.85)	(8.99)	(8.88)	(8.90)	—
Female	54.50	54.63	52.70	51.53	47.41	46.53	41.52	37.50	—
	(8.38)	(7.58)	(7.12)	(8.70)	(9.42)	(10.01)	(8.32)	(8.03)	—
Total	53.82	53.84	53.31	50.30	46.60	44.80	40.21	37.58	—
	(8.32)	(7.95)	(7.44)	(8.97)	(9.62)	(9.68)	(8.67)	(8.41)	—
1970									
Male	53.81	52.71	53.47	53.42	53.32	52.47	41.86	36.38	35.27
	(7.93)	(8.81)	(7.46)	(8.14)	(7.36)	(9.38)	(7.50)	(7.06)	(8.54)
Female	55.20	55.16	53.06	54.19	52.22	49.00	43.86	39.24	36.21
	(7.51)	(7.84)	(7.68)	(8.15)	(7.69)	(8.06)	(8.42)	(5.64)	(6.95)
Total	54.59	54.11	53.23	53.80	52.72	50.65	42.93	37.72	35.72
	(7.67)	(8.29)	(7.55)	(8.11)	(7.52)	(8.83)	(8.03)	(6.56)	(7.75)
1977									
Male	54.21	55.17	53.84	52.31	52.68	49.31	43.28	37.70	33.96
	(7.95)	(7.11)	(9.81)	(8.86)	(9.71)	(9.74)	(8.17)	(8.51)	(6.60)
Female	56.18	56.85	55.58	51.00	50.46	48.63	45.84	40.24	34.29
	(9.33)	(6.87)	(7.44)	(10.18)	(9.77)	(8.75)	(8.99)	(9.46)	(6.60)
Total	55.20	56.06	54.70	51.61	51.61	48.96	44.62	38.90	34.14
	(8.65)	(6.98)	(8.71)	(9.54)	(9.74)	(9.18)	(8.65)	(9.00)	(6.55)
1984									
Male	54.89	56.52	56.70	55.27	51.64	50.78	46.48	41.61	38.80
	(8.05)	(6.27)	(6.03)	(6.16)	(8.19)	(8.11)	(8.71)	(5.92)	(8.71)
Female	56.55	54.51	58.00	57.33	57.18	51.56	52.07	47.30	40.85
	(7.16)	(8.33)	(6.25)	(6.16)	(6.39)	(8.19)	(8.11)	(8.40)	(7.02)
Total	56.00	55.27	56.56	56.58	53.62	51.11	47.37	43.41	38.19
	(7.46)	(7.42)	(6.11)	(6.21)	(7.56)	(8.10)	(8.40)	(7.41)	(7.82)
1991									
Male	53.70	56.52	57.64	56.53	54.08	52.41	48.69	46.39	38.73
	(8.04)	(6.02)	(6.51)	(6.36)	(7.56)	(7.87)	(8.32)	(8.70)	(6.82)
Female	55.36	55.41	54.34	56.49	55.58	52.67	50.97	48.48	43.60
	(6.46)	(8.21)	(5.72)	(6.49)	(6.69)	(8.03)	(8.19)	(9.07)	(9.01)
Total	55.18	55.38	57.82	57.00	55.67	51.93	50.61	46.86	39.79
	(7.28)	(7.37)	(6.09)	(6.41)	(7.25)	(7.92)	(8.38)	(8.85)	(8.00)
1998									
Male	56.25	55.63	56.46	54.60	54.86	55.38	50.92	46.92	44.77
	(5.81)	(6.59)	(6.58)	(7.21)	(8.38)	(7.12)	(7.88)	(7.94)	(7.35)
Female	55.36	55.41	54.34	56.49	55.58	52.67	50.97	48.48	43.60
	(5.86)	(7.12)	(7.49)	(7.33)	(6.42)	(7.80)	(6.72)	(8.14)	(7.82)
Total	55.71	55.53	55.30	55.55	55.25	54.15	50.94	47.79	44.18
	(5.78)	(6.79)	(7.02)	(7.31)	(7.36)	(7.51)	(7.44)	(8.01)	(7.55)

TABLE 4.2 Continued

					Age				
	25	32	39	46	53	60	67	74	81
Summed Over All Measurement Occasions									
Verbal Meaning									
Male	52.04	53.53	54.25	52.57	51.45	49.31	45.28	41.20	39.26
	(8.29)	(7.94)	(8.13)	(8.76)	(9.57)	(10.32)	(9.60)	(9.24)	(8.87)
Female	53.72	53.95	53.62	54.38	52.02	49.53	46.72	43.56	39.37
	(7.84)	(7.88)	(8.05)	(8.19)	(8.91)	(9.18)	(9.34)	(9.42)	(9.00)
Total	53.00	53.75	53.91	53.51	51.75	49.43	46.00	42.42	39.31
	(8.07)	(7.91)	(8.09)	(8.51)	(9.22)	(9.73)	(9.49)	(9.39)	(8.92)
Spatial Orientation									
Male	59.26	57.06	57.07	54.48	52.29	50.49	47.33	43.86	42.21
	(9.39)	(8.17)	(8.11)	(8.40)	(8.46)	(8.76)	(7.89)	(7.78)	(6.85)
Female	55.06	53.95	51.47	50.67	48.31	45.91	43.11	40.67	38.33
	(9.44)	(8.18)	(9.15)	(9.19)	(8.58)	(7.98)	(7.87)	(7.05)	(6.94)
Total	56.86	55.39	54.08	52.50	50.19	48.10	45.22	42.28	40.23
	(9.61)	(8.31)	(9.11)	(9.01)	(8.75)	(8.66)	(8.15)	(7.59)	(7.15)
Inductive Reasoning									
Male	57.29	55.90	54.67	51.59	49.41	47.22	43.19	41.12	39.27
	(7.90)	(7.92)	(8.30)	(8.35)	(8.87)	(8.90)	(7.85)	(7.13)	(6.24)
Female	58.90	57.26	54.89	53.94	50.50	47.34	44.65	41.95	39.12
	(7.55)	(7.43)	(7.61)	(8.59)	(8.95)	(8.44)	(8.48)	(7.49)	(6.28)
Total	58.21	56.63	54.79	52.81	49.99	47.29	43.92	41.54	39.19
	(7.74)	(7.68)	(7.93)	(8.55)	(8.92)	(8.66)	(8.20)	(7.32)	(6.25)
Number									
Male	50.19	52.85	53.02	52.94	52.42	51.44	48.89	46.81	45.00
	(8.86)	(11.14)	(10.23)	(9.97)	(11.41)	(10.79)	(9.51)	(9.49)	(8.94)
Female	49.72	50.66	50.91	51.34	50.65	49.61	47.63	46.09	42.79
	(8.64)	(8.60)	(8.93)	(9.66)	(9.79)	(10.17)	(9.11)	(9.09)	(9.18)
Total	49.92	51.67	51.89	52.11	51.49	50.48	48.26	46.46	43.87
	(8.73)	(9.90)	(9.61)	(9.83)	(10.61)	(10.50)	(9.33)	(9.29)	(9.11)
Word Fluency									
Male	53.81	52.23	52.79	51.13	50.03	48.36	45.56	43.04	40.70
	(9.84)	(9.13)	(9.26)	(9.52)	(10.32)	(8.85)	(9.48)	(8.90)	(7.90)
Female	54.29	55.01	52.97	53.13	51.63	50.24	47.05	45.73	43.10
	(9.42)	(9.59)	(8.89)	(9.52)	(9.05)	(9.47)	(8.88)	(9.11)	(8.28)
Total	54.08	53.73	52.89	52.17	50.87	49.34	46.30	44.37	41.93
	(9.60)	(9.47)	(9.06)	(9.56)	(9.70)	(9.22)	(9.21)	(9.10)	(8.17)
Index of Intellectual Ability									
Male	55.26	55.47	55.48	53.29	51.53	49.37	45.08	41.59	39.03
	(8.42)	(8.10)	(8.20)	(8.21)	(9.68)	(9.37)	(8.79)	(8.45)	(7.58)
Female	55.15	55.05	53.43	53.34	50.84	48.18	44.76	41.96	37.96
	(8.36)	(7.80)	(7.58)	(8.65)	(8.99)	(8.92)	(8.83)	(8.37)	(7.68)
Total	55.20	55.24	54.38	53.32	51.17	48.75	44.93	41.77	38.48
	(8.37)	(7.93)	(7.94)	(8.44)	(9.32)	(9.15)	(8.80)	(8.40)	(7.64)
Index of Educational Aptitude									
Male	53.53	54.42	54.67	52.51	51.03	48.70	44.42	40.67	38.59
	(8.06)	(7.79)	(7.92)	(8.54)	(9.46)	(10.03)	(9.27)	(8.83)	(8.39)
Female	55.35	55.09	54.20	54.58	51.78	48.94	45.95	42.80	38.65
	(7.60)	(7.61)	(7.71)	(8.22)	(8.96)	(8.96)	(9.16)	(9.12)	(8.22)
Total	54.57	54.78	54.42	53.58	51.43	48.82	45.19	41.73	38.62
	(7.84)	(7.69)	(7.80)	(8.43)	(9.20)	(9.48)	(9.20)	(9.00)	(8.28)

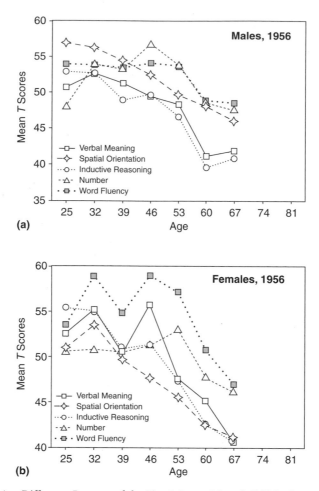

FIGURE 4.4 *Age Difference Patterns of the Five Primary Mental Abilities by Gender for the First (1956) and Last (1998) Cross-Sectional Comparisons.*

study participants, much greater shifts can be observed. In young adulthood, females now show higher performance on Spatial Orientation than was the case some 42 years ago. For this ability, the peak age for women is now in midlife. For the women, age differences in Number ability have virtually disappeared, and the peak age for Verbal Meaning has moved to the early 50s.

Absolute age differences across the adult life span, observed at any given point, have been reduced over time, but remain substantial for most abilities. However, there has been a sharp reduction of age differences in performance observed until the late 60s are reached. For example, for Verbal Meaning the absolute difference between ages 25 and 81 currently amounts to 0.8 *SD* for both men and women. But the absolute difference between ages 25 and 67 has been reduced from 0.8 to 0.2 *SD* for men and from 1.2 to 0.1 *SD* (or virtually no difference) for women.

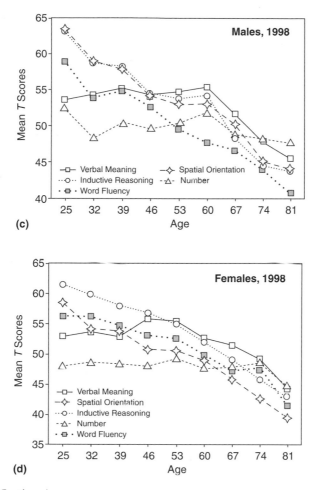

FIGURE 4.4 *Continued.*

Age Difference Patterns Across Abilities   Age difference data are not directly relevant to testing propositions about ontogenetic change. Such data, however, when examined in the context of cross-sectional sequences, are quite appropriate for testing the proposition of invariance in age difference patterns over time. Given certain assumptions, they are also the data of choice to evaluate the magnitude of cohort differences and time-of-measurement (period) effects.

Throughout our study, we have questioned whether age difference patterns remain invariant over time and have concluded that statistically significant shifts in such patterns can be observed. This conclusion is based in part on finding Age × Time interactions in time-sequential analyses and Cohort × Time interactions in cross-sequential analyses (Schaie & Hertzog, 1983; Schaie, Labouvie, & Buech, 1973; Schaie & Strother, 1968c).

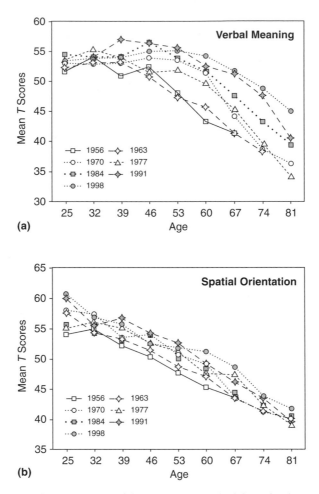

FIGURE 4.5 *Age Difference Patterns of the Primary Mental Abilities for the Total Sample by Test Occasion.*

To examine shifts in age profiles as well as the peak ages across the seven cross-sectional studies, mean values for each study across age for the five PMAs and the composite indexes are graphed in figure 4.5. What seems most apparent is that means observed at the same ages tend to rise to progressively higher levels for successive cohorts attaining a given age. This is clearly the case for Verbal Meaning, Spatial Orientation, and Inductive Reasoning as well as for the composite indexes. Successively lower levels are attained for successive cohorts on Number; the cohort pattern for Word Fluency is less clearly defined.

For Verbal Meaning there has been a general increase in performance level at all ages. Most noteworthy, however, are performance increases at the older ages. For ages 60 to 74 years, these increases amount to a full standard deviation over

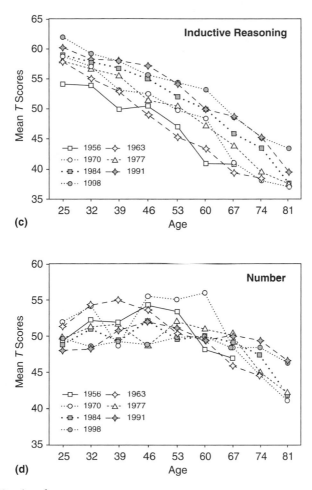

FIGURE 4.5 *Continued.*

a 42-year period. Equally dramatic, at 81 years of age, performance has increased by approximately 1 *SD* over the 28 years monitored for this age group.

Somewhat smaller increases across time, averaging approximately 0.3 *SD*, were observed for Spatial Orientation until 53 years of age. At ages 60 and 67 years, there was a gain of 0.5 *SD*, with less improvement (0.2 *SD*) for the two oldest age groups. Inductive Reasoning also showed large rises in performance over time at comparable ages (averaging about 0.7 *SD*), whereas Number and Word Fluency showed complex changes involving curvilinear patterns of age differences.

The summary indexes of Intellectual Ability and Educational Aptitude also showed significant reductions in age differences at all comparable ages. Changes in performance level are discussed in greater detail in chapter 6, with explicit discussions of cohort and period effect.

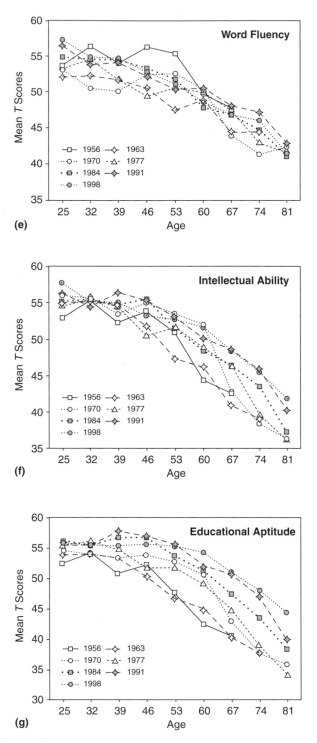

FIGURE 4.5 *Continued.*

Table 4.2 also contains means and standard deviations by age and gender summed across all observations. These values represent the averages for all seven replications over a 42-year period. Correlations among the five basic abilities by age group and for the total sample are reported in appendix A-4.1.

Expanded Cognitive Data

The expanded cognitive battery described in chapter 3 was administered in Cycles 5, 6, and 7, except for the Perceptual Speed measures of Finding A's and Identical Pictures, which were first introduced during the fourth cycle. Cross-sectional analyses for these cycles were consequently done both at the level of individual measures and at the latent construct level to determine within-ability and across-ability age difference patterns (see Schaie & Willis, 1993).

Most of the major longitudinal studies of adult development in the past collected only very limited data that speak to the issues of generalizability of findings within and across domains in the area of intellectual functioning (e.g., Busse, 1993; Costa & McCrae, 1993; Eichorn, Clausen, Haan, Honzik, & Mussen, 1981; Rott, 1990; Schaie, 1983b; Schmitz-Scherzer & Thomae, 1983; Shock et al., 1984; Siegler, 1983). Cross-sectional data may actually be quite instructive with respect to this issue because such data allow us to draw *concurrent* comparisons of age difference patterns within and across domains without requiring attention to the thorny methodological issues associated with comparisons across time (see chapter 2).

There are likely to be substantial life stage differences in adulthood in the degree to which levels of performance for different ability markers are equivalent both within and across ability domains. First I examine the extent to which patterns of age differences are congruent within a particular ability domain by describing age difference patterns for six psychometric abilities (see Schaie & Willis, 1993). These abilities broadly sample higher-order constructs, such as those espoused by Horn (1982). Thus, fluid intelligence is represented by the ability of Inductive Reasoning, Verbal Ability and Numeric Ability stand as representatives of crystallized intelligence, and mental rotation is represented by our Spatial Ability construct. Verbal Memory and Perceptual Speed are examined as ability samplers for the memory and speed domains, respectively. Next, consideration is therefore given to the age difference patterns *across* the various ability domains.

What is at issue is the question of whether patterns of age differences in ability remain invariant for multiple markers of the primary mental abilities. This issue is addressed again in chapter 8, in which several studies are reported that examine invariance across age and time by means of structural analyses (see Schaie et al., 1989, 1998), and it is shown that configural invariance (i.e., number of factors and factor pattern) is preserved across widely differing age groups. Here, we examine shifts of different marker variables at different life stages, an effect observed a long time ago in cross-sectional studies of the Wechsler Adult Intelligence Scale (Cohen, 1957).

The reasons for such shifts may be sought in such contextual variables as shifts in educational exposure to the skills embodied in a particular marker variable or latent construct and the impact of slowing in perceptual and/or motor speed that may differentially affect various markers. For example, we know that conditions of instructions and speededness imposed by time limits differentially affect performance on the PMA and Educational Testing Service vocabulary tests (Hertzog, 1989). Likewise, it is known that there have been generational shifts in instruction in quantitative skills that should affect numerical performance for different cohorts. For other abilities, congruence would be expected across the entire life span until the 80s are reached. At that late stage, the differential memorization demands as well as the relative motor complexity of answer sheet as compared with disposable booklet formats might result in differential efficiency of a given marker.

Age-difference patterns appear generally invariant across sex within domains (albeit there is strong evidence for overall gender differences in level of performance), but it is not a foregone conclusion that such invariance holds for all abilities or for all markers of a given ability. Gender differences will therefore be examined, and results are reported separately by gender when warranted.

The issue of the generalizability of markers within domains is particularly important for age comparative studies. For valid cross-sectional comparisons, it must be shown that an observed variable provides a reasonable representation of the developmental trajectory of the latent construct to be marked. If this is the case, then a single marker may suffice. But if there is wide discrepancy in developmental trajectories for multiple markers, we would then be forced to multiply mark the construct, providing differential weights for the markers at different life stages. The data presented here provide some guidance on these matters.

All scores on the observed variables were rescaled into T-score form ($M = 50$; $SD = 10$) using parameters for the total sample at first test ($N = 2,476$). Factor scores for the six intellectual abilities were computed using factor regression weights based on a previously determined best-fitting factor model (Schaie et al., 1991).

Age Difference Patterns Within Ability Domains

The age difference patterns for the observed markers of the six primary ability domains (in standardized form) are reported in table 4.3. Means and standard deviations are given separately by gender and for the total age/cohort groupings. This table also reports averages over the three data points. Correlations among the variables in the extended battery by age group and for the total sample can be found in appendix A-4.2.

The age difference gradients graphed in figure 4.6, comparing the markers for each latent construct, represent averages over three cohorts assessed at the same age. Results with respect to congruence among the patterns for the different operations measuring the ability constructs are described in the following paragraphs.

The new markers of the Inductive Reasoning factor have very similar age profiles, with an overall age difference of about 2 SD from the youngest to the oldest age cohort. Significant age differences from the youngest (peak) age appear by age 46 for all three tests. Gender differences were not significant for Letter Series, but favored women for Word Series and men for Number Series. A significant overall increase in performance level across the three assessment times was found only for Letter Series.

TABLE 4.3 Means and Standard Deviations for the Expanded Ability Battery by Sample and Gender

	Age								
	25	32	39	46	53	60	67	74	81
Inductive Reasoning									
Letter Series									
1984									
Male	60.22	57.66	55.60	53.73	49.17	48.21	44.11	39.64	36.20
	(6.53)	(8.31)	(8.60)	(7.54)	(8.20)	(8.70)	(8.30)	(6.00)	(7.39)
Female	54.92	55.96	55.81	51.80	49.97	49.66	44.94	42.19	38.06
	(9.31)	(8.98)	(8.07)	(8.06)	(8.00)	(8.76)	(7.63)	(6.58)	(7.48)
Total	57.57	56.81	55.70	52.77	49.57	47.43	44.53	40.91	37.13
	(8.54)	(8.57)	(8.27)	(7.88)	(8.08)	(8.75)	(7.92)	(6.42)	(7.35)
1991									
Male	56.56	58.69	57.92	55.26	50.74	47.47	45.15	41.34	37.34
	(9.76)	(6.91)	(7.77)	(7.40)	(8.75)	(6.00)	(8.72)	(8.97)	(6.26)
Female	60.06	57.30	56.56	55.55	53.30	47.82	47.32	42.67	36.00
	(9.10)	(8.10)	(6.07)	(9.93)	(7.67)	(8.06)	(9.16)	(7.24)	(7.31)
Total	58.31	57.99	57.24	55.41	52.02	47.65	46.23	42.01	36.67
	(9.48)	(7.60)	(6.96)	(8.93)	(8.26)	(7.17)	(8.99)	(8.11)	(6.80)
1998									
Male	64.67	58.14	57.25	53.84	51.10	51.08	45.07	42.54	39.70
	(6.62)	(7.65)	(7.62)	(7.27)	(8.07)	(7.45)	(8.24)	(7.34)	(4.79)
Female	59.80	59.25	55.96	54.66	52.27	47.58	44.60	41.77	38.30
	(5.71)	(6.72)	(7.83)	(7.82)	(8.00)	(6.43)	(8.01)	(9.16)	(5.05)
Total	62.23	58.70	56.61	54.25	51.68	49.33	44.83	42.16	38.99
	(6.44)	(7.19)	(7.73)	(7.53)	(8.01)	(7.17)	(8.11)	(8.35)	(4.92)
Word Series									
1984									
Male	59.00	56.68	54.57	53.31	48.72	48.07	43.23	39.26	32.27
	(6.20)	(8.18)	(7.84)	(7.12)	(8.33)	(7.98)	(9.16)	(7.64)	(6.34)
Female	55.77	56.40	57.04	53.29	51.46	48.45	45.65	43.84	36.62
	(9.13)	(8.32)	(8.02)	(7.19)	(6.70)	(8.15)	(8.68)	(8.29)	(7.46)
Total	57.38	56.54	55.80	53.30	50.09	48.26	44.44	41.55	34.45
	(8.06)	(8.17)	(8.01)	(7.13)	(7.65)	(8.05)	(8.95)	(8.29)	(7.23)
1991									
Male	55.41	56.41	54.41	55.00	50.47	47.84	44.51	40.00	33.47
	(8.60)	(7.23)	(8.51)	(6.33)	(8.64)	(6.79)	(8.27)	(9.02)	(5.59)
Female	59.24	57.88	57.00	55.55	54.45	47.15	47.34	44.14	36.68
	(7.31)	(8.94)	(6.53)	(8.05)	(9.06)	(7.71)	(7.90)	(9.12)	(8.57)
Total	57.32	57.14	55.71	55.28	52.46	47.50	45.93	42.07	35.07
	(8.07)	(8.24)	(7.65)	(7.36)	(9.02)	(7.27)	(8.14)	(9.25)	(7.40)
1998									
Male	60.93	57.23	56.94	52.05	51.60	50.18	44.95	43.21	36.97
	(4.45)	(7.23)	(7.49)	(8.32)	(7.82)	(8.44)	(8.01)	(9.22)	(6.46)
Female	58.80	56.91	56.98	53.03	52.76	50.48	47.11	43.39	39.37
	(9.61)	(9.48)	(7.54)	(7.89)	(7.74)	(7.03)	(7.65)	(8.99)	(7.91)
Total	59.87	57.07	56.96	52.54	52.18	50.33	46.03	43.30	38.17
	(8.06)	(8.32)	(7.48)	(8.09)	(7.75)	(7.76)	(7.91)	(9.01)	(7.23)

(*continued*)

TABLE 4.3 Continued

					Age				
	25	32	39	46	53	60	67	74	81
Number Series									
1984									
Male	61.67	57.33	55.41	56.14	51.58	50.76	47.71	42.60	37.09
	(4.61)	(11.01)	(8.52)	(7.85)	(8.88)	(7.69)	(9.50)	(8.55)	(4.46)
Female	53.48	51.90	52.58	49.94	48.04	46.02	44.78	41.00	39.75
	(10.09)	(7.66)	(8.35)	(10.07)	(8.59)	(10.16)	(9.06)	(7.16)	(6.99)
Total	57.55	54.61	54.00	53.04	49.81	48.39	46.25	41.80	38.42
	(9.32)	(9.90)	(8.51)	(9.68)	(8.88)	(9.39)	(9.34)	(7.81)	(6.13)
1991									
Male	57.89	56.84	58.10	55.88	54.84	49.12	48.35	44.46	39.03
	(9.20)	(8.41)	(9.79)	(8.14)	(9.79)	(6.74)	(8.70)	(9.88)	(6.35)
Female	56.21	54.08	52.40	50.37	51.30	45.78	46.41	42.12	38.28
	(8.81)	(7.89)	(6.66)	(8.54)	(8.43)	(8.04)	(10.56)	(7.08)	(5.99)
Total	57.05	55.46	55.25	53.12	53.07	47.45	47.38	43.29	38.66
	(8.95)	(8.18)	(8.78)	(8.76)	(9.23)	(7.63)	(9.83)	(8.56)	(6.13)
1998									
Male	62.94	57.79	57.48	53.29	52.77	52.50	48.83	46.24	45.59
	(6.70)	(9.20)	(9.29)	(7.75)	(9.53)	(8.41)	(7.86)	(8.49)	(7.94)
Female	54.60	54.31	52.90	51.38	48.92	48.70	43.51	43.93	37.93
	(6.81)	(8.20)	(9.43)	(.36)	(7.56)	(9.19)	(7.11)	(8.22)	(7.45)
Total	58.77	56.05	55.19	52.34	50.84	50.60	46.17	45.09	41.76
	(7.85)	(8.87)	(.60)	(8.62)	(8.69)	(8.91)	(7.98)	(8.34)	(8.56)
Spatial Orientation									
Object Rotation									
1984									
Male	57.89	56.39	56.21	55.41	52.20	53.16	47.86	42.65	41.23
	(5.58)	(6.78)	(7.76)	(6.91)	(7.52)	(6.86)	(8.88)	(9.63)	(8.49)
Female	53.00	53.83	52.87	52.72	48.95	48.16	44.71	39.84	37.88
	(11.20)	(7.42)	(8.55)	(8.37)	(9.23)	(8.23)	(8.71)	(8.25)	(9.44)
Total	55.44	55.11	54.54	54.07	50.58	50.66	46.28	41.24	39.55
	(9.73)	(7.14)	(8.36)	(7.89)	(8.58)	(8.00)	(8.90)	(8.96)	(9.03)
1991									
Male	56.56	56.25	57.08	55.00	53.68	53.25	47.59	43.44	37.79
	(7.59)	(6.70)	(8.05)	(6.26)	(7.82)	(6.48)	(9.94)	(9.73)	(8.94)
Female	56.21	53.68	49.62	52.43	50.20	47.37	42.80	38.72	35.59
	(7.10)	(9.21)	(9.66)	(8.47)	(9.99)	(8.84)	(7.72)	(9.33)	(7.37)
Total	56.38	54.97	53.35	53.71	51.94	50.31	45.19	41.08	36.69
	(7.26)	(8.25)	(9.60)	(7.71)	(9.11)	(8.37)	(9.00)	(9.76)	(8.19)
1998									
Male	58.69	58.63	56.71	54.39	52.72	53.38	50.75	46.64	41.63
	(7.26)	(5.85)	(6.23)	(7.71)	(7.04)	(7.84)	(7.89)	(11.38)	(7.78)
Female	56.92	54.97	55.24	50.89	49.04	48.24	45.29	37.00	36.72
	(6.20)	(7.76)	(8.22)	(11.47)	(9.78)	(9.92)	(8.53)	(9.93)	(7.61)
Total	57.80	56.80	55.97	52.64	50.88	50.76	48.02	41.82	39.18
	(6.60)	(6.99)	(7.39)	(9.90)	(8.77)	(9.13)	(8.51)	(11.56)	(8.02)

TABLE 4.3 Continued

					Age				
	25	32	39	46	53	60	67	74	81
Alphanumeric Rotation									
1984									
Male	57.56	56.59	55.31	54.12	51.87	50.24	46.94	42.13	38.08
	(3.75)	(5.05)	(7.81)	(7.24)	(8.09)	(8.41)	(9.60)	(9.32)	(8.60)
Female	51.31	56.84	54.19	52.59	49.08	47.77	45.91	41.47	37.81
	(12.04)	(4.64)	(7.65)	(7.84)	(10.15)	(8.89)	(8.77)	(9.11)	(7.93)
Total	54.43	56.72	54.75	53.36	50.47	49.01	46.42	41.80	37.95
	(9.91)	(4.84)	(7.71)	(7.61)	(9.26)	(8.74)	(9.13)	(9.16)	(8.06)
1991									
Male	56.70	55.90	56.67	56.68	53.55	50.03	45.56	42.54	37.15
	(6.01)	(7.42)	(5.20)	(5.43)	(7.96)	(8.37)	(9.18)	(9.76)	(10.06)
Female	57.56	55.28	54.79	54.16	53.10	46.70	45.32	41.77	35.18
	(6.16)	(7.67)	(7.32)	(7.84)	(8.69)	(9.44)	(8.87)	(8.70)	(9.57)
Total	57.13	55.59	55.73	55.42	53.33	48.37	45.44	42.15	36.16
	(6.05)	(7.52)	(6.38)	(7.03)	(8.29)	(9.07)	(8.96)	(9.19)	(9.79)
1998									
Male	56.87	59.37	57.90	53.93	52.95	50.95	49.18	44.42	38.52
	(7.18)	(3.53)	(5.02)	(7.71)	(7.01)	(10.24)	(9.47)	(11.41)	(7.36)
Female	53.68	56.38	55.79	53.05	50.02	48.70	45.46	40.32	37.41
	(9.97)	(6.34)	(7.09)	(8.40)	(9.69)	(11.64)	(9.00)	(10.82)	(8.50)
Total	55.27	57.87	56.84	53.49	51.49	49.82	47.32	42.37	37.96
	(9.06)	(5.25)	(6.28)	(8.05)	(8.64)	(10.89)	(9.42)	(11.17)	(7.88)
Cube Comparison									
1984									
Male	58.44	57.06	58.47	55.81	51.81	51.00	45.26	41.87	38.27
	(8.63)	(10.26)	(8.81)	(8.45)	(7.58)	(8.46)	(7.07)	(7.91)	(7.10)
Female	56.00	51.92	51.26	49.00	46.34	45.05	43.33	41.88	39.06
	(11.50)	(7.40)	(8.47)	(7.03)	(6.99)	(7.34)	(7.27)	(5.78)	(5.46)
Total	57.22	54.49	54.86	52.41	49.07	48.02	44.29	41.87	38.67
	(10.27)	(9.40)	(9.30)	(8.32)	(7.76)	(8.39)	(7.23)	(6.76)	(6.06)
1991									
Male	59.59	58.55	61.36	56.71	53.95	50.44	45.63	44.71	38.28
	(11.19)	(9.39)	(9.38)	(7.57)	(10.44)	(7.33)	(7.36)	(7.61)	(6.01)
Female	56.32	53.78	54.21	52.20	49.70	44.95	45.59	40.74	40.48
	(9.24)	(8.23)	(8.15)	(8.17)	(8.19)	(7.31)	(7.45)	(6.08)	(5.98)
Total	57.96	56.16	57.78	54.45	51.82	47.69	45.61	42.73	39.38
	(10.19)	(8.99)	(9.45)	(8.19)	(9.53)	(7.77)	(7.37)	(7.11)	(6.05)
1998									
Male	66.67	61.43	61.43	55.11	55.83	50.84	48.07	45.38	43.28
	(9.84)	(8.17)	(8.77)	(9.47)	(8.51)	(8.80)	(7.49)	(8.56)	(5.47)
Female	56.32	57.72	54.34	52.48	49.29	47.21	45.69	42.65	42.11
	(8.04)	(8.75)	(9.18)	(9.74)	(9.03)	(8.51)	(5.17)	(4.98)	(7.49)
Total	61.49	59.57	57.88	53.80	52.56	49.03	45.88	44.01	42.19
	(10.01)	(8.59)	(9.63)	(9.66)	(9.34)	(8.79)	(6.79)	(6.84)	(6.55)

(*continued*)

TABLE 4.3 Continued

	Age								
	25	32	39	46	53	60	67	74	81
Numeric Ability									
Addition									
1984									
Male	49.56	52.42	50.87	54.03	50.69	52.71	50.71	51.98	41.85
	(5.50)	(10.06)	(9.70)	(10.52)	(10.44)	(10.68)	(10.98)	(7.13)	(7.31)
Female	47.50	51.00	52.69	52.65	52.01	50.57	51.83	49.47	46.38
	(9.23)	(10.45)	(10.45)	(10.21)	(10.06)	(9.78)	(10.08)	(9.57)	(8.16)
Total	48.53	51.71	51.78	53.34	51.35	51.64	51.27	50.72	44.11
	(8.02)	(10.19)	(10.14)	(10.33)	(10.24)	(10.18)	(10.47)	(8.60)	(7.99)
1991									
Male	45.63	48.26	51.95	52.44	49.00	47.53	48.76	47.73	44.27
	(8.36)	(7.94)	(11.02)	(8.39)	(11.64)	(7.65)	(8.48)	(10.85)	(12.76)
Female	48.94	48.78	51.20	51.96	50.72	48.49	48.84	50.58	46.68
	(9.36)	(8.37)	(8.67)	(10.82)	(8.88)	(10.40)	(10.09)	(9.45)	(11.24)
Total	47.29	48.52	51.57	52.20	49.86	48.01	48.80	49.16	45.47
	(9.01)	(8.13)	(9.84)	(9.85)	(10.28)	(9.24)	(9.40)	(10.20)	(11.98)
1998									
Male	50.75	47.79	49.23	49.21	50.91	51.10	47.58	46.24	45.90
	(12.33)	(10.17)	(9.35)	(8.54)	(11.73)	(8.98)	(10.05)	(9.66)	(9.43)
Female	46.84	49.22	49.77	48.70	49.64	47.61	49.09	47.29	45.97
	(8.32)	(7.44)	(8.68)	(11.32)	(8.45)	(8.71)	(10.78)	(9.06)	(9.11)
Total	48.80	48.50	49.50	48.95	50.27	49.35	48.33	46.77	45.93
	(10.12)	(8.99)	(8.95)	(10.00)	(10.06)	(8.97)	(10.20)	(9.26)	(9.19)
Subtraction and Multiplication									
1984									
Male	48.89	53.66	53.07	54.88	50.72	52.21	49.89	48.38	40.33
	(6.13)	(11.70)	(8.44)	(9.59)	(10.00)	(9.22)	(10.63)	(7.16)	(5.96)
Female	44.54	50.20	53.84	52.02	51.23	50.48	49.91	47.06	43.00
	(8.24)	(10.11)	(9.33)	(9.92)	(9.47)	(9.49)	(9.72)	(7.79)	(9.06)
Total	46.71	51.93	53.46	53.45	50.97	51.34	49.90	47.72	41.67
	(7.61)	(11.07)	(8.94)	(9.86)	(9.71)	(9.38)	(10.10)	(7.50)	(7.87)
1991									
Male	47.19	49.41	53.38	54.44	49.68	48.28	48.80	46.77	42.73
	(10.08)	(9.57)	(10.52)	(8.07)	(12.53)	(9.46)	(7.67)	(8.14)	(9.50)
Female	50.44	49.30	52.28	54.16	51.72	46.98	48.40	48.81	45.97
	(10.93)	(9.88)	(8.57)	(9.65)	(10.61)	(10.08)	(9.55)	(9.96)	(8.81)
Total	48.81	49.36	52.83	54.30	50.70	47.63	48.60	47.79	44.35
	(10.60)	(9.68)	(9.55)	(8.99)	(11.56)	(9.76)	(8.75)	(9.12)	(9.23)
1998									
Male	49.80	48.77	51.27	50.92	51.48	51.43	48.73	44.67	46.52
	(12.85)	(11.62)	(10.64)	(9.71)	(11.04)	(9.89)	(8.76)	(10.49)	(9.45)
Female	48.08	49.69	50.05	49.77	49.86	46.88	47.31	47.58	44.15
	(10.11)	(10.85)	(10.11)	(10.80)	(9.59)	(10.00)	(10.32)	(9.96)	(10.46)
Total	48.94	49.22	50.66	50.35	50.67	49.15	48.02	46.12	45.33
	(11.08)	(11.18)	(10.33)	(10.25)	(10.26)	(10.13)	(9.34)	(10.20)	(9.93)

TABLE 4.3 Continued

	Age								
	25	32	39	46	53	60	67	74	81
Verbal Ability									
ETS Vocabulary									
1984									
Male	50.44	48.91	50.93	51.02	51.31	52.87	51.18	49.41	41.75
	(6.54)	(7.66)	(9.94)	(9.20)	(9.20)	(8.76)	(11.25)	(11.60)	(18.40)
Female	44.92	51.72	50.71	51.83	52.52	51.09	52.54	49.78	49.94
	(13.10)	(6.54)	(8.90)	(8.43)	(8.49)	(10.25)	(9.67)	(10.07)	(10.07)
Total	47.68	50.31	50.82	51.42	51.91	51.98	51.86	49.59	45.84
	(11.05)	(7.27)	(9.33)	(8.73)	(8.84)	(9.62)	(10.44)	(10.71)	(14.53)
1991									
Male	43.67	48.00	49.03	49.08	50.24	50.50	51.07	47.59	50.85
	(8.49)	(8.12)	(8.95)	(9.24)	(9.67)	(9.18)	(9.78)	(12.13)	(11.99)
Female	41.91	43.95	52.23	52.27	53.58	49.72	52.57	49.74	49.59
	(9.35)	(12.19)	(6.32)	(8.24)	(6.65)	(9.91)	(8.07)	(10.52)	(9.96)
Total	42.79	45.98	50.63	50.68	51.91	50.11	51.82	48.66	50.22
	(8.95)	(10.79)	(7.86)	(8.75)	(8.37)	(9.53)	(8.82)	(11.32)	(10.94)
1998									
Male	44.67	48.60	47.96	48.64	48.64	51.08	49.32	48.88	50.86
	(10.20)	(9.51)	(8.99)	(10.18)	(11.39)	(10.29)	(10.00)	(11.07)	(7.83)
Female	42.72	44.53	45.18	48.98	51.53	48.63	47.31	50.45	52.48
	(9.38)	(12.19)	(10.55)	(10.23)	(7.57)	(10.45)	(10.08)	(8.79)	(7.58)
Total	43.69	46.57	46.57	48.80	50.09	49.86	48.32	49.66	51.67
	(9.61)	(10.98)	(9.92)	(10.17)	(9.58)	(10.36)	(10.02)	(9.79)	(7.68)
ETS Advanced Vocabulary									
1984									
Male	49.89	49.44	50.93	52.78	51.27	53.16	51.89	49.97	43.17
	(8.94)	(9.25)	(10.41)	(8.90)	(9.27)	(8.68)	(10.12)	(10.93)	(14.19)
Female	43.92	45.82	51.33	52.84	52.70	47.78	52.02	49.51	49.24
	(10.59)	(9.02)	(9.03)	(9.41)	(9.84)	(10.60)	(10.14)	(9.51)	(9.70)
Total	46.91	48.78	50.34	51.98	51.30	51.27	51.84	49.75	45.65
	(10.18)	(9.09)	(9.63)	(9.21)	(9.53)	(9.91)	(10.10)	(10.11)	(11.85)
1991									
Male	43.67	48.12	49.75	51.18	51.32	49.57	51.79	49.53	48.12
	(8.50)	(9.18)	(9.11)	(9.52)	(9.53)	(9.63)	(9.64)	(12.47)	(12.00)
Female	43.44	45.82	51.33	52.84	52.70	47.78	52.02	49.51	49.24
	(8.59)	(9.95)	(8.63)	(10.50)	(9.17)	(9.26)	(9.17)	(12.14)	(10.99)
Total	43.55	47.38	51.82	51.90	51.52	49.17	51.31	49.40	49.54
	(8.48)	(9.69)	(8.83)	(10.09)	(9.36)	(9.46)	(9.35)	(12.23)	(11.41)
1998									
Male	48.27	48.80	49.15	50.10	50.02	52.97	48.73	49.79	50.17
	(9.44)	(10.09)	(8.87)	(9.86)	(11.06)	(9.83)	(9.86)	(10.14)	(9.76)
Female	42.32	46.59	46.00	50.37	50.98	48.39	46.46	48.58	53.33
	(8.88)	(8.14)	(10.97)	(10.68)	(9.59)	(10.96)	(9.65)	(9.59)	(9.60)
Total	45.29	47.70	47.57	50.23	50.50	50.68	47.59	49.19	51.75
	(9.44)	(9.21)	(10.13)	(10.24)	(10.25)	(10.55)	(9.80)	(9.76)	(9.73)

(continued)

TABLE 4.3 Continued

					Age				
	25	32	39	46	53	60	67	74	81

Verbal Memory

Immediate Recall

1984

Male	59.56	53.00	52.53	49.16	47.10	46.57	44.10	38.54	34.00
	(5.25)	(7.94)	(8.72)	(8.25)	(9.21)	(8.16)	(9.69)	(8.48)	(6.18)
Female	57.38	56.32	54.87	52.46	50.11	48.61	47.86	44.18	46.00
	(8.11)	(7.53)	(7.98)	(8.45)	(8.75)	(9.44)	(9.57)	(7.34)	(7.75)
Total	58.47	54.66	53.70	50.81	48.61	47.59	45.98	41.36	40.00
	(7.02)	(7.87)	(8.36)	(8.50)	(9.08)	(8.92)	(9.78)	(8.31)	(9.24)

1991

Male	57.33	54.72	54.08	53.41	49.05	47.94	44.59	42.08	39.12
	(6.18)	(8.82)	(8.82)	(8.86)	(10.42)	(8.13)	(8.71)	(10.47)	(7.84)
Female	59.26	57.40	57.16	57.76	55.30	49.35	50.16	44.67	41.65
	(6.19)	(5.84)	(7.07)	(5.76)	(7.69)	(9.97)	(7.72)	(8.35)	(8.45)
Total	58.30	56.06	55.92	55.29	52.18	48.64	47.37	43.37	40.39
	(6.21)	(7.31)	(8.15)	(7.38)	(9.59)	(9.16)	(8.57)	(9.46)	(8.20)

1998

Male	57.33	56.37	51.66	52.87	49.57	49.71	44.34	40.96	38.38
	(7.42)	(7.90)	(8.70)	(8.57)	(7.78)	(8.35)	(8.52)	(9.54)	(8.81)
Female	59.96	58.47	54.77	55.58	54.26	50.70	47.65	45.10	41.37
	(5.09)	(6.58)	(8.79)	(7.96)	(7.47)	(8.67)	(9.73)	(9.88)	(8.25)
Total	58.64	57.42	53.21	54.22	51.92	50.20	46.00	43.03	39.87
	(6.12)	(7.28)	(8.85)	(8.35)	(7.93)	(8.45)	(9.08)	(8.87)	(8.60)

Delayed Recall

1984

Male	61.33	53.94	52.45	49.69	46.85	46.53	42.89	39.54	35.75
	(5.29)	(7.56)	(8.49)	(7.81)	(9.12)	(7.44)	(8.58)	(7.29)	(6.85)
Female	57.69	58.00	55.74	52.71	49.92	49.16	48.06	43.14	43.53
	(7.78)	(7.70)	(8.24)	(8.38)	(9.21)	(8.70)	(8.72)	(6.25)	(6.24)
Total	59.51	55.97	54.09	51.20	48.39	47.85	45.47	41.34	39.64
	(6.97)	(7.82)	(8.48)	(8.27)	(9.26)	(8.23)	(9.01)	(6.93)	(7.51)

1991

Male	57.04	54.83	53.08	51.38	46.55	45.72	43.37	42.05	38.28
	(6.21)	(9.24)	(8.05)	(9.12)	(9.93)	(7.78)	(7.06)	(9.36)	(7.88)
Female	60.88	57.20	58.51	57.00	54.80	48.88	50.77	44.14	42.03
	(6.17)	(6.04)	(6.83)	(8.12)	(8.65)	(9.23)	(7.95)	(7.66)	(6.79)
Total	58.96	56.01	55.79	54.19	50.68	47.30	47.07	43.09	40.16
	(6.43)	(7.58)	(7.91)	(8.93)	(10.08)	(8.70)	(8.40)	(8.54)	(7.52)

1998

Male	56.93	56.29	51.64	53.34	49.95	49.47	43.42	39.54	39.86
	(8.58)	(8.16)	(9.49)	(7.82)	(8.07)	(8.42)	(7.56)	(7.55)	(6.95)
Female	61.52	59.34	56.61	56.42	54.45	51.36	48.77	45.00	42.69
	(5.36)	(7.14)	(7.60)	(7.61)	(7.92)	(9.28)	(8.84)	(9.03)	(8.83)
Total	59.23	57.83	54.12	54.88	52.20	50.42	46.10	42.27	41.28
	(7.01)	(7.79)	(8.81)	(7.84)	(8.26)	(8.82)	(8.43)	(8.77)	(7.95)

TABLE 4.3 Continued

					Age				
	25	32	39	46	53	60	67	74	81
Perceptual Speed									
Identical Pictures									
1984									
Male	60.65	56.76	56.19	52.44	50.71	45.89	42.65	37.70	35.00
	(7.63)	(6.55)	(6.89)	(6.99)	(7.58)	(5.62)	(7.82)	(6.63)	(8.06)
Female	59.67	57.38	56.06	52.19	50.53	46.98	42.66	40.39	38.62
	(5.36)	(7.33)	(8.16)	(8.01)	(6.98)	(8.37)	(7.11)	(7.44)	(7.13)
Total	60.16	57.07	56.12	52.32	50.62	46.43	42.65	39.04	36.81
	(6.16)	(6.87)	(7.62)	(7.58)	(7.25)	(7.24)	(7.41)	(7.18)	(7.64)
1991									
Male	58.67	57.42	58.26	57.53	52.71	47.62	43.56	40.32	34.27
	(6.97)	(6.48)	(6.35)	(6.74)	(8.15)	(5.93)	(7.91)	(7.74)	(7.56)
Female	61.26	59.00	58.42	56.08	54.32	47.68	45.96	41.65	36.00
	(4.19)	(6.10)	(5.30)	(7.19)	(7.58)	(6.21)	(6.08)	(6.40)	(8.19)
Total	59.97	58.21	58.34	56.81	53.52	47.65	44.76	40.98	35.14
	(5.69)	(6.73)	(5.80)	(7.01)	(7.85)	(6.05)	(6.97)	(7.07)	(7.88)
1998									
Male	60.31	58.05	56.46	52.76	52.09	48.95	45.53	41.68	37.23
	(5.21)	(6.73)	(7.48)	(8.09)	(6.80)	(7.50)	(6.55)	(8.03)	(6.46)
Female	59.64	58.91	56.52	54.08	52.96	49.55	46.26	42.48	37.31
	(4.98)	(6.65)	(6.29)	(7.89)	(9.00)	(8.18)	(7.04)	(7.11)	(6.90)
Total	59.98	58.48	56.49	53.42	52.53	49.25	45.90	42.08	37.27
	(5.02)	(6.66)	(6.82)	(7.99)	(8.03)	(7.77)	(6.71)	(7.48)	(6.63)
Number									
Comparisons									
1984									
Male	49.44	52.37	51.01	49.23	47.85	46.49	44.52	40.85	36.23
	(10.57)	(8.58)	(9.22)	(8.20)	(7.18)	(7.71)	(7.87)	(6.06)	(5.86)
Female	55.38	55.38	55.06	52.31	40.90	49.30	46.41	44.51	41.25
	(8.14)	(8.70)	(8.85)	(9.97)	(7.64)	(9.12)	(8.01)	(8.28)	(6.77)
Total	52.41	53.83	53.04	50.77	49.37	47.90	45.47	42.68	38.74
	(9.33)	(8.70)	(9.20)	(9.38)	(7.56)	(8.59)	(7.98)	(7.55)	(6.76)
1991									
Male	51.93	53.97	53.23	52.12	47.55	46.31	44.29	41.68	38.19
	(8.78)	(9.00)	(10.59)	(7.53)	(9.53)	(6.22)	(7.46)	(6.31)	(7.92)
Female	62.38	56.82	58.80	55.06	53.48	50.39	47.88	45.49	41.18
	(8.29)	(8.17)	(8.46)	(9.26)	(10.09)	(9.70)	(7.51)	(8.03)	(7.49)
Total	57.15	55.40	56.02	53.59	50.51	48.35	46.08	43.59	39.68
	(9.93)	(8.60)	(9.91)	(8.66)	(10.20)	(8.55)	(7.66)	(7.45)	(7.78)
1998									
Male	59.75	58.11	53.52	50.73	49.23	50.60	45.50	43.28	40.40
	(13.95)	(11.30)	(8.98)	(8.64)	(8.87)	(9.11)	(7.75)	(7.06)	(6.56)
Female	63.80	59.97	56.50	55.06	52.74	51.18	50.29	45.45	41.33
	(9.52)	(9.94)	(8.88)	(8.89)	(8.38)	(10.77)	(7.28)	(8.37)	(6.80)
Total	61.78	59.04	55.01	52.89	50.98	50.89	47.89	44.37	40.87
	(11.46)	(10.66)	(9.55)	(9.00)	(8.74)	(9.82)	(7.89)	(7.82)	(6.64)

(*continued*)

TABLE 4.3 Continued

	Age								
	25	32	39	46	53	60	67	74	81
Finding A's									
1984									
Male	53.47	51.97	50.52	49.30	47.04	47.18	47.70	42.10	40.83
	(14.27)	(10.46)	(8.80)	(9.08)	(9.61)	(8.69)	(10.37)	(6.33)	(6.85)
Female	51.83	56.24	53.38	52.19	50.56	48.81	48.73	46.04	45.56
	(11.58)	(10.14)	(10.77)	(10.57)	(8.45)	(9.79)	(8.94)	(7.56)	(9.16)
Total	52.65	54.10	51.95	50.74	48.80	48.00	48.22	44.07	43.20
	(12.49)	(10.45)	(10.04)	(10.07)	(9.19)	(9.32)	(9.59)	(7.27)	(8.45)
1991									
Male	52.52	49.86	53.36	50.18	46.66	46.09	43.46	44.95	41.48
	(9.70)	(11.01)	(9.14)	(8.34)	(9.46)	(7.20)	(8.11)	(6.77)	(6.88)
Female	58.23	54.82	54.77	53.41	53.88	50.22	48.62	47.42	45.24
	(10.82)	(10.45)	(9.54)	(9.41)	(8.98)	(7.98)	(9.48)	(8.66)	(8.80)
Total	55.38	52.34	54.06	51.79	50.27	48.16	46.04	46.18	43.36
	(10.65)	(10.89)	(9.31)	(9.08)	(9.85)	(7.86)	(9.24)	(7.85)	(8.08)
1998									
Male	57.07	52.00	53.12	50.46	50.12	49.18	46.90	46.92	47.31
	(13.63)	(9.74)	(10.45)	(9.28)	(9.32)	(8.08)	(7.99)	(7.13)	(9.98)
Female	57.80	59.62	55.84	54.11	51.84	51.15	49.89	49.77	46.44
	(10.87)	(13.54)	(9.54)	(10.33)	(8.84)	(9.25)	(8.40)	(9.09)	(7.55)
Total	57.43	55.81	54.48	52.29	50.98	50.17	48.39	48.35	46.88
	(11.81)	(12.24)	(10.01)	(9.95)	(9.05)	(8.64)	(8.23)	(8.34)	(8.82)

Across All Measurement Occasions

	25	32	39	46	53	60	67	74	81
Letter Series									
Male	59.58	58.15	56.77	54.10	50.06	48.95	44.85	41.20	39.08
	(9.02)	(7.60)	(8.07)	(7.38)	(8.30)	(7.85)	(8.16)	(7.52)	(5.25)
Female	59.04	57.60	56.08	53.56	51.50	47.14	45.60	42.37	37.57
	(8.25)	(7.93)	(7.54)	(8.59)	(7.99)	(8.20)	(8.22)	(7.40)	(6.51)
Total	59.31	57.87	56.42	53.83	50.78	48.04	45.22	41.78	38.33
	(8.54)	(7.76)	(7.78)	(8.08)	(8.16)	(8.08)	(8.19)	(7.46)	(5.97)
Word Series									
Male	57.67	56.80	55.31	53.19	49.91	48.74	44.42	40.75	35.29
	(7.51)	(7.49)	(7.94)	(7.49)	(8.32)	(7.70)	(8.30)	(8.47)	(6.18)
Female	58.46	57.18	57.11	53.75	52.56	48.60	46.45	44.11	37.70
	(8.47)	(8.90)	(7.43)	(7.64)	(7.70)	(7.87)	(8.28)	(8.47)	(8.22)
Total	58.06	56.99	56.21	53.47	51.23	48.66	45.44	42.43	36.50
	(8.07)	(8.21)	(7.71)	(7.57)	(8.10)	(7.78)	(8.34)	(8.61)	(7.40)
Number Series									
Male	60.14	57.51	56.94	55.26	52.78	50.83	48.19	44.33	41.82
	(8.15)	(9.68)	(9.00)	(7.99)	(9.31)	(7.82)	(8.77)	(9.10)	(7.75)
Female	54.90	53.65	52.64	50.47	49.54	46.50	45.02	42.22	38.67
	(8.39)	(8.00)	(8.24)	(9.56)	(8.07)	(9.56)	(9.25)	(7.37)	(6.67)
Total	57.52	55.58	54.79	52.87	51.16	48.67	46.61	43.28	40.24
	(8.65)	(9.06)	(8.85)	(9.21)	(8.85)	(9.04)	(9.15)	(8.25)	(7.34)

TABLE 4.3 Continued

					Age				
	25	32	39	46	53	60	67	74	81
Object Rotation									
Male	57.39	57.53	56.62	54.86	52.72	53.22	48.72	44.05	40.49
	(7.18)	(6.23)	(7.27)	(7.15)	(7.50)	(7.07)	(8.90)	(10.14)	(8.32)
Female	55.76	54.39	52.94	52.14	49.66	47.99	44.35	38.85	36.54
	(7.90)	(8.27)	(8.95)	(9.31)	(9.24)	(8.68)	(8.40)	(9.01)	(8.00)
Total	56.78	55.96	54.78	53.50	51.19	50.61	46.53	41.45	38.51
	(7.62)	(7.47)	(8.42)	(8.53)	(8.56)	(8.38)	(8.91)	(9.69)	(8.37)
Alphanumeric Rotation									
Male	56.90	57.40	56.47	54.60	52.56	50.61	47.30	42.89	38.51
	(5.96)	(5.60)	(6.40)	(7.13)	(7.77)	(8.45)	(9.50)	(9.97)	(8.25)
Female	55.08	56.04	54.82	53.10	50.39	47.70	45.73	41.40	36.36
	(9.05)	(6.54)	(7.40)	(8.00)	(9.74)	(9.54)	(8.76)	(9.32)	(8.96)
Total	55.99	56.72	55.64	53.85	51.48	49.16	46.51	42.15	37.44
	(7.94)	(6.11)	(7.00)	(7.66)	(8.89)	(9.15)	(9.15)	(9.63)	(8.66)
Cube Comparison									
Male	61.47	59.10	60.19	55.74	53.39	50.81	46.23	43.85	40.51
	(10.76)	(9.37)	(9.06)	(8.65)	(8.70)	(8.32)	(7.35)	(8.03)	(6.29)
Female	56.26	54.60	52.88	50.82	47.99	45.43	44.44	41.67	40.51
	(9.16)	(8.45)	(8.72)	(8.33)	(8.05)	(7.57)	(7.07)	(5.73)	(6.45)
Total	58.87	56.85	56.53	53.28	50.69	48.12	45.34	42.76	40.51
	(10.15)	(9.16)	(9.58)	(8.81)	(8.78)	(8.36)	(7.25)	(6.95)	(6.35)
Addition									
Male	47.80	49.75	50.88	51.98	50.24	51.08	49.31	49.11	44.91
	(9.61)	(9.75)	(9.95)	(9.63)	(11.01)	(9.91)	(10.23)	(9.54)	(10.26)
Female	47.57	49.51	51.53	51.22	51.16	49.52	50.61	49.30	46.22
	(8.90)	(8.69)	(9.40)	(10.76)	(9.12)	(9.73)	(10.11)	(9.45)	(9.80)
Total	47.69	49.63	51.21	51.60	50.70	50.30	49.96	49.20	45.57
	(9.16)	(9.21)	(9.64)	(10.28)	(10.08)	(9.83)	(10.17)	(9.47)	(10.01)
Subtraction and Multiplication									
Male	48.25	50.59	52.72	53.26	50.67	51.15	49.30	46.98	44.27
	(10.32)	(11.18)	(9.72)	(9.46)	(10.87)	(9.49)	(9.40)	(8.42)	(8.96)
Female	48.56	49.66	52.26	51.85	51.07	49.02	49.00	47.89	44.55
	(10.31)	(10.16)	(9.55)	(10.21)	(9.65)	(9.82)	(9.79)	(9.09)	(9.20)
Total	48.41	50.13	52.49	52.56	50.87	50.09	49.15	47.43	44.41
	(10.27)	(10.66)	(9.62)	(9.90)	(10.25)	(9.71)	(9.59)	(98.78)	(9.05)
ETS Vocabulary									
Male	45.16	48.52	49.35	49.69	50.34	51.90	50.66	48.55	50.61
	(8.93)	(8.43)	(9.39)	(9.60)	(9.93)	(9.24)	(10.46)	(11.67)	(10.48)
Female	42.74	46.14	49.32	51.07	52.51	50.33	51.59	49.90	50.85
	(10.03)	(11.40)	(9.37)	(9.04)	(7.83)	(10.20)	(9.50)	(9.89)	(9.07)
Total	43.95	47.33	49.34	50.38	51.43	51.11	51.13	49.23	50.73
	(9.63)	(10.08)	(9.37)	(9.30)	(8.97)	(9.78)	(9.97)	(10.73)	(9.74)

(*continued*)

TABLE 4.3 Continued

	Age								
	25	32	39	46	53	60	67	74	81
ETS Advanced Vocabulary									
Male	46.12	49.05	50.66	51.26	50.72	52.55	50.64	49.66	49.60
	(9.08)	(9.45)	(9.62)	(9.43)	(9.79)	(9.18)	(9.95)	(11.35)	(11.02)
Female	43.14	46.67	48.96	51.33	51.59	48.95	50.93	49.24	50.86
	(8.96)	(9.10)	(9.78)	(10.06)	(9.59)	(10.35)	(9.96)	(10.48)	(10.26)
Total	44.63	47.86	49.81	51.35	51.15	50.75	50.78	49.45	50.73
	(9.10)	(9.33)	(9.73)	(9.78)	(9.68)	(9.97)	(9.94)	(10.86)	(10.62)
Immediate Recall									
Male	57.73	54.75	52.62	51.49	48.23	47.67	44.32	40.48	38.24
	(6.36)	(8.24)	(8.74)	(8.67)	(9.18)	(8.24)	(9.07)	(9.58)	(8.13)
Female	59.17	57.47	5.44	54.53	52.75	40.16	48.54	44.72	42.35
	(6.21)	(6.50)	(8.10)	(7.96)	(8.07)	(9.41)	(9.11)	(8.22)	(8.11)
Total	58.44	56.11	54.03	53.01	50.49	48.42	46.43	42.60	40.30
	(6.28)	(7.52)	(8.50)	(8.40)	(8.91)	(8.90)	(9.32)	(9.10)	(8.35)
Delayed Recall									
Male	57.76	55.06	52.43	51.45	47.60	47.08	43.17	40.66	38.77
	(6.92)	(8.28)	(8.66)	(8.22)	(9.09)	(7.85)	(7.89)	(8.17)	(7.40)
Female	60.53	58.12	56.61	54.86	52.54	49.51	49.01	43.95	42.49
	(6.29)	(6.85)	(7.76)	(8.30)	(8.82)	(8.92)	(8.58)	(7.48)	(7.41)
Total	59.15	56.59	54.52	53.16	50.07	48.29	46.09	42.31	40.63
	(6.67)	(7.73)	(8.43)	(8.42)	(9.27)	(8.51)	(8.74)	(7.96)	(7.61)
Identical Pictures									
Male	59.59	57.28	57.04	53.75	51.64	46.92	43.78	39.74	35.55
	(6.74)	(6.81)	(6.86)	(7.68)	(7.53)	(6.31)	(7.52)	(7.56)	(7.35)
Female	60.25	58.43	56.73	53.68	52.21	47.60	44.22	41.36	37.06
	(4.79)	(6.71)	(7.08)	(7.92)	(7.88)	(7.93)	(6.99)	(7.00)	(7.57)
Total	60.02	57.86	56.88	53.72	51.95	47.25	44.00	40.61	36.64
	(5.64)	(6.77)	(6.97)	(7.80)	(7.71)	(7.22)	(7.24)	(7.29)	(7.48)
Number Comparisons									
Male	53.61	54.96	52.71	50.55	48.19	47.31	44.74	41.76	39.00
	(11.33)	(10.17)	(9.56)	(8.15)	(8.27)	(8.00)	(7.74)	(6.37)	(7.04)
Female	61.32	57.71	56.22	53.74	52.30	49.83	47.61	45.16	41.39
	(9.34)	(9.03)	(9.37)	(9.61)	(8.52)	(9.52)	(7.80)	(8.16)	(7.09)
Total	57.46	56.33	54.46	52.15	50.19	48.57	46.18	43.46	40.20
	(10.86)	(9.69)	(9.60)	(9.13)	(8.63)	(8.91)	(7.89)	(7.57)	(7.14)
Finding A's									
Male	53.95	51.34	52.14	49.93	47.77	47.45	46.47	44.47	43.66
	(12.11)	(10.31)	(9.49)	(8.96)	(9.55)	(8.28)	(9.26)	(6.73)	(8.65)
Female	55.96	56.77	54.49	53.06	51.72	49.56	48.91	47.46	45.73
	(11.36)	(11.56)	(10.11)	(10.22)	(8.74)	(9.31)	(8.97)	(8.41)	(8.36)
Total	55.26	54.06	53.23	51.50	49.83	48.52	47.70	46.02	44.91
	(11.67)	(11.26)	(9.88)	(9.80)	(9.34)	(8.90)	(9.18)	(7.82)	(8.54)

Note. ETS, Educational Testing Service.

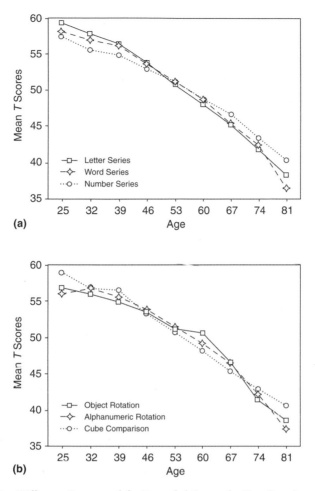

FIGURE 4.6 *Age Difference Patterns of the Expanded Battery by Test Occasion.*

(continued)

The ability profiles for the new markers of spatial orientation also showed a difference of just under 2 *SD* from the youngest to the oldest group. As for the original marker, there were significant gender differences favoring males for all three tests. Significant age differences from the youngest group were observed by age 53 for Alphanumeric Rotation, but already by age 46 for Object Rotation and Cube Comparison. On the last measure, there was also a significant gain across measurement occasions as well as a significant Sex × Age interaction that reflected the absence of sex differences in midlife (ages 39, 46, and 53).

The expanded battery contains three markers for the Perceptual Speed factor that were not measured earlier. Age differences from the youngest to the oldest group range from 1 *SD* for the Finding A's test to almost 2.5 *SD* for the Identical Pictures test. Interestingly, Identical Pictures appears to be the easiest measure for the young groups, whereas Finding A's is easier for the older groups. Gender differ-

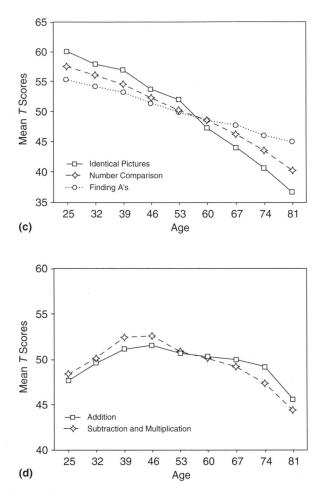

FIGURE 4.6 *Continued.*

ences favor women for all three tests. Significant age differences from the youngest group were found by age 46 for Identical Pictures and by age 53 for Number Comparison and Finding A's. Significantly higher performance levels across the three assessment points were found for Identical Pictures and for Number Comparison.

The new markers of Numeric Ability attain a peak at age 46 and then show a negative age difference of approximately 0.7 *SD* to the oldest age group. No significant gender differences were observed for either test, but there was a significant increase in performance level in 1991 for the Addition test.

The new measures of Verbal Ability have rather different profiles from the original PMA marker because they are virtually unspeeded. The profile for the 1984 testing is slightly concave for both measures, with virtually no difference in level between the youngest and oldest sample and a peak plateau from 39 to 67

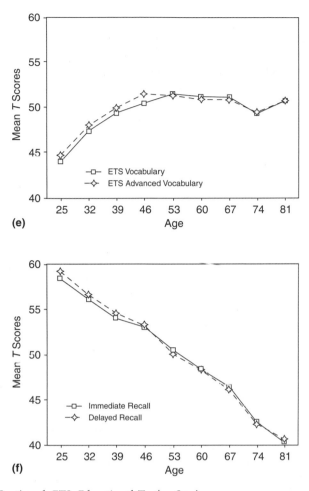

FIGURE 4.6 *Continued. ETS, Educational Testing Service.*

years of age. In contrast, the 1991 profile shows positive age differences to age 53, followed by a virtual plateau to the oldest group for both measures,

In 1998, peaks were reached at age 53 for the easier and at age 60 for the more difficult test, followed by virtual plateaus to the oldest ages. There were no significant gender differences on either test, but significantly higher overall performance levels were observed for the Advanced Vocabulary test in 1991.

Also, newly included were two measures of the Verbal Memory factor. They have quite similar profiles, with an age difference of just under 2 *SD* from the youngest to the oldest age/cohort. Significant gender differences on these measures favor women (Immediate Recall). Significant age differences from the level of the youngest group appeared by age 39 for Delayed Recall and by age 46 for Immediate Recall. Significantly higher levels of performance on the second measurement occasion were also observed.

Cross-Sectional Differences on the Latent Constructs

Both the original markers and the new tests were combined as described above, and factor scores were computed for the resulting six latent constructs. Means and standard deviations separately by gender and for the total in each age group are given in table 4.4 and are graphed across gender in figure 4.7. Table 4.4 also has means and standard deviations for the factor scores averaged over the three test occasions. Intercorrelations among factor scores by age group and for the total sample are reported in appendix A-4.3.

For four of the six factors, there are consistent negative age differences. They are statistically significant for Inductive Reasoning, Spatial Orientation, and Perceptual Speed at age 46 and for Verbal Memory at age 39. The magnitude of age difference from the youngest to the oldest group amounts to approximately 2 *SD* on average. The remaining two factors, Numeric Facility and Verbal Comprehension, have a very different profile. They both show positive age differences until midlife, with less than 0.5 *SD* negative differences thereafter, such that persons in advanced old age, on average, are at a higher level than the youngest age group. Gender differences on the latent construct measures were observed in favor of men on Spatial Orientation and in favor of women for Perceptual Speed and Verbal Memory. A higher overall performance level in 1991 was shown for Inductive Reasoning and Verbal Memory.

Practical Intelligence Data

The Basic Skills–Reading Test

The Basic Skills–Reading test was developed by the Educational Testing Service (1977) to examine whether graduating high school students had attained knowledge that was relevant to real-life tasks. The test therefore simulates textual materials representing everyday problem-solving activities. This test was given in both the fifth and sixth cycles. An overall analysis of variance of participants at first test did not detect any significant gender differences, but did result in a significant age/cohort main effect ($F[df = 8, 1953] = 142.62$, $p < .001$). As shown in table 4.5 and figure 4.8, the age difference profile is virtually flat until age 60; the first significant age difference occurs between 60 and 67 years of age. There was no significant Age × Gender interaction. Overall, there was a significantly higher level of performance in 1991 than in 1984 ($F[df = 1, 1,935] = 34.47$, $p < .001$) as well as a significant Age × Time interaction ($F[df = 1, 1,935] = 4.42$, $p < .001$). However, for a specific age group, it was only the 81-year-old level that showed a statistically significant gain across cohorts in 1991.

The Everyday Problems Test

Because of significant ceiling effects in the Basic Skills test, we decided to substitute the Everyday Problems Test (EPT; Willis, 1992b) in the 1998 cycle. Cross-sectional data by age and gender are reported in table 4.6. Intercorrelations

TABLE 4.4 Means and Standard Deviations for the Latent Construct Scores by Sample and Gender

	Age								
	25	32	39	46	53	60	67	74	81
Inductive Reasoning									
1984									
Male	60.67	57.53	55.78	54.66	49.28	48.72	43.25	38.76	35.25
	(4.61)	(8.72)	(7.51)	(6.83)	(8.34)	(7.73)	(8.41)	(6.89)	(5.70)
Female	55.08	55.88	56.50	52.37	50.74	47.09	44.60	41.42	36.19
	(8.90)	(8.71)	(7.17)	(8.01)	(7.48)	(8.27)	(8.34)	(7.18)	(6.35)
Total	57.36	56.81	56.19	53.30	50.01	47.78	44.02	40.24	35.88
	(7.83)	(8.67)	(7.30)	(7.61)	(7.93)	(8.05)	(8.37)	(7.14)	(6.03)
1991									
Male	57.19	57.79	57.00	55.44	51.29	47.13	44.70	40.74	34.86
	(9.11)	(6.47)	(8.19)	(7.35)	(9.08)	(5.40)	(8.24)	(8.93)	(5.50)
Female	59.82	57.45	56.62	55.14	53.50	46.62	46.64	41.95	34.72
	(7.98)	(7.68)	(5.11)	(8.86)	(8.35)	(8.00)	(8.99)	(7.97)	(7.09)
Total	58.66	57.59	56.81	55.27	52.42	46.85	45.83	41.38	34.79
	(8.53)	(7.14)	(6.79)	(8.23)	(8.73)	(6.92)	(8.69)	(8.41)	(6.33)
1998									
Male	64.13	58.26	57.44	52.92	51.90	51.37	45.40	42.12	39.18
	(5.32)	(7.41)	(7.30)	(6.83)	(8.48)	(7.96)	(7.61)	(8.24)	(5.63)
Female	59.40	58.06	56.25	53.90	51.86	48.61	44.86	42.13	37.76
	(5.19)	(7.03)	(7.74)	(8.27)	(7.33)	(7.31)	(7.65)	(7.76)	(6.19)
Total	61.18	58.16	58.80	53.41	51.88	50.08	45.19	42.13	38.51
	(5.67)	(7.17)	(7.53)	(7.57)	(7.84)	(7.74)	(7.59)	(7.90)	(5.89)
Spatial Orientation									
1984									
Male	59.00	57.44	57.64	55.86	52.52	52.15	46.82	41.82	38.82
	(6.42)	(6.66)	(7.62)	(7.51)	(7.41)	(7.32)	(8.11)	(8.67)	(7.17)
Female	53.69	55.52	53.75	51.93	48.38	46.70	43.98	39.69	36.88
	(12.15)	(5.72)	(8.81)	(8.00)	(8.01)	(7.79)	(7.82)	(7.61)	(6.09)
Total	55.86	56.60	55.42	53.52	50.46	49.19	45.23	40.64	37.67
	(10.35)	(6.28)	(8.51)	(8.02)	(7.97)	(8.04)	(8.05)	(8.12)	(6.49)
1991									
Male	59.00	58.00	59.41	56.82	54.23	51.29	46.24	42.85	36.69
	(7.72)	(6.97)	(7.31)	(6.14)	(8.36)	(6.64)	(8.74)	(8.74)	(7.45)
Female	58.15	54.68	52.90	52.69	50.62	45.78	42.86	38.67	34.88
	(6.91)	(8.28)	(7.94)	(8.26)	(9.29)	(7.84)	(7.74)	(7.26)	(7.46)
Total	58.52	56.07	56.15	54.39	52.38	48.22	44.29	40.71	35.77
	(7.23)	(7.88)	(8.26)	(7.70)	(8.98)	(7.78)	(8.31)	(8.24)	(7.46)
1998									
Male	62.47	60.74	49.02	54.52	53.60	51.87	49.14	44.67	40.03
	(4.94)	(5.32)	(6.20)	(7.71)	(6.35)	(7.52)	(7.83)	(9.68)	(5.53)
Female	57.12	56.03	55.41	51.69	49.47	47.73	44.26	35.96	38.29
	(6.38)	(6.62)	(8.03)	(9.45)	(8.86)	(9.43)	(7.42)	(8.37)	(7.25)
Total	59.12	58.49	57.08	53.10	51.37	49.94	47.32	41.07	38.07
	(6.38)	(6.38)	(7.43)	(8.71)	(8.03)	(8.65)	(8.00)	(9.44)	(6.68)

(*continued*)

TABLE 4.4 Continued

	Age								
	25	32	39	46	53	60	67	74	81
Perceptual Speed									
1984									
Male	58.00	55.75	55.02	52.64	49.75	46.76	43.22	36.74	32.17
	(5.39)	(5.48)	(7.15)	(6.62)	(7.44)	(6.60)	(8.86)	(6.36)	(8.62)
Female	56.23	57.88	56.27	53.55	51.66	47.98	44.42	40.90	38.00
	(7.13)	(6.73)	(7.54)	(8.29)	(6.63)	(8.60)	(7.67)	(7.48)	(6.09)
Total	56.95	56.68	55.73	53.18	50.73	47.43	43.89	39.06	35.50
	(6.40)	(6.10)	(7.38)	(7.65)	(7.08)	(7.77)	(8.21)	(7.27)	(7.71)
1991									
Male	55.74	56.14	57.46	55.38	50.45	47.28	42.93	40.29	33.31
	(8.02)	(7.60)	(7.14)	(7.28)	(9.07)	(6.34)	(8.55)	(8.22)	(7.17)
Female	61.41	57.70	59.00	56.49	55.12	48.60	47.02	42.70	36.15
	(6.68)	(7.68)	(5.66)	(7.50)	(7.65)	(7.19)	(6.87)	(7.97)	(9.59)
Total	58.90	57.04	58.23	56.04	52.85	48.01	45.29	41.52	34.77
	(7.78)	(7.63)	(6.44)	(7.39)	(8.64)	(6.81)	(7.85)	(8.14)	(8.56)
1998									
Male	60.13	57.11	56.06	52.33	51.93	47.98	44.42	40.90	38.00
	(8.54)	(7.77)	(7.71)	(8.17)	(6.94)	(7.85)	(6.99)	(7.45)	(6.89)
Female	60.32	59.78	56.69	55.26	53.73	50.27	47.74	44.00	38.22
	(6.32)	(8.74)	(7.10)	(8.54)	(8.49)	(8.57)	(7.11)	(8.39)	(8.01)
Total	60.25	58.39	56.40	53.80	52.90	49.97	46.29	43.18	38.18
	(7.12)	(8.29)	(7.36)	(8.45)	(7.83)	(8.14)	(7.09)	(7.98)	(7.38)
Numeric Facility									
1984									
Male	49.78	53.47	51.97	55.11	51.01	53.41	50.85	50.03	40.08
	(6.08)	(11.21)	(9.50)	(10.06)	(10.44)	(10.69)	(10.89)	(7.61)	(6.76)
Female	44.92	50.36	53.01	52.05	51.65	50.23	51.17	48.06	43.75
	(8.36)	(9.92)	(10.10)	(9.99)	(9.64)	(9.47)	(10.26)	(9.07)	(8.32)
Total	46.91	52.11	52.56	53.29	51.33	51.66	51.03	48.93	42.18
	(7.75)	(10.68)	(98.82)	(10.10)	(10.02)	(10.14)	(10.51)	(8.46)	(7.78)
1991									
Male	46.52	49.31	52.56	53.65	50.16	47.97	49.15	47.32	44.29
	(8.68)	(8.65)	(11.08)	(8.98)	(12.18)	(8.38)	(8.39)	(10.55)	(11.34)
Female	49.18	48.68	51.79	52.63	51.05	48.08	49.00	49.65	46.29
	(9.76)	(8.68)	(8.35)	(10.65)	(9.92)	(10.40)	(9.67)	(9.78)	(10.05)
Total	48.00	48.94	52.18	53.05	50.62	48.03	49.06	48.51	45.34
	(9.32)	(8.61)	(9.75)	(9.96)	(11.02)	(9.49)	(9.10)	(10.17)	(10.65)
1998									
Male	51.27	48.31	50.23	49.66	51.12	51.37	48.03	45.62	46.28
	(12.73)	(10.98)	(10.40)	(9.28)	(11.71)	(9.11)	(9.38)	(9.99)	(8.96)
Female	47.48	49.25	49.36	48.47	49.71	46.97	47.91	47.42	44.56
	(8.58)	(8.07)	(8.80)	(10.67)	(8.44)	(9.16)	(9.75)	(9.58)	(9.95)
Total	48.90	48.76	49.77	49.06	50.36	49.32	47.99	46.64	45.45
	(10.34)	(9.64)	(9.54)	(9.98)	(10.05)	(9.33)	(9.47)	(9.72)	(9.40)

TABLE 4.4 Continued

					Age				
	25	32	39	46	53	60	67	74	81
Verbal Comprehension									
1984									
Male	50.89	50.00	51.48	52.66	51.32	53.27	50.87	47.69	40.17
	(7.98)	(8.15)	(10.15)	(9.35)	(9.40)	(8.05)	(10.66)	(11.12)	(16.30)
Female	45.15	50.76	51.06	52.16	52.32	50.09	51.60	48.37	47.19
	(12.29)	(7.75)	(8.70)	(9.07)	(9.08)	(10.41)	(9.91)	(9.50)	(9.80)
Total	47.50	50.33	51.24	52.36	51.83	51.52	51.28	48.07	44.18
	(10.91)	(7.92)	(9.32)	(9.16)	(9.22)	(9.53)	(10.22)	(10.20)	(13.19)
1991									
Male	44.33	49.45	51.45	50.59	50.53	50.56	50.14	47.41	47.97
	(8.72)	(8.78)	(8.95)	(9.47)	(9.60)	(9.68)	(9.97)	(12.53)	(11.81)
Female	43.85	45.62	52.51	53.24	53.72	48.78	52.04	48.77	47.32
	(8.86)	(11.52)	(7.27)	(9.70)	(8.13)	(9.64)	(8.59)	(11.71)	(10.59)
Total	44.07	47.23	51.99	52.16	52.17	49.57	51.24	48.11	47.64
	(8.73)	(10.56)	(8.11)	(9.64)	(8.97)	(9.63)	(9.19)	(12.06)	(11.13)
1998									
Male	47.53	49.26	49.31	49.70	49.79	52.24	48.76	48.17	48.79
	(9.86)	(9.87)	(9.03)	(10.28)	(11.20)	(10.03)	(10.25)	(10.42)	(8.80)
Female	43.28	46.44	46.21	50.26	51.82	48.55	46.71	48.90	51.11
	(8.90)	(10.13)	(11.16)	(10.43)	(8.64)	(11.04)	(9.95)	(9.23)	(9.08)
Total	44.88	47.91	47.64	49.98	50.88	50.52	48.00	48.58	49.91
	(9.38)	(10.02)	(10.30)	(10.32)	(9.90)	(10.60)	(10.14)	(9.68)	(8.93)
Verbal Memory									
1984									
Male	61.11	53.69	52.64	49.50	46.87	46.50	43.18	38.62	34.17
	(5.49)	(7.82)	(8.80)	(8.79)	(9.29)	(7.93)	(9.09)	(7.66)	(6.41)
Female	58.00	57.64	55.64	52.73	50.03	48.72	47.89	43.43	44.27
	(8.38)	(7.77)	(8.19)	(8.49)	(8.96)	(9.20)	(9.25)	(6.90)	(6.79)
Total	59.27	55.42	54.35	51.42	48.46	47.72	45.82	41.30	39.78
	(7.35)	(7.98)	(8.56)	(8.44)	(9.23)	(8.70)	(9.45)	(7.59)	(8.27)
1991									
Male	57.44	54.97	53.87	52.50	47.76	46.78	43.66	41.80	38.09
	(6.22)	(8.93)	(8.48)	(8.68)	(10.08)	(8.03)	(7.84)	(9.98)	(7.87)
Female	60.56	57.68	58.54	57.34	55.25	49.08	50.43	44.21	41.32
	(6.32)	(5.97)	(6.96)	(6.84)	(8.42)	(9.65)	(7.87)	(8.20)	(7.53)
Total	59.18	56.54	56.21	54.36	51.60	48.06	47.57	43.05	39.76
	(6.41)	(7.42)	(8.06)	(7.96)	(9.95)	(8.98)	(8.51)	(9.13)	(7.81)
1998									
Male	57.67	56.71	51.79	53.23	49.76	49.61	43.53	39.92	38.52
	(8.20)	(8.32)	(9.12)	(8.20)	(8.00)	(8.46)	(7.90)	(8.68)	(7.96)
Female	61.24	59.28	55.96	56.15	54.49	51.00	48.09	45.10	41.96
	(5.31)	(6.81)	(8.33)	(7.93)	(7.74)	(9.09)	(9.45)	(9.31)	(8.57)
Total	59.90	57.94	54.06	54.70	52.31	50.25	45.22	42.80	40.15
	(6.67)	(7.69)	(8.90)	(8.16)	(8.17)	(8.72)	(8.75)	(9.32)	(8.36)

(*continued*)

TABLE 4.4 Continued

					Age				
	25	32	39	46	53	60	67	74	81
Across All Measurement Occasions									
Inductive Reasoning									
Male	59.84	57.88	56.66	54.16	50.46	49.04	44.30	40.33	36.76
	(8.00)	(7.54)	(7.62)	(6.97)	(8.59)	(7.47)	(8.12)	(8.08)	(5.89)
Female	58.82	57.25	56.44	53.50	51.73	47.22	45.25	41.79	36.08
	(7.43)	(7.72)	(6.92)	(8.33)	(7.69)	(8.02)	(8.42)	(7.55)	(6.68)
Total	59.25	57.56	56.54	53.79	51.11	48.07	44.79	41.12	36.41
	(7.66)	(7.62)	(7.24)	(7.77)	(8.15)	(7.81)	(8.28)	(7.81)	(6.31)
Spatial Orientation									
Male	60.02	58.81	58.57	55.55	53.22	51.91	47.45	42.88	38.36
	(6.86)	(6.41)	(7.09)	(7.33)	(7.38)	(7.20)	(8.21)	(8.92)	(6.78)
Female	56.99	55.34	54.10	52.04	49.24	46.68	43.70	38.98	35.68
	(7.97)	(7.11)	(8.38)	(8.49)	(8.58)	(8.10)	(7.71)	(7.65)	(7.07)
Total	58.24	57.07	56.15	53.57	51.18	49.14	45.51	40.77	36.99
	(7.65)	(6.97)	(8.11)	(8.18)	(8.25)	(8.11)	(8.16)	(8.46)	(7.04)
Perceptual Speed									
Male	57.43	56.36	56.02	53.11	50.50	47.58	43.88	39.38	35.04
	(7.89)	(6.98)	(7.35)	(7.44)	(7.75)	(6.94)	(8.24)	(7.63)	(7.65)
Female	60.10	58.43	57.03	54.77	53.08	48.54	45.78	42.31	37.26
	(6.81)	(7.80)	(7.06)	(8.24)	(7.55)	(8.30)	(7.45)	(7.92)	(8.38)
Total	58.99	57.40	56.57	54.04	51.84	48.10	44.86	40.97	36.18
	(7.37)	(7.46)	(7.20)	(7.93)	(7.74)	(7.70)	(7.89)	(7.91)	(8.08)
Numeric Facility									
Male	48.49	50.33	51.55	52.70	50.84	51.80	49.54	47.94	44.39
	(9.76)	(10.55)	(10.22)	(9.80)	(11.15)	(10.05)	(9.90)	(9.48)	(9.88)
Female	47.82	49.30	51.56	51.11	50.94	49.14	49.95	48.46	45.16
	(9.13)	(8.76)	(9.40)	(10.46)	(9.36)	(9.67)	(10.04)	(9.42)	(9.62)
Total	48.10	49.81	51.56	51.80	50.89	50.38	49.75	48.22	44.79
	(9.36)	(9.58)	(9.76)	(10.19)	(10.25)	(9.92)	(9.96)	(9.43)	(9.72)
Verbal Comprehension									
Male	46.43	49.56	50.75	51.08	50.72	52.46	50.01	47.69	47.03
	(9.13)	(8.91)	(9.47)	(9.77)	(9.91)	(8.91)	(10.35)	(11.44)	(11.84)
Female	43.89	47.22	49.81	51.84	52.51	49.51	50.84	48.64	48.62
	(9.45)	(10.32)	(9.59)	(9.71)	(8.72)	(10.33)	(9.70)	(10.18)	(9.96)
Total	44.94	48.38	50.24	51.51	51.64	50.89	50.44	48.21	47.84
	(9.36)	(9.69)	(9.53)	(9.71)	(9.34)	(9.79)	(10.02)	(10.77)	(10.92)
Verbal Memory									
Male	58.16	55.18	52.69	51.57	47.85	47.31	43.40	40.16	37.62
	(6.76)	(8.36)	(8.80)	(8.38)	(9.19)	(8.13)	(8.39)	(8.88)	(7.74)
Female	60.33	58.20	56.40	54.86	52.57	49.22	48.67	44.11	42.13
	(6.42)	(6.72)	(8.02)	(8.17)	(8.78)	(9.27)	(8.84)	(7.96)	(7.75)
Total	59.43	56.69	54.71	53.43	50.29	48.33	46.13	42.30	39.91
	(6.62)	(7.71)	(8.57)	(8.41)	(9.27)	(8.79)	(9.06)	(8.61)	(8.04)

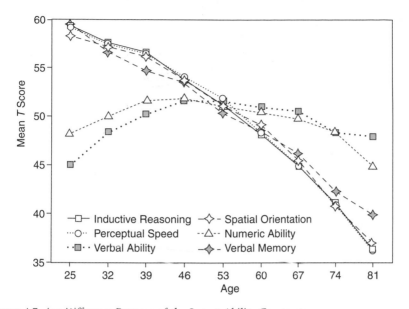

FIGURE 4.7 *Age Difference Patterns of the Latent Ability Constructs.*

TABLE 4.5 Means and Standard Deviations for the Basic Skills Test by Sample and Gender

	1984			1991		
Age	Male	Female	Total	Male	Female	Total
25	54.4	55.7	55.1	54.3	55.9	55.2
	(4.4)	(3.3)	(3.8)	(5.1)	(2.2)	(3.8)
32	55.8	54.3	55.0	56.3	54.3	55.2
	(2.1)	(6.5)	(5.0)	(2.1)	(4.2)	(3.6)
39	54.6	54.3	54.4	55.3	55.6	55.4
	(4.9)	(4.6)	(4.7)	(2.8)	(2.3)	(2.6)
46	54.2	54.0	54.1	54.8	55.0	54.9
	(3.4)	(3.9)	(3.7)	(3.0)	(3.2)	(3.1)
53	52.5	52.3	52.4	54.0	54.9	54.5
	(4.7)	(5.5)	(5.1)	(5.3)	(2.6)	(4.2)
60	52.1	51.1	51.6	52.7	51.8	52.2
	(6.2)	(6.5)	(6.4)	(7.3)	(6.4)	(6.8)
67	47.4	48.2	47.8	51.4	51.3	51.3
	(11.0)	(9.0)	(9.9)	(7.4)	(5.6)	(6.4)
74	41.2	43.2	42.2	47.8	46.9	47.3
	(12.1)	(11.0)	(11.6)	(8.4)	(8.0)	(8.1)
81	28.1	32.8	31.1	37.9	36.7	37.3
	(14.2)	(14.0)	(14.1)	(14.3)	(13.2)	(13.7)

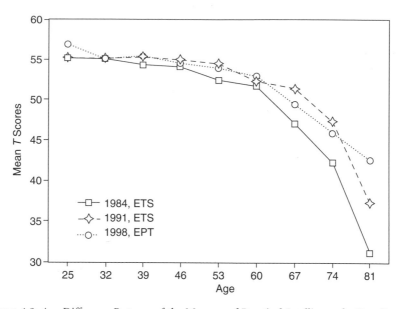

FIGURE 4.8 *Age Difference Patterns of the Measure of Practical Intelligence by Test Occasion. EPT, Everyday Problems Test; ETS, Educational Testing Service.*

among the seven subscales are reported by age group and for the total sample in appendix A-4.4.

As on the cognitive ability measures, there are age differences of approximately 2.5 *SD* from young adulthood to advanced old age. Overall age differences become significant by age 60. Women generally do better than men except at the oldest age.

Cognitive Style Data

Data on cognitive style, as measured by the TBR, were collected from the beginning of the SLS. A summary of cross-sectional data through the fourth cycle can be found in Schaie (1983b). Detailed data on the TBR subscores were provided by Schaie and Willis (1991). In this section, I provide a summary of the cross-sectional data for the latent dimensions of MCF, AF, and PS. The structural relationship between the primary mental abilities and the cognitive style constructs (see Dutta, 1992; Schaie et al., 1991) are examined in chapter 9.

Cross-sectional data on the cognitive style variables were obtained for mean ages 25 to 67 years in cycle 1, for mean ages 25 to 74 years in cycle 2, and for mean ages 25 to 81 years in the remaining cycles. To provide appropriate comparisons with the ability data, the TBR factor scores were restandardized across all seven cycles ($N = 4,837$). Table 4.7 presents means and standard deviations for the six test cycles separately by gender and for the total sample for each age level.

TABLE 4.6 Means and Standard Deviations in *T* Scores for the Everyday Problems Test by Sample and Gender, 1998 Only

	Age									
	25	32	39	46	53	60	67	74	81	88
Meal Preparation										
Male	55.20	52.00	54.89	52.35	51.60	52.15	48.89	47.12	45.29	37.37
	(8.71)	(9.48)	(5.57)	(9.19)	(9.48)	(7.77)	(10.95)	(10.90)	(11.21)	(11.48)
Female	54.52	53.49	51.89	52.70	52.48	51.60	49.38	46.02	46.02	43.61
	(6.56)	(7.84)	(9.29)	(6.48)	(7.53)	(8.17)	(7.76)	(11.66)	(10.08)	(10.69)
Total	54.86	52.75	53.39	52.52	52.04	51.87	49.14	46.58	45.66	40.49
Health Promotion										
Male	54.13	53.91	55.23	52.98	53.31	51.94	50.84	46.95	44.74	36.89
	(5.93)	(10.22)	(5.32)	(8.21)	(7.22)	(8.27)	(8.81)	(10.87)	(13.92)	(14.19)
Female	55.72	54.12	54.38	53.12	53.27	50.97	49.11	45.99	44.19	40.86
	(5.24)	(7.76)	(7.18)	(7.38)	(6.73)	(7.82)	(8.74)	(9.90)	(11.40)	(12.72)
Total	54.93	54.01	54.80	53.05	53.29	51.45	49.98	46.47	44.47	38.04
	(5.49)	(8.95)	(6.44)	(7.79)	(6.94)	(8.04)	(8.80)	(10.33)	(12.56)	(13.48)
Telephone Use										
Male	56.73	53.64	55.19	53.79	52.86	53.76	49.74	47.07	44.16	36.89
	(5.16)	(8.95)	(7.57)	(9.13)	(8.92)	(8.06)	(10.01)	(10.15)	(10.59)	(10.41)
Female	55.80	54.76	53.38	53.90	53.14	49.50	47.14	46.47	45.06	41.25
	(5.79)	(7.81)	(9.08)	(7.93)	(7.45)	(8.91)	(9.16)	(10.00)	(10.22)	(10.66)
Total	56.27	54.20	54.28	53.84	53.00	51.63	48.44	46.77	44.61	39.07
	(5.51)	(8.34)	(8.49)	(8.54)	(8.13)	(8.75)	(9.64)	(10.05)	(10.38)	(10.70)
Consumer Activities										
Male	55.00	54.13	54.14	53.28	52.61	52.79	49.97	48.18	43.88	38.30
	(4.14)	(6.83)	(5.93)	(7.96)	(8.15)	(6.93)	(8.68)	(9.78)	(13.25)	(14.39)
Female	55.40	53.08	53.89	53.21	54.05	53.00	49.21	45.73	44.59	30.20
	(4.73)	(6.95)	(6.53)	(7.15)	(5.25)	(6.86)	(9.16)	(12.37)	(13.23)	(13.94)
Total	55.20	53.61	54.02	53.25	53.33	52.89	49.59	46.95	44.23	38.75
	(4.46)	(6.88)	(6.26)	(7.55)	(6.74)	(6.88)	(8.93)	(11.24)	(13.21)	(14.01)
Financial Activities										
Male	53.73	54.51	53.44	52.86	51.32	53.06	51.77	47.12	43.61	37.11
	(4.13)	(5.36)	(6.20)	(7.56)	(8.09)	(6.43)	(8.00)	(10.45)	(12.99)	(11.79)
Female	54.60	52.94	53.29	52.27	53.34	52.43	49.06	46.93	43.36	37.50
	(5.42)	(7.04)	(7.76)	(6.79)	(6.21)	(6.73)	(9.78)	(9.97)	(11.57)	(12.71)
Total	54.17	53.73	53.37	52.55	52.33	52.75	50.41	47.02	43.49	37.31
	(4.94)	(6.32)	(7.11)	(7.18)	(7.18)	(6.58)	(9.07)	(10.17)	(12.20)	(12.29)
Household Activities										
Male	58.67	55.40	55.80	55.65	53.93	53.29	49.24	48.45	43.71	38.19
	(4.32)	(6.26)	(5.92)	(6.07)	(7.74)	(7.12)	(9.35)	(9.73)	(10.83)	(12.52)
Female	54.84	55.51	55.13	53.94	53.77	51.38	48.29	44.45	42.77	36.98
	(5.47)	(6.26)	(7.32)	(7.26)	(7.03)	(7.73)	(8.68)	(10.55)	(10.89)	(10.61)
Total	56.75	55.46	55.46	54.79	53.84	52.33	48.77	46.45	43.24	37.58
	(5.35)	(6.34)	(6.74)	(6.72)	(7.34)	(7.49)	(9.00)	(10.37)	(10.85)	(11.30)
Transportation Activities										
Male	55.00	52.20	54.01	53.91	53.23	53.62	50.58	43.85	45.13	39.67
	(4.39)	(8.83)	(6.25)	(7.58)	(7.29)	(6.20)	(9.08)	(10.30)	(12.15)	(15.68)
Female	52.96	52.88	52.39	53.50	52.17	51.19	49.32	46.32	43.27	38.57
	(6.91)	(7.48)	(7.95)	(6.91)	(7.58)	(8.31)	(8.70)	(11.61)	(12.48)	(13.49)
Total	53.98	52.54	53.20	53.70	52.70	52.41	49.95	47.58	44.20	39.12
	(6.11)	(8.10)	(7.29)	(7.24)	(7.45)	(7.44)	(8.88)	(10.10)	(12.34)	(14.79)
Total IADL Activities										
Male	57.40	54.89	56.14	54.71	53.57	53.94	50.20	46.91	42.56	33.67
	(3.50)	(7.79)	(4.66)	(7.64)	(6.19)	(6.19)	(8.28)	(9.80)	(12.01)	(13.03)
Female	56.48	55.16	54.63	54.29	54.20	51.84	48.36	44.75	42.35	36.39
	(3.85)	(6.36)	(7.77)	(5.62)	(5.09)	(6.69)	(8.12)	(10.42)	(11.37)	(12.03)
Total	56.94	55.02	55.39	54.50	53.88	52.89	49.28	45.83	42.46	35.03
	(3.70)	(7.03)	(6.65)	(6.71)	(6.37)	(6.52)	(8.23)	(10.19)	(11.64)	(12.40)

Note. IADL, instrumental activities of daily living.

TABLE 4.7 Means and Standard Deviations for the Rigidity-Flexibility Factor Scores by Sample and Gender

| | Age | | | | | | | | |
	25	32	39	46	53	60	67	74	81
Motor-Cognitive Flexibility									
1956									
Male	53.55	53.15	50.42	49.14	49.60	42.69	43.95	—	—
	(5.19)	(6.47)	(5.30)	(8.14)	(7.23)	(8.09)	(8.32)	—	—
Female	55.47	52.89	48.29	51.64	47.26	46.41	42.84	—	—
	(4.82)	(4.16)	(8.16)	(6.32)	(7.48)	(5.28)	(8.47)	—	—
Total	54.51	53.01	49.37	50.29	48.43	44.60	46.39	—	—
	(5.07)	(5.33)	(6.90)	(7.41)	(7.39)	(7.00)	(8.36)	—	—
1963									
Male	56.88	55.15	53.59	51.10	49.40	47.09	44.92	45.58	—
	(4.39)	(5.09)	(5.62)	(7.51)	(7.54)	(8.17)	(8.40)	(7.35)	—
Female	55.31	54.49	53.05	51.37	49.58	47.55	45.06	42.65	—
	(5.47)	(5.55)	(5.18)	(6.75)	(6.16)	(7.89)	(7.44)	(8.52)	—
Total	55.97	54.77	53.31	51.23	49.50	47.33	44.99	44.88	—
	(5.08)	(5.35)	(5.38)	(7.12)	(6.82)	(7.99)	(7.91)	(8.06)	—
1970									
Male	54.61	53.86	52.76	52.34	51.98	51.89	44.43	42.85	44.96
	(5.14)	(5.82)	(8.75)	(5.83)	(7.28)	(7.04)	(6.68)	(5.95)	(8.62)
Female	55.28	54.41	50.88	51.86	49.24	48.43	43.57	43.32	40.25
	(5.69)	(5.15)	(6.43)	(5.66)	(6.59)	(6.41)	(8.09)	(6.35)	(5.78)
Total	54.99	54.17	51.64	52.10	50.47	50.08	43.97	43.07	42.70
	(5.43)	(5.41)	(7.46)	(5.72)	(7.00)	(6.89)	(7.44)	(6.11)	(7.70)
1977									
Male	57.39	56.41	55.35	54.31	52.82	51.86	46.80	45.14	44.54
	(4.28)	(5.05)	(5.33)	(4.98)	(7.12)	(6.31)	(8.95)	(9.26)	(7.11)
Female	55.79	55.76	55.17	52.32	50.97	49.21	47.30	47.82	43.38
	(4.97)	(4.93)	(3.64)	(7.15)	(6.02)	(7.44)	(7.62)	(6.38)	(9.00)
Total	56.59	56.06	55.26	53.25	51.94	50.48	47.06	46.42	43.93
	(4.67)	(4.96)	(4.55)	(6.27)	(6.64)	(7.00)	(8.24)	(8.06)	(8.11)
1984									
Male	58.08	56.41	55.83	54.83	53.72	51.52	49.69	48.51	43.27
	(3.57)	(4.63)	(5.16)	(4.82)	(6.60)	(4.98)	(5.20)	(7.12)	(7.64)
Female	55.51	55.00	55.11	54.81	53.91	49.44	50.24	47.11	42.92
	(4.60)	(5.10)	(6.01)	(5.73)	(5.62)	(8.48)	(6.19)	(6.77)	(8.44)
Total	56.54	55.70	55.44	54.82	53.81	50.34	49.98	47.83	43.08
	(4.38)	(4.88)	(5.61)	(5.35)	(6.08)	(7.21)	(5.71)	(6.94)	(8.00)
1991									
Male	55.74	58.07	57.77	57.12	55.32	51.84	50.79	47.44	48.73
	(6.33)	(2.89)	(4.92)	(4.15)	(3.84)	(6.16)	(6.90)	(8.70)	(7.94)
Female	55.64	56.12	56.31	53.69	53.72	50.54	49.45	47.51	43.12
	(7.61)	(6.33)	(4.67)	(7.04)	(7.50)	(6.46)	(6.65)	(7.85)	(7.75)
Total	55.58	56.92	57.04	55.10	54.50	51.13	50.03	47.48	45.92
	(7.00)	(5.26)	(4.82)	(6.23)	(6.02)	(6.32)	(6.76)	(8.22)	(8.28)
1998									
Male	58.00	57.83	59.74	57.22	54.50	54.72	51.61	47.54	45.24
	(5.18)	(4.04)	(3.50)	(4.69)	(7.25)	(5.74)	(6.67)	(10.03)	(8.27)
Female	59.20	56.00	54.69	54.63	53.09	51.44	50.87	49.37	44.58
	(3.78)	(6.12)	(7.23)	(5.55)	(7.15)	(6.26)	(7.08)	(6.63)	(7.68)
Total	58.86	57.17	57.41	55.91	53.76	53.22	51.35	48.56	44.93
	(4.13)	(4.89)	(6.05)	(5.28)	(7.18)	(6.16)	(6.79)	(8.28)	(7.93)

TABLE 4.7 Continued

					Age				
	25	32	39	46	53	60	67	74	81

Attitudinal Flexibility

1956
Male	53.92	52.70	52.44	51.40	49.60	47.69	46.13	—	—
	(7.69)	(7.01)	(9.02)	(7.08)	(6.41)	(6.19)	(6.92)	—	—
Female	54.32	53.16	49.37	51.77	50.43	48.08	45.18	—	—
	(6.59)	(7.50)	(7.79)	(7.10)	(8.21)	(9.06)	(7.25)	—	—
Total	54.11	52.94	50.93	51.57	50.01	47.89	45.64	—	—
	(7.12)	(7.23)	(8.52)	(7.04)	(7.32)	(7.75)	(7.06)	—	—

1963
Male	63.98	53.67	53.10	50.43	48.79	47.55	44.59	42.11	—
	(9.83)	(7.33)	(6.88)	(7.96)	(7.48)	(6.57)	(8.53)	(7.30)	—
Female	52.34	51.71	51.71	51.38	49.36	48.72	45.48	42.35	—
	(8.29)	(7.90)	(7.78)	(8.58)	(8.87)	(8.13)	(8.73)	(9.10)	—
Total	53.03	52.55	52.37	50.89	49.11	48.16	45.03	42.23	—
	(5.08)	(5.35)	(7.38)	(8.26)	(8.27)	(7.42)	(8.61)	(8.22)	—

1970
Male	54.32	56.29	50.79	55.52	52.98	50.45	47.69	43.62	45.85
	(8.93)	(7.64)	(8.46)	(7.57)	(8.41)	(10.05)	(9.00)	(6.66)	(6.63)
Female	55.28	54.24	50.98	53.37	51.47	48.21	48.16	45.95	45.88
	(8.02)	(8.78)	(6.71)	(8.13)	(8.02)	(6.68)	(8.55)	(7.74)	(8.28)
Total	54.86	55.12	50.90	54.46	52.15	49.28	47.95	44.70	45.86
	(8.38)	(8.31)	(7.42)	(7.88)	(8.18)	(8.47)	(8.72)	(7.24)	(7.39)

1977
Male	56.14	56.97	53.49	55.31	51.68	53.31	45.26	47.61	42.12
	(6.61)	(6.92)	(6.05)	(7.41)	(8.15)	(8.21)	(6.67)	(8.91)	(6.24)
Female	54.46	52.70	51.92	51.43	50.32	50.92	49.65	46.91	45.69
	(9.26)	(8.22)	(8.36)	(8.57)	(8.18)	(8.52)	(7.37)	(8.11)	(6.31)
Total	55.30	54.69	52.71	53.23	51.03	52.07	47.51	47.28	44.00
	(8.02)	(7.88)	(7.28)	(8.23)	(8.14)	(8.40)	(7.33)	(8.48)	(6.47)

1984
Male	55.69	55.96	57.10	55.54	55.66	53.76	49.08	46.92	43.41
	(7.65)	(8.17)	(7.55)	(7.34)	(8.68)	(7.36)	(9.13)	(8.89)	(7.99)
Female	54.28	53.74	55.31	57.89	50.78	52.56	50.88	48.17	47.27
	(8.17)	(8.17)	(8.02)	(7.21)	(8.16)	(7.62)	(8.52)	(9.70)	(10.41)
Total	54.85	54.85	56.12	56.97	53.22	53.08	50.01	47.53	45.50
	(7.94)	(8.17)	(7.80)	(7.29)	(8.71)	(7.48)	(8.81)	(9.25)	(9.48)

1991
Male	55.85	53.43	57.85	54.26	54.97	52.19	51.93	49.12	47.58
	(7.67)	(8.85)	(5.98)	(8.48)	(9.84)	(7.76)	(8.69)	(7.17)	(9.24)
Female	55.52	55.00	56.00	55.88	56.78	54.10	53.67	49.67	49.33
	(7.63)	(7.83)	(7.49)	(8.08)	(6.40)	(6.87)	(8.65)	(7.03)	(7.20)
Total	55.67	54.35	56.92	55.22	55.90	53.24	52.92	49.40	48.45
	(7.59)	(8.24)	(6.80)	(8.23)	(8.25)	(7.29)	(8.67)	(7.06)	(8.27)

1998
Male	56.17	55.26	53.15	55.42	55.59	51.88	51.60	48.75	50.00
	(8.47)	(7.65)	(7.74)	(8.27)	(5.84)	(7.48)	(8.63)	(7.72)	(8.35)
Female	55.13	51.92	53.00	54.22	54.17	56.04	52.35	50.50	47.08
	(5.88)	(5.74)	(5.90)	(6.52)	(8.90)	(8.67)	(7.24)	(6.63)	(8.31)
Total	55.43	54.06	53.08	54.81	54.85	53.78	51.86	49.72	48.62
	(6.51)	(7.12)	(6.90)	(7.42)	(7.57)	(8.24)	(8.16)	(7.12)	(8.39)

(*continued*)

TABLE 4.7 Continued

					Age				
	25	32	39	46	53	60	67	74	81
Psychomotor Speed									
1956									
Male	50.37	48.76	50.28	50.51	47.71	43.66	42.66	—	—
	(8.45)	(7.66)	(10.50)	(9.14)	(9.81)	(8.26)	(7.49)	—	—
Female	55.82	55.32	52.23	52.57	52.03	49.27	44.66	—	—
	(6.84)	(7.87)	(7.96)	(5.86)	(7.88)	(8.05)	(6.93)	—	—
Total	53.09	52.23	51.24	51.46	49.87	49.54	43.66	—	—
	(8.11)	(8.39)	(9.32)	(7.81)	(9.10)	(8.57)	(7.24)	—	—
1963									
Male	49.38	48.00	48.45	44.92	43.31	42.09	39.59	40.58	—
	(8.55)	(8.06)	(8.15)	(7.67)	(8.02)	(7.76)	(7.01)	(6.52)	—
Female	53.07	52.54	50.62	50.49	47.00	44.97	42.59	40.80	—
	(7.80)	(6.95)	(6.91)	(7.79)	(7.93)	(8.55)	(6.85)	(5.53)	—
Total	51.52	50.61	49.59	47.65	45.40	43.60	41.08	40.69	—
	(8.29)	(7.74)	(7.57)	(8.20)	(8.15)	(8.28)	(7.06)	(5.99)	—
1970									
Male	52.87	54.43	51.47	51.89	52.02	48.26	41.33	38.30	37.69
	(6.98)	(8.83)	(9.2)	(8.23)	(8.30)	(6.86)	(7.37)	(7.02)	(6.32)
Female	57.38	55.62	52.40	55.28	54.04	49.64	45.63	43.61	40.67
	(7.62)	(7.75)	(7.61)	(7.12)	(7.01)	(7.33)	(7.01)	(5.82)	(6.92)
Total	55.41	55.11	52.02	53.56	53.13	48.99	43.65	40.77	39.12
	(7.64)	(8.19)	(8.44)	(7.84)	(7.64)	(7.10)	(7.46)	(6.98)	(6.72)
1977									
Male	51.96	56.07	51.73	49.44	49.28	45.69	44.14	36.17	36.77
	(7.74)	(8.69)	(7.88)	(8.08)	(8.48)	(8.31)	(7.16)	(5.51)	(6.11)
Female	55.21	58.45	56.94	51.22	48.35	48.66	46.86	42.15	39.69
	(10.28)	(6.51)	(7.86)	(8.09)	(6.82)	(8.25)	(7.49)	(8.20)	(6.41)
Total	53.59	57.34	54.30	50.39	48.83	47.23	45.54	39.03	38.31
	(9.16)	(7.64)	(8.24)	(8.07)	(7.70)	(8.35)	(7.41)	(7.51)	(6.39)
1984									
Male	54.77	55.59	55.52	57.25	51.12	50.88	46.03	45.43	40.14
	(9.14)	(7.32)	(6.93)	(6.69)	(8.37)	(8.73)	(7.94)	(7.40)	(8.75)
Female	58.03	57.11	59.37	57.92	56.62	52.81	50.00	48.54	41.46
	(8.36)	(7.16)	(6.13)	(6.69)	(5.72)	(7.44)	(7.98)	(6.69)	(6.26)
Total	56.72	56.35	57.62	57.66	53.88	51.97	48.09	46.94	40.85
	(8.76)	(7.21)	(6.73)	(6.64)	(7.63)	(8.02)	(8.16)	(7.18)	(7.45)
1991									
Male	61.74	61.18	62.54	60.56	58.34	54.72	51.74	48.51	42.73
	(8.60)	(7.70)	(8.10)	(9.66)	(10.31)	(7.43)	(8.18)	(7.88)	(8.66)
Female	66.55	64.10	65.85	64.12	61.10	55.26	54.15	51.86	45.24
	(5.20)	(10.36)	(5.39)	(6.89)	(7.80)	(7.90)	(8.99)	(8.73)	(7.77)
Total	64.38	62.90	64.19	62.66	59.76	55.01	53.10	50.23	43.98
	(7.29)	(9.41)	(7.03)	(8.28)	(9.16)	(7.64)	(8.68)	(8.45)	(8.26)
1998									
Male	55.50	59.57	58.47	57.40	54.75	54.56	52.40	49.25	46.28
	(8.89)	(4.82)	(6.06)	(5.58)	(7.38)	(7.78)	(8.29)	(9.37)	(6.52)
Female	63.67	60.00	58.86	59.92	57.46	55.22	51.94	52.43	48.54
	(3.52)	(4.00)	(4.76)	(6.72)	(5.84)	(7.05)	(8.36)	(7.93)	(6.43)
Total	61.33	59.72	58.65	58.67	56.16	54.86	52.24	51.02	47.35
	(6.54)	(4.49)	(5.46)	(6.28)	(6.71)	(7.40)	(8.27)	(8.66)	(6.52)

TABLE 4.7 Continued

					Age				
	25	32	39	46	53	60	67	74	81
Across All Measurement Occasions									
Motor-Cognitive Flexibility									
Male	55.99	55.66	54.88	53.41	52.17	49.90	47.51	45.97	45.58
	(5.08)	(5.25)	(6.27)	(6.73)	(7.16)	(7.75)	(7.95)	(8.13)	(8.06)
Female	55.69	54.79	53.21	52.83	50.81	48.79	46.85	46.09	42.91
	(5.50)	(5.39)	(6.35)	(6.46)	(6.92)	(7.19)	(7.88)	(7.52)	(7.86)
Total	55.82	55.19	54.01	53.11	51.46	49.32	47.19	46.03	44.24
Attitudinal Flexibility									
Male	54.87	54.71	53.87	53.51	52.32	50.62	48.04	46.12	46.04
	(8.20)	(7.67)	(7.61)	(8.05)	(8.30)	(7.98)	(8.75)	(8.11)	(8.25)
Female	54.23	53.15	52.44	53.56	51.58	50.83	49.17	47.13	47.15
	(7.89)	(7.94)	(7.72)	(8.10)	(8.51)	(8.31)	(8.72)	(8.48)	(8.13)
Total	54.51	53.87	53.12	53.54	51.93	50.73	48.61	46.62	46.60
Psychomotor Speed									
Male	53.06	53.81	53.40	51.96	50.22	47.82	45.40	42.58	40.96
	(9.05)	(9.07)	(9.55)	(9.51)	(9.86)	(9.13)	(9.04)	(8.67)	(8.08)
Female	57.59	56.80	55.1	55.81	52.85	50.18	47.74	46.45	43.19
	(8.65)	(8.51)	(8.48)	(8.61)	(8.69)	(8.62)	(8.64)	(8.50)	(7.48)
Total	55.59	55.42	54.55	53.96	51.61	49.06	46.56	44.51	42.08
	(9.10)	(8.89)	(9.07)	(9.25)	(9.35)	(8.94)	(8.91)	(8.79)	(7.85)

Table 4.7 also provides data by gender and age summarized across all seven test occasions. Intercorrelations of TBR factor scores by age group and for the total sample are reported in appendix A-4.5. Figure 4.9 provides a graphic representation of shifts in age differences over time combined across genders.

The cross-sectional data on cognitive style suggest that there is a decrease in MCF and PS for successive age/cohort groups. What is most noteworthy, however, is the fact that, until the 80s are reached, there has been an increase in flexibility and speed for successive cohorts at the same ages. This trend has led to successively later ages at which significant declines are observed. For the age groups represented on each test occasion (ages 25 to 67), there is a statistically significant Time × Age effect for both MCF and PS. MCF seems to peak in young adulthood, with lower levels prevailing as early as age 39 in our 1956 sample, but beginning only with the 60s in the most recent samples. A similar pattern is shown for PS, which in the earliest sample peaked in young adulthood, but now peaks in the early 50s. AF seems to be fairly level across age groups until the mid-40s, with decline below young adult levels observable beginning with the 60s. Again, recent cohorts show average performance that is above earlier cohorts at the same ages.

Significant overall gender differences are found for all three cognitive style factors. Women exceed men on PS, and men exceed women on MCF and AF. These gender differences generalize across age and measurement occasions.

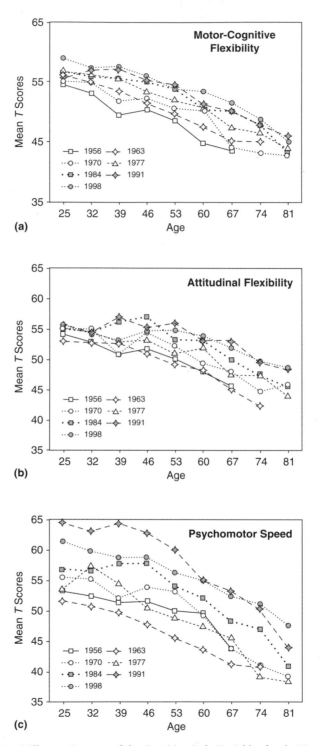

FIGURE 4.9 *Age Difference Patterns of the Cognitive Style Variables for the Total Sample by Test Occasion.*

Chapter Summary

I begin this chapter by describing three pilot studies: The first two were designed to demonstrate the applicability of the PMA test to an older population, with respect to both its level of difficulty and whether the low correlations among abilities observed in childhood would continue to prevail for adults. A third pilot study was concerned with the development of a set of psychometrically sound measurement instruments for the multiple dimensions of rigidity-flexibility that we wished to relate to cognitive abilities.

I next report findings from the 1956 baseline study, which found negative age differences on all five primary mental abilities, but showed that peak ability ages occur later than observed in the previous literature and that the differential ability patterns noted in our first pilot study could be confirmed in this representative and age-continuous investigation. Cross-sectional findings are then reported for the six measurement occasions from 1956 to 1998, involving a total of 4,851 participants. For these data sets, I describe the differential ability patterns as they have changed in magnitude and pattern across time. Whereas there are increased performance levels at most ages in successive data sets, this shift is particularly noteworthy for women. Young adult females now show markedly higher performance on Spatial Orientation than was the case 42 years earlier, age differences in Numeric Ability have virtually disappeared, and Verbal Meaning now peaks in the early 50s. The magnitude of age differences, at least until the mid-60s and early 70s, has markedly decreased. The last finding, of course, has provided a strong rationale for the abandonment of mandatory retirement ages in all occupations.

Similar data are next provided for the expanded test battery given in 1984, 1991, and 1998, including the cross-sectional analysis of age differences on the latent constructs of Inductive Reasoning, Spatial Orientation, Verbal Ability, Numeric Ability, Perceptual Speed, and Verbal Memory. For four of these more broadly sampled constructs, the earliest evidence of reliable (although modest) negative age differences was found at somewhat earlier ages: Inductive Reasoning, Spatial Orientation, and Perceptual Speed at age 53 and Verbal Memory at age 46. The remaining two factors, Numeric and Verbal Ability, showed positive age differences until midlife, and even in advanced old age were at a higher level than for the youngest age group.

Cross-sectional data are also reported for the Educational Testing Service Basic Skills test, our measure of practical intelligence, in 1984 and 1991. No significant age differences were found until age 60, but increasingly severe age differences occurred from then on. Similar findings occurred for our current measure of practical intelligence, the Everyday Problems Test.

Finally, cross-sectional data are presented for our measures of cognitive style for the latent constructs of MCF, AF, and PS. Negative age differences in MCF and AF are currently first observed at age 53, whereas such differences appear already at 46 years of age for PS. Recent cohorts show average performance that is above earlier cohorts in the flexible direction at the same ages. At all ages, women exceed men on PS, whereas men exceed women on MCF and AF.

CHAPTER FIVE

Longitudinal Studies

THIS CHAPTER REVIEWS THE CENTRAL CORE of our study, the results from the longitudinal inquiries. As indicated in the description of the database, the longitudinal studies consist of six 7-year follow-ups, five 14-year follow-ups, four 21-year follow-ups, three 28-year follow-ups, two 35-year follow-ups, and one 42-year follow-up. The presentation of each individual segment of the longitudinal studies or the data and conclusions presented elsewhere are not repeated here (Hertzog & Schaie, 1986, 1988; Schaie, 1979, 1980a, 1980b, 1980c, 1983a, 1989a, 1996b; Schaie & Hertzog, 1983, 1986; Schaie & Labouvie-Vief, 1974; Schaie & Parham, 1977; Schaie & Strother, 1968b). Instead, similar to the approach I adopted in 1996, I again attempt to integrate the entire longitudinal database to provide estimates of age changes based on the largest available number of study participants for each age interval.

One of the major objectives of attempting to forecast ontogenetic change in individuals and of generating normative data on age changes in behavior is to be able to determine whether a particular individual change remains within the average range of interindividual differences in such change or whether the observed change is excessive and thus may provide a possible indicator of behavioral pathology or neuropathology. To obtain the requisite longitudinal estimates, it seems best to average over as many cohorts and times of measurement as possible to yield data whose stability is maximized by basing it on the largest possible number of observations. In the following sections, consequently, data are aggregated, whenever possible, across two or more samples observed at the same age.

To permit comparison with the cross-sectional findings (chapter 4), the base of our mean-level estimates was set to the observed average values across all cohorts for participants tested at age 53 (the average age of our total sample). The average intraindividual age changes aggregated across all cohorts for which each age interval is available were then cumulated and added to or subtracted from these base values. In the following sections, these predicted values are provided for the total sample as well as separately by gender.

Basic Cognitive Data

The five primary mental abilities and their two composite indices for which data are available over the entire study are considered first.

Seven-Year Data

Intraindividual change estimates were computed by aggregating over all participants with data for 7-year intervals from mean ages 25 to 88 years based on 4,921 test records that were available for two points 7 years apart. Table 5.1 provides the resulting average within-participant age changes in T-score units, with positive values indicating gain from the age listed in the row to that listed in the column and negative values indicating age-associated decrement. The values in the diagonals of this table represent the observed within-group age changes. The off-diagonals are the cumulated changes obtained by summing the appropriate successive within-group values. These estimates are required to determine the ages at which decrement from some previously observed base age reaches statistical significance.

One can observe immediately that statistically significant cumulative age decrements from any previous age do not occur for any variable prior to age 60. Several variables were found to have modest increments in young adulthood and middle age. The increment above the performance level observed at age 25 remained significant for Verbal Meaning until age 67 and for Spatial Orientation and Inductive Reasoning until age 53.

It was also found that cumulative age decrement, when taken from age 25, attained statistically significant magnitudes only at age 67 for Number and Word Fluency, at age 74 for Spatial Orientation and Inductive Reasoning, and at age 81 for Verbal Meaning. The composite Index of Intellectual Aptitude showed early gain until age 46 and decline by age 60. The Index of Educational Aptitude showed gain until age 60 and decline by age 67. As compared with age 25, significant decline was not observed until age 81; however, from the peak performance at age 46, decline was observed by age 67.

Significant gender differences were found for all five abilities ($p < .01$), with women excelling on Verbal Meaning, Inductive Reasoning, and Word Fluency, and men doing better than women on Spatial Orientation and Number. There are no statistically significant gender differences in the shapes of the age gradients. However, because of the level differences, cumulative decline over the entire adult age range is somewhat greater for women than for men on Verbal Meaning and Inductive Reasoning.

A visual representation of the resultant longitudinal age gradients from age 25 to age 88 is provided in figure 5.1 for the entire sample and separately for men and women. The longitudinal gradients are centered on the aggregated mean value at age 53 (the average age of our sample).

TABLE 5.1 Cumulative Age Changes for 7-Year Longitudinal Data in *T*-Score Points

	Mean Age								
	32	39	46	53	60	67	74	81	88
Verbal Meaning									
25	1.58	2.90*	3.65*	3.96*	3.77*	2.41*	0.28	−2.82*	−8.94
32		1.32*	2.07*	2.38*	2.19*	0.83	−1.30	−4.40*	−10.52*
39			0.75	1.06	0.87	−0.49	−2.62*	−5.72*	−11.84*
46				0.31	0.12	−1.24	−3.37*	−6.47*	−12.59*
53					−0.19	−1.55*	−3.68*	−6.78*	−12.90*
60						−1.36*	−3.49*	−6.59*	−12.71*
67							−2.13*	−5.23*	−11.35*
74								−3.10*	−9.22*
81									−6.12*
Spatial Orientation									
25	1.23	1.99*	2.28*	2.06*	1.47	−0.43	−2.70*	−5.88*	−10.04*
32		0.76	1.05	0.83	0.24	−1.66	−3.93*	−7.11*	−11.27*
39			0.29	0.07	−0.52	−2.42*	−4.69*	−7.87*	−12.03*
46				−0.22	−0.81	−2.71*	−4.98*	−8.16*	−12.32*
53					−0.59	−2.49*	−4.76*	−7.94*	−12.10*
60						−1.90*	−4.17*	−7.35*	−11.51*
67							−2.27*	−5.45*	−9.61*
74								−3.18*	−7.34*
81									−4.16*
Inductive Reasoning									
25	0.72	1.37	1.66*	1.72*	1.27	−0.33	−2.53*	−4.43*	−7.52*
32		0.65	0.94	1.00	0.55	−1.05	−3.25*	−5.15*	−8.24*
39			0.29	0.35	−0.10	−1.70*	−3.90*	−5.80*	−8.89*
46				0.06	−0.39	−1.99*	−4.19*	−6.09*	−9.18*
53					−0.45	−2.05*	−4.25*	−6.15*	−9.24*
60						−1.60*	−3.80*	−5.70*	−8.79*
67							−2.20*	−4.10*	−7.19*
74								−1.90*	−4.99*
81									−3.09*
Number									
25	0.92	0.76	0.54	−0.31	−0.92	−2.90*	−5.31*	−9.15*	−13.39*
32		−0.16	−0.38	−1.23	−1.84*	−3.82*	−6.23*	−10.07*	−15.31*
39			−0.22	−1.07	−1.68*	−3.66*	−6.07*	−9.91*	−15.15*
46				−0.85	−1.46*	−3.44*	−5.85*	−9.69*	−14.93*
53					−0.61	−2.59*	−5.00*	−8.84*	−14.08*
60						−1.98*	−4.39*	−8.23*	−13.47*
67							−2.41*	−6.25*	−11.49*
74								−3.84*	−8.08*
81									−4.24*

TABLE 5.1 Continued

				Mean Age				
32	39	46	53	60	67	74	81	88

Word Fluency

25	1.03	0.77	1.12	0.53	−0.83	−2.63*	−4.75*	−7.63*	−10.41*
32		−0.26	−0.09	−0.50	−1.86*	−3.66*	−5.78*	−8.66*	−11.44*
39			0.35	−0.24	−1.60*	−3.40*	−5.52*	−8.40*	−11.18*
46				−0.59	−1.95*	−3.75*	−5.87*	−8.75*	−11.53*
53					−1.36*	−3.16*	−5.28*	−8.16*	−10.94*
60						−1.80*	−3.92*	−6.80*	−9.58*
67							−2.12*	−5.00*	−7.78*
74								−2.88*	−5.66*
81									−2.78

Intellectual Ability

25	1.38*	1.80*	1.54*	1.10	0.25	−2.02*	−4.92*	−8.73*	−14.25*
32		0.42	0.16	−0.28	−1.13	−3.40*	−6.30*	−10.11*	−15.63*
39			−0.26	−0.70	−1.55*	−3.82*	−6.72*	−10.53*	−16.05*
46				−0.44	−1.29	−3.56*	−6.46*	−10.27*	−15.79*
53					−0.85	−3.12*	−6.02*	−9.83*	−15.35*
60						−2.27*	−5.17*	−8.98*	−14.50*
67							−2.90*	−6.71*	−12.23*
74								−3.81*	−9.33*
81									−5.52*

Educational Aptitude

25	1.61*	2.84*	3.52*	3.80*	3.55*	2.05*	−0.03	−2.85*	8.60*
32		1.23*	1.91*	2.19*	1.94*	0.44	−1.64*	−4.46*	−10.21*
39			0.68	0.96	0.71	−0.79	−2.87*	−5.59*	−11.44*
46				0.28	0.03	−1.47*	−3.55*	−6.27*	−12.12*
53					−0.25	−1.75*	−3.83*	−6.55*	−12.40*
60						−1.50*	−3.78*	−6.30*	−12.15*
67							−2.28*	−4.80*	−10.65*
74								−2.85*	−8.60*
81									−5.75*

*Difference is significant at or beyond the 1% level of confidence.

Fourteen-Year Data

Longitudinal change in individuals can also be estimated using 14-year estimates. After aggregating age changes across the equivalent age ranges from the four 14-year data sets, estimates are derived similar to those given for the 7-year data. The major difference here is that all data come from 2,406 individual records that extend over 14 years; hence, these estimates are somewhat less sensitive to possible changes in rates of aging across successive cohorts, but have the disadvantage of being based on smaller samples. The resultant estimates of age changes are given in table 5.2.

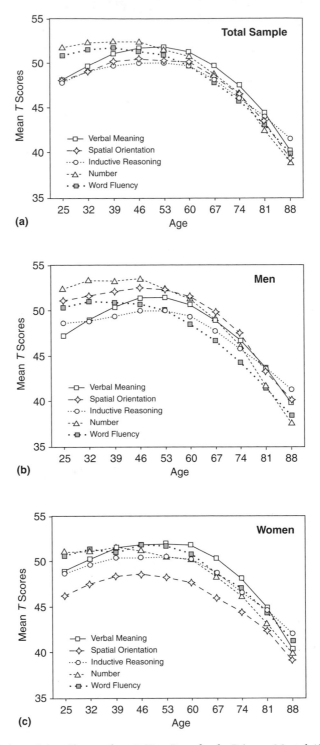

FIGURE 5.1 *Estimated Age Changes from 7-Year Data for the Primary Mental Abilities for (a) the Total Sample and (b, c) Separately by Gender.*

TABLE 5.2 Average 14-Year Longitudinal Age Changes in *T*-Score Points

Age Range	*n*	Verbal Meaning	Spatial Orientation	Inductive Reasoning	Number	Word Fluency	Intellectual Ability	Educational Aptitude
25–39	122	2.06*	1.53	0.84	0.79	1.02	1.54*	1.50
32–46	215	1.53*	1.15	0.55	−0.94	0.49	0.48	0.46
39–53	327	0.00	−0.41	0.30	−1.35**	0.15	−0.50	−0.33
46–60	410	−0.14	−1.01	−0.51	−1.60***	−1.30*	−1.35***	−1.69***
53–67	466	−1.80***	−2.11***	−1.87***	−2.91***	−2.53***	−3.10***	−3.12***
60–74	431	−3.11***	−2.79***	−3.21***	−3.86***	−2.90***	−4.28***	−4.51**
67–81	318	−4.93***	−4.87***	−3.64***	−5.73***	−4.86***	−6.38***	−7.11***
74–88	97	−6.93***	−3.07*	−4.47***	−6.61***	−5.67***	−7.58***	−9.50***

*$p < .05$. **$p < .01$. ***$p < .001$.

When age changes are examined over 14-year segments, such change becomes statistically significant for Number as early as age 53, for Word Fluency at age 60, and for the remaining three abilities at age 67. The 14-year changes were found to be significant for the Index of Intellectual Ability and the Index of Educational Aptitude by age 60.

The longitudinal age gradients resulting from these estimates are provided in figure 5.2. Note that, in contrast to figure 5.1a, the 7-year segments represent a rolling average obtained from the within-participant 14-year age changes. As a consequence, the resultant age gradients show a somewhat later attainment of

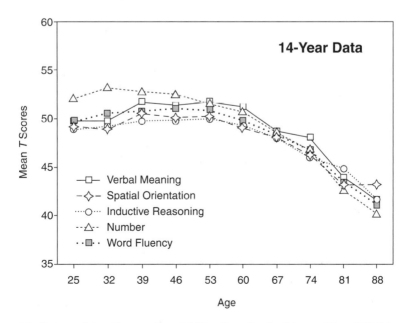

FIGURE 5.2 *Estimated Age Changes from 14-Year Data for the Primary Mental Abilities.*

peak levels of performance (in late middle age), and except for Number, decline does not become steep until the mid-70s are reached. Interestingly, in advanced old age, decline is now steepest for Verbal Meaning and Number, the two crystallized abilities.

Twenty-One-Year Data

Next, longitudinal change was estimated over a 21-year period. Data used in these estimates were limited to the test records of individuals extending over 21 years ($n = 1,266$). The individual age change estimates were based on even smaller samples. The resultant estimates of age changes are given in table 5.3.

Although we recognize that those participants remaining in the study for as long as 21 years may be an increasingly select sample, it is still interesting to point out that the rate of average decline was somewhat less for these persons. For the 21-year segments, modest but significant decrements are noted for Number and the Index of Intellectual Ability by age 60 and for the remaining variables by age 67. Cumulative decrements estimated from the three samples that cover the entire age range from 25 to 88 years amount to 0.5 SD for Verbal Meaning, 0.7 SD for Spatial Orientation and Inductive Reasoning, 1.0 SD for Number, and 0.9 SD for Word Fluency.

The longitudinal age gradients resulting from these estimates, averaging across 7-year segments, are provided in figure 5.3. Because of the longer within-cohort age ranges covered by the same participants, these gradients are even smoother than for the 14-year data; the major difference is a somewhat less steep decrement for Verbal Meaning.

Twenty-Eight-Year Data

Three data sets are available for participants who were followed for 28 years ($n = 578$). Again, data were aggregated for the comparable age ranges, and average longitudinal changes across the available 28-year ranges are given in table 5.4. In this even more select group, significant decrements over the 28-year segments are first observed for Number and the Index of Intellectual Ability by age 60; for

TABLE 5.3 Average 21-Year Longitudinal Age Changes in *T*-Score Points

Age Range	*n*	Verbal Meaning	Spatial Orientation	Inductive Reasoning	Number	Word Fluency	Intellectual Ability	Educational Aptitude
25–46	79	2.53*	2.23	0.61	−0.27	1.01	1.35	2.16
32–53	160	1.07	−0.34	−0.07	−1.62	0.15	−0.51	0.80
39–60	227	−0.54	−1.58	−0.79	−2.03***	−0.64	−1.64***	−0.72
46–67	268	−1.55**	−2.80***	−2.14***	−3.93***	−3.12**	−3.81***	−1.78***
53–74	279	−3.53***	−3.65***	−3.48***	−4.60***	−3.67***	−5.08***	−3.72***
60–81	190	−5.52***	−4.92***	−4.88***	−7.06***	−5.44***	−7.55***	−5.65***
67–88	63	−6.37***	−5.95***	−5.78***	−5.60***	−6.80***	−7.84***	−6.59***

*$p < .05$. **$p < .01$. ***$p < .001$.

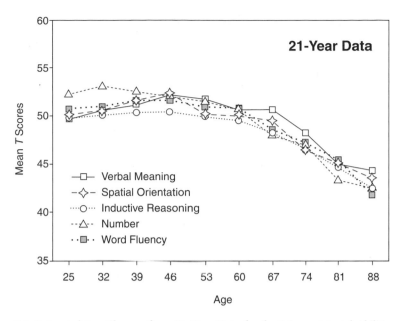

FIGURE 5.3 *Estimated Age Changes from 21-Year Data for the Primary Mental Abilities.*

Inductive Reasoning, Word Fluency, and the Index of Educational Aptitude by age 67; and for Verbal Meaning and Spatial Orientation by age 74. The estimated longitudinal gradients are shown in figure 5.4. For these participants, there was only modest average decline by age 74, with steep decline first observed by age 81.

Thirty-Five- and Forty-Two-Year Data

Two data sets contain individuals who have been followed over 35 years ($n =$ 220). Data aggregated for comparable age ranges are provided in table 5.5 and are charted in figure 5.5. In these data, significant decline is observed for Number, Word Fluency, and the Index of Intellectual Ability only by age 67 and for the remaining variables by age 74.

TABLE 5.4 *Average 28-Year Longitudinal Age Changes in T-Score Points*

Age Range	n	Verbal Meaning	Spatial Orientation	Inductive Reasoning	Number	Word Fluency	Intellectual Ability	Educational Aptitude
25–53	50	1.93	−0.33	0.61	−0.34	0.79	0.64	1.85
32–60	110	0.65	−1.99	−0.39	−2.87***	−0.64	−1.68*	0.39
39–67	132	−1.67	−1.70	−2.77***	−3.78***	−3.54***	−3.29***	−2.06**
46–74	144	−2.73***	−3.41***	−3.14***	−5.08***	−4.58***	−5.21***	−3.09***
53–81	111	−6.72***	−5.40***	−5.24***	−7.64***	−7.18***	−8.57***	−6.62***
60–88	31	−8.17***	−5.70***	−8.47***	−8.27***	−7.96***	10.24***	−8.76***

*$p < .05$. **$p < .01$. ***$p < .001$.

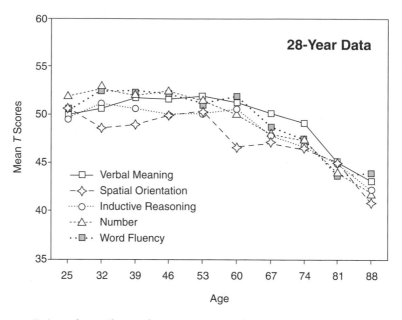

FIGURE 5.4 *Estimated Age Changes from 28-Year Data for the Primary Mental Abilities.*

Finally, 42-year data are provided for the small residual sample that has participated in our entire study ($n = 37$; see table 5.6). Findings are quite similar to those for individuals followed for 28 years. However, data on the age of statistically significant onset of decline are more difficult to interpret because of the small sample size.

Expanded Cognitive Data

Longitudinal data over 7 and 14 years are now available on the additional variables that entered the expanded test battery in 1984. In addition, this section contains the results for the longitudinal estimates of the latent ability constructs.

TABLE 5.5 Average 35-Year Longitudinal Age Changes in *T*-Score Points

Age Range	*n*	Verbal Meaning	Spatial Orientation	Inductive Reasoning	Number	Word Fluency	Intellectual Ability	Educational Aptitude
25–60	30	1.70	1.83	1.53	−0.57	0.17	1.00	1.77
32–67	56	−1.43	−3.14	−2.11	−4.50***	−4.50***	−4.46***	−1.70
39–74	63	−2.95*	−3.68**	−4.24***	−5.37***	−5.41***	−5.85***	−3.47***
46–81	53	−4.93***	−4.13**	−4.17***	−7.91***	−8.47***	−8.26***	−5.07***
53–88	18	−8.94***	−6.84**	−6.78***	−8.61***	−10.00***	−10.00***	−8.89***

*$p < .05$. **$p < .01$. ***$p < .001$.

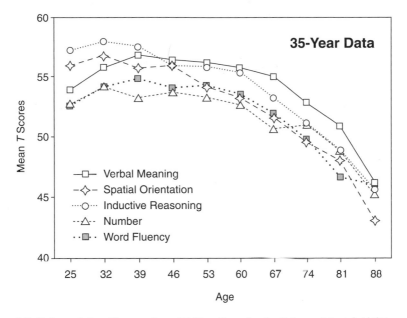

FIGURE 5.5 *Estimated Age Changes from 35-Year Data for the Primary Mental Abilities.*

Observed Variables

Intraindividual change estimates were computed for all variables added in the 1984 cycle. It should be noted that the longitudinal estimates provided in table 5.7 and the resultant longitudinal gradients over the age range from 25 to 88 years shown in figure 5.6 were limited to three data points (1984, 1991, and 1998); that is, each age segment was based on two samples followed over 7 years. However, there was a total of 2,200 observations over 7 years.

All three additional markers of Inductive Reasoning ability show significant 7-year decline only by age 67. For Spatial ability, the parallel forms for PMA Space, Object Rotation, and Alphanumeric Rotation as well as the three-dimensional rotation test, Cube Comparison, show decline by age 67. Of the new Perceptual Speed measures, Identical Pictures declines as early as age 53; Number Compari-

TABLE 5.6 Average 42-Year Longitudinal Age Changes in *T*-Score Points

Age Range	n	Verbal Meaning	Spatial Orientation	Inductive Reasoning	Number	Word Fluency	Intellectual Ability	Educational Aptitude
25–67	9	2.00	1.75	1.44	0.33	−7.22	−1.00	1.23
32–74	11	−1.18	−4.45	−2.18	−5.00	−6.64	−5.18	−1.55
39–81	11	−6.82**	−8.00**	−5.36	−9.55**	−10.71***	−12.00**	−6.91*
46–88	6	−4.66**	−8.34	−5.66	−5.34	−13.00*	−9.83**	−5.47

*$p < .05$. **$p < .01$. ***$p < .001$.

TABLE 5.7 Intraindividual Age Changes Over 7 Years for the Extended Cognitive Test Battery

	Age								
Variable	25–32 (n = 79)	32–39 (n = 123)	39–46 (n = 198)	46–53 (n = 268)	53–60 (n = 308)	60–67 (n = 378)	67–74 (n = 419)	74–81 (n = 312)	81–88 (n = 115)
Letter Series	1.19	0.77	-0.06	-0.20	-0.57	-1.45***	-1.92***	-3.13***	-1.67**
Word Series	-0.93	0.20	-0.42	-0.05	-0.63	-1.98***	-2.50***	-3.89***	-3.36***
Number Series	0.96	0.43	0.01	-0.49	-0.09	-1.56***	-1.22	-2.41***	-2.24
Object Rotation	1.49	0.11	-0.80	0.61	-0.41	-1.50**	-1.97***	-3.68***	-3.32***
Alphanumeric Rotation	0.98	1.22	-1.32	0.00	-1.19	-1.44*	-2.56***	-5.04***	-4.10***
Cube Comparison	3.17	2.03**	1.59	-0.24	-0.25	-1.30*	-1.31**	-1.75***	-2.32*
Identical Pictures	0.34	-0.83	-1.11	-1.51**	-2.05***	-3.09***	-3.74***	-4.98***	-4.91***
Number Comparison	3.15*	0.88	-0.44	-0.30	-0.55	-1.71***	-1.89***	-2.98***	-3.15***
Finding A's	1.29	0.56	0.60	0.02	-0.06	-0.53	-1.78**	-1.50	-2.73
Addition	0.26	-0.62	-0.37	-0.71	-1.07**	-1.94***	-2.49***	-4.28***	-4.97***
Subtraction and Multiplication	-0.62	-0.52	-1.15	-0.83	-1.85***	-2.37***	-2.57***	-4.22***	-5.02***
ETS Vocabulary	2.56	0.96	0.72	0.27	0.03	-0.64	-0.79	-1.21	-3.69***
ETS Advanced Vocabulary	2.51*	1.44	0.68	0.66	0.40	-0.02	-0.56	-1.62***	-2.37***
Immediate Recall	0.49	1.12	0.02	0.07	0.00	-2.31***	-1.97***	-3.79***	-3.84***
Delayed Recall	-0.67	0.39	-0.45	0.56	0.00	-1.71***	-1.92***	-2.96***	-3.35***

Note. Positive values indicate increment over time. ETS, Educational Testing Service.

*p < .05. **p < .01. ***p < .001.

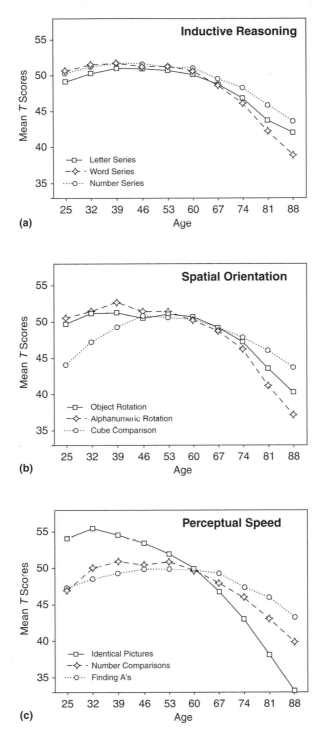

FIGURE 5.6 *Estimated Age Changes from 7-Year Data for the Expanded Test Battery. ETS, Educational Testing Service.*

(continued)

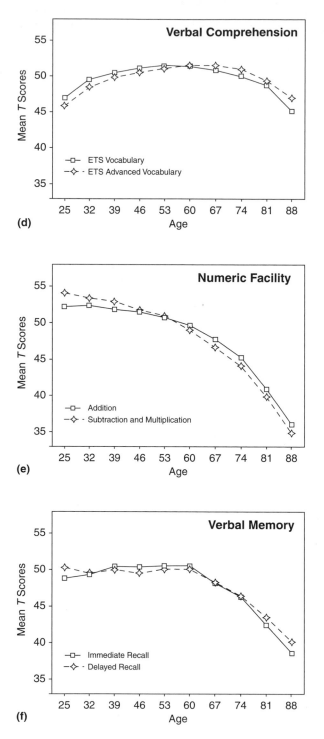

FIGURE 5.6 *Continued.*

son and Finding A's decline by age 67. Both new markers of Numeric Ability, Addition and Subtraction and Multiplication, show a significant decline by age 67. The new unspeeded Verbal tests show even longer ability maintenance than our original marker. There is a significant decline for the easier test by age 88, and for the harder test by age 81. Finally, the new Verbal Memory markers show decline by age 67.

Latent Constructs

Given the availability of multiple markers, 7-year longitudinal estimates of change within participants were computed for the latent ability constructs. The resulting estimates are provided in table 5.8, and longitudinal gradients separately by gender and for the total sample can be found in figure 5.7. These gradients are centered on the actually observed mean for the average age group in our sample (age 53). With respect to these latent construct factor score estimates, earliest reliably observed decline over 7 years occurs for Perceptual Speed and Numeric Ability by age 60; for Inductive Reasoning, Spatial Orientation, and Verbal Memory by age 67; and for Verbal Ability by age 81.

The magnitude of decline for the longitudinal data is substantially lower for several latent abilities than would be suggested by cross-sectional data. Thus, there is only a modest decline from young adulthood to advanced old age for Verbal Ability (0.4 SD). For Inductive Reasoning and Spatial Orientation, longitudinal change from age 25 to age 88 amounts to 0.8 SD. However, longitudinal estimates of change are close to cross-sectional estimates for Perceptual Speed (1.2 SD) and Verbal Memory (1.1 SD) and exceed the cross-sectional estimates for Numeric Ability (1.5 SD).

Practical Intelligence Data

This section reports intraindividual change estimates for the Basic Skills measure of practical intelligence. These estimates were based on only two data points because the Basic Skills test was replaced by the Everyday Problems Test in 1998; hence, no longitudinal data are as yet available for the latter measure. The longitudinal estimates for the Basic Skills test are reported in table 5.9 and graphed in figure 5.8. What is most noteworthy about these data is that peak performance for this measure is reached only by age 60 and that steep decline is noted only by age 81. Thereafter, decline in average performance is quite dramatic, amounting to approximately 2 SD from the 60s to the 80s. Note from the graphic presentation that there is virtually no difference in the shape of the age gradients by gender.

Figure 5.8 also provides estimates separately for four factors scores: Brief Documents, Lengthy Documents, Brief Prose, and Complex Prose. Complex Prose starts to decline in the 70s; significant decrement for the other three factors does not appear until the 80s.

TABLE 5.8 Intraindividual Age Changes Over 7 Years for the Latent Construct (Factor) Scores

					Age				
Variable	25–32 (n = 81)	32–39 (n = 123)	39–46 (n = 198)	46–53 (n = 270)	53–60 (n = 308)	60–67 (n = 378)	67–74 (n = 419)	74–81 (n = 317)	81–88 (n = 119)
Inductive Reasoning	−0.19	0.61	−0.01	−0.10	−0.44	−1.52***	−1.89***	−2.86***	−2.36***
Spatial Orientation	1.14	1.37	−0.11	0.18	−0.62	−1.38***	−1.76***	−3.53***	−3.14***
Perceptual Speed	1.19	0.16	−0.25	−0.66	−1.02***	−1.90***	−2.20***	−3.48***	−3.57***
Numeric Facility	−0.37	0.01	−0.44	−0.64	−1.15***	−2.03***	−2.57***	−4.05***	−4.03***
Verbal Comprehension	−0.47	1.05	0.40	0.27	0.10	−0.71	−0.82	−1.69***	−3.81***
Verbal Memory	−0.62	0.67	−0.06	0.36	0.00	−2.10***	−2.03***	−3.58***	−3.71***

***$p < .001$.

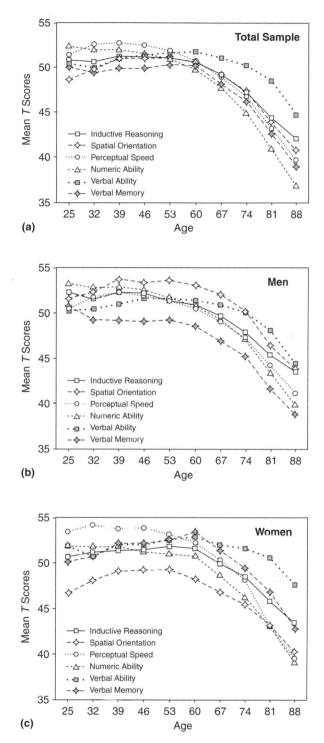

FIGURE 5.7 *Estimated Age Changes from 7-Year Data for the Latent Ability Constructs.*

TABLE 5.9 Cumulative Age Changes for the Measure of Practical Intelligence in *T*-Score Points

Mean Age	32	39	46	53	60	67	74	81	88
25	0.00	0.65	0.61	0.98	1.11	−0.11	−2.67*	−9.64*	−19.80*
32		0.65	0.61	0.98	1.11	−0.11	−2.67*	−9.64*	−19.80*
39			−0.04	0.33	0.46	−0.76	−3.32*	−10.29*	−20.45*
46				0.37	0.50	−0.72	−3.28*	−10.25*	−20.41*
53					0.13	−1.09	−3.65*	10.62*	−20.78*
60						−1.22*	−3.78*	−10.75*	−20.91*
67							−2.56*	−9.53*	−19.69*
74								−6.97*	−17.13*
81									−10.16*

*Difference is significant at or beyond the 1% level of confidence.

Cognitive Style Data

The longitudinal estimates for the cognitive style data again involve changes averaged over all six time periods and are based on all participants for whom 7-year data were available. Table 5.10 provides the longitudinal estimates and figure 5.9 graphs the longitudinal gradients for the total sample and separately by gender. First, examining the age gradients for the total sample, we note a small longitudinal increment (cumulatively about 0.2 *SD*) for both Motor-Cognitive Flexibility and Attitudinal Flexibility to age 60 and a moderate cumulative decline of 0.7 *SD* thereafter. Psychomotor Speed increases by approximately 0.5 *SD* from age 25 to a peak at age 60. In contrast to the flexibility factor, this is followed by a decline of about 1 *SD* by age 88.

Examining the longitudinal findings for the cognitive style data by gender, we note continuing gain by males on Motor-Cognitive Flexibility until about age 60, with moderate decline thereafter. Women, on the other hand, show a more modest gain until age 60, with greater decline than men thereafter. As for Attitudinal Flexibility, men show early virtual stability until about 60, with moderate decline noticeable by age 67. For women, there is a small increase in Attitudinal Flexibility from 25 to 60, with modest decline (about 0.7 *SD*) thereafter. Both men and women peak on Psychomotor Speed at age 60, with decline thereafter. Over the entire age range, men decline somewhat more than women (0.7 *SD* for men, 0.3 *SD* for women).

Chapter Summary

The presentation of the longitudinal findings begins with an examination of the within-participant estimates obtained from aggregating across participants whose data are available over 7, 14, 21, 28, 35, and 42 years. Next, 7-year longitudinal data for the additional marker variables added beginning with the 1984 data collection are considered. Longitudinal estimates are provided for the latent abil-

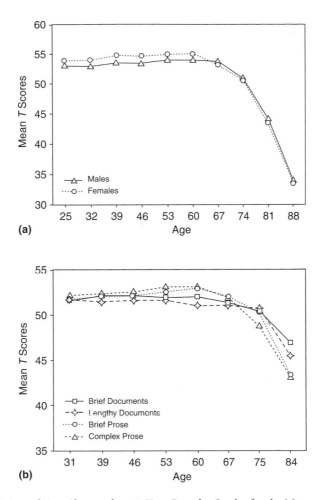

FIGURE 5.8 *Estimated Age Changes from 7-Year Data by Gender for the Measure of Practical Intelligence.*

ity construct factor scores and for the measure of practical intelligence are also provided based on 7-year data. Similar longitudinal data are then presented for the measures of cognitive style.

Longitudinal age changes are generally less pronounced than the cross-sectional data for most variables, with modest decline beginning in the early 60s and marked decline not occurring until the 80s are reached. The major exceptions to these findings occur for the Number ability, which begins to decline in the 50s. Cumulative decline is somewhat larger for men than for women on Verbal Meaning and Inductive Reasoning.

The 7-year data represent the most conservative estimates of within-participant change because they are based on large samples. Data for the same indi-

TABLE 5.10 Cumulative Age Changes for 7-Year Cognitive Style Data in *T*-Score Points

	Mean Age								
	32	39	46	53	60	67	74	81	88
Motor-Cognitive Flexibility									
25	1.38	1.73	1.96	2.00	2.01	0.79	−0.77	−3.22*	−5.42*
32		0.35	0.58	0.62	0.63	−0.59	−2.15*	−4.60*	−6.80*
39			0.23	0.27	0.28	−0.94	−2.50*	−4.95*	−7.15*
46				0.04	0.05	−1.17	−2.83*	−5.18*	7.38*
53					0.01	−1.21	−2.87*	−5.22*	−7.42*
60						−1.22*	−2.78*	−5.23*	−7.43*
67							−1.56*	−6.45*	−6.21*
74								−2.45*	−4.67*
81									2.20
Attitudinal Flexibility									
25	0.85	1.26	1.57	1.79	1.86	0.92	−0.43	−2.95*	−4.10*
32		0.41	0.72	0.94	1.01	0.07	−1.28	−3.80*	−4.95*
39			0.31	0.53	0.60	−0.34	−1.69	−4.21*	−5.36*
46				0.22	0.29	−0.65	−2.00*	−4.52*	−5.67*
53					0.07	−0.87	−2.22*	−4.74*	−5.89*
60						−0.94	−2.29*	−4.81*	−5.96*
67							−1.35*	−3.87*	−5.02*
74								−2.52*	−3.67*
81									−1.16
Psychomotor Speed									
25	1.65*	3.09*	4.04*	4.81*	4.62*	3.80*	2.11*	−0.94	−4.94*
32		1.44*	2.39*	3.16*	2.97*	2.15*	0.45	−2.59*	−6.59*
39			0.95	1.72	1.53	0.71	−0.98	−4.03*	−8.03*
46				0.77	0.58	−0.24	−1.83	−4.98*	−8.98*
53					−0.19	−1.01	−2.60*	−5.75*	−8.75*
60						−0.82	−2.39*	−5.56*	−8.56*
67							−1.69*	−4.74*	−8.74*
74								−3.05*	−7.05*
81									−4.00*

*Difference is significant at or beyond the 1% level of confidence.

viduals collected over a longer period of time (up to 42 years), who may be the select survivors of our study, show average maintenance of many abilities into the mid-70s.

For the more broadly marked ability constructs, there is an even more dramatic difference between the cross-sectional and longitudinal findings. In the longitudinal data, there is only modest decline from young adulthood to advanced old age for Verbal Ability; somewhat greater declines are seen for Inductive Reasoning, Verbal Memory, and Spatial Orientation until the 80s are reached. However, longitudinal estimates of change equal the cross-sectional ones for Per-

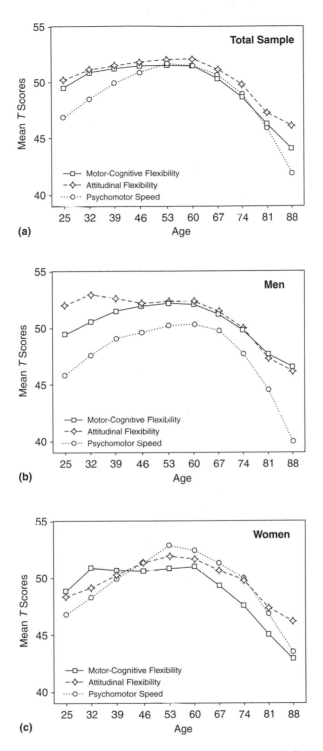

FIGURE 5.9 *Estimated Age Changes from 7-Year Data for the Cognitive Style Variables for the Total Sample and Separately by Gender.*

ceptual Speed and exceed cross-sectional estimates for Numeric Ability. The profound age decline on Numeric Ability in particular seems hidden by negative cohort trends. A peak is reached for our measure of practical intelligence by age 60, but steep decline on that measure is not observed prior to the 80s.

Finally, on the measures of cognitive style, increment is noted for Motor-Cognitive and Attitudinal Flexibility to age 60, with modest decline thereafter. Psychomotor Speed also shows small increases until age 60 and decline thereafter. However, when examined by gender, women have greater decline on Motor-Cognitive and Attitudinal Flexibility, but less decline than men on Psychomotor Speed.

CHAPTER SIX

Studies of Cohort
and Period Differences

IN MY DISCUSSION OF MAJOR METHODOLOGICAL issues addressed in the Seattle Longitudinal Study (SLS) (see chapter 2), I emphasized the desirability of obtaining separate estimates of age, cohort, and period effects. In this chapter, I address our findings regarding cohort and period differences in cognitive abilities as well as on other variables included in our study. Data regarding these matters were previously reported through the sixth study cycle (Schaie, 1983a, 1996b). Here, expanded operational definitions are provided for the computation of cohort and period effects and cumulative findings through the seventh study cycle are expanded and updated.

Studies of Cohort Differences

It is not possible to disaggregate cohort and period effects unambiguously unless relevant information has been obtained independently. However, it is possible from data such as ours to estimate cohort differences between any two cohorts over fixed time periods by comparing the performance of successive cohorts over the age ranges for which both cohorts have been observed. The cohort effects estimated in this manner, of course, will be confounded with period effects, but if series of cohort differences are computed across the same time period, each estimate will be equally affected. In our case, it is possible to generate twelve cohort differences for thirteen 7-year birth cohorts with mean birth years from 1889 to 1973.*

*Given the asymmetry of cohort representation in longitudinal studies, cohort comparisons are based on six age levels or a range of 35 years for cohorts born from 1910 to 1938; on five age levels or a range of 28 years for cohorts born from 1903 to 1945; and on four age levels or 21 years for cohorts born from 1896 to 1952. Comparisons for cohorts born in 1959, 1966, and 1973 have comparisons spanning only three, two, and one age levels, respectively.

To obtain the most stable estimates available, the average level difference between two cohorts is defined as the average of unweighted mean differences at all ages for which observations are available for the two cohorts. Thus, a cohort difference Cd is defined as

$$Cd_i = \left(\sum_j^1 (M_{ij+1} - M_{ij}) \right) / a,$$

where M_{ij} is the unweighted mean for Cohort i at age j, and a indicates the number of common ages for which observations are available for each cohort pair. Given the seven measurement occasions of the SLS, this means that cohort differences for those cohorts entering the study at an early stage can be compared at as many as six different ages; the most recently entered cohort can be compared only at the one age at which it was measured.

It should be recognized that cohort differences reported here reflect the comparison of unrelated groups of individuals. For estimates of intrafamily cohort effects, see chapter 14.

Cohort Differences in Cognitive Abilities

Cohort Differences for the Core Battery   Table 6.1 gives mean differences in *T*-score points computed for all cohort combinations in our study. This table should be read as follows: A positive value indicates that the performance of the cohort identified by the column exceeds, on average, the performance of the cohort identified by the row. A negative value means that the performance of the row (earlier-born cohort) exceeds that of the column (later-born cohort).

Comparative cohort gradients for the five abilities and the Index of Intellectual Ability are graphed in figure 6.1. It is interesting to note that the composite Index of Intellectual Ability will tend to obscure cohort differences because of differential cohort trends in the subtests; for this composite index, only the five earliest-born cohorts differ significantly from any later-born cohort, although there is a recent trend for further gain. On the other hand, when the abilities are considered separately, it becomes clear from these data that there are systematic advances in cohort level for Verbal Meaning, Spatial Orientation, and Inductive Reasoning. A significant advantage of the later-born cohorts is apparent throughout for Spatial Orientation and Inductive Reasoning. However, the cohort gradients for Verbal Meaning begin to decline slightly with the cohort born in 1959.

Very different findings, however, are seen for Number and Word Fluency. The former shows positive cohort differences up to about the 1910 cohort. Then there is a plateau and a shift to a successive lowering of performance level. Hence, the 1924 cohort exceeds both earlier- and later-born cohorts; the youngest cohorts are therefore currently at a disadvantage when compared with the older cohorts. For Word Fluency, there is a successive lowering of cohort level up to the 1938 cohort, but improvement for subsequent cohorts. Hence, for this ability, earlier cohorts have a slight advantage over the later-born ones, but beginning with the

TABLE 6.1 Mean Advantage of Later-Born Cohorts Over Earlier-Born Cohorts in *T*-Score Points

Mean Year of Birth	1896	1903	1910	1917	1924	1931	1938	1945	1952	1959	1966	1973
Verbal Meaning												
1889	−0.6	2.2	4.4*	6.7*	8.3*	8.2*	9.6*	10.0*	11.3*	9.4*	8.8*	8.8*
1896		2.8*	5.0*	7.3*	8.9*	8.9*	10.2*	10.6*	11.9*	10.0*	9.4*	9.4*
1903			2.1	4.4*	6.0*	5.9*	7.3*	7.7*	9.0*	7.1*	6.5*	6.5*
1910				2.3	3.9*	3.9*	5.2*	5.7*	6.9*	5.1*	4.4*	4.4*
1917					1.6	1.6	2.9*	3.3*	4.6*	2.7*	2.1	2.1
1924						−0.1	1.3	1.7	3.0*	1.1	0.5	0.5
1931							1.4	1.8	2.9*	1.2	0.6	0.5
1938								0.4	1.8	−0.1	−0.7	−0.7
1945									1.2	0.7	−2.6	−2.6
1952										−1.8	−2.5	−2.5
1959											−0.6	−0.6
1966												0.0
Spatial Orientation												
1889	−0.5	0.6	1.8	2.2	3.1*	3.2*	5.5*	4.8*	4.1*	4.7*	7.5*	8.1*
1896		1.1	2.3	2.6*	3.6*	3.7*	6.0*	5.3*	4.6*	5.2*	8.0*	8.6*
1903			1.2	1.5	2.5*	2.6*	4.8*	4.1*	3.4*	4.0*	6.8*	7.4*
1910				0.3	1.3	1.4	3.6*	3.0*	2.3	2.8*	5.7*	6.3*
1917					1.0	1.1	3.3*	2.7*	2.0	2.5	5.4*	6.0*
1924						0.1	2.4	1.7	1.0	1.6	4.4*	5.0*
1931							2.3	1.6	0.9	1.5	4.3*	5.0*
1938								−0.7	−1.4	−0.8	2.0	2.7*
1945									−0.0	−0.1	2.7*	3.3*
1952										0.6	5.0*	3.4*
1959											2.8*	3.5*
1966												0.6
Inductive Reasoning												
1889	−0.4	1.0	2.3	3.9*	5.8*	6.0ᵈ	8.9*	9.8*	10.3*	10.8*	11.9*	13.6*
1896		1.4	2.7*	4.3*	6.2*	6.4*	9.3*	10.2*	10.7*	11.2*	12.3*	14.0*
1903			1.3	2.9*	4.8*	5.0*	7.9*	8.8*	9.3	9.8*	10.9*	12.6*
1910				1.6	3.5*	3.7*	6.6*	7.5*	8.0*	8.5*	9.6*	11.3*
1917					1.9	2.1*	5.0*	5.9*	6.4*	6.9*	8.0*	9.7*
1924						0.2	3.1*	4.0*	4.5*	5.0*	6.1*	7.8*
1931							2.9*	3.8*	4.3*	4.8*	5.9*	7.6*
1938								0.9	1.4	1.9	3.0*	4.7*
1945									0.5	1.0	2.1	3.8*
1952										0.5	1.6	3.3*
1959											1.1	2.8*
1966												1.7

(continued)

TABLE 6.1 Continued

Mean Year of Birth	1896	1903	1910	1917	1924	1931	1938	1945	1952	1959	1966	1973
Number												
1889	0.0	0.9	3.5*	3.5*	3.7*	1.8	2.8*	1.8	1.1	−0.8	−1.0	0.6
1896		0.9	3.5*	3.5*	3.7*	1.8	2.8*	1.8	1.1	−0.8	−1.0	0.6
1903			2.6*	2.6*	2.7*	0.8	1.9	0.9	0.1	−1.7	−2.0	−0.3
1910				0.0	0.2	−1.7	−0.7	−1.7	−2.4	−4.3*	−4.5*	−2.9*
1917					0.2	−1.7	−0.7	−1.7	−2.4	−4.3*	−4.5*	−2.9*
1924						−1.9	−0.9	−1.9	−2.6*	−4.5*	−4.7	−3.1*
1931							1.1	0.0	−0.7	−2.6*	−2.8*	−1.2
1938								−1.0	−1.8	−3.6*	−3.8*	−2.2
1945									−0.8	−2.6*	−2.8*	−1.2
1952										−1.8	−2.1	−0.5
1959											−0.2	1.4
1966												1.6
Word Fluency												
1889	−2.4	−2.5	−2.4	−2.6*	−3.3*	−4.3*	−4.6*	−3.2*	−3.0*	−2.5*	−1.2	−0.4
1896		−0.2	−0.1	−0.2	−0.9	−1.9	−2.3	−0.8	−0.6	−0.2	1.1	1.9
1903			0.1	0.0	−0.8	−1.8	−2.1	−0.6	−0.5	0.0	1.3	2.1
1910				−0.1	−0.9	−1.9	−2.2	−0.7	−0.6	−0.1	1.2	2.0
1917					−0.7	−1.7	−2.1	−0.6	−0.4	0.0	1.3	2.1
1924						−1.0	−1.3	0.1	0.3	0.7	2.1	2.9*
1931							−0.3	1.1	1.3	1.7	3.0*	3.9*
1938								1.5	1.7	2.1	3.4*	4.2*
1945									0.2	0.6	1.9	2.7*
1952										0.4	1.7	2.6*
1959											1.3	2.1
1966												0.8
Index of Intellectual Ability												
1989	−0.9	0.6	3.1*	4.2*	5.0*	4.3*	6.1*	6.2*	5.6*	5.0*	5.9*	7.3*
1896		1.5	4.0*	5.1*	5.9*	5.2*	7.0*	7.1*	6.5*	5.9*	6.8*	8.2*
1903			2.5	3.7*	4.5*	3.8*	5.6*	5.7*	5.1*	4.5*	5.4*	6.8*
1910				1.1	1.9	1.2	3.7*	3.8*	3.2*	2.6*	3.5*	4.9*
1917					0.8	0.1	1.8	2.0	1.4	0.8	1.7	3.1*
1924						−0.8	1.0	1.2	0.6	0.0	0.9	2.3
1931							1.8	1.9	1.3	0.7	1.7	3.0*
1938								0.2	−0.5	−1.0	−0.1	1.2
1945									−0.6	−1.2	−0.3	1.1
1952										−0.6	0.3	1.7
1959											0.9	2.3
1966												1.4

TABLE 6.1 Continued

Mean Year of Birth	1896	1903	1910	1917	1924	1931	1938	1945	1952	1959	1966	1973
Index of Educational Aptitude												
1889	−0.6	2.0	4.2*	7.0*	8.8*	9.0*	11.0*	12.1	12.0*	11.5*	11.2*	11.7*
1896		2.6*	4.8*	7.5*	9.4*	9.6*	10.6*	12.7*	12.6*	12.1*	11.8*	12.3*
1903			2.2	4.9*	6.8*	6.9*	9.0*	10.1*	10.0*	9.1*	8.8*	9.4*
1910				2.8*	4.7*	4.8*	5.1*	6.8*	8.0*	7.9*	7.5*	8.2*
1917					1.9	2.0	4.1*	5.2*	5.1*	4.6*	4.2*	4.8*
1924						0.1	2.2	3.3*	3.2*	2.7*	2.3	2.9*
1931							2.1	3.2*	3.1*	2.6*	2.2	2.8*
1938								1.1	1.0	0.5	0.1	0.8
1945									−0.1	−0.6	−1.0	−0.3
1952										−0.5	−0.9	−0.4
1959											−0.3	0.2
1966												0.5

Note. Negative values indicate that the later-born cohort is at a disadvantage compared to the earlier-born cohort.

*$p < .01$.

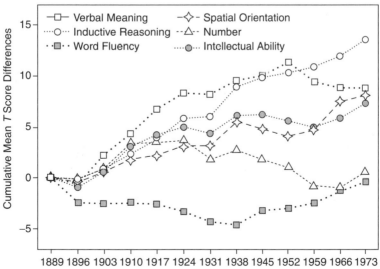

FIGURE 6.1 *Cohort Gradients for the Basic Ability Test Battery.*

cohort born in 1945, there are successive positive cohort differences for this variable also.

Not shown in figure 6.1 is the composite Index of Educational Aptitude. This index shows systematic positive cohort shifts, with a significant disadvantage for all cohorts born in 1931 or earlier. This finding has significant public policy implications and would seem to be another convincing demonstration of the importance of taking generational differences into account when planning present and future adult education activities and programs.

Cohort Differences for the Expanded Battery   In this section, I report cohort gradients for the additional ability markers used in the 1984, 1991, and 1998 testing cycles. In contrast to the rather firm data provided above, caution should be exercised in that the cohort estimates for the expanded battery provided in table 6.2 and charted cumulatively in figure 6.2 were based on a maximum of only three estimates for each cohort from mean birth years 1903 to 1973.

Cohort differences for the added markers of the Inductive Reasoning factor show the same positive linear shape observed for the original marker test. Over the cohort range from 1903 to 1973, there is a gain from 0.8 to 1 *SD*, with the largest for the ADEPT (Adult Development and Enrichment Project) Letter Series test and the least for the Number Series test.

Two of the new markers for the Spatial Orientation factor show significantly lower cohort differences from the original marker. Perhaps because of the more concrete nature of the stimulus material, cumulative cohort differences amount to only 0.1 *SD* for the Object Rotation test and to 0.3 *SD* for the Alphanumeric Rotation test. However, the new marker introducing three-dimensional rotation, the Cube Comparison test, does show a cumulative cohort difference of approximately 1.5 *SD*, which is of a magnitude similar to the cohort effect shown for the original marker.

The cohort differences for the added markers of the Perceptual Speed factor show a positive and accelerating profile. The cumulative cohort difference for Identical Pictures is only half the magnitude of cohort differences for the other measures, 0.6 *SD* as compared to 1.8 and 1.3 *SD*, respectively, for Number Comparisons and Finding A's.

The cohort differences for the added markers of Verbal Comprehension peak for the 1924 cohort, remain stable through the 1945 cohort, and show a steady decline thereafter, with modest recovery for the most recent cohort. The decline is greater for the easier vocabulary test.

The new markers for the Numeric Facility factor also attain a peak for the early cohorts, with modest decline thereafter. The declines are somewhat more pronounced than for the original marker, but there is an upward trend for the most recently born cohort on Subtraction and Multiplication.

After an initial rise from the oldest to the second-oldest cohort, there seems to be a plateau for the new vocabulary tests until the most recent baby boom cohorts, for whom a negative trend can be noted, which may be reversing in the post–baby boomers.

TABLE 6.2 Cohort Differences for the Expanded Ability Battery in *T*-Score Points

| | Inductive Reasoning | | | | | |
| | Letter Series | | Word Series | | Number Series | |
Birth Cohort	Cohort Difference	Cumulative Difference	Cohort Difference	Cumulative Difference	Cohort Difference	Cumulative Difference
1910–1903	−0.5	−0.5	0.5	0.5	0.2	0.2
1917–1910	1.7	1.2	1.8	2.3	2.3	2.5
1924–1917	0.9	2.2	1.4	3.7	1.5	4.0
1931–1924	−0.6	1.6	0.4	4.1	−0.1	3.9
1938–1931	2.1	3.6	2.6	6.7	3.2	7.1
1945–1938	1.2	4.8	0.8	7.5	−1.1	6.0
1952–1945	0.2	5.0	−1.4	6.1	0.2	6.2
1959–1952	0.3	5.3	0.9	7.0	0.3	6.5
1966–1959	0.7	6.0	−0.1	6.9	0.1	6.6
1973–1966	3.9	9.9	2.6	9.5	1.7	8.3

| | Spatial Orientation | | | | | |
| | Object Rotation | | Alphanumeric Rotation | | Cube Comparison | |
Birth Cohort	Cohort Difference	Cumulative Difference	Cohort Difference	Cumulative Difference	Cohort Difference	Cumulative Difference
1910–1903	−2.9	−2.9	−1.8	−1.8	0.7	0.7
1917–1910	1.3	−1.6	1.1	−0.7	1.8	2.5
1924–1917	−0.2	−1.8	−0.4	−1.1	1.3	3.8
1931–1924	−0.2	−0.5	1.2	0.1	0.0	3.8
1938–1931	0.9	0.4	2.2	2.3	2.0	5.8
1945–1938	−0.7	−0.3	0.1	2.4	1.7	7.5
1952–1945	−0.6	−1.0	−0.5	2.0	1.1	8.7
1959–1952	−0.4	−1.4	0.0	2.0	0.8	9.5
1966–1959	1.4	0.0	2.5	4.5	2.1	11.6
1973–1966	1.4	1.4	−1.8	2.7	3.5	15.1

| | Perceptual Speed | | | | | |
| | Identical Pictures | | Number Comparison | | Finding A's | |
Birth Cohort	Cohort Difference	Cumulative Difference	Cohort Difference	Cumulative Difference	Cohort Difference	Cumulative Difference
1910–1903	−1.7	−1.7	0.9	0.9	0.2	0.2
1917–1910	2.0	0.4	1.1	2.0	2.8	3.0
1924–1917	1.7	2.0	0.7	2.7	0.0	3.0
1931–1924	1.2	3.2	1.1	3.9	1.3	4.2
1938–1931	2.2	5.5	1.8	5.7	1.7	6.0
1945–1938	1.8	7.2	1.6	7.4	0.9	6.9
1952–1945	−0.6	6.6	1.1	8.5	1.3	8.2
1959–1952	−0.4	6.3	0.3	8.8	−0.7	7.5
1966–1959	0.0	6.3	4.2	13.0	3.1	10.6
1973–1966	0.0	6.3	4.6	17.6	2.0	12.6

(continued)

TABLE 6.2 Continued

| | Numeric Facility | | | |
| | Addition | | Subtraction and Multiplication | |
Birth Cohort	Cohort Difference	Cumulative Difference	Cohort Difference	Cumulative Difference
1910–1903	1.4	1.4	2.7	2.7
1917–1910	−0.6	0.8	0.5	3.2
1924–1917	−2.4	−1.6	−1.5	1.7
1931–1924	−1.8	−3.4	−2.1	−0.4
1938–1931	−0.1	−3.5	−0.6	−1.0
1945–1938	−0.4	−3.9	0.4	−0.6
1952–1945	−1.7	−5.6	−2.3	−2.9
1959–1952	−2.6	−8.2	−2.4	−5.3
1966–1959	−0.6	−8.6	1.0	−4.3
1973–1966	1.5	−7.3	0.1	−4.2

| | Verbal Comprehension | | | |
| | ETS Vocabulary | | ETS Advanced Vocabulary | |
Birth Cohort	Cohort Difference	Cumulative Difference	Cohort Difference	Cumulative Difference
1910–1903	4.4	4.4	3.9	3.9
1917–1910	0.3	4.7	0.9	4.8
1924–1917	0.5	5.2	−0.4	4.4
1931–1924	−2.7	2.5	−2.9	1.5
1938–1931	−0.1	2.4	0.9	2.4
1945–1938	−1.3	1.1	−0.6	1.8
1952–1945	−1.0	0.1	0.4	2.2
1959–1952	−4.2	−4.1	−2.8	−0.6
1966–1959	−2.2	−6.3	−1.5	−2.1
1973–1966	0.9	−5.4	1.7	−0.4

| | Verbal Memory | | | |
| | Immediate Recall | | Delayed Recall | |
Birth Cohort	Cohort Difference	Cumulative Difference	Cohort Difference	Cumulative Difference
1910–1903	0.4	0.4	0.5	0.5
1917–1910	0.7	1.1	1.4	2.0
1924–1917	0.5	1.6	0.4	2.3
1931–1924	−0.2	1.5	−0.2	2.1
1938–1931	2.6	4.0	2.7	4.8
1945–1938	2.1	6.2	2.3	7.1
1952–1945	0.6	6.7	1.2	8.3
1959–1952	−1.3	5.4	−0.8	7.5
1966–1959	0.8	6.2	1.3	8.7
1973–1966	0.3	6.5	0.3	9.0

Note. Negative values indicate that the later-born cohort is at disadvantage compared with the earlier-born cohort. ETS, Educational Testing Service.

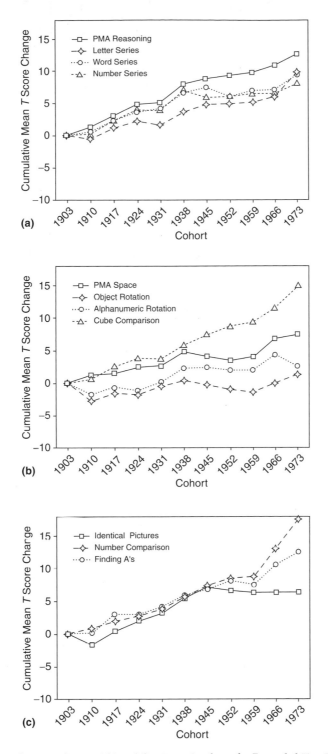

FIGURE 6.2 *Cohort Gradients within Ability Domains from the Expanded Test Battery.*
ETS, Educational Testing Service; PMA, Primary Mental Abilities.

(continued)

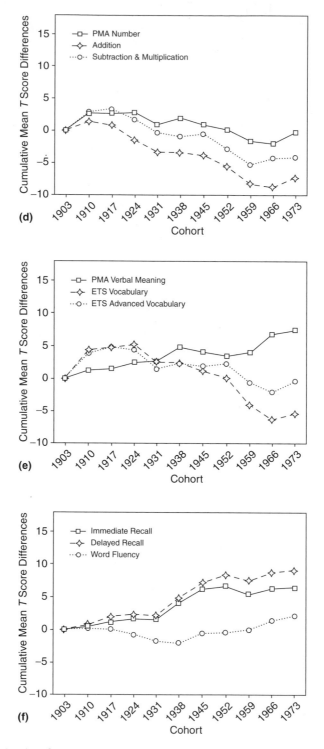

FIGURE 6.2 *Continued.*

Finally, for the measures of Verbal Memory, we observe positive cohort trends amounting to 0.6 *SD* for the Immediate Recall and 0.9 *SD* for the Delayed Recall parts of the word list memorized in this test.

Cohort Differences for the Latent Constructs Having considered differences among alternative markers of mental abilities, cohort differences at the latent construct level are now considered. Differences between adjacent cohorts were computed for the factor scores for the six latent constructs for which cross-sectional and longitudinal age differences were reported in chapters 4 and 5. The cohort difference estimates at the latent construct level are provided in table 6.3 and graphed cumulatively in figure 6.3.

For the factor scores describing the latent constructs, substantial positive and linear cohort differences are observed for the Inductive Reasoning and Perceptual Speed factors (approximately 1 *SD*). A similar, although less steep, positive difference pattern occurs for Spatial Orientation (0.6 *SD*) and Verbal Memory (0.7

TABLE 6.3 Cohort Differences for the Latent Construct Factor Scores in *T*-Score Points

Birth Cohort	*Inductive Reasoning*		*Spatial Orientation*		*Perceptual Speed*	
	Cohort Difference	Cumulative Difference	Cohort Difference	Cumulative Difference	Cohort Difference	Cumulative Difference
1910–1903	1.1	1.1	−1.9	−1.9	−0.7	−0.7
1917–1910	2.4	3.5	1.2	−0.7	2.9	2.2
1924–1917	1.3	3.7	−0.3	−1.0	1.5	3.7
1931–1924	−0.8	2.9	1.0	0.0	0.8	4.5
1938–1931	2.8	5.7	1.8	1.9	2.0	6.6
1945–1938	0.7	6.4	−0.1	1.8	1.5	8.0
1952–1945	−0.6	5.8	0.7	2.5	0.1	8.2
1959–1952	1.4	7.2	0.2	2.7	−0.7	7.4
1966–1959	0.9	8.1	2.6	5.3	1.6	9.1
1973–1966	2.5	10.6	0.6	5.9	1.4	10.4

Birth Cohort	*Numeric Facility*		*Verbal Comprehension*		*Verbal Memory*	
	Cohort Difference	Cumulative Difference	Cohort Difference	Cumulative Difference	Cohort Difference	Cumulative Difference
1910–1903	3.2	3.2	3.5	3.5	0.0	0.0
1917–1910	−0.2	3.0	1.2	4.6	1.1	1.1
1924–1917	−1.9	1.1	0.2	4.8	0.8	1.8
1931–1924	−2.4	−1.3	−2.6	2.2	−1.0	0.8
1938–1931	0.3	−1.0	0.6	2.9	2.7	3.5
1945–1938	−0.2	−1.2	−0.7	2.2	1.8	5.3
1952–1945	−2.2	−3.4	−0.7	1.4	0.9	6.2
1959–1952	−2.8	−6.2	−3.7	−2.3	−0.5	5.7
1966–1959	0.4	−5.7	−2.1	−4.3	0.7	6.4
1973–1966	0.9	−4.8	0.8	−3.5	0.7	7.1

Note. Negative values indicate that the later-born cohort is at disadvantage compared with the earlier-born cohort.

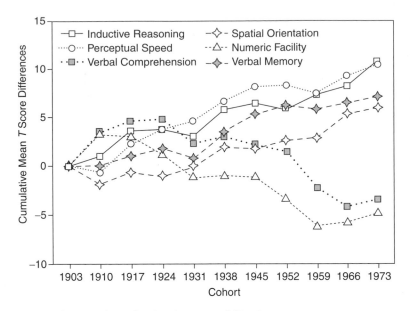

FIGURE 6.3 *Cohort Gradients for the Six Latent Ability Constructs.*

SD); a modest negative gradient (approximately 0.5 *SD*) is found for Numeric Facility, and there is a modest concave gradient with recent declines for Verbal Comprehension.

Cohort Differences on the Measure of Practical Intelligence

Our measure of practical intelligence, the Educational Testing Service (ETS) Basic Skills test, is an expression of combinations and permutations of the basic abilities in particular practical situations. It is therefore not surprising that the cohort pattern for this ability (estimated over a single 7-year interval) is rather similar to that observed for the measures of Inductive Reasoning. Indeed, inductive reasoning is the ability that seems to correlate most with the practical intelligence measure (see Willis & Schaie, 1986a). Figure 6.4 shows substantial increments in performance level for our earlier-born cohorts up to the cohort born in 1938; thereafter, the cohort gradient for practical intelligence reaches a virtual asymptote.

Cohort Differences in Cognitive Styles

We have also updated the cohort gradients for the measures of cognitive style previously reported in Schaie (1983a, 1996b). Table 6.4 provides the cumulative cohort difference estimates, which are graphed in figure 6.5. All of these measures show positive cohort effects. The Motor-Cognitive factors show a virtually linear increase in flexibility across cohorts amounting to approximately 1.2 *SD*. The Attitudinal Flexibility factor shows a smaller increment of about 0.8 *SD*, but

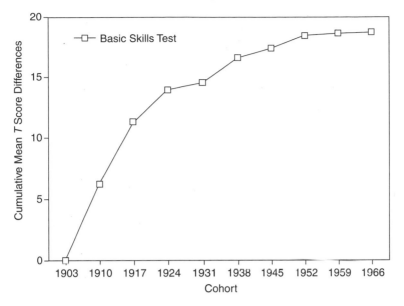

FIGURE 6.4 *Cohort Gradient for the Basic Skills Test.*

becomes virtually asymptotic with the cohort born in 1938. The cohort gradient for Psychomotor Speed shows a modest decline from the first- to the second-oldest cohort; after that, it parallels the cohort gradients for the other cognitive style measures, but beginning with the 1938 cohort, shows somewhat steeper positive increment. For this measure, the cumulative increment from the oldest to the youngest cohorts amounts to 1.4 *SD*.

Cohort Differences in Demographic Characteristics

Some data have been accumulated in the SLS on cohort shifts in the demographic characteristics of our sample. Of particular interest are data on educational level, age at first marriage, and age when the study participants' first child was born (see table 6.5 and figure 6.6). For these variables, we report both cohort differences for the entire group, and differences by gender separately. Over the cohort range represented in our study, there has been a steady increase in years of education, amounting to a difference in education of about 5.5 years between the earliest and latest cohorts studied. The increase has been approximately 1 year greater for men than for women.

Age at First Marriage   Averages declined by almost 4 years from our earliest cohort to those born in the 1930s (the lowest level was reached by men for the 1938 cohort and by women for the 1931 cohort). From that point, there has been a steady rise, which is most pronounced for women. Age of marriage of our youngest cohort had returned to the level of their grandparents and for the women had actually exceeded that of our oldest cohort.

TABLE 6.4 Mean Advantage of Later-Born Cohorts Over Earlier-Born Cohorts in *T*-Score Points

Mean Year of Birth	1896	1903	1910	1917	1924	1931	1938	1945	1952	1959	1966	1973
Motor-Cognitive Flexibility												
1889	0.3	1.4	3.6*	4.4*	5.7*	6.5*	7.8*	8.0*	8.9*	9.4*	9.0*	12.3*
1896		1.1	3.3*	4.1*	5.3*	6.2*	7.5*	7.6*	8.5*	9.0*	8.7*	12.0*
1903			2.2	3.0*	4.2*	5.1*	6.4*	6.5*	7.4*	7.9*	7.6*	10.9*
1910				0.8	2.0	2.9*	4.2*	4.3*	5.2*	5.7*	5.4*	8.7*
1917					1.2	2.1	3.4*	3.5*	4.4*	4.9*	4.6*	7.9*
1924						0.9	2.2	2.3	3.2*	3.7*	3.4*	6.7*
1931							1.3	1.4	2.3	2.8*	2.5*	5.8*
1938								0.1	1.0	1.6	1.2	4.5*
1945									0.9	1.4	1.1	4.3*
1952										0.5	0.2	3.4*
1959											−0.4	2.9*
1966												0.3
Attitudinal Flexibility												
1889	0.0	2.2	2.8*	4.4*	5.7*	5.6*	7.3*	7.7*	8.0*	6.4*	6.6*	6.4*
1896		2.2	2.8*	4.4*	5.7*	5.6*	7.3*	7.7*	9.5*	6.4*	6.6*	6.4*
1903			0.6	2.2	3.5*	3.4*	5.1*	5.5*	7.3*	4.2*	4.4*	4.2*
1910				1.6	2.9*	2.8*	4.5*	4.9*	6.7*	3.6*	3.8*	3.6*
1917					1.4	1.2	2.9*	3.3*	3.1*	2.0	2.2	2.0
1924						−0.1	1.6	2.0	2.2	0.6	0.9	0.6
1931							1.7	2.1	1.8	0.7	0.9	0.6
1938								0.4	0.6	−1.0	−0.7	−0.9
1945									0.2	−1.4	−1.1	−1.3
1952										−1.6	−1.3	−1.6
1959											0.3	0.0
1966												−0.2
Psychomotor Speed												
1889	−1.1	0.5	3.3*	5.2*	6.7*	7.6*	10.6*	12.8*	13.4*	14.8*	17.1*	14.0*
1896		1.6	4.4*	6.3*	7.8*	8.7*	11.7*	13.9*	14.5*	15.9*	18.2*	15.1*
1903			2.8*	4.7*	6.2*	7.1*	10.1*	12.3*	12.9*	13.3*	16.6*	13.5*
1910				1.9	3.4*	4.2*	7.3*	9.5*	10.1*	10.5*	13.8*	10.7*
1917					1.6	2.3	5.4*	7.6*	9.2*	8.6*	11.9*	8.8*
1924						0.8	3.8*	6.0*	7.6*	7.0*	10.3*	7.2*
1931							3.0*	5.2*	6.8*	6.2*	9.5*	6.6*
1938								2.2	4.8*	3.2*	6.5*	3.6*
1945									0.7	1.0	4.3*	1.4
1952										1.4	3.6*	0.7
1959											2.2	−0.8
1966												−3.0*

Note. Negative values indicate that the later-born cohort is at a disadvantage compared to the earlier-born cohort.

*$p < .01$.

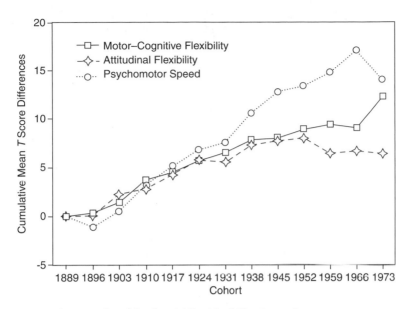

FIGURE 6.5 *Cohort Gradients for the Rigidity-Flexibility Factor Scores.*

Age at Birth of First Child   There was a decrease in age at birth of first child of about 2 years from the oldest to the 1931 cohort, followed by a steady increment of approximately 4.5 years from the lowest point to our most recent (1973) cohort. A similar pattern obtained for both sexes, although both the decrease from the oldest cohort and the increase to current cohorts were approximately 1 year greater for women.

Measures of Mobility   Other demographic characteristics that may be important in understanding cohort differences in the cognitive variables include our *measures of mobility* (changes in the location of one's home, changes of job, and changes in occupation). Average data over the 5 years preceding each reporting date were employed for these measures, which are reported across gender (table 6.6 and figure 6.7). Note that there is a very modest drop in residential and job mobility from the oldest cohort to that born in 1931; over the same cohort range, there are few cohort differences in occupational mobility. Mobility characteristics, however, increase again for the baby boomer cohorts for all three measures, with residential and job mobility changes the most pronounced.

Studies of Period (Time-of-Measurement) Differences

Just as we were able to estimate cohort differences by matching across age and assuming equivalence of period effects across cohorts, so the data can be used to estimate period (time-of-measurement) effects by matching across age and as-

TABLE 6.5 Cohort Differences for Years of Education, Age at First Marriage, and Age at Birth of First Child for Total Sample and Separately by Gender

	Years of Education					
	Males		Females		Total Sample	
Birth Cohort	Cohort Difference	Cumulative Difference	Cohort Difference	Cumulative Difference	Cohort Difference	Cumulative Difference
1896–1889	−0.60	−0.60	0.35	0.35	−0.09	−0.09
1903–1896	1.45	0.85	0.82	1.17	1.12	1.03
1910–1903	1.08	1.93	0.56	1.73	0.70	1.73
1917–1910	0.91	2.84	0.18	1.91	0.52	2.24
1924–1917	0.98	3.82	0.68	2.59	0.83	3.07
1931–1924	0.26	4.08	−0.14	2.45	0.02	3.09
1938–1931	1.00	5.08	0.95	3.40	1.00	4.09
1945–1938	0.78	5.86	0.73	4.13	0.75	4.84
1952–1945	−0.51	5.35	0.32	4.45	0.23	5.07
1959–1952	−0.22	5.14	0.31	4.76	−0.16	4.91
1966–1959	0.10	5.24	0.24	5.00	0.18	5.09
1973–1966	0.60	5.84	−0.05	4.95	0.50	5.59

	Age at First Marriage					
	Males		Females		Total Sample	
Birth Cohort	Cohort Difference	Cumulative Difference	Cohort Difference	Cumulative Difference	Cohort Difference	Cumulative Difference
1896–1889	−0.13	−0.13	−1.45	−1.45	−0.68	−0.68
1903–1896	0.93	0.80	−0.68	−2.14	0.03	−0.65
1910–1903	−1.81	−1.01	0.79	−1.35	−0.55	−1.20
1917–1910	−1.28	−2.30	−0.43	−1.78	−0.78	−1.98
1924–1917	−0.11	−2.41	−1.29	−3.07	−0.81	−2.79
1931–1924	−0.83	−3.24	−1.50	−4.57	−1.12	−3.91
1938–1931	−0.51	−3.75	0.64	−3.93	0.22	−3.69
1945–1938	1.44	−2.31	0.83	−3.10	1.01	−2.68
1952–1945	0.61	−1.70	0.76	−2.34	0.89	−1.79
1959–1952	0.53	−1.13	1.63	−0.71	0.98	−0.81
1966–1959	0.08	−1.05	0.72	0.01	0.57	−0.24
1973–1966	0.83	−0.22	0.58	0.59	0.34	0.10

TABLE 6.5 Continued

	Age at Birth of First Child					
	Males		Females		Total Sample	
Birth Cohort	Cohort Difference	Cumulative Difference	Cohort Difference	Cumulative Difference	Cohort Difference	Cumulative Difference
1896–1889	1.07	1.07	−1.20	−1.20	−0.18	−0.18
1903–1896	0.78	1.85	−0.31	−1.51	0.50	0.32
1910–1903	−0.54	1.31	1.13	−0.38	0.39	0.71
1917–1910	−1.67	−0.36	−0.46	−0.84	−0.62	0.10
1924–1917	−0.66	−1.02	−1.01	−1.85	−0.86	−0.76
1931–1924	−0.88	−1.90	−1.44	−3.29	−1.26	−2.01
1938–1931	0.28	−2.18	0.48	−2.81	0.54	−1.47
1945–1938	1.88	−0.30	1.12	−1.69	1.24	−0.23
1952–1945	−0.62	−0.92	0.90	−0.79	0.48	0.25
1959–1952	1.41	0.49	3.01	2.22	1.89	2.14
1966–1959	−0.24	0.25	−0.06	2.16	−0.24	1.90
1973–1966	1.67	1.91	0.00	2.16	0.50	2.40

Note. Negative values indicate that the level of the later cohort is lower than that of the earlier cohort.

suming equivalence of cohort effects across periods. Estimates of period effects can be obtained from the same cross-sectional sequence used for the cohort differences estimates. However, the time-sequential analysis strategy must now be used. A time-of-measurement (period) difference (Td) is defined as

$$Td_k = \left(\sum_{j}^{1} (M_{jk+1} - M_{jk}) \right)/a$$

where M_{jk} is the unweighted mean for time k at age j, and a indicates the number of common ages for which observations are available for each pair of times of measurement. In the SLS, these effects can be estimated over seven ages for the first period, eight ages for the second period, and nine ages for all subsequent periods.

The formulas for estimating average cohort and period differences seem superficially similar. However, they involve quite different data. Cohort differences are averaged differences for a given cohort pair that occur at different ages that by definition must span many time periods. The emphasis here is on obtaining the best estimate for the difference between a particular cohort pair. By contrast, period effects are averaged differences between samples of the same age over two adjacent time periods.

Period Effects for the Cognitive Abilities

The six period effects for the primary mental abilities are shown in table 6.7 for the total sample because no significant Period × Gender interactions were found.

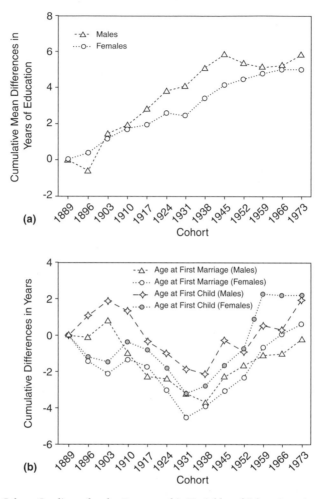

FIGURE 6.6 *Cohort Gradients for the Demographic Variables of Education, Age at First Marriage, and Age at Birth of First Child.*

Significant positive period trends are observed from 1956 to 1998 for Verbal Meaning, Spatial Orientation, and Inductive Reasoning. For Number, there is a positive trend from 1956 to 1970, but a negative trend from 1970 through 1998. For Word Fluency, a significant negative period trend occurs from 1956 to 1977, reversing to a slightly positive trend from 1977 to 1998.

Period Effects in Cognitive Styles

Similar to the period effects for the ability data, significant period effects are also observed for the measures of cognitive style. These effects are shown in table 6.8. Significant positive period effects are found for Motor-Cognitive Flexibility from

TABLE 6.6 Cohort Differences for the Mobility Measures of Changes in Homes, Jobs, and Occupational Pursuits Over the Previous 5 Years

Birth Cohort	Change of Home		Change of Job		Change of Occupation	
	Cohort Difference	Cumulative Difference	Cohort Difference	Cumulative Difference	Cohort Difference	Cumulative Difference
1896–1889	−0.10	−0.10	−0.03	−0.03	−0.23	−0.23
1903–1896	−0.04	−0.14	0.03	0.00	−0.10	−0.33
1910–1903	0.06	−0.08	0.00	0.00	0.08	−0.25
1917–1910	−0.17	−0.25	−0.05	−0.05	−0.08	−0.33
1924–1917	0.10	−0.15	−0.06	−0.11	−0.03	−0.36
1931–1924	−0.12	−0.27	−0.02	−0.13	0.07	−0.29
1938–1931	0.11	−0.16	0.16	0.03	0.20	−0.09
1945–1938	0.47	0.31	0.18	0.21	0.07	−0.02
1952–1945	0.22	0.53	0.36	0.57	0.20	0.18
1959–1952	0.18	0.71	0.29	0.86	0.05	0.23
1966–1959	0.02	0.73	−0.26	0.60	−0.07	0.16
1973–1966	−0.16	0.56	0.51	1.11	0.17	0.33

Note. Negative values indicate that the level of the later-born cohort is lower than that of the earlier-born cohort.

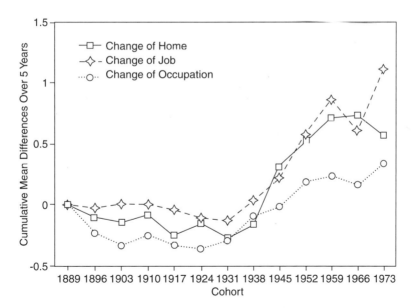

FIGURE 6.7 *Cohort Gradients for the Mobility Variables of Number of Changes in Job, Occupation, and Place of Residence.*

TABLE 6.7 Period (Time-of-Measurement) Effects for the Primary Mental Abilities in T-Score Points

	Verbal Meaning						Spatial Orientation					
	1963	1970	1977	1984	1991	1998	1963	1970	1977	1984	1991	1998
1956	0.32	2.62*	2.55*	4.69*	6.41*	6.50*	1.08	2.31*	2.13*	1.75	3.24*	3.90*
1963		2.30*	2.23*	4.37*	6.09*	6.18*		1.23	1.05	0.67	2.16*	2.82*
1970			−0.07	2.07	3.79*	3.88*			−0.18	−0.56	0.93	1.59
1977				2.14*	3.86*	3.95*				−0.38	1.11	1.77
1984					1.72	1.81					1.49	2.15*
1991						0.09						0.66

	Inductive Reasoning						Number					
	1963	1970	1977	1984	1991	1998	1963	1970	1977	1984	1991	1998
1956	0.65	2.90*	3.26*	5.21*	6.66*	7.73*	0.57	2.29*	0.33	0.04	0.58	−0.28
1963		2.25*	2.61*	4.11*	5.56*	6.63*		1.72	−0.24	−0.53	0.01	−0.86
1970			0.36	2.37*	3.77*	4.84*			−1.96*	−2.25*	−1.71	−2.57*
1977				1.95	3.27*	4.34*				−0.29	0.25	−0.61
1984					1.45	2.52*					0.54	−0.32
1991						1.07						−0.86

	Word Fluency					
	1963	1970	1977	1984	1991	1998
1956	−3.71*	−3.42*	−2.91*	−2.05*	−1.39	−1.59
1963		0.29	0.80	1.66	2.32*	−2.12*
1970			0.51	1.37	2.03*	1.83
1977				0.86	1.52	1.32
1984					0.66	0.46
1991						−0.20

	Intellectual Ability						Educational Aptitude					
	1963	1970	1977	1984	1991	1998	1963	1970	1977	1984	1991	1998
1956	0.07	2.44*	1.84	2.87*	4.36*	4.40*	0.46	2.87*	2.91*	5.26*	6.63*	7.20*
1963		2.37*	1.77	2.80*	4.29*	4.33*		2.41*	2.45*	4.80*	6.17*	6.74*
1970			−0.60	0.43	1.92	1.96*			0.04	2.39*	3.76*	4.33*
1977				1.03	2.52*	2.56*				2.35*	3.72*	4.29*
1984					1.49	1.53					1.37	1.94*
1991						0.04						0.57

*$p < .01$.

TABLE 6.8 Period (Time-of-Measurement) Effects for the Measures of Cognitive Style in *T*-Score Points

	Motor-Cognitive Flexibility						Attitudinal Flexibility					
	1963	1970	1977	1984	1991	1998	1963	1970	1977	1984	1991	1998
1956	1.93*	1.74	3.72*	3.80*	4.47*	5.30*	−0.24	1.77	1.83	3.42*	4.32*	3.67*
1963		−0.19	1.79	1.87	2.54*	2.73*		2.01*	2.07*	3.66*	4.56*	3.91*
1970			1.98*	2.06*	4.33*	5.16*			0.06	1.65	2.55*	1.90*
1977				0.08	0.75	1.58				1.59	2.49*	1.84
1984					0.67	1.50					0.90	0.35
1991						0.83						−0.65

	Psychomotor Speed					
	1963	1970	1977	1984	1991	1998
1956	−2.66*	1.03	0.23	4.13*	9.25*	7.45*
1963		3.69*	2.89*	6.79*	11.92*	10.11*
1970			−0.80	3.10*	8.22*	6.42*
1977				3.90*	9.02*	7.22*
1984					5.12*	3.32*
1991						−1.80

*$p < .01$.

1956 to 1998. However, magnitudes of effects from 1977, although still positive, do not reach statistical significance.

For Attitudinal Flexibility, positive period effects also occur that are statistically significant for effects from 1956 to 1984 and beyond, from 1977 to 1963 through 1998, from 1970 to 1991 and 1998, and from 1977 to 1991. For the Psychomotor Speed factor, a negative period difference is found from 1956 to 1963, but statistically significant positive period effects occur from 1963 through 1998, from 1970 to 1984 and beyond, from 1977 through 1998, and from 1984 to 1991 and 1998.

Period Effects in Demographic Characteristics

Finally, I provide data on period effects for the demographic variables for which cohort data are given above. Significant period effects are found for all, except for the variable of age at birth of first child. Table 6.9 provides the estimates for educational level and age at first marriage. Statistically significant period effects (in a positive direction) are found throughout except between the 1956 and 1963, between the 1984 and 1991, and between the 1991 and 1998 data collections. Period effects for age at first marriage, however, reach statistical significance only for the difference between the 1956 and all other data collections. In all these instances, there is a negative period effect from our first to the later assessment points.

TABLE 6.9 Period (Time-of-Measurement) Effects for the Demographic Variables

	Years of Education						Age at First Marriage					
	1963	1970	1977	1984	1991	1998	1963	1970	1977	1984	1991	1998
1956	−0.21	0.55	1.21*	2.11*	2.60*	2.80*	−1.34*	−1.30*	−1.67*	−1.71*	−1.21*	−1.13*
1963		0.76*	1.42*	2.32*	2.81*	3.01*		0.04	−0.33	−0.37	0.13	0.21
1970			0.66*	1.56*	2.05*	2.35*			−0.37	−0.41	0.09	0.17
1977				0.90*	1.49*	1.69*				−0.04	0.46	0.54
1984					0.59	0.79*					0.50	0.58
1991						0.20						0.08

*$p < .01$.

Statistically significant period effects are also found for the mobility measures (table 6.10). A shift toward lower residential and occupational mobility occurs between 1956 and 1963. However, period effects in the direction of greater mobility occur for residential change between the 1970 and 1977 data collections. Greater job mobility is observed from 1970 and 1977 as well as between 1963 and 1970 with respect to the data collections from 1977 to 1991. Greater occupational mobility is also seen between the 1963 to 1977 and all later data collections, as well as between 1970 to 1984 and all later data collections. However, no mobilities differences were found to be significant beginning with the 1977 cohort with respect to later cohorts.

TABLE 6.10 Period (Time-of-Measurement) Effects for the Mobility Variables

	Residential Change						Job Change					
	1963	1970	1977	1984	1991	1998	1963	1970	1977	1984	1991	1998
1956	−0.33*	−0.28	0.37*	0.26	0.38*	0.42*	−0.17	−0.07	0.22	0.19	0.24*	0.19
1963		0.05	0.70*	0.59*	0.71*	0.75*		0.10	0.39*	0.36*	0.41*	0.36*
1970			0.65*	0.54*	0.66*	0.70*			0.29*	0.26*	0.31*	0.26*
1977				−0.11	0.01	0.05				−0.03	0.02	−0.03
1984					0.12	0.16					0.05	0.00
1991						0.04						−0.05

	Occupational Change					
	1963	1970	1977	1984	1991	1998
1956	−0.29*	−0.20	−0.02	0.11	0.12	0.11
1963		0.09	0.27*	0.40*	0.41*	0.40
1970			0.18	0.31*	0.32*	0.31*
1977				0.13	0.14	0.13
1984					0.01	0.00
1991						−0.01

*$p < .01$.

Interpretation and Application of Period
Effect Estimates

Several alternative explanations can be offered for the observed period effects. They may simply represent testing effects, that is, inadvertent small but systematic changes in test administration and scoring procedures that, even with the best documentation, can easily slip into long-term longitudinal studies. Although unlikely for large samples, it is nevertheless possible that these differences represent systematic selection effects attributable to changes in the composition of the pool from which the successive samples were drawn.

An alternate explanation would be the occurrence of a systematic cohort trend, although cohort differences should only minimally affect the period estimates obtained from SLS data because, for each period difference estimate, all but two of the cohorts used are identical. Finally, of course, these findings might represent true period effects caused by systematic positive environmental impacts such as the improvement of media, increased utilization of adult education opportunities, improved nutrition, and increased participation in preventive health care programs or, in the case of negative period effects, the neglect of drill in number skills or writing exercises in educational practice.

These matters are far from trivial because longitudinal data should be adjusted for period effects to obtain age functions that can be generalized across time. In particular, the matter of period effects becomes an important problem when age functions are constructed from data gathered in short-term longitudinal studies that apply sequential data-gathering strategies.

Fortunately, however, data from cross-sectional sequences allow consideration of certain adjustments to these short-term longitudinal age functions. As indicated in chapter 2, a net age change can be obtained by subtracting the average period effect from the observed longitudinal age difference $(Ad = Lod - Td)$. If one assumes that there are no significant Age × Time interactions, then it is possible to adjust longitudinal change estimates period effect estimates such as those presented in table 6.7.

If Age × Time interactions are presumed to exist, then more complicated corrections are needed. In that case, one would compute age/time-specific time lags from cross-sectional data such as those in table 4.2 and use the resultant age/time-specific estimates of period effects to adjust the longitudinal age-change estimates. The first correction would be most appropriate for use in dealing with testing effects or true period effects occurring across all age/time levels. The second correction is appropriate for dealing with age/time-specific fluctuations. This correction would be appropriate whenever it is suspected that period effects may differentially impact different age/cohort groups. Detailed numeric examples of the adjustment procedure can be found in Schaie (1988d).

What are the consequences of making these adjustments for our longitudinal data? In a multivariate analysis of variance for the five basic abilities, I determined that, when holding age constant, there were significant main effects for time

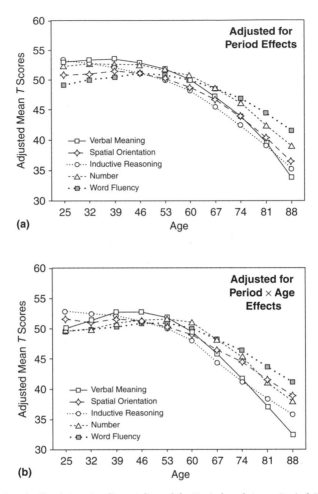

FIGURE 6.8 *Longitudinal Age Gradient Adjusted for Period and Age × Period Effects.*

(period) for all abilities as well as significant Age × Time interactions for all abilities except Spatial Orientation. I therefore made the adjustments described above for the 7-year longitudinal estimates graphed for the total sample in figure 5.1. The revised estimates are presented in figure 6.8 adjusted for (a) the average period effects and (b) age-specific period effects. These graphs have fairly similar slopes. However, the adjustments have the effect of reducing increases in young adulthood, reducing decrement in early old age, and estimating steeper decrement slopes in advanced old age. They also decrease the separation between the five abilities in young adulthood and increase the separation in old age. At the oldest age studied, the adjusted estimates result in greatest decline for Verbal Meaning and least decline for Word Fluency.

Chapter Summary

This chapter reports findings on systematic cohort trends, which generally favor later-born cohorts for variables such as Verbal Meaning, Spatial Orientation, and Inductive Reasoning. But different cohort patterns do occur, including a convex pattern favoring the middle cohorts for Number, with a currently negative trend favoring the earlier-born cohorts and a concave trend for Word Fluency, which attains a low point for the middle generations, with a recent favorable reversal.

The implication of the positive cohort differences is that when older persons are compared with their younger peers, they will, on average, show lower performance even if they have experienced little or no age decrement. On the other hand, when negative cohort differences occur, such as on Number, older persons may compare favorably with younger persons even though they may actually have declined from previous performance levels. Whether older persons are at a disadvantage in occupations requiring certain basic skills will therefore depend markedly on their relative position in the cohort succession.

At the latent construct level, positive cohort gradients (favoring more recently born cohorts) are found for Inductive Reasoning, Perceptual Speed, Verbal Memory, and Spatial Orientation. Verbal and Numeric abilities had concave cohort gradients, showing lower levels for the baby-boomer cohorts. Positive cohort gradients are also observed for our measure of practical intelligence, the measures of cognitive style, level of education, and measures of mobility. These findings are important because they suggest that as future cohorts age they will be better positioned to respond to an increasingly complex environment, given their greater education and ability to respond in a more flexible manner.

Estimates of period effects are also provided. These effects show a positive time trend for Verbal Meaning, Spatial Orientation, and Inductive Reasoning. Such secular trends imply that performance levels over time have improved for persons at all adult ages.

Finally, possible applications of the period effect estimates are considered. An example is provided of how corrections for cohort and period effects can be applied to adjust longitudinal estimates to obtain increased generalizability.

CHAPTER SEVEN

Intervention Studies

W HEN AN INVESTIGATION HAS LED to a reasonably complete description of the phenomenon under study and some of the antecedent conditions that might lead to differential outcomes are beginning to be understood, it then becomes interesting to design interventions that might modify such outcomes. In collaboration with Sherry Willis, who had previously designed and carried out a number of cognitive interventions as part of the Adult Development and Enrichment Project (ADEPT) at Pennsylvania State University in University Park (Baltes & Willis, 1982), we explored how to best take advantage of a longitudinal study to advance the methodology of cognitive interventions in older adults (see also Schaie, 1996b; Willis, 1987, 1990a, 1990b, 1992a, 2001; Willis & Schaie, 1994b).

Remediation Versus New Learning

Over the past two decades, increased attention has been given in the study of adult intelligence to the question of modifiability of intellectual performance by cognitive training procedures (see Baltes & Lindenberger, 1988; Denney & Heidrich, 1990; Giambra & Arenberg, 1980; Willis, 1985, 1987, 2001; Willis & Schaie, 1993). There has always been great interest in determining whether and how well old dogs can be taught new tricks. However, from the point of view of developmental theory and to determine the societal benefit of such interventions, it may be even more important to ask the question whether cognitive interventions can result in the remediation of reliably documented age-related decline.

The theoretical importance of this question relates to the fact that, if it is possible to show that such decline can be reversed, then grave doubt is cast on the tenability of an irreversible decrement model of aging that assumes the inevitability of normative patterns of intellectual decline for all. Irreversible decrement models of cognitive aging also generally imply that observed behavioral deficits should be isomorphic with underlying adverse physiological age changes (cf. Baltes & Lindenberger, 1997; Botwinick, 1977; Kausler, 1982; Salthouse, 1982). A demonstration of the reversal of cognitive decline, on the contrary, lends greater plausibility to the hypothesis that behavioral deficit occurring with age is more likely to be caused by specific patterns of disuse and/or neuropathology. The remediation of cognitive decline in at least some individuals would also provide support for a hypothesis postulating behavioral plasticity through life (see Baltes, 1987; Baltes & Willis, 1977).

Important practical implications also follow the demonstration of successful remediation of cognitive decline. Older individuals are often institutionalized because their intellectual competence no longer suffices for them to function independently. Cognitive interventions, if effective in the laboratory, then can lead to the development of both generalized and specific educational intervention programs that could help restore the intellectual competence of many older individuals to levels that would maintain or prolong their ability to engage at an adequate level in tasks of daily living and thus to function independently within the community (see Ball et al., 2003; Willis, 1992a, 1995, 2001).

Earlier cognitive training research strongly suggested that older adults' performance can be modified on a number of cognitive dimensions, such as memory span, inductive reasoning, cognitive problem solving, spatial egocentrism, and so on (for reviews, see Baltes & Lindenberger, 1988; Denney, 1982; Poon, Walsh-Sweeney, & Fozard, 1980; Sterns & Sanders, 1980; Willis, 1985, 1987, 1989b, 1990a; Willis & Schaie, 1994b). Training effects have also previously been shown to generalize to multiple measures of the cognitive dimension on which training occurred (Baltes & Willis, 1982).

All of the training studies prior to the interventions conducted in the context of the Seattle Longitudinal Study (SLS), however, were cross-sectional. These studies therefore could not reach any conclusions on whether the training gains represented remediation of prior cognitive decline or might represent the attainment of new performance levels (perhaps closer to the limits of their reserve capacities; see Baltes, 1993; Baltes, Dittmann-Kohli, & Kliegl, 1986) in individuals who had not experienced any cognitive decline. Obviously, addressing this distinction requires that the participants' preintervention level of functioning must be compared with data collected at earlier times. Given the availability of participants in the SLS who had been followed over time, it seemed desirable to approach this question directly. There have been three cognitive training studies within the SLS: the initial training study (1983–1984); a 7-year follow-up of training maintenance, including a booster, and replication with a new sample (1990–1991); and a 14-year follow-up, booster, and a second replication with a new sample (1997–1998) (also see Saczynski, 2001).

The 1983–1984 Cognitive Training Study

We decided to restrict the training study to those participants for whom we had at least two previous data points to obtain sufficiently large samples of participants for whom we could reliably document decline. That is, we included only those study participants who at the time of the intervention had been followed for a minimum of 14 years and who in 1983 were at least 64 years old (SLS Cohorts 1 to 5). We also decided to train on the abilities of Inductive Reasoning and Spatial Orientation, for which average decline had been documented to occur by the early 60s (see chapter 5).

Including younger study participants or attempting to train on abilities such as Verbal Meaning, for which modal decline occurs at later ages, would have resulted in an insufficient number of participants who had reliably declined. Conversely, setting an older age cutoff would have reduced the number of stable individuals needed to contrast the effects of remediation of cognitive decline with improvement from a prior stable level of functioning (Schaie & Willis, 1986b; Willis & Schaie, 1986b, 1988).

Method

Participants The 1983–1984 training phase of the SLS included 228 participants (130 women, 98 men) who were born in 1920 or earlier and who had been SLS participants at least since 1970. Their mean age was 72.8 years ($SD = 6.43$; range = 64–85 years). Mean educational level was 13.9 years ($SD = 2.90$; range = 7–20 years). There were no sex differences in age or educational level. Mean income level was $19,879 ($SD = $8,520$; range = $1,000–$33,000). All of the participants were community dwelling, and most were white. Prior to initiating the study, each participant's family physician was contacted and asked to indicate whether the participant suffered any known physical or mental disabilities that would interfere with study participation.

Classification Procedure Participants' test performances on the L. L. and T. G. Thurstone (1949) Primary Mental Abilities (PMA) Inductive Reasoning and Spatial Orientation measures were classified as having remained stable or as having declined over the 14-year interval from 1970 to pretest. The statistical criterion for the definition of decline was 1 standard error of measurement (*SEM*) or greater over the entire 14-year period (Reasoning = 4 points, Space = 6 points).* Participants were classified by defining a 1-*SEM* confidence interval about their observed 1970 score (see Dudek, 1979). Participants who in 1984 were within the confidence interval about their 1970 score were classified as stables. Those who fell below the interval were classified as decliners.

There were 106 participants (46.5% of the sample) classified as having remained stable on both ability measures; 35 participants (15.4%) had declined on Reasoning, but not on Space; 37 participants (16.2%) had declined on Space, but not on Reasoning; and 50 participants (21.9%) had declined on both measures.

*Setting the classification criterion at 1 *SEM* produces an expected misclassification rate of 16% in identifying persons as having declined when they have actually remained stable. This was adopted as a rather conservative criterion. Consequences of other intervals were reported in 1989 (Schaie, 1989c).

As would be expected, stable participants ($M = 70.9$ years; $SD = 5.35$) were some-what younger than decline participants ($M = 74.4$ years; $SD = 6.84$). Although the mean age differed significantly ($p < .001$), it is noteworthy that a wide range age range occurred for both stables (range $= 64–85$ years) and decliners (64–95 years). Decline and stable participants did not differ significantly on educational level or income.

Effects of Regression on Participant Classification   At the base point used for clas-sification (1970), there was no significant difference between participants who had been classified as stables or decliners on Space performance. However, those classified as declining on Reasoning performed, at base, significantly better ($p < .02$) than those who remained stable. Regression to the mean might therefore be a possible threat to the validity of the training study with respect to the Inductive Reasoning variable. However, the Reasoning measure has high internal consis-tency (L. L. Thurstone & Thurstone [1949] reported an r of .90 in their original studies) and long-term test-retest reliability of .80 or higher (Schaie, 1983a, 1985).

As an independent check of the plausibility of regression effects, we conducted a time-reversed control analysis (see Baltes et al., 1972; Campbell & Stanley, 1963; Schaie & Willis, 1986b). Trace lines observed in this analysis were incompatible with the presence of substantial repression effects, and classification errors as specified by our criterion of plus or minus 1 *SEM* are therefore not significantly inflated.

Participant Assignment   Participants were assigned to either Inductive Reasoning or Spatial Orientation training programs based on their performance status. Those who had declined on Reasoning but not on Space or vice versa were as-signed to the training program for the ability exhibiting decline. Participants who had remained stable on both abilities or had shown decline on both abilities were randomly assigned to one of the training programs. Spatial Orientation training participants included 50 stables (27 women, 23 men) and 66 decliners (37 women, 29 men). Inductive Reasoning training participants included 56 stables (31 women, 25 men) and 56 decliners (35 women, 21 men).

Procedure   The study involved a pretest-treatment-posttest control group design. The Inductive Reasoning training group served as a treatment control for the Spatial Orientation training group and vice versa. Participants were administered the expanded battery described in chapter 2. Training began within 1 week of pretest and involved five 1-hour individually conducted training sessions. The training sessions were conducted within a 2-week period. The majority of partici-pants were trained in their homes. Middle-aged persons with prior educational experience involving adults served as trainers. Participants were randomly as-signed to the trainers within pragmatic constraints such that each trainer worked with approximately equal numbers of stable and decline participants in each training program. On completion of training, participants were assessed within 1 week on the same measures that were administered at pretest. They were paid $150 for participating in the study.

Training Programs

The focus of the training was on facilitating the participant's use of effective cognitive strategies identified in previous research on the respective abilities. A content task analysis was conducted on the two PMA measures representing these abilities to identify relevant cognitive strategies.

Inductive Reasoning   For each item of the PMA Reasoning test, the pattern description rules used in problem solution were identified. Four major types of pattern description rules (identity, next, skip, and backward next) were identified and were a focus in training. These pattern description rules are similar to those discussed previously in the literature (Holzman, Pellegrino, & Glaser, 1982; Kotovsky & Simon, 1973; Simon & Kotovsky, 1963). Practice problems and exercises were developed based on these pattern description rules. Practice problems often involved content other than letters, so that the applicability of these rules to other content areas could be explored. For example, patterns of musical notes and travel schedules were devised based on these rules, and participants were to asked to identify the next note or destination in the series. No training problems were identical in content to test items.

Participants were taught through modeling, feedback, and practice procedures to identify these pattern description rules. Three strategies for identifying the patterns were emphasized in training: visual scanning of the series, saying the series aloud to hear the letter pattern, and underlining repeated letters occurring throughout the series. Once a hypothesis regarding the pattern type was generated, participants were taught to mark repetitions of the pattern within the series and thus to determine the next item required to fit the pattern rule.

Spatial Orientation   A content task analysis of the PMA Space test was conducted to identify the angle of rotation for each answer choice. Practice problems were developed to represent the angle of rotation identified in the task analysis (45°, 90°, 135°, and 180°). Cognitive strategies to facilitate mental rotation that were a focus in training included (a) development of concrete terms for various angles, (b) practice with manual rotation of figures prior to mental rotation, (c) practice with rotation of drawings of concrete familiar objects prior to the introduction of abstract figures, (d) participant-generated names for abstract figures, and (e) having the participant focus on two or more features of the figure during rotation. These cognitive strategies had been identified in prior descriptive research on mental rotation ability (Cooper, 1975; Cooper & Shepard, 1973; Egan, 1981; Kail, Pellegrino, & Carter, 1980).

Results of the 1983–1984 Training Study

We consider first training effects at the raw score level for the PMA Reasoning and Space tests because these are the measures for which longitudinal data were available and which served as the basis of participant classification. Second, training effects are examined at the latent construct level, that is, for the multiply marked ability factors on which training was conducted. Third, we note the proportion of participants whose decline was remediated as well as the proportion of stable participants who experienced significant improvement in functioning on the trained abilities. Fourth, we deal with the specificity of the training, that is, the question whether the training effects were indeed directed to the target abilities or whether far transfer to other abilities occurred (see Thorndike & Woodworth, 1901). Fifth, we examine the question of whether training resulted in the remediation of losses in speed and/or accuracy. The question of whether training results in shifts in ability factor structure is further examined in chapter 8.

Raw Score Analyses: Primary Mental Abilities Reasoning and Space   Training effects for the two measures with longitudinal data were analyzed with repeated measurement analyses of variance (ANOVAs), using a Training Condition (Reasoning, Space) × Status (Stable, Decline) × Gender × Occasion (Pretest, Posttest) design separately for the two tests (table 7.1). For PMA Reasoning, there were significant main effects for status ($p < .001$), gender ($p < .01$), and occasion ($p < .001$). The status and gender main effects reflect the lower scores on the target measure for decliners and men, respectively. The occasion main effect represents the retest effects occurring for both groups. With respect to the training effects of central concern, there was a significant Training × Occasion interaction ($p < .001$), indicating higher performance at posttest of those trained on Reasoning. There was a trend toward a significant fourfold interaction ($p < .09$). Post hoc tests on PMA Reasoning gain scores indicated that decliners showed greater gain than did stables. Gender and Gender × Status effects were not significant. When the Reasoning and Space training groups were compared, there were significantly greater Reasoning training effects for the target training group for stables ($p < .001$), decliners ($p < .001$), stable women ($p < .002$), and male and female decliners ($p < .001$).

For PMA Space, there were significant main effects for status ($p < .001$), gender ($p < .02$), and occasion ($p < .001$). The status and gender main effects reflect the lower scores of the decliners and women, respectively, across occasions. The occasion main effect indicates the retest effects occurring for both the Reasoning and Space training groups. As for the crucial results with respect to the training paradigm, there were significant interactions for Training × Occasion ($p < .004$) and for Training × Status × Occasion ($p < .05$). The Training × Occasion interaction indicated a significantly higher performance for the Space training group at posttest. The triple interaction with Status reflects greater training gain for the decliners at posttest. A significant Gender × Occasion interaction ($p < .05$) suggests the occurrence of larger retest effects for women. Post hoc tests on PMA Space gain scores indicated that there were significantly greater ($p < .01$) gains for decliners than for stables.

Figure 7.1 depicts the pretest–posttest gain computed from the standardized scores for the PMA Reasoning and Space tests for the four training subgroups (stable or decline on Reasoning, stable or decline on Space). Each set of bars in

TABLE 7.1 Summary of Analyses of Variance: Primary Mental Ability Raw Scores

Source	MS	df	F
Reasoning			
Training	41.03	1	0.61
Status	1,471.25	1	21.89***
Training × Status	1.34	1	0.02
Gender	483.58	1	7.20**
Training × Gender	113.73	1	1.69
Status × Gender	54.51	1	0.81
Training × Status × Gender	5.77	1	0.09
Error	67.20	221	
Occasion	857.25	1	150.24***
Training × Occasion	231.02	1	40.47***
Status × Occasion	12.24	1	2.14
Training × Status × Occasion	12.71	1	2.23
Gender × Occasion	2.77	1	0.48
Training × Gender × Occasion	0.75	1	0.13
Status × Gender × Occasion	7.24	1	1.27
Training × Status × Gender × Occasion	16.16	1	2.83
Error	5.71	221	
Space			
Training	470.12	1	2.91
Status	4,228.33	1	26.14***
Training × Status	177.70	1	1.10
Gender	922.39	1	5.70*
Training × Gender	359.65	1	2.22
Status × Gender	388.56	1	2.40
Training × Status × Gender	0.66	1	0.00
Error	161.74	221	
Occasion	2,044.16	1	90.68***
Training × Occasion	301.64	1	13.38***
Status × Occasion	49.23	1	2.18
Training × Status × Occasion	106.56	1	4.73*
Gender × Occasion	85.12	1	3.78*
Training × Gender × Occasion	55.47	1	2.46
Status × Gender × Occasion	46.55	1	2.06
Training × Status × Gender × Occasion	0.53	1	0.02
Error	22.54	221	

$*p < .05.$ $**p < .01.$ $***p < .001.$

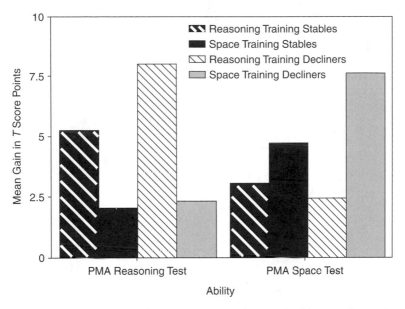

FIGURE 7.1 *Pretest-Posttest Gain for Four Training Subgroups (Stable or Decline on Reasoning, Stable or Decline on Space). PMA, Primary Mental Abilities.*

figure 7.1 compares the two subgroups trained on Reasoning with the two trained on Space; that is, each training group serves as a control for the other training condition.

Analyses at the Latent Construct Level   The factor structure of the pretest ability battery was examined via confirmatory factor analyses. An acceptable five-factor model ($\chi^2[243, N = 401] = 463.17$, $p < .01$) was obtained that represented the hypothesized primary mental ability factors of Inductive Reasoning, Spatial Orientation, Perceptual Speed, Verbal Ability, and Numeric Ability. All marker measures for Inductive Reasoning and Spatial Orientation, as predicted, had significant loadings on their respective factors. Regression weights (after orthonormal transformation) for tests loading on the Inductive Reasoning factor were as follows: PMA Reasoning = .378; ADEPT Letter Series = .213; Word Series = .298; Number Series = .111. Regression weights of tests loading on the Spatial Orientation factor were as follows: PMA Space = .260; Object Rotation = .393; Alphanumeric Rotation = .287; Cube Comparison = .060. Although the Number Series and Cube Comparison measures contributed relatively little variance to their respective factors, they were retained because they helped to obtain better definition of the factors within the broader ability space in which they were embedded. Factor scores were computed for the Inductive Reasoning and Spatial Orientation factors by standardizing ($M = 50$; $SD = 10$) the raw scores to the pretest base and then multiplying the standardized sores by their normalized regression weights.

Repeated measures ANOVAs were again performed separately on the Inductive Reasoning and Spatial Orientation factor scores using the same design applied to the PMA raw scores, that is, Training Condition (Reasoning, Space) × Status (Stable, Decline) × Gender × Occasion (Pretest, Posttest), as shown in table 7.2. For Inductive Reasoning, there were significant main effects for status ($p <$ .001) and occasion ($p < .001$). The status and gender main effects reflect the lower

TABLE 7.2 Summary of Analyses of Variance: Factor Scores

Source	MS	df	F
Inductive Reasoning			
Training	336.58	1	2.18
Status	3,038.35	1	19.66***
Training × Status	25.71	1	0.17
Gender	733.10	1	4.74*
Training × Gender	362.67	1	2.35
Status × Gender	30.31	1	0.20
Training × Status × Gender	0.08	1	0.00
Error	154.59	221	
Occasion	1,649.15	1	303.15***
Training × Occasion	205.99	1	37.86***
Status × Occasion	1.76	1	0.34
Training × Status × Occasion	7.76	1	1.43
Gender × Occasion	0.58	1	0.11
Training × Gender × Occasion	1.18	1	0.22
Status × Gender × Occasion	0.07	1	0.01
Training × Status × Gender × Occasion	1.08	1	0.20
Error	5.44	221	
Spatial Orientation			
Training	84.19	1	0.56
Status	3,884.11	1	30.10***
Training × Status	26.33	1	0.20
Gender	852.04	1	6.60**
Training × Gender	521.31	1	4.04*
Status × Gender	423.18	1	3.28
Training × Status × Gender	79.17	1	0.61
Error	129.06	221	
Occasion	1,556.41	1	195.48***
Training × Occasion	41.82	1	5.25*
Status × Occasion	9.49	1	1.19
Training × Status × Occasion	18.14	1	2.28
Gender × Occasion	4.14	1	0.52
Training × Gender × Occasion	16.27	1	2.04
Status × Gender × Occasion	0.75	1	0.09
Training × Status × Gender × Occasion	4.83	1	0.61
Error	7.96	221	

*$p < .05$. **$p < .01$. ***$p < .001$.

scores of decliners and men, respectively. The occasion main effects represent the retest effects occurring for both training groups. Specifically relevant with regard to the effects of training was the significant Training × Occasion interaction ($p <$ .001), indicating a significant training effect at posttest. No status, gender, or Gender × Status comparisons within the Reasoning training group were significant; hence, the training effect was general and not specific to status and/or gender.

For Spatial Orientation, there were significant main effects for status ($p <$ .001), gender ($p < .01$), and occasion ($p < .001$). The status and gender main effects reflect the lower scores of the decliners and women, respectively, across occasions. The occasion main effect indicates the retest effects occurring for both Reasoning and Space training groups. There were significant interactions for Training × Occasion ($p < .02$) and Training × Gender ($p < .04$). The Training × Occasion interaction indicated a significant training effect at posttest. The Training × Gender interaction indicates that overall performance on Space was higher for the target training group than for the controls for women only.

Distinguishing Between Regression and Training Effects   To exclude the possibility that regression effects might confound the results of the training study, we first examined the stability of our instruments over the interval between pretest and posttest by administering the measures over the same interval to a group of 172 participants of comparable age and socioeconomic status who did not receive any training. Stability coefficients obtained in this study were .917 for the Space factor score and .939 for the Reasoning factor score. Stabilities for the two PMA measures were .838 for Space and .886 for Reasoning. These estimates were next used to compute regressed deviation scores for our experimental participants (see Nunnally, 1982). The ANOVAs for the raw score and latent construct measures were then repeated on the adjusted scores. As would be expected in light of the high stabilities, resulting F ratios differed only trivially, and none of the previously reported findings were significantly affected.

Effects of Age, Education, and Income   Because of slight differences between subgroups in terms of demographic characteristics, we also repeated the ANOVAs, covarying on age, education, and income. Again, effects of the covariance adjustments were trivial, and none of the ANOVA findings were changed significantly.

What Is the Benefit of Cognitive Training?

The effects of cognitive training must be assessed in several ways. First, we need to know what proportion of participants showed significant gain from the intervention procedure. Next, we would like to know how successful the intervention was in remediating decline to an earlier—higher—level of functioning. Questions arise also as to whether training effects are specific to the targeted abilities or generalize to other abilities. Finally, it needs to be asked whether the training resulted in qualitative cognitive change.

Pretest-Posttest Training Improvement   The proportion of participants showing statistically reliable pretest-posttest training improvement on the PMA Reasoning or Space measure was computed. The statistical criterion for significant improvement was defined as a gain of plus or minus 1 *SEM* from pretest to posttest. The proportion of participants at the individual level with reliable training gain is shown in table 7.3. Approximately half the participants in each training group showed significant pretest-posttest improvement. Although there was a trend for a greater proportion of decline participants to show improvement in both training conditions, the difference between proportions was statistically significant only for the Space training group ($p < .01$).

Remediation of Decline   The question arises next as to what proportion of participants benefited from training sufficiently to result in a 14-year remediation to their 1970 base performance level. Two criterion levels were used to define remediation. The first level deemed remediation as having occurred when the difference between the participant's PMA posttest score and the 1970 score was 1 *SEM* or less. This is the same statistical definition used in the first place to classify participants with respect to their 14-year decline. The second criterion level was even more conservative; it defined remediation as the attainment of a PMA posttest score that was equal to or greater than the 1970 base score.

Figure 7.2 presents the proportion of decline participants attaining the remediation criteria. Of the decline participants, 62% were remediated to their predecline level if the criterion of 1 *SEM* or more is used. In both training groups, more women were returned to their 1970 score level than were men. Using the more stringent criterion of return to the 1970 base level, approximately 40% of the decline sample were returned to the performance level they had exhibited 14 years earlier. Again, the proportion of participants whose decline was fully remediated was greater for women on Space and for men on Reasoning.

Transfer-of-Training Issues   The question arises next as to whether the training effects generalize across alternative measures of the same ability dimension (*near transfer*) or whether the intervention is so general that it affects performance on abilities not specifically targeted for training (*far transfer*). Near transfer is desir-

TABLE 7.3 Proportion of Subjects Attaining Significant Pretest-to-Posttest Training Gain

| | Reasoning | | | Space | | |
Status	Men	Women	Total	Men	Women	Total
Stable	52.0	54.8	53.6	34.8	42.9	39.2
Decline	60.0	60.0	60.0	51.7	57.9	55.2
Total	55.6	57.6	56.8	44.2	51.5	48.3

Note. Significant training gain was defined as a pretest-to-posttest gain ≥ 1 *SEM* on the Primary Mental Abilities Reasoning or Space test.

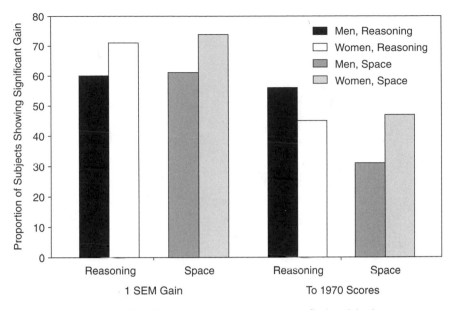

FIGURE 7.2 *Proportion of Decline Participants Attaining Remediation Criteria.*

able because it offers evidence of convergent validity; far transfer is to be eschewed if we wish to modify ability-specific behaviors rather than obtaining a Hawthorne effect that could be attributed simply to the intensive contact with our study participants.

Strong near transfer was observed for those measures most similar to the longitudinal marker (Object and Alphanumeric Rotation for the Spatial Orientation factor; Letter Series and Word Series for the Inductive Reasoning factor). With respect to far transfer, we examined pretest-posttest gains for the two target abilities as well as the dimensions of Perceptual Speed, Numeric Ability, and Verbal Ability, which had not been targets for training. Figure 7.3 shows the far transfer pattern, which confirms our training specificity hypotheses. When factor score gains are averaged for two training groups on each of the five ability dimensions, we find that each training group has significantly greater gain on the ability on which it was trained, and that there are no differences on the abilities not targeted for training. Gains for the latter abilities represent retest effects and/or small generalized training effects.

Decomposing Training Effects Into Gains in Accuracy and Speed

Performance change over time and the effect of training can be disaggregated into separate components that are attributable to participants' gains in accuracy and speed. During the longitudinal preintervention phase, decline in accuracy may occur through disuse, and gain in accuracy during training may result from

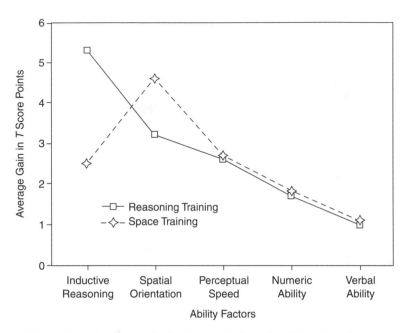

FIGURE 7.3 *Far Transfer Pattern Confirming the Training Specificity Hypotheses.*

the reactivation of appropriate problem-solving strategies. We would expect a reduction in speed of performance with increasing age, but the intensive practice during the training phase might help to speed up participants' response.

Change in accuracy for the preintervention and the pretest-posttest comparisons was obtained by the following procedures. An accuracy score was computed as the proportion of the attempted answer choices marked correctly (e.g., 1970 baseline rights/1970 items attempted). The expected accuracy score for the next test occasion was then computed, assuming that level of accuracy remained constant over the two occasions. For example, the 1984 expected score was computed as the proportion of 1970 correct responses multiplied by the 1984 number attempted. The change in accuracy then becomes the observed 1984 rights less the expected 1984 score. Subtracting the change in accuracy from the total observed score then yields the change in speed. The same procedure was used to decompose training gain, using the score of the 1984 observed rights to estimate the expected posttest accuracy score (see Willis & Schaie, 1988).

Longitudinal Change in Accuracy and Speed   The average change in speed and accuracy from 1970 to 1984 is depicted on the left side of figures 7.4 and 7.5 for Inductive Reasoning and Spatial Orientation, respectively. Because there were no significant gender differences in patterns of accuracy and speed, figure 7.4 shows change for the stable and decline participants. On Spatial Orientation, there was a significant Gender × Stability condition interaction. Data are therefore presented separately by gender and stability condition.

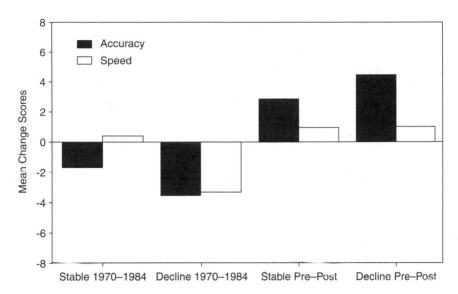

FIGURE 7.4 *Changes in Speed and Accuracy from 1970 to 1984 and for the Training Gain for Inductive Reasoning by Stability Condition.*

The 14-year decline on Inductive Reasoning can be apportioned about equally to speed and accuracy. For the stable group, a small loss in accuracy is partially compensated for by a gain in speed. No gender difference in composition of change is observed.

On Spatial Orientation, there is no significant gender difference for the entire group in the magnitude of total decline. However, a significant gender difference is found for the speed change score ($p < .03$). A greater proportion of the total decline of the men is attributable to a decrease in problem-solving speed. For the stable participants, men remained stable by compensating for a slight loss in speed by a commensurate increase in accuracy. Stable women showed a slight gain in both speed and accuracy. For the decline participants, men lost primarily in speed, whereas women declined approximately equally in both speed and accuracy.

Training Gain in Accuracy and Speed   The right side of figures 7.4 and 7.5 shows training gain decomposed into speed and accuracy in the same manner as for the longitudinal change. For Inductive Reasoning, most of the training gain was accounted for by increased accuracy; only minimal gain in speed was found. This pattern is equally true for those who declined and those who remained stable. Note, however, that the decliners recovered virtually all their loss in accuracy. No gender difference in training gain pattern was found.

On Spatial Orientation, by contrast, there is a significant gender difference in favor of women for total training gain ($p < .03$). Gain for the stable subgroup was primarily attributable to an increase in problem-solving speed, and there was

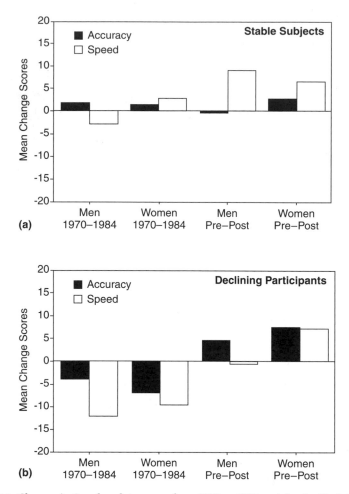

FIGURE 7.5 *Changes in Speed and Accuracy from 1970 to 1984 and for the Training Gain for Spatial Orientation by Stability Condition and Gender.*

no gender difference for this subgroup. The gender difference appears only in the decline group. Here, men show gain in accuracy but not in speed, whereas gain for the women is approximately equal for speed and accuracy.

Replication of Cognitive Training Effects

To assess the replicability of our training effects with additional samples, we also trained an additional 179 participants in 1990–1991 and an additional 190 participants in 1997–1998. All of these new trainees met the original selection criteria, but had not been trained previously (Saczinski, 2001).

Participants in the three replicates were compared to determine whether there were differences in age, education, or pretest ability. Repeated measures analysis of covariance (ANCOVA) were conducted for PMA Reasoning ($N = 586$) and Space ($N = 588$) measures as well as for Inductive Reasoning ($N = 571$) and Spatial Orientation ($N = 586$) at the factor level. Age and education were entered as covariates. The first sample had lower education than the subsequent samples ($1984 = 13.91$, $1991 = 14.48$, $1998 = 14.75$ years). No significant differences between groups were noted in age and pretest performance levels.

Analyses of the replications of the first-time training suggest that significant training effects and near transfer to alternate operational forms of the target tests can be repeatedly demonstrated. Significant effects of training in excess of pretest-posttest practice can be demonstrated as well at the latent variable level. We also replicated the finding of stronger training effects observed for Inductive Reasoning than for Spatial Orientation. In addition, we controlled for the significant covariates of age, education, and occasion by age. Table 7.4 provides the complete ANCOVA results for the factor scores across the three replicates. Figure 7.6 compares training gains under the different training conditions for the three replicates in 1983–1984, 1990–1991, and 1997–1998 for Spatial Orientation; the differences in gain between training and control groups remain quite constant over the three replicates.

Maintenance of Training

The question remains whether the effects of cognitive interventions such as ours do provide benefits that last over extended periods of time and whether it is possible to remediate further losses that occur as study participants move into advanced old age. To address these questions, the 1991 cycle included a 7-year follow-up of the original training study (see Willis & Schaie, 1992, 1994b). In 1998, we also followed a second sample over 7 years. Finally, a small sample was followed from 1984 to 1991. This section presents data that bear directly on the question of maintaining and sustaining cognitive training effects. Specifically, the question whether persons receiving brief cognitive training remain at an advantage compared with those not so trained is addressed. Second, the effects of booster training to determine the benefits of further reactivation of the abilities trained earlier are considered.

The Seven-Year Follow-up Study

Participants   All study participants who participated in the 1983–1984 training and who were known to be alive in 1990 were contacted. There were 148 trained participants who agreed to participate in the follow-up study. Of these, a total of 140 were able to complete the follow-up testing, and 132 participants received booster training. Their ages in 1990–1991 averaged 77.74 years ($SD = 4.98$; range = 71–92 years).

TABLE 7.4 Repeated Measures Analysis of Covariance for the Training Replication, Covaried for Age and Education

Source	Inductive Reasoning Factor			Spatial Orientation Factor		
	df	MS	F	df	MS	F
Between-participants effects						
Training Group	1	66.29	0.88	1	1.82	0.02
Stability Status	1	1.46	0.02	1	472.10	5.56*
Gender	1	161.72	1.99	1	1,473.23	17.35***
Replicate	1	642.39	7.90***	2	803.83	9.47***
Training Group × Stability Status	1	42.15	0.52	1	143.72	1.69
Training Group × Gender	1	263.58	3.24	1	174.25	2.05
Training Group × Replicate	2	152.12	1.87	2	73.41	0.86
Stability Status × Gender	1	14.50	0.18	1	34.24	0.40
Stability Status × Replicate	2	50.10	0.62	2	317.47	3.74*
Gender × Replicate	2	138.83	1.71	2	40.23	0.47
Education (covariate)	1	4,019.91	49.45***	1	246.45	2.90
Age (covariate)	1	15,341.95	188.74***	1	16,403.94	193.20***
Error	554	81.28		569	84.91	
Within-participants effects						
Occasion	1	162.45	41.06***	1	90.13	14.49***
Occasion × Training Group	1	297.58	75.21***	1	31.81	5.11*
Occasion × Stability Status	1	24.93	6.30*	1	55.45	8.91**
Occasion × Gender	1	0.52	0.13	1	8.41	1.35
Occasion × Replicate	2	0.21	0.05	2	33.46	5.38**
Occasion × Train × Stability Status	1	3.45	0.87	1	16.35	2.63
Occasion × Train × Gender	1	2.36	0.60	1	12.76	2.05
Occasion × Train × Replicate	2	3.45	0.87	2	3.94	0.63
Occasion × Stability Status × Gender	1	2.20	0.56	1	14.05	2.26
Occasion × Stability Status × Replicate	2	1.71	0.43	2	7.88	1.27
Occasion × Gender × Replicate	2	0.27	0.07	2	6.99	1.12
Occasion × Age	1	67.96	17.18***	1	23.41	3.76
Occasion × Education	1	14.83	3.75	1	12.90	2.07
Error	554	3.97		569	6.22	

$*p < .05.$ $**p < .01.$ $***p < .001.$

Participant Classification   All participants were assigned to the same training condition they had been assigned for the initial training: Spatial Orientation decliners (10 men, 24 women), as well as 75 Inductive Reasoning training participants, including 45 stables (17 men, 28 women) and 30 decliners (12 men, 18 women).

Study Design   The pretest-posttest design of the original training study was replicated as exactly as possible. The booster training was given for the same ability (Inductive Reasoning or Spatial Orientation) on which participants had originally been trained. Participants were assessed within 1 week of training on the same measures that were administered at pretest. They were paid $150 for participating in the study.

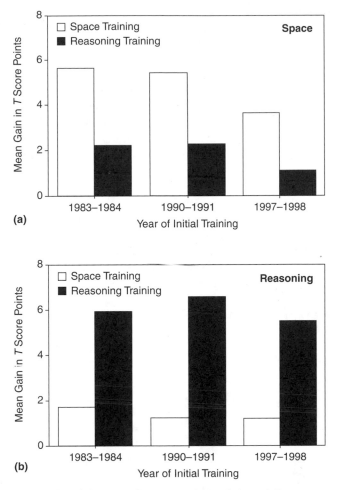

FIGURE 7.6 *Replicated Training Gain for Intervention and Control Groups.*

Results   Findings from the follow-up study are reported in three parts. First, the magnitude of the initial training for the surviving sample and the nature of attrition effects are described. Second, the maintenance of training over 7 years is considered; that is, the question whether persons receiving brief cognitive training remain at a long-term advantage over those not so trained is addressed. Third, the effects of sustaining training effects by booster training to determine the benefits of further reactivation of the abilities trained earlier are reported. For simplicity in presentation, the longitudinal markers that were applied throughout the SLS are emphasized.

Magnitude of Initial Training   During the 1983–1984 training study, significant training effects were obtained for both abilities trained. Because of attrition of approximately 40% in the follow-up studies, we recomputed training effects for the surviving sample. Overall, there was a gain of approximately 0.5 *SD* in each training program. These effects continue to be significantly greater than those for the comparison control group. However, contrary to findings in the unattrited sample, there was significantly greater effect for those participants who had been identified as decliners (see figure 7.7). These results reflect greater retention of those of the decline participants who showed significant training gain in the initial training. There was an interaction effect in retention for the stable participants. Those with greater training gain on Space also showed higher retention, but those with greater training gain on Reasoning showed lower retention.

Maintenance of Training Effects   We next consider the extent to which training gains are retained after 7 years. In 1990–1991, participants trained in 1983–1984 were functioning, on average, at their 1983–1984 pretest level on the trained ability. In contrast, the comparison group (those trained on the other ability) were functioning significantly below their 1983–1984 pretest level. As shown in figure 7.8, there was a significant maintenance of function on the trained ability even after a 7-year interval. For the total group, this was a modest effect, amounting to approximately 0.3 *SD*. Again, however, this effect was most pronounced for those participants who had been classified as decliners for purposes of the

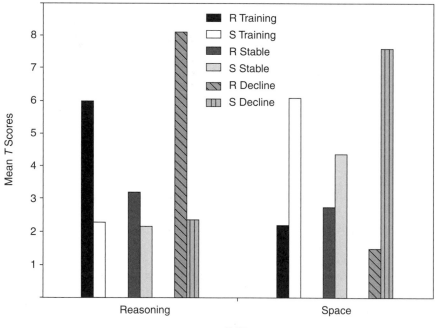

FIGURE 7.7 *Gain at Initial 1983–1984 Training for the Group Returning for Follow-Up Training. R, Reasoning; S, Space.*

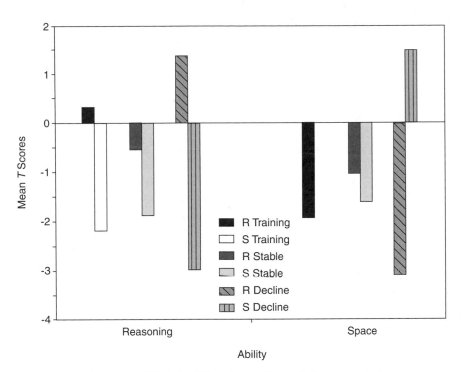

FIGURE 7.8 *Maintenance of Training Effects Over 7 Years. R, Reasoning; S, Space.*

initial training. For both abilities, these individuals, on average, still performed above their 1983–1984 pretest level, whereas their comparisons had declined further. The trained groups of decliners in 1990–1991 had an advantage of approximately 0.4 *SD* over their comparison groups. By contrast, those who had been stable in 1983–1984 were at an advantage of approximately 0.15 *SD* over their comparisons on Reasoning. The difference between the stable experimental and control groups on Space was not statistically significant.

Sustaining Training Effects Through Booster Training   When the previously trained participants were again put through the same training regimen they had experienced earlier, significant ability-specific training effects were obtained for both training conditions as well as for the subsets of participants who had been classified as having declined or remaining stable at initial training. That is, in all instances, gains from pretest to posttest were significantly larger than for the untrained comparison groups. However, the effects of the 1990–1991 booster training were of a somewhat lower magnitude in these participants, who were then 7 years older.

Of particular interest is the question of cumulative magnitude of initial and booster training when participants are compared with control groups who had the same amount of attention (by training on another ability). As shown in figure

7.9, there is a clear advantage for those participants who were originally identified as experiencing decline. After booster training, they are at an advantage of better than 0.5 *SD* over their comparison groups. The training advantage for those participants described as stable at initial training is more equivocal. It is still highly significant for Reasoning, although their advantage is more modest, but there is no significant cumulative advantage for stable participants who were trained on Space.

To show the generality of the follow-up findings beyond the prime longitudinal marker, we also computed factor scores across each set of four markers of the abilities on which we trained. Figure 7.10 shows the cumulative training effects at the latent construct level; these were quite similar to those shown in figure 7.9.

Further Analyses of the Seven-Year Follow-up

To examine the generalizability of the 7-year maintenance findings, recent analyses that expand the analysis of maintenance by growth curve modeling over the period beginning 14 years prior to training to the posttest after the 7-year follow-up are reported (Saczinski, 2001).

Participants   The maintenance replication sample included all participants initially trained in 1984 and 1991 who were available for follow-up 7 years later

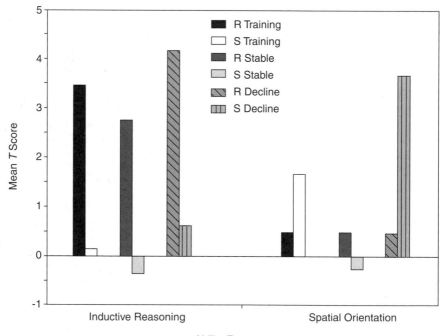

FIGURE 7.9 *Cumulative Training Effects Over Two Training Periods for the Principal Marker Variables. R, Reasoning; S, Space.*

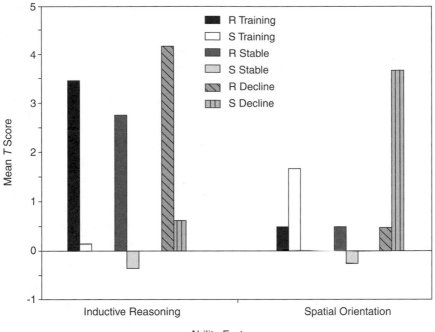

FIGURE 7.10 *Cumulative Training Effects Over Two Training Periods for the Latent Abilities. R, Reasoning; S, Space.*

(1991 or 1998, respectively). This subsample consisted of 210 participants (140 in 1984, 70 in 1991). Mean age at initial training was 70.2 years ($SD = 4.79$; range = 64–85 years). Mean educational level of this subsample was 14.3 years ($SD = 2.76$; range = 7–20 years).

An attrition analysis was conducted to determine if the total maintenance sample ($N = 210$) differed significantly from the total initial training sample ($N = 408$) with respect to age, education, and income. The follow-up subsample on average was about 2 years younger than the initial sample, but they did not differ on education or income. However, the follow-up sample had a significantly higher pretest performance at initial training than the total sample; that is, they were higher by 0.24 SD on Space and by 0.32 SD on Reasoning.

Analyses   Growth curve modeling was used to estimate parameters over a maximum of 21 years involving both training and booster interventions. Three intervals were examined: pretraining (Time 1 to Pre 1), initial training (Pre 1 to Post 1), and 7-year maintenance (Post 1 to Pre 2). Multiple group models were fit to compare participants in the Inductive Reasoning and Spatial Orientation training groups. To examine the initial training and maintenance intervals, piecewise growth models were fit to permit evaluation of multiple data trends (Bryk & Raudenbush, 1992).

Results   Although the training groups did not differ on either ability at baseline, there was a significant difference in rate of change between the two groups. For both abilities, participants in the training target group showed steeper rates of decline over the pretraining period than the comparison participants training on the other ability. This difference, of course, was a direct function of the assignment strategy.

The initial training growth models, as hypothesized, showed a significantly steeper rate for the target training compared to the other training group. Lower education, higher Motor-Cognitive Flexibility, and faster Psychomotor Speed were associated with greater training gain.

With respect to the 7-year maintenance period, it was found that there was no significant decline on the Reasoning measures for those participants training on this ability. By contrast, individuals in the Space training group did decline significantly on the Reasoning ability. On the other hand, both training groups declined significantly on Spatial ability. No covariates were identified that predicted individual differences in rate of change during the maintenance period.

Section Summary   Reexamination of the baseline through 7-year maintenance interval by growth curve modeling confirms successful initial training for both training groups, but indicates that the long-term training effect is limited to the Reasoning training with respect to reducing the rate of further decline. Figure 7.11 shows the accepted fit for the piecewise growth curve model from baseline to 7-year follow-up.

The Fourteen-Year Follow-up Study

To determine whether benefits would still remain after 14 years, we conducted another follow-up of the 1984 training study as part of the 1998 cycle. Specifically, we addressed the question whether persons receiving brief cognitive training remain at an advantage compared with those not so trained over a 14-year period, particularly if booster training is used for further reactivation of the abilities trained earlier.

Participants   All study participants who participated in the 1990–1991 training and who were known to be alive in 1997 were contacted. There were 67 trained participants who were able to complete the follow-up testing and who received booster training. Their ages in 1997–1998 averaged 82.93 years (*SD* = 4.07; range = 78–96 years).

Participant Classification   All participants were assigned to the same classification they had in 1990–1991. The surviving participants consisted of 33 Spatial Orientation participants (9 men, 24 women) and 34 Inductive Reasoning training participants (13 men, 21 women). Education and age for the attrited sample did not differ significantly from those found for the total training group in 1984.

Study Design   The pretest-posttest design of the original training study was replicated as exactly as possible. The booster training was given on the same ability

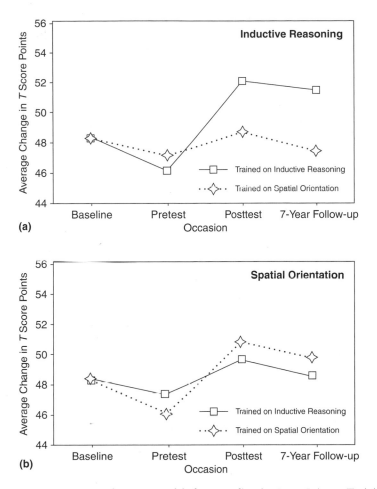

FIGURE 7.11 *Piecewise Growth Curve Models from Baseline (14 Years Prior to Training) to 7-Year Follow-Up.*

(Inductive Reasoning or Spatial Orientation) on which participants had originally been trained. Participants were assessed within 1 week of training on the same measures that were administered at pretest. They were again paid $150 for participating in the study.

Analyses   ANOVA was used to test hypotheses with respect to the combined training and maintenance design. Training Groups (2) × Occasions (6) repeated measures ANOVAs were conducted separately for the two dependent variables, followed by Tukey's HSD (honestly significant difference) post hoc tests for unequal cell sizes.

Results   The overall change within participants over the six-occasion effect was highly significant ($p < .001$). Post hoc tests also showed significant gains for each training intervention and significant 7-year declines over the intervals between the successive interventions ($p < .001$). However, the overall differences between the first pretest and the final posttest were not significant ($p > .05$), suggesting overall maintenance of performance level as a consequence of the interventions.

Of greater concern, however, is the question whether the observed maintenance of performance level is attributable to the 5-hour training program every 7 years starting with the late 60s or whether the effect is specific to the targeted training. Our findings suggest the latter interpretation because we observed significant Training Group × Occasion interactions ($p < .001$).

Post hoc tests indicated that there was maintenance for the Inductive Reasoning training group over the 14 years from first pretest to last posttest on the targeted ability but not on the other ability. However, the Spatial Orientation training group, although they did slightly better on Spatial Orientation, did show significant decline over 14 years despite the intervention (see figure 7.12).

The Role of Strategy Use in Training Success

In our efforts to understand better the mechanisms involved in obtaining improved performance through cognitive training, we investigated the role of strategy use in reasoning training with older adults (Saczynski, Willis, & Schaie, 2002). Our argument in this context was the hypothesis that the content of cognitive training interventions is largely concerned with reactivating or training participants in the use of systematic strategies to solve problems (Willis, 2001; Willis & Nesselroade, 1990).

In the study reported next, two questions were addressed: First, we asked whether increase in strategy use differed from pretest to posttest. Second, we were interested in identifying participant characteristics that might be associated with strategy use and would predict training gain on the latent construct of Inductive Reasoning.

Method

Participants   The subsample included 393 older adults (177 males, 216 females) who received their initial cognitive training in either 1984 or 1991. Mean age of the total subsample was 72.9 years ($SD = 6.41$; range = 64–95 years). Mean educational level was 14.1 years ($SD = 3.05$; range = 7–20 years). There were no significant age or educational differences between participants entering training in 1984 or 1991.

Design and Procedure   Classification and assignment to Space or Reasoning training as well as training procedures and measures used to evaluate training success have been described in the section on the first training study in this chapter. As part of the instructions, participants were encouraged to make pencil marks on test materials to help them determine serial patterns.

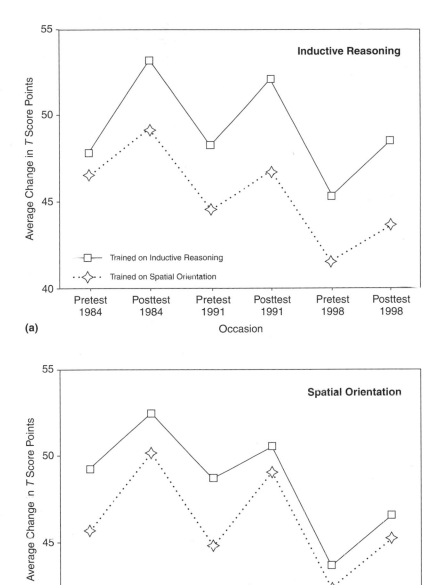

(a)

(b)

FIGURE 7.12 *Fourteen-Year Training Effects from First Pretest to Last Posttest.*

Strategy Usage Coding Procedure   The pretest and posttest protocols for the ADEPT Letter Series and the Word Series tests were coded for strategy use. Three strategies were coded: (a) slashes between repeats in patterns, (b) tick marks between skipped letters or words, and (c) underlining of repeated letters or numbers in a series. A minimum of two "strategy marks" was required for an item to be identified as representing strategy use. Coders who were blinded to the training group membership of participants achieved an interrater reliability of .87.

Analyses   Repeated measures analyses of covariance examined the effects of two training groups (Reasoning, Spatial Orientation) by two genders by decline status (stable, decline) by two replicates (1984, 1991) by three age groups (64–70, 71–77, and 78–85 years). The dependent variables were pretest and posttest strategy use. Education entered the analyses as a covariate. Hierarchical regression was used to determine the association between increased strategy use, demographic variables, and training gain.

Results

Pretest to Posttest Increase in Strategy Use   For the Letter Series test, a significant occasion by training interaction indicated significantly greater increase in strategy use after training for the target training group than for the Space training group ($p < .001$). In addition, well-educated participants, regardless of training group membership, showed greater increase in strategy than those with lower educational exposure. We also found that the youngest age group showed greater increase in strategy use than did the two older groups. No higher-order interactions proved statistically significant. Similar findings were obtained with respect to the Word Series test.

Strategy Use, Demographic Characteristics, and Training Gain   The weighted average of all four reasoning measures was used to define the latent dependent variable. Strategy use was then averaged across the two coded measures at pretest and posttest, and the interaction between training group and change in strategy use after training were entered as the first step of a hierarchical regression equation. Demographic variables (age, gender, and education) were entered in a second step. A third step added the interactions between change in strategy use and the demographic variables as well as reasoning recline status and change in strategy use.

The first step in the hierarchical regression yielded an R^2 of .204. Significant predictors of posttest gain on the Inductive Reasoning latent construct included the interaction between increase in strategy use and training group, indicating that participants who were trained on reasoning and who showed increase in strategy use also had greater training gain. Pretraining decline on the reasoning ability also turned out to be an independent significant predictor of training gain. The second step significantly increased R^2 to .217. The gain was confined to the greater posttest gain showed by younger participants. No additional increase in predictive power was obtained by the third step (see table 7.5).

TABLE 7.5 Hierarchical Regression Analysis for Variables Predicting Training Gain on the Inductive Reasoning Factor

	Step 1		Step 2		Step 3	
Predictor	B	MS	B	MS	B	MS
Training Group × Strategy Use	−0.13**	87.30	−0.08**	87.30	−0.11**	72.03
Strategy Use	0.22***	273.23	0.11***	273.23	−0.03	10.36
Training Group	2.62***	384.79	2.71***	348.79	1.05**	45.73
Reasoning Status	−0.62**	81.87	−0.76**	81.87	0.25	2.25
Age			−0.06*	48.07	−0.03	9.61
Gender		0.02		0.15	−0.14	2.69
Education			−0.03	4.31	−0.01	0.84
Strategy Use × Reasoning Status					−0.05	5.97
Strategy Use × Age					−0.01	0.13
Strategy Use × Gender					−0.05	4.77
Strategy Use × Education					0.02	8.52
R^2		0.204		0.217		0.223
ΔR^2				0.013**		0.006
df		4,376		7,373		11,369

*$p < .05$. **$p < .01$. ***$p < .001$.

Section Summary   The findings from this study suggest that there is indeed a significant role for strategy-based training in increasing training gains in cognitive interventions (cf. Verhaeghen & Marcoen, 1996). The role of strategy use was somewhat more important in the young-old than in the older group, but did not differ across educational level or decline status.

Chapter Summary

Our cognitive intervention studies allowed us to conclude that, for many persons, cognitive decline in old age may be a function of disuse rather than deterioration of the physiological substrates of cognitive behavior. A brief 5-hour training program involving individual tutorials was designed to improve the performance of participants above the age of 64 years on the abilities of Inductive Reasoning and Spatial Orientation. Participants were assigned either to training in the ability on which they had declined or randomly to one of the two training conditions if they had declined or remained stable on both abilities.

The training program used in the initial training studies succeeded in improving the performance of about two thirds of the participants. More important, of those participants for whom significant decrement had been documented, roughly 40% were returned to the level at which they had functioned 14 years earlier. Training effects were shown for the single marker for which longitudinal data were available, as well as near transfer to additional markers, indicating training improvement at the latent construct level. No far transfer was observed, demonstrating both convergent and divergent validity for the training procedures. Results of the initial training were confirmed in two replications 7 and 14 years later. Magnitudes of training effects in the replications equaled those obtained in the initial study.

Follow-up studies of cognitive training after 7- and 14-year intervals furthermore demonstrated that participants who prior to initial training had shown significant decline remained at substantial advantage over untrained comparison groups. Booster training increased the advantage of these groups further. Over 14 years, trained individuals, on average, showed maintenance from the first pretest to the last posttest on Inductive Reasoning and less decline than the comparison group on Spatial Orientation. Long-term effects for those who had remained stable at initial training differed by ability. More modest, but significant, effects were shown to prevail on Inductive Reasoning but not on Space training.

Studies of the role of strategy use in training success revealed increased use of strategies for those who gained from training, but also indicated that the young-old and those with higher levels of education were most likely to use strategies in their performance.

Findings from the training study suggest that targeted cognitive intervention programs can reverse the modest age-related decline that is likely to be related to disuse of certain cognitive skills. Booster applications of these techniques, moreover, result in reduction of age-related declines on the trained abilities. Wider applications of similar interventions may well be useful in retaining independent living status for older persons who might otherwise be institutionalized because of marginal cognitive competence.

CHAPTER EIGHT

Methodological Studies

IN THIS CHAPTER, SOME OF THE METHODOLOGICAL studies are described that were conducted either by collateral data collections or by secondary analyses of the core data archives. I begin with a concern that arose after our third cycle: We needed to shift from a sampling-without-replacement paradigm to one that involved sampling with replacement if we were to be able to continue drawing new samples not previously tested (1974 collateral study). I then discuss the issue of the aging of tests and report results from an investigation designed to determine whether switching to more recently constructed tests would be appropriate in the context of the longitudinal study (1975 collateral study). Next, I deal with the question of the effects on participant self-selection when we shifted to the current trend of offering monetary incentives to prospective study participants.

A number of secondary analyses are described that deal with experimental mortality (participant attrition) and the consequent adjustments that might be needed in our substantive findings. Next, I consider the possible effect of repeated measurement designs in understating cognitive decline and present analyses that adjust for practice effects. I then examine the issue of structural equivalence across cohorts, age, time, and gender to determine whether we can validly compare our findings. Here, I describe a number of relevant studies employing restricted (confirmatory) factor analysis designed to determine the degree of invariance of the regression of our observed variables on the latent constructs that are of interest in this study.

Changing From Sampling Without Replacement
to Sampling With Replacement
(1974 Collateral Study)

The process of maintaining longitudinal panels and supplementing them from random samples of an equivalent population base raises special problems. It has become evident, for example, that over time a sample that is representative of a given population at a study's inception will become successively less representative. This shift is caused by the effects of nonrandom experimental mortality (participant attrition) as well as reactivity to repeated testing (practice). I discuss the measurement of these effects and possible adjustment for them in a section on the effects of practice in repeated testing later in this chapter. First, however, I consider the effects of circumventing the inherent shortcomings of longitudinal studies by means of appropriate control groups.

One such possible control is to draw independent samples from the same population at different measurement points, thus obtaining measures of performance changes that are not confounded by attrition and practice factors. Such an approach, however, requires adoption of a sampling model that, depending on the size and mobility characteristics of the population sampled, involves sampling either with or without replacement. Sampling without replacement assumes that the population is fixed and large enough so that successive samples will be reasonably equivalent. Sampling with replacement assumes a dynamic population, but one for which on average the characteristics of individuals leaving the population are equivalent to those of individuals replacing them.

Although the independent random sampling approach is a useful tool for controlling effects of experimental mortality, practice, and reactivity, it requires the assumption that the characteristics of the parent population from which sampling over time is to occur will remain relatively stable. Riegel and Riegel (1972) argued that such an assumption might be flawed. They argued that "because of selective death of less able persons (especially at younger age levels) the population from which consecutive age samples are drawn is not homogeneous but, increasingly with age, becomes positively biased" (p. 308). This argument is indeed relevant for repeated sampling from the same cohorts, but not necessarily for the same age levels measured from successive cohorts. Moreover, successive samples are necessarily measured at different points in time, thus introducing additional time-of-measurement confounds.

Another problem occurs when successive samples are drawn from a population without replacement. Unless the parent population is very large, it will eventually become exhausted. That is, either all members of that population may already be included in the study or the remainder of the population is either unable or unwilling to participate. In addition, the residue of a limited population, because of nonrandom attrition, may eventually become less and less representative of the originally defined population. As a consequence, at some point in a longitudinal inquiry, it may become necessary to switch from a model of sampling without replacement to one of sampling with replacement.

Subsequent to the third Seattle Longitudinal Study (SLS) cycle, it became clear that a further random sample drawn from the remainder of the 1956 health maintenance organization (HMO) population might be fraught with the problems mentioned above. It therefore became necessary to conduct a special collateral study that would determine the effects of switching to a model of sampling with replacement. We decided to draw a random sample from the redefined population and compare the characteristics of this sample and its performance on our major dependent variables with those of the samples drawn from the original fixed population. This approach would enable us, first, to test whether there would be significant effects and, if so, second to estimate the magnitude of the differences, which could then be used for appropriate adjustments in comparisons of the later with the earlier data collections (see Gribbin et al., 1976).

Method

Participants   The original population of the HMO (in 1956) had consisted of approximately 18,000 adults over the age of 22 years. Of these, 2,201 persons had been included in our study through the third SLS cycle. The redefined population base in 1974 consisted of all of the approximately 186,000 adult members regardless of the date of entry into the medical plan (except for those individuals already included in our study). Sampling procedures similar to those described for the main study (see chapter 3) were used to obtain a sample of 591 participants, ranging in age from 22 to 88 years (in 1974).

The membership of the HMO, as of 1956, had been somewhat skewed toward the upper economic levels because many well-educated persons were early HMO joiners for principled rather than economic reasons. The membership was limited at the lower economic levels and almost devoid of minorities. Given these exceptions, the HMO membership did provide a wide range of educational, occupational, and income levels and was a reasonable match of the 1960 and 1970 census figures for the service area. By 1974, however, with the membership grown to 10 times that of the original population, there was a far greater proportion of minorities, as well as a somewhat broader range of socioeconomic levels.

Measurement Variables   Variables in the collateral study were those included in the first three SLS cycles: the primary mental abilities of Verbal Meaning (V), Spatial Orientation (S), Inductive Reasoning (R), Number (N), and Word Fluency (W) and their composites (Intellectual Ability [IQ] and Educational Aptitude [EQ]); the factor scores from the Test of Behavioral Rigidity (TBR): Motor Cognitive Flexibility (MCF), Attitudinal Flexibility (AF), and Psychomotor Speed (PS); and the attitude scale of Social Responsibility (SR) (see chapter 3 for detailed descriptions).

Design and Data Analysis   The data collected in the 1974 collateral study can be analyzed by two of the designs derived from the general developmental model (Schaie, 1965, 1977; chapter 2). Assuming that a major proportion of variance is accounted for by cohort-related (year-of-birth) differences, data may be organized into a cross-sequential format—in this instance, comparing individuals from the same birth cohorts, but drawn from two different populations. Alternatively, assuming that age-related differences are of significance, the data can be grouped according to age levels in the form of a time-sequential design—comparing individuals at the same age, but drawn not only from different birth cohorts, but also from different populations. Both designs were used in this study.

Scores for all participants were first transformed into T scores ($M = 50$; $SD = 10$) based on all samples at first test occasion from the first three SLS cycles. For the analyses by cohort, participants in both populations were grouped into 7-year birth cohorts, with mean year of birth ranging from 1889 to 1945. Because the sample from the redefined population was tested in 1974, which was 4 years subsequent to the last measurement point for the original samples, participant groupings were reorganized and mean year of birth for the new sample was shifted by 4 years to maintain equivalent mean ages for the analyses by age levels. Data were thus available for seven cohorts (mean birth years 1889 to 1945) at all times of measurement. Similarly, data were available for seven age levels (mean ages 25 to 67 years) from all occasions; specifically, observations from Cohorts 1 to 7 in 1956, cohorts 2 to 8 in 1963, and Cohorts 3 to 9 in 1970 were compared with the reorganized groupings of the participants in the 1974 testing.

Previous analyses of data from the original population samples had suggested a significant time-of-measurement (period) effect (Schaie & Labouvie-Vief, 1974; Schaie, Labouvie, & Buech, 1973). To estimate and control for these effects, trend line analyses were conducted over the first three measurement occasions, and the expected time-of-measurement effect for the 1974 sample was estimated. The coefficients of determination (degree of fit of the linear equation) ranged from .74 to .92 in both cohort and age analyses. Psychomotor Speed and Attitudinal Flexibility in the cohort analysis did not adequately fit a linear mode, but could be fitted with a logarithmic function. Estimated values for these variables were therefore obtained subsequent to such transformation. The null hypothesis with respect to the difference between observed scores from the 1974 sample and estimated scores was evaluated by means of independent t tests.

Findings From the Sampling Equivalence Study

Summary results for the comparison of data from the original and redefined populations can be found in tables 8.1 and 8.2. Significant overall differences ($p <$ .01) between samples from the two populations for both cohort and age analyses were observed on a number of variables: Verbal Meaning, Spatial Orientation, Number, Word Fluency, and the Index of Educational Aptitude. The sample from the redefined population scored somewhat lower than that from the original population, with the exception of Word Fluency, for which it scored higher. No differences were observed for the measures from the Test of Behavioral Rigidity, the Social Responsibility scale, or the composite IQ score.

Having established that differences in level between the two populations did exist on certain variables, the question next arose whether these differences prevailed across the board for all cohort/age groups or were localized at specific age levels. This was a critical issue: If there is an overall difference, then future analyses would require systematic adjustments; if the differences were confined to specific age and cohort levels, then we simply needed to take note of this in interpreting local blips in our overall data analyses. Results of the age- and cohort-specific analyses suggested that the differences were indeed local: They affected primarily members of Cohorts 4 and 5 (mean birth years 1910 and 1917, respectively), who

TABLE 8.1 Cohort Analysis of Differences Between Estimated and Observed Scores

Variable	Estimated Mean	Observed Mean	t Ratio
Verbal Meaning (V)	48.96	45.55	4.94***
Spatial Orientation (S)	47.73	45.81	3.01**
Inductive Reasoning (R)	47.31	46.63	ns
Number (N)	50.03	47.09	4.53***
Word Fluency (W)	45.75	47.40	ns
Intellectual Ability (IQ)	47.71	46.06	ns
Educational Aptitude (EQ)	48.47	45.90	3.77**
Motor-Cognitive Flexibility (MCF)	47.03	46.44	ns
Attitudinal Flexibility (AF)	8.74	48.83	ns
Psychomotor Speed (PS)	48.08	48.86	ns
Social Responsibility (SR)	49.95	49.25	ns

Note. ns, not significant.

**p < .01. ***p < .001. Means are in T scores with population mean of 50 and standard deviation of 10.

in 1974 would have been in their late 50s and early 60s. Comparisons for none of the other age/cohort levels reached statistical significance ($p < .01$).

The major conclusion of this study echoes for the investigation of developmental problems the caution first raised by Campbell and Stanley (1963) that there is always a trade-off between internal and external validity. In our case, we find that designs that maximize internal validity may indeed impair the generalizability of the phenomena studied (see also Schaie, 1978). Fortunately, the results of the 1974 collateral study suggested that such threat to the external validity of developmental designs is not equally serious for all variables or for all ages and cohorts. Hence, I do not necessarily advocate that all studies must include analyses such as the one presented in this section, but would caution the initiator of long-range studies to design data collections in a manner permitting similar anal-

TABLE 8.2 Age Analysis of Differences Between Estimated and Observed Scores

Variable	Estimated Mean	Observed Mean	t Ratio
Verbal Meaning (V)	53.36	51.02	3.74***
Spatial Orientation (S)	52.76	50.80	3.08***
Inductive Reasoning (R)	53.30	52.79	ns
Number (N)	52.64	49.70	4.83***
Word Fluency (W)	48.78	51.00	3.46***
Intellectual Ability (IQ)	52.88	51.35	ns
Educational Aptitude (EQ)	53.56	51.64	3.09**
Motor-Cognitive Flexibility (MCF)	52.41	51.35	ns
Attitudinal Flexibility (AF)	52.26	52.73	ns
Psychomotor Speed (PS)	52.98	53.87	ns
Social Responsibility (SR)	49.75	48.52	ns

Note. ns, not significant.

**p < .01. ***p < .001. Means are in T scores with population mean of 50 and standard deviation of 10.

yses for those variables when the literature does not provide appropriate evidence of external validity.

The Aging of Tests (1975 Study)

Although longitudinal designs are the most powerful approach for determining changes that occur with increasing age, they are associated with a number of serious limitations (see chapter 2; Baltes & Nesselroade, 1979; Schaie, 1973b, 1977, 1988d, 1994b). One of these limitations is the fact that outmoded measurement instruments must usually continue to be employed, even though newer (and possibly better) instruments may become available, to allow orderly comparisons of the measurement variables over time.

However, if the primary interest is at the level of psychological constructs, then specific measurement operations may be seen as no more than arbitrary samples of observable behaviors designed to measure the latent constructs (Baltes et al., 1972; Schaie, 1973b, 1988d). In this case, it might well be possible to convert from one set of measures to another if the appropriate linkage studies are undertaken. These linkage studies must be designed to give an indication of the common factor structure for both old and new measures.

Designing linkage studies require considerable attention to a number of issues. New instruments must be chosen that, on either theoretical or empirical grounds, may be expected to measure the same constructs as the old instruments. Thus, it is necessary to include a variety of tasks thought to measure the same constructs. It is then possible to determine empirically which of the new measures best describes information that was gained from the older measures so that scores obtained from the new test battery will closely reproduce the information gathered by the original measures.

The sample of participants for the linkage study must be drawn from the same parent population and should comprise individuals of the same gender and age range as those in the longitudinal study. Only in this manner can we be sure that comparable information will be gathered on the range of performance, reliability, and construct validity for both old and new measures. Given information for the same participants on both the old and new measurement variables, regression techniques can then be employed, the results of which will allow judgment whether to convert to new measures and, if so, which measures must be included in the new battery. Alternatively, study results may suggest that switching to the new measures will result in significant information loss, an outcome that would argue for retention of one or more of the old measures.

Because of the cohort effects described in this volume (see chapter 6), we began to worry as we prepared for the fourth (1977) cycle that a ceiling effect might be reached by some of the younger participants on some of the measures in the 1948 Primary Mental Abilities (PMA) battery. Although these tests have been found to be appropriate for older people (Schaie et al., 1953), the question was now raised as to whether the tests had "aged" over the time period they had been used. In other words, we were concerned whether measures retained appropriate construct validity for the more recent cohorts introduced into our study.

On the other hand, we were also concerned about the possibility that, although the test might have restricted validity for the younger cohorts, switching to a newer test might raise construct validity problems for the older cohorts. For example, Gardner and Monge (1975) found that whereas 20- and 30-year-olds performed significantly better on items entering the language after 1960, 40- and 60-year-olds performed significantly better on items entering the language in the late 1920s.

We consequently decided that it would be prudent to examine the continuing utility of the 1948 PMA version by administering this test together with a more recent PMA revision (T. G. Thurstone, 1962) and selected measures from the *Kit of Reference Tests for Cognitive Factors* published by the Educational Testing Service (ETS; French et al., 1963). The 1962 PMA was chosen because it was felt that this test would be most similar to the 1948 PMA version; the ETS tests were included with the expectation that they might account for additional variance that would reduce the information loss caused by a decision to switch the PMA test for future test occasions (see Gribbin & Schaie, 1977).

Method

Participants   The approximately 128,000 members of our HMO over the age range from 22 to 82 years (in 1975) were stratified by age and gender, and a balanced random sample in these strata was drawn. Data were collected on 242 men and women.

Measurement Variables   The test battery for this study included the five subtests of the PMA 1948 version (L. L. Thurstone & Thurstone, 1949): Verbal Meaning (V48), Spatial Orientation (S48), Inductive Reasoning (R48), Number (N48), and Word Fluency (W48). The 1962 version (T. G. Thurstone, 1962) differs from the earlier format by omitting Word Fluency; by having Number (N62) include subtraction, multiplication, and division instead of just addition; and by having Inductive Reasoning (R62) include number series and word groupings as well as the letter series that make up N48. The number of items is also increased in the Verbal Meaning (V62) test. Eight tests were added from the ETS test kit (French et al., 1963): *Hidden Patterns*, a measure of flexibility of closure; *Letter Sets*, a measure of inductive reasoning; *Length Estimation*, the ability to judge and compare visually perceived distances; *Finding A's* and *Identical Pictures*, measures of perceptual speed; *Nonsense Syllogisms*, a measure of syllogistic reasoning; *Maze Tracing*, which requires spatial scanning; and *Paper Folding*, which requires transforming the image of spatial patterns into other visual arrangements. All of the ETS tests have two parts of similar form.

Procedure   Tests were administered in a modified counterbalanced order; that is, one order presented the 1948 PMA first, followed by the ETS tests, with the 1962 PMA last. The second order presented the 1962 PMA first, followed by the ETS tests in reverse order, and ending with the 1948 PMA. A 20-minute break, with refreshments, was given after half the ETS tests had been administered.

Aging of Tests Study Findings

Regression analyses were employed to determine the relationship between the tests. For each subtest score to be predicted (that is, subtests from both versions of the PMA), scores on all subtests from the alternative version plus each part of the eight ETS tests were used as predictor variables across all participants. Because we are also concerned about the relationships among our variables by age level, similar analyses were conducted by dividing the sample into two age groups (22 to 51 and 52 to 82 years) to determine whether predictability of the tests differed by age groupings. Table 8.3 presents the R^2 (proportion of variance accounted for each subtest of the 1948 PMA, as well as the B weights (Bs, standardized regression coefficients) for each predictor variable for the younger, older, and total data sets. Similar information is provided in table 8.4 for the 1962 PMA.

As can be seen by comparing the R^2 of the comparable subtests from each PMA version, it turned out that the 1962 version was better predicted than was the 1948 version. Of the 1948 PMA tests, Verbal Meaning, Spatial Orientation, and Inductive Reasoning could be reasonably well predicted from their 1962 counterparts. However, this was not the case for Number and Word Fluency. For these subtests, only 43% and 40% of the variance, respectively, could be accounted for, suggesting that it would not have been prudent to replace these tests.

When examining findings by age level, it became clear that N48 and W48 were even less well predicted for the younger half of the sample. However, it is worth noting that W48 was better predicted for older than younger participants, and that the reverse was true for W48.

These results suggested that, by adding certain of the ETS tests, it would have been practicable to replace V48 with V62, S48 with S62, and R48 with R62 and sustain relatively little information loss. For N48 and W48, however, it was clear that replacement was not justified. By contrast, it was found that a combination of the 1948 PMA and certain of the ETS tests would allow substantial prediction of most of the reliable variance in the 1962 PMA.

In sum, it appeared that shifting to the newer version of the PMA, even with the addition of several other tests, would lead to serious problems in maintaining linkage across test occasions. Moreover, because it was possible to predict performance on the 1962 PMA well with the addition of certain ETS tests, it did not seem that any advantage was to be gained in shifting to the newer test version. We thus concluded that continued use of the 1948 PMA was justified, but we augmented the fourth cycle battery by adding the ETS Identical Pictures and Finding A's tests to be able to define an additional Perceptual Speed factor.

Effects of Monetary Incentives

Over the course of the SLS, there have been a number of subtle changes in the nature of volunteering behavior by prospective participants. In particular, our

TABLE 8.3 Regression Equations Predicting the 1948 Primary Mental Abilities (PMA)

	Verbal Meaning			Spatial Orientation			Inductive Reasoning			Number			Word Fluency		
	Y	O	T	Y	O	T	Y	O	T	Y	O	T	Y	O	T
Verbal 62	.59	.28	.50	-.17			.09	-.12		.21	.26	.26	.27		.24
Space 62	-.11	.14				.46	.58	-.13							-.11
Letter Series 62	.19	-.26	-.18	.42	-.17	.47	.43	.18			.12			.18	
Number Series 62	.39		.24	.22	.17	.14	.24	.14	.18			.12			.18
Word Groupings 62	-.23	-.18	-.24										-.13		
Number 62	.13		.13	.27		.17	-.21			.18	.31	.33			
Hidden Patterns 1	-.14	.27						.17							
Hidden Patterns 2	.22	-.14	.11		.10		.20						-.17		
Finding A's 1	-.15			.15			.09	.04	.10	.10	.11	-.11			
Finding A's 2	.19	.05							.14				.27	.14	.18
Maze Tracing 1						-.10	-.09			-.18	-.33			.16	
Maze Tracing 2	-.22	-.15	-.08		.14	.08		.25	-.13	.16	-.24	-.23	.18		
Paper Folding 1			.06		.12						-.08				
Paper Folding 2														.09	
Identical Pictures 1	.16					.26	.11	.12		.11			.18		
Identical Pictures 2			.15		.0	-.16									
Letter Sets 1	.23	.14		.15		.28	.10	.15	-.26	.14	.25	.15	.27	.14	
Letter Sets 2	.10		.11	.11	.09	.07		.19	.14					.37	.25
Line Estimation 1	-.09							.11	.04		-.11	-.11			
Line Estimation 2								-.07	-.10						
Nonsense Syllogisms 1				-.11		.11	.06			-.06		.15	.06		
Nonsense Syllogisms 2				-.08	-.04										
R^2	.65	.68	.69	.61	.72	.70	.72	.85	.84	.37	.52	.43	.45	.34	.40

Note. 62, PMA 1962; O, older; T, total; Y, younger.

TABLE 8.4 Regression Equations Predicting the 1962 Primary Mental Abilities (PMA)

	Verbal Meaning			Spatial Orientation			Inductive Reasoning			Number		
	Y	O	T	Y	O	T	Y	O	T	Y	O	T
Verbal 48	.50	.25	.41	−.10	.13					.24		.12
Space 48				.59	.51	.54	.17	.20	.10	.16		.18
Reasoning 48							.38	.35	.39	−.16	.04	−.07
Number 48	.08	.22	.13	.13			.10	.14	.10	.11	.24	.20
Word Fluency 48	.11		.10				.12		.06		.08	
Hidden Patterns 1	.13						.12				.18	
Hidden Patterns 2					.29							
Finding A's 1	.16	.18	.13	.21	.13		.11	−.10				
Finding A's 2					−.14	−.10						
Maze Tracing 1					.08	.10						.12
Maze Tracing 2	.13	.14					.19	.14		.36	.16	
Paper Folding 1				.16	−.20		−.07			.18	.09	
Paper Folding 2								.11				
Identical Pictures 1	.12	.11		.20		.13	−.10					
Identical Pictures 2			.11					.09				
Letter Sets 1							.22	.22	.22	.37	.15	.23
Letter Sets 2	−.13	−.13	−.12									
Line Estimation 1	.14						.09					
Line Estimation 2		.21	.12			.06		.14	.09	.10	.10	
Nonsense Syllogism 1			−.08				.05	.26		.13	.16	
Nonsense Syllogism 2	.19	.09	.15	.13	.08	.07	.18	.08				
R^2	.67	.67	.72	.62	.68	.73	.76	.87	.87	.63	.72	.72

Note. 48, PMA 1948; O, older; T, total; Y, younger.

original solicitation was directed toward encouraging participation by appealing to the prospective participants' interest in helping to generate new knowledge as well as in assisting their health plan in acquiring information on its membership that might help in program planning activities. As the study progressed, payments to participants in psychological studies became more frequent, and it is now virtually the rule for study participants beyond college age.

It has been well known for some time that rate of volunteering differs by age. Typically, adult volunteers tend to be younger, and when older people do volunteer, they tend to so more often for survey research than for laboratory studies (Rosenthal & Rosnow, 1975). Indeed, in our very first effort, we found a curvilinear age pattern, with middle-aged persons most likely to volunteer (Schaie, 1958c).

The increased employment of monetary incentives may have a substantial effect on the self-selection of volunteer study participants. In a study with young adult participants, MacDonald (1972) utilized three incentive conditions: (a) for pay, (b) for extra class credit, and (c) for love of science. He found that participants high in need of approval on the Marlowe-Crowne scale were more willing to volunteer than participants low in need of approval on the pay condition, but not on the other two conditions.

Because we could not find a comparable study using older adults, as part of the 1974 collateral study we attempted to determine the effects of a monetary incentive on self-selection of volunteer participants across the adult age range. Specifically, we were interested in determining whether those participants who had been promised payment differed on certain cognitive and personality factors from those who had been told that they would not be paid (see Gribbin & Schaie, 1976).

Method

Sampling and procedures for this investigation are described in the section on the 1974 collateral study. However, certain additional information relating to the monetary incentive aspects needs to be added. As part of the participant recruitment letter, half of the potential participants were informed that they would be paid $10 for their participation; no mention of payment was made in the letter to the other half. After completion of the assessment procedures, both groups were paid the participant fee. Data evaluated for the effects of monetary incentives included the five primary mental abilities, the TBR, and the 16 PF (Cattell, Eber, & Tatsuoka, 1970).

Monetary Incentives Study Findings

Of the 1,233 potential participants in each incentive category, 34% of the pay condition (P) and 32% of the no-pay condition (NP) participants volunteered to participate in the study. In both conditions, women (P = 37%; NP = 35%) were more willing to participate than men (P = 30%; NP = 29%). Peak participation occurred for participants in the age range from 40 to 68 years, with participation decreasing linearly for both those older and those younger. Nonsignificant chi-squares were obtained for age, gender, and their interaction.

No significant differences for the pay conditions were found for any of the primary mental abilities or any of the dimensions of the TBR. We did not observe any significant pay condition by gender interactions. The effect of incentive conditions on personality traits was next considered via multivariate analyses of variance of both primary source traits and the secondary stratum factors of the 16 PF. Again, none of the multivariate tests of Trait × Pay Condition or Trait × Pay Condition × Gender was statistically significant.

It thus seemed clear that offering a monetary incentive did not seem to result in biased self-selection, at least as far as measures of cognitive abilities, cognitive styles, and self-reported personality traits are concerned. In addition, it did not seem that offering a monetary incentive had any effect on recruitment rate for a relatively brief (2-hour) laboratory experiment. Of course, we do not know whether similar findings would hold for more extensive protocols such as those employed in our training studies (see chapter 7). Nevertheless, it seems safe to argue from these results that findings from studies using monetary incentives may legitimately be generalized to those that do not offer such incentives without fear that the samples will differ regarding characteristics that might be attributed to extraneous incentive conditions.

Effects of Experimental Mortality: The Problem of Participant Attrition

One of the major threats to the internal validity of a longitudinal study is the occurrence of participant attrition (experimental mortality) such that not all participants tested at T_1 are available for retest at T_2 or subsequently. In studies of cognitive aging, participant attrition may be caused by death, disability, disappearance, or failure to cooperate with the researcher on a subsequent test occasion.

Substantial differences in base performance have been observed between those who return and those who fail to be retrieved for the second or subsequent test. Typically, dropouts score lower at base on ability variables or describe themselves as possessing less socially desirable traits than do those who return (see Riegel, Riegel, & Meyer, 1967; Schaie, 1988d). Hence, the argument has been advanced that longitudinal studies represent increasingly more elite subsets of the general population and may eventually produce data that are not sufficiently generalizable (see Botwinick, 1977). This proposition can and should be tested empirically, of course. In the SLS, we have assessed experimental mortality subsequent to each cycle (for Cycle 2, see Baltes, Schaie, & Nardi, 1971; Cycle 3, Schaie, Labouvie, & Barrett, 1973; Cycle 4, Gribbin & Schaie, 1979; Cycle 5, Cooney et al., 1988; Cycle 6, Schaie, 1996b). Next, I summarize a comprehensive analysis of attrition effects across all seven cycles (see also Schaie, 1988d).

We have examined the magnitude of attrition effects for several longitudinal sequences to contrast base performance of those individuals for whom longitudinal data are available with those who dropped out after the initial assessment. In addition, we considered shifts in direction and magnitude of attrition after multiple assessment occasions.

In table 8.5, attrition data are reported as the difference in average performance between the dropouts and returnees. It will be seen that attrition effects vary across samples entering the study at different points in time. However, between T_1 and T_2, they generally range from 0.3 to 0.6 SD and must therefore be considered of a magnitude that represents at least a moderate-size effect (see Cohen & Cohen, 1975). Although attrition effects become somewhat less pronounced as test occasions multiply, they do remain of a statistically significant magnitude.

Before the reader is overly impressed by the substantial differences between dropouts and returnees, a caution must be raised. Bias in longitudinal studies because of experimental mortality depends solely on the proportion of dropouts compared to the total sample. Hence, if attrition is modest, experimental mortality effects will be quite small, but if attrition is large, the effects can be as substantial, as noted above. Table 8.6 therefore presents the actual net attrition effects (in T-score points) for our samples, showing the different attrition patterns. It is

TABLE 8.5 Difference in Average Performance at Base Assessment Between Dropouts and Returnees[a]

	Sample 1 (N = 500)	Sample 2 (N = 997)	Sample 3 (N = 705)	Sample 4 (N = 609)	Sample 5 (N = 629)	Sample 6 (N = 693)
After Test 1						
Verbal Meaning	4.07*	6.38**	6.27**	6.12**	2.85**	4.44***
Spatial Orientation	2.52**	4.00**	4.08**	4.25**	2.44**	3.01***
Inductive Reasoning	3.06**	5.28**	5.70**	6.70**	2.58**	3.87***
Number	1.97*	3.95**	5.16**	4.45**	1.91	3.71***
Word Fluency	3.06**	3.66**	4.84**	3.68**	2.28**	2.58***
After Test 2						
Verbal Meaning	1.51**	1.97**	3.71**	3.33**	6.31**	
Spatial Orientation	2.16**	1.35	5.09**	3.44**	4.44***	
Inductive Reasoning	5.14**	2.54**	5.81**	2.71**	4.63***	
Number	2.13*	1.65*	2.87**	2.05**	3.39***	
Word Fluency	2.41*	1.01	2.67**	3.43**	3.09**	
After Test 3						
Verbal Meaning	4.10**	2.30*	3.78**	7.51***		
Spatial Orientation	4.85**	0.48	4.50**	5.96***		
Inductive Reasoning	4.35**	4.73**	4.30**	7.41***		
Number	0.58	1.89	2.53**	3.55**		
Word Fluency	3.96**	1.16	2.48*	6.56***		
After Test 4						
Verbal Meaning	4.72**	6.75**	4.33**			
Spatial Orientation	3.45*	2.38	6.80***			
Inductive Reasoning	4.45*	3.15**	5.18***			
Number	1.35	1.79	0.82			
Word Fluency	4.25**	2.20	3.94*			
After Test 5						
Verbal Meaning	5.04**	8.51***				
Spatial Orientation	5.67*	7.45***				
Inductive Reasoning	3.36*	7.65***				
Number	2.44	3.66*				
Word Fluency	2.09	5.43**				
After Test 6						
Verbal Meaning	7.31***					
Spatial Orientation	4.43					
Inductive Reasoning	7.26**					
Number	3.63*					
Word Fluency	4.48*					

Note. All differences are in favor of the returnees.
[a]Data in T-score points.
*$p < .05$. **$p < .01$. ***$p < .001$.

apparent from these data that experimental mortality is largest for those test occasions when the greatest proportion of dropouts occurred (usually at T_2) and becomes smaller as panels stabilized, and the remaining attrition occurred primarily as a consequence of the participants' death or disability. However, as panels age, the magnitude of experimental mortality may increase again given the often-observed terminal decline occurring prior to death (also see Bosworth, Schaie, & Willis, 1999a).

TABLE 8.6 Attrition Effects Calculated as Difference Between Base Means for Total Sample and Returnees[a]

	Sample 1 (N = 500)	Sample 2 (N = 997)	Sample 3 (N = 705)	Sample 4 (N = 609)	Sample 5 (N = 629)	Sample 6 (N = 693)
Attrition after Test 1	38.2%	53.5%	51.9%	52.3%	32.0%	41.2%
Verbal Meaning	1.52	3.41***	2.97**	3.20**	2.85**	1.96*
Spatial Orientation	0.96	2.14**	2.12**	1.40	2.44**	1.26
Inductive Reasoning	1.17	2.82**	2.96**	2.22*	2.58**	1.57
Number	0.76	2.11**	2.68**	2.46*	1.91	1.30
Word Fluency	1.17	1.95	2.51**	2.33*	2.28**	1.24
Attrition after Test 2	25.0%	16.0%	16.5%	15.4%	25.6%	
Verbal Meaning	1.59	0.70	1.54	3.33**	3.24**	
Spatial Orientation	1.02	0.48	1.40	3.44***	1.68	
Inductive Reasoning	2.33*	0.91	1.99*	2.71***	1.61	
Number	0.93	0.59	0.98	2.05*	1.27	
Word Fluency	1.09	0.36	0.74	3.43***	1.16	
Attrition after Test 3	8.0%	7.4%	6.8%	18.3%		
Verbal Meaning	0.97	0.57	3.78***	2.89**		
Spatial Orientation	1.12	0.12	4.50***	2.30*		
Inductive Reasoning	1.03	1.14	4.30***	2.85**		
Number	0.16	0.47	2.53**	1.37		
Word Fluency	0.94	0.29	2.48*	2.54**		
Attrition after Test 4	6.6%	6.4%	6.8%			
Verbal Meaning	1.21	6.75***	1.65			
Spatial Orientation	0.86	2.38*	1.87			
Inductive Reasoning	1.14	3.15**	1.44			
Number	0.35	1.79*	0.23			
Word Fluency	1.09	2.20*	1.08			
Attrition after Test 5	5.0%	5.2%				
Verbal Meaning	5.04***	2.72**				
Spatial Orientation	5.67***	2.38*				
Inductive Reasoning	3.36**	0.95				
Number	2.44*	0.25				
Word Fluency	2.09*	1.74				
Attrition after Test 6	7.4%					
Verbal Meaning	3.66***					
Spatial Orientation	2.19*					
Inductive Reasoning	3.59***					
Number	1.79					
Word Fluency	2.21*					

Note. All differences are in favor of the returnees.
[a]Data in T-score points.
*$p < .05$. **$p < .01$. ***$p < .001$.

We can infer from these data that parameter estimates of levels of cognitive function from longitudinal studies, when experimental mortality is appreciable, could be substantially higher in many instances than would be true if the entire original sample could have been followed over time. Nevertheless, it does not follow that *rates* of change will also be overestimated unless it can be shown that there is a substantial positive correlation between base level performance and age change. Because of the favorable attrition (i.e., excess attrition of low-performing participants), the regression should result in modest negative correlations between base and age change measures. This is indeed what was found (see Schaie, 1988d, 1996b). Hence, contrary to Botwinick's (1977) inference, experimental mortality may actually result in the overestimation of rates of cognitive aging in longitudinal studies.

Effects of Practice in Repeated Testing

Longitudinal studies have been thought to reflect overly optimistic results also because age-related declines in behavior may be obscured by the consequences of practice on the measurement instruments used to detect such decline. In addition, practice effects may differ by age. We have studied the effects of practice by comparing individuals who return for follow-up with the performance of individuals assessed at the same age for the first time (Schaie, 1988d).

Practice effects estimated in this manner appear, at first glance, to be impressively large between T_1 and T_2 (up to approximately 0.4 SD), although they become increasingly smaller over subsequent time intervals (see table 8.7). The exceptions involve Verbal Meaning and Word Fluency, for which practice effects are again noted late in life. Note, however, that practice effects estimated in this manner of necessity involve the comparison of attrited and random samples. The mean values for the longitudinal samples must therefore be adjusted for experimental mortality to permit valid comparison. The appropriate adjustment is based on the values in table 8.6 (i.e., the differences between returnees and the entire sample). Because practice effects are assumed to be positive, all significance tests in table 8.7 were one tailed. Although the raw practice effects appear to be significant for most variables and samples, none of the adjusted effects reached significance except for Verbal Meaning in Sample 1 from T_1 to T_2 and from T_6 to T_7. We concluded, therefore, that practice effects do *not* tend to produce favorably biased results in the longitudinal findings of our study.

We have also examined the joint effects of attrition and history, attrition and cohort, history and practice, cohort and practice, and the joint effects of all these four potential threats to the internal validity of longitudinal studies. Designs for these analyses have been provided (Schaie, 1977), with worked-out examples in Schaie (1988d). In a data set involving two age cohorts aged 46 and 53 years at the first assessment and comparing their performance 7 years later, these effects were all significant and accounted for roughly 7% of the total variance (see Schaie, 1988d, for further details).

Controlling for Effects of Attrition and Practice
by an Independent Random Sampling Design

As indicated in chapter 2, it is possible to control for the effects of practice and attrition by examining a longitudinal sequence or sequences that use only the

TABLE 8.7 Raw and Attrition-Adjusted Effects of Practice by Sample and Test Occasion[a]

	Sample 1		Sample 2		Sample 3		Sample 4		Sample 5		Sample 6	
	Raw	Adjusted	Raw	Adjusted	Raw	Adjusted	Raw	Adjusted	Raw	Adjusted	Raw	Adjusted
From Test 1 to Test 2												
Verbal Meaning	2.81**	1.29*	4.02**	0.61	3.25**	0.28	1.21*	-1.99	0.70	-2.15	0.49	-1.47
Spatial Orientation	1.02	0.06	3.00**	0.86	2.28**	0.16	2.06**	0.66	0.24	-2.20	0.20	-1.05
Inductive Reasoning	2.03**	0.86	3.43**	0.61	2.77**	-0.19	1.33*	-0.69	0.61	-1.95	-0.07	-1.33
Number	1.02	0.26	1.29*	-0.82	3.09**	0.41	1.60*	-0.86	-0.33	-2.24	0.81	-0.49
Word Fluency	1.71*	0.54	2.94**	0.99	2.97**	0.46	1.10	-1.23	0.46	-1.86	-0.16	-1.40
From Test 2 to Test 3												
Verbal Meaning	-3.07	-4.56	3.11**	2.41**	-3.15	-4.69	0.53	-2.80	0.12	-3.12		
Spatial Orientation	-0.03	-1.05	2.05**	1.57*	1.68*	0.14	2.15*	-1.18	0.51	-1.37		
Inductive Reasoning	1.16	-1.17	2.71**	1.80*	1.93*	-0.01	-0.04	-2.67	0.94	-0.67		
Number	-0.50	-1.43	1.84*	1.25	1.13	0.15	1.51	-0.54	-0.63	-1.70		
Word Fluency	0.22	-0.87	0.41	0.05	2.15**	1.41*	0.30	-3.13	0.94	-0.22		
From Test 3 to Test 4												
Verbal Meaning	0.20	-0.77	-0.78	-1.35	1.93*	-1.85	0.96	-1.93				
Spatial Orientation	0.14	1.16	0.30	0.18	1.59	-2.91	1.98*	-0.32				
Inductive Reasoning	-0.17	-1.20	0.04	-1.10	2.64**	-1.66	0.84	-1.46				
Number	-1.03	-1.19	0.10	0.57	1.42	-1.11	1.54*	0.17				
Word Fluency	0.10	-0.84	-0.99	-1.17	2.18*	-0.30	1.03	-1.51				

202

From Test 4 to Test 5						
Verbal Meaning	0.90	−0.31	−0.38	−7.03	0.44	−1.21
Spatial Orientation	0.81	−0.05	−1.27	−3.63	1.13	−0.64
Inductive Reasoning	−0.09	−1.23	−0.79	−2.36	1.17	−0.27
Number	−1.83	−1.28	−1.63	−3.42	−0.52	−0.75
Word Fluency	−1.74	0.65	−2.16	−4.16	2.90**	1.82*
From Test 5 to Test 6						
Verbal Meaning	1.33	−4.27	−1.01	−3.73		
Spatial Orientation	1.00	−4.67	−0.55	−2.93		
Inductive Reasoning	0.89	−2.47	0.22	−0.73		
Number	−1.43	−3.37	0.09	−0.16		
Word Fluency	1.29	−0.80	−2.84	−4.68		
From Test 6 to Test 7						
Verbal Meaning	5.18***	1.52*				
Spatial Orientation	−0.15	−2.34				
Inductive Reasoning	0.20	−3.39				
Number	−1.10	−2.89				
Word Fluency	0.27	−1.55				

[a]Data in T-score points.

*$p < .05$. **$p < .01$. ***$p < .001$.

first-time data of random samples drawn from the same cohort at successive ages. Such a design, of course, requires a population frame with average membership characteristics that remain rather stable over time. Given the seven waves of data collections in the SLS, data are now available over a 42-year range for three of our study cohorts (Cohorts 5–7). It is therefore possible to construct age gradients over the age range from 25 to 81 years of age that would be controlled for effects of attrition and practice.

These gradients are obtained from table 4.2 (see chapter 4, Cross-Sectional Studies), by taking the averages at each successive age from the sample entering the study at that age for the first time. Figure 8.1a through 8.1e shows the results of these analyses for the five basic primary mental abilities. Although these data cannot be used to predict changes within individuals, they provide conservative bottom-line estimates of what the population parameters would likely be in the absence of attrition and practice effects. It should be noted that there are substantial cohort differences in these sequences. More stable estimates would require extending the sequence over additional cohorts.

Structural Equivalence

I suggest in chapter 2 that all of the comparisons across age and time as well as the gains reported for cognitive interventions depend on the assumption that structural invariance is maintained across these conditions. Very few studies have the requisite data to investigate this assumption empirically. In this section, I describe four methodological investigations that applied restricted (confirmatory) factor analysis (Mulaik, 1972) to investigate these issues. All of the analyses use the linear structural relations (LISREL) paradigm (Jöreskog & Sörbom, 1988).

Factorial Invariance Across Samples Differing in Age

In a study employing the entire set of 1,621 participants tested in 1984, we investigated the validity of the assumption that the measurement operations employed in the study are comparable across age groups (Schaie et al., 1989). The basic assumption to be tested was that each observed marker variable measures the same latent construct equally well regardless of the age of the participants assessed.

Three levels of stringency of measurement equivalence were defined: strong metric invariance, weak metric invariance, and configural invariance (see also Horn, 1991; Horn & McArdle, 1992; Meredith, 1993). The most stringent level of invariance, strong metric invariance, implies not only that the measurement operations remain relevant to the same latent construct, but also that the regressions of the latent constructs on the observed measures remain invariant across age and further that the interrelationships among the different constructs representing a domain (factor intercorrelations) also remain invariant. If invariance can be accepted at this level, then it follows that inferences can be validly drawn from age-comparative studies both for the comparison of directly observed mean

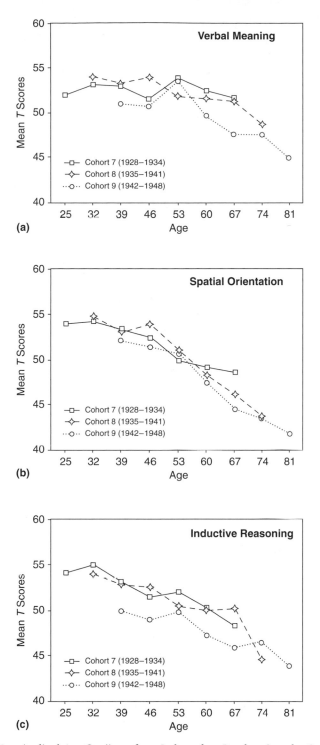

FIGURE 8.1 *Longitudinal Age Gradients from Independent Random Samples Controlling for Effects of Attrition and Practice.*

(continued)

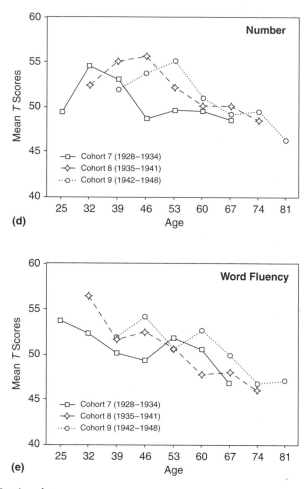

(d)

(e)

FIGURE 8.1 *Continued.*

levels and for the comparison of derived factor score means for the latent ability constructs.

A somewhat less stringent equivalence requirement, weak metric invariance, allows the unique variances and factor intercorrelations to vary across groups while requiring the regressions of the latent constructs on the observed variables to remain invariant. Given the acceptability of this relaxed requirement, it is still possible to claim that observations remain invariant across age. However, comparison of factor scores now requires that changes in the factor space (unequal factor variances and covariances) should be adequately modeled in the algorithm employed for the computation of factor scores.

For the least stringent requirement, configural invariance, we expect that the observable markers of the constructs remain relevant to the same latent construct across age (i.e., across age groups, the same variables have statistically significant loadings, and the same variables have zero loadings). However, we do not insist that the relationships among the latent constructs retain the same magnitude, and we do not require that the regression of the latent constructs on the observed variables remains invariant. If we must accept the least restrictive model, we must then conclude that our test battery does not measure the latent constructs equally well over the entire age range studied, and we must estimate factor scores using differential weights by age group.

Methods   In this analysis, we tested the hypothesis of invariance under the three assumptions outlined above for the domain of psychometric intelligence as defined by 17 tests representing multiple markers of the latent constructs of Inductive Reasoning, Spatial Orientation, Perceptual Speed, Numeric Ability, and Verbal Ability (see description of the expanded battery in chapter 2). An initial factor structure (suggested by earlier work described below [see also Schaie et al., 1987]), was confirmed on the entire sample's 1,621 study participants, yielding a satisfactory fit $[\chi^2(107, N = 1,621) = 946.62, p < .001 (GFI = .936)]$. Table 8.8 shows the factor loadings and factor intercorrelations that entered subsequent analyses. In this model, each ability is marked by at least three operationally distinct observed markers. Each test marks only one ability, except for Number Comparison, which splits between Perceptual Speed and Number, and the PMA Verbal Meaning test, which splits between Perceptual Speed and Verbal Comprehension.

The total sample was then subdivided by age into nine nonoverlapping subsets with mean ages 90 $(n = 39)$, 81 $(n = 136)$, 74 $(n = 260)$, 67 $(n = 291)$, 60 $(n = 260)$, 53 $(n = 193)$, 46 $(n = 154)$, 39 $(n = 124)$, and 29 $(n = 164)$ years. The variance-covariance matrix for each set was then modeled with respect to each of the three invariance levels specified for the overall model.

Results   As indicated in this section, model testing then proceeded at the three levels of stringency listed for determining factorial invariance:

1. *Strong metric invariance.* Model fits for the subsets were, of course, somewhat lower than for the total set but, except for ages 81 and 90 years (the oldest cohorts), were still quite acceptable. The oldest cohort, perhaps because of the small sample size, had the lowest *GFI* (.596), and the 67-year-olds had the highest (.893).
2. *Weak metric invariance.* When unique variances and the factor variance-covariance matrices were freely estimated across groups, statistically significant improvements of model fit occurred for all age groups. As in the complete metric invariance models, the poorest fit (.669) was again found for the oldest age group, with the best fit (.913) occurring for the 74-year-olds. Substantial differences in factor variances were found across the age groups. Variances increased systematically until the 60s and then decreased. Covariances also showed substantial increment with increasing age.

TABLE 8.8 Measurement Model for the 1984 Data Set

	Factor Loadings					
Variable	Inductive Reasoning	Spatial Orientation	Perceptual Speed	Numeric Facility	Verbal Comprehension	Unique Variance
PMA Reasoning	.893					.199
ADEPT Letter Series	.884					.219
Word Series	.891					.207
Number Series	.787					.381
PMA Space		.831				.309
Object Rotation		.877				.231
Alphanumeric Rotation		.831				.309
Cube Comparison		.594				.647
Finding A's			.524			.725
Number Comparison			.576	.270		.424
Identical Pictures			.832			.308
PMA Number				.838		.297
Addition				.938		.121
Subtraction and Multiplication				.865		.252
PMA Verbal Meaning				.660	.386	.254
ETS Vocabulary					.897	.195
ETS Advanced Vocabulary					.893	.203
Inductive Reasoning	—					
Spatial Orientation	.675	—				
Perceptual Speed	.777	.736	—			
Numeric Facility	.687	.584	.689	—		
Verbal Comprehension	.631	.298	.381	.552	—	

Note. All factor loadings are significant at or beyond the 0.01% level of confidence. $\chi^2(107, N = 1,621) = 946.62$. Goodness-of-fit index = .936. ADEPT, Adult Development and Enrichment Project; ETS, Educational Testing Service; PMA, Primary Mental Abilities.

3. *Configural invariance.* In the final set of analyses, factor patterns as specified in table 8.8 were maintained, but the factor patterns were freely estimated. Again, significant improvement in fit was obtained for all age groups, with the goodness-of-fit indices ranging from a low of .697 for the oldest group to a high of .930 for the 74-year-olds. Hence, the configural invariance model must be accepted as the most plausible description of the structure of this data set.

Conclusions The demonstration of configural (factor pattern) invariance is initially reassuring to developmentalists in that it confirms the hope that it is realistic to track the same basic constructs across age and cohorts in adulthood. Nevertheless, these findings give rise to serious cautions with respect to the adequacy of the construct equivalence of an age-comparative study. Given the fact that we could not accept a total-population-based measurement model at either metric or incomplete metric invariance level for any age/cohort, we had to consider the use of *single* estimators of latent constructs as problematic in age-comparative studies.

How serious is the divergence from complete metric equivalence? In the past, shifts in the interrelation among ability constructs have been associated with a differentiation-dedifferentiation theory of intelligence (see Reinert, 1970). This theory predicts that factor covariances should be lowest for the young and should increase with advancing age. As predicted by theory, we found factor covariances were lowest for our youngest age groups and increased with advancing age. Factor variances also increased until the 70s, when the disproportionate dropout of those at greatest risk again increased sample homogeneity and reduced factor variances. Because our data set for the test of complete metric invariance was centered in late midlife, it does not surprise us that discrepancies in factor covariances were confined primarily to the extremes of the age range studied (see Schaie et al., 1989). Consequently, these shifts will not seriously impair the validity of age comparisons using factor scores except at the age extremes.

Because we accept the configural invariance model as the most plausible description of our data, we must be concerned about the relative efficiency of the observed variables as markers of the latent variables at different age levels. The shift in efficiency may be a function of the influence of extreme outliers in small samples or a consequence of the attainment of floor effects in the older age groups and ceiling effects in the younger age groups when a common measurement battery is used over the entire adult life course. In this study, across age groups, for example, the Cube Comparison test becomes a less efficient marker of Spatial Orientation, whereas the PMA Space test becomes a better marker with increasing age. Likewise, the Number Comparison test (a marker of Perceptual Speed), which has a secondary loading on Numerical Ability in the general factor model, loses that secondary loading with increasing age.

These findings suggested that age comparisons in performance level on certain single markers of an ability may be confounded by the changing efficiency of the marker in making the desired assessment. Fortunately, in our case, the divergences are typically quite local in nature. That is, for a particular ability, the optimal regression weights of observable measures on their latent factors may shift slightly, but because there is no shift in the primary loading to another factor, structural relationships are well maintained across the entire age range sampled in the study.

Factorial Invariance Across Experimental Interventions

We have also investigated the stability of the expanded battery's ability structure across the cognitive training intervention described in chapter 7 (Schaie et al., 1987). This study was designed to show that the structure of abilities remains invariant across a brief time period for a nonintervention group (experimental control) and to show that the two intervention programs (Inductive Reasoning, Spatial Orientation) employed in the cognitive intervention study did not result in shifts of factor structure, a possible outcome for training studies suggested by Donaldson (1981; but see Willis & Baltes, 1981).

Methods The subset of participants used for this study included 401 persons (224 women and 177 men) who were tested twice in 1983–1984. Of these, 111 participants received Inductive Reasoning training, 118 were trained on Spatial Orientation, and 172 were pre- and posttested but did not receive any training. Mean age of the total sample in these analyses was 72.5 years ($SD = 6.41$, range = 64–95 years). Mean educational level was 13.9 years ($SD = 2.98$; range = 6–20 years). The test battery consisted of 16 tests representing multiple markers of the latent constructs of Inductive Reasoning, Spatial Orientation, Perceptual Speed, Numeric Ability, and Verbal Ability (see description of the expanded battery in chapter 2).

We first used the pretest data for the entire sample to select an appropriate factor model. Given that the training analysis classified groups by prior developmental history, we next evaluated the metric invariance of the ability factor structure across the stable and decline groups (see chapter 7). Both groups had equivalent factor loadings and factor intercorrelations [$\chi^3(243, N = 401) = 463.17$; *GFI* stable = .847, *GFI* unstable = .892]. A similar analysis confirmed the acceptability of metric invariance across gender [$\chi^2(243, N = 401) = 466.22$; *GFI* men = .851, *GFI* women = .904]. Finally, metric invariance could be accepted also across the three training conditions [$\chi^2(243, N = 401) = 511.55$; *GFI* Inductive Reasoning = .871, *GFI* Spatial Orientation = .783, controls = .902].

In the main analysis, separate longitudinal factor analyses of the pretest-posttest data were run for each of the training groups. The basic model extended the five-factor model for the pretest data to a repeated measures factor model for the pretest-posttest data. The model also specified correlated residuals to allow test-specific relations across times to provide unbiased estimates of individual differences in the factors (see Hertzog & Schaie, 1986; Sörbom, 1975).

Results Examination of the pretest-posttest factor analysis results for the control group led to the acceptance of metric invariance with an adequate model fit [$\chi^2(412, N = 172) = 574.84$; *GFI* = .833]. Freeing parameters across test occasions did not lead to a significant improvement in fit, thus indicating short-term stability of factor structure and providing a benchmark for the pretest-posttest comparisons of the experimental intervention groups.

The fit of the basic longitudinal factor model for the Inductive Reasoning training group was almost as good as for the controls [$\chi^2(412, N = 111) = 599.00$; *GFI* = .767]. It appeared that most of the difference in model fit could be attributed to subtle shifts in the relative value of factor loadings among the Inductive Reasoning markers; specifically, after training, the Word Series test received a significantly lower loading, whereas the Letter and Number Series tests received higher loadings.

The Spatial Orientation training group had a somewhat lower model fit across occasions [$\chi^2(411, N = 118) = 700.84$; $GFI = .742$]. Again, the reduction in fit was a function of slight changes in factor loading for the markers of the trained ability, with increases in loadings for PMA Space and Alphanumeric Rotation and decrease in the loading for Object Rotation.

In both training groups, the integrity of the trained factor with respect to the other (nontrained) factors remained undisturbed. Indeed, the stability of individual differences on the latent constructs remained extremely high, with the correlations of latent variables from pretest to posttest in excess of .93.

Conclusions   In this study, we first demonstrated that our measurement model for assessing psychometric ability in older adults remained invariant across gender and across subsets of individuals who had remained stable or declined over time. We next demonstrated short-term stability of factor structure (that is, impermeability to practice effects) by demonstrating strong metric invariance of factor structure for a control group. We also demonstrated high stability of the estimates of the latent constructs across test occasions.

The hypothesis of factorial integrity across experimental interventions was next tested separately for the two training groups. In each case, configural invariance was readily demonstrated. However, in each case some improvement of model fit could be obtained by allowing for shifts in the factor loadings for one of the markers of the trained ability. Nevertheless, the stability of the latent constructs also remained above .93 for the trained constructs. Perturbations in the projection of the observed variables on the latent ability factors induced by training were specific to the ability trained, were of small magnitude, and had no significant effect with respect to the relationship between the latent constructs and observed measures for the nontrained abilities. Hence, we provided support for the construct validity of both observed markers and estimates of latent variables in the training studies reported in chapter 7.

Factorial Invariance Within Samples Across Time

The 1991 data collection provided us with complete repeated measurement data on the expanded battery for 984 study participants. These data were therefore used to conduct longitudinal factor analyses within samples across time. We consequently present data on the issue of longitudinal invariance over 7 years for the total sample as well as six age/cohort groups: ages 32 to 39 ($n = 170$), 46 to 53 ($n = 128$), 53 to 60 ($n = 147$), 60 to 67 ($n = 183$), 67 to 74 ($n = 194$), and 76 to 83 ($n = 162$) years (see also Schaie et al., 1998).

Configural Invariance   We first established a baseline model (M1) that showed factor pattern invariance across time and cohort groups, the minimal condition necessary for any comparisons whether they involve cross-sectional or longitudinal data. In this, as in subsequent analyses, the factor variance-covariance matrices (ψ) and the unique variances ($\theta\varepsilon$) are allowed to be estimated freely across time and groups. The model differs from that described in the section on age-comparative analyses (also cf. Schaie et al., 1991) by setting the Word Fluency parameter on Verbal Recall to zero and by adding a gender factor that allows salient loadings for all variables. Given the complexity of this data set, this model showed a reasonably good fit: $\chi^2(3,888, N = 982) = 5,155.71, p < .001$ ($GFI = .81$; Z ratio = 1.33).

Weak Factorial Invariance   Four weak factorial invariance models were tested; the first two were nested in M1. The first model (M2) constrained the factor loadings (λ) equal across time. This is the critical test for the invariance of factor loading within a longitudinal data set. This model resulted in a slight but statistically nonsignificant reduction in fit: $\chi^2(3,990, N = 982) = 5,288.98, p < .001$ ($GFI = .81$; Z ratio = 1.33); $\Delta\chi^2(102) = 133.27, p > .01$. Hence, we concluded that invariance within groups across time can be accepted.

A second model (M3) allowed the values of the factor loadings (λ) to be free across time, but constrained equally across cohort groups. This is the test of factorial invariance for the replicated cross-sectional comparisons across cohorts. The model showed a highly significant reduction in fit compared to M1: $\chi^2(4,258, N = 982) = 5,790.65, p < .001$ ($GFI = .78$; Z ratio = 1.36); $\Delta\chi^2(370) = 634.94, p < .001$. As a consequence, this model must be rejected, and we concluded that there are significant differences in factor loadings across cohorts.

The third model (M4), which is nested in both M2 and M3, constrains the factor loadings (λ) equally across time and group. This particular model, if accepted, would demonstrate factorial invariance both within and across groups. The fit for this model was $\chi^2(4,275, N = 982) = 5,801.09, p < .001$ ($GFI = .78$; Z ratio = 1.36). The reduction in fit was significant in the comparison with M2, $\Delta\chi^2(285) = 512.11, p < .001$, but not significant when compared with M3, $\Delta\chi^2(17) = 10.44, p > .01$. This model provided further confirmation that we can accept time invariance within cohorts but cannot accept invariance across cohort groups.

Before totally rejecting factorial invariance across all cohorts, we also tested a partial invariance model (cf. Byrne et al., 1989) that constrains factor loadings across time and constrains factor loadings across all but the youngest and oldest cohorts (M5). We arrived at this model by examining confidence intervals around individual factors, $\chi^2(4,161, N = 982) = 5,484.20, p < .001$ [$GFI = .81$; Z ratio = 1.30, $\chi^2(171) = 195.22, p < .09$]. Hence, we concluded that this model can be accepted, and that we had demonstrated partial invariance across cohorts. Because we accepted model M5 (invariance across time and partial invariance across groups), we report time-invariant factor loadings separately for Cohorts 1 and 6, as well as a set of loadings for Cohorts 2 to 5 in table 8.9.

When differences in factor loadings between cohorts are examined, it is found that the significant cohort differences are quite localized. No significant differences were found on the Verbal Recall factor. Significant differences on Inductive Reasoning were found for all markers except PMA Reasoning. Significant differences on Spatial Orientation were found for all but the Object Rotation test. Loadings increased with age for Alphanumeric Rotation, but decreased for Cube Comparison. On Perceptual Speed, loadings for Number Comparison decreased

TABLE 8.9 Rescaled Solution for Multigroup Analyses

Factor/Variables	Cohort 1	Cohorts 2–5	Cohort 6
Factor Loadings			
Inductive Reasoning			
PMA Reasoning	.88	.88	.88
ADEPT Letter Series	.67*,†	.85	.98*
Word Series	.94*	.78	.88
Number Series	.62*,†	.72	.73
Spatial Orientation			
PMA Space	.60*,†	.78	.99*
Object Rotation	.82	.82	.82
Alphanumeric Rotation	.79†	.79	.52*
Cube Comparison	.24*,†	.44	.78*
Verbal Comprehension			
PMA Verbal Meaning	.36*,†	.54	.55
ETS Vocabulary	.94*,†	.86	.84
Advanced Vocabulary	.92	.92	.92
Word Fluency	.30	.39	.38
Numeric Facility			
PMA Number	.84	.86	.79*
Addition	.90	.98	.88*
Subtraction and Multiplication	.86	.86	.86
Number Comparison	.37*,†	.20	.12*
Perceptual Speed			
Identical Pictures	.61	.61	.61
Number Comparison	.34†	.49	.78*
Finding A's	.53	.51	.72
Word Fluency	.24	.32	.37
PMA Verbal Meaning	.68*,†	.44	.28
Verbal Memory			
Immediate Recall	.99	.92	.90
Delayed Recall	.87	.87	.87

Note. ADEPT, Adult Development and Enrichment Project; ETS, Educational Testing Service; PMA, Primary Mental Abilities.
*Differs significantly ($p < .01$) from Cohorts 2–5. †Differs significantly ($p < .01$) from Cohort 6 (youngest cohort). Mean ages at T_2: Cohort 1 = 32; Cohorts 2–5 = 46, 53, 60, and 67, respectively; Cohort 6 = 76.

and loadings on Verbal Meaning increased with age. The loading of Verbal Meaning on the Verbal Comprehension factor, in contrast, decreased with age. Finally, there was a significant increase for the loadings of Number Comparison on the Numerical Facility factor.

Implications for the Differentiation-Dedifferentiation Hypothesis   An interesting question long debated in the developmental psychology literature is whether differentiation of ability structure occurs in childhood and adolescence and is followed by dedifferentiation of that structure in old age (see Reinert, 1970; Werner, 1948; also see Schaie, 2000d, for details on using restricted factor analysis to test the hypothesis).

As with the tests of measurement models described in this chapter, we first added the time constraint for the factor variance-covariance matrices to our accepted measurement model (M5). The fit of this model (M6) was $\chi^2(4,287, N = 982) = 5,642.74$, $p < .001$ ($GFI = .80$; Z ratio $= 1.32$). The reduction in fit in the comparison with M5 was not significant [$\Delta\chi^2(126) = 158.51$, $p < .033$]. Hence, we concluded that this model can be accepted, and that we failed to confirm dedifferentiation over a 7-year time period.

Consistent with our earlier strategy in considering partial invariance models, we also tested the analogy of M5 for the variance-covariance differences. That is, we constrained the ψ matrices across time and for Cohorts 2 to 5, but allowed the ψs for Cohorts 1 and 6 to differ. The fit of this model (M7) was $\chi^2(4,535, N = 982) = 5,938.53$, $p < .001$ ($GFI = .79$; Z ratio $= 1.31$). This model is nested in M6. The reduction in fit in the comparison with M9 was significant, $\Delta\chi^2(248) = 295.79$, $p < .01$. This model cannot be accepted, and we concluded that there were significant differences in the factor intercorrelations across some, but not all, cohorts. Table 8.10 provides the factor intercorrelations for the accepted model.

Our findings on changes in covariance structures from young adulthood to old age lend at least partial support for the differentiation-dedifferentiation the-

TABLE 8.10 Factor Intercorrelations and Stabilities for Cohort Groups

	Cohort 1	Cohorts 2–5	Cohort 6
Intercorrelations			
Inductive Reasoning/Spatial Orientation	.64	.58	.57
Inductive Reasoning/Verbal Comprehension	.59	.54	.53
Inductive Reasoning/Numeric Facility	.55	.50	.47
Inductive Reasoning/Perceptual Speed	.79	.73	.71
Inductive Reasoning/Verbal Recall	.44	.39	.38
Spatial Orientation/Verbal Comprehension	.27	.22	.23
Spatial Orientation/Numeric Facility	.38†	.30	.28
Spatial Orientation/Perceptual Speed	.71†	.59	.55
Spatial Orientation/Verbal Recall	.29†	.21	.18
Verbal Comprehension/Numeric Facility	.27	.23	.23
Verbal Comprehension/Perceptual Speed	.40	.34	.34
Verbal Comprehension/Verbal Recall	.48	.42	.41
Numerical Facility/Perceptual Speed	.72	.63	.62
Numerical Facility/Verbal Recall	.26	.20	.19
Perceptual Speed/Verbal Recall	.45	.40	.42
Factor Stabilities			
Inductive Reasoning	.901	.949	.980
Spatial Orientation	.806†	.885	.943
Verbal Comprehension	.930	.990	.990
Numeric Facility	.878	.954	.973
Perceptual Speed	.872†	.907	.999
Verbal Memory	.672	.731	.682

†Differs significantly ($p < .01$) from Cohort 6 (youngest cohort).

ory (figure 8.2). I show magnitudes of intercorrelations for the 1984 and 1991 test occasions for a young adult cohort at ages 29 and 36 years and an old adult cohort at ages 76 and 84 years. Note that factor intercorrelations decreased slightly for 11 of 15 correlations for the young cohort, but increased for all correlations for the old cohort.

Factorial Invariance Across Gender

The 1991 and 1998 data sets described above were further examined to assess the invariance of factor structures across gender and time at various ages (Maitland et al., 2000). For this analysis, the subsets were younger adults (mean age 35.5 years, range 22–49 years; $n = 296$; 134 men, 162 women); middle-aged adults (mean age 56.5 years, range 50–63 years; $n = 330$; 154 men, 202 women); and older adults (mean age 75.5 years, range 64–87; $n = 356$; 154 men, 176 women).

Again, three models were considered. The first tested the hypothesis of time invariance of factor loadings. Next, gender invariance of the factor loadings was tested. Finally, a simultaneous test of invariance between genders and across time was examined.

The configural invariance model (M1), allowed factor loadings to be estimated freely for both gender and occasion [$\chi^2 = 2,328.81(1,296)$, $p < .001$, $GFI = 894$, comparative fit index (CFI) $= .975$]. Model M2 tested invariance across time and constraining factor loadings across occasion and estimated loadings separately for men and women [$\chi^2 = 2,371.03(1330)$, $p < .001$, $GFI = .892$, $CFI = .975$; $\Delta\chi^2 =$

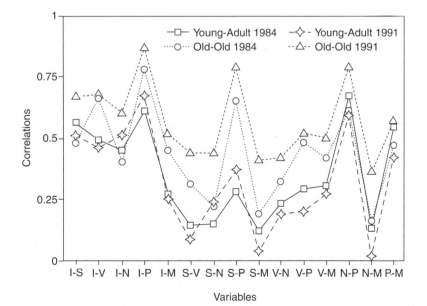

FIGURE 8.2 *Correlations Among the Latent Ability Constructs Across Time for the Youngest and Oldest Cohorts.*

42.21(34), $p > .16$]. The time invariance model did not differ significantly from the configural model. Hence, we accepted the hypothesis of time invariance of factor loadings within gender groups. Model M3 estimated the factor loadings freely across occasion and tested the hypothesis of gender invariance of factor loadings [$\chi^2 = 2,396.18$ (1330), $p < .001$, $GFI = .890$, $CFI = .974$; $\Delta\chi^2 = 67.36(34)$, $p < .001$]. The $\Delta\chi^2$ was significant, and we therefore rejected the hypothesis of gender invariance.

Because time invariance was accepted and gender invariance was not, we evaluated individual gender constraints for all cognitive tests at both time points. The only significant gender difference noted for the 20 cognitive tests was for the Cube Comparison task at T_1 ($z = -4.88$) and at T_2 ($z = -3.78$). Therefore, relaxing the equality constraint for the Cube Comparison test between genders, at both time points, provided our test of partial measurement invariance (M4). This model was compared to the configural measurement model (M1) and had an acceptable fit [$\chi^2 = 2,373.13$ (1328), $p < 0.001$, $GFI = .892$, $CFI = .974$; $\Delta\chi^2 = 44.32$ (32), $p > .07$].

Once we were able to accept the partially invariant model, we could next add the longitudinal equivalence of factor loadings. This partially invariant model (M5) tested the hypothesis of simultaneous invariance of factor loadings between genders and across time [$\chi^2 = 2,390.97$ (1346), $p < .001$, $GFI = .891$, $CFI = .974$; $\Delta\chi^2 = 62.16$ (50), $p > .12$]. This model did not differ significantly and could therefore be accepted; it proved to be the most parsimonious solution (i.e., gender and time invariance for all loadings for the cognitive tasks across 7 years with the exception of gender differences in the Cube Comparison task). Factor loadings and factor correlations for the accepted model may be found in table 8.11.

Conclusions on the Issue of Factorial Invariance

As we expected from the earlier cross-sectional analyses, we could accept invariance of factor patterns, but not of the regression coefficients, across age/cohort groups or across gender. However, gender invariance was restricted to a single cognitive task, and cohort differences were confined primarily to the youngest and oldest cohorts. Within groups, we could accept the stability of the regression weights across time at least over 7 years. These findings strongly suggested greater stability of individual differences within cohorts than across cohorts or gender, and they provided further arguments for the advantages of acquiring longitudinal data sets.

Chapter Summary

This chapter describes some of the methodological studies conducted by secondary analyses of the core data archives or through collateral data collections. The first study examined the consequences of shifting from a sampling-without-replacement paradigm to one that involved sampling with replacement. I concluded that no substantial differences in findings result; hence, the first three data collections

TABLE 8.11 Standardized Factor Loadings and Factor Correlations for the Accepted Partial Invariance Gender Model

Variable	Inductive Reasoning	Spatial Orientation	Verbal Comprehension	Numeric Facility	Perceptual Speed	Verbal Memory
Factor Loadings						
PMA Reasoning	.852					
ADEPT Letter Series	.791					
Word Series	.811					
Number Series	.660					
PMA Space		.796				
Object Rotation		.832				
Alphanumeric Rotation		.800				
Cube Comparison		.500–699[a]				
PMA Verbal Meaning			.455		.563	
ETS Vocabulary			.788			
Advanced Vocabulary			.849			
Word Fluency			.344		.406	
PMA Number				.807		
Addition				.914		
Subtraction and Multiplication				.837		
Identical Pictures					.770	
Number Comparison				.225	.532	
Finding A's					.498	
Immediate Recall						.835
Delayed Recall						.838
Factor Correlations						
Inductive Reasoning	**.963**	.706	.415	.430	.829	.540
Spatial Orientation	.779	**.918**	.170	.264	.727	.383
Verbal Comprehension	.451	.235	**.978**	.229	.184	.344
Numeric Facility	.521	.411	.264	**.940**	.423	.190
Perceptual Speed	.858	.820	.262	.554	**.960**	.562
Verbal Memory	.648	.538	.407	.323	.683	**.791**

Note. Upper triangle contains 1984 factor intercorrelations. Lower triangle contains 1991 factor intercorrelations. Bold values in the diagonal denote factor stabilities.
[a]Cube comparison freely estimated between genders (Female = .500, Male = .699). χ^2 (1,424, Female = 442, Male = 540) = 2,478.83, *GFI* = .89, *CFI* = .97. All factor loadings significant $p < .01$.

using the sampling-without-replacement approach are directly comparable to later studies using the sampling-with-replacement paradigm. The second study investigated the "aging" of tests by comparing the 1949 and 1962 PMA tests. It concluded that there was advantage in retaining the original measures. The third study considered the question of shifts in participant self-selection when changing from a nonpaid to a paid volunteer sample. No selection effects related to participant fees were observed.

A set of secondary analyses is described that dealt with the topic of experimental mortality (participant attrition) and the consequent adjustments needed for our substantive findings. Such adjustments primarily affect level of performance, but not the rate of cognitive aging. Analyses of the effect of practice occurring when the same variables are administered repeatedly showed only slight effects over 7-year intervals, but methods are presented for adjusting for the observed practice effects.

Finally, I consider the issue of structural invariance of the psychometric abilities across cohorts, gender, age, and time. Findings are presented from analyses using restricted (confirmatory) factor analysis to determine the degree of invariance of the regression of the observed variables on the latent constructs of interest in this study. Cross-sectional factor analyses resulted in a demonstration of configural (pattern) invariance, but not of strong metric invariance. These findings implied that factor regressions for young adults and the very old may require differential weighting in age-comparative studies. Another study demonstrated factorial invariance across a cognitive training intervention, confirming that cognitive training results in quantitative change in performance without qualitative shifts in factor structure. Last, I report on longitudinal factor analyses that suggested significant shifts in the variance-covariance matrices, but stability of regression coefficients linking the observed variables and latent constructs over a 7-year period. This study also examined gender equivalence in structure, which was confirmed except for one of our cognitive tasks (Cube Comparison).

CHAPTER NINE

The Relationship Between Cognitive Styles and Intellectual Functioning

THE BASE STUDY THAT LED TO THE SEATTLE Longitudinal Study (SLS) had as its primary objective the test of the hypothesis that differential age changes in abilities might be related to initial status on the dimensions of flexibility-rigidity (see chapter 1). Although the viability of this proposition had to be rejected on the basis of the initial cross-sectional data, we have since returned to this question, utilizing the longitudinal database for a more appropriate set of inquiries than was possible with the original 1956 data (see Schaie, 1958c). Before returning to a further examination of this issue, it is necessary first to determine whether our ability measures and the flexibility-rigidity factors defined by the Test of Behavioral Rigidity (TBR) do indeed represent independent constructs. After confirming this important assumption, we can then turn to the effect of flexible behavior at earlier ages in predicting maintenance of cognitive functioning in old age.

Does Flexibility-Rigidity Represent an Independent Domain?

The original multiple group factor analyses that led to the development of the TBR (Schaie, 1955; see also chapter 4) identified the independence of three latent constructs to account for the individual differences variance in the flexibility-rigidity measures. These measures were then correlated with the five primary mental abilities in our core battery, and, given the moderate positive correlations between the flexibility-rigidity factor scores and the cognitive measures, we assumed that their independence had been empirically demonstrated (Schaie, 1958c). Given the state of the art at the time of these studies, this assumption seemed reasonable. However, modern research practice requires more formal tests. The results of such formal tests were reported by Schaie et al. in 1991 (see also Dutta, 1992) and are summarized here.

Confirmation of the Test of Behavioral Rigidity Factor Structure

The TBR factor structure was reexamined using the data on 1,628 participants (743 men and 885 women) who were examined in the fifth (1984) SLS cycle. The initial model tested was based on the original factor analyses (Schaie, 1955) and was examined using the LISREL procedure (for a description of the TBR subtests, see section on measurement variables in chapter 3). Seven measures were modeled to map on three cognitive style factors: Psychomotor Speed, Motor-Cognitive Flexibility, and Attitudinal Flexibility. Several of the TBR measures represent scores derived from the same subtests; hence, their errors would be expected to correlate. For example, the Capitals test yields a speed score (Cap-NR) and a flexibility score (Cap-R). Similarly, two flexibility scores are derived from the opposites test using different scoring approaches. The four elements in the error matrix corresponding to the correlation among the measures originating from the same source data were freed. The model was first tested on a random half of the total sample and then confirmed on the second random half as well as on the total sample. This model was accepted as having an excellent fit [$\chi^2(7, N = 1,628) = 14.47$, $p < .04$; $GFI = .997$, $RMSR = 1.64$]. The measurement model for the flexibility-rigidity domain can be found in figure 9.1.

Confirmation of the Cognitive Factor Structure

In a similar manner, we also confirmed the factor structure for our expanded battery on the same sample used for the TBR analysis. Here, the initial model

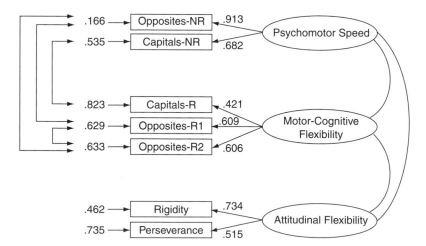

FIGURE 9.1 *Measurement Model for the Test of Behavioral Rigidity.*

was based on prior analyses, but with the addition of a Memory factor (see Schaie et al., 1987, 1989; see also chapter 8). The 20 cognitive measures were modeled as indicators of six oblique factors: Inductive Reasoning, Spatial Orientation, Verbal Ability, Numeric Ability, Perceptual Speed, and Verbal Memory. The original model had good overall fit, but for this particular sample showed stress in the specification of the Word Fluency measure. In addition to its placement on the Memory factor, this measure was therefore allowed to load as well on the Perceptual Speed and Verbal Ability factors. The model was again tested on a random half of the sample, confirmed on the second half, and then reestimated on the total sample $[\chi^2(151, N = 1,628) = 1,144.26, p < .001; GFI = .934, RMSR = 4.09]$. The accepted model was characterized by high and statistically significant loadings of all variables on their associated primary ability factors, as well as high communalities (see figure 9.2 for the resulting measurement model).

Confirmation of Distinct Domains

The hypothesis of distinct cognitive and cognitive style domains was tested by analyzing the combined covariance matrix of the 27 cognitive and flexibility-rigidity measures. An exploratory factor analysis of this matrix suggested that from 8 to 10 factors would be required to explain the total reliable variance. Hence, our first model hypothesized the 9 factors resulting from the separate domain analyses. This model essentially specifies maintenance of the original factor structures when the two batteries are combined. We again estimated this model on a random half, with subsequent confirmation on the second half. The initial estimate suggested a good fit, with comparable parameter estimates to the separate analyses. The initial indices of model fit were $\chi^2(280, N = 814) = 979.33$, $p < .001; GFI = .918; RMSR = 5.1$, for Sample 1, and $\chi^2(280, N = 814) = 1,095.73$, $p < .001; GFI = .909; RMSR = 5.66$ for Sample 2.

Cross-battery interfactor correlations were then examined, and three high correlations were identified. The Psychomotor Speed and Motor-Cognitive Flexibility factors correlated highly with inductive reasoning, and Perceptual Speed correlated highly with Psychomotor Speed. As our exploratory analyses had suggested the plausibility of an eight-factor solution and because the highest interfactor correlations were found between the two speed factors, we next examined a model combining the speed variables into a single factor. However, this model resulted in a significantly worse fit $[\Delta\chi^2(8, N = 814) = 137.29, p < .01$ in Sample 1, and $\Delta\chi^2(8, N = 814) = 121.41, p < .01$ in Sample 2] and was therefore rejected. The accepted total model has a good fit $[\chi^2(280, N = 814) = 1,116.62, p < .001;$ $GFI = .924; RMSR = 5.08]$; it is shown in table 9.1.

We concluded from these studies that rigidity-flexibility does indeed represent a domain of cognitive styles that can be distinguished from the cognitive abilities domain. The question of the reciprocal influence of these two domains first raised at the inception of the SLS (Schaie, 1958c) therefore continues to be of interest and is examined below.

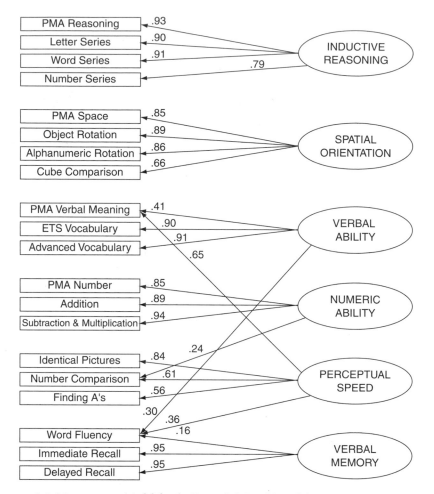

FIGURE 9.2 *Measurement Model for the Expanded Cognitive Ability Battery. ETS, Educational Testing Service; PMA, Primary Mental Abilities.*

Does Rigidity-Flexibility Affect the Maintenance of Intellectual Abilities Into Old Age?

To answer whether rigidity-flexibility affects the maintenance of intellectual abilities into old age, the concurrent relationship between rigidity-flexibility and core ability measures is examined first. Then, the cross-lagged correlations between the two domains is examined to generate hypotheses about the possible causal path between the domains. These relationships were previously examined for the first four study cycles (Schaie, 1983a, 1984b). Data presented here include all seven cycles.

Concurrent Relationships

To obtain the largest possible sample sizes, we aggregated all subjects at first test for the measures in the core battery. Table 9.2 lists correlations for all available ages. It should be noted that there are moderate-to-substantial correlations between Psychomotor Speed and all ability measures. This correlation is highest with Verbal Meaning, Reasoning, and Word Fluency. Motor-Cognitive Flexibility also correlates moderately with all ability measures, with the highest relationship found with Verbal Meaning and Reasoning. Somewhat lower correlations, mostly during midlife, are found between Attitudinal Flexibility and Verbal Meaning, Reasoning, and Word Fluency. Of considerable interest is the finding that, for all three correlates, values of the concurrent correlations typically increase from young adulthood to late midlife, but decline somewhat thereafter. These findings suggest that the reciprocal relationship between intellectual abilities in cognitive styles is particularly salient in midlife.

Predictors of Future Ability Level

From the longitudinal data on the rigidity-flexibility and cognitive ability measures, it is possible to compute cross-lagged correlations that can be used in a cautious test of the time-dependent causal relationships between the two domains. For this purpose, we use the sample first tested in 1956 over 7-, 14-, 21-, 28-, 35-, and 42-year intervals ($N = 302$, 163, 130, 97, 75, and 38, respectively). Again, the measures used are the five primary mental abilities of the core battery and the three cognitive style factor scores. For each of the six time intervals, cross-lags were corrected using Kenny's (1975, 1979) method, and significant differences between cross-lags were computed by the Pearson-Filon test. Table 9.3 shows the cross-lagged correlations for each of the six time periods.

In this sample, we find a number of predictive relationships that differ somewhat, depending on the length of time between the measurement of the predictor and criterion variables. For the 7-year interval, the causal path is from both Motor-Cognitive and Attitudinal Flexibility to the T_2 measure of Verbal Meaning. However, there is also a causal path from reasoning at T_1 to Psychomotor Speed at T_2. These paths are not found for the 14-year interval. Instead Motor-Cognitive Flexibility and Psychomotor Speed have causal paths to the T_3 measure of the Number ability. In addition, Reasoning has causal paths to Attitudinal Flexibility and Psychomotor Speed. Over the 21-year interval, there is a causal path from Motor-Cognitive Flexibility to Word Fluency, as well as a path from Spatial Orientation to Attitudinal Flexibility to Psychomotor Speed at T_4.

Significant paths are found from Spatial Orientation at T_1 to Attitudinal Flexibility at T_5. Also, there are significant paths from Verbal Meaning and Spatial Orientation to Psychomotor Speed. Across the 35-year interval, causal paths are found from Motor-Cognitive Flexibility to Number and Word Fluency and from Attitudinal Flexibility to Word Fluency. In addition, there is a significant path from Reasoning to Motor-Cognitive Flexibility. Finally, there are significant cross-lags over 42 years from Motor-Cognitive Flexibility to Spatial Orientation;

TABLE 9.1 Accepted Solution for the Combined Cognitive Styles and Cognitive Abilities

Variable	Inductive Reasoning	Spatial Orientation	Verbal Comprehension	Numeric Facility	Perceptual Speed	Verbal Memory	Psychomotor Speed	Motor-Cognitive Flexibility	Attitudinal Flexibility	Unique Variance
Factor Loadings										
PMA Reasoning	.933									.130
Letter Series	.900									.190
Word Series	.914									.164
Number Series	.791									.375
PMA Space		.848								.281
Object Rotation		.893								.202
Alphanumeric Rotation		.860								.261
Cube Comparison		.663								.560
PMA Verbal Meaning		.413			.647					.244
ETS Vocabulary			.903							.185
ETS Advanced Vocabulary			.907							.177
PMA Number				.853						.273
Addition				.944						.109
Subtraction/Multiplication				.794						.200
Identical Pictures				.852						.291
Number Comparison				.251	.601					.405
Finding A's					.542					.707

	(1)	(2)	(3)	(4)	(5)	(6)
Word Fluency	.305	.400	.131			.553
Immediate Recall			.950			.097
Delayed Recall			.946			.105
Opposites				.872		.239
Capitals				.721		.481
Capitals-R					.391	.847
Opposites-R1					.626	.608
Opposites-R2					.634	.598
R Scale					.761	.421
P Scale					.496	.754

Factor Intercorrelations

	Spatial Orientation	Verbal Ability	Numeric Ability	Perceptual Speed	Verbal Memory	Psychomotor Speed	Motor-Cognitive Flexibility	Attitudinal Flexibility
Spatial Orientation	.769							
Verbal Ability	.470	.253						
Numeric Ability	.560	.417	.368					
Perceptual Speed	.875	.774	.313	.563				
Verbal Memory	.645	.472	.370	.355	.672			
Psychomotor Speed	.863	.665	.557	.667	.913	.663		
Motor-Cognitive Flexibility	.906	.811	.507	.499	.866	.637	.840	
Attitudinal Flexibility	.546	.418	.423	.255	.531	.454	.553	.597

Note. ETS, Educational Testing Service; PMA, Primary Mental Abilities.

TABLE 9.2 Concurrent Correlations Between the Cognitive Style and Intellectual Ability Measures at First Test

Age	n	Verbal Meaning	Spatial Orientation	Reasoning	Number	Word Fluency
Motor-Cognitive Flexibility						
25	486	.16**	.29**	.26**	.12*	.17**
32	512	.20**	.23**	.33**	.15**	.16**
39	632	.35**	.27**	.41**	.13**	.26**
46	649	.50**	.29**	.48**	.27**	.36**
53	630	.43**	.31**	.48**	.28**	.23**
60	615	.46**	.29**	.49**	.31**	.31**
67	671	.51**	.33**	.53**	.27**	.33**
74	468	.45**	.29**	.42**	.32**	.36**
81	287	.39**	.27**	.44**	.29**	.12
All	4,952	.52**	.44**	.58**	.30**	.38**
Attitudinal Flexibility						
25	472	.25**	.09	.21**	.06	.10
32	506	.24**	.09	.18**	.05	.10
39	626	.28**	.14**	.22**	.03	.16**
46	642	.38**	.07	.28**	.06	.23**
53	627	.34**	.21**	.33**	.12*	.25**
60	612	.32**	.12*	.30**	.12*	.28**
67	670	.36**	.17**	.33**	.15**	.19**
74	466	.33**	.10	.34**	.23**	.21**
81	284	.30**	.11	.19**	.15*	.15*
All	4,905	.41**	.26**	.39**	.16**	.29**
Psychomotor Speed						
25	488	.52**	.21**	.56**	.33**	.50**
32	512	.44**	.15**	.48**	.14**	.38**
39	635	.49**	.14**	.55**	.18**	.39**
46	649	.62**	.21**	.60**	.23**	.40**
53	632	.66**	.24**	.64**	.33**	.47**
60	615	.66**	.26**	.61**	.39**	.45**
67	673	.68**	.31**	.64**	.44**	.50**
74	470	.68**	.25**	.61**	.46**	.52**
81	288	.64**	.22**	.59**	.50**	.50**
All	4,962	.68**	.40**	.69**	.36**	.54**

*$p < .01$. **$p < .001$.

from Attitudinal Flexibility to Number and Word Fluency; from Psychomotor Speed to Verbal Meaning, Number, and Word Fluency; and from Reasoning to Motor-Cognitive Flexibility.

One of the difficulties in interpreting these analyses is the successive attrition of the long-term sample, so that sample sizes may be too small to stable cross-lags. However, most of the causal paths clearly lead from the cognitive style measures to the intellectual abilities.

TABLE 9.3 Cross-Lagged Correlations Between the Cognitive Style and Intellectual Ability Variables

	Motor-Cognitive Flexibility	Attitudinal Flexibility	Psychomotor Speed
Over 7 Years (1956–1970) (N = 302)			
	1956	1956	1956
Verbal Meaning 1963	.49*	.42*	.58
Spatial Orientation 1963	.42	.26	.25
Reasoning 1963	.52	.29	.54
Number 1963	.31	.20	.45
Word Fluency 1963	.39	.33	.49
	1963	1963	1963
Verbal Meaning 1956	.37	.43	.66
Spatial Orientation 1956	.35	.20	.34
Reasoning 1956	.45	.42	.68*
Number 1956	.28	.16	.44
Word Fluency 1956	.27	.32	.53
Over 14 Years (1956–1970) (N = 163)			
	1956	1956	1956
Verbal Meaning 1970	.41	.31	.53
Spatial Orientation 1970	.37	.19	.21
Reasoning 1970	.46	.24	.45
Number 1970	.29*	.17	.50*
Word Fluency 1970	.29	.29	.46
	1970	1970	1970
Verbal Meaning 1956	.47	.38	.61
Spatial Orientation 1956	.31	.14	.31
Reasoning 1956	.49	.40*	.60*
Number 1956	.21	.16	.42
Word Fluency 1956	.33	.29	.42
Over 21 Years (1956–1977) (N = 130)			
	1956	1956	1956
Verbal Meaning 1977	.35	.32	.56
Space 1977	.30	.16	.22
Reasoning 1977	.37	.32	.44
Number 1977	.23	.13	.51
Word Fluency 1977	.25*	.31	.45

(*continued*)

TABLE 9.3 Continued

	Motor-Cognitive Flexibility	Attitudinal Flexibility	Psychomotor Speed
Over 21 Years (1956–1977) (N = 130)			
	1977	1977	1977
Verbal Meaning 1956	.32	.41	.68
Space 1956	.25	.21	.30
Reasoning 1956	.44	.35	.57*
Number 1956	.27	.12	.46
Word Fluency 1956	.16	.35	.43
Over 28 Years (1956–1984) (N = 97)			
	1956	1956	1956
Verbal Meaning 1984	.33	.41	.38
Spatial Orientation 1984	.37	.32*	.21
Reasoning 1984	.41	.25	.37
Number 1984	.28	.14	.36
Word Fluency 1984	.18	.34	.36
	1984	1984	1984
Verbal Meaning 1956	.31	.39	.57*
Spatial Orientation 1956	.40	.17	.41*
Reasoning 1956	.40	.34	.51
Number 1956	.23	.12	.49
Word Fluency 1956	.19	.26	.39
Over 35 Years (1956–1991) (N = 75)			
	1956	1956	1956
Verbal Meaning 1991	.32	.36	.45
Space 1991	.44	.20	.04
Reasoning 1991	.31	.32	.34
Number 1991	.33*	.19	.36
Word Fluency 1991	.17*	.39*	.31
	1991	1991	1991
Verbal Meaning 1956	.26	.36	.42
Space 1956	.39	.10	.18
Reasoning 1956	.48*	.39	.44
Number 1956	.07	.00	.28
Word Fluency 1956	−.10	.18	.30

TABLE 9.3 Continued

	Motor-Cognitive Flexibility	Attitudinal Flexibility	Psychomotor Speed
Over 42 Years (1956–1998) (N = 38)			
	1956	1956	1956
Verbal Meaning 1998	.11	.39	.49*
Spatial Orientation 1998	.43*	.16	.22
Reasoning 1998	.27	.26	.45
Number 1998	.28	.19*	.53*
Word Fluency 1998	.19	.38*	.33*
	1998	1998	1998
Verbal Meaning 1956	.17	.16	.33
Spatial Orientation 1956	.26	.04	.10
Reasoning 1956	.48*	.31	.36
Number 1956	.18	−.26	.29
Word Fluency 1956	.01	−.14	−.06

*$p < .05$. Cross-lags followed by asterisks are significantly greater than their falsifications.

Relationships Between the Latent Ability Constructs and the Cognitive Style Measures

Of interest also is a repetition of these analyses for the relationship of the cognitive styles and the latent cognitive ability measures. The latter data are available only for the 1984, 1991, and 1998 cycles.

Concurrent Relationships

The relevant correlations are provided in table 9.4. For Motor-Cognitive Flexibility, the strongest concurrent relationships are shown with Inductive Reasoning, Perceptual Speed, and Spatial Orientation; Attitudinal Flexibility has modest correlations with all ability factors except Numeric Ability. There are substantial correlations for Psychomotor Speed with all ability factors; these are strongest for Perceptual Speed and Inductive Reasoning and weakest with Numeric and Verbal Abilities. The concurrent correlations for the factor scores follow the age pattern described in the preceding section. They are fairly weak in young adulthood and increase with advancing age.

Predictors of Future Ability Level

The 7- and 14-year cross-lags are available for those study participants for whom latent ability construct scores are available in both 1984 and 1991 as well as the

TABLE 9.4 Concurrent Correlations Between the Cognitive Style and Intellectual Ability Latent Construct Measures

Age	n	Inductive Reasoning	Spatial Orientation	Perceptual Speed	Numeric Ability	Verbal Ability	Verbal Memory
Motor-Cognitive Flexibility							
25	184	.25**	.21*	.15	.12	.17	.24**
32	220	.42**	.37*	.26**	.25*	.25**	.19*
39	305	.37**	.38**	.24**	.22**	.20**	.04
46	362	.48**	.33**	.46**	.31**	.28**	.20**
53	354	.44**	.32**	.39**	.26**	.37**	.16**
60	405	.47**	.35**	.38**	.26**	.35**	.25**
67	481	.48**	.38**	.32**	.27**	.37**	.19**
74	399	.48**	.36**	.40**	.25*	.40**	.25**
81	260	.42**	.28**	.31**	.28**	.39**	.25**
All	2,970	.62**	.55**	.56**	.30**	.32**	.43**
Attitudinal Flexibility							
25	166	.19	−.01	.11	.06	.14	.18
32	211	.26**	.11	.19*	.08	.39**	.32**
39	297	.17*	.06	.22**	.10	.28**	.13
46	356	.13	.04	.12	.10	.22**	.13
53	347	.28**	.17*	.25**	.09	.24**	.15*
60	399	.14*	.06	.15*	.05	.26**	.25**
67	475	.23**	.14*	.18**	.07	.27**	.20**
74	392	.26**	.08	.22**	.14*	.33**	.18*
81	250	.28**	.21**	.33**	.24**	.42**	.26**
All	2,893	.37**	.28**	.36**	.15**	.30**	.33**
Psychomotor Speed							
25	184	.47**	.24**	.64**	.45**	.26**	.52**
32	221	.47**	.26**	.58**	.32**	.35**	.36**
39	308	.36**	.14*	.50**	.33**	.30**	.34**
46	365	.46**	.28**	.56**	.40**	.47**	.42**
53	359	.54**	.18**	.65**	.43**	.50**	.37**
60	409	.49**	.26**	.64**	.41**	.50**	.39**
67	481	.62**	.38**	.68**	.54**	.52**	.42**
74	399	.62**	.31**	.70**	.47**	.54**	.43**
81	260	.57**	.47**	.73**	.65**	.57**	.45**
All	2,986	.70**	.53**	.77**	.45**	.41**	.59**

*p < .01. **p < .001.

subset that was retested in 1998. These cross-lags are shown in table 9.5. Cross-lag differences significant at or beyond the 1% level of confidence occur for all three cognitive style measures from T_1 to the latent construct measure of Numeric Ability in 1991. However, we also found significantly larger cross-lags from the Inductive Reasoning and Perceptual Speed factor score at T_1 to Psychomotor Speed in 1991.

TABLE 9.5 Cross-Lagged Correlations Between the Cognitive Style
and Intellectual Ability Latent Factor Scores

	Motor-Cognitive Flexibility	Attitudinal Flexibility	Psychomotor Speed
Over 7 Years (1984–1991) (N = 1,121)			
	1984	1984	1984
Inductive Reasoning 1991	.59	.33	.60
Spatial Orientation 1991	.52	.25	.40
Perceptual Speed 1991	.54	.33	.66
Numeric Facility 1991	.33*	.19*	.50*
Verbal Comprehension 1991	.35	.26	.43
Verbal Memory 1991	.42	.32	.49
	1991	1991	1991
Inductive Reasoning 1984	.61	.31	.69*
Spatial Orientation 1984	.51	.27	.48
Perceptual Speed 1984	.51	.33	.77*
Numeric Facility 1984	.23	.07	.42
Verbal Comprehension 1984	.30	.21	.42
Verbal Memory 1984	.39	.28	.54
Over 14 Years (1984–1998) (N = 713)			
	1984	1984	1984
Inductive Reasoning 1998	.52	.29	.55
Spatial Orientation 1998	.44	.17	.31
Perceptual Speed 1998	.45	.25	.56
Numeric Facility 1998	.31	.14	.46*
Verbal Comprehension 1998	.33	.24	.48*
Verbal Memory 1998	.28	.27	.41
	1998	1998	1998
Inductive Reasoning 1984	.55	.32	.60
Spatial Orientation 1984	.45	.23	.38
Perceptual Speed 1984	.45	.35	.67*
Numeric Facility 1984	.42	.01	.35
Verbal Comprehension 1984	.32	.22	.34
Verbal Memory 1984	.31	.28	.47

$*p < .01$. Cross-lags followed by asterisks are significantly greater than their falsifications.

Over the 14-year period, significant cross-lags were found from Psychomotor Speed at T_1 to Numeric and Verbal Ability at T_3. In the opposite direction, there was a significant cross-lag from Perceptual Speed at T_1 to Psychomotor Speed at T_3.

Chapter Summary

In this chapter, we first present evidence on the distinctiveness of the cognitive styles of Motor-Cognitive Flexibility, Attitudinal Flexibility, and Psychomotor Speed from the domain of psychometric intelligence as measured in the SLS. Results of separate and joint factor analyses for the three cognitive style and six psychometric ability constructs leads us to conclude that these domains are indeed separate.

We next consider the concurrent and predictive relationships for the two domains utilizing the cognitive style and core battery primary mental ability variables over 7, 14, 21, 28, 35, and 42 years. We conclude that the concurrent relationships increase into young old age and then decline again. We also examine similar data for the latent ability constructs over 7- and 14-year periods.

The predictive direction was identified to lead from the cognitive style measures to the ability measures of Verbal Meaning, Number, and Word Fluency in the core battery and to the latent construct measures of Verbal and Numeric Ability. However, there are inconsistencies over different time intervals, and occasional paths in the core battery from Verbal Meaning to Psychomotor Speed and from Reasoning to Motor-Cognitive Flexibility are found.

For the latent constructs, causal paths are identified from the measures of cognitive style to Numeric Ability over 7 and 14 years and from Psychomotor Speed to Verbal Ability over 14 years. However, there are also significant cross-lags from Inductive Reasoning and Perceptual Speed to Psychomotor Speed.

CHAPTER TEN

Health and Maintenance
of Intellectual Functioning

A N EXAMINATION OF ANTECEDENTS of individual differences in the maintenance or decline of intellectual functioning would surely begin by inquiring into the impact of health on cognition. As shown here, however, it does not necessarily follow that the relationship between health and intellectual functioning is unidirectional. Reviews of the literature (see Elias, Elias, & Elias, 1990; Siegler, 1988) suggest that the relationship indeed may be reciprocal: a healthy body facilitating intellectual competence, and competent behavior facilitating the maintenance of health. In this chapter, I consider both. I first report our efforts to assess health histories in a manner suitable for relating them to behavioral development. Second, I consider the diseases that seem to affect the maintenance of cognitive functions. Third, I describe our work on the study of health behaviors. Finally, I return to the role of intellectual functioning as a predictor of physical health, as a predictor of medication use, and as a possible early indicator of impending mortality.

The Analysis of Health Histories

One of the interesting aspects of our panel of study participants is the fact that all panel members, during their time of participation in our study, received all of their health care (with the rare exception of emergency procedures when away from home) from the health maintenance organization (HMO) that forms the base of our sampling frame. Virtually complete records are therefore available on the frequency and kinds of illnesses requiring medical care, as well as anecdotal records of treatment history. Subsequent to the third study cycle, we were finally able to obtain the necessary resources to take advantage of the existence of these records for our study participants (Schaie, 1973a). We have worked intensively with the medical and research staff of the HMO to develop procedures designed to quantify the health records of our panel in such a way that it is possible to index them in terms of both the age of the individual and the points in time when incidents of ill health occurred.

We soon discovered that, although most physicians generate voluminous medical histories, only a few have experience or interest in retrieving data from such histories, particularly in a form that lends itself to research. At the time we became interested in this problem, a number of formal ways existed to code medical data. We elected to use the American version of the international system sponsored by the World Health Organization (U.S. Public Health Service, 1968). Unfortunately, as others interested in abstracting from medical records (e.g., Hurtado & Greenlick, 1971) have found, it is quite difficult to relate descriptive disease categories to individual outcome parameters. To do so requires the specialized services of medical record librarians, who must detect and decipher the information required for such coding.

Incidents and Episodes

If there is interest in relating medical histories to outcomes of a nonmedical nature, moreover, concern must also be given to the issue of incidents and episodes of medical care in addition to simply recording diagnostic entries. Such an approach was first used by Solon and associates (Solon, Feeney, Jones, Rigg, & Sheps, 1967; Solon et al., 1969). For our purposes, we decided to code data for our panel members with respect to incidents of a given disease condition and to apply the episode or "spell of illness" approach.

Severity Ratings

If there is concern with the impact of disease on behavior, we must also deal with the relative significance of a particular diagnostic condition as it affects the life of the person experiencing that condition. That is, we would like to assign a "severity" weight to particular diagnostic entities. A special study was therefore conducted to obtain such weights (Parham, Gribbin, Hertzog, & Schaie, 1975).

In this study, the health records for 150 participants were coded for a 14-year period. Although the eighth edition of the *International Classification of Diseases* (ICDA-8; U.S. Public Health Service, 1968) contains over 8,000 disease classifications, only about 820 were actually encountered in our sample. By collapsing and overlapping categories, we further reduced this number to 448 of the most frequently occurring classifications. Then, 12 physicians Q-sorted these classifications on an 11-point severity scale ranging from benign to extremely severe. The physicians were asked to rate severity according to the long-range impact of the particular disease on the general health and well-being of the patient. The 448 categories were divided into four decks of 112 cards each, on which the disease name and a brief description were typed. Each physician Q-sorted two of these decks; a total of four physicians sorted each deck. Interrater reliabilities for the disease severity ratings ranged from .82 to .90. Average weights were then computed, and these severity weights were used in some of the analyses described in this chapter.

Computerized Approaches and Changes in Coding Methods

Fortunately, our collaborating HMO shifted to an automated patient record systems shortly after our sixth data collection. This means that future analyses related to health and disease will be able to benefit from the use of computerized databases; our manual coding utilized ICDA Version 8, and the automated coding utilizes ICDA Version 9. Although no simple transformation programs have been available to us, it turns out that this is not a major problem for our analyses because our data aggregations utilize primarily the first two digits of the diagnostic code, which remain similar across versions.

Age and Health Histories

Before discussing our data, I first must consider how a disease model can be related to the study of cognitive aging. A model then is explicated that might explain the complex relationship between health breakdown and decline in cognitive functioning.

How Meaningful Is the Disease Model?

I begin by raising the question whether it is reasonable to expect a direct relationship between raw indices of disease diagnoses (or incidence of medical care) and behavioral outcomes (e.g., Wilkie & Eisdorfer, 1973). I follow here the lead of Aaron Antonovsky, who has addressed this question in some detail. He held that the social or behavioral scientist dealing with the consequences of physical illness should not be concerned with the particular physiological dimensions involved in a disease, but should rather address the behavioral and social consequences embedded in the concept of "breakdown."

More specifically, Antonovsky (1972) argued that there are basically four dimensions of breakdown that deserve attention. First, a disease may or may not be directly painful to the individual; second, it may or may not handicap individuals in the exercise of their faculties or performance of social roles; third, it can be characterized along the dimension of acuteness-chronicity with respect to its possible threat to life; and fourth, it is or is not recognized by society's medical institutions as requiring care under the direction of such institutions.

A very similar system of classification can be suggested with respect to the impact a particular disease may have on cognitive functions, particularly if medical histories are reclassified in terms of the degree of breakdown presented therein rather than in terms of the specific disease represented by the history.

Although we must pursue the impact of specific diseases on behavior, we should also be conscious of the possibility that it may not be fruitful to insist on a direct connection between specific diseases and behavior. It would therefore be better to organize information on illness and the utilization of medical care in terms of more psychologically meaningful organizing principles, such as the concept of breakdown. Such an approach would reduce the conceptual dilemma of having to distinguish between the contribution of the actual disease process and the manner in which the individual responds to the disease condition. It is often the latter that may be the more direct mediator of the behavioral consequences, at least at the macrolevel most easily accessible to observation and analysis.

Health Breakdown and Cognitive Functioning

Given the methods of coding described in this chapter concerning the analysis of disease histories (as well as modification of these methods for application to computerized data), we can first study the impact of specific diseases in relation to cognitive change. Next, the cumulative impact of health trauma can also be charted in at least two ways. First, a cumulative index of physical health breakdown can be assigned, which is simply the summation of all incidents observed as weighted by their impact on the life of each study participant. Second, we can graph the average level of breakdown at each measurement point for which behavioral data are available and relate the slope of physical health states to the slope of observed cognitive change.

Throughout these analyses, it is just as necessary as it was with the cognitive data to be concerned with the effects of cohort differences in the utilization of medical care as well as with the tendency of previous episodes of ill health to elicit different patterns of subsequent ill health than would be true if the occurrence of health breakdown were the first. Fortunately, our system of data acquisition permits a reasonable modicum of controls.

Diseases That Affect Maintenance of Cognitive Functioning

The first two analyses bearing on the question of how disease might affect cognitive functioning involved relatively small data sets. The first focused on the relation of cardiovascular disease (CVD) and maintenance of intellectual functioning; the second attempted to include a somewhat broader spectrum of diseases.

Cardiovascular Disease and Intelligence

In our first effort to chart the relationship between CVD and maintenance of cognitive functioning systematically (Hertzog et al., 1978), we studied the health records of 156 study participants tested in 1956 and 1963, of whom 86 also participated in the 1970 testing. For this study, participants were classified as having the diagnoses of hypertension, atherosclerosis (constriction of arterial pathways by fatty deposits), hypertension and atherosclerosis, cerebrovascular disease, miscellaneous CVD, and benign CVD or as having no evidence of CVD.

After exclusion of participants who had only hypertension and those with benign CVD, the remaining participants with CVD were then compared with those without CVD. It was first noted that there was an excess of persons with CVD among the dropouts at the 1970 test occasions, thus making CVD a major factor in experimental mortality (see chapter 8). The CVD dichotomy was then related by analyses of variance to the maintenance of intellectual performance over time.

Significant main effects favoring the participants without CVD were found for Verbal Meaning, Inductive Reasoning, Number, and the composite indices, as well as Motor-Cognitive Flexibility. However, an increase in the additional risk over time was found only for Psychomotor Speed. Breaking down CVD into subgroups, greater risk for those affected over time occurred for those with atherosclerosis and cerebrovascular disease for the Space and Number tests as well as for the composite IQ and the Psychomotor Speed measure. However, those with hypertension without other manifestations of CVD actually improved over time.

Application of Structural Equations Methods to the Study of Relationships Between Disease and Cognition

The next set of analyses of the health data was conducted for a doctoral dissertation by Stone (1980). She examined a sample of 253 participants for whom psychological and health data were available at three time points: 1963, 1970, and 1977. Disease codes were aggregated into 16 systemic categories, of which 11 were sufficiently well represented to warrant investigation. These were as follows:

1. Diseases of the blood and blood-forming organs
2. Diseases of the circulatory system
3. Endocrine, nutritional, and metabolic disorders
4. Diseases of the digestive system
5. Diseases of the genitourinary system
6. Infectious diseases
7. Diseases of the musculoskeletal system and of connective tissues
8. Diseases of the skin and subcutaneous tissues
9. Neoplasms
10. Diseases of the nervous system
11. Diseases of the respiratory system.

Structural models were examined to link illness variables to Primary Mental Abilities (PMA) performance. Because there was little covariation among disease entities, separate structural models were tested for those categories that were well represented for all three time periods. Three of the concatenated disease categories listed in this section appeared to be significant predictors of time-related change in intellectual functioning: circulatory disorders, neoplasms, and musculoskeletal disorders. However, when the sample was divided by age into halves (35 to 58 and 59 to 87 years at T_3), the relationship held for both age groups only for circulatory disease, and the other two variables were significant only in the older group. Interestingly, there was an unexpected positive relationship between diagnosed neoplasms at T_2 and intelligence at T_3. It might be speculated that the more able persons were more likely to seek earlier diagnosis and had better opportunities for effective treatment, thus increasing their survival rate. Another possible problem with the findings was the failure to disaggregate diagnoses of neoplasms into malignant and benign types (see next section).

More Comprehensive Analyses of the Effects of Disease on Cognition

Our most complete analysis of the prevalence of disease and its impact on cognitive functioning thus far was conducted as part of the dissertation research of Ann Gruber-Baldini (1991a) for a sample of 845 participants for whom data were available through the completion of the fifth cycle (1984). These participants entered and departed the Seattle Longitudinal Study (SLS) at various measurement points (1956, 1963, 1970, 1977), but all had at least two points of measurement. Analyses either organized data by age at testing or utilized the 1970–1977 period, for which most of the participants had complete data.

Disease Occurrence

One goal of this analysis was to utilize the data from the HMO medical records to assess patterns of disease occurrence, prevalence and incidence of diseases, comorbidity of chronic disease conditions, and the progression and complications of disease categories (Gruber-Baldini, 1991b). Findings from HMO records were comparable to rates in other studies using self-report methods. Diseases increased in prevalence, incidence (except for neoplasms), and comorbidity with age. Arthritis was the most prevalent condition, followed by vision problems, neoplasms, and hypertension. Differences were found in rates of disease occurrence for men and women and in rates across time periods. Women had higher rates of arthritis, benign CVD, benign neoplasms, essential hypertension, osteoporosis and hip fractures, and depression. Males had higher frequency of more serious conditions (in terms of risk of mortality), such as atherosclerosis, cerebrovascular disease, and malignant neoplasms. The number of physician contacts and hospital days was more frequent in the latest measurement period, whereas the average number of chronic conditions in the sample peaked during the period from 1964 to 1970.

Rates of chronic conditions varied by time of measurement as well as age. Overall, arthritis, benign CVD, neoplasms, and osteoporosis peaked from 1957 to 1963 (the first measurement period), but all others peaked from 1970 to 1977. Rates from 1977 to 1984 appear to be lower than for other periods for arthritis, vision problems, and benign CVD. This period had lower rates of conditions even when rates were examined only for the age range 60 to 67 years. However, participants with data from 1977 to 1984 were members of a training study in the SLS and may have been a more select sample because they were able to undergo five 1-hour sessions of cognitive training (see chapter 7). Also, differences because of cohort effects in risk factors associated with medical utilization were confounded with time of measurement.

Average age of disease onset occurred after 50 years for all chronic conditions. Rheumatoid arthritis, benign CVD, and nonmalignant neoplasms have earlier disease onset; osteoarthritis, atherosclerosis, cerebrovascular disease, and malignant neoplasms have average onset after age 60 years.

Impact of Diseases on Cognitive Functioning

The impact of diseases on cognitive functioning was examined longitudinally by three sets of analyses (Gruber-Baldini, 1991a). The first included logistic regression and event history analyses predictors for the occurrence of and age at onset of significant cognitive decline. The second used latent growth curve models (LGMs; McArdle & Anderson, 1990; McArdle & Hamagami, 1991) to examine longitudinal patterns of PMA functioning from ages 53 to 60 years. The third examined a LISREL (linear structural relations) path model for the direct effects of diseases on cognitive level and change and for indirect effects on level and change through measures of inactive lifestyle (leisure activities and an obesity measure).

Overall Health   Prior research suggested that ratings of poor overall health predict lowered cognitive functioning. In the current study, measures of the number of chronic conditions, total number of physician visits, and number of hospital days were examined. The number of chronic conditions had negative influences on cognitive level for Verbal Meaning, Number, and Word Fluency and predicted greater decline on Verbal Meaning and Number. However, the age of experiencing significant decline occurred later for persons with more chronic conditions on Number and Word Fluency. A greater number of physician visits predicted an increased hazard of cognitive decline for Reasoning and a later age of onset of decline for number. Physician visits were positively correlated with arthritis episodes, and arthritis was predictive of lower cognitive level on a number of the PMA measures. Hospitalization had no significant impact on PMA functioning except that it was positively correlated with number of physician visits, number of chronic conditions, and number of episodes for some chronic diseases (especially arthritis), all of which were predictive of PMA performance.

Cardiovascular Disease   Research on the relation of specific diseases and cognitive functioning has focused mostly on CVD, particularly on hypertension. This research has found mixed results with respect to the direction of influence of hypertension on cognition. Most studies in the literature suggested that more severe CVD (atherosclerosis, cerebrovascular disease, etc.) has a negative impact on cognitive functioning. However, much of the prior research was cross-sectional. Longitudinal studies in this area have often involved small samples, have included a limited number of testing occasions (i.e., fewer than three points), have failed to compare hypertension groups with groups with more severe CVD, and did not have information on cognitive functioning prior to disease onset.

In the analyses summarized here, multiple CVD groups were examined for the influence of the disease on cognitive functioning. Results suggest that atherosclerosis is associated with lower cognitive functioning and greater decline on Space and Number. LGM results suggest, however, that less decline occurred for Verbal Meaning in people with atherosclerosis; the decline occurred after the age of 60 years and resulted in little level difference at age 81 years in groups with and without atherosclerosis. Cerebrovascular disease was also negatively associated with cognitive level and increased the risk of and amount of cognitive decline (although the age of onset of significant decline was later than average for Spatial Orientation in the event history analyses).

The LGM results suggest that hypertensives with other CVD complications performed worse over time than uncomplicated hypertensives and normotensives. Noncomplicated hypertensives had higher performances and less decline than complicated hypertensives and normotensives. The total number of hypertension episodes predicted increased hazard of significant decline and overall level on Word Fluency, but significantly later decline onset for Spatial Orientation and Reasoning. Also, hypertension was the only significant disease predictor for people under the age of 60 years in the path models (again predicting lower performance and negative change over time for Word Fluency). Miscellaneous CVD predicted earlier decline on Word Fluency. Results from logistic and event history models suggest that miscellaneous CVD predicted less decline and later onset on Spatial Orientation. However, miscellaneous CVD also indirectly predicted (through leisure activities involving phone calls, game playing, and daydreaming) decreased Spatial Orientation level and change over time. Persons with miscellaneous CVD also performed at lower levels on reasoning from ages 53 to 81 years, although their onset of decline was later than for people free of miscellaneous CVD. Benign CVD was associated with a lower rate of cognitive decline.

Thus, the more serious CVD conditions (atherosclerosis and cerebrovascular disease) have generally negative influences, and benign CVD has more positive influences on cognition. Miscellaneous CVD and hypertension appear to fall between serious and benign CVD, with uncomplicated hypertensives maintaining higher cognitive functioning. Studies are needed to confirm the differences between CVD groups on a different longitudinal sample.

Diabetes   Studies on the influence of diabetes have shown a negative impact of diabetes on functioning. However, these studies have also been cross-sectional and did not screen subjects for complications from other chronic diseases. We had available only a limited number of diabetics ($n = 51$) and thus were not able to examine the longitudinal pattern of functioning for this group by LGM analyses. However, other types of analysis showed that diabetes had an indirect positive effect on Inductive Reasoning level and longitudinal change (mediated via the measure of body mass index). It is conceivable again that long-term survivors like those included in our study who are functioning at high intellectual levels may be able to manage their chronic conditions more adequately. These findings contradict prior findings and need to be replicated.

Arthritis   Only a few prior studies have examined the influence of arthritis on cognitive functioning, despite the high prevalence of this disease among the aged. Results from the LGM analyses suggest that arthritics have lower functioning and greater decline on Verbal Meaning, Spatial Orientation, and Inductive Reasoning. Logistic regression results, however, found that arthritis presented a lower proportional hazard of decline for Spatial Orientation and later average onset of significant decline on Verbal Meaning, Spatial Orientation, and Reasoning. Also, LISREL path models showed that arthritis had a direct negative effect on Spatial Orientation level and change from 1970 to 1977, and an indirect negative effect (through diversity of leisure activities) on Number and Word Fluency levels and change (less decline). Dividing arthritics by age of occurrence, LGM results indicate that persons who developed arthritis after the age of 60 years had lower levels and experienced greater decline on Verbal Meaning. However, persons with arthritis before age 60 years had lower levels and greater decline on Inductive Reasoning. A mixed pattern resulted for Spatial Orientation, with arthritics before age 60 years experiencing greater decline, whereas the post-60 years group had lower overall levels of functioning by age 81 years. Future studies may need to examine longitudinally the separate effects of rheumatoid arthritis and osteoarthritis—subdiagnoses of arthritis that differ by age of diagnosis—on cognition to clarify the results of arthritis influences on cognitive level and cognitive change.

Neoplasms   In prior research on neoplasms, Stone (1980) found positive effects of neoplasms on cognitive performance in the SLS, but used a global measure of neoplasms (the entire ICDA category). The analyses described here employed more specific categories, considering differences between malignant and benign neoplasms and between skin (the most frequent neoplasms) and other neoplasms. Results suggest that the positive effects found by Stone might be caused by the large frequency of benign neoplasms in the neoplasms category. Benign neoplasms (not skin) were found to produce earlier onset of decline, but less overall decline. Malignant neoplasms and benign skin neoplasms had indirect (through activity factors) negative influences on performance. Results of the influence of neoplasms on cognition might be specific to combinations of type (malignant versus nonmalignant) and location (skin, bone, etc.). Small subsample sizes again limit detailed examination of these effects.

Other Chronic Conditions   Other conditions found to be related to cognitive functioning included osteoporosis and hip fractures and sensory problems. Osteoporosis and hip fractures were predictive of earlier decline on Word Fluency. Hearing impairment was associated with an increased risk of experiencing Verbal Meaning decline, but was associated with better performance and later decline on Space. Vision difficulties predicted later age at onset of decline for Verbal Meaning and Space.

The Study of Health Behaviors

There is wide agreement that healthy lifestyles are important with regard to the onset of disease, the prevention of disability, and mortality. In 1993, we began to develop a health behavior questionnaire (HBQ), which was first administered as a mail questionnaire and subsequently was administered as part of the 1996 family study as well as the 1998 cycle of the SLS. A number of investigations have been concerned with the attempt to dimensionalize the questionnaire empirically by factor analysis (Maier, 1995), to study the invariance of the resulting dimension across time and different groups (Maitland, 1997), and to investigate some possible antecedents of positive health behaviors (Maier, 1995; Zanjani, 2002). Some of this work is summarized in this section.

Dimensions of Health Behaviors

The first question we raised was whether separate health practices can be aggregated into more general categories. We asked whether there is an overall positive health orientation or healthy lifestyle that results in the adoption of fairly global health behaviors (Maier, 1995). Health behavior theorists hold diverging opinions on the validity of a "healthy lifestyle" hypothesis. Some subscribe to this hypothesis by arguing that "it is reasonable to regard the presence of multiple co-occurring health behaviors as well established" (Vickers, Conway, & Hervig, 1990, p. 377). Others are more skeptical and claim that "research has not yet identified statistically significant clusters of health practices" (Ory, Abeles, & Lipman, 1992, p. 17). To answer this question, it was necessary to determine the latent structure of the HBQ and to contrast this structure with a single-factor hypothesis.

Participants   The HBQ was administered by mail. All longitudinal and family study participants tested in 1990–1991 were mailed the HBQ in 1993. The return rate for this survey was 82.5%. Altogether, the total sample used in this analysis was comprised of 2,491 HBQ respondents (longitudinal $n = 1,568$; family $n = 923$). There were 1,444 females and 1,047 males. Their age range in 1993 was 24 to 96 years ($M = 57.5$; $SD = 16.2$), and their years of education ranged from 6 to 20 years ($M = 15.10$; $SD = 2.7$). Participants rated their health as good ($M = 2.05$; $SD = 0.89$) on a 6-point Likert scale (1 = "very good," 6 = "very poor").

Results   Questionnaire items were packaged into 30 indicator variables and fitted to an eight-factor model specifying the dimensions of

1. Not smoking
2. Alcohol abstention
3. Avoiding unhealthy food
4. Healthy food preparation
5. Exercise
6. Wearing seat belts

7. Dental care
8. Medical checkups

Two additional factors were specified and named health status and positive health perceptions. Given the large sample size, the sample was divided into a calibration sample and a cross-validation sample. The calibration sample had a good fit ($\chi^2 = 948.70$, $df = 371$, $RMSEA = .0354$, $GFI = .950$, $CFI = .947$). A two-group model was then tested to determine the equivalence of the calibration and cross-validation sample constraining factor loadings, variances, and covariances across groups. No significant differences between groups were found. Tables 10.1 and 10.2 report the factor loadings for the accepted health behavior model.

Next, five competing second-order models were examined to determine whether a more parsimonious model might suffice. Of these models, ranging from one to five factors, the three-factor model had the best fit, but it fit significantly worse than the accepted eight-factor model. As a consequence, a series of analyses was conducted also to determine how well the accepted eight-factor model would fit health behaviors in different age groups. The total sample ($N = 2,491$) was split into four age groups: young adults (24–44 years, $n = 645$), middle-aged adults (45–64 years, $n = 877$), young-old adults (65–74 years, $n = 521$), and old-old adults (75–96 years, $n = 448$). The structural model fit well across the different age groups.

Summary and Conclusions   We had initially endorsed the "healthy lifestyle" hypothesis and attempted to explain associations among many singular practices by a smaller, more parsimonious set of higher-order dimensions. The identification of eight primary health behavior domains lent preliminary support to the healthy lifestyle hypothesis. However, it should be noted that each of the eight primary domains of health behaviors describes a relatively narrow set of health practices.

An examination of the associations among primary health behavior domains provided a more stringent test for the healthy lifestyle hypothesis. Although associations among primary domains were in the expected positive direction, they were quite low in magnitude. A model that used a single hierarchical dimension (preventive health behavior) to explain associations among primary domains resembled the healthy lifestyle hypothesis most closely. This model was rejected by the data, as were models that allowed for two or three hierarchical dimensions. Hence, we did not find support for the healthy lifestyle hypothesis. Study findings rather suggested that health behaviors are adopted more individually, and that individuals who take favorable health actions in one domain will not necessarily comply with recommended practices in other domains.

Invariance of Health Behavior Dimensions Across Groups

Of immediate concern is the question whether the structural properties of our HBQ remained invariant across groups differing in gender and age. This section reports results of relevant analyses conducted by Maitland (1997). In this study, the eight health behavior and two health status factors defined by Maier (1995)

TABLE 10.1 Accepted Eight-Factor Model for Health Behaviors

Indicator	Not Smoking	Alcohol Abstention	Avoid Unhealthy Food	Food Preparation	Exercise	Seat Belt Use	Dental Care	Medical Checkups	Unique Variance
Current smoker	.87								.25
Amount smoked	.94								.11
Alcohol consumption		.87							.24
Amount alcohol		.93							.13
Amount caffeine			.28						.92
Beef consumption			.53						.72
Veal consumption			.20						.96
Lamb consumption			.18						.97
Pork consumption			.55						.70
Egg yolk consumption			.37						.86
Eat without butter				.31					.90
Read sodium labels				.58					.67
Buy low sodium				.66					.56
Cook low sodium				.23					.95
Read fat labels				.76					.42
Buy low fat				.83					.31
Cook without butter				.33					.89

Exercise hours/week	.76				.43
Exercise frequency	.85				.28
Seat belt (highway)		.87			.25
Seat belt (town)		.93			.14
Teeth brushing			.40		.84
Teeth flossing			.53		.72
Dental visit			.40		.84
Vision checkup				.31	.91
Hearing checkup				.31	.90
Physical checkup				.58	.66
Cholesterol checkup				.54	.71
Colon/rectal checkup				.57	.67
Flu shots				.47	.78

TABLE 10.2 Two-Factor Model for Health Status

Indicator	Self-Reported Positive Objective Health Status	Positive Health Perceptions	Unique Variance
Number of doctor visits	.48		.78
Days in hospital	.40		.84
Need assistance for stairs[a]	.53		.72
Use walker	.47		.78
Good health (self-rating)		.78	.40
Decline in health (self-rating)[a]		.57	.68
Good vision (self-rating)		.27	.93
Good hearing (self-rating)		.29	.91

[a]These items were reverse coded, with higher values reflecting better health.

were fitted across parent-offspring and adult sibling dyads. In addition, similarities and differences in health behaviors and health status within families were examined at the latent construct level.

Participants   There were a total of 441 parent-offspring dyads. A single offspring was matched to each parent, selecting the oldest offspring available. Ages of the participants included in this study for the parents were $M = 66.24$, $SD = 9.51$, range 43 to 88 years; for the offspring, these values were $M = 38.42$, $SD = 8.91$, range 22 to 63 years. The cross-gender dyadic combinations were 72 father-son, 121 father-daughter, 68 mother-son, and 180 mother-daughter. The mean age difference between parents and offspring was 27.93 years ($SD = 5.45$).

When multiple sibling pairs were available, the two siblings closest in age were included. There were 320 sibling pairs. Ages for Sibling 1 were $M = 57.07$, $SD = 14.65$ years; for Sibling 2, the ages were $M = 56.75$, $SD = 14.38$ years. There were 46 brother-brother pairs, 110 sister-sister pairs, and 166 brother-sister pairs. The mean age difference for the sibling dyads was 5.51 years ($SD = 3.96$).

Analyses   Five levels of invariance were tested using the LISREL protocol. These included the three levels of configural invariance, weak invariance, and strong invariance described in chapter 2. In addition, a β-constrained model was tested that constrained factor loading and covariates (age, gender, education) across groups; ψ-constrained models tested the equivalence of factor variance-covariance matrices across groups.

Factorial Invariance: Health Behaviors   Findings for the total parent-offspring sample resulted in an acceptable configural invariance fit [$\chi^2(df = 1,498$, $n = 441$ dyads$) = 2,090.78$, $p < .001$; $GFI = .87$; Z ratio $= 1.39$]. However, the test of weak factorial invariance resulted in a significantly worse fit [$\chi^2(df = 1,517$, $n = 441$ dyads$) = 2,198.48$, $p < .001$; $GFI = .84$; Z ratio $= 1.45$; $\Delta\chi^2(df = 19) = 107.7$]. This means that the same number of factors and the salient factor patterns could be fitted across both generations, but that the factor loadings could not be constrained across groups.

An acceptable fit was also found for the sibling sample [$\chi^2(df = 1,498, n = 322$ dyads) = 1,988.13, $p < .001$; $GFI = .84$; Z ratio = 1.33]. Subsequent model tests for weak invariance, β-constrained, and strong invariance models did not result in significant reductions in fit, although the ψ-constrained model did. Hence, we accepted the strong invariance model for the siblings [$\chi^2(df = 1,560, n = 322$ dyads) = 2,089.53, $p < .001$; $GFI = .83$; Z ratio = 1.33; $\Delta\chi^2(df = 62) = 101.40, p > .05$]. This means that we can accept invariance across sibling pairs as well as invariance of the latent means across the dyads.

Factorial Invariance: Health Status   The assumption of configural invariance could be confirmed for the parent-offspring sample [$\chi^2(df = 174, n = 441$ dyads) = 483.10, $p < .001$; $GFI = .91$; Z ratio = 2.77]. The weak invariance model constraining equal factor loadings across the two generations could also be accepted [$\chi^2(df = 180, n = 441$ dyads) = 499.65, $p < .001$; $GFI = .91$; Z ratio = 2.77; $\Delta\chi^2(df = 6) = 14.61, p > .05$]. However, a test of the strong invariance model showed loss in fit, and it had to be rejected.

The basic configural invariance model for the siblings resulted in acceptable fit statistics [$\chi^2(df = 174, n = 322$ dyads) = 402.96, $p < .001$; $GFI = .90$; Z ratio = 2.31]. Successive tests led to the acceptance of the strong invariance model constraining factor loadings, covariates, and latent means [$\chi^2(df = 192, n = 322$ dyads) = 440.34, $p < .001$; $GFI = .89$; Z ratio = 2.29; $\Delta\chi^2(df = 18) = 37.38, p > .05$].

Latent Health Behavior Differences   The latent mean comparisons between parents and their adult offspring resulted in some expected as well as unexpected findings. The adult children were less likely to smoke, exercised less, and used their seat belts less often than their parents.

Older parents were more likely to abstain from alcohol and have medical checkups than did younger parents. Gender effects suggested that mothers were less likely to smoke or use alcohol and more likely to avoid unhealthy food, show concern for food preparation, use seat belts more frequently, and have more regular dental care than did fathers. Higher levels of education were related to greater alcohol use, more exercise, and better dental care.

Older offspring smoked more and ate more unhealthy food, but they also had more regular medical checkups and claimed that they were more cautious about food preparation. Daughters were more likely to abstain from alcohol and show concern for healthy food preparation, and they had better dental care and more frequent medical checkups than did the sons. Among the offspring, higher level of education was associated with nonsmoking, avoiding unhealthy food, greater seat belt use, and better dental care.

There were no significant latent mean differences among sibling dyads. However, among the siblings, age covaried significantly with more careful food preparation, more exercise, better dental care, and more frequent medical checkups, but older siblings were also more likely to smoke, Gender effects indicated that sisters were less likely to smoke, and more likely to abstain from alcohol use, have greater seat belt use, and have better dental care than was true for brothers.

Latent Health Status Differences   The offspring reported higher levels of positive health status, most likely because of the age difference between them and their parents. However, there were no differences for positive health perceptions. No significant gender effects were noted, but higher education predicted more positive health perceptions among the parents.

For the sibling sample, there was an age effect, with the older sibling reporting worse health. A modest gender effect occurred, with males more likely to report worse health status.

Antecedents of Health Behaviors

It is of obvious interest to explore what might be the behavioral and contextual factors that have an impact on health behavior. With the relevant data available in our study, we explored the extent to which level of cognitive ability, family influence in the family of origin and the current family, as well as personality factors might influence the adoption of good health behaviors (cf. Zanjani, 2002). Hierarchical regression analysis was used to fit a model for the full sample and for the four age groups. Results are presented by health behavior dimension, and the proportion of variance accounted for as well as statistically significant predictors ($p < .05$) are indicated.

Participants   This study used a sample of 979 (454 males, 525 females 525) SLS participants in the sixth wave (1991). The sample was subdivided into four age groups: 207 young adults from 22 to 42 years old ($M = 34.73$; $SD = 5.38$); middle-aged adults from 43 to 62 years old ($M = 52.76$; $SD = 5.72$); 221 young-old adults from 63 to 72 years old ($M = 67.00$; $SD = 2.84$); and 147 old-old adults from 73 to 87 years old ($M = 77.81$; $SD = 3.55$).

Measures   The 8 health behavior dimensions described here were the dependent variables; the 6 cognitive factor scores, the 8 family environment scales (see chapter 16), and the 13 personality factor scales (see chapter 12), as well as some social network variables and demographic indicators were the independent predictor variables.

Nonsmoking Domain   Significant predictors for the total sample were higher education, threat reactivity (timidity), being married, frequent club attendance, and a recreation-oriented current family environment. No single predictor was significant across all age groups. For young adults, higher levels of Threctia and higher levels of income were implicated. For the middle-aged adults, higher level of childhood family conflict and higher levels of education became salient. For the young-old, nonsmoking was associated with frequent club attendance and current recreational family orientation. In the old-old, nonsmoking was associated with higher levels of Verbal Ability and higher levels of Threctia.

Alcohol Use Domain   For the total sample, lower alcohol use was associated with higher levels of Affectothymia (being outgoing). However, this predictor reached statistical significance only for the young adult and young-old groups.

Food Consumption Domain   Healthy food consumption practices in the total sample were associated with higher levels of Affectothymia, higher levels of Premsia (tender-mindedness), and being female. These characteristics were also significant for the young adults. For the middle-aged, the only significant characteristic was being single. In the young-old, knowing more neighbors well enough to visit was associated with healthy food consumption. In the old-old, significant characteristics were higher level of Numeric Ability, lower level of Verbal Memory, and being single.

Food Preparation Domain   Use of healthy food preparation methods for the total sample was associated with lower levels of Verbal Ability, higher levels of Affectothymia, lower levels of Low Self-Esteem, higher levels of Honesty, lower levels of Inflexibility, being married, visiting more neighbors, and having fewer children living at home. None of the predictors were significant across all age groups. Significant characteristics for the young adults were higher levels of Affectothymia, being married, visiting more neighbors, and having fewer children living at home. Those for the middle-aged were higher levels of Affectothymia, lower levels of Low Self-Esteem, and visiting more neighbors. For the young-old, salient characteristics were lower levels of Low Self-Esteem and lower Community Involvement. For the old-old, the significant predictors were lower Verbal Ability, lower Inflexibility, higher Community Involvement, and higher Achievement Orientation in their current family environment.

Exercise Domain   In the total sample, engagement in high levels of exercise was associated with lower Superego Strength, visiting more neighbors, fewer children living at home, greater church attendance, higher Recreational Orientation in their current family, and higher income levels. For the young adults, predictors were limited to visiting more neighbors, fewer children at home, and higher Recreational Orientation in the current family.

For the middle-aged, exercise behavior was associated only with higher levels of their current family's Recreational Orientation. In the young-old, exercise behavior was associated with higher levels of Recreational Orientation and visiting more neighbors. Salient characteristics for the old-old were high levels Achievement Orientation in their childhood family, higher Untroubled Adequacy, higher Interest in Science, and visiting more neighbors.

Seat Belt Use Domain   Seat belt use was associated in the total sample with higher levels of Affectothymia, fewer grandchildren, and less time being visited. In the young adults, salient predictors were higher level of current family Cohesion, higher Affectothymia, higher Political Concern, and less time being visited. For the middle-aged, the only significant predictor was higher level of Recreational Orientation in the current family. The only significant predictor for the young-old was higher level of club attendance. Predictors for the old-old were visiting more neighbors, less club attendance, and fewer grandchildren.

Dental Care Domain For the total sample, greater use of dental care was associated with lower levels of Spatial Ability, higher Numeric Ability, fewer grandchildren, fewer siblings, higher levels of current family Organization, higher education, higher income, and being female. In young adults, however, the only significant predictors were higher income and being female. In the middle-aged, salient characteristics were higher Verbal Ability, lower Superego Strength, fewer siblings, greater current family Organization, and being female. Significant predictors for the young-old were higher Cultural Orientation in their childhood family and visiting more neighbors. Significant characteristics for the old-old were fewer grandchildren and higher levels of education.

Medical Checkup Domain For the total sample, greater use of medical checkups was characterized by lower levels of Verbal and Spatial abilities, lower Verbal Memory, higher level of Honesty, visiting more neighbors, higher club attendance, fewer children at home, more grandchildren, and higher levels of current family Organization. There were no significant predictors for the young adults or the old-old. For the middle-aged, medical checkups were associated with lower levels of Cohesion and greater Expressivity in their childhood family, lower Verbal Memory, visiting more neighbors, and fewer children at home. Significant predictors for the young-old were higher levels of Conservatism and more visits with neighbors.

Summary The most striking finding from these analyses is that there are no predictors of health behaviors consistent across different health behavior domains or across different life stages. What is also clear is that our extensive system of predictors account for only limited proportions of variance in the occurrence of positive health behaviors, and it again varies substantially across health behavior domains and age groups. To illustrate this, we report findings of proportions of variance by health behavior domain and age group in table 10.3.

Intellectual Functioning as a Predictor of Physical Health

We have also investigated the reverse side of the coin, more specifically, whether we can demonstrate that our measures of cognitive abilities and cognitive style might be useful in predicting the occurrence and onset of physical disease (Maitland, 1993).

Our first analysis (Maitland & Schaie, 1991) involved a sample of 370 subjects (169 males, 201 females; mean age 66.5 years) who were studied between 1970

TABLE 10.3 Total Proportions of Variance in Health Behaviors Accounted for in Health Behaviors From Cognitive Abilities, Family Environment, Personality Factors, Social Network Characteristics, and Sociodemographic Factors (R^2)

Health Behavior Domain	Young Adults	Middle Aged	Young-Old	Old-Old	Total Sample
Smoking	.134	.047	.153	.090	.054
Alcohol use	.041	.000	.044	.000	.017
Food consumption	.126	.014	.021	.107	.044
Food preparation	.125	.042	.058	.180	.091
Exercise	.107	.064	.176	.235	.110
Seat belt use	.155	.024	.032	.125	.024
Dental care	.084	.124	.059	.125	.116
Medical checkups	.000	.085	.064	.000	.141

and 1984. Two logistic regression models were tested. In the first model, all subjects diagnosed as having CVD were contrasted with normal controls. Age, gender, education, Attitudinal Flexibility, and decline in Spatial Ability were identified as significant predictors of the CVD condition $[\chi^2(13) = 80.96, p < .001]$. When examined separately by gender, age and Attitudinal Flexibility were significant for the females $[\chi^2(12) = 39.02, p < .001]$, whereas age, Attitudinal Flexibility, and education were significant predictors of CVD for males $[\chi^2(12) = 44.67, p < .001]$.

The second model included only those subjects who developed a CVD condition after the second data point. The prediction model for recent occurrence of conditions implicated age, Attitudinal Flexibility, decline in Psychomotor Speed, Spatial Ability decline, and decline in Reasoning Ability were significant $[\chi^2(13) = 43.14, p < .001]$. Separately by gender, age, decline of Reasoning Ability, and decline in Word Fluency were significant for males $[\chi^2(12) = 29.13, p < .01]$, whereas Attitudinal Flexibility was the only significant predictor for females. Lifestyle predictors of change in activity level and smoking surprisingly did not contribute to the prediction of recent CVD in this particular sample.

The most interesting finding from this analysis is the establishment of an association between the cognitive style measure of Attitudinal Flexibility and the presence of CVD regardless of time of onset of the disease. Explanations for these findings would be that very rigid participants may already have dropped out of the study prior to the onset of CVD or that rigid individuals might be more attentive to their health behaviors and thus more likely to avoid disease outcomes.

In a second analysis, as part of a master's thesis Maitland (1993) extended these findings to the possible effects of behaviors on the occurrence of arthritic disease and applied survival analysis to the prediction of the occurrence of both cardiovascular and arthritic disease. In this sample, women were more likely than men to have arthritis, but measures of social status, obesity, and smoking were not significant predictors. Greater Attitudinal Flexibility and decline of Psychomotor Speed were associated with preexisting arthritis, whereas declines in Spatial and Reasoning abilities were predictive of the occurrence of arthritis.

Life table and survival analysis methods were used to predict age of onset of cardiovascular and arthritic disease. Declines in Verbal and Reasoning abilities predicted later occurrence of first diagnosis of CVD; high levels of Spatial Ability were associated with earlier onset. For the arthritic participants, greater declines in Verbal and Spatial abilities, as well as higher level of education and Psychomotor Speed base levels, were associated with later ages of disease onset; decline in Psychomotor Speed and low baseline function on Spatial Ability predicted earlier onset.

Effects of Social Support on Illness

Another influence that might affect the onset, course, and outcome of illness is the broad spectrum of social support. In this study, we investigated the extent to which both actual social networks and perceived social environments relate to health outcomes and service utilization in the middle to older years. The study of the relationship between social support and disease at older ages is important because the elderly are at greatest risk for almost all morbidity and mortality outcomes.

In the following analyses, we address these issues by applying both variable-oriented and individual-oriented approaches to contribute further information on the relation between social environment and health (cf. Bosworth, 1994; Bosworth & Schaie, 1997).

Methods

Participants The subsample used in the following analyses consists of 387 participants (173 men and 214 women) who participated in the sixth cycle (1991) data collection; the participants had a mean age of 58.3 years (range 36 to 82 years) for those whose medical records were abstracted. Their mean health care characteristics in 1991 were as follows: Primary care visits, $M = 3.6$, $SD = 1.6$, range 2–10; hospital days, $M = 1.7$, $SD = 5.3$, range 0–50; medication usage, $M = 1.9$, $SD = 2.0$, range 0–11; total annual health care cost, $M = \$3,203$, $SD = \$2,270$, range \$465–\$11,835.

Measures Included in this analysis as predictors were structural social network measures from the Life Complexity Index and perceived social environment measures from the family environment scales (see chapters 3, 11, and 16). Health outcome variables included number of diagnoses, number of disease episodes, number of hospital visits over a 1-year period (1991), the number of medications used regularly for at least 1 month, and an estimate of total annual health expenditures for each study participant.

Analyses Structural equation modeling using LISREL VIII (Jöreskog & Sörbom, 1993) were used to evaluate the model shown in figure 10.1. As an alternate

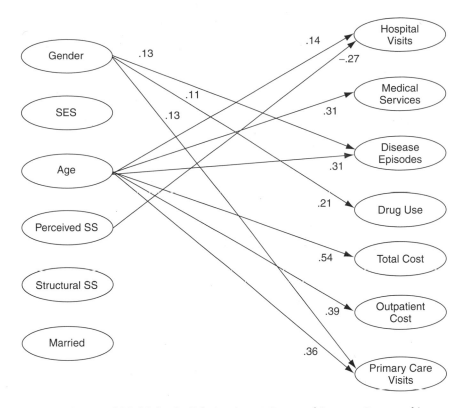

FIGURE 10.1 *Structural Model for the Relation Among Structural Support, Demographic Factors, and Health Care Outcomes. SES, Socioeconomic Status; SS, Social Support.*

approach, cluster analysis using the agglomerative method with cosine similarities was used to cluster individuals on the constructs of perceived social environment and social networks (cf. Blashfild, 1976).

Results

Structural Equation Modeling   Confirmatory factor analysis of the model in figure 10.1 showed a quite satisfactory fit, $\chi^2(df = 199, n = 387) = 329.25, p < .001$; $GFI = .936$; $RMSEA = .046$. Increased social networks were negatively correlated with hospital visits, and being unmarried was negatively correlated with higher estimated total health care costs, outpatient costs, and number of primary care visits. Increased favorable perceptions of social environment was negatively correlated with lower estimated primary care costs. Increased age was positively correlated with all health care variables, and lower socioeconomic status was negatively correlated with increased number of disease episodes, medications used, and estimated health care utilization.

As shown in figure 10.1, females had more physician visits, used a more medications, and had more primary care visits. The magnitude of perceived social relations was negatively related to number of hospital and primary care visits. Advanced age predicted greater health problems.

Differences between married and unmarried adults were examined using multiple group structural equations modeling. The model was the same as for the total group except for the exclusion of marital status. Married women had more disease episodes, greater medication usage, and more outpatient care visits than married men. For married persons, age was negatively related to all health variables; structural social networks were negatively related total health care costs, outpatient costs, and primary care visits. For unmarried persons, age was positively related to health care variables; magnitude of perceived social environment was negatively related to disease episodes. The models separately by marital status are shown in figure 10.2.

Cluster Analyses   Four clusters were retained for each of the structural social network and perceived social network data. It was found that the cluster that had significantly lower levels of social interaction also had the highest estimated health

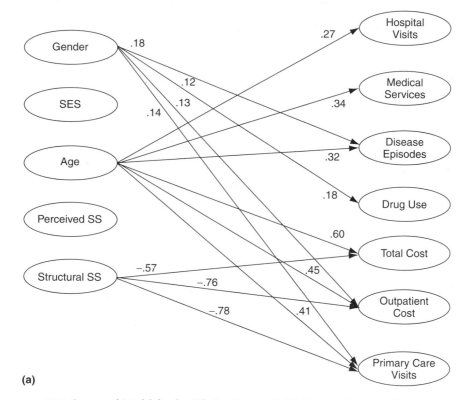

(a)

FIGURE 10.2 *Structural Model for the Relation Among Social Support, Demographic Factors, and Health Care Outcomes by Marital Status: (a) Married; (b) Unmarried. SES, Socioeconomic Status; SS, Social Support.*

care costs even though they had higher church attendance than the other clusters. The two clusters that had the most positive health outcomes were also the younger members of the sample.

With respect to the perceived social environment clustering, it was found that the cluster with the most health problems was characterized by low levels of education and low levels of intellectual-cultural and recreational orientations in their current families. These individuals could be described as socially isolated. The two clusters with the least health problems had high levels of family cohesion and expressiveness.

Summary   These analyses confirm that married persons tend to have fewer physical health problems than unmarried persons, and that higher socioeconomic status is also associated with better health. On the other hand, we account for relatively little variance in health outcomes from more extensive structural support systems. However, perceived support appears to be important in those individuals who are married as well as for those clusters of individuals who are experiencing more serious health problems. These findings underline the importance of developing typologies of subsets of individuals who exhibit different causal mechanisms for outcomes of interest.

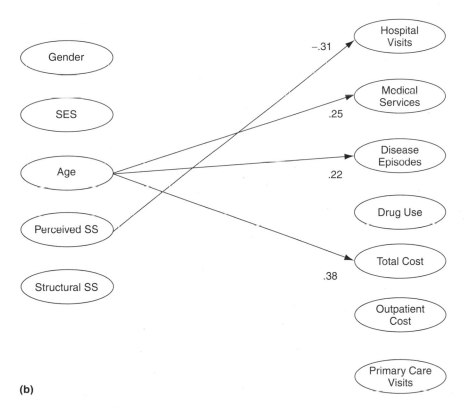

(b)

FIGURE 10.2 *Continued.*

Effects of Cognition on Medication Use

We have been able to obtain access to the medication use of our study participants because most of our participants receive their prescription medications from the collaborating HMO. These data began to be automated in the 1980s and prescription data were obtained for the 4-month window prior to our test administrations. We have not yet been able to develop appropriate models of how we should correct our cognitive test findings for medication use. However, we have been able to begin initial studies of the impact of cognition on medication use. In this section, we report findings on the effects of cognition on understanding the purpose of one's medication at different ages (cf. Bosworth, Schaie, & Willis, 1999b).

Background

Although a majority of older adults understand the purpose of their medication, many individuals do not for various reasons. A study of a large sample residing in a rural community found that as many as 90% of all reported drug purposes were considered accurate (Semla, Lemke, Helling, Wallace, & Chrischelles, 1991). But other studies have found smaller percentages of individuals who understood the purpose of their medication (e.g., O'Connell & Johnson, 1992). Much of this research is problematic because of a lack of uniform description of what constitutes patient knowledge, and operational definitions of patient knowledge vary significantly in published research. *Medication knowledge* in this study is defined as a general understanding of the purpose of the medication.

Considerable attention has also focused on the relationship between cognitive function and compliance (Morrell, Park, & Poon, 1989; Park, Willis, Morrow, Diehl, & Gaines, 1994). A major cause of noncompliance may be related to cognitive function, particularly among older adults. Older adults may have difficulty understanding what they are to do with their medication or, if they do understand, remembering what to do with it.

Despite the attention on the relationship between cognitive function and compliance, few have examined the relationship between cognitive level of functioning and simply understanding the therapeutic purpose of one's medication. A basic understanding of the therapeutic function of prescription medications is necessary, but not sufficient, to ensure compliance in medication use.

There remains a paucity of information regarding the correlates of the knowledge of therapeutic purpose of medications used among adults, and research is lacking on identifying predictors of misidentification of medication purpose across the life span. In addition, despite the information on the ramifications of medication noncompliance, there is a lack of information on understanding the purpose of one's medication and its relation to health outcome and service utilization.

The SLS provides an opportunity to examine individuals' therapeutic understanding of their medication for a large, sociodemographically diverse group of adults across the life span and to examine whether knowledge of one's medication mediates the relationship between cognition and health status and service utilization.

This study was designed to explore four issues: First, we investigated medication usage patterns across the life span of adults who are members of an HMO. Second, we examined participants' knowledge of the therapeutic function of their prescription medications. Third, we examined the relationship of level of cognitive abilities and sociodemographic variables with understanding the purpose of one's medication. Fourth, we were interested in whether the understanding of the therapeutic purpose of one's medication mediated the relationship between cognition and health outcome and service utilization.

Methods

Participants   Prescription medication use was examined in a sample of 816 males and 986 females ($N = 1,802$) with a mean age of 59.7 years (range 22–94 years) at the time data were collected in 1991. The perceived therapeutic purpose (PTP) of CVD medication was examined in a subsample of 110 males and 82 females ($n = 192$) with a mean age of 68.99 years (range 35–92 years). The PTP of nonsteroidal antiinflammatory medications (NSAIDs) was examined in a subsample of 60 males and 56 females ($n = 116$) with a mean age of 66.37 years (range 31–92 years).

Procedures   All participants were asked to bring all medications taken regularly for at least 1 month to the session at which their cognitive function was assessed. The name of the medication, dosage level, subjects' perceived purpose for the medication, and physicians' instructions were recorded by the examiner. Each medication was assigned a drug code based on the American Hospital Formulary Service (1991) coding scheme. CVD and NSAID medication categories were examined because they are two of the most commonly prescribed types of drugs (Baum, Kennedy, Knapp, Juergens, & Faich, 1988).

Cognitive Measures   The psychometric tests used in this study included three dimensions of mental abilities: Verbal Memory, Inductive Reasoning, and Verbal Comprehension. These were measured by the PMA Verbal Meaning and Reasoning tests and by the Immediate and Delayed Recall tests. Various demographic and personal information was extracted from the Life Complexity Index, including age, family income, and education (see chapter 3 for details).

Health Outcome Measures   In 1993, participants rated their health on a 6-point Likert scale (1 = very good to 6 = very poor). Individuals also reported the number of doctor visits and hospital stays for 1993. Number of medications in 1991 was also considered. Estimated total care costs for 1991 were based on a Chronic Disease Score (CDS). The CDS was based on empirically derived weights based on age, gender, and pharmacy utilization of the HMO's pharmacies. These weights were then used to calculate a predicted score for total care costs (Clark, Von Korff, Saunders, Baluch, & Simon, 1995).

Analyses   Individual PTPs were classified according to whether they corresponded to the actual therapeutic purpose (ATP) of CVD and NSAID medications. The ATP of medication purposes listed by participants were often broad responses. If the PTP did not correspond with the ATP of the medication, the response was categorized as inaccurate. For example, if an individual used a CVD medication and reported the PTP as "hypertension," the response was coded as correct. If an individual used CVD medication but reported it was used for the treatment of gout, the response was coded as incorrect. To avoid overrepresentation of individuals who may take two of the same types of medications, only the individual's first reported medication was included in analyses and then used to determine the sociodemographic variables and cognitive abilities that may be risk factors for misunderstanding the purpose of one's medication.

First, age, gender, income, and education were modeled. Then each individual cognitive ability (i.e., PMA Verbal Meaning, PMA Inductive Reasoning, Immediate Recall and Delayed Recall) was added to assess the magnitude of increased prediction above the influence of sociodemographic factors. The final model tested assumed that accurately reporting the purpose of one's medication is dependent first on sociodemographic variables (i.e., age, gender, income, and education), then on Verbal Ability, Inductive Reasoning, and finally Verbal Memory.

Measurement Model   Multiple measures of Verbal Meaning, Semantic Memory, and Inductive Reasoning were treated as latent variables with three to four indicators. Age, income, education, and gender were entered as manifest variables; they were unique factors in and of themselves. The observed dependent variables were treated as latent variables to assess whether they were impacted by cognitive functioning, gender, education, income, age, and medication knowledge.

Results: Medication Usage

Participants were classified by frequency of drug use. Given the low frequency of multiple drug use, subjects who used seven or more drugs were combined. Medication usage was examined across ten 7-year age cohorts that corresponded to the data collection intervals of this study. Analyses of variance and covariance were used to assess the difference between cohorts and medication use as well as the relationship of medication use and demographic variables, controlling for age.

Lack of any current medication usage was reported by 41% of the sample ($n = 731$). The average number of medications reported by the remaining subjects was 1.68. There was a significant difference in number of drugs used by age cohort [$F(9, 1,756) = 23.21$, $p < .001$]. Medication usage increased significantly for successively older age cohorts.

A significant main effect for gender when controlling for age was obtained for the number of drugs consumed [$F(1, 1,761) = 127.33$, $p < .001$]. Females used significantly more drugs ($M = 1.92$; $SD = 2.03$) than males ($M = 1.31$; $SD = 1.77$).

Participants were then split into three levels of education: high school and less, college level (12–16 years), and graduate level (more than 16 years of education). Participants with different levels of education also differed in the number of drugs consumed when controlling for age and gender [$F(4, 1,759) = 68.93$, $p < .001$]. Individuals with less than a high school education used more drugs ($M = 1.92$), followed by those with some college education ($M = 1.67$); least use was by those with some graduate education ($M = 1.33$). A significant difference was also found for income level when controlling for age [$F(2, 1,763) = 101.23$, $p < .001$]. Those with incomes lower than $30,000 used more medications ($M = 2.01$; $SD = 2.10$) than those with higher incomes ($M = 1.4$; $SD = 1.76$).

Results: Perceived Therapeutic Purpose

Cerebrovascular Disease Medications   Of those who reported the use of a CVD medication, 90% accurately reported its therapeutic purpose. There was a significant negative correlation between age and accurately understanding the purpose of one's CVD ($r = -.18$, $p < .01$); increased age was associated with greater understanding. Those individuals who reported accurate responses were 7 years older on average (accurate $M = 69.56$ years; inaccurate $M = 62.84$ years) and had used the medication for approximately 21 months longer (accurate $M = 62.81$ months; inaccurate $M = 42.06$ months). Individuals who reported inaccurate responses used less medications on average ($M = 2.56$) than those who responded accurately ($M = 3.44$).

Verbal Ability, Inductive Reasoning, Immediate Recall, and Delayed Recall failed to be significant risk factors for misunderstanding the purpose of one's medication. However, individuals who were younger and male and had lower levels of education and income were more likely to be inaccurate.

Nonsteroidal Antiinflammatory Medications   The PTP for 84% of those who reported using NSAIDs was correct. A significant negative correlation between age and accurately understanding the purpose of one's NSAIDs was observed ($r = -.30$, $p < .001$); increased age was associated with greater understanding. In addition, length of use of an NSAID was negatively correlated with knowing the purpose of the NSAID ($r = -.25$, $p < .001$). Those individuals who reported accurate responses used the medication for approximately 40 months longer (accurate $M = 62.77$ months; inaccurate $M = 23.22$ months) and were eleven years older on average (accurate $M = 68.07$ years; inaccurate $M = 57.28$ years). Individuals who reported inaccurate responses used fewer medications on average ($M = 2.71$) than those who responded accurately ($M = 3.09$).

Age and length of use were significant predictors of understanding the purpose of NSAIDs. Once sociodemographic factors were controlled, performance on Verbal Meaning and Inductive Reasoning did not add significant risk of inaccuracy. However, both Immediate and Delayed Recall accounted for differences in knowing the purpose of one's NSAIDs. In fact, low performance on Delayed and Immediate Recall placed subjects at an increased risk of 24% and 19%, respectively, in misinterpreting their medication's purposes.

Summary

This study found significant age differences in medication use, with older adults using more medications than younger adults. However, lower medication usage than observed in other studies was found (e.g., Lamy, Salzman, & Nevis-Olsessen, 1992). The low levels of medication usage reported here have occurred because of three possible reasons: First, identification of low levels of medication usage could be an artifact of the method by which reports of drug usage were obtained. Although subjects may have been prescribed and may have purchased many other drugs, they were asked to report only those drugs that they were using regularly for at least 1 month prior to the survey. Second, low levels of medication use may be a function of the philosophy of practice of the HMO. HMOs emphasize ambulatory and preventive care. Members of this HMO may therefore represent an unusually healthy group who require less medication (Gold, Jolle, Kennedy, & Tucker, 1989). Third, because this population, on average, is relatively well educated and financially affluent (Schaie, 1996b), better health practices and life-styles may have led to lower medication use.

Women were found to use more medications than men, as has also been shown in previous research. Women are more likely to encounter types of illness, problems, and conditions that are amenable to drug therapy (e.g., hypertension and menopause). Gender differences in the number of medications used may also result from differences in health behaviors. Women are more likely to seek medical attention then men; women accounted for about 60% of all office visits and for a majority of the visits in each age group except for the youngest (U.S. Department of Health and Human Services, 1992).

An examination of PTP indicated that individuals who reported using CVD and NSAID medications were generally correct in reporting the purpose of their medications. However, no evidence was found for the hypothesis that community-dwelling older adults have lower congruence between PTP and ATP of one's medication, specifically CVD and NSAIDs medications, than do younger adults. In fact, they were more accurate than their younger peers.

Despite the increased number of medications and likely increased complexity of prescribed regimen, older adults understood the purpose of their medication better than younger adults. Similar findings have been obtained in the compliance literature; age had no adverse effects on compliance (e.g., Lorenc & Branthwaite, 1993).

We did find differences in the length of time individuals were using their medications. There was an approximately 40-month difference between accurate and nonaccurate NSAID users and a 21-month difference between accurate and nonaccurate CVD medication users. As hypothesized, the longer an individual has been taking a medication, the less likely the person is to forget the purpose of it.

There was evidence that a lack of understanding of the therapeutic purpose of one's medication does have health consequences in this study. In the CVD model, medication knowledge was predictive of increased health care costs, decreased self-reported rating of health, and increased hospital visits. In contrast, in the

NSAIDs model, a lack of medication knowledge was associated only with increased health care amount.

Cognitive Decline and the Prediction of Mortality

Thus far, we have dealt with issues concerned with the relation of disease and cognition and with the cognitive and environmental influences that may affect morbidity. We now turn to the issue of the role of cognitive and sociodemographic risk factors in the prediction of mortality.

Background

Lower cognitive performance in older adults has long been associated with earlier mortality (cf. Berg, 1996; Bosworth & Schaie, 1999; Maier & Smith, 1999; Small & Bäckman, 1997). Although the evidence is fairly consistent, it has not been clear whether this association holds true across different abilities or whether the association is affected by gender, education, or age.

Three classes of theories have been offered for the association between cognitive decline and mortality. The first class includes the implication of early cognitive impairment, general systems decline, and disease (Swan, Carmelli, & LaRue, 1995). All of these might be detected early by cognitive tests because these tests assess the integrity and efficiency of the central nervous system (Muscovith & Winocur, 1992).

The second type of theories suggests that decline in cognitive function may have an indirect role in affecting general health. Intact memory, for example, is required to follow any treatment regimen. Also, decline in perceptual speed may reflect the primary aging of the central nervous system, which reduces adaptive capability in general, hence increasing susceptibility to a number of internal and external events that increase the probability of death (e.g., Swan et al., 1995).

A third class of theories would suggest that low cognitive test performance may be an indicator of general cognitive disturbance that can be attributed to diseases that affect the brain only indirectly. Such diseases would include cardiovascular problems as well as metabolic or toxic disturbances,

We have previously dealt with these issues in the context of the popular construct of terminal decline and the issue of participant attrition (e.g., Cooney et al., 1988). Given the 7-year interval of assessment, we cannot directly deal with short-term decline occurring shortly before death. Rather, we deal with the question of the extent that cognitive functions can predict mortality from cognitive and other variables available to us at the last assessment point prior to death.

The analyses reported in this section address three questions: First, we ask whether there is a general relationship between cognitive function and risk of mortality when controlled for gender, education, and age. We hypothesized that Psychomotor Speed would most likely show the highest relationship with mortality. Second, we ask whether the relationship between cognition and mortality operates differentially by age. Third, we consider whether magnitude of decline over the last two measurement points available to us indicates increased risk of mortality (cf. Bosworth, Schaie, & Willis, 1999a; Bosworth, Schaie, Willis, & Siegler, 1999).

Methods

Participants   These analyses include the 601 decedent SLS participants (342 males and 259 females) whose date of death could be established by December 1995. A control group of 609 survivors (296 males and 313 females) who were last assessed in 1991 was selected whose members were within 2 years of age and within 1 year of education of the decedents.

Measures   The following analyses included the basic PMA battery (Verbal Meaning, Spatial Orientation, Inductive Reasoning, Number, and Word Fluency); immediate and delayed Verbal Memory; perceptual speed (Finding A's, Identical Pictures, and Number comparison); and the Psychomotor Speed measure from the Test of Behavioral Rigidity. Demographic information included participants' age, gender, and years of education.

Analyses   The SAS PHREG procedure was used to compute Cox's semiparametric proportional hazard models assessing the effects of level cognitive performance and cognitive decline on the probability of mortality. it is then possible to compute odds ratios that will represent probability of mortality given level and decline of cognitive performance.

Hierarchical models were estimated successively introducing variables hypothesized to confound the association between cognitive performance and mortality. Groups of independent variables were introduced in the following order: (a) with cognitive performance at last measurement categorized as quartiles as the only variable in the model; (b) with the addition of sociodemographic factors (age, gender, education); and (c) Psychomotor Speed. Psychomotor Speed was treated as a covariate for all other cognitive measures. However, Psychomotor Speed was included in the model as an independent predictor of mortality. Dummy codes represented each quartile of cognitive performance, and the reference point for each individual cognitive ability was performance in the top 25th percentile. The use of dummy codes followed the conventional practice in previous studies using self-rated health (Bernard et al., 1997; Idler & Kasl, 1991). Age also was categorized by quartiles, and the youngest quartile was used as the reference age category. Education was categorized by less than 11 years of education, 12 to 15 years of education, and 16 years of education or more. The last category was used as the reference category for education.

Because we were operating in a Thurstonian framework, we were interested in ability-specific change. Hierarchical analyses were first conducted for level of cognitive performance for all participants. Then, decline in cognitive level, as assessed by difference scores, was assessed in a similar hierarchical fashion as the level models. Finally, analyses were conducted in a similar hierarchical fashion except they were stratified by age; a median split was used to categorize the old-old (=74 years of age) and younger adults (=73 years of age).

Results

Level of Cognitive Performance at Last Measurement   Examining the unadjusted association between cognition and mortality, participants in the lower 50th percentile on Spatial Ability, Delayed Recall, Immediate Recall, Psychomotor Speed, and Identical Pictures had a significantly higher risk of mortality than those in the top 25th percentile on these measures. Individuals who performed in the lower 25th percentile of Verbal Meaning and Numerical Ability had a significantly higher risk relative to their reference categories. Significant odds ratios ranged from 1.38 to 2.32 for the lowest percentile of performance (table 10.4). The odds ratios for many of the cognitive abilities decreased after adjusting for sociodemographic factors. This excess risk of low levels of Verbal Meaning, Numerical Ability, Spatial Ability, and Psychomotor Speed ceased to be a significant predictor of mortality once demographic factors were adjusted. However, low levels of Verbal Memory (Immediate Recall, Delayed Recall) and a measure of perceptual speed (Identical Pictures) remained significantly related to a higher probability of mortality after adjusting for sociodemographic factors. However, once Psychomotor Speed was introduced into the model, only Identical Pictures remained significantly related to mortality.

Decline in Cognitive Performance   The influence of cognitive decline on mortality/survival is shown in table 10.5. Greater magnitude of decline was related to increased risk of mortality. Participants who had the greatest magnitude of 7-year decline in Verbal Meaning, Spatial Ability, Inductive Reasoning, and Psychomotor Speed had a 63%, 113%, 50%, and 97% greater likelihood, respectively, for mortality relative to their reference category even after adjusting for sociodemographic factors and psychomotor speed.

Level of Decline in Cognitive Performance by Age Group   We next stratified participants by median age. The oldest adults were 75 to 95 years of age or older, and the younger adults were 34 to 74 years of age. Level of performance on Identical Pictures remained a significant predictor of mortality for both age groups. However, the relationship appeared to be more substantial among older adults, with those individuals in the lowest 50th percentile having a significant risk of mortality. Among the younger sample, only those in the bottom 25th had a significant risk of mortality compared to their reference categories. Examining the odds ratios, younger adults who had significant declines in Spatial Ability and/or Inductive Reasoning had a greater risk of mortality than older adults. Older adults who had significant declines in Verbal Meaning and Psychomotor Speed had greater risks of mortality than the younger group (see table 10.6).

Summary

Level of cognitive function was related to subsequent mortality, but the relationship of performance level and early mortality varied across abilities. Lower levels of crystallized abilities, spatial abilities, Verbal Memory, and perceptual speed as

TABLE 10.4 Odds Ratios and Confidence Intervals for Level of Performance

Independent Variables	Model I OR (95% CI)	Model II OR (95% CI)	Model III OR (95% CI)
Age			
(≤25th percentile)		1.00	1.00
(26th–50th percentile)		ns	ns
(51st–75th percentile)		1.53 (1.19, 1.98)	1.53 (1.18, 1.98)
(≥76 percentile)		2.17 (1.67, 1.82)	2.16 (1.66, 2.81)
Gender (male)		1.35 (1.14, 1.60)	1.35 (1.14, 1.60)
≥16 years of education		1.00	1.00
12–15 years of education		ns	ns
Less than high school (≤11 years)		1.26 (1.03, 1.53)	1.27 (1.04, 1.56)
Verbal Meaning			
(51st–75th percentile)	ns	ns	ns
(26th–50th percentile)	ns	ns	ns
(≤25th percentile)	1.67 (1.33, 2.08)	ns	ns
Numeric Ability			
(51st–75th percentile)	ns	ns	ns
(26th–50th percentile)	ns	ns	ns
(≤25th percentile)	1.42 (1.14, 1.78)	ns	ns
Spatial Ability			
(51st–75th percentile)	ns	ns	ns
(26th–50th percentile)	1.32 (1.04, 1.69)	ns	ns
(≤25th percentile)	1.38 (1.08, 1.75)	ns	ns
Delayed Recall			
(51st–75th percentile)	ns	ns	ns
(26th–50th percentile)	1.84 (1.05, 3.25)	1.88 (1.03, 3.42)	ns
(≤25th percentile)	1.97c(1.09, 3.56)	ns	ns
Immediate Recall			
(51st–75th percentile)	ns	ns	ns
(26th–50th percentile)	1.96 (1.10, 3.48)	1.58 (1.07, 3.67)	ns
(≤25th percentile)	1.87 (1.07, 3.25)	ns	ns
Psychomotor Speed			
(51st–75th percentile)	ns	ns	ns
(26th–50th percentile)	1.30 (1.02, 1.66)	ns	ns
(≤25th percentile)	1.51 (1.18, 1.92)	ns	ns
Identical Pictures			
(51st–75th percentile)	ns	ns	ns
(26th–50th percentile)	1.75 (1.14, 2.67)	2.08 (1.31, 3.32)	2.07 (1.30, 3.31)
(≤25th percentile)	2.32 (1.56, 3.45)	2.80 (1.75, 4.80)	2.73 (1.64, 4.56)

Note. CI, confidence interval; ns, not significant; OR, odds ratio.

well as declines in Verbal Meaning, Spatial Ability, Inductive Reasoning, and Psychomotor Speed were significant predictors of mortality. Level of cognitive performance was related to mortality, but Psychomotor Speed mediated the relationship for many of these cognitive variables. Seven-year decline in cognitive performance was a better predictor of subsequent survival than level of performance at last measurement, even after adjusting for demographic factors and psychomotor speed. Overall, the pattern of results in this study indicates that not all cognitive abilities are equally affected by terminal change or directly associated

TABLE 10.5 Relative Risk Ratios and Confidence Intervals for 7-Year Change Before Death

Independent Variables	Model I OR (95% CI)	Model II OR (95% CI)	Model III OR (95% CI)
Age			
(≤25th percentile)		1.00	1.00
(26th–50th percentile)		ns	ns
(51st–75th percentile)		ns	ns
(≥76 percentile)		1.73 (1.19, 2.53)	1.67 (1.12, 2.48)
Gender (male versus female)		1.37 (1.06, 1.71)	1.33 (1.01, 1.75)
≥16 years of education		1.00	1.00
12–15 years of education		ns	ns
≤11 years		1.35 (1.01, 1.79)	1.38 (1.03, 1.85)
Verbal Meaning			
(51st–75th percentile)	ns	ns	ns
(26th–50th percentile)	ns	ns	ns
(≤25th percentile)	1.74 (1.19, 2.47)	1.68 (1.14, 2.47)	1.63 (1.10, 2.43)
Spatial Ability			
(51st–75th percentile)	ns	ns	ns
(26th–50th percentile)	1.95 (1.32, 2.88)	1.96 (1.32, 2.89)	1.94 (1.31, 2.87)
(≤25th percentile)	2.09 (1.40, 3.12)	2.13 (1.43, 3.19)	2.13 (1.43, 3.19)
Reasoning			
(51st–75th percentile)	ns	ns	ns
(26th–50th percentile)	ns	ns	ns
(≤25th percentile)	1.45 (1.02, 2.07)	1.48 (1.03, 2.13)	1.50 (1.05, 2.16)
Psychomotor Speed			
(51st–75th percentile)	1.75 (1.12, 2.59)	1.71 (1.12, 2.59)	1.71 (1.12, 2.60)
(26th–50th percentile)	2.06 (1.37, 3.10)	2.02 (1.34, 3.05)	2.05 (1.34, 3.13)
(≤25th percentile)	2.10 (1.42, 3.12)	1.97 (1.32, 2.94)	1.97 (1.29, 3.00)

*All odds ratios (ORs) are with reference to participants in the top quartile, except for variables for which another quartile is set to 1.00. CI, confidence interval; ns, not significant.

with mortality after adjusting for age, gender, level of education, and Psychomotor Speed.

The relationship of Psychomotor Speed with mortality was one of the most consistent findings in this study, and the findings regarding Psychomotor Speed are similar to those reported by Birren (1968) and Kleemeier (1962): A significant decline in Psychomotor Speed is a risk factor for subsequent mortality. This study also indicated that some of the relationship observed between cognitive function and mortality may be mediated by Psychomotor Speed, a measure of perceptual speed. There is growing evidence that perceptual speed is an important contributor to the decline in cognitive performance that occurs in many tasks (Earles & Salthouse, 1995; Salthouse, 1993). Perceptual speed has been suggested as a general mechanism underlying age-related differences on many cognitive tasks, including reasoning and spatial cognition (Mayr & Kliegel, 1993; Salthouse, 1985).

Only a few studies have analyzed memory in relation to survival. Our finding that Verbal Memory is related to survival agrees with the results of Deeg, Hoff-

TABLE 10.6 Odds Ratios and Confidence Intervals for Level
of Performance by Age Group

Independent Variables	Young (34–74 years), OR (95% CI)	Old (75–95 years), OR (95% CI)
Identical Pictures		
(51st–75th percentile)	*ns*	*ns*
(26th–50th percentile)	*ns*	2.57 (1.16, 5.25)
(≤25th percentile)	2.80 (1.02, 7.66)	2.93 (1.40, 6.14)
Change Verbal Meaning		
(51st–75th percentile)	*ns*	*ns*
(26th–50th percentile)	*ns*	1.84 (1.07, 3.19)
(≤25th percentile)	*ns*	1.80 (1.06, 3.06)
Change Spatial Ability		
(51st–75th percentile)	*ns*	*ns*
(26th–50th percentile)	2.48 (1.30, 4.72)	1.65 (1.01, 2.71)
(≤25th percentile)	1.75 (1.42, 5.33)	1.72 (1.03, 2.87)
Change Reasoning Ability		
(51st–75th percentile)	*ns*	*ns*
(26th–50th percentile)	*ns*	*ns*
(≤25th percentile)	1.85 (1.04, 3.28)	*ns*
Change Psychomotor Speed		
(51st–75th percentile)	*ns*	*ns*
(26th–50th percentile)	*ns*	2.64 (1.49, 4.70)
(≤25th percentile)	*ns*	2.67 (1.27, 4.07)

Note. Age, gender, education level adjusted; OR, odds ratio; CI, confidence interval;
ns = not significant.

man, and van Zonneveld (1990); Small and Bäckman (1997); and the Göteborg
Longitudinal Study (Johansson & Berg, 1989).

Verbal Meaning is known to be less sensitive to age than most other cognitive
abilities, and vocabulary performance may be sensitive to the disease processes
primarily responsible for death in the present deceased participants (Bosworth &
Schaie, 1999; Cooney et al., 1988).

There was also evidence that decline in Spatial Ability, a measure of visualization ability, was related to mortality. Few studies have included Spatial Ability
and examined its relationship with mortality. Survivors had significantly higher
mean levels of Spatial Ability than decedents, but did not show significant decline
over time (Bosworth & Schaie, 1999).

The association between cognitive performance and subsequent mortality in
younger adults (<73 years) differed from older adults. Declines in age-related
cognitive functions (i.e., Spatial and Reasoning abilities) were more of a risk
factor among younger adults, whereas Verbal Meaning (crystallized ability) and
two types of perceptual speed represented greater risk factors among adults older
than 75 years. A possible explanation for this association between cognitive function and mortality between the two age groups might be found in the different

age-related trajectories of these variables. That is, adults tend to decline earlier on visualization and fluid abilities than on crystallized abilities. Nevertheless, this relationship among age, cognition, and mortality may explain why past research has reported that certain age groups may appear more likely to exhibit terminal change than others (Bosworth & Schaie, 1999; Cooney et al., 1988).

Chapter Summary

This chapter discusses the manner in which physical disease may affect the maintenance of function and how disease onset might be affected by behavioral antecedents and concomitants. A series of studies is described that relates the role of disease and intellectual functioning in the SLS. The first study implicated CVD as associated with earlier onset of decline of intellectual functioning. Decline in Psychomotor Speed was also identified as a risk factor for the occurrence of CVD. However, when hypertensives were disaggregated, they did not show any increased risk of cognitive decline.

The second study, concerned with the structural relationship between disease processes and maintenance of intellectual functioning, also implicated cardiovascular and musculoskeletal conditions as leading to excess risk for cognitive decline. Surprisingly, the diagnosis of neoplasms was negatively correlated with cognitive decline.

A more comprehensive analysis has extended these findings to the disease categories of diabetes, neoplasms, and arthritis as well as to a measure of overall health. Overall health status as measured by number of chronic disease diagnoses was found to have a negative effect on the abilities of Verbal Meaning, Number, and Word Fluency. The more serious CVD conditions (atherosclerosis and cerebrovascular disease) have generally negative influences, whereas benign CVD (including uncomplicated hypertension) has a slightly positive influence on cognition. Diabetes was correlated positively with intellectual functioning, perhaps reflecting the survival of those who can manage this condition more intelligently. The onset of arthritis was associated with timing of cognitive decline on Inductive Reasoning and Spatial abilities. When neoplasms were disaggregated into benign and malignant forms, the malignant cases were associated with cognitive decline.

New studies of self-reported health behaviors identified eight latent dimensions: not smoking, alcohol abstention, avoiding unhealthy food, healthy food preparation, wearing seat belts, dental care, and medical checkups. We had to reject a healthy lifestyle hypothesis and instead conclude that positive health behaviors are adopted on a behavior-specific basis, and that they differ across gender and age groups. Factor-analytic studies of the invariance of the health behavior construct across groups suggest that the factor patterns appear to be invariant across both parent-offspring and sibling dyads. However, different factor weights are required for a good fit for parents and offspring; a strong invariance model (constraining factor loadings and latent means) can be fitted to the sibling sample. Studies of personality characteristics and demographic factors as antecedents of health behaviors resulted in age- and domain-specific patterns that accounted for only a limited proportion of variance in the health behaviors.

The impact of our behavioral measures as predictors was also considered for the occurrence of and the age of onset of CVD and arthritis. As expected, higher levels of cognitive functioning and of education were generally associated with later disease onset, but the picture is complex, not uniform across all abilities.

Studies of structural and perceived social support confirm that married persons tend to have fewer physical health problems than unmarried persons, and that higher socioeconomic status is associated with better health. But, we account for limited variance in health outcomes from more extensive structural support systems. By contrast, perceived support is important for married persons and for those experiencing more serious health problems.

We also studied the effect of cognition on medication use. As found in other studies, women and the elderly used more medication, even though in this well-educated population average medication use was lower than typically found. Most participants were aware of the therapeutic purpose of their medications, and older participants did not differ from younger persons in this respect. There was no effect of cognitive variables on misperception of therapeutic purpose, although participants who were young, male, or with a lower level of education and income were more likely to be inaccurate.

Finally, we examined cognitive level at last assessment as well as 7-year change in performance as predictors of mortality. Lower levels of performance on crystallized abilities, Spatial Ability, Verbal Memory, and perceptual speed, as well as 7-year declines on Verbal Meaning, Spatial Orientation, Inductive Reasoning, and Psychomotor Speed were associated with earlier mortality. However, decline in fluid abilities was a better predictor of mortality in the young-old; declines in crystallized abilities and Psychomotor Speed were better predictors of mortality in the old-old.

CHAPTER ELEVEN

Lifestyle Variables That Affect Intellectual Functioning

W E HAVE COLLECTED DATA ON SOME LIMITED demographic characteristics of our participants from the very beginning of our study. It was not until 1974, however, that we began to engage systematically in an exploration of what we then termed our participants' microenvironment as a possible source of influences that would help us to understand individual differences in cognitive aging (DeFrias, 1998; Gribbin et al., 1980; Nguyen, 2000; Schaie, 1996b; Schaie & Gribbin, 1975; Schaie & O'Hanlon, 1990).

We constructed a survey instrument named the Life Complexity Inventory (LCI) that was designed to measure various aspects of our participants' immediate environment. This questionnaire was originally administered in the spring of 1974 as a structured interview in home visits to 140 of the participants who had taken part in the first three study cycles. The data from this interview were then clustered, and eight distinct dimensions were identified (Gribbin et al., 1980). Variables comprising these item clusters are shown in table 11.1. Subsequent to the analyses described next, we made minor changes in the interview scheme and converted it to a survey instrument that has been used systematically beginning with the 1977 data collection.

The term *disengaged* used in the following discussion refers to the tendency of many older persons to reduce environmental stress and perhaps compensate for perceived losses in competence by reducing their interaction with other persons as well as reducing their active participation in community and their social participation (see Cumming & Henry, 1961; Havighurst, Neugarten, & Tobin, 1968).

In the initial analysis of the LCI, significant gender differences were found for two clusters. As expected, women had higher scores on the homemaker role cluster, and surprisingly, they also scored higher on the disengagement cluster than the men. With respect to age differences, we found the younger participants

TABLE 11.1 Variables Comprising Life Complexity Inventory Item Clusters

Social status
  High level of education
  High present and previous income
  High present and previous occupational
    status
  Perceived time pressure
  Reads many magazines
  Large number of rooms in home
Subjective dissatisfaction with life status
  High present and retrospective dissatisfaction
    with life
  High present and retrospective dissatisfaction
    with job success
  Few friends
Noisy environment
  Living now and previously close to freeways
    or airports
  Living in a noisy environment and bothered
    by it
  Present and past environment filled with traf-
    fic noise
Family dissolution
  High number of changes in residence in past
    5 years
  Spouse lost by death
  Living in multiple-unit dwelling
  Living in neighborhood with large elderly pop-
    ulation
  Widowed or not married

Semipassive engagement with the environment
  Retrospective upper-middle-class lifestyle
  Many home-related activities
  Many friends with diverse interests
Disengagement from interaction with the envi-
  ronment
  High number of passive activities
  Few changes of occupation
  More advanced age
  Many solitary activities
  Few past and present hours spent reading
  Low involvement in people-related activities
  Low present and past involvement in work ac-
    tivities
Maintenance of acculturation
  High number of fiction and nonfiction books
    read
  High number of college or adult education
    courses taken
  Higher number of weeks spent in educational
    activities
Female homemaker role
  Younger than spouse
  Widowed or not married
  Much time spent in homemaking activities
  Much time spent in solitary activities
  Much time spent in working with hands
  Never in military service
  High on unnecessary conversation

scored higher on social status, whereas older participants were more disengaged and were more likely to score high on the family dissolution cluster.

Lifestyle Characteristics and Cognitive Functioning: Initial Analyses

We examined the relationship between lifestyle characteristics and maintenance of cognitive function in a number of different ways. We began by clustering individuals in terms of their cluster scores on the LCI variables and were able to identify four types of individuals with distinct lifestyle characteristics who also differed markedly in maintaining high levels of cognitive performance (Gribbin et al., 1980; Schaie, 1984b).

Over both 7- and 14-year periods, we found that there was least decline for those persons who had high socioeconomic status and who were fully engaged in interaction with their environment. Next were those fully engaged persons who had average socioeconomic status. Substantial decline was shown by persons who were relatively passive in their interaction (those we called semiengaged). Finally, it was the widowed women who had never had a career of their own and who showed a disengaged lifestyle who were most likely to show excess decline.

These differences in maintenance of cognitive ability level of the lifestyle types were statistically significant for all abilities except Number; they were also significant for the factor measures of cognitive style. In particular, high social status has positive predictive value, whereas disengagement has negative predictive value for the abilities. Maintenance of acculturation is a positive predictor of Word Fluency, Attitudinal Flexibility, and Psychomotor Speed, and family dissolution negatively predicts future performance on most variables. Finally, centrality of the homemaker role predicts positively to Psychomotor Speed but negatively to Spatial Orientation.

Lifestyle Characteristics and Cognitive Functioning: More Recent Analyses

The relationship between environmental factors and cognitive functioning has been examined in three doctoral dissertations and one master's thesis conducted in my laboratory. The first dissertation (Stone, 1980) was concerned primarily with the structural relations among environmental factors, health, and cognition (see chapter 10). The second (O'Hanlon, 1993) is of particular interest as it focused primarily on the environmental factors. The third (Nguyen, 2000) was concerned with family similarities in lifestyles. I begin by describing O'Hanlon's analysis, which included data for 1,376 participants who completed the LCI as part of the 1977 data collection. It also included a subset of 779 persons for whom LCI data were available in both 1977 and 1984. Findings from this work are summarized next.

Dimensions of Leisure Activities

In the O'Hanlon study (1993), initial analyses focused on developing empirical dimensions for the 30 leisure activities included in the LCI (see also Maitland, O'Hanlon, & Schaie, 1990). An initial series of exploratory and confirmatory factor analyses determined that 17 of these activities had sufficient commonalities to permit the development of a six-factor model. The resulting factors were Household Activities, Social Activities, Educational-Cultural Activities, Fitness Activities, Solitary Activities, and Communicative Activities. The model was estimated on a random half of the 1977 participants and confirmed on the other random half, maintaining excellent fit [$\chi^2(df = 100) = 155.56$, $p < .001$; $GFI = .974$; $AGFI = .965$; $RMSR = .03$]. Maximum likelihood factor loading estimates and factor intercorrelations for the accepted model are given in table 11.2.

Factor scores were then calculated and a 2 (gender) × 9 (cohort) multivariate analysis of variance (MANOVA) was run to determine whether there were significant differences by age/cohort and gender. Women had significantly higher means on the Social, Solitary, and Household Activities factors; men had higher scores

TABLE 11.2 Measurement Model for Life Complexity Inventory Activities

	House-hold	Social	Educational/Cultural	Fitness	Solitary	Commu-nication	Unique Variance
Factor Loadings							
Variable							
Cooking	.807						.348
Household chores	.733						.463
Shopping	.427	.261					.654
Being visited		.682					.535
Visiting others		.696					.516
Social life and parties		.363	.288				.701
Educational activities			.625				.609
Cultural activities			.565				.681
Self-improvement			.504				.745
Participant in sports			.386				.851
Physical fitness				.618			.618
Outdoor hobbies				.301	.194		.848
Solitary games or hobbies					.487		.763
Handicrafts				.603			.637
Discussion and talking					.749		.440
Daydreaming and reminiscing						.533	.715
Writing correspondence	.296					.356	.710
Factor Intercorrelations							
Factor							
Household							
Social	.431						
Educational-Cultural	.199	.400					
Fitness	−.022	.375	.485				
Solitary	.406	.478	.300	.200			
Communication	.360	.709	.588	.452	.380		

Note. All factor loadings are significant at or beyond the .01% level of confidence. From O'Hanlon (1993).

on the Fitness factor. No significant gender differences occurred for the Social and Communicative Activities factors. Age differences were significant between the most extreme age groups for all factors except Solitary Activities. The youngest cohorts had generally higher mean levels of participation in leisure activities than did the oldest cohorts.

Relationship Between Leisure Activities and Cognitive Functioning

Correlations between the activity factors and the Primary Mental Abilities (PMA) core variables were low to modest. The highest significant correlations were those of Verbal Meaning with Educational-Cultural ($r = .37$) and Communications ($r = .25$); Spatial Orientation with Communications ($r = .19$); Reasoning with Educational-Cultural ($r = .26$) and Communications ($r = .27$); and Word Fluency with Educational-Cultural ($r = .27$) and Communications ($r = .24$).

Dimensions of the Life Complexity Inventory

Another series of factor analyses was conducted to determine the latent dimensions of the LCI. The variables included a broad spectrum of environmental dimensions as well as the factor scores derived from the leisure activity analyses described in the preceding section. Again, the basic analyses were run on a random half of the 1977 samples, with verification of the best-fitting factor model on the remaining half. The model that was finally accepted includes 30 variables and eight factors [$\chi^2(df = 373) = 986.09$, $p < .001$; $GFI = .912$; $AGFI = .890$; $RMSR = .05$]. The environmental factors identified were Prestige, Social Status, Leisure Activities, Physical Environment, Mobility, Intellectual Environment, Social Network, and Work Characteristics. Maximum likelihood factor loading estimates and factor intercorrelations for the accepted model are given in table 11.3.

Factor scores were calculated for the eight latent lifestyle dimensions; again, a 2 (gender) × 9 (cohort) MANOVA was run to determine gender and age/cohort differences. It was found that men had significantly higher scores than women on the Prestige, Social Status, and Work factors. Women had significantly higher scores on the Leisure Activities factor, but no significant sex differences were found for Physical Environment, Mobility, Intellectual Environment, and Social Network. Age/cohort differences were significant for all factors except for Physical Environment.

In general, age differences were in favor of the younger cohorts. For the Social Status factor, there was a significant difference between the youngest cohort (mean age 25 years) and the three oldest cohorts (mean ages 67 years and older); none of the other cohorts differed significantly. With respect to the Leisure Activities factor, all other cohorts were significantly above the level of the oldest cohort (mean age 81 years). On the Intellectual Environment factor, the middle-aged cohorts (mean ages 39 to 53 years) were significantly above the two oldest cohorts. The youngest cohort was also above the level of the oldest cohort. With respect to the Mobility factor, the youngest cohort (mean age 25 years) was significantly above all other cohorts. Those in early middle age (cohorts with mean ages 32 and 39 years) were also significantly more mobile than all cohorts above a mean age of 60 years.

Considering the Prestige factor, it is interesting to note that the cohort in early middle age (mean age 32 years) exceeded the level of persons who were in their 60s or older. In addition, the middle-aged exceeded the oldest cohorts. Not surprisingly, all cohorts exceeded the two oldest cohorts on the Work factor. The Social Status factor, however, showed a rather different pattern. Here, the highest level was shown by the cohort with a mean age of 46 years, which was significantly higher than all but the two adjacent cohorts.

Finally, we observed a significant Gender × Cohort interaction for the Mobility factor. Women had lower means for all cohorts except one of the middle-aged

TABLE 11.3 Measurement Model for Life Complexity Inventory Lifestyle Dimensions

Variable	Prestige	Social Status	Leisure	Physical Environment	Mobility	Intellectual Environment	Social Network	Work Characteristics	Unique Variance
Factor Loadings									
Education	.770								.390
Occupation	.758								.426
Marital status		.538							.765
Home ownership		.535							.782
Income		.549						.359	.362
Number of rooms		.711							.608
Fitness			.349						.839
Educational-cultural activities		.436	.468					.307	.621
Communicative activities			.712						.512
Social activities			.626						.667
Solitary activities			.395						.888
Household activities			.532						.805
Air quality				.690					.516
Trees in neighborhood				.694					.526
Noise level				-.371					.861
Changes in jobs					.777				.447
Changes in homes					.588			.324	.659
Changes in occupations					.377				.774
Books in home						.546			.704

				h^2
Art objects in home	.495			.758
Magazines read	.358			.871
Educational course taken	.383			.852
Confidants		.384		.857
Meetings attended		.523		.726
Visits outside neighborhood		.376		.860
Reading (proportion of activities)			.488	.761
Work status (working/retired)			.831	.342
Work under pressure			.536	.707
Workplace (indoors/out)			-.698	.470
Working with people			.395	.834

Factor Intercorrelations

Factor	Prestige	Social Status	Leisure Activities	Physical Environment	Mobility	Intellectual Environment	Social Network	Work Characteristics
Prestige								
Social Status	.299							
Leisure Activities	.084	.106						
Physical Environment	.359	.351	.078					
Mobility	.093	-.179	.128	-.081				
Intellectual Environment	.593	.411	.422	.366	-.028			
Social Network	.019	-.048	.266	.111	-.312	.173		
Work Characteristics	.492	.330	-.173	.140	.177	.320	-.355	

Note. All factor loadings are significant at or beyond the .01% level of confidence. From O'Hanlon (1993).

cohorts (mean age 46 years). For this cohort, women exceeded men in Mobility level.

Relationship Between Lifestyle Factors and Intellectual Abilities

Again the lifestyle factor scores were correlated with the core mental abilities. Three factors showed strong ability correlates: Prestige, Social Status, and Work Characteristics. These three were positively correlated with the ability scores, with correlations ranging from .27 to .51. Lower, but still significant, correlations were found for the Leisure, Intellectual Environment, and Physical Environment factors. There were no significant correlations with the extent of the participants' Social Network.

As an alternative approach, O'Hanlon (1993) also investigated the characterization of our participants in terms of their lifestyle profiles. Using cluster analysis, she identified 11 clusters of persons who had similar profiles, but differed from other cluster types in certain salient characteristics. Participant type was then entered as an independent variable in the MANOVA of cognitive abilities.

This analysis identified three clusters with members who performed significantly worse on the mental abilities than did member of other clusters. Individuals in these same cluster types also scored lower than those in other clusters on various permutations of environmental factors. The adverse factors typically represented low scores on the Prestige, Social Status, and Work Characteristics or on the Intellectual and Physical Environment factors. By contrast, the participant cluster characterized by above-average scores on the Prestige, Social Status, Intellectual Environment, and Work Characteristics factors also performed significantly better than other cluster types on Verbal Meaning, Space, Reasoning, and Word Fluency. In addition, the cluster that exhibited moderately high Mobility and Intellectual Environment scores scored significantly above average on Verbal Meaning, Space, and Reasoning abilities.

Longitudinal Analyses of the Lifestyle Variables

A series of confirmatory factor analyses determined whether the LCI dimensions developed on the basis of the 1977 sample would be maintained longitudinally over a 7-year period. Confirmatory models constraining factor loading across time, for the participants still available in 1984, were tested for both the leisure activities data and for the lifestyle factors described above. The structure of the leisure activities remained invariant by the most stringent criteria (invariance of patterns, loadings, and error variances across time). The lifestyle latent variable structure was somewhat less stable. However, it was possible to accept the equivalence of factor patterns across times (configural invariance).

A 2 (gender) × 9 (cohort) repeated measurement MANOVA was next run to determine whether there was longitudinal stability in mean levels. No statistically significant changes in mean level were found over the 7-year period for any of the leisure activities factors for any of the gender or age/cohort groupings.

When a similar analysis was conducted for the eight LCI lifestyle factors, however, several significant findings emerged. A significant Gender × Time effect was found only for the Work Characteristics factor, with women showing an increase at the second time of measurement. Significant Time × Age/Cohort interactions were found for Social Status, with the two youngest cohorts gaining significantly on this factor over the 7 years; all other cohorts remained stable. With respect to the Mobility factor, there was a significant increase in mobility over time for the four youngest cohorts and reduced mobility for all other cohorts. The youngest four cohorts also showed a significant increase on the Work factor, whereas the cohort with a mean age of 53 years at base measurement decreased significantly over the 7 years.

Effects of Retirement on the Lifestyle Variables

A final series of analyses examined the question whether stability in the lifestyle variables might be influenced by the marked lifestyle changes brought about by retirement. The longitudinal sample was divided into three groups: those who reported that they were working in both 1977 and 1984; those who were working in 1977, but were retired in 1984; and those who had retired prior to 1977. Repeated measurement MANOVAs were then run crossing gender, work status, and time of measurement.

The effects of greatest interest with respect to the leisure activities are those concerned with the question of whether retirement significantly affects participation in leisure activities. The Retirement Status × Time interaction was indeed significant. For those recently retired, there was a significant increase in Social Activities, Solitary Activities, and Household Activities. On the other hand, both the long-term retired and working groups showed decline over time in Social Activities, and the working group declined in Household Activities.

Similar analyses were conducted for the LCI lifestyle factors. There was an overall increase over time for the Work factor, as well as several significant Retirement Status × Time interactions. On the Prestige factor, the working group showed an increase over time, and the retired groups showed a decrease. Consistent with the analyses of the leisure activities, the Leisure factor showed a significant increase for the recently retired, but decreases for those working and for the long-term retirees. With respect to Mobility, those working showed an increase, those recently retired remained stable, and the long-term retirees decreased. Finally, on the Work factor, as expected, the recently retired showed a significant decrease, whereas those still working showed an increase.

Family Similarity in Lifestyle Characteristics

In an effort to explore the structure of intergenerational cohesion, Nguyen (2000) confirmed the structural invariance of the lifestyle dimensions identified by O'Hanlon (1993) and then examined similarities and differences between parents and their adult offspring and between adult siblings.

Method

Participants   The subset from the SLS included in the following analysis included participants of the 1989 and 1996 family studies who were matched against members of the longitudinal panel who participated in either 1984 or 1996 waves. A total of 1,012 parent-offspring pairs were matched. These included 216 father-son, 268 father-daughter, 206 mother-son, and 412 mother-daughter pairings. The following ages applied to this sample: parents, $M = 67.6$, $SD = 10.0$, range = 41 to 92 years; offspring, $M = 43.4$, $SD = 10.3$, range 22 to 72 years. The mean age difference between parents and offspring was 24.2 years. The sample was divided into two age groups consisting of those with parents who were younger or older than 65 years.

In a similar manner, 655 sibling pairs were identified. Of these, 121 were brother-brother pairs, 239 sister-sister pairs, and 295 brother-sister pairs. Average ages for the siblings were as follows: longitudinal study members, $M = 57.2$, $SD = 14.9$ years; relatives, $M = 59.8$, $SD = 14.8$ years. The average age difference within sibling pairs was 2.6 years. This sample was also divided into two age groups according to whether the older sibling was either younger or older than 65 years.

Measures   Six of the dimensions from the LCI determined by O'Hanlon (see section on dimensions of the LCI) were included in this analysis: Prestige, Social Status, Physical Environment, Intellectual Environment, Social Network, and Work Complexity.

Analyses   Multiple group restricted factor analyses (LISREL 8.14; Jöreskog & Sörbom, 1993) were used to test factorial invariance (see chapter 2). Tests of invariance were conducted for the total samples as well as the various specific relationship subsets. Family similarity was then examined by comparing the within-dyad concordance of the lifestyle factors.

Results

Structural Invariance   An initial analysis within the parent-offspring dyads specified a configural invariance baseline model for which a reasonable fit was obtained ($\chi^2 = 1{,}514.56$, $df = 580$, $RMSEA = .04$, $GFI = .93$). The test of weak invariance, the constraining factor loading across groups, resulted in a significant decrease in fit ($\Delta\chi^2 = 68.69$, $df = 13$, $p < .01$). Hence, configural invariance was accepted as the best fit. Lifestyle characteristics for which loadings could not be constrained across generations included marital status, home ownership, living characteristics, social network, and work characteristics.

Configural invariance was also the accepted model for the father-son, father-daughter, mother-son, and mother-daughter subsets, as well as for the subgroups of older and younger parent-offspring dyad sets.

Next examined was the structural similarity between sibling dyads. The accepted baseline model had a reasonable fit (χ^2 1,036.20, $df = 580$, $RMSEA = .04$, $GFI = .93$). Again, a test of weak factorial invariance resulted in a significant decrease in fit ($\Delta\chi^2 = 39.24$, $df = 13$, $p < .01$) and therefore had to be rejected. Lifestyle characteristics that could not be fit across sibling dyads included home ownership neighborhood, social network, and work characteristics.

In contrast to the parent-offspring results, it was possible, however, to accept weak factorial invariance for the sister-sister and brother-brother, but not for the brother-sister, dyads. Weak factorial within-dyad invariance could also be accepted for the older, but not for the younger, sibling dyads.

Similarity of Lifestyle Factors   Intergenerational and within-generation lifestyle similarity was next examined by considering the magnitudes of factor correlations across dyads. These concordance coefficients are reported in table 11.4. The parent-offspring correlations were quite modest, ranging from 0.11 to 0.35. The highest subgroup correlations occurred for mother-daughter dyads and the lowest for father-daughter dyads. Little difference was found between age groups.

Somewhat greater similarity, ranging from 0.12 to 0.48, was found within sibling dyads. Concordance within sibling dyads was highest for sister-sister and lowest for brother-brother pairs. Slightly higher concordance was found for older as compared to younger sibling pairs.

Summary

Structural invariance of lifestyle factors was limited to the configural invariance level between parent-offspring pairs, but weak invariance could be accepted for sister-sister and brother-brother dyads. Family similarity as measured by concordance of factor correlations was quite modest, but again greater within sibling than parent-offspring pairs.

Effects of Work Characteristics and Retirement Status on Cognitive Functioning

Further analyses of the relation of the effect of work and retirement on cognitive functioning were conducted by DeFrias (1998). This work was informed by Schooler's (1987, 1990) environmental complexity hypothesis. Schooler argued that environmental complexity is determined by the stimulus variability and intensity of demands of an individual's environment. Deleterious cognitive effects may arise by overexposure to routine or nonstimulating settings. On the other hand, immersion in environments that demand continued use and practice of intellectual skills may favorably affect cognitive maintenance into old age. Some empirical support for the disuse perspective suggests that involvement in intellectually stimulating activities may buffer against decline in cognitive functioning (Hultsch, Hertzog, Dixon, & Small, 1998; Kohn et al., 1983; Schooler, Mulatu, & Oates, 1999). A potentially moderating role of the timing of retirement on the above relationship is also supported by other studies (Avolio & Waldman, 1990, 1994; Avolio, Waldman, & McDaniel, 1990; DeFrias & Schaie, 2001; Dutta, Schulenberg, & Lair, 1986).

TABLE 11.4 Concordance of Lifestyle Factors Within Family Dyads

	Parent-Offspring Dyads					Sibling Dyads			
Factor	Father-Son	Father-Daughter	Mother-Son	Mother-Daughter	All Dyads	Sister-Sister	Sister-Brother	Brother-Brother	All Siblings
Prestige	.36*	.20*	.35*	.34*	.35*	.56	.40*	.39*	.48*
Social Status	.24*	-.04	-.02	.17*	.03	.23*	-.07	.05	.12*
Physical Environment	-.08	-.03	.19*	.19*	.11	.04	.08	-.08	.05
Intellectual Environment	.01	.21	-.17	.40*	.09	.35	.42*	.14	.32*
Social Network	.21*	.02	.17	.21	.20*	.58*	.13	-.04	.27*
Work Complexity	.13	.11	.15	.05	.11*	.14	.30	.27	.24*

*p < .05.

In the following sections, I first report the effects of work characteristics on change in cognitive abilities over a 7-year period; second, I examine the potentially moderating role of the timing of retirement on this relationship; and third, I ask whether there are gender differences in the environment-cognition relationship.

Methods

Participants   The subsample included in these analysis met the following criteria: In 1984, participants were between the ages of 55 and 70 years, so that by 1991 they had reached the minimum eligibility age for Social Security pensions; all participants were working in 1984. Based on these criteria, these analyses included 164 participants (93 men and 71 women) who in 1984 had a mean age of 60.17 years ($SD = 3.92$; range 55–70 years). Their mean educational level in 1984 was 15.1 years ($SD = 2.8$; range 8–20). The median income in 1984 was $36,324. In 1984, the participants worked in a number of different occupations, ranging from blue collar to professional ($Mdn = 3.0$; range 1–5). By 1991, 60% of the participants were retired.

Measures   Cognitive abilities include the five measures from our basic ability battery (Verbal Meaning, Spatial Orientation, Inductive Reasoning, Number, and Word Fluency) as well as the measure of Immediate Recall. Three global indicators of work characteristics include number of hours spent reading and writing, working with one's hands, and dealing with other people. More specific indicators measure number of persons interacted with, speed at which work is controlled, doing the same or different tasks, and length of time required to complete an average task (see discussion of LCI above and chapter 3 for further details).

Analyses   Two analytic techniques were utilized. First, a confirmatory factor analysis using LISREL 8.3 (Jöreskog & Sörbom, 1993) was performed on the LCI work variables using a larger SLS sample. The factors extracted from the analyses represent the three work constructs (Complexity, Control, and Routine) used in further analyses. Second, a 2 (gender) × 2 (retirement status) × 2 (work level) × 2 (occasion) repeated measures multivariate analysis of covariance (MANCOVA) with age and education as the covariates was performed on the six cognitive measures.

Results

Confirmatory Factor Analysis of Work Characteristics From the Life Complexity Inventory   The fit of a three-factor model was tested to create summary work-related variables for use in further analyses. To obtain more stable parameter estimates, we tested the expected three-factor model in a larger SLS sample ($n = 1,567$). The three factors were labeled Complexity, Control, and Routine. Variables marking the Complexity factor were reading/writing, dealing with people, and number of employees. Variables marking the Control factor were speed control and working under time pressure. Variables marking the Routine factor were working with hands, routinization of tasks, and task duration.

The three-factor model was estimated by maximum likelihood methods using the correlation matrix presented in table A-11.1 in the appendix. In addition to the chi-square statistic, which is sensitive to sample size, other fit indices include the comparative fit index (*CFI*; Bentler, 1990), *GFI* (Jöreskog & Sörbom, 1993), and *RMSEA* (Steiger, 1990). Based on these indices, the model fits the data reasonably well: $\chi^2 = 80.97$, $df = 17$, $CFI = .92$, $GFI = .99$, $RMSEA = .05$. All LCI items loaded significantly onto their expected factors (see table 11.5). Composite factor scores were then created by summing across the indicator variables and calculating an average score. These composite scores were used in further MANCOVA analyses.

Change in Cognitive Abilities by Gender, Retirement Status, and Work Characteristics A four-way (2 Gender × 2 Retirement Statuses × 2 Work Levels × 2 Occasions) repeated measures MANCOVA was used to examine change over 7 years in cognitive abilities. Three separate models were examined, one for each work factor (i.e., Complexity, Control, and Routine). The covariates used for these analyses were age and education to partial out the variance explained by these variables before analyzing the influence of retirement status and work level on change in cognitive abilities. The combined cognitive scores were significantly affected by a retirement status by Job Complexity interaction, an occasion by Job Complexity interaction, an occasion by gender by retirement status by Job Complexity interaction, and a gender by Routine interaction.

Univariate tests revealed significant main effects for retirement status on Immediate Recall and Job Complexity on Immediate Recall. The group not retired scored higher on Immediate Recall than the retired group. The group with high Job Complexity scored higher than the group with low Job Complexity. The low Routine group declined on Spatial Orientation over the 7-year period; the group with high Job Complexity experienced no reliable change over the same time period. The group with low Job Complexity also declined in Word Fluency.

TABLE 11.5 Standardized Factor Loadings for Life Complexity Inventory Work Factors

Variable	Complexity	Control	Routine
Reading/writing	.34*	—	—
Dealing with people	.52*	—	—
Number of employees	.51*	—	—
Speed control	—	.47*	—
Working under time pressure	—	.91*	—
Working with hands	—	—	.40*
Routinization of tasks	—	—	.46*
Task duration	—	—	.25*

*$p < .05$.

Among the group already retired, those who had been involved in relatively low Control jobs experienced decline in Number performance; those in jobs with relatively high Control remained stable. Among the not-retired group, women scored lower than men on Spatial Orientation.

Summary   These analyses provide evidence for the beneficial impact of Job Complexity and Control over aspects of work for the maintenance of cognitive performance. Interestingly, in select relations those workers in relatively routine jobs outperformed workers in jobs involving changing task demands. Perhaps there is a balance between level of task demand and the maintenance of cognitive functioning, especially in the presence of decline in cognitive resources with aging. Nonetheless, some of our findings support the notion that occupational self-direction and delayed retirement are conducive to slowing the process of cognitive decline evident in the sixth and seventh decades of the life span.

Low occupational self-direction was associated with cognitive decline, perhaps because of a lack of full use of one's abilities. Given the increase in individual differences in late adulthood, training programs might perhaps help older adults prolong their competency levels in the workforce until later ages. Successful aging in the domain of work (cf. Abraham & Hansson, 1995; Schaie & Schooler, 1998), as with other contexts (cf. Freund & Baltes, 1998), depends on an optimal match between the changing demands of the work contexts and the skills available to the worker. Some combinations of work contexts and individual capabilities may well be uniquely synergistic.

Chapter Summary

The LCI has been used since 1974 to characterize the microenvironment of participants in the SLS. Early analyses of this instruments identified eight lifestyle factors that were related to our measures of intellectual abilities. Four participant types were identified: the affluent fully engaged, those of average socioeconomic status who were fully engaged, the semiengaged, and widowed homemakers. The first two groups maintained their levels of intellectual functioning or even showed modest improvement over 7 and 14 years; the other two groups showed significant decline—substantial for the widowed homemakers.

More recent analyses utilized larger samples to establish six dimensions of the leisure activities contained in the LCI: Household Activities, Social Activities, Educational-Cultural Activities, Fitness Activities, Solitary Activities, and Communicative Activities. Factor scores for these dimensions was included in the analysis of the remaining LCI variables, with an eight-factor lifestyle dimensions structure emerging: Prestige, Social Status, Leisure Activities, Physical Environment, Mobility, Intellectual Environment, Social Network, and Work Characteristics. Women exceeded men on the Social, Solitary, and Household Activities factors; men scored higher on the Fitness factor. The youngest age group exceeded the oldest group on all factors except Solitary Activities. The younger cohorts scored higher in Leisure Activities. Men exceeded women on the Prestige, Social Status, and Work lifestyle factors; women scored higher on Leisure Activities.

Low-to-modest positive correlations were found between amount of leisure activity and levels of cognitive functioning. Positive lifestyle characteristics were also correlated with high levels of cognitive functioning, with the dimensions of Prestige, Social Status, and Work Characteristics showing the highest correlations. Longitudinal stability was demonstrated at the metric invariance level for the leisure activities factors and at the configural invariance level for the lifestyle dimensions.

Family similarity in lifestyles was examined for parent-offspring and sibling dyads. Factorial invariance was observed at the configural level for the parent-offspring dyads and at the weak factorial invariance level for the siblings. Family similarity was greater within than across generations and greatest for mother-daughter and sister-sister pairs.

Finally, we examined the effects of work characteristics and retirement on cognitive functions. Complex work situations and low routinization of the workplace support maintenance of cognitive functions; retirement is enhancing for those in routine jobs, but less favorable for those who have experienced challenging and complex job situations. No significant level changes occurred over 7 years for the Leisure Activities. However, there was an increase over time for women on Work Characteristics. The two youngest cohorts gained significantly on Prestige, and there was an increase in Mobility and Work Characteristics for the four youngest cohorts, with reduced Mobility for all others. Retirement increased Leisure Activities for the recently retired, with a reduction of activities for those working or retired for a substantial time. As expected, the retired showed a decrease in Work and Prestige; the opposite pattern prevailed for those still working after 7 years.

CHAPTER TWELVE

The Sequential Study
of Personality Traits
and Attitudes

ALTHOUGH THE STUDY OF PERSONALITY has not been the central focus of the Seattle Longitudinal Study (SLS), a large body of data on a limited number of personality traits and attitudes was acquired almost incidentally. These data come primarily from the Test of Behavioral Rigidity (TBR; Schaie, 1955, 1960; Schaie & Parham, 1975). As mentioned in chapter 3, when I constructed the TBR questionnaire that provided the base for our latent construct of Attitudinal Flexibility, I included as masking items a set of 44 items from the Social Responsibility scale of the California Psychological Inventory (Gough, 1957; Gough et al., 1952). The sequential data (cross-sectional and longitudinal) on this scale are, of course, of interest in their own right in chronicling stability and change on this trait over the adult age range and time period covered by our study.

I soon realized, moreover, that personality and/or attitudinal true-and-false questionnaire items are likely to carry information on other personality characteristics than the particular traits for which they were originally selected. Hence, we began to engage in item factor analyses of the entire set of 75 items contained in the TBR questionnaire (see Maitland et al., 1992; Schaie, 1996b; Schaie & Parham, 1976).

In this chapter, I first report findings with respect to the directly observed trait of social responsibility. I then describe the work on personality traits derived from the 75 TBR questionnaire items. Next I provide preliminary data on recent work relating the TBR-derived personality factors to the NEO. Finally, I describe new work on the Center for Epidemiologic Studies–Depression Scale (CES-D) questionnaire used as a subjective measure of depression in our study participants older than 60 years.

Social Responsibility

Initial cross-sectional findings for the Social Responsibility scale were reported on the base-level study (Schaie, 1959b), and sequential models have been applied to this scale on data from the first three cycles (Schaie & Parham, 1974). In the following sections, I report data over all seven study occasions and use the format employed for the cognitive data.

Cross-Sectional Findings

Means and standard deviations by gender for the total sample are reported by test occasion in table 12.1. As can be seen from figure 12.1, there is a tendency for the cross-sectional data to suggest relatively lower responsibility levels until early midlife and from then on what seem to be occasion-specific age differences. That is, for the early cohorts, lower levels are shown into old age, whereas for the more recent cohorts, there seem to be favorable trends for the oldest groups.

Longitudinal Findings

The longitudinal data reported here were averaged across all participants within each 7-year age segment over all periods for which appropriate 7-year data are available. By contrast to the cross-sectional data, the longitudinal estimates provided in table 12.2 and graphed in figure 12.2 separately by gender suggest that there is a modest gain in Social Responsibility until age 74 years, followed by a minimal decline thereafter. A gender difference in favor of women occurs until age 46 years.

Cohort and Period Effects

When examined over all seven waves, cohort effects for the Social Responsibility scale are not very pronounced. There is a modest concave pattern, but it is only the 1952 cohort that has a significantly lower level of Social Responsibility than some of the other cohorts (see table 12.3). With respect to secular trends, it appears that Social Responsibility was at a nadir at the 1977 measurement occasion. Significant overall decline in reported Social Responsibility was found from 1956 to 1977, whereas a significant increase occurred from 1977 through 1998 (see table 12.4).

Other Personality Traits

An item factor analysis of the 75 TBR questionnaire items using all available data from the 1963 and 1970 data collections resulted in the acceptance of a 19-factor structure. The resultant factors were matched by content to Cattell's (1957) personality taxonomy. Of the factors, 13 appeared to me to be substantively simi-

TABLE 12.1 Means and Standard Deviations for the Social Responsibility Scale by Sample and Gender

	Age								
	25	32	39	46	53	60	67	74	81
1956									
Male	46.24	48.58	51.78	49.49	54.11	48.86	52.95	—	—
	(11.01)	(8.43)	(9.25)	(8.78)	(8.72)	(11.03)	(8.73)	—	—
Female	49.79	52.59	51.80	53.37	53.89	52.97	49.53	—	—
	(10.05)	(8.69)	(10.02)	(10.35)	(9.22)	(8.64)	(9.15)	—	—
Total	48.02	50.70	51.79	51.28	54.00	50.97	51.24	—	—
	(10.62)	(8.74)	(9.56)	(9.66)	(8.91)	(10.02)	(9.05)	—	—
1963									
Male	49.14	49.08	48.72	49.32	47.11	48.69	46.23	48.68	—
	(10.23)	(11.93)	(10.21)	(10.03)	(11.84)	(10.67)	(10.41)	(11.26)	—
Female	49.90	50.49	52.35	50.59	51.14	50.41	51.03	45.90	—
	(9.27)	(10.38)	(8.42)	(9.18)	(8.13)	(10.51)	(10.95)	(8.24)	—
Total	49.58	49.89	50.63	49.94	49.39	49.59	48.61	47.26	—
	(9.64)	(10.05)	(9.45)	(9.62)	(10.08)	(10.58)	(10.91)	(9.86)	—
1970									
Male	46.29	51.32	48.91	51.14	51.28	51.47	48.00	48.83	48.62
	(10.82)	(6.71)	(11.10)	(7.98)	(8.59)	(8.02)	(9.24)	(8.67)	(7.64)
Female	46.68	50.84	51.14	51.65	51.84	52.71	51.00	51.88	49.04
	(9.84)	(7.76)	(9.08)	(7.95)	(10.10)	(9.62)	(8.80)	(9.83)	(11.53)
Total	46.51	51.05	50.24	51.39	51.58	52.12	49.62	50.25	48.82
	(10.20)	(7.27)	(9.94)	(7.92)	(9.40)	(8.86)	(9.08)	(9.30)	(9.61)
1977									
Male	42.46	45.79	49.57	45.28	49.90	47.26	49.23	47.63	44.31
	(11.26)	(7.66)	(9.23)	(10.35)	(7.88)	(9.43)	(8.06)	(10.77)	(9.89)
Female	45.00	45.52	49.61	47.57	49.11	49.55	48.29	47.03	49.47
	(10.06)	(10.99)	(8.77)	(11.92)	(9.02)	(9.58)	(12.83)	(10.97)	(11.40)
Total	43.73	45.65	49.59	46.51	49.52	48.45	48.74	47.34	47.07
	(10.66)	(9.50)	(8.94)	(11.20)	(8.40)	(9.51)	(10.75)	(10.79)	(10.94)
1984									
Male	43.96	46.48	52.07	51.38	49.17	50.58	48.67	47.55	48.38
	(10.96)	(9.79)	(9.03)	(10.88)	(12.50)	(9.35)	(10.64)	(11.65)	(9.66)
Female	47.10	46.15	48.11	52.65	49.09	52.24	50.43	47.91	52.62
	(10.80)	(8.54)	(11.29)	(7.99)	(7.99)	(8.44)	(11.58)	(9.36)	(8.02)
Total	45.88	46.31	49.91	52.15	49.12	51.51	49.58	47.73	50.72
	(10.88)	(9.10)	(10.44)	(9.17)	(10.41)	(9.04)	(11.11)	(10.54)	(8.95)
1991									
Male	45.19	44.39	51.92	51.47	51.56	51.50	54.52	52.61	53.85
	(10.68)	(12.51)	(9.92)	(9.68)	(10.78)	(9.44)	(8.67)	(12.00)	(8.03)
Female	44.82	48.65	49.87	53.24	51.65	52.74	55.13	53.72	53.64
	(10.45)	(11.00)	(10.97)	(7.62)	(7.92)	(10.21)	(10.76)	(8.66)	(7.34)
Total	44.98	46.90	50.90	52.52	51.60	52.18	54.87	53.18	53.74
	(10.46)	(11.74)	(10.44)	(8.51)	(9.36)	(9.82)	(9.86)	(10.38)	(7.63)

(continued)

TABLE 12.1 Continued

					Age				
	25	32	39	46	53	60	67	74	81
1998									
Male	46.40	49.44	50.29	51.88	50.46	51.39	54.24	53.29	53.97
	(10.06)	(9.40)	(10.71)	(11.18)	(10.62)	(9.25)	(8.64)	(8.08)	(8.20)
Female	42.76	48.78	48.48	52.34	51.06	50.42	52.63	54.45	54.26
	(8.52)	(9.41)	(10.90)	(10.43)	(9.92)	(9.61)	(8.99)	(9.48)	(7.73)
Total	44.12	49.12	49.33	50.11	50.79	50.94	53.63	53.95	54.11
	(9.18)	(9.34)	(10.79)	(10.76)	(10.19)	(9.37)	(8.76)	(8.83)	(7.91)
Across All Measurement Occasions									
Male	45.91	48.05	50.23	50.07	50.22	49.87	50.45	49.57	50.21
	(10.79)	(10.01)	(10.01)	(10.03)	(10.46)	(9.74)	(9.78)	(10.70)	(9.30)
Female	47.12	49.33	50.42	51.58	51.16	51.52	51.32	50.18	51.89
	(10.06)	(9.89)	(9.84)	(9.48)	(8.94)	(9.66)	(10.65)	(9.87)	(9.43)
Total	46.58	48.75	50.33	50.86	50.72	50.73	50.89	49.88	51.06

lar to one of the trait ends of the Cattell taxonomy; the remaining factors appeared to be primarily attitudinal in nature (see table 12.5). The factor scores estimated for these factors were then subjected to analyses of variance utilizing sequential strategies. Given the availability of only two points in time, these analyses had to be limited to the cross-sequential and time-sequential strategies. By comparing results from these alternative analyses, it was possible to identify three types of developmental pattern for the personality traits: biostable, acculturated, and biocultural (see Schaie & Parham, 1976).

A Classification Model for Personality Traits

Three types of personality traits were distinguished that are thought to have differential developmental patterns: biostable, acculturated, and biocultural traits.

Biostable traits represent a class of behaviors that may be genetically determined or constrained by environmental influences that occur early in life, perhaps during a critical imprinting period. These traits typically show systematic gender differences at all age levels, but are rather stable across age, whether examined in cross-sectional or longitudinal data. *Acculturated* traits, conversely, appear to be overdetermined by environmental events occurring at different life stages and tend to be prone to rather rapid modification in response to sociocultural change. These traits usually do not display systematic gender differences. Their age differences rarely form systematic patterns and can usually be resolved into generational shifts and/or secular trend components on sequential analysis. *Biocultural* traits display ontogenetic trends with expression that is modified either by generational shifts or by sociocultural events that affect all age levels in a

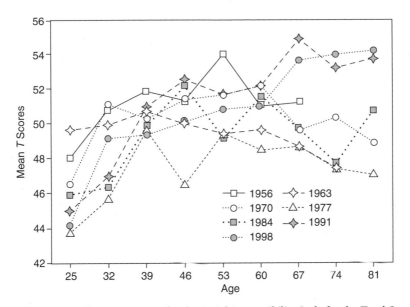

FIGURE 12.1 *Age Difference Patterns for the Social Responsibility Scale for the Total Sample by Test Occasion.*

TABLE 12.2 Cumulative Age Changes for the Scale of Social Responsibility in *T*-Score Points (*N* = 4,665)

	Mean Age								
	32	39	46	53	60	67	74	81	88
25	2.27	3.01*	3.80*	3.88*	4.29*	5.12*	5.65*	4.79*	4.18*
32		0.74	1.53	1.61	2.02	2.75*	3.38*	2.52	1.91
39			0.79	0.87	1.28	2.01	2.64*	1.78	1.17
46				0.08	0.49	1.22	1.85	0.59	0.38
53					0.41	1.14	1.77	0.51	0.30
60						0.83	1.36	0.10	−0.11
67							0.53	−0.73	−0.94
74								−0.86	−1.47
81									−0.61

*Difference is significant at or beyond the 1% level of confidence.

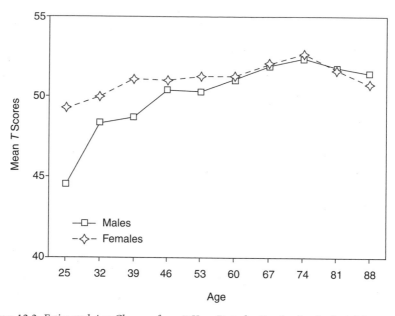

FIGURE 12.2 *Estimated Age Changes from 7-Year Data by Gender for the Social Responsibility Scale.*

TABLE 12.3 Mean Advantage of Later-Born Cohorts Over Earlier-Born Cohorts on the Social Responsibility Scale in *T*-Score Points

	1896	1903	1910	1917	1924	1931	1938	1945	1952	1959	1966	1973
						Mean Year of Birth						
1889	−0.5	−0.4	−0.5	0.2	1.4	0.2	1.7	−0.1	−1.2	0.2	0.9	0.0
1896		0.1	0.0	0.7	1.9	0.7	2.2	0.4	−0.7	0.7	1.4	0.5
1903			−0.1	0.6	1.8	0.6	2.1	0.3	−0.8	0.6	1.3	0.4
1910				0.7	1.9	0.7	2.2	0.4	−0.7	0.7	1.4	0.5
1917					1.2	0.0	1.5	−0.3	−1.4	0.0	0.7	−0.2
1924						−1.2	0.3	−1.5	−2.6*	−1.2	−0.5	−1.4
1931							1.5	−0.3	−1.4	0.0	0.7	−0.2
1938								−1.8	−2.9*	−1.5	−0.8	−1.7
1945									−1.1	0.3	1.0	0.1
1952										1.4	2.1	1.2
1959											0.7	−0.2
1966												−0.9

Note. Negative values indicate that the later-born cohort is at a disadvantage compared to the earlier-born cohort.
*$p < .01$.

TABLE 12.4 Period (Time-of-Measurement) Effects
for the Scale of Social Responsibility in *T*-Score Points

	1963	1970	1977	1984	1991	1998
1956	−1.51	−0.72	−3.49*	−1.68	0.32	−0.22
1963		0.79	−1.98	−0.18	1.82	1.29
1970			−2.77*	−0.96	1.04	0.57
1977				1.81	3.81*	3.28*
1984					2.00	1.47
1991						−0.53

*$p < .01$.

similar fashion. Cross-sectional data for such traits would typically show Age ×
Gender interactions.

Biostable Traits   Four subtypes are possible for the biostable traits:

1. *Gender differences only.* Such traits would seem to be overdetermined
   by genetic variance, probably located on the sex chromosome. The
   only trait that fit this paradigm in our study was Premsia (tender-mindedness, which was higher for women), but even that gender difference
   was barely significant and must be treated with caution. We suggest
   that it is probably unreasonable to expect to find personality traits that
   fit the purely inherited category without ambiguity.
2. *Period differences only.* Such traits also appear to be overdetermined by
   genetic variance, but they are modified in their expression by secular
   sociocultural trends. In our analysis, this type of trait was represented
   by Untroubled Adequacy, which showed a decrease over the 7 years
   monitored.

TABLE 12.5 List of 19 Personality Traits from the Test
of Behavioral Rigidity Questionnaire

A+, Affectothymia	Q1−, Conservation of Temperament
D+, Excitability	Q2−, Group Dependency
E+, Dominance	Q3−, Low Self-Sentiment
G+, Superego Strength	Honesty
H+, Threctia	Interest in Science
I+, Premsia	Flexibility
J+, Coasthenia	Financial Support of Society
L+, Protension	Political Concern
M−, Praxernia	Community Involvement
O−, Untroubled Adequacy	

Note. Signs represent the unidimensional pole of the Cattell factor represented by these scales.

3. *Cohort differences only.* These traits are not subject to transient environmental influences, but seem to reflect generation-specific patterns in early training or socialization procedures. This would seem to be the modal pattern for those traits that are indeed determined by early socialization. The traits matching this category observed in our study were Threat Reactivity, Coasthenia, expressed Honesty, Interest in Science, and Community Involvement.

4. *Period and cohort differences.* A final subtype involves development of a trait in response to early socialization as well as to transient sociocultural impact. Both Praxernia and Group Dependence followed that pattern in our study.

Acculturated Traits   It is the acculturated traits that display no gender difference, but may show a variety of combinations of age changes and/or period and cohort differences. Six possible subtypes can be identified:

1. *Age changes only.* This type of trait reflects social roles that are determined by universals that underlie stage models of human development (see Piaget, 1972; Schaie, 1977–1978; Schaie & Willis, 2000b) and that are rather impermeable to cohort differences or secular trends. The only trait that met these criteria was Humanitarian Concern, which showed increase with age.

2. *Age changes and cohort differences.* Such traits are mediated by life stage changes in universally determined life roles, which in turn are modified by generational shifts in early socialization practices. Identification of traits of this type was not possible in this data set because a cohort-sequential data matrix would have been required for their identification.

3. *Age changes and period differences.* Such traits are determined by universally prescribed life roles that are impermeable to early socialization practices, but are subject to transient secular impacts for persons of all ages. It is difficult to imagine that a trait could have such attributes, and none of those included in our study fit this pattern.

4. *Cohort differences only.* Such traits are not subject to ontogenetic change, but instead their development is mediated by generation-specific patterns of early socialization practices. This pattern prevailed for Affectothymia, Superego Strength, Protension, and Low Self-Sentiment. Except for Superego Strength, it is conceivable, however, that these traits could also have fit Subtype 2 above if we had the appropriate data to test for the presence of both age and cohort differences.

5. *Period differences only.* Such traits are not age related and are independent of shifts in early socialization practices. However, they are affected by sociocultural impact for all age levels. Dominance and Financial Support of Society fit this pattern.

6. *Cohort and period differences.* Non-age-related traits may be modified both by specific patterns of early socialization and by transient sociocultural changes that affect individuals at all ages. In our study, it was the Flexibility factor that showed these characteristics, displaying a general pattern toward greater flexibility across cohorts, accompanied by additional increase in flexibility across the periods monitored.

Biocultural Traits   Biocultural traits are overdetermined by genetic variance and consequently show significant gender differences, but also are modified in their expression because of universally experienced life stage expectancies or the effects of early socialization experiences. Three subtypes were identified:

1. *Age changes only.* Such traits are characterized by clear ontogenetic "programs" that seem to be impermeable to cohort differences or sociocultural change. Our only example of this type was Excitability, which systematically increased with age.
2. *Age changes and cohort differences.* Such traits, in addition to systematic ontogenetic shifts, are modified in level by generation-specific socialization practices. Again, our data set did not permit clear identification of such traits; it is probably unlikely that they exist.
3. *Age changes and period differences.* Such traits have clear ontogenetic programs, but are amenable to modification because of specific environmental interventions that affect persons at all ages. The only trait that fit this criterion in our study was Premsia.

Our principal conclusion from this analysis was that age-related change in personality traits was quite rare, but that cohort and period differences were common and would lead to the spurious reporting of lack of stability for personality traits when reliance is primarily on cross-sectional data.

More Recent Analyses of the Personality Data

Although we continued to collect the personality item data at all subsequent test occasions, if only to be able to measure the cognitive style of Attitudinal Flexibility, we did not go beyond the work summarized above until the late 1980s.

The original work on the personality items had been conducted by then state-of-the-art methods of exploratory factor analysis that did not allow adequate tests of the number of nonrandom factors represented in the item pool or allow formal tests confirming the invariance of factor structures over time.

Results of more recent item factor analyses are now summarized. Then, cross-sectional and longitudinal findings on the developmental patterns of factor scores for the resultant latent constructs are considered, followed by analyses focusing on the relationship of the derived scales to other constructs investigated in the SLS (see Maitland et al., 1992; Maitland & Schaie, 1991; Maitland, Willis, &

Schaie, 1993; Schaie et al., 1991; Schaie, Willis, et al., 2004; Willis, Schaie, & Maitland, 1992).

Reassessment of Item Factor Structure

Contemporary analysis techniques (using linear structural relations [LISREL] 7) were used to confirm the factor structure identified in the earlier work (Schaie & Parham, 1976). The database for this analysis included the 2,515 test records used in the original study as well as an additional 2,811 tests accumulated in the 1977 and 1984 cycles. When confirmatory factor analysis was used to assess the fit for the 19-factor model determined in the exploratory analyses, it was determined that the data had been overfitted, resulting in several factors with extremely high factor intercorrelations. Further consideration of the number of factors unambiguously represented in the data resulted in an acceptable 13-factor model with good fit $[\chi^2(df= 1,191) = 3,548.16$, $p < .001$; $GFI = .945$; $RMSR = .007]$. The 13-factor model was then tested on the participants assessed in 1977 and 1984, and it continued to show an acceptable fit $[\chi^2(df= 1,191) = 4,302.98$, $p < .001$; $GFI = .941$; $RMSR = .007]$. A two-group analysis further investigated factorial invariance across time by constraining factor loadings and factor variance-covariance matrices to be equal across the two data sets. This analysis also yielded an acceptable fit $[\chi^2(df= 2,512) = 6,910.00$, $p < .001$; $GFI = .945$; $RMSR = .007]$.

The 13-factor model includes 8 factors that can be mapped on the Cattell (1957; Cattell et al., 1970) taxonomy of personality dimensions: Affectothymia, Superego Strength, Threctia, Premsia, Untroubled Adequacy, Conservatism of Temperament, Group Dependency, and Low Self-Sentiment. The remaining five factors are best described as attitudinal traits and were labeled Honesty, Interest in Science, Inflexibility, Political Concern, and Community Involvement.

The factors that were mapped on one end of the trait continuum described by Cattell have been described as follows (Cattell et al., 1970):

Affectothymia—Outgoing, warmhearted, easygoing, participating tendencies
Superego Strength—Conscientious, persistent, moralistic, staid
Threctia—Shy, timid, restrained, threat sensitive
Premsia—Tender-minded, sensitive, clinging, overprotected
Untroubled Adequacy—Self-assured, placid, secure, complacent, serene
Conservatism of Temperament—Respecting traditional ideas, tolerant of traditional difficulties
Group Dependency—A "joiner" and sound follower, group adherence
Low Self-Sentiment—Uncontrolled, lax, follows own urges, careless of social rules

The additional five attitudinal traits may be described as follows:

Honesty—Endorsement of items that reflect personal beliefs of honesty
Interest in science—Endorsement of an item couplet that reflects interest in science

Inflexibility—Endorsement of items that reflect lack of tolerance for disruption of routines

Political Concern—Reflects attitudes toward other countries

Community Involvement—Endorsement of positive attitudes about citizenship and civic responsibilities

Intercorrelations among the 13 personality factors are reported for the total sample and by age group in the appendix (see table A-12.1).

Age and Gender Differences in Personality Traits and Attitudes

Cross-sectional data were available across the age range from mean age 25 to mean age 81 years from 4,200 participants at first test in Study Cycles 1 through 7. The overall multivariate analysis of variance yielded overall gender [Rao's $R(13, 4,170) = 62.19$, $p < .001$] and age [Rao's $R(104, 28,726) = 10.14$, $p < .001$] effects. The interaction between age and gender was not significant. Overall means by age group are given in table 12.6.

Gender Differences   Univariate follow-up tests found gender differences significant at or beyond the .01 level of confidence, with higher overall scores for women on Group Dependency, Interest in Science, Inflexibility, and Political Concern. Overall means for men were higher on Interest in Science, Premsia, and Superego Strength.

Age Differences   All univariate follow-up tests found significant age differences at or beyond the .001 level of confidence. The cross-sectional age differences are shown in figure 12.3. Because of the absence of an overall Age × Gender interaction, they are shown only for the total group without regard to gender. Seven of the factors show increases with age, which are most pronounced for Inflexibility and Untroubled Adequacy and smallest for Superego Strength and Interest in Science. Six factors show decreases with age differences, most pronounced for Group Dependency and Honesty and smallest for Premsia (tender-mindedness).

Age Changes in Personality Traits

When we aggregate within-participant age changes over each 7-year period in our study, we can obtain direct estimates of average age changes. For the personality data, we were able to base our estimates on all participants entering the study in 1963, 1970, 1977, 1984, 1991, and 1998 who were followed up at least once. This resulted in 4,193 observations covering the age range from 25 to 88 years. Given the large number of observations, we did obtain overall within-participant change over 7 years on all variables except for Low Self-Esteem and Interest in Science. *T*-score means for the 13 personality factors are reported in table 12.7.

TABLE 12.6 Means and Standard Deviations for the 13 Personality Factors by Age, Averaged Across All Measurement Occasions

	Age								
	25 (n = 381)	32 (n = 450)	39 (n = 560)	46 (n = 589)	53 (n = 530)	60 (n = 505)	67 (n = 542)	74 (n = 433)	81 (n = 210)
Affectothymia	50.32 (8.49)	51.07 (8.25)	51.59 (8.00)	51.14 (9.02)	51.83 (8.41)	50.66 (9.10)	49.14 (10.03)	47.87 (11.41)	48.11 (10.32)
Superego Strength	49.10 (9.57)	48.96 (10.10)	49.68 (9.85)	48.60 (9.42)	49.66 (10.35)	49.77 (9.90)	50.93 (9.95)	52.85 (9.85)	50.88 (9.88)
Threctia	49.39 (10.38)	50.52 (9.62)	51.91 (8.70)	51.34 (9.36)	50.38 (9.96)	49.84 (10.21)	49.09 (10.73)	47.18 (11.44)	47.00 (11.63)
Premsia	50.88 (9.89)	51.07 (10.23)	50.56 (10.05)	50.36 (10.35)	50.34 (10.32)	49.78 (10.18)	48.92 (10.44)	47.97 (10.65)	49.71 (10.66)
Untroubled Adequacy	45.03 (10.78)	47.37 (11.11)	48.33 (10.35)	48.64 (9.93)	49.51 (9.63)	50.87 (8.94)	51.56 (9.08)	51.94 (8.75)	53.42 (7.66)
Conservatism	48.12 (10.64)	48.30 (10.51)	48.70 (10.08)	50.06 (9.76)	48.92 (10.42)	50.94 (9.66)	52.31 (9.79)	53.52 (9.68)	52.18 (9.45)
Group Dependency	53.61 (10.61)	52.35 (10.34)	51.20 (10.31)	50.79 (10.22)	50.09 (10.35)	48.74 (9.79)	48.46 (9.86)	47.53 (9.10)	45.54 (7.75)
Low Self-Esteem	52.44 (10.30)	51.63 (10.10)	51.24 (10.17)	50.97 (10.12)	50.95 (10.24)	49.58 (9.48)	48.33 (9.38)	47.51 (8.89)	47.63 (8.81)
Honesty	51.77 (9.67)	52.54 (10.26)	52.45 (9.44)	52.28 (9.91)	50.91 (9.91)	49.53 (10.14)	47.59 (9.39)	45.90 (9.16)	45.16 (8.70)
Interest in Science	47.85 (8.53)	48.86 (9.60)	49.23 (9.88)	50.10 (10.21)	50.43 (10.13)	50.89 (10.49)	50.39 (10.55)	51.26 (10.73)	49.24 (9.88)
Inflexibility	46.17 (8.05)	46.38 (8.49)	47.18 (8.43)	47.43 (9.01)	48.70 (9.20)	50.52 (10.45)	53.47 (10.25)	56.23 (10.20)	56.40 (10.20)
Political Concern	45.54 (11.93)	47.27 (10.61)	48.57 (10.13)	50.63 (9.39)	50.11 (9.60)	51.51 (9.10)	51.61 (9.07)	52.93 (7.88)	52.98 (7.42)
Community Involvement	48.22 (10.07)	49.52 (10.27)	49.37 (9.87)	49.50 (9.51)	49.70 (9.85)	50.19 (9.83)	51.42 (9.85)	52.34 (9.52)	53.56 (9.19)

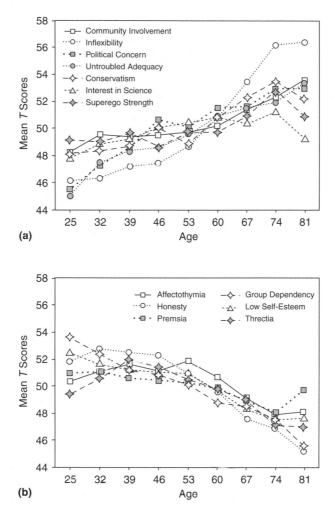

FIGURE 12.3 *Age Difference Patterns on the 13 Personality Factor Scores.*

Longitudinal age patterns on the personality variables are, of course, generally quite stable. However, there were significant occasion effects for four of the personality traits and two of the attitudinal measures. In addition, there were significant Occasion × Age group interactions for four of the personality traits and for three of the attitudinal measures. Figure 12.4 charts the estimates of longitudinal changes in personality traits obtained from these data, anchoring all age gradients on the observed values at age 53. For ease of inspection, I have grouped separately the traits that show increment over age and time in the top part of the figure and those that show a decremental trend in the bottom part.

Most noteworthy are modest within-participant increases with age in Superego Strength, Untroubled Adequacy, and Honesty. Smaller increases with age were

TABLE 12.7 Longitudinal Estimates of *T*-Score Means for the 13 Personality Factors[a]

	Age									
	25	32	39	46	53	60	67	74	81	88
Affectothymia	50.58	51.57	51.94	52.23	51.83	51.59	51.22	50.35	48.32	43.70
Superego Strength	46.04	47.63	49.25	49.24	49.66	50.26	50.84	51.52	52.64	51.89
Threctia	48.52	49.51	49.72	50.05	50.38	51.04	51.44	52.43	52.64	52.14
Premsia	51.12	49.59	49.92	50.47	50.34	49.91	49.59	48.30	47.48	46.83
Untroubled Adequacy	45.73	47.68	48.09	48.52	49.51	48.81	48.40	48.38	48.12	50.00
Conservatism	48.62	48.43	48.65	48.70	48.92	48.09	50.07	51.08	51.98	52.63
Group Dependency	50.47	49.83	49.91	50.33	50.09	49.82	49.16	48.64	48.80	47.61
Low Self-Esteem	50.05	50.39	51.18	51.09	50.95	50.90	50.57	50.45	49.59	49.10
Honesty	46.00	47.95	50.01	50.64	50.91	51.07	52.59	52.90	53.88	51.70
Interest in Science	48.89	49.96	49.72	50.08	50.43	50.31	49.87	49.71	49.54	49.89
Inflexibility	50.04	50.17	49.69	49.39	48.70	48.17	48.76	48.49	50.27	51.69
Political Concern	49.34	49.55	49.78	50.10	50.11	48.86	48.50	48.54	46.90	46.60
Community Involvement	50.88	51.93	51.30	50.85	49.70	49.98	49.70	50.16	49.74	49.08

[a]Centered on observed values at age 53.

also noted for Threctia and Conservatism. Equally interesting is the decline in Affectothymia in advanced old age. Premsia and Group Dependency show small systematic declines across the entire adult age range; Political Concern begins to show systematic decline from midlife on. Age trends for Low Self-Sentiment, Interest in Science, Inflexibility, and Community Involvement were not statistically significant.

Cohort and Period Differences in the Personality Factors

Cohort Differences   As for our ability measures, these age differences confound cohort and maturational changes. We therefore computed cohort differences in the manner described in chapter 6 (see table 12.8), and chart the resulting cohort gradients in figure 12.5. Figure 12.5a shows the six traits characterized by positive cohort differences or by convex patterns that remain negative until the turn of the century, followed by a positive trend. Group Dependency reaches a peak for the 1938 cohort and declines somewhat thereafter. Low Self-Sentiment is highest in the 1955 cohort. Honesty declines until the 1910 cohort, and then rises linearly. Premsia increases to an asymptote for the 1952 cohort, with slight decline thereafter. Affectothymia reaches an asymptote for the 1938 cohort, with some decline thereafter. Threctia remains virtually flat.

Figure 12.5b shows the seven traits that have systematic decreases or concave patterns with increments for the early cohorts, followed by substantial decline. These include Superego Strength and Conservatism, with the lowest point reached by the 1966 cohort. Untroubled Adequacy reaches its highest level for the 1910 cohort, with linear decline thereafter. Community Involvement shows steady decline, with a low point for the 1952 cohort, with some decline thereafter.

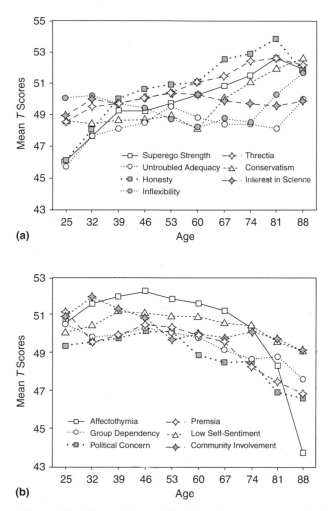

FIGURE 12.4 *Estimated Age Changes From 7-Year Data for the 13 Personality Factor Scores.*

Political Concern and Interest in Science reached a peak before the turn of the century, with decline peaking for the 1966 cohort. Finally, Inflexibility after an early peak also declined steadily with the low point for the 1952 cohort.

Period Differences   We next examine whether the 13 personality factors are affected by secular trends (period effects). Cumulative period effects were computed using the same approached illustrated for the cognitive variables in chapter 6. These period effects are listed in table 12.9. Positive period effects were found for Premsia/, Untroubled Adequacy, Superego Strength, and Interest in Science (the last three only from 1956 to 1963). Inflexibility increased from 1956 to 1963, but then decreased with a low point in 1991. Negative period effects occurred

TABLE 12.8 Cohort Differences for the 13 Personality Factors in *T*-Score Points

Birth Cohort	Cohort Difference	Cumulative Difference	Cohort Difference	Cumulative Differences	Cohort Difference	Cumulative Difference	Cohort Difference	Cumulative Difference
	Affectothymia		*Superego Strength*		*Threctia*			
1896–1889	1.11	1.11	0.01	0.01	−1.31	−1.31		
1903–1896	−0.10	1.01	−1.39	−1.38	−1.12	−2.43		
1910–1903	1.10	2.11	−0.25	−1.63	1.54	−0.89		
1917–1910	0.88	2.99	−0.94	−2.57	0.94	0.05		
1924–1917	0.73	3.72	−1.06	−3.63	1.10	1.15		
1931–1924	−0.25	3.47	0.82	−2.81	−0.33	0.82		
1938–1931	0.90	4.37	−1.52	−4.33	0.59	1.41		
1945–1938	−1.23	3.14	0.69	−3.64	−1.92	−0.51		
1952–1945	0.08	3.22	1.06	−2.58	1.41	0.90		
1959–1952	−0.48	2.74	0.10	−2.48	−1.09	−0.19		
1966–1959	0.37	3.11	−2.38	−4.86	−1.31	−1.50		
1973–1966	−1.73	1.38	4.56	−0.30	1.20	−0.30		
	Premsia		*Untroubled Adequacy*		*Conservatism*			
1896–1889	1.54	1.54	3.81	3.81	−0.28	−0.28		
1903–1896	1.32	2.86	0.68	4.49	−2.64	−2.72		
1910–1903	1.06	3.92	−0.55	3.94	−0.02	−2.74		
1917–1910	0.69	4.61	−0.53	3.41	−0.46	−3.20		
1924–1917	0.92	5.53	−0.47	2.94	0.68	−2.52		
1931–1924	−1.52	4.01	−1.68	1.26	0.13	−2.39		
1938–1931	0.72	4.73	−2.38	−1.12	−1.14	−3.53		
1945–1938	0.15	4.88	−2.37	−3.49	−0.36	−3.89		
1952–1945	0.90	5.78	−0.62	−4.01	−1.86	−5.75		
1959–1952	−1.98	3.80	−0.68	−4.78	0.86	−4.89		
1966–1959	1.02	4.82	0.37	−4.41	−0.88	−5.77		
1973–1966	0.00	4.82	−2.40	−6.81	2.50	−3.27		
	Group Dependency		*Low Self-Esteem*		*Honesty*			
1896–1889	−0.24	−0.24	0.15	0.15	−2.82	−2.82		
1903–1896	0.44	0.20	0.36	0.51	0.01	−2.81		
1910–1903	1.24	1.44	1.10	1.61	−0.33	−3.14		
1917–1910	−0.34	1.10	1.22	2.83	1.27	−1.87		
1924–1917	0.44	1.54	−0.20	2.63	1.49	−0.38		
1931–1924	0.28	1.82	−1.49	1.15	1.08	0.70		
1938–1931	3.25	5.07	1.26	2.41	2.86	3.56		
1945–1938	−0.30	4.77	−0.96	1.55	2.24	5.80		
1952–1945	−1.60	3.17	1.67	3.22	0.64	6.44		
1959–1952	1.52	4.69	−1.41	1.81	−1.19	5.25		
1966–1959	−1.06	3.63	0.40	2.21	0.86	6.11		
1973–1966	0.12	3.75	0.05	2.26	0.58	6.69		
	Interest in Science		*Inflexibility*		*Political Concern*		*Community Involvement*	
1896–1889	2.31	2.31	3.93	3.93	2.93	2.93	−0.11	−0.11
1903–1896	0.28	2.59	−1.32	2.61	−0.73	2.20	−2.81	−2.92
1910–1903	−2.16	0.43	0.04	2.65	−0.82	1.38	−2.13	−5.05
1917–1910	0.55	0.98	−2.80	−0.15	0.16	1.54	−1.01	−6.06
1924–1917	−0.64	0.34	−2.81	−2.86	−0.30	1.24	−0.78	−6.84
1931–1924	−0.47	−0.13	0.34	−2.52	−1.27	−0.03	0.17	−6.67
1938–1931	−1.43	−1.56	−2.00	−4.52	−0.03	−0.06	0.00	−6.67
1945–1938	0.76	−0.80	−2.22	−6.74	−1.30	−1.36	−0.01	−6.68
1952–1945	−1.03	−1.83	−1.40	−8.14	−1.16	−2.52	−0.62	−7.30
1959–1952	0.09	−1.74	2.58	−5.56	1.83	−0.69	1.60	−5.70
1966–1959	−0.79	−2.53	−0.33	−5.91	−2.76	−3.45	−1.12	−6.82
1973–1966	−0.52	−3.05	0.70	−5.21	2.07	−1.38	1.07	−5.75

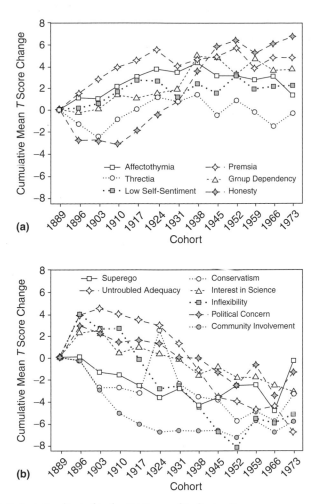

FIGURE 12.5 *Cohort Gradients for the 13 Personality Factor Scores.*

for Threctia (from 1956 to 1970), Conservatism (1956 to 1984), Community Involvement and Group Dependency (from 1956 to 1963), and Political Concern (from 1970 to 1977, and from 1991 to 1998). No significant period effects were found for Affectothymia and Low Self-Sentiment.

The NEO Personality Inventory

To extend the range of personality data in the SLS and to have a direct measure of the big five personality traits, a mail administration of the NEO-PI-R personality inventory was conducted in 2001. The questionnaire was sent to the 1,796 partici-

TABLE 12.9 Period Differences for the 13 Personality Factors in *T*-Score Points

Period	Period Difference	Cumulative Difference	Period Difference	Cumulative Difference	Period Difference	Cumulative Difference	Period Difference	Cumulative Difference
	Affectothymia		*Superego Strength*		*Threctia*			
1963–1956	−1.69	−1.69	2.49**	2.49**	−1.66	−1.66		
1970–1963	2.02*	0.33	−1.52	0.97	−1.47	−3.13***		
1977–1970	−1.32	−0.99	−0.43	0.45	1.20	−1.93		
1984–1977	0.42	−0.54	−0.85	−0.31	1.36	−0.57		
1991–1984	1.72	−1.18	−0.91	−1.22	−0.58	−1.15		
1998–1991	−0.93	−0.25	0.73	−0.49	0.64	−0.51		
	Premsia		*Untroubled Adequacy*		*Conservatism*			
1963–1956	−0.13	−0.13	5.76***	5.76***	−2.86**	−2.86**		
1970–1963	0.45	0.32	−1.79	3.97***	0.60	−2.26*		
1977–1970	1.41	1.73	−3.08***	0.89	−2.06*	−4.32***		
1984–1977	1.08	2.91**	−1.34	−0.45	−0.74	−5.06***		
1991–1984	0.02	2.93**	−0.40	−0.85	0.01	−5.05***		
1998–1991	0.38	3.31***	−0.61	−1.46	0.09	−4.97***		
	Group Dependency		*Low Self-Sentiment*		*Honesty*			
1963–1956	−2.44*	−2.44*	−0.56	−0.56	−4.85***	−4.85***		
1970–1963	1.88	−0.56	1.48	0.92	2.18*	−2.67**		
1977–1970	−0.44	−1.00	−1.10	−0.18	0.69	−1.98*		
1984–1977	1.60	0.60	0.40	0.22	2.75**	0.77		
1991–1984	0.43	1.03	0.68	0.90	0.42	1.19		
1998–1991	0.02	1.05	0.55	1.45	0.77	1.96*		
	Interest in Science		*Inflexibility*		*Political Concern*		*Community Involvement*	
1963–1956	3.36***	3.36***	2.75**	2.75**	−0.32	−0.32	−4.01***	−4.01***
1970–1963	−0.63	2.73**	−2.34*	0.41	−0.06	−0.38	0.51	−3.50***
1977–1970	−1.05	1.68	−1.04	−0.63	−1.60	−1.98*	0.11	−3.39***
1984–1977	−1.59	0.09	−2.97**	−3.60***	0.79	−1.19	−0.14	−3.51***
1991–1984	−0.08	0.01	−0.58	−4.18***	0.21	−0.98	−0.56	−4.12***
1998–1991	−0.26	−0.25	0.24	−3.94***	−1.20	−2.18*	0.20	−3.92***

*$p < .05$. **$p < .01$. ***$p < .001$.

pants of the 1998 SLS wave for whom current addresses were available. Completed questionnaires were returned by 1,501 participants (83.6% return rate).

The scales in this inventory (Costa & McCrae, 1992) are described as follows:

Neuroticism (N). This scale contrasts adjustment or emotional stability with maladjustment or neuroticism

Extraversion (E). Extraverts are not only sociable, but also assertive, active, and talkative. Introverts are reserved and independent, and they prefer to be alone.

Openness (O). Open individuals are curious and willing to entertain novel ideas and unconventional values. They experience positive and negative emotions more intensely than do closed individuals.

Agreeableness (A). Agreeable persons are altruistic, sympathetic to others, and eager to help, expecting others to be equally helpful in return. Disagreeable persons are egocentric, skeptical of others' intentions, and competitive rather than cooperative.

Conscientiousness (C). High scorers are scrupulous, punctual, and reliable. Low scorers do not necessarily lack moral principles, but are less exacting in applying them, more hedonistic, and more lackadaisical in working toward their goals.

Cross-Sectional Findings

Significant age differences were found for all five factors ($p < .01$), and there were significant gender differences ($p < .001$) for all factors except Conscientiousness. Women scored higher than men on all four factors. Neuroticism declines to age 60 and then remains level. Extraversion shows an early peak at age 32 years and then declines steadily. Openness declines linearly from 39 years of age. Agreeableness increases linearly with age; Conscientiousness increases slightly to age 60 years and then declines moderately. Means and standard deviations for the five NEO factors (standardized to a mean of 50 and *SD* of 10) are reported in table 12.10 and graphed in figure 12.6. Intercorrelations among the five NEO scales for the total sample and by age group are reported in the appendix (see table A-12.2).

Longitudinal Findings

Although observed longitudinal findings are not yet available, we were able to employ extension analysis (described in chapter 2) to postdict scores on the NEO for 1991 by projecting the observed NEO into the 13-factor personality space for 1998 (also see Schaie, Willis, et al., 2004). This analysis was based on the 1,171 participants who had data on the NEO and the 1998 personality factor scores. Factor loadings of the NEO scales on the 13 personality factors are reported in table 12.11.

Estimation procedures involved computing NEO scores by multiplying the 13 factor scores by weights obtained from the orthonormalized factor loadings in table 12.11 and restandardizing resulting scores to a mean of 50 and standard deviation of 10. Within-participant changes over 7 years were then computed and aggregated across successive 7-year age cohorts. The resulting longitudinal age gradients were then centered on average scores at age 53 years and are depicted in figure 12.7. Considerable caution is in order in interpreting the findings using these NEO proxy estimates. However, they do represent within-participant change data across much of the adult life span.

Although cross-sectional data usually depict few personality differences across adulthood, these data suggest much more dramatic developmental trends. For neuroticism, we see a sharp increase until midlife, with virtual stability thereafter. Openness shows a modest increase until age 46 years, a plateau until the late 60s, and a decline thereafter. Extraversion shows a steady decline from the 40s.

TABLE 12.10 Means and Standard Deviations for the NEO Personality Questionnaire, by Age and Gender, Administered in 2001

	Age									
	25	32	39	46	53	60	67	74	81	88
Neuroticism										
Male	57.80	49.61	51.10	49.89	49.40	47.11	47.23	48.02	47.38	49.21
	(8.94)	(11.23)	(10.88)	(9.97)	(10.46)	(9.63)	(10.24)	(7.70)	(8.96)	(7.17)
Female	56.92	52.36	54.23	52.24	50.27	48.99	48.67	50.13	49.32	48.00
	(10.36)	(9.84)	(11.24)	(10.96)	(9.77)	(9.47)	(9.22)	(8.63)	(8.53)	(6.91)
Total	57.18	51.20	53.13	51.33	49.91	48.19	48.06	49.27	48.52	48.39
	(9.84)	(10.50)	(11.19)	(10.64)	(10.06)	(9.57)	(9.68)	(8.32)	(8.74)	(6.96)
Extraversion										
Male	52.30	52.36	50.44	49.40	49.57	49.85	48.90	47.99	46.11	45.21
	(14.26)	(11.84)	(11.19)	(10.93)	(10.23)	(8.82)	(10.38)	(9.03)	(9.87)	(9.90)
Female	51.96	55.24	52.14	51.35	51.02	50.26	49.81	48.59	48.58	46.52
	(9.54)	(8.43)	(10.17)	(10.62)	(9.82)	(9.70)	(9.44)	(8.85)	(8.60)	(7.97)
Total	52.06	54.03	51.54	50.59	50.42	50.08	49.42	48.34	47.56	46.10
	(10.90)	(10.07)	(10.56)	(10.77)	(10.00)	(9.36)	(9.85)	(8.92)	(9.21)	(8.57)
Openness										
Male	56.30	51.18	53.25	51.99	49.05	48.59	47.33	44.70	43.10	41.58
	(8.21)	(9.83)	(9.48)	(10.51)	(9.84)	(9.96)	(9.83)	(9.17)	(8.97)	(9.67)
Female	52.38	52.95	52.70	52.64	53.12	51.31	49.18	48.70	47.08	44.38
	(9.40)	(9.31)	(9.66)	(9.58)	(10.42)	(9.44)	(9.39)	(8.47)	(9.64)	(7.57)
Total	53.53	52.21	52.89	52.39	51.43	50.14	48.39	47.07	45.43	43.47
	(9.13)	(9.54)	(9.58)	(9.94)	(10.37)	(9.74)	(9.61)	(8.96)	(9.55)	(8.32)
Agreeableness										
Male	38.70	43.64	44.31	46.12	45.88	46.66	48.49	46.29	49.06	47.16
	(14.27)	(8.99)	(13.22)	(8.63)	(9.96)	(9.73)	(9.11)	(9.37)	(8.63)	(9.12)
Female	47.33	49.77	49.46	50.65	52.85	53.82	54.01	53.68	54.74	56.35
	(10.43)	(8.49)	(10.02)	(10.07)	(9.45)	(9.04)	(8.76)	(8.14)	(7.72)	(7.08)
Total	44.79	47.19	47.65	48.89	49.95	50.74	51.65	50.67	52.39	53.39
	(12.14)	(9.19)	(11.49)	(9.78)	(10.25)	(9.98)	(9.31)	(9.38)	(8.55)	(8.85)
Conscientiousness										
Male	45.00	48.59	50.16	49.46	50.30	51.06	50.53	50.29	49.49	50.76
	(9.75)	(12.28)	(10.87)	(10.30)	(10.61)	(10.02)	(10.57)	(9.04)	(10.21)	(8.55)
Female	48.83	50.07	49.74	50.39	49.78	51.48	50.73	48.79	48.86	49.82
	(11.14)	(10.49)	(10.51)	(10.92)	(10.02)	(9.20)	(8.81)	(8.38)	(9.07)	(9.69)
Total	44.18	49.45	49.89	50.03	50.00	51.30	50.64	49.40	49.12	50.07
	(10.62)	(11.26)	(10.62)	(10.68)	(10.25)	(9.55)	(9.59)	(8.67)	(9.54)	(9.27)

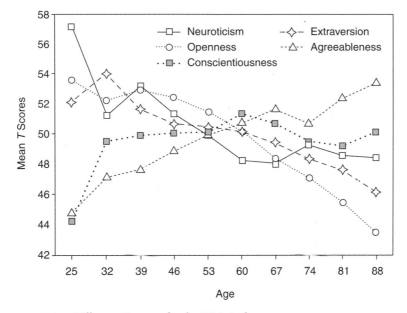

FIGURE 12.6 *Age Difference Patterns for the NEO Scales.*

TABLE 12.11 Standardized Factor Loadings for the NEO on the 13 Personality Factors

	Neuroticism	Extraversion	Openness	Agreeableness	Conscientious
Affectothymia	.293***	.141	.027	.057	.323***
Superego Strength	.455**	.380**	.157	.557***	.371***
Threctia	.087	.108	.134	.346***	.127*
Premsia	.198	.438***	.790***	.352***	.107
Untroubled Adequacy	.386**	.429***	.199	.346*	.330**
Conservatism	.458**	.296*	.081	.193	.498***
Group Dependency	.090	.023	.065	.080	.089
Low Self-Esteem	.072	.496***	.437***	.324***	.333***
Honesty	.010	.032	.061	.267***	.072
Interest in Science	.000	.066*	.038	.057	.003
Inflexibility	.463***	.197*	.246**	.131	.423***
Political Concern	.011	.014	.046	.045	−.007
Community Interest	.278**	.272**	.100	.284**	.264***

$*p < .05. **p < .01. ***p < .001.$

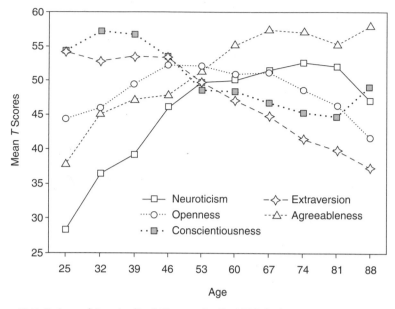

FIGURE 12.7 *Estimated Longitudinal Changes for the NEO Scales.*

Agreeableness shows a steep increment with age. Finally, Conscientiousness declines until the 50s, followed by a virtual plateau.

Depression in Old Age

As part of our neuropsychology studies of our older participants, we have collected data on the CES-D (Radloff, 1977; Radloff & Teri, 1986). The scale was developed as a short inventory for measuring depressive symptoms in the general population, although most clinicians would argue that it measures psychological distress rather than clinical depression. We report here cross-sectional data on a set of 494 study participants who ranged in age from 57 to 95 years. For comparison with our other data, this sample was divided into five age groups with mean ages of 60, 67, 74, 81, and 88 years. Table 12.12 provides means and standard deviations by age and gender. Although we did not find any significant gender differences or Age × Gender interaction, there was a trend ($p < .10$) toward higher depression scores with advancing age.

A 3-year follow-up study of 286 participants of the neuropsychology study yielded a stability coefficient of .582 for the depression scale. However, change in level of the depression score over the 3-year interval was not statistically significant.

TABLE 12.12 Means and Standard Deviations for the Center
for Epidemiologic Studies–Depression Scale Questionnaire
by Age and Gender (in Raw Scores)

	Age				
	60 (n = 76)	67 (n = 122)	74 (n = 143)	81 (n = 112)	88 (n = 41)
Male	7.15	6.33	7.62	8.28	11.06
	(6.42)	(5.76)	(5.91)	(7.07)	(7.89)
Female	6.55	7.95	8.02	9.74	7.20
	(7.36)	(6.61)	(6.64)	(7.59)	(5.48)
Total	6.82	7.31	7.85	9.09	8.71
	(6.91)	(6.31)	(6.33)	(7.36)	(6.71)

Chapter Summary

Although the primary objectives of the SLS did not originally address the study of personality per se, we have collected a substantial corpus of data on the adult development of personality and attitudinal traits. We have explicitly studied the attitudinal trait of Social Responsibility, have derived other personality traits and attitudes from the TBR questionnaire, and have recently added the NEO as a measure of the big five personality factors and the CES-D as a measure of depression.

Cross-sectional data on the measure of Social Responsibility suggested the presence of an Age × Cohort interaction, with lower Social Responsibility in old age in the earlier cohorts, but a reversal in the more recent cohorts. When aggregate longitudinal data are examined, however, we conclude that there is modest gain in Social Responsibility until age 74 years. Women show greater social responsibility than men until age 46 years, but the age gradients for both genders coincide thereafter. Only modest cohort differences were found, with the lowest Social Responsibility level shown by the 1952 cohort. However, there were significant secular trends displaying an overall decline in Social Responsibility from 1956 to 1977 and a significant rise thereafter.

Item factor analyses of the 75-item TBR questionnaire originally resulted in the identification of 19 personality factors (based on data from the first three cycles) that were assigned to a personality trait taxonomy of biostable, biocultural, and acculturated traits. A more recent confirmatory factor analysis of our entire data set found a 13-factor solution was more parsimonious. The factors identified were Affectothymia, Superego Strength, Threctia, Premsia, Untroubled Adequacy, Conservatism of Temperament, Group Dependency, Low Self-Sentiment, Honesty, Interest in Science, Inflexibility, Political Concern, and Community Involvement.

Significant cross-sectional age differences were found for all 13 personality factors. However, these differences can largely be explained by a pattern of positive and negative cohort differences. Far fewer significant within-participant age changes were found. Most noteworthy were modest within-participant increases with age in Superego Strength, Untroubled Adequacy, Honesty, Threctia, and Conservatism. Age-related declines were found for Affectothymia, Premsia, and Political Concern. No age trends were found for Low Self-Sentiment, Interest in Science, Inflexibility, and Community Involvement.

On the NEO, negative age differences are found for Neuroticism, Extraversion, and Openness, and positive age differences for Agreeableness and Conscientiousness did not differ significantly by age group. Estimated longitudinal age changes suggest rather different life course patterns. Here, Neuroticism and Openness show increases until midlife, with stability thereafter; Extraversion has a concave pattern of increment until midlife, with a decrease in old age; Agreeableness shows steep age-related increments; and Conscientiousness declines until midlife, with stability thereafter.

Finally, the CES-D data for our older participants showed a trend toward modest increase in psychological distress with increasing age.

CHAPTER THIRTEEN

Influences of Personality
on Cognition

THERE HAVE BEEN MANY SUGGESTIONS that the study of cognition and aging might be advanced by introducing personality constructs as possible covariates that might explain some proportion of age-related changes and differences in cognitive performance. In the earlier literature (cf. Mischel, 1973), it was often argued that most measures of personality traits were not sufficiently stable or did not show high enough correlations with cognitive measures to make it likely that they could account for substantial proportions of age-related variance. The former criticism has largely been addressed by more recent rigorous measurement development (e.g., Costa & McCrae, 1992), but the latter concern requires further empirical investigations.

In chapter 12, I reported our findings on age differences and age changes on the 13 personality factors that we derived from the Test of Behavioral Rigidity questionnaire. We also have reported age difference and estimated longitudinal data on the NEO Personality Inventory (Costa & McCrae, 1992). In this chapter, I report new analyses that speak to the influences of these personality variables in accounting for parts of the individual differences in cognitive performance (cf. Schaie, Willis, et al., 2004).

Studying the Relation Between Personality
and Cognition

Participants

Included in the analyses reported in this chapter are three different subsets from the Seattle Longitudinal Study (SLS). The first set used for the analyses of concurrent relationships between personality factors and cognitive abilities was the 1,761 participants who were assessed during the SLS seventh data collection and for whom we obtained both personality and cognitive ability scores. The second set used for the longitudinal analyses was the 1,055 participants who have personality factor and cognitive scores in both 1991 and 1998. Of these participants, 667 had scores also in 1984, 419 in 1977, 285 in 1970, and 157 in 1963. The third set was 1,501 participants who completed the NEO and who also had 1998 cognitive ability scores.

Measures

The measures include the cognitive ability scores, the cognitive factor scores, and the five NEO factor scores, as described in chapters 3 and 12.

Procedures

The TBR questionnaire (from which the 13 personality factor scores are derived) was administered either as part of the cognitive group testing sessions or as part of a take-home package. The NEO was administered as a mail survey.

Concurrent Relationships

We first examined concurrent relationships between the TBR personality factors and the NEO with the measures of the six latent ability constructs.

Test of Behavioral Rigidity Personality Factors

Stability of Personality Factor Scores   As an initial step, we conducted an analysis of the stability of the 13 personality factors over time. Included in this analysis were the 1,055 participants who had retest data over at least 7 years. All stability coefficients were statistically significant ($p < .01$). The 7-year stabilities ranged from .32 for Affectothymia to .71 for Group Dependency. The 14-year stabilities ranged from .33 for Affectothymia to .69 for Interest in Science. The 21-year stabilities ranged from .20 for Affectothymia to .67 for Group Dependency. The 28-year stabilities ranged from .24 for Political Concern to .65 for Interest in Science, and the 35-year stabilities ranged from .29 for Honesty to .66 for Group Dependency. Average stability coefficients were .59 over 7 years; .54 over 14 years; .49 over 21 years; .46 over 28 years; and .45 over 35 years (see table 13.1).

We also examined the 7-year stabilities separately for four age groups: young adult (age 29–49 years; $N = 182$); middle-aged (age 50–63 years; $N = 276$); young-old (age 64–77 years; $N = 379$); and old-old (age 78 years and older; $N = 182$). All ages are given for the second measurement occasion. Average stability coefficients over 7 years were .54 for the young adults, .58 for the middle-aged, .60 for the young-old, and .57 for the old-old. These stabilities ranged from somewhat lower to comparable values frequently seen in the personality literature (cf. Roberts & DelVecchio, 2000).

TABLE 13.1 Stability of the Personality Factor Scores

Factor	7 Years, 1991–1998 (N = 1,065)	14 Years, 1984–1998 (N = 667)	21 Years, 1977–1998 (N = 419)	28 Years, 1970–1998 (N = 285)	35 Years, 1963–1998 (N = 157)
Affectothymia	.318	.334	.205	.318	.297
Superego Strength	.588	.482	.440	.368	.415
Threctia	.696	.574	.545	.556	.452
Premsia	.589	.499	.487	.524	.514
Untroubled Adequacy	.643	.595	.597	.534	.441
Convervatism	.689	.613	.566	.586	.391
Group Dependency	.708	.653	.673	.631	.661
Low Self-Esteem	.675	.626	.483	.480	.482
Honesty	.500	.386	.362	.288	.291
Interest in Science	.694	.694	.653	.680	.604
Inflexibility	.570	.585	.529	.508	.530
Political Concern	.441	.475	.377	.236	.376
Community Interest	.595	.555	.415	.317	.357

Note. All stability coefficients are statistically significant at $p < .01$.

Concurrent Relation Between Personality and Ability Factors   The concurrent correlations are provided in table 13.2. Correlations ranged from small to modest. Consistently highest relationships for all abilities occurred with Conservatism (−), Untroubled Adequacy (+), and Group Dependency (−). Additional correlations significant at or beyond the .001 level of confidence were found for Inductive Reasoning with Affectothymia (+), Threctia (−), Premsia (+), Low Self-Esteem (−), Honesty (+), Interest in Science (+), Inflexibility (−), Political Concern (+),

TABLE 13.2 Concurrent Correlations of Personality Factor Scores and Cognitive Abilities

Factor	Inductive Reasoning	Spatial Orientation	Perceptual Speed	Numeric Facility	Verbal Comprehension	Verbal Memory
Affectothymia	.169***	.098***	.179***	.067**	.228***	.128***
Superego Strength	.059*	.017	.054*	.002	.102***	.035
Threctia	−.096***	−.118***	−.074**	.040	−.009	−.063**
Premsia	.235***	.192***	.198***	.068**	.108***	−.154***
Untroubled Adequacy	.290***	.199***	.255***	.084**	.257***	.247***
Convervatism	−.369***	−.257***	−.342***	−.144***	−.372***	−.307***
Group Dependency	−.216***	−.076**	−.216***	−.228***	−.299***	−.174***
Low Self-Esteem	−.136***	−.112***	−.096***	−.006	−.137***	−.091***
Honesty	−.082**	−.061*	−.089***	.009	.024	.088**
Interest in Science	.090***	.120***	.087***	−.010	.116***	.035
Inflexibility	−.116***	−.081***	−.150***	−.075**	−.081***	−.123***
Political Concern	.142***	.069**	.120***	.054*	.192***	.125***
Community Interest	−.120***	−.143***	−.140***	−.024	.080***	−.105***

$*p < .05.$ $**p < .01.$ $***p < .001.$

and Community Interest (−); for Spatial Orientation with Affectothymia (+), Threctia (−), Premsia (+), Low Self-Esteem (−), Interest in Science (+), Inflexibility (−), and Community Interest (−); for Perceptual Speed with Affectothymia (+), Premsia (+), Low Self-Esteem (−), Interest in Science (+), Inflexibility (−), Political Concern (+), and Community Interest (−); for Verbal Comprehension with Affectothymia (+), Superego Strength (+), Premsia (+), Low Self-Esteem (−), Interest in Science (+), Inflexibility (−), Political Concern (+), and Community Interest (+); and for Verbal Memory with Affectothymia (+), Premsia (−), Inflexibility (−), Political Concern (+), and Community Interest (−).

We also computed ordinary least squares (OLS) regressions of the ability factor scores on the personality factor scores (see table 13.3). Multiple Rs ranged from .27 for Numeric Facility to .49 for Verbal Comprehension. Proportions of variance accounted for by personality in the ability factors were approximately 20% for Inductive Reasoning, 11% for Spatial Orientation, 18% for Perceptual Speed, 7% for Numeric Facility, 24% for Verbal Comprehension, and 14% for Verbal Memory.

The NEO

Concurrent correlations were computed also between the five scales of the NEO Personality Inventory (table 13.4). Again, correlations ranged from small to modest. Consistently highest relationships for all abilities (except Numeric Facility) occurred with Openness. Additional correlations significant at or beyond the .001 level of confidence were found for Inductive Reasoning with Extraversion (+) and Agreeableness (−); for Spatial Orientation with Agreeableness (−); for Percep-

TABLE 13.3 Concurrent Ordinary Least Squares Regression of Personality Factor Scores on Cognitive Abilities (β Weights)

Factor	Inductive Reasoning	Spatial Orientation	Perceptual Speed	Numeric Facility	Verbal Comprehension	Verbal Memory
Affectothymia	.041	.017	.072**	.015	.083***	.023
Superego Strength	−.109***	−.126***	−.104***	−.035	.024	−.109***
Threctia	−.038	−.059*	−.027	.034	.014	−.027
Premsia	.092***	.088**	.054	.034	−.045	.018
Untroubled Adequacy	.145***	.084**	.081**	−.001	.082**	.114***
Convervatism	−.253***	−.177***	−.242***	−.119***	−.294***	−.225***
Group Dependency	−.140***	−.019	−.143***	−.206***	−.210***	−.108***
Low Self-Esteem	−.001	.010	.026	.036	−.060*	.009
Honesty	−.038	−.019	−.013	.009	.036	.053*
Interest in Science	.024	−.083***	−.056*	−.052*	.042	−.020
Inflexibility	−.013	−.013	−.068**	−.025	.031	−.061*
Political Concern	.001	−.022	−.017	−.009	.033	.011
Community Interest	−.051*	−.100***	−.085***	−.020	.154***	−.050*
Multiple Rs	.443	.336	.422	.267	.491	.370
R^2	.196	.106	.178	.071	.241	.137

*$p < .05$. **$p < .01$. ***$p < .001$.

TABLE 13.4 Concurrent Correlations of NEO Scores and Cognitive Abilities

Factor	Inductive Reasoning	Spatial Orientation	Perceptual Speed	Numeric Facility	Verbal Comprehension	Verbal Memory
Neuroticism	.025	.045	.004	−.052	−.067**	−.001
Extraversion	.093***	.051	.150***	.101***	−.012	.134***
Openness	.294***	.177***	.318***	.053	.355***	.316***
Agreeableness	−.090***	−.143***	−.016	.000	.036	.042
Conscientiousness	−.053	−.022	.037	.090***	−.082**	.037

**$p < .01$. ***$p < .001$.

tual Speed with Extraversion (+); for Numeric Facility with Extraversion (+) and Conscientiousness (+); and for Verbal Memory with Extraversion (+).

OLS regressions of the ability factor scores on the NEO scales are shown in table 13.5. Multiple Rs range from .12 for Numeric Facility to .40 for Verbal Comprehension. Proportions of variance accounted for by the NEO personality factors in the ability factors were approximately 10% for Inductive Reasoning, 6% for Spatial Orientation, 12% for Perceptual Speed, 2% for Numeric Facility, 16% for Verbal Comprehension, and 12% for Verbal Memory.

Relationship of the NEO and Cognitive Training

The relationship between the five NEO scales and gains from cognitive training (see chapter 7) has recently been examined by Boron (2003). No relationship was observed for the Spatial Orientation training. However, significant effects were found for the Inductive Reasoning training. There was an overall significant contribution of variance from the Agreeableness and Neuroticism factors, with high scores associated with reliable training gain. Further, there was an association between training gain and low scores on openness. In view of the fact that training gain was most pronounced for individuals with previous cognitive decline, it may follow that individuals with a personality profile of high Agreeableness and

TABLE 13.5 Ordinary Least Squares Regressions of Cognitive Abilities on NEO Scores (β Weights)

Factor	Inductive Reasoning	Spatial Orientation	Perceptual Speed	Numeric Facility	Verbal Comprehension	Verbal Memory
Neuroticisim	.003	.027	.058	.005	−.152***	.058
Extraversion	−.005	−.004	.03	.074*	−.200**	.021
Openness	.300***	.187***	.310***	.024	.414***	.314***
Agreeableness	−.096***	−.144***	−.028	−.018	−.001	.033
Conscientiousness	−.036	.014	.057*	.073*	−.098***	.030
Multiple Rs	.314	.234	.339	.123	.405	.347
R^2	.095	.055	.115	.015	.164	.120

*$p < .05$. **$p < .01$. ***$p < .001$.

Neuroticism but low Openness may be at higher risk for cognitive decline given that this profile may lead to a lower likelihood of seeking intellectual stimulation.

Longitudinal Relationships

We next examined the longitudinal relationship between personality factors and current cognitive performance. The assumption here was that personality is relatively stable, and that one would therefore expect a long-term effect on cognition. We examined this hypothesis using personality predictors that preceded the current cognitive performance by 7, 14, 21, 28, and 35 years.

OLS regressions of the ability factor scores obtained in 1998 on each of the personality factor scores were computed using personality factor scores obtained in 1963, 1970, 1977, 1984, and 1991. The pattern of statistically significant predictors remained fairly constant across increasing time intervals, although the p levels declined with shrinking sample sizes. Group dependency (−) was the strongest personality predictor for most abilities, followed by Conservatism (−), Untroubled adequacy (+), Premsia (+), and Low Self-Esteem (−).

Table 13.6 reports regression coefficients and proportions of variance accounted for in the 1998 cognitive ability factors by earlier standing on the 13 personality factors. The proportions did not vary markedly across the increasing length of the prediction interval. Average proportion of cognitive ability variance predicted was 15.8% over 7 years, 13.6% over 14 years, 13.0% over 21 years, 15.5% over 28 years, and 14.8% over 35 years. The predictability was highest for Verbal Comprehension (20% to 37%) and lowest for Spatial Orientation (7% to 13%) and Numeric Facility (6% to 15%).

Chapter Summary

Interestingly, we showed that there are modest but significant concurrent relationships between personality trait measures and ability construct that account for up to 20% of shared variance. Both our 13 personality factor measures and the NEO could be related to the cognitive ability constructs, albeit the 13-factor measure accounted for more of the shared variance than did the NEO. The personality dimensions that were most substantively related to high performance on cognitive ability factors were high Untroubled Adequacy, low Conservatism, and low Group Dependency from the 13 personality factors measure and high scores of Openness on the NEO.

We were also able to show that there is moderate stability across time for the personality measures that is fairly comparable with the stability found in much of the personality literature (cf. Roberts & DelVecchio, 2000). It might be argued, therefore, that prediction of cognitive change over age would benefit from the inclusion of personality traits as predictors of distal levels of cognitive perfor-

TABLE 13.6 Predictive Ordinary Least Squares Regression of Personality Factor Scores on Cognitive Abilities (β Weights)

Factors	7 Years, 1991–1998 (N = 986)	14 Years, 1984–1998 (N = 588)	21 Years, 1977–1998 (N = 384)	28 Years, 1970–1998 (N = 245)	35 Years, 1963–1998 (N = 144)
Inductive Reasoning 1998					
Affectothymia	.010	−.047	.005	−.020	.118
Superego Strength	.128***	.112**	.072	−.067	−.025
Threctia	−.064*	−.060	.013	.080	−.010
Premsia	.059*	.062	.079	.182**	.133
Untroubled Adequacy	.164***	.191***	.138*	.075	−.008
Conservatism	−.217***	−.116**	−.106	−.124	.037
Group Dependency	−.140***	−.193***	−.243***	−.197**	−.298**
Low Self-Esteem	−.050	.012	.063	−.063	−.113
Honesty	.047	−.020	−.111*	.007	.022
Interest in Science	.019	.036	.022	.114	−.028
Inflexibility	−.004	.003	.037	.070	−.006
Political Concern	.002	.034	−.078	−.065	−.050
Community Interest	−.082**	−.075	−.003	.079	−.042
Multiple Rs	.443***	.399***	.383***	.359**	.342
R^2	.197	.159	.147	.129	.117
Spatial Orientation 1998					
Affectothymia	−.022	−.042	−.089	−.113	.109
Superego Strength	.150***	.076	.011	−.084	.048
Threctia	−.059	−.085*	−.035	−.045	−.213
Premsia	.078*	.096*	.070	.098	.144
Untroubled Adequacy	.082*	.037	.036	−.007	−.177
Conservatism	−.215***	−.109*	.001	−.019	.155
Group Dependency	−.020	−.080*	−.106*	−.102	−.230**
Low Self-Esteem	.037	.003	.022	−.011	−.059
Honesty	−.073*	−.020	−.130*	.026	−.013
Interest in Science	.066*	.058	.078	.166*	.055
Inflexibility	−.004	.052	.001	.092	−.026
Political Concern	−.039	−.038	−.113*	−.045	−.048
Community Interest	−.091*	−.124**	−.029	−.019	−.180*
Multiple Rs	.360***	.287***	.258***	.279***	.358
R^2	.130	.083	.066	.078	.128
Perceptual Speed 1998					
Affectothymia	.045	−.001	.040	.027	.141
Superego Strength	.098**	.093*	.057	−.048	−.004
Threctia	−.057	−.106**	−.042	.118	.004
Premsia	.032	.057	−.010	.149*	.090
Untroubled Adequacy	.146***	.146**	.079	.020	.073
Conservatism	−.212***	−.111*	−.062	−.167*	.066
Group Dependency	−.124***	−.181***	−.210***	−.194**	−.323***
Low Self-Esteem	.009	−.028	.051	−.023	−.091
Honesty	−.063*	−.013	−.098	−.043	−.032
Interest in Science	−.008	.008	−.047	.009	−.049

(continued)

TABLE 13.6 Continued

Factors	7 Years, 1991–1998 (N = 986)	14 Years, 1984–1998 (N = 588)	21 Years, 1977–1998 (N = 384)	28 Years, 1970–1998 (N = 245)	35 Years, 1963–1998 (N = 144)
Inflexibility	−.040	.015	−.032	.052	.126
Political Concern	−.012	.033	−.086	−.058	−.053
Community Interest	−.074*	−.122**	−.111*	.011	−.197*
Multiple Rs	.413***	.384***	.333***	.347**	.422**
R^2	.170	.147	.111	.120	.178
Numeric Facility 1998					
Affectothymia	−.043	−.027	−.050	.000	.058
Superego Strength	.052	.026	.042	−.029	−.165
Threctia	−.003	−.062	−.048	.098	.051
Premsia	.019	.017	−.050	.153*	−.031
Untroubled Adequacy	.082*	.060	.069	.071	−.033
Conservatism	−.081*	−.023	.019	−.043	.048
Group Dependency	−.177***	−.203***	−.146**	−.169**	−.200*
Low Self-Esteem	−.020	−.035	−.083	−.109	−.206*
Honesty	.006	.016	−.030	−.029	.054
Interest in Science	−.062*	−.069	−.136**	−.060	−.064
Inflexibility	−.007	−.011	−.018	.027	−.163
Political Concern	.021	.036	.060	−.023	.061
Community Interest	−.064	−.047	−.068	.059	−.065
Multiple Rs	.255***	.257***	.250*	.297***	.386
R^2	.065	.066	.063	.088	.149
Verbal Comprehension 1998					
Affectothymia	.033	.018	.197***	.158**	.176
Superego Strength	−.001	.034	.008	−.108	−.028
Threctia	−.007	−.047	.023	.039	.038
Premsia	.007	−.057	−.078	.025	−.043
Untroubled Adequacy	.141***	.174**	.152**	.210***	.067
Conservatism	−.294***	−.247***	−.206***	−.261***	−.152
Group Dependency	−.211***	−.307***	−.303***	−.271***	−.305***
Low Self-Esteem	.057	.019	.052	−.092	−.048
Honesty	.063*	.009	−.066	.000	.055
Interest in Science	.054*	.082*	.075	.052	−.041
Inflexibility	.077**	.057	.015	.060	−.049
Political Concern	.079**	.010	−.016	.081	−.115
Community Interest	.087**	.080*	.131**	.141**	.008
Multiple Rs	.517***	.509***	.536***	.609***	.453**
R^2	.267	.260	.287	.371	.205
Verbal Memory 1998					
Affectothymia	−.024	−.031	.091	−.002	.040
Superego Strength	.128***	.119**	.112*	−.030	.032
Threctia	−.020	−.049	.088	.156*	.063
Premsia	.040	.015	.040	.215**	.083
Untroubled Adequacy	.137***	.165***	.112	.092	.103
Conservatism	−.109**	−.120**	−.129*	−.147*	−.143

TABLE 13.6 Continued

Factors	7 Years, 1991–1998 (N = 986)	14 Years, 1984–1998 (N = 588)	21 Years, 1977–1998 (N = 384)	28 Years, 1970–1998 (N = 245)	35 Years, 1963–1998 (N = 144)
Group Dependency	−.155***	−.136***	−.130**	−.120	−.179
Low Self-Esteem	.016	.049	.040	−.052	−.067
Honesty	−.056	.024	−.083	−.047	−.071
Interest in Science	−.009	−.007	.018	.105	.037
Inflexibility	.028	−.063	−.007	−.066	.123
Political Concern	.033	−.054	−.001	.076	.023
Community Interest	−.073*	−.054*	.021	.052	.000
Multiple Rs	.346***	.351***	.323***	.382***	.336
R^2	.120	.123	.104	.146	.113

$*p < .05.$ $**p < .01.$ $***p < .001.$

mance. This argument is bolstered by the fact that some of the personality-cognition relations could be established over as long as a 35-year interval.

Perhaps most important, we also demonstrated that even though the SLS did not originally focus on the assessment of personality traits, it was possible to utilize suitable estimation procedures that permitted longitudinal analyses bearing on the contributions of personality constructs in understanding adult cognition.

CHAPTER FOURTEEN

Family Studies of Intellectual Abilities in Adulthood

OUR INTEREST IN STUDYING INTRAFAMILY RELATIONSHIPS began serendipitously because membership in a health maintenance organization is usually held on a family rather than an individual basis. Our sampling procedures therefore yielded subsamples of married couples. More recently, exposure to the behavior genetics literature suggested that the Seattle Longitudinal Study (SLS) would be a natural vehicle for studying family similarity in the general (nontwin) population, and we began to gather data systematically on many adult children and siblings of our longitudinal panel members.

Married Couples

Similarity between married couples has usually been examined in the context of marital assortativity. Previous researchers have found significant correlations between spouses on a number of cognitive abilities and personality dimensions (see Murstein, 1980; Zonderman, Vandenberg, Spuhler, & Fain, 1977). The observed similarity was typically explained as based on initial couple similarity, the convergence of abilities over the marriage, the divorce of couples who are dissimilar, or confounds because of age-related trends (Price & Vandenberg, 1980). Cross-sectional research designs have dominated research in this field, and findings are thus based on comparisons of similarity within couples of different marriage durations. By contrast, we were able to examine a longitudinal sample of married couples for whom we could investigate change in couple similarity over time on our measures of cognitive abilities and cognitive styles (Gruber & Schaie, 1986; Gruber-Baldini et al., 1995).

This study addressed four questions. First, we asked to what degree couples' scores are similar on cognitive and cognitive style measures and whether spousal similarity varies across abilities. Second, we raised the question whether further convergence occurs as couples remain married for long periods of time. Third, we inquired whether the observed level of similarity is attributable to spousal similarity on background variables such as age and education. Fourth, we examined whether convergence is a product of changes of both spouses or whether one spouse is more likely to move closer to the other's level of functioning over time.

Methods

Participants   We were able to identify 169 married couples with both partners participating in at least two SLS waves. Couples entered the study in 1956, 1963, or 1970. Data are available over 7 years for 150 couples, over 14 years for 106 couples, and over 21 years for 66 couples. At initial testing, participants ranged from 22 to 79 years of age. The participants included in the 21-year analyses (mean age 42.31 years) were slightly younger than those in the 7-year (mean age 44.94 years) and 14-year (mean age 43.18 years) data sets. There were no significant differences in educational, income, and occupational characteristics.

Measures   Variables included in the couples analyses consist of the five Primary Mental Abilities (PMA) subtests (Verbal Meaning, Spatial Orientation, Inductive Reasoning, Number, and Word Fluency), the composite indices of Intellectual Ability and Educational Aptitude, the three factor scores from the Test of Behavioral Rigidity (Motor-Cognitive Flexibility, Attitudinal Flexibility, and Psychomotor Speed), and the questionnaire scale of Social Responsibility.

Results of the Couples Study

The initial correlations among spouses were statistically significant for Verbal Meaning, Inductive Reasoning, and Word Fluency as well as the Index of Educational Aptitude and the Social Responsibility scale in all three data sets. The correlations remained significant when controlling for age and educational level of the spouses. Changes (increases) in similarity among couples across time were significant for Verbal Meaning and the Index of Intellectual Ability as well as for the factor scores in Attitudinal Flexibility.

Examination of cross-lag panel correlations suggested that the question of which spouse has more influence on the other may be ability and time specific. The earlier Inductive Reasoning scores of the husbands positively influenced their wives' Inductive Reasoning scores 7 years later, and wives' Verbal Meaning scores influenced their husbands' Verbal Meaning scores 14 years later.

When couples were divided according to which spouse had the higher initial score, the lower spouses' Attitudinal Flexibility influenced the higher spouses' Motor-Cognitive Flexibility 7 years later. When both age and education were controlled, the higher functioning spouses' Word Fluency had a positive effect on the lower functioning spouses' Word Fluency and Verbal Meaning scores over both 7 and 14 years.

Couples were also classified on the basis of whether they became more similar or more different or had not significantly changed in magnitude of similarity over a 7-year interval. Couples who became more similar on the ability variables had husbands with higher occupational levels. Couples whose similarity did not change significantly over time had husbands with fewer changes of profession. Couples who became more dissimilar over time had husbands who changed professions more frequently.

Relevance of the Seattle Longitudinal Study to Developmental Behavior Genetics

Developmental behavior genetics has recently begun to focus on change. This is often surprising to those developmentalists who tend to associate the adjectives *genetic* and *stable*. However, longitudinally stable characteristics do not necessarily have a hereditary base, and genetically influenced characteristics are not necessarily stable (Plomin, 1986). The identification of genetic sources of developmental change is important because change prevails over continuity for most aspects of development. For this reason, a major task for developmental behavior genetics is to explain longitudinal change as well as continuity. It should be emphasized that only longitudinal studies are able to assess genetic change and continuity.

A second issue receiving attention by developmental behavior geneticists is that of nonshared environmental influence. In general, behavioral genetic research provides the best available evidence for the importance of environmental influences. This is because environmental influences have been found to make individuals in the same family as different from one another as are pairs of individuals selected at random from the population. In other words, psychologically relevant environmental influences make individuals in a family different from, not similar to, one another (see Plomin & Daniels, 1987).

The relevance of this issue to our research lies in the usefulness of parent-offspring comparisons for identifying specific sources of nonshared environmental influence by relating experiential differences within pairs to behavioral differences within the pairs. The key question in environmental research is why individuals in the same family are so different from each other. This question can only be addressed by studies that include more than one individual per family (Plomin & Daniels, 1987).

Developmental Behavior Genetics and Adulthood

From a behavioral genetic perspective, relatively little is known about the origins of individual differences in cognitive abilities, personality, and adjustment during the last half of the life span (McClearn & Vogler, 2001; Plomin & McClearn, 1990). As our analyses have demonstrated, there are vast individual differences in intellectual change across adulthood, ranging from early decrement for some persons to maintenance of function into very advanced age for others; a basic and fundamental research goal therefore must be to account for this individuality in aging. Most behavior genetic research in adulthood involves offspring in their late teens, typically toward the end of high school or at the time of military induction (see Plomin, 1986). In the handful of studies that included older adults, the average age of the sample was typically in the 20s or 30s, and the age range was so great that it was difficult to conduct cross-sectional analyses of family resemblance as a function of age.

The first systematic behavior genetic study in middle and old age was organized by Franz Kallman and Gerhard Sander (1948, 1949) in the 1940s. Over 1,000 pairs of twins in New York were studied biennially, with a primary emphasis on physical aspects of aging. Psychological tests were administered to 75 identical and 45 fraternal twin pairs between the ages of 60 and 89 years who were selected for cognitive testing on the basis of concordance for relatively good health, lack of institutionalization, and literacy (Kallman, Feingold, & Bondy, 1951). The results were analyzed in terms of intrapair differences rather than correlations: Identical twins showed significantly smaller intrapair differences than fraternal twins, with the exception of memory tests involving simple recall of recent material, suggesting the importance of genetic influence on individual differences in cognitive functioning later in life. Small samples of surviving twins were studied again in 1955 (Jarvik, Kallman, Falek, & Kleber, 1957) and 1967 (Jarvik, Blum, & Varma, 1971). In 1967, when the surviving intact pairs were from 77 to 88 years old, 19 pairs (13 identical and 6 fraternal) were studied again by seven tests of cognitive abilities. This longitudinal sample, however, was so small as to vitiate the comparison of identical and fraternal twin correlations.

Perhaps the major behavior genetic studies of older adults, with participants obtained from the Swedish twin registry, are currently being conducted in Sweden with a sample of twins reared apart and matched twins reared together (for a major review of the Swedish twin studies, see Pedersen & Liechtenstein, 2000; Smedby, Lundberg, & Sørensen, 2000). In the aging twin study, questionnaire data on personality and many other variables were collected for over 300 pairs of twins reared apart and matched pairs of twins reared together, with an age range from 50 to 80 years (Pedersen et al., 1991; Pedersen & Reynolds, 1998; Plomin, Pedersen, Nesselroade, & Bergeman, 1988). The second phase of this study involves individual biomedical and behavioral testing of 50 pairs each of identical and fraternal twins reared apart and matched pairs of identical and fraternal twins reared together. A second wave of testing occurred after 3 years, and a third wave occurred 6 years after initial testing (Finkel, Pedersen, McClearn, Plomin, & Berg, 1996; Finkel, Pedersen, Plomin, & McClearn, 1998).

By contrast, the research reported here capitalizes on the longitudinal design of the SLS to offer an "instant" longitudinal study of parents and offspring from young adulthood through middle age. Because parents and offspring share family environment as well as heredity, our family design cannot unambiguously disentangle the contributions of heredity and shared environment on familial resemblance. The family design used here, however, has some important advantages over twin and adoption designs. Twins have environmental experiences in common to a much greater extent than do first-degree relatives; furthermore, twin studies estimate higher-order genetic interactions (i.e., epistasis) unique to identical twins. Thus, the results of twin studies may not generalize to the usual case of first-degree relatives in terms of either environmental or genetic factors. Early-adopted individuals are rare, difficult to find later in life, and may differ from nonadopted individuals in terms of the family environments they experience. Also, adoptees are often selectively placed in their adoptive families, which attenuates the separation of genetic and environmental influences when the adoption design is used (Plomin, 1983).

Family studies are valuable because first-degree relatives represent the population to which we wish to generalize the results of behavioral genetic investigations. Furthermore, family studies provide upper-limit estimates of genetic influence—that is, additive genetic influence cannot exceed estimates based on first-degree relatives. Although familial resemblance could reflect family environment as well as shared heredity, which is why estimates of genetic influence are called upper-limit estimates, it appears that shared environmental influences are of negligible importance to personality, psychopathology, and cognitive abilities after adolescence (Plomin, 1987; Plomin & Daniels, 1987). In other words, the important environmental factors in development are no more experienced in common by individuals in the same family than they are for pairs of individuals picked at random from the population. Thus, as a first approximation, it is not unreasonable to assume that familial resemblance later in life is primarily mediated genetically.

Our study is a reasonable first step in understanding the etiology of individual differences in functioning later in life, even if a conservative interpretation is taken, in the sense that familial resemblance is not interpreted as exclusively genetic in origin. The family design asks the extent to which individual differences are caused by familial factors, whether genetic or environmental, and it provides upper-limit estimates of genetic and shared family environmental influences.

The long-term longitudinal nature of the SLS provides a unique opportunity to study relatives tested at roughly the same age; differences in same-age comparisons of sibling resemblance and parent-offspring resemblance as a function of year of birth yield a novel test of cohort effects. In addition to these same-age comparisons, the SLS data archives make it possible to trace parent-offspring resemblance forward in time by comparing same-age resemblance of parents and offspring to resemblance when the parents are 7, 14, 21, 28, and 35 years older.

Hypotheses That Were Investigated

Because behavior genetic data during the last half of the life span are sparse, it was not possible to propose well-founded hypotheses that could be tested with our data. However, four categories of hypothesis were delineated and addressed in this investigation:

1. *Family similarity in cognitive abilities will be found throughout adulthood, and the relationship will be stronger for verbal ability than for other cognitive abilities.* It is expected that at least modest parent-offspring correlations will be found for all cognitive abilities. However, we also expect that greater similarity will be found for verbal ability. Although evidence is not good that any specific cognitive ability is more heritable than any other (DeFries, Vandenberg, & McClearn, 1976), there

is some evidence that shared family environmental factors are greater for verbal abilities than for other cognitive abilities (Plomin, 1987). This hypothesis seems reasonable when the possibilities for training and modeling are considered, for example, for vocabulary as compared with spatial ability. For this reason, we predict that familial resemblance will be greater for the two verbal tests Verbal Ability and Word Fluency than for other abilities. Further, if this effect is caused by shared family environment, we would expect the effect to diminish with age.

2. *Familial resemblance in cognitive abilities is expected to increase from early adulthood to middle adulthood.* It is generally assumed that nonnormative experiences increase in importance during development (Baltes, Reese, & Lipsitt, 1980), which would lead to the prediction that familial resemblance for cognitive abilities should decrease during adulthood. However, four recent behavior genetic studies of adoptive siblings all indicated that shared family environmental influences that affect general cognitive ability are of negligible importance after adolescence (Plomin, 1987). This means that the environmental component of familial resemblance does not appear to change during adulthood. In contrast, there is some evidence that genetic influence increases in importance during adulthood (Pedersen, 1996; Plomin & Thompson, 1987). If genetic influence increases, we are led to the counterintuitive (from an environmental perspective) hypothesis that familial resemblance in cognitive abilities increases later in life, decades after family members have left their shared family environment. To test this hypothesis, familial resemblance will be examined as a function of age.

3. *Familial influences are expected to exert long-term effects on cognitive abilities throughout the adult life course.* If it is assumed that shared environmental influences are relatively unimportant in adulthood (implying that such influences do not contribute to family resemblance), one would not expect to find—strictly from an environmental perspective—familial resemblance with either same-age or cross-age comparisons. However, there is increasing evidence that genetic influence on cognitive abilities shows substantial continuity throughout adulthood (Plomin & Thompson, 1987). For example, model-fitting analyses of adoption data have indicated that genetic effects in childhood are highly correlated with genetic effects in adulthood for IQ (DeFries, Plomin, & LaBuda, 1987). This leads to the prediction that long-term familial (presumably genetic) effects will produce familial resemblance in cognitive abilities even when one family member is assessed at a very different age from another family member. This hypothesis can be tested by assessing family resemblance cross-sectionally over a wide range of ages as well as longitudinally within the same data set. The simplest analytic approach to this problem is to test whether familial resemblance differs as a function of the interval at which the family members were assessed (see also Schaie, 1975, for alternative methods of analysis).

4. *Cohort effects will be seen in that parent-offspring correlations will be greater for earlier cohorts of adult offspring.* The striking finding that shared family environmental influence is negligible for cognitive ability after adolescence has been studied only in recent cohorts. Earlier cohorts will show greater shared family environmental influence if the influence of the family on cognitive scores has declined or if the importance of extrafamilial influences such as television has

increased. Older and younger cohorts of parent-offspring relatives yield the same expectation of genetic similarity unless the magnitude of assortative mating has changed (see section Married Couples; and see Gruber-Baldini et al., 1995). As a test of the hypothesis of cohort effects, parent-offspring resemblances were assessed as a function of year of birth.

Parents and Adult Offspring

Parent-offspring similarities have traditionally been studied in young adult parents and their children. In this section, I describe longitudinal data collected on similarity of parents and adult offspring considered specifically as a function of the age of parent-offspring pairs when studied (see Schaie, Plomin, et al., 1992; Schaie et al., 1993).

Methods

Participants   The participants in this study consisted of the adult offspring (aged 22 years or older in 1990) of members of the SLS panels and their target relatives. Those members who participated in the fifth cycle of the SLS had a total of 3,507 adult children. Of these, 1,416 adult children (701 males, 715 females) resided in the Seattle metropolitan area.

The adult offspring were recruited in two ways: (a) A letter containing an update report on the SLS was sent to all study participants tested in 1983–1984. This letter also announced the family resemblance study and requested that panel members provide names and addresses of siblings and offspring. A recruitment letter was then sent to all offspring thus identified. (b) We also searched the participating health maintenance organization records to identify offspring and siblings of longitudinal panel members who had dropped out because of death or illness. Offspring of some panel members were also identified because they were included in their parents' service contracts. Surviving spouses were also identified in the same manner and were used as informants to obtain addresses for offspring of deceased panel members.

We were able to test 531 adult offspring. Of these study participants, 439 (82.7%) resided in the Seattle metropolitan area; the remaining 92 (17.3%) were scattered throughout the United States and Canada. The offspring in 1990 ranged in age from 22 to 74 years ($M = 40.43$; $SD = 10.45$). Target parents ranged in age from 39 to 91 years at the time they were last tested in 1984 ($M = 63.66$; $SD = 10.89$). All participants were community-dwelling individuals when tested. This data set included 99 father-son pairs, 211 mother-daughter pairs, 115 father-daughter pairs, and 106 mother-son pairs. Data on age and sex distribution by subset are provided in table 14.1.

Measures   The test battery administered to the participants in this study is a subset of measures administered to their parents. It includes the PMA tests of Verbal Meaning, Spatial Orientation, Inductive Reasoning, Number, and Word

TABLE 14.1 Age and Sex Distribution of Parent-Offspring Study Participants

Age Range	Parents (1984)			Offspring (1990)		
	Male	Female	Total	Male	Female	Total
22–28	—	—	—	21	30	51
29–35	—	—	—	52	96	48
36–42	—	11	11	48	82	30
43–49	15	27	42	43	55	98
50–56	34	63	97	25	34	59
57–63	56	59	115	14	17	31
64–70	49	69	118	3	6	9
71–77	35	52	87	2	3	5
79–84	16	28	44	—	—	—
85–91	9	8	17	—	—	—
Total	214	317	531	208	323	531

Fluency. In addition, the Educational Testing Service (ETS) Finding A's test was included as a measure of perceptual speed, and the Test of Behavioral Rigidity was used to assess cognitive styles.

Procedure   Potential participants who agreed to participate were scheduled by telephone for group assessment sessions. Size of the groups ranged from 5 to 20, depending on the age of the participants. The testing sessions lasted approximately 2.5 hours plus a take-home package of questionnaires requiring approximately an additional hour of effort. Each session was conducted by a psychometrist, aided by a proctor whenever more than 5 participants were tested simultaneously. Participants were paid $25 for their participation.

Analyses   Regression analyses were employed to analyze parent-offspring resemblance and to determine the extent to which familial resemblance differs as a function of other variables, such as age and testing interval, as well as other variables such as gender, time of measurement, and demographic factors (DeFries & Fulker, 1985; Ho, Foch, & Plomin, 1980; Zieleniewski, Fulker, DeFries, & LaBuda, 1987). This least-squares model fitting represents a straightforward approach to the analysis of such simple designs as the family design, in which we do not attempt to differentiate genetic and environmental components of variance. For example, we may regress out the effects of parent and offspring age to obtain net estimates of the parent-offspring correlations. Alternatively, we may ask the question whether the family similarity differs as a function of offspring age. Using hierarchical multiple regression (Cohen & Cohen, 1975), we regressed the parent's score on three predictors: (a) the offspring's score, (b) the offspring's age, and (c) the interaction between offspring age and performance. A significant standard partial regression coefficient for the interaction of offspring score and age indicates that family resemblance differs as a function of offspring age.

Estimation of Genetic Parameters   In addition to these straightforward analyses of familial resemblance and its interaction with other variables, genetic analyses can be conducted if the assumption is made that shared environment does not contribute to familial resemblance, in other words, if it is assumed that familial resemblance is caused solely by hereditary factors. As indicated here, this appears to be a reasonable assumption for cognitive abilities in adulthood; however, the novelty of this conclusion and the need for more data to confirm it limit the following genetic analyses to exploratory ventures rather than precise estimates of genetic parameters. If the assumption is made that shared environment does not contribute to familial resemblance in cognitive abilities, doubling parent-offspring correlations provides estimates of heritability—the proportion of phenotypic variance that can be explained by genetic variance (see also Plomin, DeFries, & McClearn, 1980). If, for example, a same-age parent-offspring correlation of .30 were obtained for the PMA Spatial Orientation test, it would suggest a heritability of .60 if shared environment does not contribute to the parent-offspring similarity. The rest of the variance is nongenetic; some of the nongenetic variance involves error of measurement, and the remainder is caused by nonshared environment. The regression analyses described above provide estimates of heritability across ages, with interactions between familial resemblance and age defining age trends in heritability.

It should again be emphasized that heritability is a descriptive statistic and thus will change as the relative contributions of genetic and environmental influences change in different populations or during development. These statistics imply no more precision than do other descriptive statistics; as for all descriptive statistics, standard errors of estimate need to be consulted to evaluate precision. Most important, heritability does not imply immutability: It simply refers to the proportion of observed interindividual variance in a population that is caused by genetic differences among individuals.

Results of the Parent-Offspring Study

Findings on parent-offspring similarity are first presented in terms of the correlation of parental performance with that of their offspring, as well as of adjusted coefficients when the regression of parental and offspring age on the dependent variables has been removed. Next, the stability of parent-offspring correlations across time (and age) is considered. The possible effect of shared environment is then reported by considering the correlation of intensity of current contact between parents and offspring. Age/cohort differences in the magnitude of parent-offspring correlation are also examined. Finally, the magnitudes of generational differences in level within families and changes in the magnitude of these differences for successive cohort groupings are considered.

Parent-Offspring Correlations   As shown in table 14.2 and figure 14.1, parent-offspring correlations for the total sample were statistically significant ($p < .05$) for all variables studied except for the trait measure of Social Responsibility. Among the ability measures, correlations were highest for Inductive Reasoning,

TABLE 14.2 Correlation of Parents and Offspring

	Total (N = 531)	Father-Son (N = 99)	Mother-Daughter (N = 211)	Father-Daughter (N = 115)	Mother-Son (N = 106)
Verbal Meaning	.14**	.22*	.18**	.00	.09
Space	.24***	.10	.22**	.32***	.27**
Reasoning	.28***	.17	.32***	.34***	.40***
Number	.19***	.24*	.19**	.20*	.12
Word Fluency	.27***	.18	.33***	.20*	.19*
Finding A's	.10*	−.09	.20**	.12	.12
Intellectual Ability	.26***	.13	.30***	.37***	.20*
Educational Aptitude	.20***	.26*	.23**	.13	.16
Motor-Cognitive Flexibility	.29***	.07	.25***	.43***	.36***
Attitudinal Flexibility	.13**	.08	.09	.20	.21*
Psychomotor Speed	.21***	.17	.23***	.04	.36***
Social Responsibility	.00	−.07	−.02	.09	.06

*p < .05. **p < .01. ***p < .001.

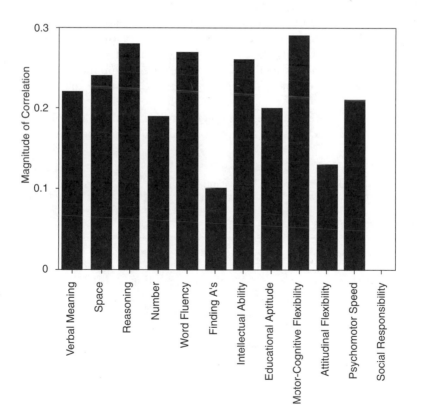

FIGURE 14.1 *Parent-Offspring Correlations.*

Word Fluency, and the Intellectual Ability composite measure. They were lowest for the measures of Perceptual Speed (the Finding A's test) and Verbal Meaning. Among the cognitive style measures, correlations were highest for Motor-Cognitive Flexibility and lowest for Attitudinal Flexibility.

Because of the wide age range among parents and offspring (and to model the assumption of equal ages), we partialed out the effects of parent and offspring age. The correlations adjusted for age at the most recent test are provided in table 14.3 and figure 14.2. Subsequent to the age adjustment, all but the measures of Perceptual Speed and Social Responsibility remain statistically significant ($p <$ .01). However, the magnitudes of the correlations change somewhat, with Word Fluency and Verbal Meaning now displaying the highest ability correlations, along with the composite indices of Intellectual Ability and Educational Aptitude. Both Motor-Cognitive Flexibility and Psychomotor Speed continue to show higher family resemblance than does Attitudinal Flexibility.

The correlational findings are not uniform across subsets. When raw parent-offspring correlations are examined (table 14.2 and figure 14.1), statistically significant correlations ($p < .05$) between fathers and sons are found only for Verbal Meaning, Number, and Educational Aptitude. For the mother-daughter set, however, statistically significant correlations ($p < .05$) are found for all variables except Attitudinal Flexibility and Social Responsibility. Correlations between fathers and daughters are statistically significant ($p < .05$) for Spatial Orientation, Inductive Reasoning, Number, Word Fluency, the Index of Intellectual Ability, and Motor-Cognitive Flexibility. Finally, for the mother-son set, statistically significant ($p < .05$) correlations are found for Spatial Orientation, Inductive Reasoning, Word Fluency, Intellectual Ability, Motor-Cognitive Flexibility, and Psychomotor Speed.

When age of parent and offspring is controlled, further differences between subsets are observed (see table 14.3). Statistically significant correlations ($p < .05$)

TABLE 14.3 Correlation of Parents and Offspring Adjusted for Age at Test

Variable	Total	Father-Son	Mother-Daughter	Father-Daughter	Mother-Son
Verbal Meaning	.25***	.30***	.30***	.10	.21*
Space	.15**	.04	.10	.27**	.16*
Reasoning	.21***	.19*	.21**	.28***	.31**
Number	.21***	.25**	.22**	.24*	.11
Word Fluency	.27***	.22*	.35***	.21*	.13
Finding A's	.07	−.12	.15*	.11	.08
Intellectual Ability	.29***	.21*	.31***	.43***	.17*
Educational Aptitude	.29***	.34**	.32***	.18*	.25*
Motor-Cognitive Flexibility	.21**	.04	.16*	.39***	.22*
Attitudinal Flexibility	.15**	.10	.10	.11	.23*
Psychomotor Speed	.21***	.19*	.25***	.01	.26***
Social Responsibility	.00	−.03	−.04	.11	.03

*$p < .05$. **$p < .01$. ***$p < .001$.

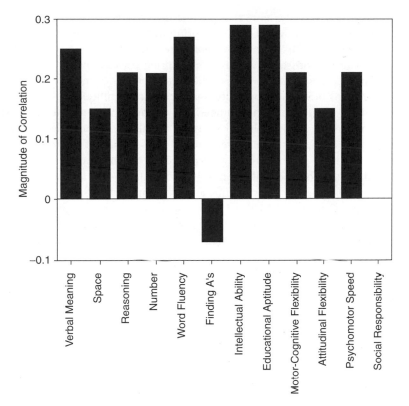

FIGURE 14.2 *Parent-Offspring Correlations Adjusted for Age.*

between fathers and sons are now found for Verbal Meaning, Word Fluency, Inductive Reasoning, Number, Intellectual Ability, Educational Aptitude, and Psychomotor Speed. For the mother-daughter set, however, statistically significant correlations ($p < .05$) continue to be found for all variables except Spatial Orientation, Attitudinal Flexibility, and Social Responsibility. Correlations between fathers and daughters remain statistically significant ($p < .05$) for the same variables as for the raw correlations. For the mother-son set, statistically significant correlations ($p < .05$) are now found for Verbal Meaning, Spatial Orientation, Inductive Reasoning, the composite indices, Motor-Cognitive Flexibility, Attitudinal Flexibility, and Psychomotor Speed.

Stability of Parent-Offspring Correlations Over Time   One of the critical issues in studying family similarity in adulthood is to determine whether such similarity remains stable or changes as the distance in age at time of assessment between parent and offspring increases. To examine stability of correlations with a sufficiently large sample, we considered for this analysis only those parent-offspring pairs for whom at least four data points (1963, 1970, 1977, and 1984) were available for the parents, yielding a set of 162 participant pairs tested 6, 13, 20, and

27 years apart, respectively. Note that, for the first data point, parents were close to the same age as that at which their offspring were tested in 1990. The first half of table 14.4 and figure 14.3 show the stability results in terms of raw correlations. Note that there is good stability of parent-offspring correlations for all variables. For this data set, however, values for Social Responsibility do not reach statistical significance at any time point; for Attitudinal Flexibility, significance is reached only for the 1963 comparison, and for Number, it is reached only for 1970 and 1984.

For comparability with the initial analyses, age also was controlled for in the stability analyses. Relevant data are reported in the second half of table 14.4. The observed stability of parent-offspring correlations remains impressive. After age adjustment, values for Social Responsibility continue to fail to reach statistical significance. All values are now significant for Number, but Spatial Orientation is significant only for the 1963 and 1977 comparisons, Motor-Cognitive Flexibility reaches significant levels only in 1977 and 1984, and Attitudinal Flexibility is significant only in the 1963 comparison.

TABLE 14.4 Parent-Offspring Correlations as a Function of Time[a]

Variable	Parents Tested In			
	1963	1970	1977	1984
Verbal Meaning	.24**	.22**	.19*	.20**
Space	.26**	.17*	.30***	.22**
Reasoning	.29***	.34***	.32***	.33***
Number	.13	.16*	.14	.20**
Word Fluency	.36***	.22**	.31***	.29***
Finding A's	—	—	.18*	.21**
Intellectual Ability	.24**	.25**	.23**	.25**
Educational Aptitude	.25**	.27**	.21**	.27**
Motor-Cognitive Flexibility	.14	.10	.27**	.23**
Attitudinal Flexibility	.16*	.12	.13	.11
Psychomotor Speed	.40***	.35***	.42***	.40***
Social Responsibility	.01	.09	.12	.07
Standardized Regression Coefficients Adjusted for Parent and Offspring Age				
Verbal Meaning	.26**	.26**	.23**	.26**
Space	.20*	.10	.26**	.13
Reasoning	.24**	.30***	.27**	.29**
Number	.15*	.17*	.18*	.24**
Word Fluency	.36***	.22**	.31***	.29***
Finding A's	—	—	.15*	.18*
Intellectual Ability	.25**	.26**	.26**	.28***
Educational Aptitude	.10	.05	.23**	.20*
Attitudinal Flexibility	.15*	.11	.11	.12
Psychomotor Speed	.38***	.32***	.42***	.38***
Social Responsibility	.00	.08	.10	.06

[a]Offspring ages in 1990 were approximately equal to parental age in 1963; age differences increased for each successive data point.
*p < .05. **p < .01. ***p < .001.

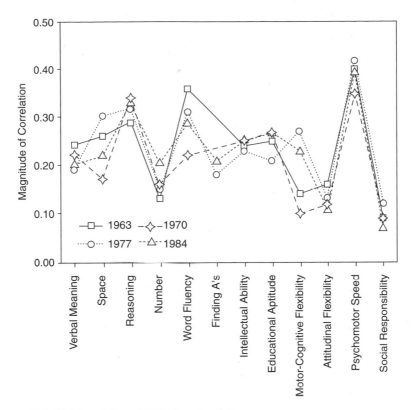

FIGURE 14.3 *Stability of Parent-Offspring Correlations.*

Effects of Current Family Contact   All offspring were asked to indicate on a multiple-item Likert scale questionnaire the intensity of their current contact with their parents. As can be seen from table 14.5, intensity of contact was slightly greater for daughters than sons; contact was greatest for the mother-daughter and lowest for the father-son sets; the last two sets differed significantly ($p < .01$). Degree of contact, however, did not significantly correlate with the age of parent or offspring.

Magnitudes of parent-offspring resemblance adjusted for age were reexamined to consider the effect of contact. This analysis led to slight upward adjustment of some coefficients, but all significant regressions for intensity of contact were neg-

TABLE 14.5 Contact of Parents and Offspring

Variable	Total	Father-Son	Mother-Daughter	Father-Daughter	Mother-Son
Mean contact	19.01	17.81	19.72	19.17	18.51
SD	3.60	4.09	3.23	3.45	3.64

Note. Contact score is the sum of 7 Likert scale items; total sum can range from 0 to 41. Actual observed range 2 to 28.

ative. That is, parent-offspring resemblance was greater with *less* contact. Significant statistical effects of contact ($p < .05$) were found for the total sample only for Verbal Meaning, Spatial Orientation, Number, and Attitudinal Flexibility.

Age/Cohort Differences in Parent-Offspring Correlations   The magnitude of parent-offspring correlations is next considered as a function of age/cohort membership. Because most of our participants (whether parents or adult offspring) were assessed at ages for which stability of cognitive performance is the rule rather than the exception (see Schaie, 1983a), it makes sense to organize these data by cohort rather than by age. For this reason, we divided the total sample into a youngest cohort ($N = 199$; birth years 1955 to 1968), a middle-aged cohort ($N = 228$; birth years 1931 to 1954), and an older cohort ($N = 104$; birth years before 1931).

As can be seen from table 14.6 and figure 14.4, there are substantial differences in pattern and magnitude of correlations. Parent-offspring correlations for the youngest cohort are statistically significant ($p < .05$) for all variables but Perceptual Speed, Attitudinal Flexibility, and Psychomotor Speed; for the middle-aged cohort, correlations are statistically significant ($p < .05$) for all variables except for Motor-Cognitive Flexibility. For the oldest cohort, however, correlations are statistically significant ($p < .05$) only for Inductive Reasoning, Word Fluency, Intellectual Ability, and Motor-Cognitive Flexibility. Correlations rise generally from the older to the youngest cohorts. However, the correlations drop across cohorts for Inductive Reasoning and Motor-Cognitive Flexibility and show a curvilinear pattern for Psychomotor Speed.

In sum, it does not appear that there are significant differences between the younger and the middle cohort, but there might well be lower relationships for

TABLE 14.6 Parent-Offspring Correlations as a Function of Cohort

	Cohort Grouping		
Variable	Youngest, 1955–1968 ($N = 199$)	Middle Aged, 1931–1954 ($N = 228$)	Older, Before 1931 ($N = 104$)
Verbal Meaning	.21**	.23**	.05
Space	.22**	.16**	.11
Reasoning	.18**	.29***	.26***
Number	.18**	.25***	.16
Word Fluency	.26***	.29***	.25**
Finding A's	.12	.21**	.02
Intellectual Ability	.22**	.27***	.26**
Educational Aptitude	.14*	.06	.45***
Motor-Cognitive Flexibility	.14*	.06	.45***
Attitudinal Flexibility	.13	.16*	.07
Psychomotor Speed	.04	.36***	.04
Social Responsibility	.20**	.13*	.07

*$p < .05$. **$p < .01$. ***$p < .001$.

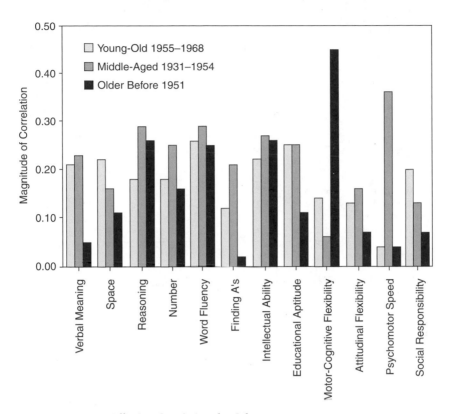

FIGURE 14.4 *Parent-Offspring Correlations by Cohort.*

the older cohort, albeit this last finding might be shaky because of the smaller size of the older group.

The effect of offspring age on family resemblance was tested directly in the total sample by regressing parent performance scores on the interaction of offspring age and offspring performance while controlling for the offspring performance and for the age main effects (hierarchical multiple regression; see Cohen & Cohen, 1975). Only two statistically significant interactions ($p < .05$) were found. They suggest that older offspring showed greater resemblance in Perceptual Speed and Motor-Cognitive Flexibility.

Cohort Differences Between Parents and Offspring   To permit comparison with previously determined population values, mean level scores were standardized to T scores ($M = 50$; $SD = 10$). The average parent-offspring differences were then computed in T-score points (see table 14.7). Note first that there are statistically significant level differences ($p < .001$) for all variables. Raw differences are in favor of the offspring, except differences for Number and Social Responsibility, which favor the parents.

Because of average within-participant age changes, the raw differences must be adjusted before comparison with population cohort differences. This was done

TABLE 14.7 Parent-Offspring Generational Differences in Performance Level[a]

Variable	Parent-Offspring Difference	Expected Age Difference	Net Difference	Population Difference
Verbal Meaning	2.75***	1.01	1.74**	2.28**
Space	5.06***	1.31*	3.75***	−0.78
Reasoning	6.45***	1.77**	4.68***	2.99***
Number	−1.83***	3.04***	−4.87***	−4.26***
Word Fluency	1.73***	2.46**	−0.73	0.56
Finding A's	2.36***	9.06***	−6.70***	3.55***
Intellectual Ability	2.86***	1.52*	1.34	−0.79
Educational Aptitude	6.73***	−0.53	7.26***	5.43***
Motor-Cognitive Flexibility	6.73***	−0.53	7.26***	5.43***
Attitudinal Flexibility	2.33***	2.03**	0.30	4.42***
Psychomotor Speed	9.19***	3.15***	6.04***	3.22***
Social Responsibility	−3.89***	0.23	−4.12***	−9.43***

[a]Positive values are in favor of the offspring. All values are T scores with a population mean of 50 and standard deviation of 10, computed on the basis of 3,442 study participants at first test, except for Finding A's, which is based on 1,628 participants.
*$p < .05$. **$p < .01$. ***$p < .001$.

by computing the average within-participant age changes found over the range of mean ages for our parents and offspring (using the relevant information provided in Schaie, 1983a). These values are found in the third column of table 14.7, with adjusted net differences in the fourth column. After age adjustment, differences are no longer statistically significant for Spatial Orientation, Word Fluency, the Index of Intellectual Ability, and Attitudinal Flexibility. The direction of differences in the remaining variables remains as before the age adjustment.

The fifth column of table 14.7 provides population cohort differences over the mean birth years represented by our parents and offspring (also obtained from Schaie, 1983a). Inspection of the fourth and fifth columns of table 14.7 (and figure 14.5) therefore allows comparison of population cohort difference estimates with those found for our "natural" cohort. The cohort difference estimates are quite comparable, except for four noteworthy exceptions:

1. Spatial Orientation provides a significant cohort difference in the present study, but not in the population for similar birth years.
2. Perceptual Speed in the natural cohort favors the offspring, but in the population estimate shows an advantage for older cohorts.
3. We find no significant difference in Attitudinal Flexibility in this study, but population values argue for an advantage for younger cohorts.
4. The Social Responsibility difference favoring the older cohort is less than half the value estimated for the population.

We finally address the question whether parent-offspring performance differences might be affected by cohort groupings. Using the cohort subsets described at the beginning of this section, we report raw mean differences in table 14.8 and

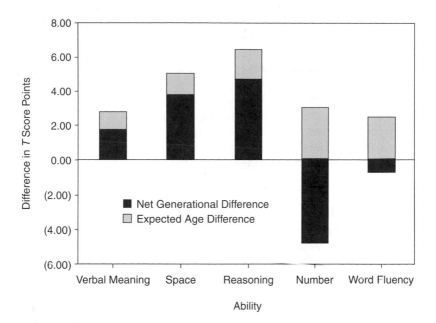

FIGURE 14.5 *Generational Differences Between Parents and Offspring in* T-*Score Points.*

TABLE 14.8 Performance Differences Between Parents
and Offspring as a Function of Cohort Grouping

	Cohort Grouping		
Variable	Youngest, 1955–1968 (N = 199)	Middle Aged, 1931–1954 (N = 228)	Older, Before 1931 (N = 104)
Verbal Meaning	−1.83**	3.83***	9.82***
Space	4.49***	4.57***	7.48***
Reasoning	3.73***	7.56***	9.49***
Number	−5.43***	1.37	2.43**
Word Fluency	−0.74	3.22***	3.89**
Finding A's	2.40*	2.73**	1.40
Intellectual Ability	−0.58	3.85***	7.68***
Educational Aptitude	−0.48	4.98***	10.10***
Motor-Cognitive Flexibility	4.38***	7.06***	10.18***
Attitudinal Flexibility	−0.49	2.70***	7.30***
Psychomotor Speed	6.09***	10.75***	11.99***
Social Responsibility	−6.11***	−3.60***	0.13

Note. Values in *T* scores (see table 14.7 note).
*p < .05. **p < .01 ***p < .001.

figure 14.6. As would be expected because of the increase in age of the parents for the groups, differences here are least for the youngest cohort and greatest for the older cohort. Nevertheless, even in the youngest group, differences in favor of the offspring remain significant for Spatial Orientation, Inductive Reasoning, Number, Perceptual Speed, Motor-Cognitive Flexibility, and Psychomotor Speed; differences in Verbal Meaning, Number, and Social Responsibility favor the parents. For the middle group, all variables favor the offspring, except for Number (nonsignificant difference) and Social Responsibility (which favors the parents). For the older cohort, all differences, except Perceptual Speed and Social Responsibility, significantly favor the offspring.

Summary and Conclusions   Significant family similarities were observed for our total sample for all ability measures except Perceptual Speed and the cognitive style measures. The magnitude of correlations for the ability measures are comparable to those found between young adults and their children (DeFries, Ashton, et al., 1976). Like the DeFries et al. study, we also found differences in resemblance across subsets. For example, same-gender pairs showed higher correlations

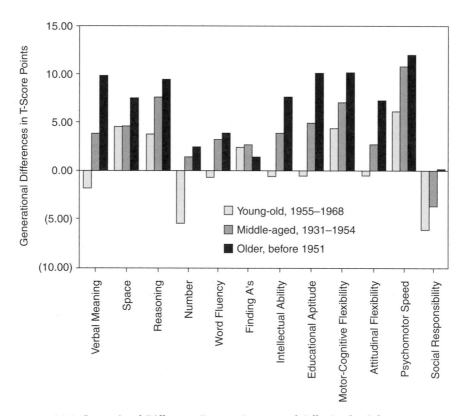

FIGURE 14.6 *Generational Differences Between Parents and Offspring by Cohort.*

on Verbal Meaning, Number, and Word Fluency, but opposite-gender pairs showed it on Spatial Orientation, Inductive Reasoning, and Motor-Cognitive Flexibility. Greater similarity was also found between mother-offspring pairs than between father-offspring pairs on Inductive Reasoning and Psychomotor Speed. Moreover, higher parent-offspring correlations were found for daughters than for sons, suggesting at least the possibility that females may experience greater shared environmental influences than males. Our first hypothesis also argued for the possible effect of early shared environment on offspring performance on Verbal Meaning and Word Fluency. After age adjustment, these were indeed the abilities that showed the greatest parent-offspring similarity.

If shared environmental influences are relatively unimportant in adulthood, then similarity within parent-offspring pairs should remain reasonably constant in adulthood across time and age. Our data strongly support this proposition for all variables that displayed significant parent-offspring correlations. Indeed, parent-offspring correlations measured at approximately the same age of parent and offspring and when those ages were 20 years apart had similar magnitudes.

It has been argued that family similarity should decrease with age because of the increasing amount of nonnormative, nonshared environment expected as adult life progresses. Counterintuitively, no such decrease in similarity could be observed. Indeed, for two variables, there was evidence for increasing similarity as a function of offspring age. This finding makes good sense for our Perceptual Speed variable. Most of our younger offspring typically have not yet experienced age-related decline on this variable, whereas some of their parents have. Both older offspring and parents may have experienced sufficient decline so that again their observed similarity is increased. The other variable showing an age effect was Motor-Cognitive Flexibility. In this instance, our cross-sectional data may confound substantial cohort effects that could have spuriously inflated the offspring age effect.

Further evidence supporting the absence of shared environmental effects on family similarity is provided by our analyses of the intensity of current parent-offspring contact. All of the few observed significant, but very modest, effects of contact on parent-offspring resemblance in performance (for Verbal Meaning, Spatial Orientation, Number, and Attitudinal Flexibility) were in a negative direction.

We had suspected that cohort effects in parent-offspring correlations would result in higher correlations for earlier cohorts because of a decline in shared environmental influence attributed to an increase in extrafamilial influences in more recent cohorts. This proposition could be supported only for the attitudinal trait of Social Responsibility (systematic cohort differences on this variable have previously been reported; see Schaie & Parham, 1974). For the cognitive abilities, again counterintuitively, there seems to be stability or even an increase in family similarity for more recent cohorts. As in the population estimates (Schaie, 1990b) and in other studies (see Sundet, Tambs, Magnus, & Berg, 1988), nonlinear cohort trends were also observed. One plausible explanation for the increase in family similarity in successive cohorts might be the decrease of intrafamilial differences in level of education from our oldest cohort grouping to our youngest.

Finally, we asked whether level differences within families equaled or approximated differences found for similar cohort ranges within a general population sample (see Schaie, 1990b; Willis, 1989a). Comparable differences were the rule, but there were some noteworthy exceptions. Thus, the population estimates underestimated the advantage of the offspring cohort for Spatial Orientation and Psychomotor Speed, but overestimated that advantage for Perceptual Speed. On the attitudinal trait of Social Responsibility, however, the estimated cohort difference in favor of the parent cohort was far greater in the population than that observed in the natural cohort. When broken down by cohort groupings, it became clear that cohort differences became generally smaller for the more recently born parent-offspring pairs, with the exception of increasing differences in favor of the parent generation for Number and Social Responsibility.

Rate of Cognitive Change Across Generations

An important policy-relevant aspect of our generational studies is the possibility of asking whether the rate of aging has changed across successive generations. Recent policy debates in the United States and Europe, for example, have been concerned with the question whether Social Security and other pension systems will remain viable when the baby boomers reach retirement ages. Some have argued that the easiest fix for this problem would be to raise the age at which pensions are now paid (cf. Crystal & Shea, 2002). However, such a fix depends on the assumption that the next generation is able to work to later ages because the rate of aging has slowed, that is, whether the next generation will decline physically and mentally more slowly than did their parents (Schaie, 1995, 2000a; Schaie & Willis, 2000b).

The most direct test of whether the rate of cognitive aging has slowed is provided by the comparison of persons with their biologically related adult offspring at approximately the same ages. It has recently been possible to assemble a data set that meets this condition. The data set contains 496 participants (248 parent-offspring dyads; 89 sons and 159 daughters). To obtain approximate age equivalence, we compared the 1970 and 1977 test scores of the parents with the 1990 and 1997 test scores of the adult offspring.

To examine whether the generational differences vary by age level, we further subdivided the data sets into three groups by average age of each dyadic pair as follows: up to 44 years of age ($n = 62$; $M = 40.4$, range 31–44); 45 to 59 years of age ($n = 128$; $M = 51.8$, range 45–59); and 60 years or older ($n = 58$; $M = 65.5$, range 60–82). We then conducted a repeated measurement analysis of variance with 3 Age levels × 2 Generations × 2 Occasions × 6 test variables (Verbal Meaning, Spatial Orientation, Reasoning, Number, Word Fluency, and Psychomotor Speed) and controlled for the gender of parent and offspring by removing variance associated with their main effect and their interaction with the other variables of interest. Individuals are treated as replicates within parent-offspring dyads. Post hoc tests of interaction effects used the most conservative Tukey's HSD (honestly significant difference) procedure. Table 14.9 lists the analysis of variance results for all of the effects involving generational differences.

TABLE 14.9 Analysis of Variance Effects for Generations

Effect	df	Mean Squares	F Ratios
Generations	1, 236	3,647.16	13.36***
Generations × Age Group	2, 236	1,350.00	4.95**
Generations × Occasions	1, 236	413.46	20.40***
Generations × Variables	5, 1,180	2,776.08	51.53***
Generations × Age Group × Occasion	2, 236	19.53	0.96
Generations × Age Group × Variables	10, 1,180	108.77	2.02*
Generations × Occasions × Variables	5, 1,180	56.98	3.49**
Generations × Age Group × Occasions × Variables	10, 1,180	11.25	0.69

$*p < .05.$ $**p < .01.$ $***p < .001.$

Despite the multidirectional nature of the generation effects (Schaie, 1996b; Schaie, Plomin, et al., 1992; Willis, 1989a), the main effect for generation is highly significant. That is, there is an overall gain in level of performance from the parent to the offspring generation. Moreover, there is a significant interaction between age group and generation [F ($df = 2,236$) = 4.95, $p < .01$]. That is, a significant overall generational difference is found only at the oldest age level (60 years or older). We next examine the significant overall interaction of generation by variable [F ($df = 5$, 1,180) = 51.83, $p < .001$]. Significant effects in favor of the younger generation are found for Spatial Orientation, Reasoning, and Psychomotor Speed and in favor of the older generation for Number.

For testing hypotheses about generational differences in rate of change, our primary concern is with the interactions involving generational differences and change over time. The overall interaction between generations and occasion (the rate of change) is highly significant [F ($df = 1,236$) = 20.27, $p < .001$]. There is a significant overall decline over 7 years in the older, but not in the younger, generation [F (2.236) = 20.40, $p < .001$]. The overall 7-year rate of change also differs across age groups and variable [F ($df = 5$, 1,180) = 3.49, $p < .01$]. This interaction reflects primarily the greater decline in number for the older generation.

It is instructive also to examine the change patterns by generation for each variable, as shown by figure 14.7. The interaction between rate of change and level of performance may be critical for the prediction of practical consequences of these changes. It is noteworthy that performance levels for the parent generation are tightly clustered. By contrast, levels of performance for the offspring generation are quite dispersed, with highest performance levels on Inductive Reasoning and lowest on the Number ability.

Information is presented also on differences in within-generation change patterns separately for the oldest group in figure 14.8 because generational differences are most profound at ages above 60 years. Note particularly that there are average decremental changes for this age group in the parent generation for all six variables. For the offspring generation, however, there is gain for Verbal Meaning and Psychomotor Speed and virtual stability for Reasoning and Space, and decline is found only for the Number and Word Fluency abilities.

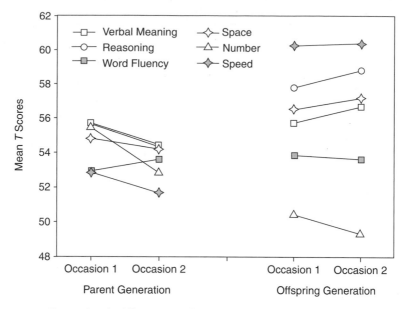

FIGURE 14.7 *Generational Differences in Change Over 7 Years.*

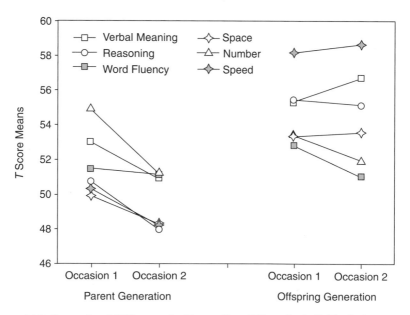

FIGURE 14.8 *Generational Differences in Change Over 7 Years for Individuals Over Age 60.*

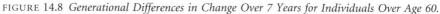

Adult Siblings

As part of the family study described here, we identified a total of 1,799 siblings, including 779 brothers and 1,020 sisters of our panel members. We were able to assess a total of 304 siblings, resulting in 45 brother-brother pairs, 102 sister-sister pairs, and 157 brother-sister pairs. The newly assessed siblings in 1990 ranged in age from 22 to 89 years ($M = 58.26$; $SD = 14.56$). Target siblings ranged in age from 24 to 89 years when tested in 1984 ($M = 53.26$; $SD = 13.95$). All study participants were community-dwelling individuals when tested (see Schaie et al., 1993).

Sibling Correlations

In the case of the siblings, the performance of the target sibling is regressed on the index case (the sibling assessed in 1990). The raw correlations are shown in the second column of table 14.10. Sibling correlations are statistically significant ($p < .01$) for all variables studied except for Perceptual Speed and the trait measure of Social Responsibility. Among the ability measures, correlations are highest for Inductive Reasoning and Verbal Meaning, as well as for the composite measures. They are lowest for the measures of Perceptual Speed (the Finding A's test), Space, and Word Fluency. Among the cognitive style measures, correlations are highest for Motor-Cognitive Flexibility and lowest for Attitudinal Flexibility.

Again, adjustment is needed for the age of siblings to meet assumptions for heritability estimates. The standardized regression coefficients adjusted for the age of both siblings can be found in the third column of table 14.9. Subsequent to the age adjustment, all but the measures of Perceptual Speed and Social Responsibility remain statistically significant ($p < .05$). However, the magnitudes of the correlations change somewhat, with Verbal Meaning and Number now dis-

TABLE 14.10 Sibling Correlations

Variable	Raw	Age Adjusted
Verbal Meaning	.337***	.256***
Space	.256***	.150***
Reasoning	.470***	.212***
Number	.266***	.262***
Word Fluency	.270***	.201***
Finding A's	.068	.032
Intellectual Ability	.351***	.219***
Educational Aptitude	.381***	.239***
Motor-Cognitive Flexibility	.316***	.129*
Attitudinal Flexibility	.163**	.109*
Psychomotor Speed	.290***	.138**
Social Responsibility	−.044	−.033

*$p < .05$. **$p < .01$. ***$p < .001$.

playing the highest ability correlations. Correlations for the cognitive style measures are reduced and are now of about equal magnitude.

Stability of Sibling Correlations Over Time

Regression coefficients adjusted for age of both siblings were also computed between the index sibling and the performance of the target sibling in 1963, 1970, 1977, and 1984. Because of the relatively small number of pairs for which all four data points were available ($N = 72$), the demonstration of stability is not quite as good as for the parent-offspring pairs. Relevant data are provided in table 14.11. There is strong evidence for the stability of sibling concordance for Number and Psychomotor Speed. Stable trends seem to prevail as well for Space, Reasoning, and the composite indices.

Summary and Conclusions

Just as for parent-offspring pairs, substantial adult family similarity can be documented also for the sibling pairs. The two exceptions to this finding are the attitudinal trait of Social Responsibility and the measure of Perceptual Speed, neither of which seems to display heritable characteristics. In general, parent-offspring and sibling correlations are of similar magnitude. However, after controlling for age, sibling correlations are somewhat lower than those observed for the parent-offspring pairs. Stability data for the siblings can be strongly confirmed only for the variables of Number and Psychomotor Speed. Trends comparable to those observed for the parent-offspring pairs for other variables probably failed to reach significance because of the limited power of the longitudinal sibling sample.

TABLE 14.11 Sibling Correlations as a Function of Time Adjusted for Age of Both Siblings

| Variable | Target Siblings Tested In | | | |
	1963	1970	1977	1984
Verbal Meaning	.153	.114	.124	.191*
Space	.107	.204*	.169	.303**
Reasoning	.157	.239*	.244*	.043
Number	.408***	.276**	.388***	.368***
Word Fluency	.052	.061	.155	.012
Finding A's	—	—	.107	.085
Intellectual Ability	.177	.176	.235*	.164
Educational Aptitude	.135	.124	.116	.124
Motor-Cognitive Flexibility	−.018	−.039	−.046	−.075
Attitudinal Flexibility	.115	.070	.211**	.022
Psychomotor Speed	.304**	.259*	.357***	.285**
Social Responsibility	.063	.178	.194*	.149

*$p < .05$. **$p < .01$. ***$p < .001$.

Chapter Summary

Married couples were studied for as long as 21 years. They showed significant initial within-couple correlations on Verbal Meaning, Inductive Reasoning, and Word Fluency, the Index of Educational Aptitude, and Social Responsibility, even when controlling for age and education. Spousal similarity increased by length of marriage on Verbal Meaning, the Index of Intellectual Ability, and Attitudinal Flexibility. Several reciprocal cross-lag effects were found over time, with husbands influencing wives on Inductive Reasoning and wives influencing husbands on Verbal Meaning. The higher-functioning spouse influenced positively the performance level of the lower-functioning spouse over time on Word Fluency and Motor-Cognitive Flexibility.

Studies of families involved adult parents and their adult offspring as well as adult siblings. Significant correlations (averaging about .30) were found for all mental abilities (except for Perceptual Speed) for parent-offspring pairs, with somewhat lower correlations for the siblings. The within-family correlations were of a magnitude similar to those found in parent-offspring studies at younger ages. Some significant differences were found in the magnitude of correlations between same-sex and opposite-sex parent-offspring pairs, and higher parent-offspring correlations were found for daughters than for sons. The stability of parent-offspring correlations remained high over 7, 14, and 21 years and was not affected by the degree of family contact. Significant within-family cohort ability differences were found in favor of the offspring generation, but generational differences became smaller for more recently born parent-offspring pairs.

CHAPTER FIFTEEN

Subjective Perceptions
of Cognitive Change

RESEARCH ON INTELLECTUAL AGING has usually focused on the objective assessment of study participants' performance. However, there is also some recent interest in the examination of participants' subjective appraisal of their cognitive performance. Subjective assessments of perceived competence are thought to play an important role in the process of intellectual aging. Some studies have linked personal expectations of performance on tests or in real-life situations to actual performance on cognitive tasks (see M. E. Lachman, 1983; Schaie et al., 1994; Willis & Schaie, 1986a). Several studies examining concurrent relationships between intellectual self-efficacy and ability performance have reported that both young and elderly adults are fairly accurate in estimating their intellectual performance (M. E. Lachman & Jelalian, 1984; J. L. Lachman, Lachman, & Thronesbery, 1979; Perlmutter, 1978). Both age groups, moreover, have been found to make more accurate predictions for tests on which they exhibit higher levels of performance (M. E. Lachman & Jelalian, 1984).

The relationship between perceived and actual performance may also be complicated by age and gender differences. Researchers have differed on the question of whether older adults over- or underestimate their performance on abilities on which they perform poorly. There has been some speculation (e.g., Bandura, 1981, 1982) that the elderly underestimate their performance. However, findings from other studies (M. E. Lachman & Jelalian, 1984) indicate that the elderly consistently overestimate their performance on measures of fluid abilities. Furthermore, researchers examining concurrent relationships between self-efficacy and ability performance often interpret their findings to suggest that age differences in self-efficacy are ability specific. Hence, these studies imply that the elderly do not subscribe to global negative perceptions of their intellectual competence.

Most previous studies have focused on the concurrent relationships between perceived competence and its objective measurement (Cornelius & Caspi, 1986;

M. E. Lachman & Jelalian, 1984; M. E. Lachman, Steinberg, & Trotter, 1987). By contrast, in the Seattle Longitudinal Study (SLS), we asked our study participants to compare their 1984 performance on five mental abilities with their performance 7 years earlier (Schaie et al., 1994). Parts of this study were replicated in a master's thesis by Roth (2001), who studied congruence types for our 1991 study participants who rated their performance 7 years earlier. For those who had been in the study on three occasions, Roth also investigated the stability of congruence types over 14 years. In a separate study, we have also assessed participants' perception of short-term improvement as a function of participating in cognitive training activities.

Perception of Cognitive Change Over Seven Years

Participants were asked to rate whether they thought that their current performance was better, the same, or worse; their responses are referred to as perceiver types. Participants were then categorized in a typology based on the congruence between their perceived and actual performance change over time. Three congruence types were identified: realists, optimists, and pessimists.

The questions to be asked were as follows:

1. Are there age and gender differences in perceiver types (better, the same, worse)?
2. Do participants' current levels of ability performance differ by perceiver type?
3. How accurately can participants evaluate change in their performance on the five cognitive abilities (congruence between reported perception and actual performance)?
4. Do participants predict with the same accuracy for all abilities?
5. Are there age and gender differences in congruence types (realists, optimists, pessimists)?
6. Does current level of ability performance differ by congruence type?
7. Does the magnitude of the actual ability change (1977 to 1984) differ by congruence type?

Methods

Participants The subsample selected for this particular study was those individuals who were tested in 1977 and who returned for the next assessment in 1984. This criterion resulted in a sample of 837 participants (383 men and 454 women) with a mean age in 1984 of 68.36 years ($SD = 13.34$; range 29–95) and a mean educational level of 14.14 years ($SD = 3.07$). To examine possible age differences among perceiver and congruence types, the sample was divided into three subsets by age in 1984: younger (29 to 49 years; $M = 41.76$; $SD = 5.20$), middle-aged (50 to 70 years; $M = 60.63$; $SD = 5.73$), and older adults (71 to 95 years; $M = 77.24$, $SD = 5.74$).

Procedure   After completing the five Primary Mental Abilities (PMA) tests (Verbal Meaning [V], Spatial Orientation [S], Inductive Reasoning [R], Number [N], Word Fluency [W]), study participants answered the PMA Retrospective Questionnaire. This questionnaire reminded the participants that they had taken the same five ability tests several years earlier and asked them to reflect on how their performance on the tests just completed (in 1984) compared with their earlier performance (in 1977). Participants evaluated their relative performance for each of the five abilities using a 5-point scale with the categories (1) much better today, (2) better today, (3) about the same, (4) worse today, (5) much worse today. Because of the small number of persons who chose the extreme categories (1 or 5), these categories were collapsed into a 3-point scale, resulting in three perceiver types: better, same, and worse.

Creation of Congruence Types   Study participants were classified according to how their actual PMA performance had changed between the two test occasions on each of the five abilities. Difference scores between the 1977 and 1984 performance were computed, and participants were classified into groups showing reliably higher, similar, or lower performance for each ability. The classification criteria for a positive or negative change were that the participant in 1984 performed at least 1 *SEM* below or above his or her 1977 performance (see Dudek, 1979; Schaie, 1989c).

Cross-tabulations between actual performance change and perceived performance change were next examined. Based on the patterns in these tables, the sample was then categorized into three congruence types for each ability: pessimists, individuals who perceived greater negative change or less improvement in performance relative to their actual change (1977 to 1984); realists, those individuals who accurately predicted change or stability; optimists, those who perceived greater positive change or stability than indicated by their actual performance (see table 15.1).

Age and Gender Differences in Perceiver Types

The proportion of participants who reported that their performance had improved over time ranged from 13.3% for Spatial Orientation to 22.3% for Induc-

TABLE 15.1 Schema for Classification Into Congruence Types

| | *Reported Change* | | |
	Better	Same	Worse
Actual change			
Improved	R	P	P
Same	O	R	P
Declined	O	O	R

Note. O, optimist; P, pessimist; R, realist.

tive Reasoning. Those who reported that their performance had remained the same ranged from 47.3% for Spatial Orientation to 71.5% for Verbal Meaning. Those who reported themselves as having performed worse than on the previous test occasion ranged from 8.4% for Verbal Meaning to 39.4% for Spatial Orientation.

For the total sample, there was a significant relationship between age and perceiver type for four of the five abilities. On both Verbal Meaning and Inductive Reasoning, more young participants than old reported that they had become better, whereas more old participants than young reported having become worse; the middle-aged were in between [$\chi^2(V)(4, N = 818) = 58.35, p < .001; \chi^2(R)(4, N = 818) = 45.18, p < .001$]. On Spatial Orientation, young participants reported more improvement than did both the old and the middle-aged, and the old reported more decline than did either the young or middle-aged [$\chi^2(4, N = 818) = 13.61, p < .01$]. However, on Number, the age relationship was reversed, with more older individuals reporting that they remained stable or improved and more younger persons reporting that they got worse, with the middle-aged in between [$\chi^2(4, N = 819) = 27.51, p < .001$].

The relationship between age and perceiver type was similar across genders except for a Gender × Perceiver Type interaction for Spatial Orientation [$\chi^2(2, N = 818) = 21.05, p < .001$]. On that ability, the proportion of men and women who reported having become better did not differ, but more men than women reported having remained the same, and more women than men reported having gotten worse.

Perceiver Type Differences in Current Primary Mental Abilities Scores

Differences were examined for participants who had reported that they remained stable, improved, or declined regardless of the accuracy of their report. A 3 (perceiver type) × 2 (age group) × 2 (gender) analysis of variance (ANOVA) was run separately for each ability (see table 15.2 for the associated means). Significant type differences were found for Spatial Orientation [$F(df = 2, 813) = 37.33, p < .001$] and for Word Fluency [$F(df = 2, 811) = 31.49, p < .001$]. In both instances, PMA scores were highest for individuals who had reported positive change, in between for those reporting no change, and lowest for those reporting negative change.

Significant Perceiver Type × Age interactions were also found for Spatial Orientation [$F(df = 2, 813) = 3.53, p < .01$] and Number [$F(df = 2, 811) = 2.23, p < .05$]. The Type × Age interaction for Spatial Orientation indicated that, although there was virtually no performance difference among the three types for the old group, in the young group those who perceived themselves to have improved indeed performed much better than those who perceived themselves to have declined. The Type × Age interaction for Number conversely indicated that, whereas there was little difference in performance among the types for either the young or the middle-aged, older adults who perceived themselves to have declined performed at a lower level than did those who perceived themselves to have im-

TABLE 15.2 Mean *T* Scores for Current Performance Levels by Perceiver Type by Ability, Age Group, and Gender

	Males			Females			Total		
	Better	Same	Worse	Better	Same	Worse	Better	Same	Worse
Verbal Meaning									
Young	57.00	56.53	61.00	56.82	58.40	53.67	56.91	57.47	57.33
Middle-aged	56.09	54.37	52.57	53.24	54.37	51.58	54.67	54.37	52.76
Old	43.86	46.03	39.73	47.25	46.68	42.63	45.55	46.35	41.18
Total	52.31	52.31	51.10	52.44	53.15	49.29	52.38	52.73	50.20
Spatial Orientation									
Young	63.21	58.17	55.58	61.25	57.25	48.32	62.23	57.71	51.95
Middle-aged	54.58	56.87	49.08	54.05	52.82	46.74	54.32	54.85	47.91
Old	43.92	47.92	43.26	45.25	44.67	41.97	44.59	46.29	42.62
Total	53.90	54.32	49.31	53.52	51.58	45.67	53.71	52.95	47.49
Inductive Reasoning									
Young	57.67	57.50	61.62	61.11	58.11	61.14	59.39	57.80	61.38
Middle-aged	53.07	53.52	53.19	52.26	54.45	56.58	52.66	53.99	54.89
Old	45.11	44.90	45.33	47.43	45.29	44.58	46.27	45.10	44.96
Total	51.95	51.97	53.38	53.60	52.62	54.10	52.78	52.30	53.74
Number									
Young	48.80	52.07	58.12	50.22	50.51	46.12	49.51	51.29	52.12
Middle-aged	53.98	52.23	50.64	48.71	49.98	51.00	51.34	51.10	50.82
Old	51.23	48.75	44.32	50.50	47.11	45.31	50.87	47.93	44.82
Total	51.34	51.02	51.02	49.81	49.20	47.48	50.57	50.11	49.25
Word Fluency									
Young	57.00	52.06	50.58	57.90	56.05	52.58	57.45	54.06	51.58
Middle-aged	56.29	50.23	46.98	52.41	53.08	45.49	54.35	51.65	46.23
Old	46.58	46.09	36.92	53.91	47.09	44.43	50.24	46.59	40.68
Total	53.30	49.46	44.83	54.74	52.07	47.50	54.01	50.77	46.16

proved. Significant triple interactions, moreover, were found for Number [$F(df = 4, 811) = 2.75$, $p < .05$] and Word Fluency [$F(df = 4, 811) = 3.98$, $p < .01$]. The triple interaction on Number reflects the fact that, whereas both older adult males and females who perceived themselves to have declined performed at lower levels than those who perceived themselves to have improved, young males showed the opposite pattern; young males who perceived themselves to have declined actually had higher mean scores than those who perceived themselves to have improved or remained stable. The triple interaction on Word Fluency reflects the finding that men who perceived themselves to have improved or declined showed greater age differences in performance than women; however, the Age × Gender difference in performance was not found for those who perceived themselves as remaining stable.

Correlation Between Perceived and Observed Change

Although the correlations between perceived and actual change for the same ability (convergent validity) were statistically significant ($p < .001$) and for the most part were larger than cross-ability correlations (divergent validity), they were quite small (see table 15.3). Indeed, significantly larger correlations were found among ratings of perceived change across abilities, suggesting that the ratings of perceived change are associated with global perceptions of change in intellectual functioning in addition to the actual observed change on the target ability.

Given the categorical nature of the judgment of perceived change, the correlations do not necessarily give a good picture of the accuracy of the respondents' perceptions. We therefore proceeded next with analyses of the congruence types.

Congruence Types

Total Sample   Proportions of each congruence type by ability are shown in figure 15.1. Assuming that the expected chance probability of assignment to one of the three response congruence types was .33, chi-square analyses determined that assignment to type differed significantly from chance at or above the 5% level of confidence. Approximately half the participants were realistic in their perception of change or stability over the 7-year period. Participants were most accurate (realistic) in estimating stability or change on the Verbal Meaning test. The highest proportion of pessimists (overestimation of decline) occurred for Spatial Orientation (34%), and pessimists were the fewest for Verbal Meaning (10.3%). Approximately 30% of the sample were optimistic (underestimation of decline) about their performance change for all abilities except Spatial Orientation.

Consistency in congruence types across the five PMA tests was examined, but no consistent pattern was evident. Some study participants who were categorized as pessimistic for one ability were likely to be realistic on another and possibly optimistic on a third. There are 120 possible permutations of congruence types across all five abilities, and virtually all possible permutations were observed. The most frequent permutation ($N = 30$) was the pattern of realism across all five abilities.

By Age and Gender   Gender differences in the distribution of congruence types were found for only one ability, Spatial Orientation. Here, a greater proportion

TABLE 15.3 Correlations Between Perceived and Actual Change

	Perceived Change				
	Verbal Meaning	Spatial Orientation	Inductive Reasoning	Number	Word Fluency
Actual change					
Verbal Meaning	.112***	.056	.080*	.046	.012
Spatial Orientation	.068	.206***	.055	−.045	.037
Inductive Reasoning	.101**	.035	.141***	.047	−.030
Number	.151***	.076*	.123***	.134***	.064
Word Fluency	.083*	.015	.041	−.039	.210***

*$p < .05$. **$p < .01$. ***$p < .001$. Convergent validities in bold.

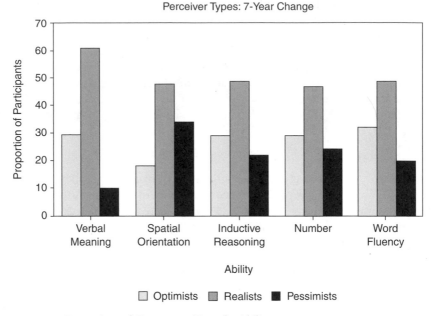

FIGURE 15.1 *Proportions of Congruence Types by Ability.*

of women were pessimistic about change in their spatial ability than men [$\chi^2(2,$ $N = 818) = 6.4$, $p < .05$].

Regarding age, a greater proportion of the oldest group of participants was more pessimistic than the young and middle-aged about change in their Verbal ability [$\chi^2(2, N = 818) = 19.1$, $p < .01$] and Inductive Reasoning ability [$\chi^2(2, N = 818) = 13.8$, $p < .05$]. However, a greater proportion of the oldest group was realistic in the assessment of performance change on the Number test [$\chi^2(2, N = 753) = 26.02$, $p < .001$].

Congruence Type Differences in Current Ability Scores

Differences among congruence types in the 1984 PMA scores were also examined by means of 3 (congruence type) × 3 (age group) × 2 (gender) ANOVAs conducted separately for each of the five abilities (see table 15.4 for associated means). Significant differences by type were found for Verbal Meaning [$F(df = 2, 798) = 11.36$, $p < .001$] and for Inductive Reasoning [$F(2, 795) = 3.76$, $p < .02$]. Both realists and pessimists had significantly higher 1984 Verbal Meaning scores than optimists. Realists' 1984 Inductive Reasoning scores were significantly higher than those of pessimists.

Significant age main effects occurred for all variables. Gender main effects favored men for Spatial Orientation and Number, but favored women for Word Fluency. The only significant Age × Gender interaction occurred for Word Flu-

TABLE 15.4 Mean T Scores for Current Performance Levels by Congruence Type, Age Group, and Gender

	Males			Females			Total		
	P	R	O	P	R	O	P	R	O
Verbal Meaning									
Young	60.00	56.66	56.04	57.86	59.51	55.06	58.93	58.08	55.55
Middle-aged	53.14	54.95	54.04	54.52	55.45	50.53	53.83	55.20	52.29
Old	44.46	46.57	41.50	46.72	46.97	43.68	45.49	46.77	42.59
Total	52.53	52.73	50.53	53.03	53.98	49.75	52.78	53.35	50.14
Spatial Orientation									
Young	58.69	57.46	61.40	53.31	54.83	53.96	56.00	56.14	57.66
Middle-aged	54.18	54.67	53.71	48.65	50.60	52.91	51.42	52.63	53.31
Old	45.85	46.82	42.67	43.54	42.94	42.79	44.69	44.88	42.73
Total	52.91	52.98	52.59	48.50	49.46	49.87	50.70	51.22	51.23
Inductive Reasoning									
Young	60.25	59.92	56.73	55.93	60.81	60.29	58.08	60.37	58.51
Middle-aged	52.87	54.13	52.58	56.14	54.74	53.06	54.36	54.44	52.82
Old	42.72	46.33	45.62	43.25	46.38	46.32	42.99	46.36	45.97
Total	51.85	53.46	51.64	51.77	53.98	53.33	51.81	53.72	52.43
Number									
Young	50.62	52.38	52.53	50.26	49.83	49.86	50.44	51.10	51.19
Middle-aged	51.47	51.42	54.15	48.52	51.22	48.49	50.00	51.32	51.32
Old	48.79	48.21	45.62	46.95	46.67	47.33	47.87	47.44	51.19
Total	50.30	50.67	50.77	48.58	49.24	48.56	49.80	50.07	49.60
Word Fluency									
Young	53.59	51.67	55.50	57.05	55.25	56.00	55.31	53.46	55.75
Middle-aged	49.57	51.42	51.72	51.52	52.23	49.79	50.55	51.82	50.76
Old	39.41	44.10	45.53	48.24	47.37	50.04	43.82	45.74	47.79
Total	47.52	49.06	50.92	52.27	51.61	51.94	50.28	50.52	51.07

Note. O, optimists; P, pessimists; R, realists.

ency, reflecting greater age differences for women between the younger and middle-aged groups and for men between the middle-aged and old groups.

Congruence Type Differences in Magnitude of Ability Change

Differences among congruence types in magnitude of ability change (1977 to 1984) were examined via 3 (congruence type) × 3 (age group) × 2 (gender) ANOVAs conducted separately for each ability (see table 15.5 for the associated mean changes). Significant type differences were found for all abilities: Verbal Meaning [$F(df = 2, 798) = 105.59$, $p < .001$], Spatial Orientation [$F(df = 2, 798) = 53.47$, $p < .001$], Inductive Reasoning [$F(df = 2, 795) = 60.83$, $p < .001$], Number [$F(df = 2, 801) = 53.28$, $p < .001$], and Word Fluency [$F(df = 2, 796) = 47.40$, $p < .001$]. For all abilities, each type differed significantly from the others in magnitude of change. As would be expected from the type definitions, the optimists experienced greater average decline (respectively less gain) than either realists or pessi-

TABLE 15.5 Mean *T* Scores for Magnitude of Change from 1977 to 1984 by Congruence Type, Ability, Age Group, and Gender

	Males			Females			Total		
	P	R	O	P	R	O	P	R	O
Verbal Meaning									
Young	−8.83	−0.43	1.35	−7.57	−0.65	2.53	−8.20	−0.54	1.94
Middle-aged	−5.53	0.70	3.55	−3.20	0.53	5.35	−4.27	0.62	4.45
Old	−3.54	1.68	8.63	−0.50	3.13	8.43	−2.02	2.39	8.53
Total	−5.90	0.64	4.51	−3.76	1.01	5.44	−4.83	0.82	4.97
Spatial Orientation									
Young	−1.81	−0.19	3.85	−2.11	1.26	5.25	−1.96	0.53	4.55
Middle-aged	−3.32	2.07	6.00	0.29	2.85	3.87	−1.51	2.46	4.69
Old	0.09	3.02	7.00	0.51	4.51	8.58	0.30	3.77	7.79
Total	−1.68	1.63	5.62	−0.44	2.87	5.74	−1.06	2.25	5.68
Inductive Reasoning									
Young	−3.50	−0.18	2.09	−3.93	0.26	1.66	−3.71	0.04	1.87
Middle-aged	−1.70	0.71	4.58	−2.28	1.12	3.47	−1.99	0.92	4.02
Old	−0.06	1.44	4.38	0.31	2.27	6.35	0.13	1.86	5.37
Total	−1.75	0.66	3.68	−1.97	1.22	3.83	−1.86	0.94	3.76
Number									
Young	−1.42	0.16	1.88	−1.71	1.80	2.48	−1.56	0.98	2.18
Middle-aged	−0.97	1.49	2.74	−1.91	1.04	4.97	−1.44	1.27	3.86
Old	−2.07	1.94	6.44	−1.80	1.81	2.48	−1.94	1.88	5.80
Total	−1.48	1.20	3.69	−1.81	1.55	4.20	−1.65	1.37	3.94
Word Fluency									
Young	−2.41	0.61	1.75	−4.90	0.67	2.78	−3.66	0.64	2.27
Middle-aged	−1.48	0.57	4.41	−3.02	2.03	5.03	−2.25	1.30	4.72
Old	1.56	2.78	5.88	−2.53	1.19	4.89	−0.49	1.98	5.38
Total	−0.78	1.32	4.01	−3.48	1.29	4.23	−2.13	1.31	4.12

Note. Negative values represent mean gain from 1977 to 1984. O, optimists; P, pessimists; R, realists.

mists, and the pessimists experienced objectively the least decline. The difference between pessimists and optimists exceeded 1 *SD* for all abilities and was greatest for Verbal Meaning.

A Congruence Type × Age interaction was found for Verbal Meaning [$F(df = 2, 798) = 3.18$, $p < .001$]. The young pessimists gained significantly more over time than did the middle-aged or old pessimists. Likewise, the old optimists declined significantly more than did their young and middle-aged counterparts. Also, the young realists gained significantly more over time than did the middle-aged and old realists. A significant Congruence Type × Gender interaction occurred for Word Fluency [$F(df = 2, 796) = 3.01$, $p < .05$]. This interaction reflected significantly greater gain over time for the female than the male pessimists. Finally, a significant triple interaction was obtained for Spatial Orientation [$F(df = 4, 798) = 2.62$, $p < .05$]. This interaction reflects significant gain over time for the male pessimists, but stability for the female pessimists.

Summary and Conclusions

We assumed in this study that community-dwelling adults are capable of making appropriate judgments of change in performance on cognitive tests taken 7 years apart. It could be argued that what the participants actually do is more likely to be a projection of their feelings about change in their cognitive competence, with the current test providing no more than a projective stimulus for the expression of such feelings. However, the data suggest that much more systematic judgments are made.

Perceptions of age-related change in ability functioning were examined for three age groups (young, middle-aged, and older adults). Furthermore, a typology was proposed for examining the congruence between perceptions of change and actual age-related change in intellectual functioning. The typology categorized three congruence types: realists, those who correctly estimated change or stability; pessimists, those who thought they had declined more than they actually had; and optimists, those who thought they did better than the objective data reflected. We were able to verify this typology by showing that the three groups differed significantly in absolute magnitude of change in the expected direction on all five abilities; that is, pessimists declined the least or gained, optimists declined the most, and realists were in between.

With respect to participants' perception of change in ability functioning (regardless of the accuracy of perceptions), we found that a greater proportion of older adults than young or middle-aged adults perceived themselves to have declined on three of the abilities studied (Verbal Meaning, Reasoning, Spatial Orientation). For Number ability, by contrast, a significantly smaller proportion (18%) of older adults perceived themselves to have declined than young adults (38%). No Age × Perceiver Type interaction was found for Word Fluency.

There are two possible implications of these findings. Prior research findings (M. E. Lachman & Jelalian, 1984) were supported in that age differences in perceptions turned out to be ability specific; the old did not hold global perceptions of universal decline across all abilities. Second, the findings suggest a possible cohort effect in ability perceptions. Given our finding on the multidirectionality of cohort differences in Number ability (see chapter 6), it is interesting to note that the older group in the perceptions study represents those cohorts whose Number ability was particularly high compared with more recent cohorts, which may contribute to the age differences in perception of decline on Number ability found in the study.

When perceptions of cognitive change over 7 years were compared with objectively measured change (congruence typology), we found that approximately half our sample could accurately categorize their performance change over time, albeit that the correct attribution in most instances turned out to be their judgment that no change had occurred. Participants were not only aware of their concurrent levels of performance, but they could make reasonably accurate estimates of change in performance over a 7-year period. However, study participants did not predict change in their performance with equal accuracy across all the abilities measured.

The variables of age and gender were found to moderate accuracy of perceptions of ability change (i.e., congruence typology). Women were more pessimistic than men regarding their decline on Spatial Orientation. In our society, women, particularly older women, frequently report themselves to be less competent at tasks involving Spatial Orientation, such as map reading and giving directions. Our findings suggest that women's overly pessimistic views of decline in Spatial Orientation ability (compared with those of men) may be fostered by negative gender stereotypes because their individual performance profiles do not warrant such pessimism. Finally, the old (compared with the young) were more pessimistic regarding age-related decline in their verbal and Inductive Reasoning abilities than the performance data would support. Of particular concern is the pessimism of the elderly regarding decline in their verbal ability. Because verbal ability remains relatively stable into old age (see chapter 5), it seems reasonable that most older adults should feel fairly confident of their verbal skills.

Stability of Congruence Types

The stability of the congruence types discussed here over a 14-year period was examined in a master's thesis by Roth (2001). This study replicated congruence types for a second 7-year period (1984–1991) and examined the consistency of membership in the same congruence type over the 14-year period. It also examined the relation of performance level and change over time to both congruence type and consistency of congruence type.

Methods

Participants   The subsample for the following analyses included those individuals who had complete data on the five basic primary mental abilities in 1977, 1984, and 1991 and who had completed the retrospective PMA performance questionnaire. This sample consisted of 588 participants (264 males, 324 females). The participants' mean age in 1977 was 51.1 years ($SD = 12.09$; range 22–79). The sample was divided into three age/cohort groups by their base age in 1977. The age categories were young adult ($n = 121$, mean age = 33.23 years; $SD = 4.66$; range 20–39); middle-aged ($n = 308$, mean age = 50.61 years; $SD = 5.34$; range 40–59); and older adults ($n = 159$, mean age = 65.49 years; $SD = 4.20$; range 60–79).

Measures   The following analyses included the five basic PMA measures of Verbal Meaning, Spatial Orientation, Inductive Reasoning, Number, and Word Fluency; the PMA Retrospective Questionnaire; and the three factor scores from the Test of Behavioral Rigidity: Motor-Cognitive Flexibility, Attitudinal Flexibility, and Psychomotor Speed (see chapter 3).

Analyses   As in the earlier studies, participants were classified as having remained stable, having gained, or having lost by using the criterion of 1 *SEM* to determine change from 1977 to 1984 and from 1984 to 1991. Cross-tabulations were then

made between actual change and perceived change, and participants were classified as pessimists, who underestimate positive change or overestimate negative
change; optimists, who overestimate positive change or underestimate negative
change; and realists, who accurately estimate their observed change.

For the determination of consistency of congruency type across time, participants were classified into a five-category typology:

1. Participants who were pessimists over both time periods
2. Participants who were realists over both time periods
3. Participants who were optimists over both time periods
4. Participants who changed toward pessimism
5. Participants who moved toward optimism

Consistency of Congruence Types Over Time

Distribution of Congruence Types   The first step in the consistency analysis was
to replicate the 1984 findings with respect to congruency type for the 1984–1991
time interval. Assignment to congruence types differed significantly from chance
for all five abilities [$\chi^2(V)(df=1,588) = 232.64$, $p < .001$; $\chi^2(S)(df=1,588) = 92.92$,
$p < .001$; $\chi^2(R)(df=1,588) = 306.56$, $p < .001$; $\chi^2(N)(df=1,588) = 56.80$, $p < .001$;
$\chi^2(W)(df=1,588) = 56.90$, $p < .001$]. Almost half of all participants were realistic
in their estimation of change, except for Inductive Reasoning, for which the majority of participants were pessimistic. Proportions of congruence types for each
ability and broken down by age and gender are shown in table 15.6.

Significant gender differences in congruency types were found for Verbal
Meaning, with a greater proportion of women than men optimistic about their
change on Verbal Meaning. Significant age differences were observed for Inductive Reasoning, with more young adults pessimistic than older adults, more older
adults optimistic than younger adults, and more middle-aged participants realistic than either younger or older adults.

Age differences were significant also for Spatial Orientation, with young adults
more realistic or optimistic than middle-aged adults. Finally, older adults were
more pessimistic than young adults, both young and old adults were more optimistic than the middle-aged, and more middle-aged were realistic than were older
adults.

Distribution of Consistency in Congruence Types   Patterns of change across the
two time periods were next cross-tabulated. Again, chi-square analyses indicated
that assignment to consistency patterns differed significantly from chance for all
five abilities [$\chi^2(V)(df=4,588) = 270.84$, $p < .001$; $\chi^2(S)(df=4,588) = 223.95$, $p <$
.001; $\chi^2(R)(df=4,588) = 466.96$, $p < .001$; $\chi^2(N)(df=4,588) = 102.630$, $p < .001$;
$\chi^2(W)(df=1,588) = 123.33$, $p < .001$]. Table 15.7 gives the proportion of each of
the five consistency in congruence patterns for every ability.

Overall, for Verbal Meaning, about 37% of the sample remained realistic;
about 36% became more pessimistic. For Spatial Orientation, more than 40%
became more pessimistic, and 25% remained realistic. For Inductive Reasoning,

TABLE 15.6 Proportions of 1991 Congruence Types by Ability, Age, and Gender

	Males			Females			Total		
	P	R	O	P	R	O	P	R	O
Verbal Meaning									
Young	0.0	58.3	41.7	1.8	56.1	42.1	1.0	57.1	41.9
Middle-aged	4.0	67.5	28.6	5.4	61.1	33.6	4.7	64.0	31.3
Old	4.7	64.1	31.3	10.5	40.8	48.7	7.9	51.4	40.7
Total	3.4	64.7	31.9	6.0	54.6	39.4	4.8	59.2	36.0
Spatial Orientation									
Young	7.5	62.3	30.2	10.4	5.2	34.3	9.2	58.3	32.5
Middle-aged	24.4	51.9	23.7	18.3	49.1	32.5	21.1	50.3	28.6
Old	26.8	43.7	29.6	18.4	49.4	32.2	22.2	46.8	31.0
Total	21.6	51.7	26.6	16.7	30.5	32.8	18.0	51.0	30.1
Inductive Reasoning									
Young	65.4	25.0	9.6	83.3	15.2	1.5	75.4	19.5	5.1
Middle-aged	66.2	26.2	7.7	70.4	22.8	6.8	68.5	24.3	7.2
Old	51.5	27.3	21.2	65.1	18.1	16.9	59.1	22.1	18.8
Total	62.1	26.2	11.7	71.7	19.9	8.4	67.4	22.7	9.8
Number									
Young	30.0	42.0	28.0	32.8	44.8	22.4	31.6	43.6	24.8
Middle-aged	27.5	47.3	25.2	24.2	50.3	25.5	25.7	49.0	25.3
Old	25.4	52.1	22.5	17.9	48.8	33.3	21.3	50.3	28.4
Total	27.4	47.6	25.0	24.4	48.7	26.9	25.7	48.2	26.1
Word Fluency									
Young	26.4	47.2	26.4	23.9	37.3	38.8	25.0	41.7	33.3
Middle-aged	19.3	51.9	28.9	24.4	46.4	29.2	22.1	48.8	29.0
Old	11.3	53.5	35.2	20.7	40.2	39.1	16.5	46.2	37.3
Total	18.5	51.4	30.1	23.3	42.9	33.9	21.2	46.6	32.2

Note. O, optimists; P, pessimists; R, realists.

more than 55% became more optimistic. For Number, about 30% became more pessimistic, and about 25% became more optimistic. For Word Fluency, 30% became more pessimistic, 25% became more optimistic, and 25% remained realistic.

Significant gender differences in the distribution of consistency patterns were found only for Inductive Reasoning, with more women becoming more optimistic over time than men.

Significant age differences were observed for Inductive Reasoning, for which more middle-aged and older adults either remained pessimistic or became more pessimistic than did younger adults. Also, young adults became more optimistic than middle-aged adults, and both the young and middle-aged became more optimistic than the old adults.

For Verbal Meaning, more young adults remained realistic than did either the middle-aged or old. Older adults became more pessimistic than did the younger and middle-aged adults, and more middle-aged and older adults became more optimistic than did the young adults.

TABLE 15.7 Proportions of Consistency in Congruence Patterns by Ability, Age, and Gender

	Remained Pessimists			Remained Optimists			Remained Realists			Became More Pessimistic			Became More Optimistic		
	M	F	T	M	F	T	M	F	T	M	F	T	M	F	T
Verbal Meaning															
Young	0.0	1.8	1.0	40.4	36.8	38.5	12.8	17.5	15.4	36.2	31.6	29.2	10.6	12.3	11.5
Middle-aged	0.0	1.4	0.7	40.6	38.8	42.1	4.8	6.8	5.9	30.2	38.8	30.6	19.0	14.3	16.5
Old	1.6	2.6	2.1	32.8	21.1	26.4	7.8	10.5	9.3	34.4	46.1	29.9	23.4	19.7	21.4
Total	1.4	1.8	1.2	41.4	33.6	37.1	7.2	10.0	8.7	32.5	39.3	30.1	18.6	15.4	16.8
Spatial Orientation															
Young	5.8	4.5	5.0	25.0	25.4	25.2	5.8	7.3	6.7	48.1	53.7	51.3	15.4	9.0	11.8
Middle-aged	10.4	7.1	8.6	27.4	21.4	24.1	7.4	4.8	5.9	31.9	47.0	40.3	23.0	19.6	21.1
Old	13.7	6.9	9.5	28.2	24.1	25.9	7.0	10.3	8.9	31.0	36.9	34.2	21.1	21.8	21.5
Total	10.1	6.5	8.1	27.1	23.0	24.8	7.0	6.8	6.9	34.9	45.7	40.9	20.9	18.0	19.3
Inductive Reasoning															
Young	15.4	9.1	11.9	13.5	7.6	10.2	3.8	0.0	1.7	5.8	4.5	5.1	61.5	78.8	71.2
Middle-aged	14.6	19.4	17.2	16.9	10.0	13.1	0.0	1.3	0.7	13.1	12.5	12.8	55.4	56.9	56.2
Old	22.7	24.1	23.5	13.6	4.8	8.7	9.1	1.2	4.7	21.2	24.1	22.8	33.3	45.8	40.3
Total	16.9	18.4	17.8	15.3	8.1	11.3	3.2	1.0	2.0	13.7	13.9	13.8	50.8	58.6	55.1
Number															
Young	18.4	18.2	18.3	26.5	22.7	24.3	12.2	7.6	9.6	24.5	31.8	28.7	18.4	19.7	19.1
Middle-aged	8.5	14.1	11.6	28.7	30.1	29.5	9.3	5.5	7.2	29.5	33.1	31.5	24.0	17.2	20.2
Old	11.8	3.6	7.3	30.9	22.9	26.5	5.9	13.3	9.9	26.5	31.3	29.1	25.0	28.9	27.2
Total	11.4	12.2	11.8	28.9	26.6	27.6	8.9	8.0	8.4	27.6	32.4	30.3	23.2	20.8	21.9
Word Fluency															
Young	13.2	7.5	10.0	28.3	20.9	24.2	11.3	9.0	10.0	20.8	35.8	29.2	26.4	26.9	26.7
Middle-aged	5.9	6.6	6.3	25.2	25.3	25.2	11.1	9.0	10.0	31.1	30.1	30.6	26.7	28.9	27.9
Old	2.9	6.9	5.1	22.9	20.7	21.7	15.7	14.9	15.3	27.1	32.3	29.9	31.4	25.3	28.0
Total	6.6	6.9	6.7	25.2	23.1	24.0	12.4	10.6	11.4	27.9	21.9	30.1	27.9	27.3	27.7

Note. F, females; M, males; T, total.

Level of Cognitive Ability and Congruence Types

Seven-Year Effect of Congruence Type   Performance levels on the primary mental abilities in 1991 were next related to congruence type in 1977 by means of a 3 (1977/1984 congruence type) × 3 (age group) × 2 (gender) ANOVA, separately for each ability. This analysis examined the impact of congruence type on performance level after a 7-year interval. Significant congruence type differences in performance level were observed for Verbal Meaning [$F(2, 588) = 8.79, p < .001$]; Inductive Reasoning [$F(2, 588) = 15.35, p < .001$]; Number [$F(2, 588) = 3.73, p < .05$]; and Word Fluency [$F(2, 588) = 3.44, p < .05$]. Pessimists performed better than realists or optimists on Inductive Reasoning. However, realists and optimists performed better than pessimists on Verbal Meaning. In addition, optimists performed better than realists on Number and Word Fluency.

No Congruence Type × Gender interaction was found. However, there were significant Congruence Type × Age interactions for Verbal Meaning and Word Fluency. For Verbal Meaning, both the young and old pessimists performed significantly below the optimists and realists; there were no differences in congruence types for the middle-aged. On Word Fluency, old pessimists performed better than old realists or optimists, and middle-aged pessimists did less well than the other types. Table 15.8 provides standardized means for the 1991 cognitive ability performance by 1984/1991 congruence type, age, and gender.

Effect of Consistency of Congruence Type   Differences in 1991 cognitive ability levels were further examined in terms of the congruence consistency patterns by means of a 5 (consistency in congruence type) $\times$ 3 (age group) $\times$ 2 (gender) ANOVA separately for each ability. Significant performance differences by consistency patterns were found for Verbal Meaning [$F(4, 588) = 906$, $p < .001$]; Inductive Reasoning [$F(4, 588) = 9.27$, $p < .001$]; and Number [$F(4, 588) = 3.96$, $p < .01$]. On Verbal Meaning, those who remained realistic performed better than all other groups. Those who remained pessimists or who became more optimistic performed significantly better than all other groups on Inductive Reasoning, and participants who remained optimists did better on the Number ability.

The Gender $\times$ Congruence pattern interaction was significant only for Spatial Orientation. Although gender differences in favor of men are usually found for

TABLE 15.8 Standardized Means for 1991 Cognitive Ability Performance by Congruence Type, Age, and Gender

	Males			Females			Total		
	P	R	O	P	R	O	P	R	O
Verbal Meaning									
Young	—	52.84	53.36	40.54	57.55	55.09	41.00	55.40	54.30
Middle-aged	50.02	51.66	52.15	49.85	52.86	50.50	49.85	52.26	51.15
Old	23.34	48.86	41.51	34.98	43.01	43.02	31.82	45.22	42.51
Total	40.06	50.60	49.67	42.30	51.85	49.00	41.59	51.22	49.27
Spatial Orientation									
Young	59.95	58.94	60.63	52.37	52.70	54.12	55.09	55.60	56.77
Middle-aged	56.63	52.80	53.93	46.74	49.51	48.64	51.86	51.04	50.53
Old	44.94	46.16	42.98	42.74	42.88	41.25	43.89	44.26	42.06
Total	52.90	52.78	52.15	49.26	48.49	47.88	49.65	50.42	49.57
Inductive Reasoning									
Young	58.25	56.44	48.95	58.57	55.71	52.86	58.35	56.00	46.97
Middle-aged	53.24	46.67	43.23	51.93	50.50	41.79	52.39	48.56	42.43
Old	44.85	38.24	39.11	43.59	39.83	39.54	43.97	38.97	39.14
Total	52.49	46.29	42.23	51.55	48.76	41.00	51.93	47.49	41.65
Number									
Young	54.14	47.25	52.50	51.42	49.91	52.65	54.37	52.56	55.65
Middle-aged	51.95	52.81	54.86	48.01	50.40	50.80	48.18	51.14	51.88
Old	47.45	45.35	46.18	42.06	45.08	51.29	48.23	42.99	47.73
Total	51.25	49.54	52.13	47.82	48.89	51.29	49.44	49.17	51.65
Word Fluency									
Young	50.85	50.22	53.10	57.45	54.90	56.98	52.68	48.78	52.62
Middle-aged	47.43	51.07	51.93	48.61	51.18	51.84	49.93	51.48	52.60
Old	50.84	41.65	45.36	46.95	44.43	49.53	44.94	46.17	49.45
Total	49.00	48.22	50.03	50.10	50.14	52.35	49.67	49.20	51.38

Note. O, optimists; P, pessimists; R, realists.

this ability, the gender differences were not significant for those individuals who consistently remained either realists or optimists. Again, we provide standardized means for the 1991 performance level by congruence consistency pattern, age, and gender (see table 15.9).

Magnitude of Cognitive Change and Congruence Types

Seven-Year Change in Abilities and Congruence Types   Of concern also is the effect of congruence type on cognitive change over 7 years. This effect was analyzed by means of a 3 (congruence type) × 3 (age group) × 2 (gender) ANOVA separately for each of the five abilities. Statistically significant effects of congruence type on magnitude of change over 7 years were found for Verbal Meaning [$F(2, 588) = 14.77$, $p < .001$]; Inductive Reasoning [$F(2, 588) = 11.24$, $p < .001$]; and Word Fluency [$F(2, 588) = 3.84$, $p < .05$]. Optimists improved; pessimists and realists declined on Verbal Meaning and Inductive Reasoning. Also, there were no significant congruence type by age or gender interactions. Magnitudes of change were fairly similar to those reported in table 15.5.

TABLE 15.9 Standardized Means for 1991 Ability Scores by Consistency in Congruency Types

	Remained Pessimists			Remained Optimists			Remained Realists			Became More Pessimistic			Became More Optimistic		
	M	F	T	M	F	T	M	F	T	M	F	T	M	F	T
Verbal Meaning															
Young	—	40.5	40.5	55.6	57.7	56.7	51.7	51.5	51.5	52.9	57.5	55.3	48.7	57.5	53.8
Middle-aged	—	54.1	54.1	52.5	54.6	53.5	53.8	50.8	51.9	51.3	51.6	41.5	50.1	47.5	48.9
Old	22.2	33.1	29.6	50.7	45.6	48.5	32.3	41.7	38.1	43.5	43.6	50.1	41.0	36.7	38.9
Total	22.2	43.1	39.6	48.5	53.7	53.2	46.7	48.5	47.8	49.5	50.0	49.8	46.9	45.4	46.1
Spatial Orientation															
Young	54.6	58.2	56.4	56.0	57.4	56.8	61.8	58.2	59.5	61.2	51.3	55.3	62.4	45.9	55.3
Middle-aged	55.8	43.9	50.3	52.0	52.6	52.3	49.7	48.9	49.4	54.3	48.4	50.5	56.6	47.2	51.8
Old	45.7	38.5	42.8	45.2	42.6	43.9	39.1	43.8	42.1	46.4	42.9	44.3	43.7	41.6	42.5
Total	52.1	44.4	48.7	50.8	50.9	50.8	48.8	48.9	48.8	54.3	47.9	50.3	53.9	45.3	49.4
Inductive Reasoning															
Young	59.2	61.9	60.4	58.0	51.7	55.4	47.6	—	47.6	49.8	55.3	52.6	57.3	58.4	58.0
Middle-aged	52.5	53.5	53.1	45.7	54.2	49.3	—	40.8	40.8	45.3	45.4	45.3	53.1	51.2	52.1
Old	47.1	45.0	45.9	39.3	35.9	38.3	39.1	31.8	38.0	38.7	39.5	39.1	42.0	43.1	42.7
Total	51.9	51.4	51.6	46.4	50.8	48.2	41.2	37.8	40.3	43.0	43.3	43.2	52.2	51.6	51.9
Number															
Young	58.6	50.8	54.1	48.5	50.3	49.5	55.2	61.5	58.1	50.3	50.2	50.3	45.2	50.8	48.5
Middle-aged	55.6	47.6	50.2	50.2	49.8	49.9	59.6	49.0	55.0	53.5	51.6	52.4	52.5	50.2	51.4
Old	47.3	39.5	45.2	47.5	45.2	53.0	46.4	49.0	50.1	43.7	50.5	47.7	45.3	43.1	44.0
Total	54.2	47.9	50.6	49.1	48.8	49.0	57.2	51.5	54.2	50.4	51.1	50.8	49.2	47.7	48.4
Word Fluency															
Young	53.7	55.6	54.5	50.3	55.7	52.9	52.0	54.6	53.3	53.6	57.1	56.0	48.4	56.5	53.0
Middle-aged	44.2	51.4	48.4	50.8	53.2	52.1	52.9	51.8	52.3	50.7	51.6	51.2	50.9	48.0	49.2
Old	59.0	46.2	49.4	39.4	42.7	41.1	43.8	48.1	46.1	45.2	50.0	48.1	45.2	46.0	45.6
Total	49.8	51.0	50.5	47.9	51.1	49.6	49.6	50.0	50.3	49.7	52.5	51.3	48.7	49.2	49.0

Note. F, females; M, males; T, total.

Seven-Year Change in Abilities and Consistency Patterns   Possible effects of the different consistency patterns in congruence type on cognitive change over 7 years were investigated by a 5 (consistency pattern) $\times$ 3 (age group) $\times$ 2 (gender) ANOVA for each ability. Significant effects of congruence type on magnitude of change over 7 years were found for all abilities: Verbal Meaning [$F(4, 588) = 27.03$, $p < .001$]; Spatial Orientation [$F(4, 588) = 22.11$, $p < .001$]; Inductive Reasoning [$F(4, 588) = 27.03$, $p < .001$]; Number [$F(4, 588) = 19.67$, $p < .010$]; and Word Fluency [$F(4, 588) = 24.52$, $p < .001$]. For all abilities, participants who remained pessimists or became more pessimistic had significantly greater positive change than did realists, in contrast to optimists or those becoming more optimistic who experienced negative changes. There were no significant congruence type by age or gender interactions. Table 15.10 therefore reports mean changes by consistency pattern only for the total sample.

Summary

In the analyses in this section, study participants were classified by congruence types for two 7-year periods, as well as for consistency in congruency over the two periods. Performance levels for the three types (pessimists, realists, optimists) differed by ability. Thus, pessimists did better in Inductive Reasoning, and Optimists excelled on Verbal Meaning. However, optimists tended to show greater positive change over time than did pessimists and realists. On the other hand, when consistency of congruency was examined it, was the pessimists or those becoming more pessimistic who showed greater improvement over time; those who were optimists or became more optimistic actually experienced negative cognitive changes.

Perception of Short-Term Cognitive Change and of Training Effects

Perceptions of change in cognitive functioning over a brief period of time were examined for the five basic primary mental abilities as part of the intervention

TABLE 15.10 Mean *T*-Score Change from 1984 to 1991 in Ability Scores by Consistency in Congruence Types

	Remained Pessimists	Remained Optimists	Remained Realists	Became More Pessimistic	Became More Optimistic
Verbal Meaning	−1.50	−0.41	−2.53	4.09	−5.63
Spatial Orientation	1.89	−0.85	−6.55	2.61	−5.60
Inductive Reasoning	0.98	−0.98	−1.36	1.35	−1.86
Number	0.71	−2.12	−2.94	2.04	−4.62
Word Fluency	2.85	−2.35	−3.86	1.98	−6.22

studies described in chapter 7. Here, the question of interest was whether participants can accurately perceive short-term shifts in cognitive performance occurring between repetitions of the same test over a period of 2 to 4 weeks; another question was whether participants who were given cognitive training in a specific ability were more likely to perceive change accurately than those not so trained.

Methods

Participants   Three subsamples selected for this study included those individuals who had taken the PMA battery twice as part of the intervention study. There were 399 participants (177 men and 222 women) with a mean age in 1984 of 72.55 years ($SD = 6.87$; range 64–95); 310 participants (136 men and 174 women) with a mean age in 1991 of 75.2 years ($SD = 6.31$; range 64–93), and 346 participants (143 men and 203 women) with a mean age in 1998 of 76.19 years (SD 6.95; range 64–95).

Procedure   After completing the five PMA tests (Verbal Meaning, Spatial Orientation, Inductive Reasoning, Number, and Word Fluency) during the posttest, study participants again answered the PMA Retrospective Questionnaire. Participants were reminded that they had taken the same five ability tests several weeks earlier and were asked to indicate how their performance on the tests just completed (at posttest) compared with their earlier performance (at pretest). Participants evaluated their relative performance for each of the five abilities using a 5-point scale with the categories (1) much better today, (2) better today, (3) about the same, (4) worse today, (5) much worse today. Again, only a few persons chose the extreme categories (1 or 5), and these categories were collapsed into a 3-point scale, resulting in three perceiver types: better, same, and worse.

Creation of Congruence Types   Study participants were classified according to how their actual PMA performance had changed from pretest to posttest on each of the five abilities. Difference scores between the two test occasions were computed, and participants were classified into groups showing reliably higher, similar, or lower performance for each ability. The classification criteria for a positive or negative change were that the participant at posttest performed at least 1 *SEM* below or above his or her pretest performance (see Dudek, 1979; Schaie, 1989c). Based on the cross-tabulations between actual performance change and perceived performance change, the samples were again categorized into the three congruence types (pessimists, realists, and optimists) for each ability, as described in table 15.1.

Results of the Perception of Training Effects Study

Gender and Secular Differences in Perceived Change   The proportions of study participants indicating that they had improved, remained stable, or become worse from pre- to posttest are shown in table 15.11. No significant gender effects were observed in the 1984 study. However, in 1991 there was a significant gender effect

TABLE 15.11 Proportion of Study Participants Reporting
Perceived Change in Performance From Pretest to Posttest
by Ability and Gender

	1984 Study			1991 Study		
	Better	Same	Worse	Better	Same	Worse
Verbal Meaning						
Males	20.1	51.7	38.3	30.2	53.7	16.2
Females	17.6	46.6	35.8	27.6	51.2	21.3
Total	18.7	48.9	32.4	28.7	52.3	19.0
Spatial Orientation						
Males	18.8	53.4	27.8	29.4	42.6	27.9
Females	21.7	48.4	16.6	19.0	37.4	43.7
Total	20.4	50.6	29.0	23.6	39.7	36.8
Inductive Reasoning						
Males	22.6	44.1	33.3	24.3	51.5	24.3
Females	16.7	39.2	44.1	32.8	42.5	24.7
Total	19.3	41.4	39.3	29.0	46.4	24.5
Number						
Males	41.2	35.6	23.2	22.6	62.1	15.3
Females	33.3	42.8	23.9	16.7	59.5	23.8
Total	36.8	39.6	23.6	19.2	60.6	20.2
Word Fluency						
Males	30.1	46.6	23.3	54.4	36.8	8.8
Females	23.5	46.2	30.3	37.9	50.0	12.1
Total	26.4	46.4	27.2	45.2	44.2	10.6

for Spatial Orientation $[\chi^2(2, N = 310) = 9.22, p < .01]$ that reflected more men than women perceiving positive change and more women than men perceiving negative change. Likewise, a significant gender effect for Word Fluency $[\chi^2(2, N = 310) = 8.37, p < .01]$ indicated that men perceived positive change more frequently than women, whereas women perceived lack of change more frequently than males. In 1998, we also found a significant gender effect for Spatial Orientation $[\chi^2(2, N = 346) = 9.10, p < .01]$, reflecting more women perceiving negative change than did men.

There were also some interesting secular differences in perceived change. These differences involved an increase of positive perceptions from 1984 to 1991, as well as linear decline in negative perceptions for Verbal Meaning from 1984 through 1991. Inductive Reasoning and Word Fluency also showed a linear increase in positive perceptions and a decrease in negative perceptions over this period. Spatial Orientation had an increase in negative perceptions and Number increased the proportion that reported no change.

Correlation Between Perceived and Observed Change   The correlations between perceived and actual change for the same ability (convergent validity) were statistically significant on all three occasions only for Inductive Reasoning and Word Fluency. In addition, there was a significant correlation for Spatial Orientation in

1984 and 1998 and for Number in 1991 and 1998. These correlations, however, were small even though, for the most part, they were larger than cross-ability correlations (divergent validity; see table 15.12). As for the ratings over the 7-year period, significantly larger correlations were again found among ratings of perceived change across abilities, giving further credence to the conclusion that ratings of perceived change are associated with global perceptions of change in intellectual functioning in addition to the actually observed change on the target ability.

Congruence Types   Figure 15.2 shows proportions of each congruence type from pre- to posttest by ability and occasion. Again, assuming that the expected chance probability of assignment to one of the three response congruence types was .33, chi-square analyses determined that assignment to type differed significantly from chance at the 1% level of confidence. In 1984, approximately 40% to 50% of the participants were realistic in their perception of change or stability from pre- to posttest. Participants were most accurate (realistic) in estimating stability or change on the Verbal Meaning and Spatial Orientation tests and least realistic on Inductive Reasoning and Number. The highest proportion of optimists was found for Number (36.6%) and the lowest for Verbal Meaning (18.7%). A pessimistic assessment of performance change was highest for Inductive Reasoning (39.3%) and lowest for Number (23.6%).

TABLE 15.12 Correlations Between Perceived and Actual Change From Pretest to Posttest

	Perceived Change				
	Verbal Meaning	Spatial Orientation	Inductive Reasoning	Number	Word Fluency
Actual Change					
Verbal Meaning	**.034**	−.022	.000	−.031	−.020
	−.023	−.128*	−.066	−.028	−.022
	.065	.044	.051	.021	−.045
Spatial Orientation	−.007	**.198*****	−.050	−.026	.004
	.055	**.001**	.032	.045	.047
	.033	**.131***	.059	.027	.044
Inductive Reasoning	.012	.107*	**.199*****	.048	.049
	−.066	−.082	**.242*****	−.020	.015
	.064	.018	**.218*****	−.019	−.027
Number	.070	−.050	.030	**.015**	−.076
	.054	−.033	.009	**.222*****	−.025
	−.075	.030	.054	**.107***	.025
Word Fluency	.031	.018	.017	−.012	**.323*****
	.018	−.050	.059	.040	**.234*****
	.023	−.077	.012	.078	**.251*****

Note. First value is for the 1984 study, second value for the 1991 study, and third value for the 1998 study.
*p < .05. ***p < .001. Convergent validities are bold.

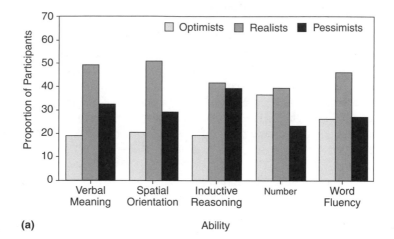

(a) Ability

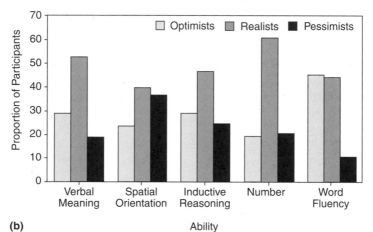

(b) Ability

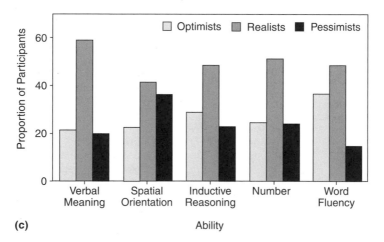

(c) Ability

FIGURE 15.2 *Proportions of Perceiver Types from Pretest to Posttest for the (a) 1984, (b) 1991, and (c) 1998 Training Studies.*

Secular shifts were also found in the perceiver types. In 1991, proportions of realistic perceivers had increased, with a low of 39.7% for Spatial Orientation and a high of 60.6% for Number. The highest proportion of optimists now occurred for Word Fluency (45.26%), and the lowest proportion remained for Number (19.2%). Likewise, the highest proportion of pessimists now occurred for Spatial Orientation and the lowest for Word Fluency.

By 1998, the lowest proportion of realists continued to occur for Spatial Orientation (41.3%); the highest proportion of realists shifted to Verbal Meaning (59.2%). The highest proportion of optimists continued for Word Fluency (36.8%), with the lowest for Verbal Meaning (21.1%) and Spatial Orientation (22.3%). Most pessimists were found for Spatial Orientation and least for Word Fluency (14.8%).

Accuracy of Perceived Change on Trained Ability   A final question is whether study participants who are trained on a particular ability are likely to perceive greater positive change on that ability than a control group, as well as whether their perception of change (given the fact that they receive feedback during training) is more accurate than that of the controls. Indeed, on all three occasions the trained group reported significantly greater positive change than did the control group. The effect was more robust for the Inductive Reasoning training [χ^2 1984(2, $N = 228$) = 15.45, $p < .001$; χ^2 1991(2, $N = 310$) = 34.89, $p < .001$; χ^2 1998 (2, $N = 346$) = 19.88, $p < .001$] than for the Spatial Orientation training [χ^2 1984(2, $N = 228$) = 5.88, $p < .05$; χ^2 1991(2, $N = 310$) = 5.54, $p < .06$; χ^2 1998(2, $N = 346$) = 7.96, $p < .05$]. However, there were no significant differences between those trained and their controls with respect to perceiver type.

Chapter Summary

In this chapter, I examined the accuracy of adults' perceptions regarding an issue of increasing concern as we get older—whether our intellectual abilities are actually declining. These concerns were investigated by evaluating the accuracy of participants' assessment of intellectual change over 7 years. The findings suggest that perceptions of ability decline are not limited to old age, but that there are also young and middle-aged individuals who perceive that their cognitive abilities have declined. These perceptions vary across abilities, age, and gender.

Subjective report of performance change was compared with actual observed change over 7 years. If participants thought that they had changed less than they actually did, they were designated as optimists; if they perceived change status correctly, they were called realists; and if they declined less than they reported, they were designated as pessimists. Frequency of assignment to these three congruence types varied by age and gender. For some abilities, women tended to be more likely to underestimate their performance, as did older study participants. However, accuracy of prediction was not strongly related to ability level. Thus, it appears that stereotypes of universal intellectual decline with increasing age do not seem to be supported either by adults' perceptions or by the accuracy of their estimates.

We replicated the 7-year retrospective data for a second 7-year period in 1991 and investigated the stability of the congruence types identified in this study over a 14-year period. Performance levels for the three congruence types (pessimists, realists, optimists) differed by ability. Pessimists performed better on Inductive Reasoning, and optimists excelled on Verbal Meaning. However, optimists tended to show greater positive change over time than did pessimists or realists. However, when consistency of congruency over time was examined, it was the pessimists or those becoming more pessimistic who showed greater improvement over time; those who were optimists or became more optimistic experienced negative cognitive changes.

We also evaluated judgments of short-term change after repeated testing and training interventions spanning a 4-week period for three different training occasions (see chapter 7). Accuracy of prediction was modest, and it varied by ability, but was greatest on the ability on which the participants had actually been trained. Frequencies of congruence types showed secular changes, with an increase in the proportion of realists and decrease in the proportion of pessimists.

CHAPTER SIXTEEN

Influences of Family Environment on Cognition

THE PURPOSE OF THIS CHAPTER IS TO REPORT data on family similarity in the perception of individuals' family environments and to contrast differences in perceptions within parent-offspring pairs (across generations) to differences within sibling pairs (within generations). We then examine influence of family environments on current levels of cognitive performance.

Parent-offspring similarity has traditionally been studied in young adult parents and their children, and sibling studies have primarily involved children and adolescents. In this chapter, we report data from the Seattle Longitudinal Study (SLS) on the similarity of perceptions of family environments of parents and their adult offspring and the similarity in such perceptions of adult siblings reported in adulthood. Perceptions of family environments are considered both with respect to the family of origin (i.e., the family setting experienced by our study participants when they lived with their own parents) and with respect to the current family (i.e., their family unit at the time these data were collected). Included in this chapter also are analyses of the relation of perceived family environments to reported current intensity of contact between parent and offspring and between sibling pairs (cf. Schaie & Willis, 1995).

The argument is then made that we can compare the impact of heritability of cognitive performance by examining correlations between parent-offspring and sibling dyads to the shared and unique effects of childhood and current family environments as measured by participants' reports of their family of origin and current family environments.

The Measurement of Family Environments

Our efforts to measure these perceptions were motivated by the fact that it is extremely difficult to measure current environments objectively, and it is of course virtually impossible to obtain such information directly over the quality of environments that pertained at earlier life stages of our study participants. We therefore decided that it was necessary to infer environmental quality by asking our participants to rate both their current environments and their retrospection of the family environment they experienced within their biological family of origin.

We first examine the usefulness of family environment perceptions to measure environmental heterogeneity. That is, we ask the structural question whether the same dimensions can be used by participants across and within families to describe their current families and their families of origin. We next examine the substantive issues whether we can demonstrate the existence of generational patterns or secular trends in the perception of family characteristics. We do this by testing whether the strength of family similarity in perception is greater with respect to *shared* than to *unshared* environments. This question, moreover, is examined for parent-offspring pairs who have shared the same environment, but did so at different life stages, and for sibling pairs who have shared the same environment at the same life stage. To the extent that we can demonstrate differential strength of perceptions within similar environments as opposed to different environments, we also provide indirect evidence supporting the construct validity of measures of the perceived family environment as indicators of actual family environments.

Our measures of family environment (as described in chapter 3) are derived from the work of Moos and Moos (1986), who constructed a 90-item true-and-false family environment scale measuring 10 different dimensions (each measured by nine items), 3 of which they described as relationship, 5 as personal growth, and the remaining 2 as system maintenance and change dimensions. The purpose of this scale was to provide an assessment instrument to that could be used to examine environmental context of adaptation (Moos, 1985, 1987). We adapted the scale for8 of these dimensions for our purposes by selecting five items per dimension and presenting each statement in Likert scale form (1 = strongly disagree, 2 = somewhat disagree, 3 = in between, 4 = somewhat agree, 5 = strongly agree).

Two forms of the Family Environment Scale were constructed: The first asked that the respondents rate their family of origin (i.e., past tense statement with respect to the parental family); the second form requested the same information (in present tense) with respect to the current family. On each form, respondents were also asked to indicate the membership of both their families of origin and their current families. They were then instructed to do the ratings with respect to the family grouping identified by them. In other words, for the parents this implied rating the "empty nest" family. In recognition of the fact that significant numbers of our young adult and older study participants lived by themselves, an alternate form was constructed that allowed participants to define their current family as those individuals (whether or not related by blood or marriage) who the respondent considered as his or her primary reference group and with whom the respondent interacted at least on a weekly basis.

A confirmatory factor analysis (using LISREL [linear structural relations] 7) was conducted on a random half of the sample of relatives for both forms to determine whether the retained items clustered on the factors described by Moos (1985, 1987). The obtained fit for the family of origin [$\chi^2(701) = 1,235.56$, $p <$ .001; $GFI = .842$; $RMS = .084$] and the current family [$\chi^2(701) = 1,254.48$, $p <$ .001; $GFI = .839$; $RMS = .089$] was then confirmed on the second random half for the family of origin ($\chi^2(701) = 1,266.05$, $p < .001$; $GFI = .842$; $RMS = .090$] and the current family [$\chi^2(701) = 1,357.07$, $p < .001$; $GFI = .829$; $RMS = .089$]. Factor intercorrelations for both scales are shown in table 16.1. Although we obtained a good fit for the primary dimensions, we failed to reproduce the higher-order structure postulated by Moos. Our analyses were therefore limited to Moos's primary dimensions.

Data relevant to the analyses in this chapter include family members of SLS panel members who participated in the 1984 data collection. These persons were tested in 1989–1990 and were matched with the panel members who were still in the panel in 1991. Subsequent to matching target participants and their relatives, we were able to identify 452 parent-offspring and 207 sibling pairs for whom complete data is available, for a total sample of 1,318 individuals. These consist of 85 father-son, 110 father-daughter, 96 mother-son, 161 mother-daughter, 28 brother-brother, 106 brother-sister, and 73 sister-sister pairings. The reduction in sample size occurred because of substantial attrition in the number of study members whose relatives we had been able to assess earlier; among the older study members attrition was attributable primarily to death or sensory and motor disabilities that precluded further assessment or questionnaire response.

Average age of the parents was 70.26 years ($SD = 9.24$), and it was 39.94 years ($SD = 8.64$) for the offspring. The parents averaged 14.46 years of education ($SD = 2.86$) as compared to 15.56 years of education ($SD = 2.41$) for their children. Total family income averaged $24,681 for the parents and $26,841 for the offspring, respectively. Average number of children was 3.53 for the parental and 1.45 for the offspring generation.

Average ages for the siblings were 63.23 years ($SD = 12.78$) for the longitudinal study members and 61.06 years ($SD - 13.16$) for their relatives. The target siblings averaged 14.90 years of education ($SD = 3.25$) as compared to 14.62 years of education ($SD = 2.78$) for their brothers or sisters. Average incomes were $26,416 for the longitudinal study members and $25,682 for their siblings. Average number of children was 3.09 for the longitudinal participants and 2.69 for their siblings.

Similarity of Perceptions of Parents and Their Adult Offspring

Three sets of relationships can be considered. The first is the correlations between family environment perceptions of parents and offspring with respect to their family of origin, their nonshared and temporally distinct environment. The second concerns the correlation of perceptions of the current families, of parents and adult offspring, the nonshared but temporally concurrent environment. Finally, there is the correlation of the offspring's perception of their family of origin with their parent's perception of the parent's current family, the shared environ-

TABLE 16.1 Intercorrelation of Family Environment Scales (Values for Family of Origin Above Diagonal, Values for Current Family Below Diagonal)

	Cohesion	Expressivity	Conflict	Achievement Orientation	Intellectual-Cultural	Active-Recreational	Organization	Control
Cohesion		.860	.664	.372	.434	.524	.272	-.133
Expressivity	.837		.341	.339	.483	.515	.033	-.208
Conflict	.565	.323		.065	.161	.210	.256	-.286
Achievement Orientation	.274	.239	.009		.430	.369	.333	.289
Intellectual-Cultural Orientation	.492	.562	.251	.234		.659	.056	-.130
Active-Recreational Orientation	.448	.453	.093	.445	.606		.138	-.038
Organization	.346	.235	.346	.234	.149	.186		.393
Control	-.013	-.121	-.155	.209	-.216	.006	.448	

ment. The first two sets of relationships involve comparisons of the same life stage across generations, but representing different families for each generation. The third set of relationships is concerned with the perceived similarity of the family environment within the same family across generations. In comparing correlational patterns (magnitude of correlations) across generations, within life stages, and across different gender pairings, a generalized maximum likelihood test is employed to test the statistical significance of differences between correlation patterns.

Family of Origin   For the total sample, significant, but modest, correlations between parents and offspring are found for the dimensions of Cohesion, Expressivity, Conflict, Intellectual-Cultural, Organization, and Control (see table 16.2). The highest overall correlation amounted to .294 for Conflict. When analyzed separately by gender pairing, a significantly different pattern is found for the correlations for the father-daughter and mother-daughter combinations [$\chi^2(8) = 24.71$, $p < .01$]. The relationships for Cohesion and Active-Recreational Orientation remain significant only for mothers and daughters, that for Expressivity only between fathers and daughters, for Intellectual-Cultural Orientation between mothers and their children (regardless of gender), and for Organizational between fathers and their children. The relationship for Conflict holds for all gender pairings; that for Control holds for all except the mother-son pairings.

Current Family   Somewhat lower correlations are found when our participants' perceptions of their current families were compared across the two generations. Overall, correlations were significantly lower for the current family correlations than for the family of origin correlations for the father-son [$\chi^2(8) = 17.71$, $p < .05$] and mother-daughter [$\chi^2(8) = 12.46$, $p < .05$] combinations. However, significant overall correlations also were observed here for the dimensions of Cohesion, Intellectual-Cultural, Organization, and Control (see table 16.3). When gender pairings were considered, additional significant correlations were found for mothers and daughters on Expressivity and for fathers and daughters on Conflict.

TABLE 16.2 Correlation Between Parents and Offspring in Their Perceptions of Family Environment in Their Family of Origin

	Total Sample	Fathers/ Sons	Fathers/ Daughters	Mothers/ Sons	Mothers/ Daughters
Cohesion	.204***	.201	−.011	.191	.310***
Expressivity	.142*	.139	.268**	.088	.088
Conflict	.294***	.208*	.292**	.306**	.307***
Achievement Orientation	.093	.088	−.011	−.002	.206**
Intellectual-Cultural	.231***	.109	.177	.351***	.276***
Active-Recreational	.084	.043	.056	.036	.151*
Organization	.213***	.405***	.291***	.142	.119
Control	.151***	.230*	.244**	−.052	.154*

*$p < .05$. **$p < .01$. ***$p < .001$.

TABLE 16.3 Correlation Between Parents and Offspring in Their Perceptions of Family Environment in Their Current Family

	Total Sample	Fathers/ Sons	Fathers/ Daughters	Mothers/ Sons	Mothers/ Daughters
Cohesion	.108*	.015	.106	.145	.147
Expressivity	.044	−.194	.038	.031	.172*
Conflict	.087	.094	.226*	.051	.023
Achievement Orientation	.098	−.083	−.047	.274**	.114
Intellectual-Cultural	.266***	.283**	.297**	.200*	.284***
Active-Recreational	.156**	.144	.090	.228*	.154*
Organization	.184**	.123	.178	.191	.233**
Control	.105*	−.092	.232*	.083	.131

$^*p < .05.$ $^{**}p < .01.$ $^{***}p < .001.$

The relationship for Achievement Orientation remained significant only for mother-son pairings, for Active-Recreational Orientation for mothers and their children (regardless of gender), for mothers and daughters on Organization, and for fathers and daughters on Control. However, the correlational patterns did not differ significantly across pairings.

Similarity of Perceived Family Environment Across Generations   Here, the magnitude of the relationship between the parents' current environment and their offsprings' perception of their family of origin is investigated. This is presumably the same family at different life stages, when the offspring were part of the parental family, and that same family now in its postparental phase. Even though the actual family composition has, of course, changed, we found that correlations were substantially higher for this comparison and were statistically significant for the total sample for all dimensions (see table 16.4). Statistically significant correlations were found also for all gender pairings for the Intellectual-Cultural, Active-Recreational, Organization, and Control dimensions.

TABLE 16.4 Correlation Between Parents' Perception of Their Current Family and Offsprings' Perception of Their Family of Origin

	Total Sample	Fathers/ Sons	Fathers/ Daughters	Mothers/ Sons	Mothers/ Daughters
Cohesion	.207***	.305**	.178	.133	.242**
Expressivity	.101*	.007	.145	.072	.131
Conflict	.206***	.234*	.241*	.072	.230**
Achievement Orientation	.217***	.282**	.012	.257*	.263**
Intellectual-Cultural	.374***	.377***	.361***	.378***	.391***
Active-Recreational	.293***	.247*	.334***	.379***	.253***
Organization	.368***	.419***	.387***	.456***	.313***
Control	.194***	.228*	.185*	.225*	.184*

$^*p < .05.$ $^{**}p < .01.$ $^{***}p < .001.$

Significant correlations were found for same gender (father-son and mother-daughter) pairings for Cohesion and for all but mother-son pairings for Conflict. Correlational patterns did not differ significantly by gender pairing. However, these correlations were significantly higher than those found for the family of origin ratings across the two generations' ratings for the total sample [$\chi^2(8) = 31.38$, $p < .001$] as well as the father-son [$\chi^2(8) = 17.71$, $p < .05$], father-daughter [$\chi^2(8) = 15.51$, $p < .05$], mother-son [$\chi^2(8) = 22.88$, $p < .001$], and mother-daughter [$\chi^2(8) = 15.80$, $p < .05$] gender pairings. They were also significantly higher than the cross-generational correlations for their current families for the total sample [$\chi^2(8) = 30.87$, $p < .001$] and for the father-son [$\chi^2(8) = 29.95$, $p < .001$] gender pairing.

Similarity of Perceptions of Siblings

The sibling comparisons were, of course, made within the same generation. However, it should be noted that for the siblings the ratings for the family of origin reflect perceptions of the same family at the same life stage; ratings of the current family reflect membership in different families. Because of the small sample size for brother-brother pairings ($N = 28$), gender-specific data are provided only for the brother-sister and sister-sister pairings.

Family of Origin   Statistically significant correlations were found for all family dimensions, ranging from a low of .191 for Achievement Orientation to a high of .491 for the Intellectual-Cultural dimension. Correlational patterns did not differ significantly by gender pairings, and the correlational values remained significantly different from zero, except for Achievement Orientation, which did not reach significance for the brother-sister pairs (see table 16.5).

Current Family   The comparison of siblings' perceptions of their current families yielded few significant correlations. Overall, low but significant correlations were

TABLE 16.5 Correlation Between Siblings' Perception of Their Family of Origin

	Total Sample	Brothers/Sisters	Sisters/Sisters
Cohesion	.390***	.427***	.370***
Expressivity	.251***	.277**	.220*
Conflict	.457***	.428***	.430***
Achievement Orientation	.169*	.119	.307**
Intellectual-Cultural	.491***	.486***	.473***
Active-Recreational	.366***	.301**	.381***
Organization	.414***	.430***	.489***
Control	.215**	.183*	.253*

Note. Because of the small sample size, correlations are not reported for the brother-brother subset.
*$p < .05$. **$p < .01$. ***$p < .001$.

found for the Intellectual-Cultural and Organization dimensions. However, when broken down by gender pairings, only the correlation between brothers and sisters for the Intellectual-Cultural dimension remained significant (see table 16.6). Magnitudes of correlations for the perception of current families were significantly lower than for the family of origin for the total sample [$\chi^2(8) = 51.11$, $p < .001$], as well as for the brother-sister [$\chi^2(8) = 30.96$, $p < .001$] and sister-sister [$\chi^2(8) = 21.87$, $p < .01$] pairings.

Prediction of Offsprings' Perception of Their Current Family Environment

Next we considered the extent to which parental perceptions of family environment, and the offsprings' perception of the environment prevailing in their family of origin, as well as to what extent contact between offspring and parents affects the offsprings' perception of their current family environment. Table 16.7 provides the relevant β weights and multiple correlations. The magnitude of the relationship was highly significant, and between 20% and 25% of the variance in perceptions of current family environment can be accounted for. Note that the major significant predictor for each dimension of the current family environment was the corresponding dimension in the offsprings' perception of their family of origin. However, in each case, one or more parental perception of their current or original family contributed significantly to the variance in the offsprings' perception. Interestingly, however, frequency of contact with parents (see chapter 13) contributed little variance to these predictions (see table 16.7).

Prediction of Contact Between Parents and Offspring

Do perceptions of family environments of parents and offspring, both current and in their family of origin, influence their reports of frequency of intrapair contact? Reports of frequency of contact were provided by both parents and

TABLE 16.6 Correlation Between Siblings' Perception of Their Current Family

	Total Sample	Brothers/Sisters	Sisters/Sisters
Cohesion	.072	−.013	.003
Expressivity	−.015	−.099	−.052
Conflict	.095	.098	.029
Achievement Orientation	.070	.059	.120
Intellectual-Cultural	.201**	.193*	.172
Active-Recreational	.099	.086	.103
Organization	.134*	.045	.146
Control	.015	.026	.028

Note. Because of the small sample size, correlations are not reported for the brother-brother subset.
*p < .05. **p < .01.

TABLE 16.7 Regression Analyses Predicting Offsprings' Perception of Their Current Family Environment (β Weights: $p < .05$)

	Cohesion	Expressivity	Conflict	Achievement Orientation	Intellectual-Cultural	Active-Recreational	Organization	Control
Offspring family of origin								
Cohesion	.284						-.160	
Expressivity	.142		.367					
Conflict				.383			.142	
Achievement Orientation					.271		-.130	.167
Intellectual-Cultural						.215		-.157
Active-Recreational							.268	
Organization								.302
Control								
Parent family of origin								
Cohesion			-.154				-.169	
Expressivity								
Conflict						-.114		
Achievement Orientation								
Intellectual-Cultural								
Active-Recreational	.131		.134			.141	.110	
Organization								
Control		.174						-.124
Parent current family								
Cohesion		.169						
Expressivity								
Conflict		-.111						
Achievement Orientation								
Intellectual-Cultural					.107		-.138	-.139
Active-Recreational								
Organization								
Control								
Contact with parent				.116		.101		
Multiple correlation	.392	.407	.434	.446	.431	.414	.478	.486

offspring. The offspring reported slightly more contacts than did their parents ($p <$ .05). The difference in reported contact by the two generations was greatest for the father-son pairings, but the greatest frequency of contact was reported by both parents and offspring for the mother-daughter pairing. There was a significant correlation between contact reported by parents and offspring, but its magnitude ($r = .388$) was low enough to suggest that different aspects of family perception might influence contact as reported by parents and offspring. Frequency of specific types of contacts is provided in figure 16.1.

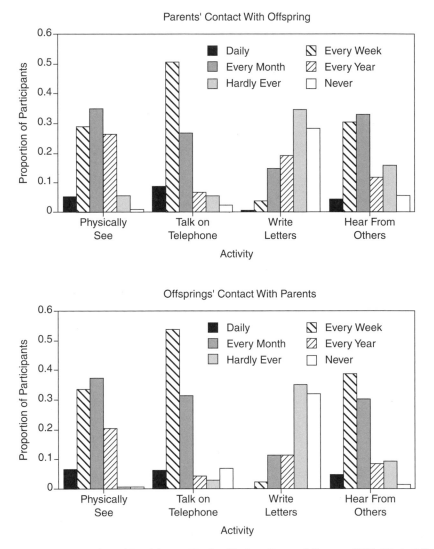

FIGURE 16.1 *Proportion of Participants Having Various Types of Contacts With Their Offspring or Parents.*

Approximately 57% of the parents and 50% of the offspring described the nature of their relationship as "very close." An additional 29% of the parents and 35% of the offspring described it as "close"; 9% of the parents and 11% of the offspring rated the relationship as "in between"; 3% of parents and offspring rated it as "somewhat close"; and only 1.5% of parents and offspring rated it as "not close at all."

Almost a fourth of the variance in contact can be predicted from perceptions of family environments. However, the only variable accounting for significant variance in common to parents and offspring is that of Cohesion as rated for the parental family of origin (the grandparental family for the offspring). The other significant predictors for the offsprings' reports of contact with parents are high Cohesion in the offspring family of origin, high Control in their current family, low Achievement Orientation in the parental family of origin, and low Organization in the current parental family. By contrast, significant predictors for Contact as reported by parents are low Conflict and high Active-Recreational Orientation in their families of origin, high Cohesion and low Expressivity in their current family, as well as high Achievement and Active-Recreational Orientation, low Organization, and high Control in their offsprings' perception of the parental family (see table 16.8).

Magnitude of Differences in Perceptions of Family Environment

Generational Differences   The focus now shifts to the question of differences in perceptions of family environment both within families across generations and in the perception of differences between our study participants' parental and current families. Because of the wide age range of the participants and to adjust for possible differences in the age span between individual parent-offspring pairs, we covaried on age of both parents and offspring. A multivariate analysis of covariance (MANCOVA) design was used in which parental gender and offspring gender were the between-participant effects, generations (parents/offspring) and family stage (family of origin/current family) were treated as within-participant effects, and the family environment dimensions were treated as dependent variables.

Table 16.9 gives results of the overall MANCOVA, which was then followed by univariate tests for the significant effects of interest. Main effects significant at or beyond the 5% level of confidence were obtained for gender of offspring, generations, and family stage. Two-way interactions were significant for parental gender by family stage and for generations by family stage. There were also significant three-way interactions for parental gender by generations by family stage and for offspring gender by generations by family stage.

Univariate tests indicated that the main effect for offspring sex was significant only for the dimension of Achievement Orientation ($p < .01$), with men reporting a higher overall level of Achievement Orientation. The main effect for generations was significant for six dimensions ($p < .001$). The offspring reported lower overall levels of family Cohesion, Organization, and Conflict, but greater Achievement,

TABLE 16.8 Regression Analyses Predicting Parent-Offspring Contact (β Weights: $p < .05$)

	Contact as Perceived By	
	Offspring	Parents
Parent family of origin		
Cohesion	.179	.251
Expressivity		
Conflict		−.148
Achievement Orientation	−.119	
Intellectual-Cultural		
Active-Recreational		.165
Organization		
Control		
Parent current family		
Cohesion		.159
Expressivity		−.146
Conflict		
Achievement Orientation		
Intellectual-Cultural		
Active-Recreational		
Organization	−.119	
Control		
Offspring family of origin		
Cohesion	.297	
Expressivity		
Conflict		
Achievement Orientation		
Intellectual-Cultural		.115
Active-Recreational		.165
Organization		−.119
Control		.124
Offspring current family		
Cohesion		
Expressivity		
Conflict		
Achievement Orientation		
Intellectual-Cultural		
Active-Recreational		
Organization		
Control	.126	
Multiple Correlation	.453	.451

Intellectual-Cultural, and Active-Recreational Orientation. The family stage main effects were also significant ($p < .001$) for all dimensions except Achievement Orientation. Higher levels of Cohesion, Expressivity, Conflict, Intellectual-Cultural, and Active-Recreational Orientation were reported for the current family; a higher level of Control was attributed to the family of origin.

The parental gender by family stage interaction was statistically significant for the Cohesion ($p < .01$), Conflict ($p < .05$), Intellectual-Cultural ($p < .01$), and

TABLE 16.9 Multivariate Analysis of Variance of Family Environment Dimensions for Parental Gender, Offspring Gender, Generations, and Family Stages

Effect	Rao's R
Parental gender	0.98
Offspring gender	2.18*
Generations	32.91***
Family stages	110.02***
Parental Gender × Offspring Gender	0.72
Parental Gender × Generations	1.16
Parental Gender × Generations	1.91
Parental Gender × Family Stages	2.46**
Offspring Gender × Family Stages	1.52
Generations × Family Stages	8.47***
Parental Gender × Offspring Gender × Generations	0.69
Parental Gender × Offspring Gender × Family Stages	0.92
Parental Gender × Generations × Family Stages	2.46**
Offspring Gender × Generations × Family Stages	2.20*
Parental Gender × Offspring Gender × Generations × Family Stages	1.25

*$p < .05$. **$p < .01$. ***$p < .001$. $df = 8, 422$.

Organization ($p < .01$) dimensions. Mothers reported significantly lower Cohesion and Conflict for family of origin than for the current family. Their family of origin was also described as significantly lower in Active-Recreational Orientation, and they reported greater Control for the current family.

The generations by family stage interaction is of particular interest for our purposes. Here, statistically significant effects were obtained for Achievement Orientation ($p < .001$), Intellectual-Cultural Orientation ($p < .001$), and Control ($p < .01$). Mean scores for these dimensions by generation and family stage are shown in figure 16.2. Achievement Orientation in the current family was rated significantly lower by the parents than by the offspring. Not only was Intellectual-Cultural Orientation rated lower for the family of origin, but it was rated lowest in the parents' family of origin. Level of Control was reported to be greatest by the parents for their family of origin and was about equally low for the current family of both generations.

Gender differences further complicate the findings with respect to generational/family stage differences in family perceptions. Significant triple interaction for parental gender by generations by family stage ($p < .01$) were found for the Intellectual-Cultural Orientation, Organization, and Control. Intellectual-Cultural Orientation in their present family was perceived to be higher by mothers than by fathers; Organization was perceived as greater in their current family by sons than by daughters; and Control was seen to be greater in the current family by fathers than by mothers. A significant triple interaction for offspring gender by generations by family stage ($p < .001$) was found for Expressivity. In the last instance, daughters reported greater Expressivity in their current family than did sons.

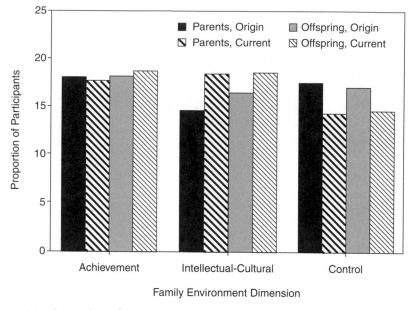

FIGURE 16.2 *Interactions of Generation and Family Stage Effects.*

Cohort Differences   For a better understanding of possible intrafamily shifts in perceptions of family environments of successive cohorts, we repeated the analyses in this section by adding four levels of cohort groupings. In terms of the years of birth of the offspring, these were those born prior to 1941 and those born between 1941 and 1947, 1948 and 1954, and 1955 and 1968. Three significant interactions involving cohort grouping were found: cohort by family stage ($p <$ .01), cohort by parental gender by family stage ($p < .05$), and cohort by generation by family stage ($p < .01$).

Significant univariate effects for the cohort by family stage interaction were found for Cohesion ($p < .01$) and conflict ($p < .001$). Perceptions of both dimensions for the current family environment did not differ, but there was a linear decline for successive cohorts in perceptions of Cohesion and Conflict in the family of origin. With respect to the triple interaction of cohort by parental gender by family stage, significant univariate effects were found for Expressivity ($p <$ .001) and Achievement Orientation ($p < .05$). These effects seem to be accounted for primarily by significant drops in Expressivity in the current family for the men in the most recent cohort, with a concomitant significant increase for the women in that cohort.

For Achievement Orientation, the effects reflect a slight but systematic drop for males in the family of origin and an increase for females in the current family. Finally, the triple interaction for cohort by generation by family stage was statistically significant ($p < .05$) for Intellectual-Cultural Orientation and Organization. The former effect reflects primarily a significant increase in Intellectual-Cultural Orientation from the oldest to the youngest cohort within the family of origin.

The latter reflects the fact that, although there was a general decline in perceived family organization, this decline apparently reversed for the current families of the most recent cohort.

Differences Within Sibling Pairs   Differences in siblings' perceptions of family environment were analyzed with a MANCOVA design in which target and relative gender were the between effects, and target versus relative status and family stage (family of origin/current family) were treated as within effects, again with the family dimensions treated as dependent variables. Table 16.10 provides results of the overall MANCOVA, which was followed by univariate tests for the significant effects of interest. Main effects significant at or beyond the 5% level of confidence were obtained for target versus relative status and family stage. A significant two-way interaction was found for target gender by status. None of the higher-order interactions was statistically significant.

Univariate main effects for study status (i.e., whether the respondents were members of the longitudinal panel or their relatives) were statistically significant for the dimensions of Expressivity ($p < .01$), Intellectual-Cultural Orientation ($p < .05$), Active-Recreational Orientation ($p < .01$), and Control ($p < .01$). Our original study participants reported higher levels of Expressivity as well as Intellectual-Cultural and Active-Recreational Orientations across family of origin and current family than did their siblings. However, the relatives reported a higher overall level of Control. As for the parent-offspring panel, siblings also reported significant differences in family environment between their family of origin and their current family for all dimensions. Higher levels of Cohesion, Expressivity, Conflict, Intellectual-Cultural, and Active-Recreational Orientation were reported for

TABLE 16.10 Multivariate Analysis of Variance of Family Environment Dimensions for Target Sibling Gender, Relative Sibling Gender, Target Versus Relative Status, and Family Stages

Effect	Rao's R
Target gender	1.32
Relative gender	1.64
Status	2.96**
Family stages	41.98***
Target Gender × Relative Gender	0.95
Target Gender × Status	2.41*
Target Gender × Family Stages	0.75
Relative Gender × Status	1.94
Relative Gender × Family Stages	0.99
Status × Family Stages	1.70
Target Gender × Relative Gender × Status	0.71
Target Gender × Relative Gender × Family Stages	1.88
Target Gender × Status × Family Stages	0.98
Relative Gender × Status × Family Stages	1.00
Target Gender × Relative Gender × Status × Family Stages	1.65

*$p < .05$. **$p < .01$. ***$p < .001$. $df = 8, 189$.

the current family; Achievement Orientation, Organization, and Control were rated higher in the family of origin. The target gender by status orientation was only marginally significant for Cohesion, with women from the longitudinal study reporting greater family Cohesion than did the other groupings.

Summary for the Study of Similarities in Family Environment

The availability of a loyal panel of long-term research participants such as that in our longitudinal studies of adult competence simplifies the logistics of acquiring family data, hence our successful effort to recruit good-size panels of adult offspring and siblings of our longitudinal study participants. However, when we began to consider the relevance of the SLS as a potential vehicle for studies of family similarity, it became apparent that, although we had available to us extensive longitudinal data on cognitive performance, we had no direct measures of our study participants' family environments. Although one must always be careful in accepting the veracity of subjective data, particularly when it is retrospective in nature, there is substantial evidence of the utility of perceptions of behavioral dimensions (e.g., in the literature on personal efficacy in adults, e.g., M. E. Lachman, 1989), and we have previously obtained useful evidence on our own study participants' ability to retrospect on their prior performance in the cognitive area (Schaie et al., 1994).

In earlier work with adolescent siblings, Plomin and Daniels (1987) had successfully employed a true-and-false derivative of the Moos and Moos (1986) Family Environment Scales to assess perceptions of the common family environment. It seemed sensible, therefore, to employ these measures for our adult family studies. However, on closer review, the materials in the original scales were deemed too lengthy, and we proceeded with the development of briefer forms that employed Likert scales and were phrased in such a fashion as to be useful for the assessment of families of origin and current families. The psychometric work on these scales mentioned here suggested that we have maintained the dimensionality of the original Family Environment Scales both for retrospective and current reports and have thus created appropriate instruments to obtain data relevant to the questions raised here.

What we have done, then, is to obtain evidence with respect to similarities and differences within and across generations in the perception of eight basic dimensions of family environment. Our data could have been arrayed in a variety of complex ways (for an alternative approach, cf. Rossi, 1989). We elected to analyze data for our adult siblings with respect to within-generation similarities and differences and by studying parent-offspring pairs to determine these relations across generations. Moreover, for each of these analyses, we contrast perceptions of the family of origin and current family (as a within-participant variable). Because of the possibility of shifts in these relationships for successive cohorts, similar to those we have often reported for cognitive variables (cf. Schaie, 1990b), we also elected to include a cohort variable, classifying our offspring into those born prior to World War II, those born during the war years and immediately thereafter, and into the early and late baby boomers.

Our first and most dramatic conclusion is that there is a clear differentiation for parents, offspring, and siblings in the perceived level of all family dimensions between the family of origin and the current family. Obviously, the distance in time was greater for the parents than for the offspring, a factor in part controlled by covarying on respondents' age. Nevertheless, it seems clear that our respondents perceived shifts in the quality of family environments over their own life course. They saw their current families as not only more cohesive and expressive, but also characterized by more conflict than was true for their families of origin. What these changes reflect, of course, may simply express generally greater openness and engagement in family interactions. More intensive family interactions may also be represented by the reported increase in Intellectual-Cultural and Active-Recreational Orientation from the family of origin to the current family. Concomitant with these shifts as well is the overall perception of lower levels of perceived Control, family Organization, and Achievement Orientation. Perhaps these judgments are another way of characterizing the increasing complexity of modern American families (cf. Elder, 1981; Elder & Rudkin, 1995; Hareven, 1982).

Combined with continuing reports of ever-lower reported levels of social responsibility (cf. Schaie & Parham, 1974), this may well mean that the perceived role of the family is changing from that of a primary socialization agent (operating on behalf of the larger society) to a more effective support system for the needs of the individual family member. When our parent-offspring sample was broken down into four distinct cohort groups, we noted further that the shift in perceived family level occurred primarily for perceptions of the family of origin, with much greater stability for perceptions of the current family. This is reasonable because judgments of the current family occurred at one point in time; judgments with respect to the family of origin necessarily reflected different secular periods for which successive cohorts described their early family experiences.

The second conclusion, with respect to within-family similarity in the perception of family environments, is that sibling (particularly sister-sister) pairs share substantial variance in the perception of their family of origin (i.e., the family they shared in childhood and adolescence) over all family dimensions that we examined. However, this commonality did not extend to their perception of their current (nonshared) families. The only exception to this finding was a low correlation for Intellectual-Cultural Orientation and family organization. The reported similarity of early environments might support the contention that retrospective perceptions of families over a long time interval represent the validation of the veracity of these perceptions. On the other hand, the shared variance may simply indicate currently shared (and perhaps idealized) perceptions about the childhood family. However, the lack of similarity between current environments might reflect the fact that siblings do not seem to seek to replicate these early family environments.

Third, in spite of the lack of similarity of current family environments in siblings, we found that the best predictor for the level of each dimension of the current family was the corresponding level reported by each person for his or her family of origin. Perhaps perceptions of the family environment of origin may be one of the factors entering into marital assortativity, even though such perceptions may differ for and may differentially affect the perceptions of current family environments by different siblings.

Fourth, supporting evidence for the continuity of family values and behaviors (cf. Bengtson, 1986) is provided by our finding of substantial correlations between the parents' description of their current family environment and their offsprings' description of their family of origin. Even though there is a substantial time gap in the period rated, these two ratings do refer to the same parental family unit. These relationships were particularly strong for the three dimensions most closely reflective of value orientations (Achievement, Intellectual-Cultural, and Active-Recreational) and for family organization.

Fifth, differences in perceived family environment and the magnitude of similarity across generations will differ by gender pairing and by dimensions, although it is not surprising that the strongest relationships are observed within mother-daughter and sister-sister pairings, even though frequency of contact is only slightly greater than for other relationship combinations.

Sixth, it appears that the intensity (frequency) of contact between parents and offspring has virtually no impact on the similarity of reported family environments. However, there were family environment dimensions (particularly level of Cohesion) that could predict almost a fourth of the variance in the total family contact scores.

Finally, we suggest that the hierarchy of the magnitude of shared perceptions, from low correlations when describing nonshared environments to moderately high correlations when describing commonly experienced environments, provides at least indirect evidence for the contention that self-descriptions of family environments (perceptions) may well be useful indicators of the actually experienced environments.

Another feature of this work has been to show the viability of a system of describing family environments as they affect both within- and across-generation family similarity. As found earlier with respect to cognitive similarity, we were also able to show substantial shared variance with respect to the perceptions of the family of origin. This finding has important implications for behavior genetic studies because it increases the plausibility of using retrospective perceptions as estimates of early shared environments. For the study of intergenerational continuity, our data support earlier literature (cf. Bengtson, 1975) that successive generations tend to evaluate their family environments in rather similar terms. Nevertheless, there is also strong evidence that perceived environments in the newly formed families of the offspring generation are not simply replications of their families of origin but may well represent the outcome of restructured family relations (cf. Green & Boxer, 1985). Hence, the perceived differences in family environments in the current families of successive generations, as well as the substantial differences reported within generations between the perceived environments in their families of origin and their current families, extend the concept of developmental plasticity (Lerner, 1984; Magnusson, 1998) from the level of individual behavior to developmental plasticity in the value system ascribed to whole family units.

Influences of Family Environment on Cognition

An extensive literature has dealt with the relative contribution of inherited predispositions and the influence of both the shared and unique experiences occurring within the family of origin on cognitive functioning in children. Much of this work is derived from twin studies because behavior geneticists have used the twin model as the most convincing paradigm to investigate heritability of intelligence and many other traits (cf. Plomin, 1986). However, because twins represent a rather atypical subset of the general population, the role of family environments has also been investigated in parent-offspring and sibling pairs (e.g., Defries, Vandenberg, et al., 1976). Most studies reported that roughly half of the individual difference variance in cognitive functioning is attributable to heritability. Very little variance, on the other hand, has been attributed to shared family environments. In fact, it has been argued that the environment in the family of origin has quite unique influence on different siblings (Plomin & Daniels, 1987).

Relatively little is known about the origin of individual differences in the later half of the life span as they might relate to inherited predispositions or to early influences transmitted through the family environment. Again, twin studies dominate (e.g., Jarvik et al., 1971; Pedersen, 1996, 2000; Plomin et al., 1988; Rowe & Plomin, 1981), and it is difficult to extrapolate to the more typical case of family similarities among nontwins.

We now present findings from the SLS that may inform us on the relative contribution of heritability of certain cognitive traits and the extent to which current cognitive performance may be attributed to family influences that are shared with other family members during early life as well as the influences of the nonshared family setting currently experienced by our participants (also see Schaie & Zuo, 2001).

Methods

Participants   For the purpose of studying the influence of environmental factors on cognition, we were able to construct a data set that consisted of 537 parent-offspring and 294 sibling pairs for whom complete data are available, a total sample of 1,662 individuals. These consist of 106 father-son, 118 father-daughter, 115 mother-son, 198 mother-daughter, 51 brother-brother, 139 brother-sister, and 104 sister-sister pairings.

Average age of the parents was 70.59 years ($SD = 10.37$), and it was 41.76 years ($SD = 10.46$) for the offspring. The parents averaged 14.22 years of education ($SD = 2.75$) as compared to 15.64 years of education ($SD = 2.49$) for their children. Total family income averaged $25,002 for the parents and $26,841 for the offspring.

Average ages for the siblings were 60.75 years ($SD = 14.42$) for the longitudinal study members and 59.62 years ($SD = 14.77$) for their relatives. The target siblings averaged 15.04 years of education ($SD = 2.80$) as compared to 14.90 years of education ($SD = 2.72$) for their brothers or sisters. Average incomes were $29,361 for the longitudinal study members and $25,682 for their siblings.

Measures   The test battery administered to the participants in this study included the basic Primary Mental Abilities battery (Verbal Meaning, Space, Reasoning, Number, and Word Fluency and the IQ and EQ [Index of Educational Aptitude] indices derived therefrom), as well as the three cognitive style factor scores (Motor-Cognitive Flexibility, Attitudinal Flexibility, and Psychomotor Speed). Family of origin and current family measures were also available for all participants. Included also was the personality trait of Social Responsibility. All measures are described in chapter 3.

Analysis Details   A general linear regression model was fitted to associate each dependent variable (current Primary Mental Abilities and Test of Behavior Rigidity scores) with the significant independent variables. The model was initially chosen by a stepwise model selection procedure. To include all potentially significant independent variables, the level for entering the model was set at an α of $p < .10$. With independent variables selected from the initial screening step, the linear regression model was then fitted, and independent variables with $p > .05$ were excluded from the final model.

After selecting the optimal regression model, several hierarchical regression analyses then assessed the proportion of variance explained by successive blocks of independent variables. The independent variables were classified into four blocks: Block 1 contains the static familial variables (i.e., parents' or siblings' performance on the corresponding cognitive variable, as well as their level of educational attainment). Block 2 includes the significant variables for characterizing the shared early environment (i.e., parents' or siblings' perception of the family of origin of the targeted offspring or sibling). Block 3 includes the significant variables characterizing the nonshared early environment (i.e., the offsprings' or targeted siblings' perception of their family of origin). Block 4 includes the significant variables characterizing the targeted participants' perception of their current (nonshared) environment. The proportion of variance accounted for by each block after the first is the increment in R^2.

Family Influences Shared With Parents

In the parent-offspring data set, significant heritability was found for the five primary mental abilities and the derived summative indices, as well as for Motor-Cognitive Flexibility and Psychomotor Speed. In addition, parental education regressed significantly on adult offspring performance on Spatial Orientation, Inductive Reasoning, and the composite cognitive induces as well as on Motor-Cognitive and Attitudinal Flexibility. However, only one of the regression coefficients for the abilities and one coefficient for the regression of social responsibility on the parental perceptions of their current family environment (the estimate of shared environment) was significant. It seems that the time since our adult offspring shared the current family of their parents was simply too long to have the parents' current environment serve as a surrogate for the early shared environment (see table 16.11).

Nevertheless, there were a number of significant regressions for the offsprings' perception of the family of origin (the unique experience of their early environment). These regressions, at least for the cognitive abilities, accounted for as much or more variance than the participants' perception of their current environment. Cohesion related positively to Spatial Orientation and Social Responsibility. Expressivity was negatively related to Verbal Meaning, Spatial Orientation, Motor-Cognitive Flexibility, and Psychomotor Speed as well as the indices of Intellectual Ability and Educational Aptitude. Perceived Conflict related positively to Number and negatively to Word Fluency. Achievement Orientation related positively to Number. Intellectual-Cultural Orientation related positively to Verbal Meaning and Social Responsibility. Organization related negatively to Inductive Reasoning. Finally, perceived Control related negatively to Verbal Meaning, Spatial Orientation, and the index of Educational Aptitude.

Significant regressions for the effect of the current environment of the offspring were also found. Cohesion related positively to Word Fluency and the IQ and Educational Aptitude indices, but negatively to Spatial Orientation. Expressivity related positively to Verbal Meaning, Inductive Reasoning, Attitudinal Flexibility, and Psychomotor Speed. Conflict related positively to Social Responsibility. Achievement Orientation related positively to Psychomotor Speed, but negatively to Attitudinal Flexibility. Intellectual-Cultural Orientation related positively to Verbal Meaning, Educational Aptitude, Attitudinal Flexibility, Psychomotor Speed, and Social Responsibility. Active-Recreational Orientation related positively to Spatial Orientation. Organization related negatively to the IQ index and Attitudinal Flexibility. Control related positively to Social Responsibility, but negatively to Attitudinal Flexibility.

Family Influences Shared With Siblings

Significant heritabilities were again observed for all primary mental abilities and their composite indices, as well as for Motor-Cognitive Flexibility, Attitudinal Flexibility, and Psychomotor Speed (see table 16.12). Siblings' educational level yielded significant regressions for Spatial Orientation and Inductive Reasoning. Substantial regressions were also found for the shared environment in the family of origin. Cohesion negatively influenced Word Fluency, Intellectual Ability, and Psychomotor Speed. Expressivity related negatively to Verbal Meaning, but positively to Psychomotor Speed. Achievement Orientation related positively to Motor-Cognitive Flexibility and Social Responsibility. Intellectual-Cultural Orientation related positively to Verbal Meaning, Word Fluency, Intellectual Ability, and Motor-Cognitive Flexibility. Active-Recreational Orientation related positively to Number. Organization related negatively to Spatial Orientation and Motor-Cognitive Flexibility. Finally, Control related positively to Spatial Orientation.

TABLE 16.11 Regression Coefficients for Parent-Offspring Study

Predictors	Verbal Meaning	Spatial Orientation	Inductive Reasoning	Number	Word Fluency	IQ	EQ
Parents' ability (heritability)	.149	.176	.239	.180	.256	.229	.191
Parent's education		.156	.134			.117	.118
Parent's perception							
Cohesion							
Expressivity	.088						
Conflict							
Achievement							
Intellectual-Cultural				−.129			
Active-Recreational							
Organization							
Control							
Offspring's perception of family of origin							
Cohesion		.134					
Expressivity	−.213		−.163			−.130	−.217
Conflict				.095	−.146		
Achievement				.090			
Intellectual-Cultural	.141						
Active-Recreational	−.110		.107				
Organization			−.088				
Control	−.131	−.139					−.130
Offspring's perception of current family							
Cohesion		−.134			.115	.126	.168
Expressivity	.154		.110				
Conflict							
Achievement							
Intellectual-Cultural	.099						.119
Active-Recreational							
Organization		−.109					
Control					−.103		

Predictors	Motor-Cognitive Flexibility	Attitudinal Flexibility	Psychomotor Speed	Social Responsibility
Parents' status (heritability)	.112		.204	
Parent's education	.142	.129		
Parent's perception				
Cohesion				
Expressivity				
Conflict				.138
Achievement				
Intellectual-Cultural				
Active-Recreational				
Organization	.112			
Control				
Offspring's perception of family of origin				
Cohesion				.164
Expressivity	−.124		−.106	
Conflict				
Achievement				
Intellectual-Cultural				
Active-Recreational				−.132
Organization				
Control				
Offspring's perception of current family				
Cohesion				
Expressivity		.148	.146	
Conflict				.082
Achievement		−.159	.088	
Intellectual-Cultural		.155	.106	.256
Active-Recreational	.129			
Organization		−.147		
Control		−.128		.113

Note. EQ, Index of Educational Aptitude.

All regression coefficients reported are significant at or beyond the .05 level of confidence.

TABLE 16.12 Regression Coefficients for Sibling Study

Predictors	Verbal Meaning	Spatial Orientation	Inductive Reasoning	Number	Word Fluency	IQ	EQ
Target sibling's ability (heritability)	.209	.163	.295	.122	.230	.218	.269
Sibling's education		.115	.123				
Target sibling's perception							
Cohesion					-.252	-.218	
Expressivity	-.174						
Conflict			-.155				
Achievement							
Intellectual-Cultural	.194				.171	.205	
Active-Recreational				.158			
Organization		-.179					
Control		.265					
Sibling's perception of family of origin							
Cohesion							
Expressivity			-.233			-.148	
Conflict	-.119						-.140
Achievement							
Intellectual-Cultural							
Active-Recreational			.142		.153	.163	
Organization				-.126			
Control							
Sibling's perception of current family							
Cohesion				.190			
Expressivity	.179		.176				.161
Conflict							
Achievement							
Intellectual-Cultural	.180		.139		.125	.125	.211
Active-Recreational	-.206	.139	-.215			-.191	-.227
Organization		-.195					
Control							

Predictors	Motor-Cognitive Flexibility	Attitudinal Flexibility	Psychomotor Speed	Social Responsibility
Target sibling's status (heritability)	.241	.226	.268	
Target sibling's perception				
Cohesion			-.203	
Expressivity			.138	
Conflict	-.150			
Achievement	.224			.159
Intellectual-Cultural			.173	
Active-Recreational				
Organization	-.147			
Control				
Sibling's perception of family of origin				
Cohesion	-.161		-.148	.202
Expressivity				
Conflict				
Achievement				
Intellectual-Cultural				
Active-Recreational			.107	
Organization				
Control				-.113
Sibling's perception of current family				
Cohesion				
Expressivity	.182		.142	
Conflict	-.126			
Achievement	.173		.149	-.166
Intellectual-Cultural				.372
Active-Recreational		.200		
Organization	-.226	-.123		
Control		-.194		

Note. EQ, Index of Educational Aptitude.

All regression coefficients reported are significant at or beyond the .05 level of confidence.

Smaller but significant contributions were provided by the siblings' unique perceptions of the family origin. These include a positive correlation of cohesion with Social Responsibility, but a negative correlation with Motor-Cognitive Flexibility and Psychomotor Speed. There was a negative relation between Expressivity and Inductive Reasoning as well as the Index of Intellectual Ability, Conflict related negatively to Verbal Meaning and the measure of Intellectual Aptitude. Active-Recreational Orientation related positively to Inductive Reasoning, Word Fluency, and Intellectual Aptitude as well as to Psychomotor Speed, and Control related negatively to Social Responsibility.

Significant regressions were also found for the influences of perceptions of the current family environment. Here, Cohesion related positively to Number. Expressivity related positively to Verbal Meaning, Inductive Reasoning, Educational Aptitude, Motor-Cognitive Flexibility, and Psychomotor Speed. Conflict related negatively to Motor-Cognitive Flexibility. Achievement orientation related positively to Motor-Cognitive Flexibility and Psychomotor Speed, but negatively to Social Responsibility. Intellectual-Cultural Orientation related positively to Verbal Meaning, Inductive Reasoning, Word Fluency, the composite indices, Motor-Cognitive Flexibility, and Psychomotor Speed, but negatively to Social Responsibility. Active-Recreational Orientation related positively to Spatial Orientation and Attitudinal Flexibility, but negatively to Verbal Meaning, Inductive Reasoning, and the composite indices. Organization related negatively to Spatial Orientation, Motor-Cognitive Flexibility, and Attitudinal Flexibility. Control related negatively to Attitudinal Flexibility.

Proportions of Individual Differences Accounted for by Familial Influences, Shared Early Environment, Unique Early Environment, and Current Environment

The critical issue in this analysis, of course, is the determination of the extent to which individual differences in cognitive performance in adulthood can be allocated to familial influences (including heritability) and shared early environment and how much is because of the unique influences of early and current family environments.

Parent-Offspring Data   When we disaggregate perceived environmental from static familial influences, we find that the former account for relatively small proportions of variance, ranging from 1.7% for Attitudinal Flexibility to 7.5% for Inductive Reasoning. No such influences can be found for Attitudinal Flexibility and Social Responsibility. Because of the lack of temporal coincidence in the parental ratings for the offspring families of origin, we find only trivial influences for the perceptions of the shared early family environment. Significant, but fairly small, proportions of individual differences in cognition in adulthood are accounted for by the unique offspring perceptions of the family of origin. These range from 1.7% for the Number ability to 9.5% for Verbal Meaning. No effects of the unique early environment are found for Attitudinal Flexibility. Current family environment influences range from 1.2% for Inductive Reasoning to

10.9% for Attitudinal Flexibility. The only dependent variable not significantly affected is the Number ability. Detailed findings are shown in table 16.13.

Sibling Data   We first note that static familial influences range from zero for Social Responsibility and Motor-Cognitive Flexibility to a high of 10.2% for Inductive Reasoning. Contributions of early shared environment range from zero for Attitudinal Flexibility to 9.3% for Attitudinal Flexibility. Perceptions of the unique early environment range from zero for Spatial Orientation and Attitudinal Flexibility to 7.4% for Inductive Reasoning. Current environment influences range from 1.6% for Word Fluency to 16.6% for Social Responsibility.

The total contribution of all family environment sources ranges from a low of 7.7% for Number to a high of 25% for Motor-Cognitive Flexibility. When we consider the joint effect of static familial influences and early shared environment, the proportion of explained individual differences ranges from a low of 2.5% for Social Responsibility to a high of 16% for Psychomotor Speed. For the primary mental abilities, these values are Verbal Meaning 11.2%; Spatial Orientation 14.2%; Number 4%, and Word Fluency 12.6%. Table 16.14 shows the detailed breakdown into the various sources of variance.

Summary of the Analyses of the Impact of Family Environment on Cognition

Given the assumption that individual's perceptions of family environments are reasonable representations of such environments, we find that a significant impact of shared early environment on adult cognitive performance can be demonstrated in sibling but not in parent-offspring dyads. This discrepancy is readily explained by the fact that the parental family perceptions must be measured by inquiring about their current family (which in most cases is the family of origin

TABLE 16.13 Proportion of Variance by Source for Parent-Offspring Study

Variables	Familial	Shared Early Environment	Unique Early Environment	Unique Current Environment
Verbal Meaning	2.2	0.8	9.5	3.4
Spatial Orientation	5.5	—	3.7	3.0
Inductive Reasoning	7.5	—	4.6	1.2
Number	3.2	1.7	1.7	—
Word Fluency	6.6	—	2.1	1.3
IQ	6.6	—	1.7	2.6
EQ	5.0	—	6.4	4.2
Motor-Cognitive Flexibility	3.3	1.3	1.5	1.7
Attitudinal Flexibility	1.7	—	—	10.9
Psychomotor Speed	2.6	—	1.1	4.0
Social Responsibility	—	1.5	4.4	9.2

Note. EQ, Index of Educational Aptitude.

TABLE 16.14 Proportion of Variance by Source for Sibling Study

Variables	Familial	Shared Early Environment	Unique Early Environment	Unique Current Environment
Verbal Meaning	4.4	6.8	1.4	10.7
Spatial Orientation	4.0	10.2	—	5.7
Inductive Reasoning	10.2	2.4	7.4	9.7
Number	1.5	2.5	1.6	3.6
Word Fluency	5.3	9.3	2.3	1.6
IQ	4.8	9.0	4.8	5.2
EQ	7.2	—	2.0	12.2
Motor-Cognitive Flexibility	5.8	9.4	2.6	13.0
Attitudinal Flexibility	5.1	—	—	9.3
Psychomotor Speed	7.2	8.8	3.3	4.2
Social Responsibility	—	2.5	5.4	16.6

Note. EQ, Index of Educational Aptitude.

of the offspring). On the other hand, the siblings' perception of their family of origin involves retrospection to that time interval mostly shared with the target sibling. By contrast, influences of the unique early environment (involving the participant's own retrospection) and current environment yielded significant proportions of variance in adult cognitive performance in both the parent-offspring and sibling samples. Findings from these analyses have been replicated in a master's thesis by Ledermann (2003), utilizing structural equation modeling procedures on a more recent family data set.

Significant differences in both static familial characteristics and shared early environment estimates between same-gender and cross-gender pairs were again noted (also see chapter 13). Although subsamples were too small to provide stable estimates, heritability estimates were generally higher in same-gender pairs; the effect of shared early environment was greater in cross-gender pairs for most (but not all) variables.

What then were the family environment dimensions that were most salient in predicting adult cognitive performance? As far as the early environment was concerned, there was a clear positive effect of a strong intellectual-cultural family orientation. On the other hand, high levels of family cohesion had a negative effect.

High expressivity estimates from the unique perceptions of the early environment also seemed to have negative effects on several cognitive variables; the unique perception of high Active-Recreational Orientation had a positive impact. By contrast, positive influences on cognitive performance and positive cognitive styles of the current family environment involved primarily high levels of Cohesion, Expressivity, and Intellectual-Cultural Orientation coupled with low levels of family organization.

Chapter Summary

This chapter provides information on the similarity of perceptions of family environments of parents and their adult offspring and the similarity in such perceptions of adult siblings reported in adulthood. Perceptions of family environments include the family of origin (i.e., the family setting experienced when study participants lived with their own parents) and with respect to their current family (i.e., their family unit at the time data were collected). These data are then used to compare the impact of heritability and environmental influences on cognitive performance by examining correlations between parent-offspring and sibling dyads to the shared and unique effects of childhood and current family environments.

Different versions of the Moos Family Environment Scale were constructed to assess the perceptions of our study participants with respect to their family of origin and their current family, as well as allowing participants to define their current family as those individuals with whom they interact most closely.

We conclude that there is a clear differentiation for parents, offspring, and siblings in the perceived level of all family dimensions between the family of origin and the current family. The current families not only are seen as more cohesive and expressive, but also are characterized by more conflict than was true for their families of origin. In addition, there is the perception of lower levels of perceived Control, family organization, and Achievement Orientation.

Siblings share a great many perceptions of their family of origin, but not of their current families. But in spite of the lack of similarity of current family perceptions, the best predictor of the current family environment is the corresponding perception of their family of origin.

Evidence supporting the continuity of family values and behaviors is provided by substantial correlations between the parents' description of their current family environment and their offsprings' description of their family of origin. These relationships were strongest for the perceptions of Achievement, Intellectual-Cultural, and Active-Recreational Orientation and for family organization.

Perceived family environment and the magnitude of similarity across generations differ by gender pairing and by dimensions. Strongest relationships are found within mother-daughter and sister-sister pairings. Nevertheless, intensity of contact between parents and offspring has virtually no impact on the similarity of reported family environments.

With respect to the impact of shared early environment on adult cognitive performance, we demonstrate such a relationship in sibling, but not in parent-offspring, dyads. Significant differences in both static familial characteristics and shared early environment estimates between same-gender and cross-gender pairs are also noted. Heritability estimates are generally higher in same-gender pairs; the effect of shared early environment is greater in cross-gender pairs for most variables.

The family environment dimensions most salient in predicting adult cognitive performance are as follows: Shared perceptions of the early environment revealed a positive effect of a strong Intellectual-Cultural family orientation, but a negative effect of high family Cohesion. On the other hand, unique perceptions of the early environment implicated positive effects of an Active-Recreational Orientation; high Expressivity seemed to have negative effects on several cognitive variables. Current family environments that had positive influences on cognitive performance and cognitive styles were characterized by high levels of Cohesion, Expressivity, and Intellectual Cultural Orientation as well as low levels of family organization.

CHAPTER SEVENTEEN

The Role of Longitudinal Studies
in the Early Detection
of Dementia

ALTHOUGH THE Seattle Longitudinal Study (SLS) was designed to focus on cognitive changes in normal community-dwelling populations, it is inevitable that a prospective study of aging will eventually include in its successive follow-up cycles individuals who are beginning to show cognitive impairment and eventually may develop full-blown symptoms of dementia. The early detection of excess risk for the eventual development of dementia may have significant value in planning the deployment of prophylactic pharmaceutical and behavioral interventions as such techniques are beginning to emerge from the laboratory.

As an ever-larger proportion of our study participants is entering the age range at which some incidence of cognitive impairment is to be expected, we have begun to focus more directly on this issue by including an added battery of neuropsychological measures that has been administered since 1997 to most of our study participants 60 years of age or older (cf. chapter 3). To monitor the early stages of cognitive impairment, this battery is administered in 3-year intervals. We have also obtained blood samples from our older study participants that are genotyped to determine the participants' apolipoprotein E (ApoE) genotypes to study possible excess rates of age change for individuals who bear one or both of the high-risk alleles.

Finally, we have studied the projection of standard neuropsychological assessment measures conventionally used by clinicians into the primary mental ability space by means of extension analysis (cf. chapter 2). This allows us to postdict estimated scores of the neuropsychological measures at earlier points in time and thus conduct longitudinal analyses to determine how far back we could have predicted risk for cognitive impairment.

In this chapter, we first provide some initial results of our work with the ApoE genetic marker of dementia as it relates to cognitive decline. We then describe our studies involving the neuropsychological assessment of a community-dwelling sample of older adults who have not previously been identified as suffering from cognitive impairment. Preliminary results are also given for a 3-year follow-up assessment. We then describe the extension analyses that link the clinical measures with our psychometric battery for the study of normal aging. Finally, we report analyses of studies that obtain postdicted estimates of earlier performance on the neuropsychological measures and speak to the possibility of early detection of risk for cognitive impairment.

Genetic Markers of Dementia

Background

There have been a number of interesting findings by geneticists regarding the relation of ApoE allele combinations to the likelihood of occurrence and the time of onset of Alzheimer's disease. There are six possible ApoE genotypes, commonly referred to as $\varepsilon_{2/2}$, $\varepsilon_{2/3}$, $\varepsilon_{2/4}$, $\varepsilon_{3/3}$, $\varepsilon_{3/4}$, and $\varepsilon_{4/4}$. The most common genotype is the $\varepsilon_{3/3}$ combination (Poduslo & Yin, 2001; Saunders, 2000).

Specifically, the presence of the ε_4 allele has been linked to the disease in a dose-dependent manner. That is, there may be some predictive power for a single ε_4 allele, but high predictive power for the presence of the double ε_4 allele (cf. Saunders et al., 1993). Moreover, a meta-analysis across a large number of ApoE studies found significant associations between the ApoE ε_4 allele and Alzheimer's disease in white, African American, Hispanic, and Chinese subpopulations in the United States (Farrer et al., 1997). In addition, presence of the ε_2 allele has been linked to lower low-density lipoprotein (LDL) cholesterol levels as well as lower total/high-density lipoprotein (HDL) cholesterol ratios; the latter may in turn be related to health outcomes that influence the severity of age-related decline and possibly the likelihood of an eventual diagnosis of dementia.

The *ApoE* Gene and Cognitive Decline

In this section, I report results of some preliminary analyses of a subsample from the SLS for whom we obtained ApoE genotypes and for whom we have at least 7-year longitudinal cognitive data. The analyses were to determine whether there is differential age-related decline in cognitive abilities that depends on membership in a given allele combination (Kennet, Revell, & Schaie, 1999; Kennet & Schaie, 1998).

Participants ApoE genotypes were determined for 678 SLS participants (44.2% male, 55.8% female) who at their last cognitive test in 1998 averaged 68.5 years of age and for whom $\varepsilon_{2/2} = 4$ (0.59%), $\varepsilon_{2/3} = 91$ (13.42%), $\varepsilon_{2/4} = 20$ (2.95%), $\varepsilon_{3/3} = 397$ (58.55%), $\varepsilon_{3/4} = 149$ (21.98%), and $\varepsilon_{4/4} = 17$ (2.51%). These frequencies are roughly comparable to those reported in other studies of European and North American populations (cf. Parasuraman, Greenwood, & Sunderland, 2002).

Measures   Dependent variables in these analyses were the six mental ability factor scores of Inductive Reasoning, Spatial Orientation, Numeric Facility, Verbal Ability, and Verbal Memory (see chapter 3).

Analyses   Data were analyzed by analyses of covariance (ANCOVAs), controlling for participant age, to examine the effect of ApoE allele combinations. ApoE combination is treated as a categorical variable (the $\varepsilon_{2/2}$ combination was omitted because of its low frequency of occurrence in our sample).

Results   The ANCOVA yielded a significant overall effect for differences among allele combinations [Rao's R $(df = 30, 2,666) = 1.55$, $p < .03$]. Univariate follow-ups resulted in significant allele combination differences for the Inductive Reasoning and Verbal Memory factors ($p < .01$). There were no significant gender or Gender × Allele combination effects. Age differences among allele combinations were significant, but only for the $\varepsilon_{4/4}$ combination as compared to all others. Seven-year declines in the cognitive factor scores are shown in table 17.1. Greatest decline was shown for both Inductive Reasoning and Verbal memory by the $\varepsilon_{2/4}$ combination; least decline was observed for the $\varepsilon_{2/3}$ combination. On average, there was also a trend for greater decline for the combined group of individuals with at least one ε_4 allele.

Neuropsychological Assessment of Dementia in a Community-Dwelling Sample

Background

Specific measurement systems that are utilized to assess cognitive status, cognitive change across age, and the detection of cognitive deficits differ markedly depending on whether the investigators' interest is focused on the study of normal aging or on the detection and diagnostic definition of neuropathology.

TABLE 17.1 Cognitive Decline Over 7 Years in T Scores by Apolipoprotein E Allele Combination

	Allele Combination				
Cognitive Factor	$\varepsilon_{2/3}$ ($n = 91$)	$\varepsilon_{3/3}$ ($n = 397$)	$\varepsilon_{2/4}$ ($n = 20$)	$\varepsilon_{3/4}$ ($n = 149$)	$\varepsilon_{4/4}$ ($n = 17$)
Inductive Reasoning	−1.12	−1.74	−4.60***	−1.72	−1.65
Spatial Orientation	−1.93	−1.43	−2.35*	−1.11	0.47
Verbal Ability	−0.11	−0.38	−0.10	−0.38	0.18
Numeric Facility	−1.91	−2.02*	−3.70***	−1.75	−1.00
Perceptual Speed	−2.30*	−2.19*	−4.05***	−1.87	−2.12*
Verbal Memory	−0.65	−1.86	−6.25***	−2.08*	−3.88***

*$p < .051$. ***$p < .001$.

To study normal aging, it has generally been necessary to construct assessment batteries suitable for measurement across the entire adult life span, hence requiring stimulus material across a wide range of difficulty. Measures typically used . for this purpose come from derivatives of L. L. Thurstone's (1938) work on defining primary mental abilities for the detailed study of normal intelligence (e.g., Ekstrom et al., 1976; Horn, 1982; Schaie, 1985) or from the various forms of the Wechsler-Bellevue scales and derivatives (Kaufman, Kaufman, McLean, & Reynolds, 1991; Matarazzo, 1972).

Measures used by neuropsychologists (with the exception of the Wechsler scales, for which use overlaps both camps), however, are typically designed to have relatively low ceilings and bottoms because they are used to chart deficit from the point in time when it was first noticed to the end point of death or total inability to respond to psychological measures. A neuropsychological battery commonly used in North America for the diagnosis of dementia was developed by the Consortium to Establish a Registry for Alzheimer's Disease (CERAD) (Morris et al., 1989, 1993; Welsh et al., 1994).

In this section, I report findings from a subsample of community-dwelling participants in the SLS to whom we administered the CERAD battery. In the following sections, I then report the projection of this battery developed for the detection of dementia into the normal mental ability factor space. Regression equations are then provided that allow postdiction of indicators of possible risk of dementia by considering study participants' longitudinal psychometric data at an age when neuropsychological assessment would not have been feasible or productive. The effectiveness of utilizing the longitudinal psychometric data and the longitudinal change on the estimated neuropsychological data are then evaluated against the criterion of dementia ratings made by neuropsychologists (also see Schaie, Caskie, et al., 2004).

Methods

Participants   The subsample consisted of 499 adults (211 men, 288 women) who were part of the SLS seventh wave data collection in 1997–1998 and who ranged in age from 60 to 97 years ($M = 73.07$; $SD = 8.30$) at the time of their neuropsychological assessment. For the age/cohort group comparisons, we subdivided the sample into a young-old group (age range 60–69 years, $n = 180$; 73 males, 107 females; $M = 64.23$; $SD = 3.54$), an old-old group (age range 70–79 years, $n = 205$; 90 males, 115 females; $M = 74.61$; $SD = 2.85$), and a very old group (age range 80–95 years, $n = 114$; 48 males, 66 females; $M = 84.26$; $SD = 3.76$). Educational levels of the sample ranged from 7 to 20 years ($M = 15.04$; $SD = 2.77$). Participants were included in the neuropsychology studies only if they had been tested on the Primary Mental Abilities (PMA) battery on at least one previous occasion (7 years earlier).

Measures   The variables included in the following analysis were the 20 subtests and 6 factor scores of the SLS cognitive battery, the CERAD battery, selected tests from the Wechsler Adult Intelligence Scale–Revised (WAIS-R) and the Wechsler Memory Scale–Revised (WMS-R), and some other commonly used neuropsychological assessment instruments (see chapter 3 for descriptions of the individual measures).

Neuropsychologist Ratings   Because the SLS studies community-dwelling samples, no psychiatric examinations or clinical dementia ratings were available. Instead, we relied on a research protocol involving a two-step procedure for rating of neuropsychological functional status. First, participants were evaluated against a screening algorithm to determine whether there were characteristics that might result in a rating of cognitive impairment in a neuropsychological case conference. The screening algorithm utilized cutoff scores based on previous research on the association of cutoff criteria and cognitive dysfunction (Crum et al., 1993; LaRue, 1992; Spreen & Strauss, 1991). The cutoff criteria for the selected tests were as follows:

1. Mini-Mental State Examination (MMSE) score below 27
2. Mattis Dementia Rating Scale score below 130
3. Trail B score time longer than 180 seconds
4. An age-adjusted scaled score less than 7 for any of the following: WAIS-R Vocabulary, WAIS-R Comprehension, WAIS-R Block Design, and WAIS-R Digit Symbol

As a second step, those records that met the algorithm's screening criteria were then examined in greater detail by two neuropsychology consultants. In the consensus conferences, scores on the neuropsychological tests and tester's report of observed sensory limitations and current or previous health problems were considered. Participants received one of the following ratings:

1. The participant is normal.
2. The participant is not demented at this time, but has one or more characteristics that suggest further monitoring is indicated.
3. The participant is probably demented.
4. The participant is definitely demented.

The neuropsychological ratings identified 354 participants (70.9%) as normal, 111 participants (22.2%) who required monitoring, 22 participants (4.4%) who were probably demented, and 12 (2.4%) who were definitely demented. There were no significant gender differences in the proportions of individuals assigned to the different rating classifications. As expected, there were significant age differences between rating groups. The group requiring monitoring was approximately 4 years older than those in the normal group, and those in the demented categories were 8 years older than the those in the normal group. There were no educational differences between the normal and demented groups, but the "monitor" group had approximately 1 year less education on average than both the normal and demented groups. Mean Center for Epidemologic Studies–Depression Scale (CES-D) scores for the four groups were 7.26, 8.92, 11.41, and 12.02, respectively in order of declining function. Reported mean instrumental activities of daily living (IADL) complaints were 0.83, 1.01, 2.05, and 3.00, respectively in order of declining function.

Analysis Plan   The data analysis plan involved first the confirmation of the factor structure for the PMA measures. Second, an extension analysis was conducted to determine the relation of the neuropsychology measures to the primary mental abilities. Third, the regressions of the primary mental abilities on the neuropsychology measures were used to estimate neuropsychology measures for prior SLS occasions. Fourth, change scores for the primary mental abilities and the estimated neuropsychology scores were computed from 1984 to 1991 and from 1991 to 1994, and participants were classified as to whether they had experienced reliable decline or not.

Transformations   For ease of comparisons, all raw data were transformed to *T* scores with a mean of 50 and a standard deviation of 10. Four neuropsychological variables with skewness greater than 2.00 were normalized using a McCall transformation (Garrett, 1966). The normalized variables were Fuld Retrieval, the MMSE, Mattis grand total, and Trails A. Also, values above 300 seconds on Trails B were trimmed to a value of 300 before *T*-score transformation.

Descriptive Data

An analysis of variance of the neuropsychology measures determined that there were statistically significant overall differences for gender, age group, and the Age × Gender interaction ($p < .001$). Univariate follow-up analyses showed significant age group difference for all 17 variables. As expected, higher scores were consistently observed for the young-old as compared to the two older groups and for the old-old compared to the very old. Gender differences were significant at or beyond the 1% level of confidence for the Fuld Retrieval test, the Fuld Rapid Verbal Retrieval test, the Word List Recall, and the Mattis total score; all differences favored women. Age × Gender interactions were significant for the WAIS-R Vocabulary test and the Mattis total score. For both variables, there were significant age group differences for the men, but not for the women.

Descriptive data for the CERAD variables included in this study are provided in table 17.2. Because information on a community-dwelling sample on this extensive database may be of broader interest, means and standard deviations are reported in raw score form by gender and age/cohort group as well as for the total sample. The intercorrelations among the 17 primary mental ability measures and the 17 neuropsychology measures are provided in the appendix (table A-17.1).

Stability and Change Over Three Years

We have completed a 3-year follow-up of the original administration of the neuropsychological test battery and provide here a preliminary report on the retest stability of the battery as well as information on average change over 3 years.

Participants   The 3-year follow-up sample consisted of 286 adults (114 men, 172 women) who were part of the SLS seventh wave data collection in 1997–1998 and who ranged in age from 60 to 98 years ($M = 74.30$; $SD = 7.94$) at the time of their neuropsychological assessment. For the age/cohort group comparisons, we subdivided the sample into a young-old group (age range 60–69 years, $n = 86$; 34 males, 52 females; $M = 64.84$; $SD = 2.51$), an old-old group (age range 70–79 years, $n = 120$; 49 males, 71 females; $M = 74.63$; $SD = 2.89$); and a very old group (age range 80–98 years, $n = 80$; 31 males, 49 females; $M = 83.96$; $SD = 3.98$). Educational level of the sample ranged from 8 to 20 years ($M = 15.21$; $SD = 2.75$).

Procedures   All follow-up participants were assessed within 1 month of the third anniversary of their original test administration. Testing was conducted in the participants' homes in the same manner as for the original test administration.

Retest Stability   The 3-year stability of the neuropsychology battery ranged from modest to quite satisfactory, although it was generally lower than the retest stabilities reported for the SLS cognitive abilities battery. Stability coefficients ranged from a low of .481 for the Mattis total score to a high of .883 for the WAIS Digit Symbol test. Stability coefficients for all 17 measures are provided in table 17.3.

Three-Year Changes in Performance Level   A 2 (gender) × 3 (age/cohort level) multivariate analysis of variance was conducted for the follow-up data set. Significant main effects were found for age group, gender, and test occasions as well as for the Age Group × Occasion interaction (Rao's $R < .001$). However, the Age Group × Gender, Occasion × Gender, and the triple interaction were not statistically significant. It is therefore the Age Group × Occasion interaction that is of particular interest because it reflects age/cohort differences in change over time. Table 17.3 provides information from the univariate follow-up tests to indicate average changes in raw score units over the 3-year interval. The univariate effects indicated significant change over time for all of the WAIS subtests, Trails B, the Mattis, and Verbal Recall. Differential change by age level was significant at or below the 5% level of confidence for all neuropsychology measures except for the Mattis, WAIS Block Design, Verbal Fluency, and Word Recall measures. Table 17.3 provides the raw score differences for the total sample and by age group.

In summary, the neuropsychology battery had moderate-to-good stability over 3 years. Significant age changes were in a positive direction for the young-old. For the old-old, there were still some positive changes (Word List Recall, WAIS Vocabulary, WAIS Comprehension, Mattis total), but significant negative changes were found for the WAIS Digit Symbol test. Even the very old gained on the WAIS Vocabulary and Comprehension test, but declined significantly on Boston Naming, WAIS Digit Symbol, Trails B, Fuld Retrieval, and Fuld Verbal Retrieval tests.

Projecting the CERAD Battery Into the Primary Mental Abilities Construct Space

An important application of confirmatory factor analysis, as described in chapter 2, is the method of extension analysis (Dwyer, 1937; Tucker, 1971).

TABLE 17.2 Raw Score Means and Standard Deviations for the Neuropsychology Battery

Variable	Young-Old Age			Old-Old Age			Very Old Age			Total		
	Males	Females	Total	Males	Females	Total	Males	Females	Total	Males	Females	Total
CERAD												
Boston Naming	14.64	14.53	14.58	14.30	14.30	14.30	13.83	13.41	13.59	14.31	14.18	14.24
	(0.63)	(0.70)	(0.68)	(1.01)	(0.91)	(0.95)	(1.52)	(1.48)	(1.50)	(1.09)	(1.09)	(1.09)
MMSE	28.62	28.87	28.77	27.82	28.50	28.20	27.40	27.61	27.52	28.00	28.43	28.25
	(1.46)	(1.43)	(1.45)	(2.94)	(1.65)	(2.33)	(2.56)	(2.37)	(2.44)	(2.47)	(1.83)	(2.13)
Praxis (Delayed)	8.76	8.49	8.60	8.08	7.51	7.76	6.08	6.02	6.04	7.86	7.54	7.67
	(1.98)	(2.28)	(2.16)	(2.23)	(2.73)	(2.53)	(3.50)	(2.93)	(3.17)	(2.69)	(2.78)	(2.74)
Verbal Fluency	21.47	21.19	21.30	18.11	18.67	18.42	17.17	16.61	16.84	19.06	19.13	19.10
	(5.83)	(5.03)	(5.35)	(4.90)	(4.84)	(4.86)	(6.16)	(4.85)	(5.42)	(5.79)	(5.21)	(5.45)
Word List (Recall)	7.62	8.47	8.12	6.49	7.37	6.99	5.65	6.66	6.23	6.69	7.62	7.23
	(1.81)	(1.79)	(1.84)	(2.10)	(1.95)	(2.06)	(2.50)	(2.42)	(2.49)	(2.22)	(2.13)	(2.21)
WAIS-R												
Digit Span	16.01	16.23	16.14	15.53	14.66	15.04	13.92	14.83	14.45	15.33	15.28	15.30
	(3.69)	(4.31)	(4.06)	(4.48)	(3.40)	(3.93)	(3.89)	(3.90)	(3.91)	(4.15)	(3.93)	(4.02)
Vocabulary	58.15	54.57	56.02	53.84	55.19	54.60	50.67	53.67	52.40	54.61	54.61	54.61
	(6.98)	(8.52)	(8.10)	(8.83)	(9.03)	(8.95)	(13.11)	(9.18)	(11.05)	(9.82)	(8.86)	(9.27)
Comphrension	24.42	22.43	23.24	23.42	22.90	23.12	21.54	22.29	21.97	23.34	22.58	22.90
	(3.73)	(4.61)	(4.37)	(4.50)	(4.52)	(4.51)	(5.00)	(4.80)	(4.87)	(4.48)	(4.61)	(4.57)
Block Design	32.14	29.37	30.49	27.08	25.01	25.91	19.60	19.85	19.75	27.13	25.45	26.16
	(8.30)	(8.91)	(8.75)	(8.78)	(7.90)	(8.34)	(8.07)	(7.88)	(7.92)	(9.62)	(9.01)	(9.30)
Digit Symbol	49.85	50.51	50.24	41.57	42.29	41.98	32.02	35.80	34.19	42.27	43.88	43.20
	(9.65)	(10.46)	(10.12)	(8.65)	(9.90)	(9.36)	(10.77)	(9.75)	(10.32)	(11.58)	(11.54)	(11.57)

Other Neuropsychology Measures

Measure												
WMS-R Immediate	28.82	29.15	29.02	24.31	26.12	25.33	22.52	23.82	23.33	25.47	26.74	26.21
	(6.64)	(6.90)	(6.78)	(7.69)	(6.80)	(7.24)	(8.60)	(7.90)	(8.20)	(7.95)	(7.36)	(7.63)
WMS-R Delayed	24.66	23.97	24.25	18.21	20.83	19.68	16.17	17.79	17.11	19.99	21.30	20.74
	(8.31)	(7.78)	(7.99)	(8.39)	(7.94)	(8.22)	(9.87)	(9.05)	(9.40)	(9.36)	(8.46)	(8.87)
Trails A	35.32	35.48	35.41	45.39	42.08	43.52	61.90	54.35	57.56	45.66	42.40	43.78
	(15.63)	(15.42)	(15.46)	(17.82)	(14.28)	(15.97)	(40.21)	(22.24)	(31.23)	(26.07)	(18.18)	(21.90)
Trails B	80.00	87.76	84.61	109.05	106.43	107.56	158.23	147.72	152.17	109.97	108.68	109.22
	(29.36)	(46.70)	(40.65)	(52.83)	(45.61)	(48.76)	(71.12)	(69.12)	(69.84)	(58.68)	(56.64)	(57.45)
Fuld Retrieval	44.34	46.21	45.45	42.38	43.33	42.92	37.45	39.34	38.82	41.94	43.63	42.91
	(4.02)	(2.71)	(3.42)	(4.96)	(4.47)	(4.70)	(10.41)	(8.35)	(9.32)	(6.85)	(5.65)	(6.24)
Fuld Rapid Verbal Retrieval	65.42	74.10	70.58	59.21	66.75	63.46	51.79	60.20	56.60	59.68	68.04	64.50
	(10.58)	(13.08)	(12.83)	(11.24)	(11.62)	(12.02)	(15.83)	(11.64)	(14.16)	(13.19)	(13.26)	(13.85)
Mattis Total	139.27	139.55	139.44	136.19	138.83	137.67	131.58	136.42	134.39	136.21	138.55	137.56
	(4.51)	(3.99)	(4.24)	(12.01)	(4.39)	(8.68)	(10.63)	(5.38)	(8.33)	(10.09)	(4.64)	(7.53)

Note. CERAD, Consortium to Establish a Registry for Alzheimer's Disease; MMSE, Mini-Mental State Examination; WAIS-R, Wechsler Adult Intelligence Scale–Revised; WMS-R, Wechsler Memory Scale–Revised.

TABLE 17.3 Average Raw Score Change Over Three Years for the Neuropsychology Battery

Variable	Young-Old Age (n = 86)	Old-Old Age (n = 120)	Very Old Age (n = 80)	Total (n = 286)	Retest Stability
CERAD					
Boston Naming	0.01	0.12	−0.33**	−0.06	.593
MMSE	0.29	0.17	−0.43	0.00	.523
Praxis (Delayed)	0.78*	−0.27	0.18	0.23	.502
Verbal Fluency	0.08	0.17	−1.31	−0.34	.602
Word List (Recall)	0.25	0.76***	0.27	0.58***	.565
WAIS-R					
Digit Span	1.38***	0.31	0.71	1.21***	.737
Vocabulary	6.46***	6.72***	4.71***	5.86***	.766
Comprehension	5.21***	3.80***	3.96***	4.35***	.511
Block Design	1.90*	1.56	1.46	1.58***	.749
Digit Symbol	0.12	−1.86***	−2.85***	−1.53***	.883
Other Neuropsychology Measures					
WMS-R Immediate	0.07	0.93	−1.63	−0.25	.701
WMS-R Delayed	0.10	0.78	−1.71	−0.27	.753
Trails A[a]	−6.47**	−1.90	2.51	−1.95	.584
Trails B[a]	−3.71	7.13	21.86***	8.43**	.627
Fuld Retrieval	0.47	0.10	−2.01**	−0.48	.708
Fuld Rapid Verbal Retrieval	2.25	−0.14	−3.62**	−0.49	.746
Mattis Total	2.10***	2.06***	0.53	1.60***	.481

Note. CERAD, Consortium to Establish a Registry for Alzheimer's Disease; MMSE, Mini-Mental State Examination; WAIS-R, Wechsler Adult Intelligence Scale–Revised; WMS-R, Wechsler Memory Scale–Revised.
[a]The Trails test is scored in seconds; a positive score needs to be interpreted as an adverse change.
*$p < .05$. **$p < .01$. ***$p < .001$. Positive values reflect gain over time. All stability coefficients are significant ($p < .001$).

To conduct an optimal extension analysis, it is necessary to have a sample for whom data are concurrently available both on a set of measures with dimensionality (i.e., latent constructs) that has been well established and on the other measures with relation to these constructs that is to be studied. For our purposes, we began with the psychometric abilities battery that has been employed in the SLS since 1983. We then added the CERAD as well as other neuropsychological measures we wished to relate to the psychometric ability dimensions.

Redetermination of the Primary Mental Ability Factor Structure

The fit of the six-factor structure for the 20 primary mental ability tests employed in the SLS (Schaie et al., 1991) was assessed for the subsample used in the following analyses. All factor models were estimated using the full information maximum likelihood procedure implemented in Amos 4.0 (Arbuckle & Wothke, 1999). This procedure estimates the model parameters from the raw data matrix rather than from a covariance or correlation matrix.

It was necessary to remove the Perceptual Speed factor and related observed measures from these analyses because of the speeded nature of all other tests included to avoid pulling off excessive individual difference variances on the speed factor. The PMA battery minus the three perceptual speed tests was therefore recomputed for the remaining 17 variables and five factors based on the sample used in the present study. The fit for the reduced five-factor solution was $\chi^2(df = 108, N = 499) = 536.08$, $p < .001$, $CFI = .99$, $RMSEA = .09$, $TLI = .98$. Standardized factor loadings were significant for all salient values reported by Schaie et al. (1991).

Extension Analyses for the Neuropsychology Measures

In the extension analysis, factor loadings were constrained to the unstandardized values from the confirmatory factor analysis solution for the cognitive variables for this sample. Factor loadings for the neuropsychological measures were then freely estimated providing information on the projection of these measures into the previously established five-factor cognitive factor structure. Because multiple scores from several of the neuropsychology tests were used, three residual covariances were estimated: Trails A with Trails B, Fuld Retrieval with Fuld Rapid Verbal Retrieval, and WMS-R Immediate with WMS-R Delayed. Factor variances for the five latent cognitive factors were fixed to unity. Error variances for the 34 observed variables were freely estimated.

The neuropsychological assessment measures, when extended into the psychometric abilities factor structure, as might be expected, generally spread over two or more of the psychometric ability domains (see table 17.4). All measures, except for the WAIS-R Digit Span, Vocabulary, Comprehension, and Block Design scales, had significant loadings on the Verbal Memory factor. Of the last scales, Digit Span, Vocabulary, and Comprehension had their largest extensions into the Verbal Comprehension factor; Block Design extended most prominently into the Spatial Ability factor.

Most measures also had a secondary loading on the Spatial Ability factor, except for the Wechsler Memory Immediate Recall, the WAIS-R Digit Span scale, and the MMSE. Several measures also had secondary and/or tertiary loadings on the Inductive Reasoning and Numeric Ability factors. The negative loadings found for Trails were expected because, for that measure, a large score (time to completion) is in the unfavorable direction.

The Postdiction of Neuropsychology Measures From the Primary Mental Ability Scores

To determine risk for the occurrence of dementia in old age prior to the occurrence of clinically diagnosable symptoms, it is necessary to find a way of estimating what the study participants' scores would have been at earlier ages if these tests could have been administered. This requires an exercise in postdiction.

TABLE 17.4 Standardized Loadings of Neuropsychological Tests on Cognitive Factors Allowing Correlated Errors for Subtests of Fuld, WMS-R, and Trails

Neuropsychology Test	Reasoning	Spatial	Verbal	Number	Memory
Boston Naming Test—CERAD	−.11	.41***	.29***	−.16**	.11*
Fuld Retrieval[a]	−.05	.28***	−.01	−.02	.58***
Fuld Rapid Verbal Retrieval	.00	.16**	.25***	.09*	.37***
Mattis Grand Total[a,b]	−.04	.21***	.34***	.03	.29***
WMS-R Immediate Total	.13	.11	.33***	−.19***	.33***
WMS-R Delayed Total	.02	.17**	.26***	−.15**	.47***
WAIS-R Digit Span	.30***	−.10	.31***	.11*	−.05
WAIS-R Vocabulary	−.16**	.13**	.93***	−.08*	.04
WAIS-R Comprehension	−.22**	.22***	.74***	−.11*	.08
WAIS-R Block Design	.17*	.50***	.13**	−.02	.06
WAIS-R Digit Symbol	.19**	.37***	−.11**	.25***	.23***
MMSE[a]	.13	.00	.19***	.15**	.30***
Verbal Fluency	−.10	.24***	.41***	−.07	.24***
Word List Recall	−.20**	.20***	.07	−.06	.71***
Praxis Delayed Total	−.03	.42***	.10*	−.09	.31***
Trails A[a]	−.10	−.41***	.07	−.07	−.18***
Trails B[c]	−.23**	−.34***	.02	−.15***	−.17***

Note. CERAD, Consortium to Establish a Registry for Alzheimer's Disease; MMSE, Mini-Mental State Examination; WAIS-R, Wechsler Adult Intelligence Scale–Revised; WMS-R, Wechsler Memory Scale–Revised.
[a]Normalized with McCall transformation. [b]Extreme low values trimmed to 102. [c]Extreme high values trimmed to 300.
*p < .05. **p < .01. ***p < .001.

Estimation Procedures

We first estimated T scores on the neuropsychology measures from the PMA factor scores for the concurrent occasion using factor weights obtained by orthonormal transformation of the values in table 17.4. We then obtained information on the relation between the estimated and the actually observed T scores. Table 17.5 reports the correlations between the observed and estimated neuropsychology test scores as well as the multiple correlations between the concurrent PMA tests and the neuropsychology tests, both with and without including age and education as predictors. As can be seen, the values from the extension analyses are somewhat more conservative because they attenuate for error of measurement.

We conclude that we can validly estimate scores on the neuropsychology tests from scores on the five PMA factors on the basis of the following considerations: First, all correlations between estimated and observed neuropsychology scores are significant at the .001 confidence level. Second, the correlations between the observed and estimated correlations for the neuropsychology measures approach the reliable variance of the tests (see chapter 3). Third, the correlations between observed and estimated scores are also within the first decimal for alternate ordinary least squares (OLS) regression estimates for most measures. However, the extension analysis-derived estimates are preferred because they adjust for error of measurement (Tucker, 1971). Hence, it seemed reasonable to attempt backward

TABLE 17.5 Concurrent Prediction of Neuropsychology Tests From the Primary Mental Ability Factors, Ordinary Least Squares (OLS) Regression, and Extension Analyses

Neuropsychology Test	Mulple Rs From OLS Regression	Multiple Rs From OLS Regression Including Age and Education	Correlation of Estimated Scores From Extension Analysis
Boston Naming Test—CERAD	.406	.452	.363
Fuld Retrieval	.594	.615	.584
Fuld Rapid Verbal Retrieval	.595	.600	.574
Mattis Grand Total	.570	.511	.542
WMS-R Immediate Total	.573	.578	.526
WMS-R Delayed Total	.604	.611	.578
WAIS-R Digit Span	.483	.489	.461
WAIS-R Vocabulary	.752	.765	.746
WAIS-R Comprehension	.538	.562	.532
WAIS-R Block Design	.678	.703	.639
WAIS-R Digit Symbol	.731	.819	.708
MMSE	.580	.586	.550
Verbal Fluency	.519	.566	.499
Word List Recall	.612	.626	.607
Praxis Delayed Total	.516	.521	.501
Trails A	.558	.569	.512
Trails B	.680	.704	.664

Note. CERAD, Consortium to Establish a Registry for Alzheimer's Disease; MMSE, Mini-Mental State Examination; WAIS-R, Wechsler Adult Intelligence Scale–Revised; WMS-R, Wechsler Memory Scale–Revised.

All values are statistically significant, $p < .001$.

prediction (postdiction) to estimate what our participants' earlier scores on the neuropsychology battery might have been if we had had the opportunity to measure them 7 and 14 years earlier.

We next used the factor weights from the extension analyses to estimate (postdict) T scores for the neuropsychology tests for our data collections that occurred 7 (1991) and 14 years (1984) prior to the direct measurement on the neuropsychology tests.

Decline in Neuropsychology Measures by Age Group

Mean values by age group (young-old, old-old, very old) are provided in table 17.6 for the three estimated data points. Age declines significant at the .01 level of confidence are observed in the young-old group over a 14-year interval (1984–1998) for all measures except the Mattis. However, significant decline on the WAIS-R Vocabulary scale is observed only over the second 7-year interval, from 1991 to 1998.

In the old-old group, significant change over 7 years from 1984 to 1991 is found for WAIS-R Digit Symbol, Praxis Delayed Total, Trails A, and Trails B.

TABLE 17.6 Predicted Neuropsychology Test Score Means for 1984, 1991, and 1998 by Age Group

Neuropsychology Test	Young-Old			Old-Old			Very Old		
	1984	1991	1998	1984	1991	1998	1984	1991	1998
Boston Naming Test	60.03	59.59	55.49^{a,b}	56.99	55.74	50.73^{a,b}	52.50	49.91^a	43.52^{a,b}
Fuld Retrieval	58.22	59.84	54.83^{a,b}	55.53	54.57	49.70^{a,b}	53.27	51.31	44.63^{a,b}
Fuld Rapid Verbal Retrieval	57.36	58.76	54.18^{a,b}	55.42	54.57	49.94^{a,b}	53.11	51.43	44.96^{a,b}
Mattis Grand Total	53.19	54.16	54.31	51.72	51.09	50.52	49.25	47.67	45.02^{a,b}
WMS-R Immediate Total	56.94	58.03	53.80^{a,b}	55.63	54.81	50.30^{a,b}	53.08	51.49	45.06^{a,b}
WMS-R Delayed Total	57.41	58.84	54.21^{a,b}	55.46	54.60	49.84^{a,b}	53.24	51.54	45.04^{a,b}
WAIS-R Digit Span	57.67	57.72	54.20^{a,b}	55.52	55.16	50.52^{a,b}	51.18	50.21	44.86^{a,b}
WAIS-R Vocabulary	52.64	52.95	51.42^b	53.09	53.27	50.98^{a,b}	51.36	51.09	47.44^{a,b}
WAIS-R Comprehension	53.82	54.21	52.19^{a,b}	53.78	53.78	50.93^{a,b}	51.55	50.94	46.78^{a,b}
WAIS-R Block Design	61.50	60.90	56.52^{a,b}	57.22	55.89	50.65^{a,b}	52.62	49.50^a	43.31^{a,b}
WAIS-R Digit Symbol	61.59	61.63	56.31^{a,b}	58.22	56.53^a	50.57^{a,b}	53.58	50.35^a	43.12^{a,b}
MMSE	57.56	58.88	54.21^{a,b}	55.71	54.85	49.90^{a,b}	53.22	51.48	45.00^{a,b}
Verbal Fluency	56.52	57.14	53.77^{a,b}	55.24	54.78	50.70^{a,b}	52.43	51.02	45.24^{a,b}
Word List Recall	57.73	59.43	54.55^{a,b}	55.20	54.31	49.54^{a,b}	53.08	51.33	45.05^{a,b}
Praxis Delayed Total	61.29	61.70	56.35^{a,b}	57.50	55.95^a	50.33^{a,b}	53.45	50.34^a	43.09^{a,b}
Trails A	61.94	61.66	56.69^{a,b}	57.64	56.14^a	50.53^{a,b}	53.08	50.00^a	43.04^{a,b}
Trails B	62.07	61.88	56.72^{a,b}	57.87	56.31^a	50.37^{a,b}	52.77	49.69^a	42.71^{a,b}

Note. All values are in *T*-score units scaled on the total 1998 sample (mean = 50, SD = 10). MMSE, Mini-Mental State Examination; WAIS-R, Wechsler Adult Intelligence Scale–Revised; WMS-R, Wechsler Memory Scale–Revised. [a]Significant decline in performance from baseline (1984 score) at .01 level of confidence. [b]Significant decline from 1991 performance.

Significant 14-year changes (1984–1998) occur for all measures accept the Mattis. These can be attributed primarily to the many significant declines occurring during the period from 1991 to 1998. Finally, in the very old group, significant 7-year changes from 1984 to 1991 are found for the Boston Naming Test, WAIS-R Block Design, and Digit Symbol scales as well as Praxis Delayed Total, Trails A, and Trails B. Significant 14-year changes are found for all measures.

Predicting Risk of Dementia From Young Adulthood and Middle Age Primary Mental Ability Assessments

The next step in this analysis was to examine the effectiveness of utilizing longitudinal change data on the primary mental abilities and estimated neuropsychology data in predicting the ratings made by our neuropsychologists.

We first examine change over the most proximal 7 years from 1991 to 1998. Then we reach back another 7 years and examine changes occurring from 1984 to 1991. Longitudinal change is considered both for the PMA factor scores (computed from the actual observations) and for the estimated neuropsychology measures. In each instance, we first contrast all participants rated as having some suspicious characteristics against the normal participants (Rating 1 vs. combined

Ratings 2, 3, and 4). We then contrast only those individuals who were identified as probably or definitely demented against the normal group (Ratings 1 vs. Ratings 3 and 4).

In tables 17.7 through 17.10, we consequently distinguish between Normal (Rating 1), Suspect (Ratings 2, 3, and 4), and Demented (Ratings 3 and 4) individuals. Because there were no significant sex by rating category or age group by rating category interactions, data are reported only for the total sample. In each case, mean longitudinal change is reported in T-score points. Perhaps of greater practical interest, however, are the proportion of individuals who show reliable decline (defined as a drop that is greater than 1 SE from T_1) and the odds ratios between the normal and diagnosed groups.

Changes Over the Most Proximal Seven Years (1991–1998)

Primary Mental Abilities Factor Scores   Table 17.7 shows average declines in T-score points, proportions of the rating groups who declined significantly over 7 years, and the odds ratios of these proportions contrasting the normal and rating groups. Because all of the participants in this analysis were over 60 years of age (mean age 73 years at the time they were rated), it is not surprising that significant average age changes were observed on all of the factor scores. There is a significant interaction between magnitude of 7-year change and rating group for all factor scores except Inductive Reasoning. As expected, greater change is observed for the groups rated as other than normal. When all individuals with some suspicious characteristics are contrasted with normal individuals, significant odds ratios are obtained only for the Verbal Comprehension and the Verbal Recall factors. However, when only those rated as probably or definitely demented are contrasted with the normal individuals, significant odds ratios are found for all estimated neuropsychology measures.

Estimated Neuropsychology Scores   Data for the estimated neuropsychology scores may be found in table 17.8. Again, significant interactions are found between magnitude of 7-year change and rating groups, with greater change for both suspect and demented categories. Odds ratios are statistically significant for the suspect group for all neuropsychology scores except the Boston Naming Test and for Word List Recall. All odds ratios are significant for the demented group. It is noteworthy that the odds ratios for the estimated neuropsychology measures are substantially larger than those for the psychometric factor scores.

Changes Over the Earlier Seven-Year Period (1984–1991)

Having established that we can provide meaningful estimates over the most proximal 7 years (1991–1998) prior to the actual neuropsychological assessment of our study participants, we then reached further back to determine the effectiveness of this procedure in identifying individuals at risk at an earlier point in

TABLE 17.7 Mean Decline in *T*-Score Points, Proportion of Participants Declining from 1991 to 1998, and Odds Ratios of Diagnosed Versus Normal Groups for the Primary Mental Abilities Factor Scores

Factor	Mean Decline			Proportion Declining			Odds Ratios	
	Normal	Suspect	Demented	Normal	Suspect	Demented	Suspect	Demented
Inductive Reasoning	3.77	4.41	6.24	53.9	59.6	72.7	1.10	1.35*
Spatial Orientation	3.47	4.41	5.95	40.9	47.2	58.8	1.15	1.44*
Numeric Facility	3.15	4.09	7.26	37.8	44.4	64.7	1.17	1.71**
Verbal Comprehension	1.42	2.55	6.03	21.3	37.3	61.8	1.75*	2.90***
Verbal Recall	4.13	6.39	10.57	34.5	46.5	64.7	1.30**	1.88***

*$p < .05$. **$p < .01$. ***$p < .001$.

TABLE 17.8 Mean Decline in *T*-Score Points, Proportion of Participants Declining from 1991 to 1998, and Odds Ratios of Diagnosed Versus Normal Groups for the Estimated Neuropsychology Scores

Factor	Mean Decline			Proportion Declining			Odds Ratios	
	Normal	Suspect	Demented	Normal	Suspect	Demented	Suspect	Demented
Boston Naming Test	4.26	5.84	8.67	50.3	55.9	78.6	1.11	1.40*
Fuld Retrieval	5.23	7.81	13.13	37.3	50.4	66.7	1.35**	1.79***
Fuld Rapid Verbal Retrieval	4.21	6.44	11.23	40.5	57.4	75.8	1.48***	1.70***
Mattis Grand Total	-0.80	2.44	5.53	13.1	34.0	57.6	2.60***	4.34***
WMS-R Immediate Total	3.42	6.41	10.14	43.3	59.6	87.9	1.36***	2.02***
WMS-R Delayed Total	4.48	7.28	12.00	41.6	55.3	75.8	1.33**	1.82***
WAIS-R Digit Span	2.31	5.05	6.88	41.6	52.5	60.6	1.26*	1.32*
WAIS-R Vocabulary	-0.39	1.82	1.50	21.1	35.5	57.6	1.68***	2.73***
WAIS-R Comprehension	0.26	2.56	2.74	23.6	39.0	60.6	1.65***	2.56***
WAIS-R Block Design	5.06	5.83	8.73	47.3	58.9	66.7	1.24*	1.41*
WAIS-R Digit Symbol	5.73	7.64	12.21	57.0	73.0	90.6	1.28***	1.59***
MMSE	4.33	7.34	12.00	42.2	56.0	81.8	1.33**	1.94***
Verbal Fluency	2.26	4.80	6.82	37.6	55.3	75.8	2.67***	2.01***
Word List Recall	5.02	7.67	13.04	38.5	44.5	63.6	1.24	1.65**
Praxis Delayed Total	5.89	7.47	12.05	47.3	64.4	75.8	1.36***	1.60***
Trails A	5.42	6.74	10.47	41.6	58.2	69.7	1.40***	1.68**
Trails B	5.76	7.32	11.53	53.0	67.4	81.8	1.27**	1.54***

Note. MMSE, Mini-Mental State Examination; WAIS-R, Wechsler Adult Intelligence Scale–Revised; WMS-R, Wechsler Memory Scale–Revised.
*$p < .05$. **$p < .01$. ***$p < .001$.

TABLE 17.9 Mean Decline in *T*-Score Points, Proportion of Participants Declining from 1984 to 1991, and Odds Ratios of Diagnosed Versus Normal Groups for the Primary Mental Abilities Factor Scores

Factor	Mean Decline			Proportion Declining			Odds Ratios	
	Normal	Suspect	Demented	Normal	Suspect	Demented	Suspect	Demented
Inductive Reasoning	0.50	0.44	1.81	20.0	19.0	31.0	0.95	1.54
Spatial Orientation	1.28	1.50	1.54	22.2	24.0	26.9	1.08	1.21
Numeric Facility	1.54	1.98	3.69	25.8	33.0	46.2	1.32	1.79*
Verbal Comprehension	−0.21	−0.12	1.42	9.8	12.4	23.1	1.26	2.35*
Verbal Recall	−0.29	1.26	3.00	2.0	2.1	3.8	1.08	1.96

*p < .05.

412

TABLE 17.10 Mean Decline in T-Score Points, Proportion of Participants Declining from 1984 to 1991, and Odds Ratios of Diagnosed Versus Normal Groups for the Estimated Neuropsychology Scores

Factor	Mean Decline			Proportion Declining			Odds Ratios	
	Normal	Suspect	Demented	Normal	Suspect	Demented	Suspect	Demented
Boston Naming Test	1.22	1.54	2.85	21.3	22.7	30.8	1.07	1.45
Fuld Retrieval	−0.01	1.39	2.96	16.5	33.0	38.5	1.99***	2.33***
Fuld Rapid Verbal Retrieval	−0.02	1.21	3.27	12.6	22.7	42.3	1.80*	3.36***
Mattis Grand Total	0.07	0.93	2.81	20.1	28.9	53.8	1.44	2.68***
WMS-R Immediate Total	0.05	1.13	3.50	14.5	20.5	46.2	1.42	3.17***
WMS-R Delayed Total	−0.06	1.31	3.35	13.4	30.9	46.2	2.31***	3.45***
WAIS-R Digit Span	0.30	0.28	2.50	16.9	14.4	26.9	0.88	1.59
WAIS-R Vocabulary	−0.20	−0.08	1.69	12.6	16.5	30.8	1.31	2.44**
WAIS-R Comprehension	−0.10	0.13	2.12	13.4	15.5	30.8	1.15	2.30*
WAIS-R Block Design	1.44	1.70	1.92	24.8	25.8	26.9	1.03	1.06
WAIS-R Digit Symbol	1.35	1.88	3.27	20.1	26.8	42.3	1.33	2.11**
MMSE	0.01	1.21	3.38	15.0	29.9	38.5	2.00**	2.57**
Verbal Fluency	0.14	0.70	2.85	14.2	17.5	42.3	1.24	2.99***
Word List Recall	−0.19	1.39	3.27	15.0	30.9	42.3	2.07***	2.83***
Praxis Delayed Total	1.06	1.86	2.92	23.6	29.9	38.5	1.27	1.63
Trails A	1.37	1.78	2.46	21.3	29.9	34.6	1.41	1.63
Trails B	1.31	1.82	2.92	21.3	27.8	38.5	1.31	1.81

Note. MMSE, Mini-Mental State Examination; WAIS-R, Wechsler Adult Intelligence Scale–Revised; WMS-R, Wechsler Memory Scale–Revised.
*$p < .05$. **$p < .01$. ***$p < .001$.

time by studying the predictive effectiveness of change over the preceding 7-year period.

Primary Mental Abilities Factor Scores   Table 17.9 shows data on change in the PMA factor scores from 1984 to 1991 (the end point is now 7 years prior to the actual administration of the neuropsychology tests). Participants at $T_1 = 1984$ in this analysis were in their late 50s. Hence, decline over 7 years was not significant for any PMA factor for the normal and suspect groups. However, significant odds ratios were found for the demented group ($p < .05$) for Numeric Facility and Verbal Comprehension.

Estimated Neuropsychology Scores   Results for the estimated neuropsychology scores are given in table 17.10. Significant interactions between the magnitude of 7-year decline and rating group were found for all measures except the Boston Naming Test, WAIS-R Digit Span, WAIS-R Block Design, Praxis Delayed total, and part A of the Trail-Making Test. Significant odds ratios when contrasting the suspect with the normal group were found for the estimated scores of the Fuld Retrieval, the Delayed Wechsler Memory, the MMSE, and the Word List Recall. Significant odds ratios contrasting the demented with the normal group were obtained for all measures except Boston Naming, WAIS-R Digit Span, WAIS-R Block Design, Praxis Delayed total, and part A of the Trail-Making test.

Implications of the Postdiction Analyses

Our findings suggest that it is possible to obtain useful estimates of what individuals' status on neuropsychological measures might have been at earlier points in time had we been able to measure them instantly. Findings indicate that, for this community-dwelling sample, age-related declines would have been found over 14 years in all age groups (except for the Mattis) and for a few neuropsychological measures over 7 years in the old-old and very old age groups.

A major criterion for the utility of the analyses presented here is, of course, whether the backward estimation of neuropsychological measures can contribute to the detection of potential risk of dementia at an earlier point in time when the direct identification by a neuropsychological battery would not be practical because of expected ceiling effects. The criterion used by us for this purpose was the well-established procedure of consensus ratings by neuropsychologists.

Our results suggest first that significant individual change on PMA test performance over the 7 years preceding neuropsychological evaluation has predictive value for identifying individuals who will be rated by neuropsychologists as mentally impaired. More important, although there is some predictability directly from the psychometric test battery, there is better prediction from the estimated neuropsychology test scores. Further, we can also successfully predict current diagnostic status from change in the estimated neuropsychology measures from 14 years to 7 years prior to the actual administration of the neuropsychology battery.

Another interesting advantage of the approach taken here is that, in contrast to the actual neuropsychology tests, the estimated scores have no ceiling because they are scaled from the midpoint of the total population. Removing the ceiling limitation for the estimated neuropsychology tests may well be a major reason for the greater outcome efficacy of the estimated neuropsychology scores over the direct measures of change in the primary mental abilities.

Efforts to develop programs for the prevention or arrest of dementia at early stages will depend heavily on the early identification of those at risk before clinical symptoms begin to appear. This chapter presents a novel approach that takes advantage of existing longitudinal data to identify individuals at risk by postdicting performance on neuropsychological tests 7 and 14 years prior to neuropsychological assessment.

Chapter Summary

Some initial results are provided for our work with the ApoE genetic marker of dementia as it relates to cognitive decline. We confirmed excess decline over 7 years in persons over age 60 years who possess the $\varepsilon_{2/4}$ allele combination on the cognitive abilities of Inductive Reasoning and Verbal Memory, with a trend toward excess decline in Perceptual Speed. The $\varepsilon_{2/3}$ allele combination, moreover, showed less-than-average decline on these abilities.

Studies are next described that involve the neuropsychological assessment of a community-dwelling sample of older adults who have not previously been identified as suffering from cognitive impairment. Higher performance levels were found for the young-old as compared to the old-old and very old groups. Significant gender differences in favor of women were found for the Fuld Retrieval test, the Fuld Rapid Verbal Retrieval test, the Word List Recall, and the Mattis total score. Preliminary results are also given for a 3-year follow-up assessment. Moderate-to-good stabilities were obtained for the neuropsychology battery. The observed 3-year change was positive for the young-old and partially positive for the old-old, but significant decrements were found for the very old subgroup.

Extension analyses are then described that link the clinical measures with our psychometric battery for the study of normal aging. Most measures had significant loadings on the Verbal Memory factor. The exceptions were the WAIS-R Digit Span, Vocabulary, and Comprehension, with primary loadings on the Verbal Comprehension factor; and Block Design, which loaded most prominently on the Spatial Ability factor. Several measures also had secondary and/or tertiary loadings on Spatial Ability, Inductive Reasoning, and Numeric Ability.

Finally, analyses are reported on studies that use the results of the extension analyses to obtain postdicted estimates of earlier performance on the neuropsychological measures. The postdicted neuropsychology scores allow tests of the possibility of early identification of risk for an eventual clinical diagnosis of dementia. Results of these studies suggest that data from psychometric tests suitable for a normal community-dwelling population can predict high risk for dementia 7 and 14 years prior to the identification of cognitive impairment by neuropsychologists.

CHAPTER EIGHTEEN

Summary and Conclusions

THE READER HAS accompanied me through the highlights of a scientific journey, now covering over 45 years, that I pursued with the help and support of many colleagues and students. The focus of this journey throughout was to gain a clearer understanding of the progress of adult development of the cognitive abilities and the many influences that make for such great individual differences in life trajectories. What now remains is to attempt a succinct statement of what I think can be concluded from these studies. I begin by reviewing what we have learned in the context of the five questions regarding the life course of intellectual competence raised in the introductory chapter. I then summarize the conclusions reached from our efforts at intervening in the normal course of adult cognitive development, as well as the findings from our efforts to learn more about adult cognition in a developmental behavior, genetic, and/or family context. I then discuss findings from our extensions into identifying the genetic and environmental influences that shape adult intellectual development. In that context, I return to the heuristic model I started with in chapter 1 and suggest where our concerns must next turn. Finally, I provide information on how to access certain limited data sets from the Seattle Longitudinal Study (SLS) that I am making available for use by qualified researchers and college teachers for secondary analyses or instructional purposes.

The Course of Adult Intellectual Development

Although the development of intellectual competence in childhood and adolescence follows a rather uniform path, with new stages of competence and differentiation of functioning occurring within a relatively narrow band with respect to age, the same cannot be said for the life course of adult intelligence. And, of course, in contrast to the major external criterion in early life—the child's ability to master the educational and socialization systems of our public and private schools—adult intellectual competence can be referenced to an almost infinite multiplicity of outcome variables.

Although I have tried to address many of these issues with the studies described in this volume, I have nevertheless maintained a relatively narrow focus, limited to a number of basic questions assessed in considerable depth. Hence, there are many questions we could have asked our study participants had we been satisfied with narrower age ranges and smaller samples, but that our strategies involving a large data set placed beyond our reach. Unfortunately, one cannot go backward in a longitudinal study to expand one's inquiry, although one can always add new variables or ask questions in more sophisticated ways as a study progresses. This is what I believe we have done and, building on our rich data set, is what we shall continue to do to be able to answer new questions that will arise as time passes. Of course, one can use statistical approaches that allow estimation of variables that were not directly observed in the past, leading to the interesting theme of postdiction. Here, then, are my conclusions as they seem appropriate at the present stage of our inquiry.

Does Intelligence Change Uniformly Through Adulthood, or Are There Different Life Course Ability Patterns?

The answer to this question remains quite unambiguous: Neither at the level of analysis of the tests actually given nor at the level of the inferred latent ability constructs do we find uniform patterns of developmental change across the entire ability spectrum. I continue therefore to warn those who would like to assess change in intellectual competence by means of an omnibus IQ-like measure that such an approach will not be helpful to the basic researcher or to the thoughtful clinician. I have reported some overall indices of intellectual and educational aptitude because they are of some theoretical interest, but I do not think that such global measures have practical utility in monitoring changes (or differences) in intellectual competence for individuals or groups.

At any particular time, a cross-sectional snapshot of age difference profiles for different abilities will be largely influenced by the interaction of cohort differences and age changes for any given ability. My work in the 1950s began with the observation that there were differences in the age difference patterns for the five abilities measured in our core battery. However, only by observing longitudinal data averaged over multiple cohorts can one reach definitive conclusions about whether the nature of these differences is part of a developmental process of change in adulthood that will be observed whenever the perturbations of time and place are removed. Any single ability measure, moreover, may be unduly influenced by the form and speededness of the particular test. More stable conclusions are therefore likely to be based on ability profiles that compare estimates of the latent ability constructs. The following conclusions are based on the data presented in chapter 5.

From the extensive data on the original core battery, I conclude that Verbal Meaning, Space, and Reasoning attain a peak plateau in midlife, from the 40s to the early 60s, whereas Number and Word Fluency peak earlier and show very modest decline beginning in the 50s. In contrast to our earlier conclusions, it now seems apparent on the basis of larger samples the steepness of late-life decline is greatest for Number and least for the measure of Reasoning ability. Verbal Meaning (recognition vocabulary) declines last, but also shows steeper decline than the other abilities from the 70s to the 80s. These findings are observed whether the large number of observations of individuals followed over 7 years are aggregated or whether the smaller data sets for those individuals followed over 14, 21, 28, and 35 years are examined.

For the more limited data on the latent construct estimates (obtained only in the fifth through seventh study cycles), it appears that peak ages of performance are still shifting, and that we now see these peaks occurring in the 50s for Inductive Reasoning and Spatial Orientation and in the 60s for Verbal Ability and Verbal Memory. By contrast, Perceptual Speed peaks in the 20s and Numeric Ability in the late 30s. Even by the late 80s, declines for Verbal Ability and Inductive Reasoning are modest, but they are severe in very old age for Perceptual Speed and Numeric Ability, with Spatial Orientation and Verbal Memory in between.

Again, I must caution that these are average patterns of age change profiles. Individual profiles depend to a large extent on individual patterns of use and disuse and on the presence or absence of neuropathology. Indeed, virtually every possible permutation of individual profiles has been observed in our study (see Schaie, 1989a, 1989b).

At What Age Is There a Reliably Detectable Decrement in Ability, and What Is Its Magnitude?

For some ability markers, significant but extremely modest average changes have been observed in the 50s. Nevertheless, I continue to maintain that individual decline prior to 60 years of age is almost inevitably a symptom or precursor of pathological age changes. On the other hand, it is clear that by the mid-70s significant average decrement can be observed for all abilities, and that by the 80s, average decrement is severe except for Verbal Ability.

From the largest longitudinal data set, the aggregated changes over 7 years in the core battery, I conclude that statistically significant decrement occurs for Number and Word Fluency by age 60 years and for Space and Reasoning by age 67 years, but for Verbal Meaning only by 81 years of age. For the composite indices, average statistically significant decrement is first observed at age 60 years for the Index of Intellectual Ability and at age 67 years for the Index of Educational Aptitude.

At the latent construct level, statistically significant decrement is first observed by age 60 years for Spatial Ability, Numeric Ability, and Perceptual Speed; by age 67 years for Inductive Reasoning; and by age 74 years for Verbal Ability and Verbal Memory.

The average magnitude of age-related decrements during the 7-year period when they first become statistically significant is quite small, but it becomes increasingly larger as the 80s are reached. The difference in performance for the core battery between age 25 years and the age at which the first decrement is observed is less than 0.3 SD. However, by 88 years of age, that difference amounts to 0.75 SD for Reasoning; approximately 1 SD for Verbal Meaning, Space, and Word Fluency; and as much as 1.5 SD for Number. For the latent construct measures, initial declines are even smaller (between 0.10 and 0.25 SD). The cumulative change from 25 to 88 years of age differs widely by ability domain. Because of gains in midlife, it is virtually zero for Verbal Ability; ranges from 0.6 to 0.8 SD for Inductive Reasoning, Verbal Memory, and Spatial Orientation; and amounts to approximately 2 SD for Numeric Ability and Perceptual Speed.

From these data, I conclude that it is during the period of the late 60s and 70s that many people begin to experience noticeable ability declines. Even so, it is not until the 80s are reached that the average older adult will fall below the middle range of performance for young adults. There are some occupations for which speed of performance is important, but because broad individual differences in the speededness of behavior exist, even here there is substantial overlap in the performance of young and old workers until the 80s are reached. This conclusion is reached even independent of the possibility that compensatory effects of experience in many skilled trades and professions may lessen the effect of age declines in the basic cognitive skills. Hence, it turns out that for decisions relating to the retention of individuals in the workforce, chronological age is not a useful criterion for groups and certainly not for individuals. This conclusion has, of course, been the rationale for largely abandoning mandatory retirement in the United States.

What Are the Patterns of Generational Differences, and What Is Their Magnitude?

Throughout our studies, I have been cognizant not only of the fact of individual aging, but also of the fact that there have been profound changes in environmental support and societal context that must be part of shaping individual development. I have tried to document the impact of these changes on intellectual development by charting cohort (generational) differences in the intellectual performance measures. These studies have clearly demonstrated that there are substantial generational trends in intellectual performance. As documented in chapter 6, these trends amount to as much as 1.5 SD across the 70-year cohort span that we have investigated.

For the core battery, the form of these generational trends is positive for Verbal Meaning, Space, and Reasoning, but it is concave for Number (with peak performance for the 1924 cohort and decline thereafter) and is convex for Word Fluency (with lowest performance for the 1931 cohort and return to the level of the 1889 baseline cohort thereafter).

In the case of the latent construct estimates, equally substantial positive cohort gradients were observed for Inductive Reasoning, Perception, Spatial Orientation, and Verbal Memory. However, at the factor level, the cohort gradient for Verbal Ability takes a concave form, presumably because the additional markers of this construct are less speeded than our original single measure. Interestingly, decline is observed here for the baby boomer cohorts, particularly the trailing edge of that group. Numeric Ability at the latent construct level peaks with the 1917 cohort, shows a negative trend until the 1959 cohort, with some modest gain for the post–baby boomers.

An understanding of these cohort differences is important to account for the discrepancy between the longitudinal (within-participant) age changes and the cross-sectional (between-group) age differences reported in chapter 4. In general, I conclude that cross-sectional findings will overestimate within-individual declines whenever there are positive cohort gradients and will underestimate decline in the presence of negative cohort gradients. Curvilinear cohort gradients will lead to temporary dislocations of age difference patterns and will over- or underestimate age changes, depending on the direction of differences over a particular time period.

Because of these cohort effects, our most recent cross-sectional data suggest much steeper declines on Verbal Meaning, Space, and Reasoning than are found in the longitudinal data and show far less decline on Number (see figure 4.4). Similar findings also obtain for the latent construct measures (see figure 4.7). The slowing of the cohort difference trend suggests that, in the next 20 or 30 years, concurrently measured age differences will become substantially smaller over that age range for which there is little or no within-participant decline. This is fortunate because there is a need to retain people to higher ages in the labor force because of the demographic reality of the aging of the baby boomers. Stereotypes about age decline will obviously be reinforced less in the absence of the dramatic shifts in ability base levels that were observed for cohorts entering adulthood in the first half of the 20th century.

What Accounts for Individual Differences in Age-Related Change in Adulthood?

Throughout this volume I have stressed the vast individual differences in intellectual change across adulthood. Some individuals, either because of the early onset of neuropathology or the experience of particularly unfavorable environments, begin to decline in their 40s, whereas a favored few maintain a full level of functioning into very advanced age.

Not all individuals decline in lockstep. Indeed, although linear or quadratic forms of decline may best describe the average aging of large groups, individual decline appears to occur far more frequently in a stairstep fashion. Individuals will have unfavorable experiences to which they respond with a modest decline in cognitive functioning, but then tend to stabilize for some time, perhaps repeating this pattern several times prior to their demise. To be sure, the sequence of decline of abilities is not uniform across individuals, but may depend in any one individual on the circumstances of use and disuse of particular skills. Thus, in actuarial studies of our core battery, we have observed that virtually all individuals had significantly declined on one ability by age 60 years, but that virtually no one had declined on all five abilities even by 88 years of age.

Certainly, genetic endowment will account for a substantial portion of individual differences (see chapter 16 for circumstantial evidence of heritability of adult intelligence). Nevertheless, there are many other important sources of individual differences in intellectual aging that have been implicated in our studies.

To begin with, the onset of intellectual decline seems markedly affected by the presence or absence of several chronic diseases. As discussed in chapter 10, cardiovascular disease, diabetes, neoplasms, and arthritis are all involved as risk factors for the occurrence of cognitive decline, as is a low level of overall health. On the other hand, high levels of cognitive functioning seem to be associated with survival after malignancies and late onset of cardiovascular disease and arthritis. Those persons who function at high cognitive levels are also more likely to seek earlier and more competent medical intervention in the disabling conditions of late life. They also are more likely to comply effectively with preventive and ameliorative regimens that tend to stabilize their physiological infrastructure. Perhaps even more important, they are less likely to engage in high-risk lifestyles, and they will respond more readily to professional advice that maximizes their chances for survival and reduction of morbidity. On the other hand, there does not seem a high relation between cognitive competence and systematic adoption of effective health behaviors. However, the more able individuals tend to engage in more effective medication use.

My interest next turned to environmental circumstances that might account for individual differences in cognitive aging. Early candidates for investigation were all those aspects of the environment that are likely to enhance intellectual stimulation (see Schaie & Gribbin, 1975; Schaie & O'Hanlon, 1990).

From the data presented in chapter 11, I conclude that the onset of intellectual decline is often postponed for individuals who live in favorable environmental circumstances, as would be the case for those persons characterized by a high socioeconomic status. These circumstances include above-average education, histories of occupational pursuits that involve high complexity and low routine, and the maintenance of intact families. Likewise, risk of cognitive decline is lower for persons with substantial involvement in activities typically available in complex and intellectually stimulating environments. Such activities include extensive reading, travel, attendance at cultural events, pursuit of continuing education activities, and participation in clubs and professional associations.

It is not surprising that intact families, our most important individual support system, reduce risk of cognitive decline. What was less obvious is the finding that cognitive decline is also less severe for those married to a spouse with high cognitive status. Our studies of cognitive similarity in married couples suggest that the lower-functioning spouse at the beginning of a marriage tends to maintain or increase his or her level vis-à-vis the higher-functioning spouse (see chapter 12).

From the very beginning of our study, we have pursued the question whether the cognitive style of rigidity-flexibility might be associated with differential intellectual aging. I now conclude that an individual's self-report of a flexible personality style at midlife and flexible performance on objective measures of motor-cognitive perseveration tasks do indeed reduce the risk of cognitive decline (see chapter 9). The implication of these findings is that individuals who find themselves having developed rigid response patterns in midlife would be well advised to take advantage of psychological therapeutic interventions that could lead to a more flexible response when it is needed to cope with the vicissitudes of advanced age.

Aging effects on many cognitive abilities tend to be confounded with the perceptual and response speed required to process the tasks used to measure these abilities. Thus, individuals who remain at high levels of perceptual speed are also at an advantage with respect to the maintenance of such other abilities.

Finally, those individuals who rate themselves as satisfied with their life's accomplishment in midlife or early old age seem to be at an advantage. Some individuals tend to deny the inescapable fact that some cognitive losses will occur with advancing age in almost everyone and may therefore avoid constructive lifestyle modifications while they are still feasible. People who overestimate their cognitive losses are frequently those who are still functioning well. But excessive pessimism about one's rate of aging can also result in self-fulfilling prophecies if the consequence of such attitudes is a reduction of their active participation in life (see chapter 15).

I have used event history methods to develop life tables for the occurrence of decline events on the five single ability markers in the core battery, and I developed a calculus that allows estimation of the most probable age by which an individual can expect to experience decline on each of these abilities (Schaie, 1989a). The most highly weighted variables in this calculus that predict earlier-than-average decline were found to be a significant decrease in flexibility during the preceding 7-year period, low educational level, male gender, and low satisfaction with success in life.

Can Intellectual Decline With Increasing Age Be Reversed by Educational Intervention?

Once adult intellectual development has been described and a number of antecedents of individual differences have been identified, it then becomes useful to think about ways in which normal intellectual aging might be slowed or reversed.

In conjunction with Sherry Willis, who analyzed these issues and developed training programs that could be applied to our study samples, we began to initiate a series of cognitive interventions. In contrast to training young children, for whom it can be assumed that new skills are conveyed, older adults are likely to have access to the skills being trained but through disuse have lost their proficiency. Longitudinal studies are therefore particularly useful in distinguishing individuals who have declined from those who have remained stable. In the former, training should result in remediation of loss; in the latter, we are dealing with the enhancement of previous levels of functioning, perhaps compensating for the cohort-based disadvantage of older persons.

Results from our cognitive interventions allow the conclusion that cognitive decline in old age is, for many older persons, likely to be a function of disuse rather than of the deterioration of the physiological or neural substrates of cognitive behavior. In the initial studies, a brief 5-hour training program succeeded in improving the performance of about two thirds of the participants on the abilities of Spatial Orientation and Inductive Reasoning.

The average training gain amounted to roughly 0.5 SD. Even more dramatically, of those for whom significant decrement could be documented over a 14-year period, roughly 40% were returned to the level at which they had functioned when first studied. The analyses of structural relationships among the ability measures prior to and after training further allow the conclusion that training did not result in qualitative changes in ability structures and is thus highly specific to the targeted abilities.

The literature is replete with cognitive interventions that show significant pre–postintervention gains, but often also report diminution of training effects after brief time intervals. Our follow-up of cognitive training over 7- and 14-year periods (including further booster training) has demonstrated that those participants who showed significant decline at initial training do remain at a substantial advantage over untrained comparison groups. Long-term effects for those who had remained stable at initial training differed by ability. Significant effects were shown to prevail on the intervention for Inductive Reasoning, but not on the Spatial Orientation training. Finally, replication of initial training with new samples confirmed the magnitudes of the training effects obtained in the initial study.

Some might ask how these interventions on laboratory tasks relate to real-life issues. Clearly, the showing of substantial relationships between performance on psychometric ability tests and the measure of practical intelligence or everyday problem solving suggest that these training interventions may be quite useful in a broad sense. The cost of institutionalization for individuals who are only marginally incompetent to live independently because of relatively low levels of intellectual competence is high. Modest educational interventions similar to those described in this volume, on the other hand, are quite inexpensive. As a consequence, some of the interventions developed in the course of our study have been included in a large-scale field trial to see whether they can raise competencies sufficiently to keep many elders independent for a longer period as well as to enhance the quality of their lives.

Methodological Advances in the Seattle Longitudinal Study

The SLS has not only provided empirical data, but has also been a vehicle for introducing methodological innovations, as well as introducing to developmental psychology methods common in other disciplines but only rarely used in psychology. These contributions are briefly summarized here.

Design Innovations

The conversion of the SLS from a single-occasion cross-sectional study to a multi-cohort longitudinal study was accompanied by the introduction of the age-cohort-period model into psychological developmental research (Schaie, 1965). This was followed by developing the distinction between cross-sectional and longitudinal sequences and the concept of following the same individuals over time or collecting successive random samples from the same cohorts (Schaie & Baltes, 1975). Early on, methodological studies were conducted to provide examples of how to address the issue of sampling with or without replacement and the role of monetary incentives in recruiting study participants. Following the introduction of restricted factor analysis by Karl Jöreskog, the SLS was one of the first developmental studies to switch to a design measuring behavioral change at the latent construct level. Hence, we were also the earliest users of structural equation models to test propositions regarding factorial invariance of cognitive abilities in both cross-sectional and longitudinal data sets.

The SLS was also one of the first psychological studies to apply event history and life table methods to the study of adult development. Another first was the application of longitudinal designs to cognitive training paradigms, as well as the development of family similarity paradigms for adult parent-offspring and sibling dyads. Most recently, we have introduced the concept of postdiction to utilize methods of extension analysis to estimate data for previous measurement occasions in longitudinal studies by developing algorithms based on the concurrent relationship between measurement batteries, parts of which were not administered on earlier occasions.

Test Construction Activities

Any extensive study eventually requires some measurement development. Measures specifically constructed for use in the SLS include both expansions of previously existing tests and the construction of new tests. Thurstone's Science Research Associates (SRA) Primary Mental Abilities (PMA) test was expanded, made more user friendly for adults, and named the Schaie-Thurstone Adult Mental Abilities Test. The Moos Family Environment Scales were adapted and reformatted for work across the adult life span for studying perceptions of current families as well as families of origin. A measure of cognitive styles, the Test of Behavior Rigidity (TBR), was newly constructed to measure the dimensions of Motor-Cognitive Flexibility, Attitudinal Flexibility, and Psychomotor Speed. In addition, 13 latent personality factor scores were derived from this test. Also newly constructed were three self-report inventories: The first, the Life Complexity Inventory, includes extensive demographic information, lifestyle variables, leisure use, and complexity characteristics of the individual's work and home environments. The second, the Health Behavior Questionnaire, gathers information on subjective perceptions of health status, preventive behaviors, nutrition, and substance use as well as utilization of preventive health care.

The third is the PMA Retrospective Questionnaire, used in our studies of the congruence of objective cognitive change and its subjective perception. All of these instruments have been normed by age and gender, and a variety of validity and/or reliability studies have been conducted for them.

Family Similarity in Adult Intellectual Development

Going beyond the study of age in single individuals, we began to be interested in the effects of cognitive aging within families. We began these studies by tracing the impact of shared environment on similarity in intellectual functioning in married couples. Our studies provide some support for the notion of marital assortativity in mate selection by demonstrating substantial within-couple correlations. These relationships persist over time (in our study, over as long as 21 years) and indeed in some instances increase in the direction of the spouse who was the higher functioning at base level.

More recently, influenced by developments in the behavior genetics literature, we began to assess the adult children and siblings of our longitudinal participants. Significant adult parent-offspring similarities were observed for our total sample for all ability measures (except Perceptual Speed) and for the cognitive style measures. The magnitudes of correlation are comparable to those found between young adults and their children. However, same-gender pairs showed higher correlations on Verbal Meaning, Number, and Word Fluency; opposite-gender pairs higher correlations were on Spatial Orientation, Inductive Reasoning, and Motor-Cognitive Flexibility.

Our data strongly support the hypothesis that if shared environmental influences are relatively unimportant in adulthood, then similarity in parent-offspring pairs should remain reasonably constant in adulthood across time and age.

Given our interest in generational differences in ability, we asked whether level differences within families equaled or approximated differences found for similar cohort ranges in a general population sample. Comparable differences were indeed found to be the rule, but there were some exceptions. The general population estimates underestimated the advantage of the offspring cohort for Spatial Orientation and Psychomotor Speed, but overestimated that advantage for Perceptual Speed.

More recently, we addressed differences in the rate of cognitive change across generations. This issue is of considerable importance as most industrialized nations are beginning to consider adjusting the age of eligibility for their old-age pension systems to compensate for the increasingly adverse ratio of workers to those not in the workforce. Such efforts must avoid simply moving from retirement for reasons of age to retirement by reason of disability. It becomes critical, therefore, to know whether age declines in ability occur at a slower rate for successive generations. Our comparison across parents and biologically related offspring for changes in the decade of the 60s have found that there is indeed a slowing of decline over this age period. Although the parents showed modest but significant decline, there was no statistically significant decline for the second generation except on the variable of Number ability.

Substantial family similarity was documented also for the adult sibling pairs. In general, parent-offspring and sibling correlations were of similar magnitude. However, after controlling for age, sibling correlations were somewhat lower than those observed for the parent-offspring pairs. Interestingly, stability of sibling correlations across time and age was not as strong as for the parent-offspring data.

The Role of Personality and Lifestyle Characteristics

When our study began, there was considerable pessimism regarding the possibility that personality variables might be able to influence the life course of intelligence. Nevertheless, I thought early on that it would be useful to collect data on the adult development of possibly cognition-relevant personality and attitudinal traits. We therefore explicitly studied the attitudinal trait of Social Responsibility, derived other personality traits and attitudes from the TBR questionnaire, and added the NEO to measure the big five personality factors and the Center for Epidemologic Studies–Depression Scale (CES-D) as an indicator of psychological distress or depression.

Longitudinal data suggest a very modest gain in Social Responsibility with age until age 74 years. Women show greater social responsibility than men until age 46 years, but the age gradients for both genders coincide thereafter. Only modest cohort differences were found, with the lowest Social Responsibility level shown by the 1952 cohort. Interestingly, however, there were significant secular trends, with an overall decline in self-reports of Social Responsibility from 1956 to 1977 and a significant rise thereafter.

Item factor analyses of the 75-item TBR questionnaire have resulted in a fairly parsimonious 13-factor solution. The factors identified were Affectothymia, Superego Strength, Threctia, Premsia, Untroubled Adequacy, Conservatism of Temperament, Group Dependency, Low Self-Sentiment, Honesty, Interest in Science, Inflexibility, Political Concern, and Community Involvement. Although significant cross-sectional age differences were found for all 13 personality factors, fewer significant within-individual age changes were found. Most noteworthy were modest within-individual increases with age in Superego Strength, Untroubled Adequacy, Honesty, Threctia, and Conservatism. Age-related declines were found for Affectothymia, Premsia, and Political Concern. No age trends were found for Low Self-Sentiment, Interest in Science, Inflexibility, and Community Involvement.

Our studies with the NEO resulted in findings of negative age differences for Neuroticism, Extraversion, and Openness and a positive age difference for Agreeableness. Conscientiousness did not differ significantly by age group. Estimated longitudinal age changes suggested rather different life course patterns. Here, Neuroticism and Openness showed increases until midlife, with stability thereafter; Extraversion had a concave pattern of increment until midlife, with a decrease in old age; Agreeableness showed steep age-related increments; Conscientiousness declined until midlife, with stability thereafter. The CES-D data for our older participants showed a trend toward modest increase in psychological distress with increasing age.

Interestingly, we can show that there are modest but significant concurrent relationships between personality trait measures and ability constructs that account for up to 20% of shared variance. Both our 13 personality factor measures and the NEO could be related to the cognitive ability constructs. The personality dimensions that showed the highest relationship with high performance on the latent cognitive ability factors were high Untroubled Adequacy, low Conservatism, and low Group Dependency from the measurement of the 13 personality factors and high scores of Openness on the NEO.

Given reasonable stability across time for our personality measures, we might argue, therefore, that prediction of future cognitive change over age would benefit from the inclusion of personality traits as predictors of distal levels of cognitive performance. At least in the SLS, it was possible to show that some of the personality-cognition relations could be found over as long as a 35-year interval.

Early Detection of Risk for Dementia

At the inception of the SLS, not enough was known about mechanisms and prevalence of dementia in population samples to warrant including prediction of future cognitive impairment in our study design. However, advances in relevant sciences and the acquisition of complex longitudinal-sequential data have opened the possibility of seriously addressing the identification of risk for dementia utilizing cognitive data collected long before clinically noticeable symptoms of impairment become apparent.

We reported in this volume initial results of our work with the apolipoprotein E (ApoE) genetic marker of dementia as it relates to cognitive decline. We confirmed excess decline over 7 years in persons over age 60 years who possess the $\varepsilon_{2/4}$ allele combination on the cognitive abilities of Inductive Reasoning and Verbal Memory with a trend toward excess decline in Perceptual Speed. The $\varepsilon_{2/3}$ allele combination, moreover, showed less-than-average decline on these abilities.

Studies were then considered that involved the neuropsychological assessment (with an expanded Consortium to Establish a Registry for Alzheimer's Disease [CERAD] battery) of a community-dwelling sample of older adults who were not known to suffer from clinically diagnosable cognitive impairment. Age differences, favoring the young-old, were found on this battery in our normal sample. Significant gender differences in favor of women were found for the Fuld Retrieval test, the Fuld Rapid Verbal Retrieval test, the Word List Recall, and the Mattis total score. Preliminary results for a 3-year follow-up assessment yielded moderate-to-good stabilities for the neuropsychology battery. The observed 3-year changes were positive for the young-old and partially positive for the old-old, but significant decrements were found for the very old subgroup.

We were able to link the measures used in clinical practice with our psychometric battery for the study of normal aging. Most measures had their primary loadings on our Verbal Memory factor. However, the Wechsler Adult Intelligence Scale–Revised (WAIS-R) Digit Span, Vocabulary, and Comprehension scales had their primary loadings on the Verbal Comprehension factor, and the WAIS-R Block Design loaded most prominently on the Spatial Ability factor. Several neuropsychological measures also had secondary and/or tertiary loadings on Spatial

Ability, Inductive Reasoning, and Numeric Facility. We were able to use the neuropsychological data to identify participants in our study who appeared to have reached early cognitive impairment or who had indications that future monitoring will identify such impairment.

Finally, we were able to develop algorithms by means of extension analyses that allow us to obtain postdicted estimates of earlier performance and permit tests of the hypothesis that it may be possible to identify those at risk for an eventual clinical diagnosis of dementia. These algorithms are based on knowledge of the concurrent relationship of neuropsychological measures with our psychometric assessment battery and applied to earlier psychometric measures. Results of these studies suggest that data from psychometric tests suitable for a normal community-dwelling population can predict high risk for dementia as long as 7 and 14 years prior to the identification of cognitive impairment by a neuropsychologist.

Relationship of the Empirical Data
to the Conceptual Model

Having begun my exposition of findings from the SLS by providing a conceptual model, I now attempt to identify as clearly as possible where to find both methods and substantive data relevant to the relationships posited in that model. The model offered in chapter 1 is, of course, primarily a heuristic guide to our comprehensive research program. I reproduce it again as figure 18.1 so that the reader will be able to compare it directly with the submodels that have directly guided specific research efforts conducted as part of the SLS. However, I have numbered each of the proposed causal paths so that I can specify more conveniently where data used for estimating a given path or relevant for the understanding of a particular path may be located in this volume.

To make the relationship between the conceptual model and the empirical data more comprehensible, I have divided the overall model into four submodels (see figure 18.2). The first submodel is concerned with the heritable and contextual variables that directly affect the life course of cognitive functioning. This model represents not only the longitudinal study of cognition over the adult life course, but also indicates our efforts to assess the relative impact of heritability and environmental influences.

The second model includes influences that originate in the early family environment that result in social status and lifestyle factors that influence late-life cognitive functioning. It represents our work on charting the individual's micro-environment and the resultant lifestyle factors that make the difference in achieving successful aging.

The third model tracks the influences of chronic disease as moderated by lifestyles and midlife cognitive functioning on late-life cognitive functioning. This model represents our efforts to take advantage of our collaboration with a health maintenance organization to account for the effects of chronic disease on cognitive aging.

The fourth model charts the relation between genetic predisposition and late-life cognitive functioning to result in the detection of neuropathology at eventual

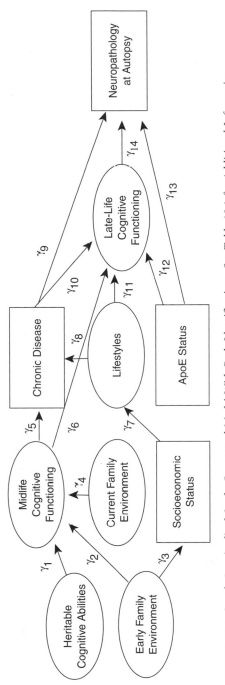

FIGURE 18.1 *Seattle Longitudinal Study Conceptual Model With Path Identifications. See Table 18.1 for Additional Information.*

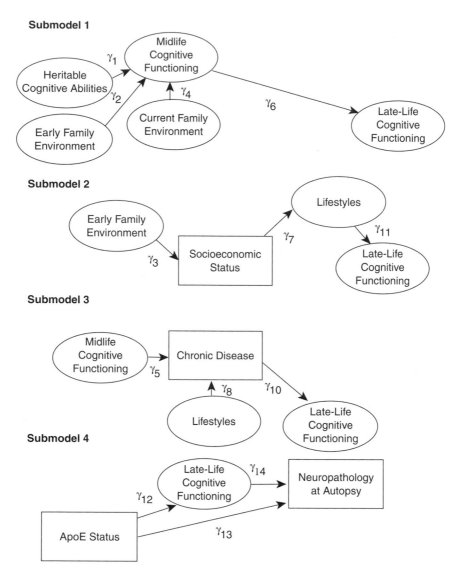

FIGURE 18.2 *Submodels With Path Identifications. See Table 18.1 for Additional Information.*

TABLE 18.1 Location of Evidence for Relationships Specified in the Conceptual Model

Path	Path Description	Location in Volume
γ_1	Heritable abilities–midlife cognition	Chapters 14 and 16
γ_2	Early environment–midlife cognition	Chapter 16
γ_3	Early environment–socioeconomic status	Chapter 11
γ_4	Current environment–midlife cognition	Chapter 16
γ_5	Midlife cognition–chronic disease	Chapter 10
γ_6	Midlife cognition–late-life cognition	Chapters 5, 9, and 13
γ_7	Socioeconomic status–lifestyles	Chapter 11
γ_8	Lifestyles–chronic disease	Chapter 10
γ_9	Chronic disease–neuropathology	Data being collected
γ_{10}	Chronic disease–late-life cognition	Chapter 10
γ_{11}	Lifestyles–late-life cognition	Chapters 10 and 11
γ_{12}	ApoE status–late-life cognition	Chapter 17
γ_{13}	ApoE status–neuropathology	Data being collected
γ_{14}	Late-life cognition–neuropathology	Data being collected

Note. ApoE, apolipoprotein E.

autopsy. The evidence for these paths is as yet incomplete as we are still in the process of collecting relevant data. Table 18.1 indicates the specific chapters that provide evidence for each of these paths in some detail.

What We Still Need to Learn

Although we have learned a lot about adult intellectual development in our journey that now extends over 45 years, I am very conscious of the fact that many questions remain that can be addressed by further analyses of our database and the data currently being collected (with funding from the National Institute on Aging that currently extends through 2005). Current data collections include completion of the acquisition of a third-generation sample, conducting 7- and 14-year follow-up data collections on the family study, as well as acquiring new participants in that study. The objectives of a new proposal currently pending review will be to conduct a further longitudinal follow-up and acquisition of an eighth data wave to permit monitoring of age-related change in additional cohorts, with particular emphasis on the baby boomers. Also included will be further emphases on biological markers of aging and the relation of cognitive change to changes in brain structure and functioning.

New Questions to Be Asked

The questions to be asked next can be loosely grouped under the following topics:

1. *Differences in rate of aging across generations.* We report in this volume favorable data on the slowing of the rate of cognitive decline across bio-

logically related parent-offspring dyads during the seventh decade of life. New data will permit examining this phenomenon over a 14-year period and into the eighth age decade.

2. *Cross-cultural generalizability of differential patterns of cognitive aging.* We have previously conducted pilot studies in China that suggested both similarities and differential patterns as compared with American samples (see Dutta et al., 1989; Schaie, Nguyen, Willis, Dutta, & Yue, 2001). These studies should be replicated and extended to other cultures, including larger samples of American ethnic minorities.

3. *Effects of retirement on the maintenance of cognitive functioning in old age.* The cognitive effects of retirement seem to be positive for those in routine jobs, but retirement leads to lower functioning in those retiring from complex jobs (see DeFrias & Schaie, 2001; Dutta et al., 1986). These results may well have been affected by the abandonment of mandatory retirement and therefore need to be replicated with more current data.

4. *Relation of psychometric and practical intelligence.* Further studies are needed to determine the predictive value of laboratory measures of cognition to functioning in the community. To do so, longitudinal data need to be acquired for objective measures of instrumental activities of daily living (IADLs).

5. *Psychometric abilities and early detection of risk for dementia.* The work reported in this volume is encouraging enough to suggest further work on the relation between measures used for the description of normal aging and neuropsychological measures used to detect neuropathology.

6. *Brain-behavior relationships.* Cognitive changes with normal aging need to be related to structural and functional changes in the brain. We need to know whether early cognitive declines in midlife represent changes in brain structure and function. We also need to know whether those individuals who gain in cognitive performance in midlife differ in brain morphology from those who remain stable or decline.

7. *Neuropathology detected at postmortem.* The delineation of the relationship of documented long-term behavior change to structural changes in the brain needs to be continued. Of particular interest will be individuals who retained competent behavior close to their demise even though neuropathology is identified at postmortem.

Providing Archival Data for Other Investigators

There is no way that my associates and I will ever be able to fully explore all of the implications of the rich data that we have been privileged to collect. I have therefore begun to develop a public use archive for use by qualified researchers and college teachers for secondary analyses or instructional purposes. This archive is available at http://geron.psu.edu/sls. Here I describe its content and provide instruction on how it can be accessed.

The data archive currently contains all PMA and TBR scores for the first four waves of the study, plus a limited number of demographic descriptors. The files have been stripped of any personal information and of the original identification numbers to make it impossible to identify any particular individual. Altogether, there were 2,813 participants at first occasion. Of these, 1,058 returned for a second assessment, 494 returned for a third occasion, and 121 for a fourth occasion. The data set consequently consists of four cross-sectional files and six longitudinal files.

Those interested in using the archive should access the SLS Web site at http://geron.psu.edu/sls. The following steps should be taken:

1. Select the "For Researchers" button.
2. Select "Measures" to become familiarized with the variable provided.
3. Select "Objectives."
4. Select "SLS Datasets."
5. Select "New User Setup."
6. Print access application form and submit as indicated.

Approved users will then be given a time-limited password that will allow them to download data sets of interest.

Some Final Words

A broadly conceived longitudinal study, far from becoming outdated and obsolete, can often provide the basis for new and exciting questions that could not have been formulated given the state of the art at the study's inception. This volume has provided an account of the many ways in which the original questions proliferated into an extensive program of studies of adult cognitive development and of the many influences that led to the vast individual differences in developmental trajectories. This exciting voyage of discovery has provided me with the basis for my own exciting scientific career and an opportunity to train several cohorts of successful graduate students. As I have moved from being the contemporary of my youngest study participants to that of the older participants, it has also continued to provide encouragement for me in my continuing efforts to shed further light on the dynamics of adult development. Hence, I do not yet consider my work done, and I hope that the reader will anticipate future installments in the account of this odyssey as eagerly as I do.

Appendix

TABLE A-4.1 Intercorrelations for the Basic Ability Battery by Age Group and for the Total Sample

	25 (n = 488)	32 (n = 516)	39 (n = 633)	46 (n = 648)	53 (n = 616)	60 (n = 571)	67 (n = 640)	74 (n = 448)	81 (n = 284)	Total (n = 4,844)
					Age					
Verbal Meaning–Space	.261	.241	.253	.307	.383	.387	.413	.370	.342	.473
Verbal Meaning–Reasoning	.564	.568	.543	.633	.688	.678	.681	.688	.622	.706
Verbal Meaning–Number	.400	.319	.325	.305	.404	.461	.514	.501	.535	.459
Verbal Meaning–Word Fluency	.468	.412	.402	.463	.470	.422	.457	.523	.386	.534
Space–Reasoning	.465	.402	.391	.444	.449	.440	.460	.402	.394	.598
Space–Number	.319	.226	.200	.234	.318	.286	.375	.236	.268	.327
Space–Word Fluency	.249	.190	.157	.162	.198	.206	.286	.239	.122	.349
Reasoning–Number	.468	.353	.323	.313	.459	.466	.481	.508	.509	.440
Reasoning–Word Fluency	.428	.369	.350	.387	.418	.383	.429	.469	.288	.511
Number–Word Fluency	.393	.187	.263	.312	.361	.333	.357	.333	.310	.364

TABLE A-4.2 Intercorrelations for the Expanded Ability Battery by Age Group and for the Total Sample

					Age					
	25	32	39	46	53	60	67	74	81	Total
	(n = 153)	(n = 203)	(n = 335)	(n = 383)	(n = 340)	(n = 345)	(n = 376)	(n = 233)	(n = 157)	(n = 2,525)
PMA Reasoning–Letter Series	.695	.732	.673	.710	.770	.766	.771	.753	.702	.833
PMA Reasoning–Word Series	.635	.699	.687	.667	.741	.723	.790	.727	.718	.819
PMA Reasoning–Number Series	.541	.552	.475	.558	.575	.615	.623	.592	.517	.680
PMA Reasoning–PMA Verbal	.477	.462	.361	.529	.516	.565	.598	.637	.632	.620
PMA Reasoning–Identical Depiction	.362	.267	.386	.438	.414	.365	.456	.435	.441	.650
PMA Reasoning–Number Comparison	.339	.442	.321	.362	.455	.468	.488	.416	.475	.577
PMA Reasoning–Finding A's	.444	.352	.291	.364	.377	.367	.372	.381	.439	.456
PMA Reasoning–Word Fluency	.358	.288	.279	.378	.310	.373	.434	.416	.282	.484
PMA Reasoning–Immediate Recall	.353	.197	.233	.292	.357	.325	.355	.401	.372	.524
PMA Reasoning–Delayed Recall	.337	.199	.240	.248	.315	.336	.360	.386	.286	.520
PMA Reasoning–PMA Space	.445	.431	.426	.381	.392	.338	.413	.347	.335	.562
PMA Reasoning–Object Rotation	.391	.362	.315	.368	.269	.318	.385	.337	.419	.543
PMA Reasoning–Alphanumeric Rotation	.430	.312	.291	.364	.352	.330	.463	.315	.408	.571
PMA Reasoning–Cube Comparison	.571	.387	.387	.390	.349	.392	.375	.324	.278	.576
PMA Reasoning–ETS Vocabulary	.340	.407	.342	.371	.438	.445	.471	.499	.341	.273
PMA Reasoning–Advanced Vocabulary	.388	.412	.314	.406	.398	.463	.455	.535	.393	.299
PMA Reasoning–PMA Number	.426	.404	.370	.428	.374	.459	.380	.411	.450	.358
PMA Reasoning–Addition	.421	.412	.384	.422	.355	.441	.349	.328	.385	.352
PMA Reasoning–Subtraction and Multiplication	.347	.370	.342	.418	.429	.427	.400	.405	.447	.413
Letter Series–Word Series	.674	.605	.639	.643	.675	.667	.728	.697	.607	.785
Letter Series–Number Series	.595	.588	.516	.610	.599	.631	.666	.569	.464	.700
Letter Series–PMA Verbal	.490	.456	.311	.492	.455	.516	.544	.530	.438	.569
Letter Series–Identical Pictures	.380	.251	.336	.432	.423	.293	.401	.311	.360	.624
Letter Series–Number Comparison	.359	.364	.310	.342	.340	.434	.429	.415	.302	.545
Letter Series–Findings A's	.269	.340	.266	.333	.422	.292	.379	.361	.374	.436

(continued)

437

TABLE A-4.2 Continued

| | Age | | | | | | | | | Total |
	25 (n=153)	32 (n=203)	39 (n=335)	46 (n=383)	53 (n=340)	60 (n=345)	67 (n=376)	74 (n=233)	81 (n=157)	(n=2,525)
Letter Series–Word Fluency	.336	.278	.254	.366	.309	.358	.413	.436	.182	.469
Letter Series–Immediate Recall	.255	.317	.261	.357	.360	.333	.341	.369	.359	.527
Letter Series–Delayed Recall	.293	.226	.257	.339	.315	.336	.322	.356	.300	.524
Letter Series–PMA Space	.381	.425	.412	.373	.404	.386	.449	.253	.319	.565
Letter Series–Object Rotation	.255	.426	.354	.412	.286	.357	.366	.259	.234	.539
Letter Series–Alphanumeric Rotation	.394	.384	.301	.390	.370	.358	.420	.293	.306	.567
Letter Series–Cube Comparison	.567	.398	.423	.381	.395	.377	.363	.276	.261	.583
Letter Series–ETS Vocabulary	.333	.399	.309	.370	.396	.472	.409	.462	.287	.245
Letter Series–Advanced Vocabulary	.380	.425	.312	.422	.380	.523	.461	.460	.358	.291
Letter Series–PMA Number	.356	.348	.351	.407	.362	.440	.370	.447	.353	.335
Letter Series–Addition	.336	.359	.318	.373	.306	.398	.315	.351	.263	.312
Letter Series–Subtraction and Multiplication	.306	.355	.301	.402	.394	.368	.398	.433	.245	.381
Word Series–Number Series	.457	.459	.406	.507	.531	.469	.567	.564	.428	.628
Word Series–PMA Verbal	.448	.357	.341	.452	.512	.485	.611	.576	.633	.594
Word Series–Identical Pictures	.264	.240	.364	.436	.432	.389	.439	.394	.475	.636
Word Series–Number Comparison	.389	.339	.332	.339	.372	.490	.460	.446	.464	.560
Word Series–Finding A's	.364	.360	.290	.333	.412	.315	.449	.318	.469	.452
Word Series–Word Fluency	.350	.269	.227	.414	.338	.320	.463	.401	.317	.479
Word Series–Immediate Recall	.288	.221	.185	.292	.396	.286	.345	.452	.372	.511
Word Series–Delayed Recall	.338	.112	.204	.226	.302	.298	.343	.410	.333	.498
Word Series–PMA Space	.402	.295	.324	.377	.330	.299	.413	.304	.370	.531
Word Series–Object Rotation	.321	.229	.239	.381	.269	.293	.330	.336	.383	.517
Word Series–Alphanumeric Rotation	.311	.234	.207	.334	.297	.344	.427	.354	.368	.545
Word Series–Cube Comparison	.458	.297	.344	.423	.396	.352	.407	.219	.332	.559
Word Series–ETS Vocabulary	.305	.293	.265	.299	.412	.361	.453	.442	.390	.236
Word Series–Advanced Vocabulary	.363	.294	.252	.334	.359	.360	.452	.422	.413	.256

										(continued)
Word Series–PMA Number	.413	.333	.400	.386	.369	.404	.399	.405	.496	.353
Word Series–Addition	.374	.359	.370	.381	.354	.417	.359	.298	.389	.341
Word Series–Subtraction and Multiplication	.358	.391	.304	.361	.416	.398	.401	.390	.506	.403
Number Series–PMA Verbal	.416	.329	.278	.410	.427	.388	.513	.475	.332	.498
Number Series–Identical Pictures	.309	.170	.212	.322	.297	.234	.372	.326	.211	.496
Number Series–Number Comparison	.242	.320	.171	.274	.271	.281	.321	.292	.378	.430
Number Series–Finding A's	.386	.291	.211	.259	.287	.221	.348	.214	.277	.363
Number Series–Number Fluency	.329	.189	.251	.240	.257	.310	.290	.302	.164	.384
Number Series–Immediate Recall	.214	.219	.193	.160	.259	.274	.198	.281	.139	.392
Number Series–Delayed Recall	.239	.081	.211	.139	.230	.278	.205	.293	.150	.394
Number Series–PMA Space	.355	.329	.298	.357	.451	.355	.487	.226	.382	.507
Number Series–Object Rotation	.266	.368	.279	.376	.311	.296	.350	.200	.288	.470
Number Series–Alphanumeric Rotation	.323	.303	.280	.346	.347	.281	.400	.191	.293	.482
Number Series–Cube Comparison	.489	.358	.325	.363	.365	.377	.409	.303	.202	.515
Number Series–ETS Vocabulary	.342	.348	.246	.262	.400	.380	.358	.472	.230	.253
Number Series–Advanced Vocabulary	.354	.346	.338	.337	.413	.389	.414	.503	.267	.305
Number Series–PMA Number	.414	.469	.393	.416	.420	.411	.416	.392	.480	.390
Number Series–Addition	.431	.480	.380	.427	.372	.375	.334	.266	.364	.365
Number Series–Subtraction and Multiplication	.451	.497	.445	.466	.451	.388	.432	.335	.422	.449
PMA Verbal–Identical Pictures	.454	.287	.274	.374	.402	.432	.484	.539	.572	.539
PMA Verbal–Number Comparison	.190	.220	.222	.282	.281	.429	.484	.487	.536	.449
PMA Verbal–Finding A's	.327	.214	.242	.294	.400	.282	.363	.468	.513	.392
PMA Verbal–Word Fluency	.477	.363	.345	.474	.415	.397	.464	.437	.363	.492
PMA Verbal–Immediate Recall	.429	.349	.292	.342	.381	.381	.337	.466	.310	.468
PMA Verbal–Delayed Recall	.394	.260	.282	.275	.368	.370	.320	.466	.281	.447
PMA Verbal–PMA Space	.235	.223	.158	.235	.319	.272	.376	.352	.357	.406
PMA Verbal–Object Rotation	.303	.299	.164	.326	.249	.309	.345	.367	.415	.447
PMA Verbal–Alphanumeric Rotation	.316	.300	.167	.344	.388	.304	.374	.362	.341	.472
PMA Verbal–Cube Comparison	.426	.259	.164	.175	.171	.291	.358	.338	.334	.393
PMA Verbal–ETS Vocabulary	.750	.702	.604	.707	.657	.612	.583	.493	.490	.540
PMA Verbal–Advanced Vocabulary	.705	.711	.601	.704	.653	.620	.584	.518	.528	.555
PMA Verbal–PMA Number	.372	.321	.297	.312	.340	.359	.411	.423	.447	.368

TABLE A-4.2 Continued

	25 (n = 153)	32 (n = 203)	39 (n = 335)	46 (n = 383)	53 (n = 340)	60 (n = 345)	67 (n = 376)	74 (n = 233)	81 (n = 157)	Total (n = 2,525)
PMA Verbal–Addition	.287	.323	.296	.367	.305	.369	.390	.342	.455	.364
PMA Verbal–Subtraction and Multiplication	.275	.324	.332	.405	.368	.394	.463	.449	.461	.432
Identical Pictures–Number Comparison	.331	.308	.369	.429	.333	.421	.475	.452	.479	.578
Identical Pictures–Finding A's	.266	.280	.281	.360	.297	.321	.330	.400	.411	.427
Identical Pictures–Word Fluency	.340	.298	.182	.272	.242	.266	.335	.288	.337	.437
Identical Pictures–Immediate Recall	.314	.368	.211	.260	.287	.289	.223	.324	.327	.500
Identical Pictures–Delayed Recall	.305	.319	.179	.215	.279	.196	.232	.326	.240	.502
Identical Pictures–PMA Space	.276	.290	.334	.318	.317	.319	.364	.334	.394	.533
Identical Pictures–Object Rotation	.371	.131	.216	.301	.257	.289	.363	.395	.422	.532
Identical Pictures–Alphanumeric Rotation	.371	.139	.205	.305	.305	.367	.355	.421	.461	.567
Identical Pictures–Cube Comparison	.388	.222	.296	.347	.308	.303	.369	.265	.357	.556
Identical Pictures–ETS Vocabulary	.362	.233	.181	.228	.192	.199	.195	.233	.311	.100
Identical Pictures–Advanced Vocabulary	.285	.224	.153	.238	.194	.236	.191	.225	.275	.119
Identical Pictures–PMA Number	.130	.222	.272	.271	.123	.128	.244	.280	.309	.197
Identical Pictures–Addition	.185	.221	.329	.312	.166	.228	.284	.287	.359	.245
Identical Pictures–Subtraction and Multiplication	.157	.167	.259	.300	.220	.258	.350	.351	.339	.307
Number Comparison–Finding A's	.488	.400	.417	.398	.424	.440	.374	.396	.493	.493
Number Comparison–Word Fluency	.216	.232	.121	.280	.220	.233	.286	.323	.365	.370
Number Comparison–Immediate Recall	.245	.267	.255	.246	.264	.273	.280	.285	.357	.436
Number Comparison–Delayed Recall	.324	.160	.264	.218	.230	.265	.282	.230	.358	.433
Number Comparison–PMA Space	.237	.218	.231	.171	.245	.186	.312	.145	.252	.400
Number Comparison–Object Rotation	.181	.065	.175	.244	.119	.180	.211	.180	.388	.380
Number Comparison–Alphanumeric Rotation	.216	.020	.113	.259	.246	.244	.263	.162	.415	.413
Number Comparison–Cube Comparison	.190	.229	.138	.199	.120	.205	.320	.120	.263	.396
Number Comparison–ETS Vocabulary	.045	.082	.162	.062	.155	.189	.228	.120	.150	.074
Number Comparison–Advanced Vocabulary	.088	.186	.112	.053	.116	.192	.137	.136	.206	.081

Number Comparison–PMA Number	.433	.288	.426	.362	.363	.406	.457	.491	.636	.382
Number Comparison–Addition	.527	.371	.502	.482	.456	.504	.510	.543	.691	.462
Number Comparison–Subtraction and Multiplication	.492	.386	.482	.492	.454	.520	.498	.630	.697	.501
Finding A's–Word Fluency	.365	.245	.243	.308	.284	.263	.289	.235	.318	.359
Finding A's–Immediate Recall	.167	.246	.349	.235	.358	.200	.280	.206	.249	.365
Finding A's–Delayed Recall	.211	.177	.290	.252	.345	.162	.306	.209	.306	.365
Finding A's–PMA Space	.331	.022	.180	.230	.187	.193	.216	.118	.180	.302
Finding A's–Object Rotation	.250	-.091	.139	.315	.157	.164	.118	.154	.221	.280
Finding A's–Alphanumeric Rotation	.202	.024	.091	.316	.215	.238	.191	.222	.299	.320
Finding A's–Cube Comparison	.242	-.004	.106	.158	.184	.105	.237	.190	.320	.286
Finding A's–ETS Vocabulary	.194	.098	.209	.204	.304	.129	.219	.178	.235	.152
Finding A's–Advanced Vocabulary	.227	.093	.151	.222	.275	.154	.262	.204	.265	.171
Finding A's–PMA Number	.433	.241	.341	.253	.297	.186	.241	.351	.321	.277
Finding A's–Addition	.398	.333	.382	.327	.320	.284	.284	.323	.371	.326
Finding A's–Subtraction and Multiplication	.425	.339	.357	.346	.373	.286	.324	.382	.418	.371
Word Fluency–Immediate Recall	.411	.318	.310	.284	.223	.416	.325	.363	.400	.439
Word Fluency–Delayed Recall	.391	.354	.297	.256	.238	.418	.327	.353	.331	.437
Word Fluency–PMA Space	.281	.265	.107	.166	.172	.167	.271	.164	.083	.326
Word Fluency–Object Rotation	.277	.226	.137	.216	.141	.147	.217	.174	.144	.328
Word Fluency–Alphanumeric Rotation	.265	.395	.085	.155	.197	.209	.273	.177	.206	.357
Word Fluency–Cube Comparison	.256	.207	.136	.172	.080	.157	.217	.044	.070	.312
Word Fluency–ETS Vocabulary	.355	.313	.425	.410	.333	.425	.447	.425	.406	.335
Word Fluency–Advanced Vocabulary	.408	.274	.443	.400	.367	.454	.447	.447	.404	.358
Word Fluency–PMA Number	.396	.294	.279	.270	.325	.265	.278	.267	.330	.293
Word Fluency–Addition	.231	.317	.285	.357	.326	.287	.281	.275	.375	.315
Word Fluency–Subtraction and Multiplication	.197	.253	.256	.342	.375	.251	.289	.343	.372	.343
Immediate Recall–Delayed Recall	.856	.844	.847	.835	.858	.868	.840	.855	.839	.886
Immediate Recall–PMA Space	.180	.088	.103	.106	.111	.040	.097	.119	-.030	.309
Immediate Recall–Object Rotation	.262	.231	.080	.166	.059	.074	.129	.148	.079	.339
Immediate Recall–Alphanumeric Rotation	.218	.222	.095	.226	.147	.140	.091	.248	.138	.379
Immediate Recall–Cube Comparison	.213	.196	.132	.206	.108	.067	.059	.049	.046	.346
Immediate Recall–ETS Vocabulary	.362	.327	.355	.316	.350	.409	.271	.388	.298	.242

(continued)

TABLE A-4.2 Continued

					Age					
	25 (n = 153)	32 (n = 203)	39 (n = 335)	46 (n = 383)	53 (n = 340)	60 (n = 345)	67 (n = 376)	74 (n = 233)	81 (n = 157)	Total (n = 2,525)
Immediate Recall–Advanced Vocabulary	.312	.340	.360	.328	.326	.465	.334	.381	.292	.275
Immediate Recall–PMA Number	.178	.229	.139	.072	.152	.208	.182	.201	.348	.176
Immediate Recall–Addition	.231	.189	.161	.109	.158	.224	.170	.100	.353	.184
Immediate Recall–Subtraction and Multiplication	.197	.178	.212	.160	.227	.224	.191	.188	.328	.251
Delayed Recall–PMA Space	.185	.111	.077	.088	.063	.054	.073	.118	-.022	.311
Delayed Recall–Object Rotation	.205	.213	.076	.142	.043	.052	.082	.113	.063	.333
Delayed Recall–Alphanumeric Rotation	.222	.205	.091	.199	.106	.100	.107	.264	.071	.377
Delayed Recall–Cube Comparison	.242	.167	.089	.164	.060	.049	.088	.145	.032	.352
Delayed Recall–ETS Vocabulary	.302	.307	.326	.254	.331	.370	.265	.360	.212	.203
Delayed Recall–Advanced Vocabulary	.300	.272	.328	.270	.323	.419	.302	.365	.266	.235
Delayed Recall–PMA Number	.231	.122	.135	.052	.087	.207	.148	.200	.314	.147
Delayed Recall–Addition	.283	.128	.167	.110	.125	.220	.158	.106	.360	.173
Delayed Recall–Subtraction and Multiplication	.264	.098	.202	.152	.221	.229	.192	.176	.332	.243
PMA Space–Object Rotation	.615	.597	.661	.724	.685	.685	.671	.763	.576	.750
PMA Space–Alphanumeric Rotation	.436	.429	.487	.530	.572	.540	.580	.610	.464	.646
PMA Space–Cube Comparison	.519	.571	.485	.456	.433	.477	.452	.305	.188	.593
PMA Space–ETS Vocabulary	.207	.211	.086	.132	.192	.182	.311	.151	.266	.115
PMA Space–Advanced Vocabulary	.229	.213	.157	.175	.258	.222	.275	.200	.231	.156
PMA Space–PMA Number	.332	.170	.251	.239	.293	.266	.277	.211	.249	.253
PMA Space–Addition	.211	.227	.262	.237	.224	.234	.234	.164	.158	.231
PMA Space–Subtraction and Multiplication	.146	.168	.199	.200	.262	.215	.248	.124	.193	.254
Object Rotation–Alphanumeric Rotation	.569	.658	.649	.673	.660	.593	.656	.712	.630	.745
Object Rotation–Cube Comparison	.258	.379	.426	.402	.300	.416	.396	.301	.242	.529
Object Rotation–ETS Vocabulary	.236	.337	.115	.248	.120	.172	.211	.136	.120	.120
Object Rotation–Advanced Vocabulary	.235	.350	.158	.278	.137	.190	.231	.204	.099	.155
Object Rotation–PMA Number	.233	.187	.265	.257	.217	.276	.191	.133	.275	.231

	1	2	3	4	5	6	7	8	9	10
Object Rotation–Addition	.208	.176	.241	.260	.196	.214	.146	.099	.286	.217
Object Rotation–Subtraction and Multiplication	.191	.119	.238	.234	.263	.208	.221	.118	.370	.273
Alphanumeric Rotation–Cube Comparison	.257	.276	.343	.362	.288	.386	.430	.406	.280	.527
Alphanumeric Rotation–ETS Vocabulary	.286	.269	.111	.204	.228	.186	.226	.163	.190	.129
Alphanumeric Rotation–Advanced Vocabulary	.321	.266	.142	.249	.260	.221	.267	.221	.147	.171
Alphanumeric Rotation–PMA Number	.263	.239	.159	.284	.257	.208	.226	.166	.328	.231
Alphanumeric Rotation–Addition	.255	.226	.165	.194	.220	.173	.197	.081	.289	.210
Alphenumeric Rotation–Subtraction and Multiplication	.238	.168	.201	.162	.265	.248	.250	.112	.362	.278
Cube Comparison–ETS Vocabulary	.346	.142	.003	.062	.081	.095	.122	.029	.014	.019
Cube Comparison–Advanced Vocabulary	.352	.226	.099	.140	.057	.182	.102	.046	-.009	.070
Cube Comparison–PMA Number	.322	.142	.207	.170	.171	.260	.195	.095	.145	.183
Cube Comparison–Addition	.315	.128	.150	.141	.147	.191	.170	.042	.202	.171
Cube Comparison–Subtraction and Multiplication	.278	.099	.177	.160	.165	.248	.201	.089	.279	.235
ETS Vocabulary–Advanced Vocabulary	.760	.798	.789	.821	.787	.794	.787	.845	.843	.807
ETS Vocabulary–PMA Number	.226	.244	.195	.189	.237	.290	.256	.237	.276	.231
ETS Vocabulary–Addition	.170	.207	.225	.208	.153	.161	.219	.136	.165	.190
ETS Vocabulary–Subtraction and Multiplication	.112	.231	.265	.256	.234	.175	.259	.186	.163	.217
Advanced Vocabulary–PMA Number	.234	.212	.146	.122	.229	.209	.230	.227	.306	.209
Advanced Vocabulary–Addition	.180	.173	.166	.128	.197	.136	.190	.143	.213	.174
Advanced Vocabulary–Subtraction and Multiplication	.129	.204	.224	.190	.264	.166	.260	.202	.194	.214
PMA Number–Addition	.796	.799	.840	.783	.830	.823	.807	.776	.735	.806
PMA Number–Subtraction and Multiplication	.647	.676	.712	.662	.740	.683	.748	.728	.725	.705
Addition–Subtraction and Multiplication	.799	.823	.808	.812	.828	.798	.818	.803	.837	.814

Note. ETS, Educational Testing Service; PMA, Primary Mental Abilities.

TABLE A-4.3 Intercorrelations for the Cognitive Factor Scores

	Age									Total
	25 (n = 153)	32 (n = 203)	39 (n = 335)	46 (n = 383)	53 (n = 340)	60 (n = 345)	67 (n = 376)	74 (n = 233)	81 (n = 157)	(n = 2,525)
Inductive Reasoning–Spatial Orientation	.600	.511	.480	.540	.488	.484	.543	.384	.508	.686
Inductive Reasoning–Perceptual Speed	.631	.568	.540	.645	.635	.602	.680	.629	.617	.771
Inductive Reasoning–Numeric Ability	.490	.510	.458	.525	.482	.518	.450	.460	.483	.436
Inductive Reasoning–Verbal Ability	.473	.477	.407	.476	.518	.573	.560	.621	.466	.389
Inductive Reasoning–Verbal Memory	.378	.271	.289	.330	.387	.368	.373	.468	.338	.560
Spatial Orientation–Perceptual Speed	.537	.293	.346	.465	.418	.443	.501	.442	.575	.654
Spatial Orientation–Numeric Ability	.343	.238	.286	.305	.318	.304	.284	.156	.410	.301
Spatial Orientation–Verbal Ability	.405	.370	.163	.270	.260	.280	.342	.240	.252	.227
Spatial Orientation–Verbal Memory	.287	.237	.118	.203	.097	.105	.123	.187	.054	.408
Perceptual Speed–Numeric Ability	.536	.476	.559	.520	.461	.467	.519	.535	.578	.463
Perceptual Speed–Verbal Ability	.538	.476	.475	.484	.512	.512	.515	.484	.522	.388
Perceptual Speed–Verbal Memory	.467	.443	.409	.382	.446	.386	.401	.452	.414	.601
Numeric Ability–Verbal Ability	.436	.272	.265	.243	.276	.261	.311	.264	.255	.281
Numeric Ability–Verbal Memory	.270	.187	.198	.139	.189	.258	.205	.182	.384	.228
Verbal Ability–Verbal Memory	.405	.368	.400	.343	.385	.495	.357	.462	.327	.329

TABLE A-4.4 Intercorrelations for the Everyday Problems Test by Age Group and for the Total Sample

	25 (n = 40)	32 (n = 96)	39 (n = 163)	46 (n = 218)	53 (n = 222)	60 (n = 224)	67 (n = 266)	74 (n = 271)	81 (n = 224)	88 (n = 71)	Total (n = 1,795)
Meals–Health	.337	.576	.582	.292	.298	.316	.392	.381	.536	.554	.507
Meals–Phone	.338	.578	.326	.315	.375	.365	.442	.465	.492	.548	.505
Meals–Consumer	-.106	.509	.401	.264	.418	.299	.395	.466	.462	.566	.499
Meals–Financial	.045	.389	.310	.353	.298	.344	.406	.418	.590	.576	.508
Meals–Household	.364	.421	.420	.357	.437	.400	.485	.457	.471	.448	.535
Meals–Transport	-.041	.477	.322	.490	.322	.273	.361	.505	.575	.513	.514
Health–Phone	.067	.427	.417	.325	.288	.383	.313	.418	.479	.530	.498
Health–Consumer	-.191	.649	.410	.246	.353	.196	.295	.416	.525	.462	.505
Health–Financial	-.072	.298	.422	.336	.287	.255	.327	.514	.524	.515	.523
Health–Household	.199	.409	.427	.334	.348	.337	.353	.414	.354	.442	.505
Health–Transport	.122	.323	.399	.320	.348	.390	.259	.483	.519	.412	.494
Phone–Consumer	-.090	.352	.321	.296	.318	.261	.316	.350	.456	.466	.460
Phone–Financial	.021	.290	.321	.373	.214	.266	.437	.443	.525	.424	.499
Phone–Household	.017	.261	.347	.411	.303	.337	.363	.430	.439	.419	.509
Phone–Transport	-.137	.309	.420	.385	.334	.374	.443	.409	.534	.500	.509
Consumer–Financial	.240	.422	.488	.444	.363	.336	.302	.500	.485	.519	.542
Consumer–Household	.021	.417	.406	.344	.352	.333	.381	.396	.445	.477	.520
Consumer–Transport	-.112	.524	.402	.369	.254	.224	.269	.459	.566	.693	.520
Financial–Household	.271	.441	.492	.449	.298	.368	.468	.420	.504	.536	.562
Financial–Transport	.176	.414	.505	.423	.272	.303	.394	.504	.557	.472	.540
Household–Transport	.552	.389	.356	.411	.287	.397	.361	.496	.510	.566	.544

TABLE A-4.5 Intercorrelations for the Test of Behavioral Rigidity Factor Scores

| | Age | | | | | | | | | |
	25 (*n* = 487)	32 (*n* = 516)	39 (*n* = 631)	46 (*n* = 648)	53 (*n* = 615)	60 (*n* = 571)	67 (*n* = 640)	74 (*n* = 449)	81 (*n* = 280)	Total (*n* = 4,837)
Motor-Cognitive Flexibility with Attitudinal Flexibility	.131	.213	.183	.275	.242	.284	.286	.228	.176	.341
Motor-Cognitive Flexibility with Psychomotor Speed	.141	.211	.298	.410	.348	.361	.411	.380	.249	.465
Attitudinal Flexibility with Psychomotor Speed	.218	.292	.242	.345	.349	.325	.330	.281	.271	.383

TABLE A-11.1 Intercorrelations Among Life Complexity Inventory Work Variables

Variable	1	2	3	4	5	6	7
1. Reading/writing							
2. Dealing with people	.20						
3. Number of employees	.16	.26					
4. Speed control	.03	.04	.11				
5. Working under time pressure	.08	.17	.20	.43			
6. Working with hands	−.09	.00	−.01	.11	.11		
7. Routinization of tasks	−.05	−.08	−.12	.06	−.01	.19	
8. Task duration	−.05	−.14	−.01	.02	−.02	.10	.11

TABLE A-12.1 Intercorrelations for the 13 Personality Factor Scales

					Age					
	25 (n = 381)	32 (n = 450)	39 (n = 560)	46 (n = 589)	53 (n = 530)	60 (n = 505)	67 (n = 338)	74 (n = 542)	81 (n = 433)	Total (n = 4,200)
Affectothymia–Community Involvement	-.024	-.051	-.059	-.111	-.096	-.162	-.139	-.092	-.143	-.113
Affectothymia–Conservatism	.147	.049	.006	-.058	-.009	-.021	-.038	-.128	-.068	-.039
Affectothymia–Group Dependency	.147	.191	.162	.151	.137	.182	.164	.124	.151	.170
Affectothymia–Honesty	.189	.221	.218	.267	.294	.255	.228	.236	.196	.258
Affectothymia–Inflexibility	-.188	-.298	-.245	-.335	-.346	-.328	-.316	-.340	-.361	-.334
Affectothymia–Interest in Science	-.100	-.148	-.136	-.184	-.159	-.170	-.124	-.203	-.193	-.160
Affectothymia–Low Self-Esteem	.060	.102	.119	.159	.196	.131	.176	.170	.142	.158
Affectothymia–Political Concern	.103	.152	.081	.151	.101	.126	.117	.138	.000	.088
Affectothymia–Premsia	.091	.103	.095	-.026	.037	.096	.094	.050	.031	.071
Affectothymia–Superego Strength	-.167	-.184	-.145	-.230	-.160	-.205	-.203	-.200	-.252	-.203
Affectothymia–Threctia	.202	.336	.295	.336	.384	.379	.274	.352	.321	.335
Affectothymia–Untroubled Adequacy	.091	.016	.080	-.001	-.012	-.065	.015	-.028	.029	-.012
Community Involvement–Conservatism	.061	.111	.103	.093	.123	.198	.117	.135	.148	.137
Community Involvement–Group Dependency	-.207	-.146	-.157	-.114	-.192	-.254	-.268	-.273	-.287	-.220
Community Involvement–Honesty	-.308	-.150	-.209	-.288	-.281	-.277	-.285	-.373	-.345	-.282
Community Involvement–Inflexibility	.266	.207	.194	.267	.266	.301	.334	.326	.340	.300
Community Involvement–Interest in Science	-.019	-.071	-.124	-.030	.083	-.035	-.018	-.027	.075	-.017
Community Involvement–Low Self-Esteem	-.255	-.108	-.152	-.231	-.226	-.302	-.383	-.331	-.270	-.260
Community Involvement–Political Concern	.239	.263	.217	.211	.203	.247	.061	.165	.094	.214
Community Involvement–Premsia	-.060	-.063	-.024	.055	-.103	-.040	-.036	-.037	-.083	-.047
Community Involvement–Superego Strength	.090	.020	.015	.082	.058	.096	.154	.077	.130	.088
Community Involvement–Threctia	-.072	-.019	-.043	-.047	-.134	-.090	-.059	-.100	-.144	-.089
Community Involvement–Untroubled Adequacy	.179	.154	.154	.209	.279	.228	.179	.240	.222	.222
Conservatism–Group Dependency	-.169	-.063	-.113	-.106	-.075	-.124	-.054	-.095	-.170	-.131
Conservatism–Honesty	.052	.040	-.068	-.048	-.076	-.028	-.035	.013	-.134	-.066
Conservatism–Inflexibility	.179	.119	.233	.141	.174	.149	.179	.140	.117	.208

	C1	C2	C3	C4	C5	C6	C7	C8	C9	C10
Conservatism–Interest in Science	.074	-.123	-.026	-.150	.022	-.044	-.059	-.043	-.008	-.033
Conservative–Low Self-Esteem	-.134	-.085	-.155	-.096	-.025	-.123	-.103	-.109	-.079	-.126
Conservatism–Political Concern	.275	.194	.255	.192	.133	.220	.049	.081	.186	.208
Conservatism–Premsia	-.223	-.125	-.192	-.180	-.150	-.148	-.177	-.174	-.199	-.183
Conservatism–Superego Strength	.025	.040	.062	-.012	.033	-.021	.033	.091	-.080	.042
Conservatism–Threctia	.019	.029	-.053	.008	-.070	-.012	-.056	-.061	-.133	-.051
Conservatism–Untroubled Adequacy	.111	.078	.143	.061	.067	.086	.011	.036	.108	.109
Group Dependency–Honesty	.261	.199	.257	.285	.346	.347	.363	.310	.441	.332
Group Dependency–Inflexibility	-.273	-.186	-.197	-.215	-.240	-.237	-.304	-.311	-.324	-.294
Group Dependency–Interest in Science	-.099	-.104	-.050	-.137	-.181	-.098	-.044	-.052	-.079	-.108
Group Dependency–Low Self-Esteem	.398	.347	.338	.293	.317	.423	.332	.371	.456	.371
Group Dependency–Political Concern	-.178	-.064	-.066	-.048	-.086	-.178	-.110	-.130	-.123	-.142
Group Dependency–Premsia	.130	.064	.083	-.009	.114	.091	.008	.022	.105	.074
Group Dependency–Superego Strength	-.350	-.347	-.292	-.338	-.310	-.276	-.286	-.192	-.271	-.308
Group Dependency–Threctia	.198	.048	.111	.072	.061	.149	.109	.142	.209	.129
Group Dependency–Untroubled Adequacy	.005	-.146	-.135	-.083	-.225	-.128	-.111	-.216	-.251	-.174
Honesty–Inflexibility	-.387	-.406	-.378	-.428	-.489	-.434	-.458	-.481	-.463	-.478
Honesty–Interest in Science	-.113	-.159	-.141	-.209	-.216	-.198	-.159	-.156	-.198	-.180
Honesty–Low Self-Esteem	.192	.098	.158	.243	.243	.194	.303	.169	.257	.232
Honesty–Political Concern	-.064	-.066	-.034	-.017	.027	-.105	-.093	-.139	-.067	-.095
Honesty–Premsia	.062	.051	.123	.025	.100	.079	.052	.036	.066	.075
Honesty–Superego Strength	-.270	-.056	-.135	-.190	-.214	-.217	-.310	-.170	-.287	-.217
Honesty–Threctia	.123	.162	.180	.208	.227	.300	.246	.236	.284	.239
Honesty–Untroubled Adequacy	-.219	-.291	-.209	-.216	-.208	-.236	-.291	-.331	-.196	.285
Inflexibility–Interest in Science	.238	.077	.237	.219	.220	.219	.211	.191	.185	.209
Inflexibility–Low Self-Esteem	-.171	-.106	-.189	-.228	-.228	-.245	-.300	-.310	-.279	-.266
Inflexibility–Political Concern	.116	.095	.156	.127	.029	.148	.097	.055	.077	.160
Inflexibility–Premsia	-.187	-.172	-.189	-.025	-.160	-.160	-.172	-.124	-.205	-.167
Inflexibility–Superego Strength	.177	.169	.148	.190	.210	.196	.265	.182	.208	.220
Inflexibility–Threctia	-.169	-.247	-.203	-.231	-.290	-.290	-.255	-.233	-.439	-.281
Inflexibility–Untroubled Adequacy	.235	.242	.201	.199	.159	.321	.236	.287	.223	.285

(continued)

449

TABLE A-12.1 Continued

					Age					
	25 (n = 381)	32 (n = 450)	39 (n = 560)	46 (n = 589)	53 (n = 530)	60 (n = 505)	67 (n = 338)	74 (n = 542)	81 (n = 433)	Total (n = 4,200)
Interest in Science–Low Self-Esteem	.027	.028	.056	-.022	-.074	-.034	-.029	-.024	.039	-.020
Interest in Science–Political Concern	-.022	.070	-.044	-.022	-.024	-.049	-.015	-.079	-.087	-.006
Interest in Science–Premsia	-.125	-.107	-.057	.011	-.059	-.156	-.119	-.136	-.104	-.095
Interest in Science–Superego Strength	.260	.178	.183	.223	.278	.247	.202	.174	.278	.224
Interest in Science–Threctia	-.151	-.170	-.183	-.121	-.167	-.153	-.249	-.105	-.212	-.168
Interest in Science–Untroubled Adequacy	-.095	.012	-.047	-.015	.035	-.031	-.014	-.015	-.023	-.002
Low Self-Esteem–Political Concern	.055	-.038	-.055	-.009	-.037	-.174	-.126	-.030	-.188	-.087
Low Self-Esteem–Premsia	.123	.071	.102	-.048	.011	-.034	-.013	-.019	.033	.034
Low Self-Esteem–Superego Strength	-.154	-.146	-.212	-.166	-.167	-.150	-.190	-.116	-.130	-.177
Low Self-Esteem–Threctia	.013	-.016	.051	.044	.128	.070	.043	.034	.053	.065
Low Self-Esteem–Untroubled Adequacy	-.062	-.052	-.046	-.048	-.106	-.122	-.139	-.101	-.139	-.115
Political Concern–Premsia	-.001	-.015	-.031	.059	-.062	-.039	-.017	.046	-.072	-.027
Political Concern–Superego Strength	.002	-.080	.000	-.043	-.070	-.033	-.062	-.076	-.084	-.026
Political Concern–Threctia	.049	.027	.063	.013	.107	.037	-.009	.020	-.052	.016
Political Concern–Untroubled Adequacy	.177	.242	.188	.137	.152	.077	.224	.144	.089	.206
Premsia–Superego Strength	-.139	-.143	-.127	.007	-.069	-.102	-.100	-.108	-.039	-.099
Premsia–Threctia	.149	.057	.090	.042	.044	.049	.123	.071	.155	.089
Premsia–Untroubled Adequacy	-.004	.012	-.027	.063	-.029	-.016	.030	.026	-.075	-.012
Superego Strength–Threctia	-.096	-.122	-.146	-.074	-.112	-.131	-.117	-.115	-.181	-.130
Superego Strength–Untroubled Adequacy	-.023	-.011	-.052	.062	.000	.065	.058	.068	-.014	-.037
Threctia–Untroubled Adequacy	.087	-.008	.113	-.037	.016	-.041	-.040	-.119	-.051	-.025

TABLE A-12.2 Intercorrelations for the NEO Personality Questionnaire Scales

| | \multicolumn{11}{c}{Age} | | | | | | | | | | |
	25 (n=34)	32 (n=145)	39 (n=308)	46 (n=419)	53 (n=388)	60 (n=333)	67 (n=338)	74 (n=331)	81 (n=227)	88 (n=59)	Total (n=2,582)
Neuroticism–Extraversion	-.127	-.291	-.361	-.440	-.350	-.335	-.407	-.254	-.249	-.202	-.319
Neuroticism–Openness	-.080	.092	-.058	-.128	-.131	-.081	-.157	-.045	-.040	-.202	-.048
Neuroticism–Agreeableness	-.034	-.150	-.225	-.262	-.297	-.190	-.204	-.155	-.282	-.277	-.247
Neuroticism–Conscientiousness	-.064	-.504	-.445	-.472	-.465	-.513	-.452	-.455	-.522	-.559	-.476
Extraversion–Openness	.113	.332	.246	.397	.465	.323	.430	.393	.540	.004	.400
Extraversion–Agreeableness	-.154	.128	.017	.182	.105	.048	.128	.139	.161	.087	.078
Extraversion–Conscientiousness	.134	.133	.339	.214	.277	.146	.422	.365	.258	.207	.266
Openness–Agreeableness	-.099	.055	.051	.161	.139	.107	.115	.166	.069	.076	.067
Openness–Conscientiousness	-.096	-.109	.045	.000	.014	-.084	.102	.076	-.028	-.036	.007
Agreeableness–Conscientiousness	-.074	.067	.046	.110	.125	.194	.197	.111	.266	.048	.131

451

TABLE A-17.1 Intercorrelations Among the Psychometric and Neuropsychology Measures (N = 499)

Correlations Among the Neuropsychology Measures

Measure	2	3	4	5	6	7	8	9	10	11	12	13	14	15	16	17
1. PMA Reasoning	.78	.81	.63	.56	.54	.54	.52	.65	.35	.38	.47	.44	.50	.48	.49	.27
2. ADEPT Letter Series		.75	.64	.51	.48	.49	.51	.56	.33	.36	.46	.40	.46	.42	.47	.45
3. Word Series			.60	.51	.51	.51	.49	.61	.37	.38	.44	.41	.48	.48	.49	.47
4. Number Series				.46	.41	.43	.48	.53	.27	.30	.46	.48	.51	.35	.33	.34
5. PMA Space					.77	.66	.55	.46	.22	.22	.35	.33	.33	.27	.25	.23
6. Object Rotation						.70	.51	.49	.24	.19	.32	.30	.32	.27	.26	.24
7. Alphanumeric Rotation							.52	.50	.25	.20	.32	.32	.36	.29	.32	.32
8. Cube Comparison								.42	.10	.13	.33	.32	.38	.28	.23	.21
9. PMA Verbal Meaning									.52	.53	.47	.48	.52	.50	.51	.47
10. ETS Vocabulary II										.79	.23	.21	.25	.37	.35	.27
11. ETS Vocabulary IV											.23	.21	.25	.46	.39	.32
12. PMA Number												.82	.72	.35	.26	.26
13. ETS Addition													.81	.38	.28	.28
14. Subtraction/Multiplication														.38	.28	.33
15. PMA Word Fluency															.38	.43
16. Immediate Recall																.90
17. Delayed Recall																

Correlations Between the Neuropsychology and Psychometric Measures

Measure	1	2	3	4	5	6	7	8	9	10	11	12	13	14	15	16	17
18. Boston Naming	.27	.26	.29	.24	.30	.31	.27	.26	.34	.27	.24	.11	.06	.12	.19	.23	.23
19. Fuld Retrieval	.41	.39	.44	.24	.28	.33	.30	.21	.42	.20	.20	.22	.23	.26	.32	.54	.57
20. Fuld Rapid Retrieval	.46	.39	.50	.29	.26	.27	.34	.24	.51	.31	.35	.29	.34	.36	.59	.50	.50
21. Mattis Total	.44	.42	.44	.30	.35	.33	.30	.20	.44	.33	.37	.30	.28	.32	.39	.47	.44
22. WMS-R Immediate	.42	.44	.44	.28	.27	.26	.23	.19	.40	.35	.37	.16	.14	.17	.29	.47	.45
23. WMS-R Delayed	.42	.46	.41	.31	.28	.29	.24	.22	.40	.32	.38	.18	.16	.22	.33	.46	.54
24. WAIS-R Digit Span	.37	.34	.41	.34	.25	.20	.20	.15	.34	.33	.35	.35	.20	.26	.40	.53	.25

Measure	19	20	21	22	23	24	25	26	27	28	29	30	31	32	33	35
25. WAIS-R Vocabulary	.42	.40	.31	.28	.26	.26	.20	.50	.65	.73	.23	.24	.25	.45	.41	.35
26. WAIS-R Comprehension	.30	.32	.27	.36	.22	.20	.16	.37	.44	.51	.14	.15	.19	.29	.32	.29
27. WAIS-R Block Design	.57	.53	.53	.56	.51	.52	.52	.50	.27	.27	.34	.33	.36	.33	.37	.35
28. WAIS-R Digit Symbol	.62	.59	.52	.49	.48	.50	.51	.62	.19	.19	.43	.51	.58	.42	.45	.27
29. MMSE	.40	.45	.35	.26	.23	.26	.22	.44	.33	.33	.39	.33	.38	.36	.47	.44
30. Verbal Fluency	.36	.33	.29	.25	.28	.25	.24	.43	.36	.41	.14	.18	.25	.37	.40	.34
31. Word List Recall	.31	.30	.17	.20	.19	.19	.14	.37	.18	.24	.14	.16	.21	.30	.59	.60
32. Praxis Delayed	.40	.40	.36	.38	.36	.36	.31	.39	.19	.21	.20	.19	.26	.30	.38	.38
33. Trails A	-.46	-.46	-.35	-.41	-.40	-.41	-.40	-.44	-.13	-.12	-.27	-.30	-.34	-.36	-.34	-.33
34. Trails B	-.59	-.59	-.50	-.46	-.50	-.48	-.46	-.59	-.25	-.24	-.42	-.44	-.47	-.40	-.42	-.40

Correlations Among the Neuropsychology Measures

Measure	19	20	21	22	23	24	25	26	27	28	29	30	31	32	33	35
18. Boston Naming	.26	.29	.29	.31	.28	.13	.32	.30	.33	.27	.24	.32	.22	.32	-.28	-.34
19. Fuld Retrieval		.54	.44	.46	.51	.21	.27	.25	.37	.50	.42	.35	.62	.47	-.39	-.48
20. Fuld Rapid Retrieval			.45	.41	.45	.29	.43	.33	.41	.54	.40	.51	.44	.37	-.45	-.47
21. Mattis Total				.41	.40	.31	.50	.46	.36	.43	.41	.34	.39	.36	-.30	-.40
22. WMS-R Immediate					.90	.21	.45	.39	.32	.31	.42	.40	.53	.50	-.24	-.35
23. WMS-R Delayed						.17	.44	.37	.33	.34	.44	.42	.59	.43	-.25	-.36
24. WAIS-R Digit Span							.36	.30	.29	.28	.32	.17	.14	.14	-.24	-.30
25. WAIS-R Vocabulary								.69	.39	.26	.34	.44	.29	.33	-.21	-.32
26. WAIS-R Comprehension									.37	.23	.29	.36	.29	.31	-.21	-.26
27. WAIS-R Block Design										.55	.38	.38	.28	.46	-.46	-.52
28. WAIS-R Digit Symbol											.37	.38	.39	.41	-.60	-.62
29. MMSE												.31	.40	.33	-.27	-.40
30. Verbal Fluency													.35	.31	-.28	-.36
31. Word List Recall														.44	-.24	-.32
32. Praxis Delayed															-.30	-.42
33. Trails A																.57

Note. ADEPT, Adult Development and Enrichment Project; ETS, Educational Testing Service; MMSE, Mini-Mental State Examination: PMA, Primary Mental Abilities; WAIS-R, Wechsler Adult Intelligence Scale–Revised; WMS-R, Wechsler Memory Scale–Revised.

All correlations are significant at the .05 level of confidence.

References

Abraham, J. D., & Hansson, R. O. (1995). Successful aging at work: An applied study of selection, optimization, and compensation through impression management. *Journals of Gerontology: Psychological Sciences, 50B,* P94–P103.

Adam, J. (1978). Sequential strategies and the separation of age, cohort, and time-of-measurement contribution to developmental data. *Psychological Bulletin, 85,* 1309–1316.

Alwin, D. F., & Jackson, D. J. (1981). Applications of simultaneous factor analysis to issues of factorial invariance. In D. J. Jackson & E. F. Borgatta (Eds.), *Factor analysis and measurement* (pp. 249–278). London: Sage.

American Hospital Formulary Service. (1991). *AHFS: Drug information.* Bethesda, MD: Author.

American Society of Hospital Pharmacists. (1985). *Drug information 85.* Bethesda, MD: Author.

Anastasi, A. (1976). *Psychological testing* (4th ed.). New York: Macmillan.

Antonovsky, A. (1972). Breakdown: A needed fourth step in the conceptual armamentarium of modern medicine. *Social Science and Medicine, 6,* 537–544.

Arbuckle, J. L., & Wothke, W. (1999). *Amos 4.0 user's guide.* Chicago: Small Waters.

Atkinson, R. C., & Shiffrin, R. M. (1971). The control of short-term memory. *Scientific American, 221,* 82–90.

Avolio, B. J., & Waldman, D. A. (1990). An examination of age and cognitive test performance across job complexity and occupational types. *Journal of Applied Psychology, 75,* 43–50.

Avolio, B. J., & Waldman, D. A. (1994). Variations in cognitive, perceptual, and psychomotor abilities across the working life span: Examining the effects of race, sex, experience, education, and occupational type. *Psychology and Aging, 9,* 430–442.

Avolio, B. J., Waldman, D. A., & McDaniel, M. A. (1990). Age and work performance in non-managerial jobs: The effects of experience and occupational type. *Academy of Management Journal, 33,* 407–422.

Balinsky, B. (1941). An analysis of the mental factors of various age groups from nine to sixty. *Genetic Psychology Monographs, 23,* 191–234.

Ball, K., Berch, D. B., Helmers, K. F., Jobe, J. B., Leveck, M. D., Marsiske, M., Morris, J. N., Rebok, G. W., Smith, D. M., Tennstedt, S. L., Unverzagt, F. W., & Willis, S. L. (2002). Cognitive training interventions with older adults. ACTIVE: A randomized controlled trial. *Journal of the American Medical Association, 288,* 2271–2281.

Baltes, P. B. (1968). Longitudinal and cross-sectional sequences in the study of age and generation effects. *Human Development, 11,* 145–171.

Baltes, P. B. (1987). Theoretical propositions of life-span developmental psychology: On the dynamics between growth and decline. *Developmental Psychology, 23,* 611–626.

Baltes, P. B. (1993). The aging mind: Potential and limits. *Gerontologist, 33,* 580–594.

Baltes, P. B., Dittmann-Kohli, F., & Kliegl, R. (1986). Reserve capacity of the elderly in aging-sensitive tests of fluid intelligence: Replication and extension. *Psychology and Aging, 1,* 172–177.

Baltes, P. B., & Lindenberger, U. (1988). On the range of cognitive plasticity in old age as a function of experience: 15 years of intervention research. *Behavior Therapy, 19,* 283–300.

Baltes, P. B., & Lindenberger, U. (1997). Emergence of a powerful connection between sensory and cognitive functions across the adult life span: A new window to the study of cognitive aging. *Psychology and Aging, 12,* 12–21.

Baltes, P. B., & Nesselroade, J. R. (1979). History and rationale of longitudinal research. In J. R. Nesselroade & P. B. Baltes (Eds.), *Longitudinal research in the study of behavior and development* (pp. 1–39). New York: Academic Press.

Baltes, P. B., Nesselroade, J. R., Schaie, K. W., & Labouvie, E. W. (1972). On the dilemma of regression effects in examining ability level-related differentials in ontogenetic patterns of adult intelligence. *Developmental Psychology, 6,* 78–84.

Baltes, P. B., Reese, H. W., & Lipsitt, L. P. (1980). Life-span developmental psychology. *Annual Review of Psychology, 31,* 65–100.

Baltes, P. B., Reese, H. W., & Nesselroade, J. R. (1977). *Life-span developmental psychology: Introduction to research methods* (pp. 219–251). Monterey, CA: Brooks/Cole.

Baltes, P. B., Schaie, K. W., & Nardi, A. H. (1971). Age and experimental mortality in a seven-year longitudinal study of cognitive behavior. *Developmental Psychology, 5,* 18–26.

Baltes, P. B., Staudinger, U. M., & Lindenberger, U. (1999). Lifespan psychology: Theory and application to intellectual functioning. *Annual Review of Psychology, 50,* 471–507.

Baltes, P. B., & Willis, S. L. (1977). Towards psychological theories of aging and development. In J. E. Birren & K. W. Schaie (Eds.), *Handbook of the psychology of aging* (pp. 128–154). New York: Van Nostrand Reinhold.

Baltes, P. B., & Willis, S. L. (1982). Enhancement (plasticity) of intellectual functioning in old age: Penn State's Adult Development and Enrichment Project (ADEPT). In F. I. M. Craik & S. E. Trehub (Eds.), *Aging and cognitive processes* (pp. 353–389). New York: Plenum.

Bandura, A. (1981). Self-referent thought: A developmental analysis of self-efficacy. In J. H. Flavell & L. Ross (Eds.), *Social cognitive development: Frontiers and possible futures* (pp. 200–239). New York: Cambridge University Press.

Bandura, A. (1982). Self-efficacy mechanism in human agency. *American Psychologist, 37,* 122–147.

Baum, L., Kennedy, D. L., Knapp, D. E., Juergens, J. P., & Faich, J. P. (1988). Prescription drug use in 1984 and changes over time. *Medical Care, 26,* 105–114.

Bayley, N., & Oden, M. H. (1955). The maintenance of intellectual ability in gifted adults. *Journal of Gerontology, 10,* 91–107.

Bengtson, V. L. (1975). Generation and family effects in value socialization. *American Sociological Review, 40,* 358–371.

Bengtson, V. L. (1986). Sociological perspective on aging, the family and the future. In M. Bergener (Ed.), *Perspectives on aging: The 1986 Sandoz lectures in gerontology* (pp. 237–262). New York: Academic Press.

Bengtson, V. L., Schaie, K. W., & Burton, L. (Eds.). (1995). *Adult intergenerational relations: Effect of societal changes.* New York: Springer.

Bentler, P. M. (1990). Comparative fit indices in structural models. *Psychological Bulletin, 107,* 238–246.

Berg, S. (1996). Aging, behavior , and terminal decline. In G. L. Maddox & E. W. Busse (Eds.), *Aging: The universal human experience* (pp. 411–417). New York: Springer Publishing Co.

Bernard, S. L., Kinkade, J. E., Konrad, T. R., Arcury, T. A., Rabiner, D. J., Woomert, A., DeFriese, G. H., & Ory, M. G. (1997). Predicting mortality from community surveys of older adults: The importance of self-rated functional ability. *Journals of Gerontology: Social Sciences, 52B,* S155–S163.

Bernstein, E. (1924). Quickness and intelligence. *British Journal of Psychology, 3*(7), 1–37.

Binet, A., & Simon, T. (1905). Méthodes nouvelles pour le diagnostic du niveau intellectuel des anormaux. *L'Année Psychologique, 11,* 191.

Birkhill, W. R., & Schaie, K. W. (1975). The effect of differential enforcement of cautiousness in the intellectual performance of the elderly. *Journal of Gerontology, 30,* 578–583.

Birren, J. E. (1968). Increments and decrements in the intellectual states of the aged. *Psychiatric Research Reports, 23,* 207–214.

Blashfild, R. K. (1976). Mixture models tests of cluster analysis accuracy of four agglomerative models. *Psychological Bulletin, 83,* 377–388.

Blieszner, R., Willis, S. L., & Baltes, P. B. (1981). Training research in aging on the fluid ability of inductive reasoning. *Journal of Applied Developmental Psychology, 2,* 247–265.

Boron, J. B. (2003). *The effects of personality on cognitive ability, training gains, and strategy use in adults in the Seattle Longitudinal Study.* Unpublished master's thesis, Pennsylvania State University, University Park.

Bosworth, H. B. (1994). *Dimensions of social support and health outcomes in the Seattle Longitudinal Study.* Unpublished master's thesis, Pennsylvania State University, University Park.

Bosworth, H. B. (1996). *Terminal change: A longitudinal and cross-sectional examination of confounding factors.* Unpublished doctoral dissertation, Pennsylvania State University, University Park.

Bosworth, H. B., & Schaie, K. W. (1997). The relationship of social environment, social networks, and health outcomes in the Seattle Longitudinal Study: Two analytical approaches. *Journals of Gerontology: Psychological Sciences, 52B,* P197–P205.

Bosworth, H. B., & Schaie, K. W. (1999). Survival effects in cognitive function, cognitive style, and sociodemographic variables in the Seattle Longitudinal Study. *Experimental Aging Research, 25,* 121–139.

Bosworth, H. B., Schaie, K. W., & Willis, S. L. (1999a). Cognitive and sociodemographic risk factors for mortality in the Seattle Longitudinal Study. *Journals of Gerontology: Psychological Sciences, 54B,* P273–P282.

Bosworth, H. B., Schaie, K. W., & Willis, S. L. (1999b, November). *Perceived therapeutic purpose of medication use: The effects of cognitive abilities: Sociodemographic factors, and health care service and utilization.* Paper presented at the annual meeting of the Gerontological Society of America, San Francisco.

Bosworth, H. B., Schaie, K. W., Willis, S. L., & Siegler, I. C. (1999). Age and distance to death in the Seattle Longitudinal Study. *Research on Aging, 21,* 723–738.

Botwinick, J. (1977). Intellectual abilities. In J. E. Birren & K. W. Schaie (Eds.), *Handbook of the psychology of aging* (pp. 580–605). New York: Van Nostrand Reinhold.

Botwinick, J., & Arenberg, D. (1976). Disparate time spans in sequential studies of aging. *Experimental Aging Research, 2,* 55–61.

Brooks, J., & Weintraub, M. (1976). A history of infant intelligence testing. In M. Lewis (Ed.), *Origins of intelligence* (pp. 19–58). New York: Plenum.

Browne, M. W., & Cudeck, R. (1993). Alternate ways of assessing model fit. In K. A. Bollen & J. S. Long (Eds.), *Testing structural equation models.* (pp. 136–162). Newbury Park, CA: Sage.

Bryk, A. S., & Raudenbush, S. W. (1992). *Hierarchical linear models: Applications and data analysis.* Thousand Oaks, CA: Sage.

Buss, A. R. (1979–1980). Methodological issues in life-span developmental psychology from a dialectical perspective. *International Journal of Aging and Human Development, 10,* 121–163.

Busse, E. W. (1993). Duke longitudinal studies of aging. *Zeitschrift für Gerontologie, 26,* 123–128.

Byrne, B. M., Shavelson, R. J., & Muthén, B. (1989). Testing for the equivalence of factor covariance and mean structures: The issue of partial measurement invariance. *Psychological Bulletin, 105,* 456–466.

Cahn, D. A., Salmon, D. P., Butters, N., Wiederholt, W. C., Corey-Bloom, J., Edelstein, S. L., & Barrett-Connor, E. (1995). Detection of dementia of the Alzheimer type in a population-based sample: Neuro-psychological test performance. *Journal of the International Neuropsychological Society, 1,* 252–260.

Campbell, D. T., & Stanley, J. C. (1963). Experimental and quasi-experimental designs for research in teaching. In N. L. Gage (Ed.), *Handbook of research on teaching* (pp. 171–246). Skokie, IL: Rand McNally.

Cattell, R. B. (1957). *Personality and motivation structure and measurement.* New York: World Book.

Cattell, R. B. (1963). Theory of fluid and crystallized intelligence: A critical experiment. *Journal of Educational Psychology, 54,* 1–22.

Cattell, R. B., Eber, H., & Tatsuoka, M. M. (1970). *Handbook for the 16 PF.* Champaign, IL: Institute for Personality and Ability Testing.

Charness, N., & Schaie, K. W. (Eds.). (2003). *Impact of technology on the aging individual.* New York: Springer.

Chown, S. M. (1959). Rigidity—A flexible concept. *Psychological Bulletin, 56,* 195–223.

Clark, D. O., Von Korff, M., Saunders, K., Baluch, W. M., & Simon, G. E. (1995). A chronic disease score with empirically derived weights. *Medical Care, 33,* 783–795.

Cohen, J. (1957). The factorial structure of the WAIS between early adulthood and old age. *Journal of Consulting Psychology, 21,* 283–290.

Cohen, J., & Cohen, P. (1975). *Applied multiple regression/correlation analysis for the behavioral sciences.* New York: Academic Press.

Commons, M. L., Sinnott, J. D., Richards, F. A., & Armon, C. (Eds.). (1989). *Beyond formal operations: Vol. 2. Adolescent and adult development models.* New York: Praeger.

Cook, T. C., & Campbell, D. T. (1979). *Quasi-experiments: Design and analysis issues for field settings.* Chicago: Rand McNally.

Cooney, T. M., Schaie, K. W., & Willis, S. L. (1988). The relationship between prior functioning of cognitive and personality dimensions and subject attrition in longitudinal research. *Journals of Gerontology: Psychological Sciences, 43,* P12–P17.

Cooper, L. B. (1975). Mental transformations of random two-dimensional shapes. *Cognitive Psychology, 7,* 20–43.

Cooper, L. B., & Shepard, R. N. (1973). Chronometric studies of rotation of mental images. In W. G. Chase (Ed.), *Visual information processing* (pp. 75–96). New York: Academic Press.

Cornelius, S. W., & Caspi, A. (1986). Self-perceptions of intellectual control and aging. *Educational Gerontology, 12,* 345–357.

Cornelius, S. W., Willis, S. L., Nesselroade, J. R., & Baltes, P. B. (1983). Convergence between attention variables and factors of psychometric intelligence in older adults. *Intelligence, 7,* 253–269.

Costa, P. T., Jr., & McCrae, R. R. (1992). *Revised NEO Personality Inventory (NEO PI-R).* Odessa, FL: Psychological Assessment Resources.

Costa, P. T., Jr., & McCrae, R. R. (1993). Psychological research in the Baltimore Longitudinal Study of Aging. *Zeitschrift für Gerontologie, 26,* 138–141.

Cronbach, L. J. (1970). *Essentials of psychological testing* (3rd ed.). New York: Harper and Row.

Crum, R. M., Anthony, J. C., Bassett, S. S., & Folstein, M. F. (1993). Population-based norms for the Mini-Mental State Examination by age and education level. *Journal of the American Medical Association, 269,* 2386–2391.

Crystal, S., & Shea, D. (Eds.). (2002). *Focus on economic outcomes in later life.* New York: Springer.

Cumming, E., & Henry, W. (1961). *Growing old: The process of disengagement.* New York: Basic.

Cunningham, W. R. (1978). Principles for identifying structural differences: Some methodological issues related to comparative factor analysis. *Journal of Gerontology, 33,* 82–86.

Cunningham, W. R. (1991). Issues in factorial invariance. In L. M. Collins & J. L. Horn (Eds.), *Best methods for the analysis of change* (pp. 106–113). Washington, DC: American Psychological Association.

Deeg, D. J. H., Hoffman, A., & van Zonneveld, R. J. (1990). The association between change in cognitive function and longevity in Dutch elderly. *American Journal of Epidemiology, 132,* 973–982.

DeFrias, C. M. (1998). *Work characteristics, cognitive performance and retirement.* Unpublished master's thesis, Pennsylvania State University, University Park.

DeFrias, C. M., & Schaie, K. W. (2001). Perceived work environment and cognitive style. *Experimental Aging Research, 27,* 67–81.

DeFries, J. C., Ashton, G. C., Johnson, R. C., Kusi, A. R., McClearn, G. E., Mi, M. P., Rashad, M. N., Vandenberg, S. G., & Wilson, J. R. (1976). Parent-offspring resemblance for specific cognitive abilities in two ethnic groups. *Nature, 261*(5556), 131–133.

DeFries, J. C., & Fulker, D. W. (1985). Multiple regression of twin data. *Behavior Genetics, 15,* 467–473.

DeFries, J. C., Plomin, R., & LaBuda, M. (1987). Genetic stability of cognitive development from childhood to adulthood. *Developmental Psychology, 23,* 4–12.

DeFries, J. C., Vandenberg, S. G., & McClearn, G. E. (1976). The genetics of specific cognitive abilities. *Annual Review of Genetics, 10,* 197–207.

Denney, N. W. (1982). Aging and cognitive changes. In B. B. Wolman (Ed.), *Handbook of developmental psychology* (pp. 807–827). Englewood Cliffs, NJ: Prentice-Hall.

Denney, N. W., & Heidrich, S. M. (1990). Training effects on Raven's Progressive Matrices in young, middle-aged, and elderly adults. *Psychology and Aging, 5,* 144–145.

Donaldson, G. (1981). Letter to the editor. *Journal of Gerontology, 36,* 634–636.

Dudek, F. J. (1979). The continuing misinterpretation of the standard error of measurement. *Psychological Bulletin, 86,* 335–337.

Dutta, R. (1992). *The relationship between flexibility-rigidity and the Primary Mental Abilities.* Unpublished doctoral dissertation, Pennsylvania State University, University Park.

Dutta, R., Schulenberg, J. E., & Lair, T. J. (1986, April). *The effect of job characteristics on cognitive abilities and intellectual flexibility.* Paper presented at the annual meeting of the Eastern Psychological Association, New York.

Dutta, R., Yue, G. A., Schaie, K. W., Willis, S. L., O'Hanlon, A. M., & Yu, L. C. (1989, November). *Age difference patterns in primary mental abilities in China and the U.S.A.* Paper presented at the annual meeting of the Gerontological Society of America, Minneapolis, MN.

Dwyer, P. S. (1937). The determination of the factor loadings of a given test from the known factor loadings of other tests. *Psychometrika, 2,* 173–178.

Earles, H. L., & Salthouse, T. A. (1995). Interrelation of age, health and speed. *Journals of Gerontology: Psychological Sciences, 50B,* P33–P41.

Educational Testing Service. (1977). *Basic Skills Assessment Test—Reading.* Princeton, NJ: Author.

Egan, D. E. (1981). An analysis of spatial orientation performance. *Intelligence, 5,* 85–100.

Eichorn, D. H., Clausen, J. A., Haan, N., Honzik, M. P., & Mussen, P. H. (1981). *Present and past in middle life.* New York: Academic Press.

Ekstrom, R. B., French, J. W., Harman, H., & Derman, D. (1976). *Kit of factor-referenced cognitive tests* (rev. ed.). Princeton, NJ: Educational Testing Service.

Elder, G. H., Jr. (1981). History of the family: The discovery of complexity. *Journal of Marriage and the Family, 43,* 489–519.

Elder, G. H., Jr., & Rudkin, L. (1995). Intergenerational continuity and change in rural America. In V. L. Bengtson, K. W. Schaie, & L. Burton (Eds.), *Societal impact on aging: Intergenerational perspectives* (pp. 30–60). New York: Springer.

Elias, M. F., Elias, J. W., & Elias, P. K. (1990). Biological and health influences upon behavior. In J. E. Birren & K. W. Schaie (Eds.), *Handbook of the psychology of aging* (3rd ed., pp. 79–102). New York: Academic Press.

Epstein, N. B., Baldwin, L. M., & Bishop, D. S. (1983). The McMaster family assessment device. *Journal of Marital and Family Therapy, 9,* 171–180.

Epstein, N. B., Bishop, D., Ryan, C., Miller, I., & Keitner, G. (1993). The McMaster model: View of health family functioning. In F. Walsh (Ed.), *Normal family processes* (pp. 138–160). New York: Guilford.

Farer, L. A., Cupples, A., Haines, J. L., Hyman, B., Kukull, W. A., Mayeux, R., et al. (1997). Effects of age, sex, and ethnicity on the association between apolipoprotein E genotype and Alzheimer disease. *Journal of the American Medical Association, 278,* 1349–1356.

Finkel, D., Pedersen, N. L., McClearn, G. E., Plomin, R., & Berg, S. (1996). Cross-sequential analysis of genetic influences on cognitive ability in the Swedish Adoption/Twin Study of Aging. *Aging Neuropsychology and Cognition, 3,* 84–99.

Finkel, D., Pedersen, N. L., Plomin, R., & McClearn, G. E. (1998). Longitudinal and cross-sectional twin data on cognitive abilities in adulthood: The Swedish Adoption/Twin Study of Aging. *Developmental Psychology, 34,* 1400–1413.

Folstein, M. F., Folstein, S. E., & McHugh, P. R. (1975). Mini-Mental State: A practical method for grading the cognitive state of patients for the clinician. *Journal of Psychiatric Research, 12,* 189–198.

French, J. W., Ekstrom, R. B., & Price, L. A. (1963). *Kit of reference tests for cognitive factors.* Princeton, NJ: Educational Testing Service.

Freund, A. M., & Baltes, P. B. (1998). Selection, optimization, compensation as strategies of life management: Correlations with subjective indicators of successful aging. *Psychology and Aging, 13,* 531–543.

Fuld, P. A. (1977). *Fuld Object-Memory Evaluation.* Woodsdale, IL: Stoelting Company.

Galton, F. (1869). *Hereditary genius.* London: Macmillan.

Gardner, E. F., & Monge, R. H. (1975). Adult age differences in cognitive abilities and educational background. *Experimental Aging Research, 3,* 337–383.

Gardner, H. (1993). *Creating minds.* New York: Basic Books.

Garrett, H. E. (1946). A developmental theory of intelligence. *American Psychologist, 1,* 372–378.

Garrett, H. E. (1966). *Statistics in psychology and education* (6th ed.). New York: McKay.

George, L. K., Siegler, I. C., & Okun, M. A. (1981). Separating age, cohort, and time of measurement: Analysis of variance and multiple regression. *Experimental Aging Research, 7,* 297–314.

Giambra, L. M., & Arenberg, D. (1980). Problem solving, concept learning and aging. In L. W. Poon (Ed.), *Aging in the 1980s* (pp. 253–259). Washington, DC: American Psychological Association.

Gilewski, M. J., & Zelinski, E. M. (1988). The Memory Functioning Questionnaire (MFQ). *Psychopharmacology Bulletin, 24,* 665–670.

Glenn, N. D. (1976). Cohort analysts' futile quest: Statistical attempts to separate age, period and cohort effects. *American Sociological Review, 41,* 900–904.

Glenn, N. D. (1981). Age, birth cohort, and drinking: An illustration of the hazards of inferring effects from cohort data. *Journal of Gerontology, 36,* 362–369.

Gold, M., Jolle, M., Kennedy, T. L., & Tucker, A. M. (1989). Pharmacy benefits in health maintenance organizations. *Health Affairs, 8,* 182–190.

Gonda, J., Quayhagen, M., & Schaie, K. W. (1981). Education, task meaningfulness and cognitive performance in young-old and old-old adults. *Educational Gerontology, 7,* 151–158.

Gough, H. G. (1957). *The California Psychological Inventory.* Palo Alto, CA: Consulting Psychologists Press.

Gough, H. G., McCloskey, H., & Meehl, P. E. (1952). A personality scale for social responsibility. *Journal of Abnormal and Social Psychology, 42,* 73–80.

Green, A. L., & Boxer, A. M. (1985). Daughters and sons as young adults: Restructuring the ties that bind. In N. Datan, A. Green, & H. Reese (Eds.), *Lifespan developmental psychology: Intergenerational relationships* (pp. 125–149). Hillsdale, NJ: Erlbaum.

Gribbin, K., & Schaie, K. W. (1976). Monetary incentive, age, and cognition. *Experimental Aging Research, 2,* 461–468.

Gribbin, K., & Schaie, K. W. (1977, November). *The aging of tests: A methodological problem of longitudinal studies.* Paper presented at the annual meeting of the Gerontological Society, San Francisco.

Gribbin, K., & Schaie, K. W. (1979). Selective attrition in longitudinal studies: A cohort-sequential approach. In H. Orino, K. Shimada, M. Iriki, & D. Maeda (Eds.), *Recent advances in gerontology* (pp. 549–551). Amsterdam, Netherlands: Excerpta Medica.

Gribbin, K., Schaie, K. W., & Parham, I. A. (1980). Complexity of life style and maintenance of intellectual abilities. *Journal of Social Issues, 36,* 47–61.

Gribbin, K., Schaie, K. W., & Stone, V. (1976, August). *Ability differences between established and redefined populations in sequential studies.* Paper presented at the annual meeting of the American Psychological Association, Washington, DC.

Gruber, A. L., & Schaie, K. W. (1986, November). *Longitudinal-sequential studies of marital assortativity.* Paper presented at the annual meeting of the Gerontological Society of America, Chicago.

Gruber-Baldini, A. L. (1991a). *The impact of health and disease on cognitive ability in adulthood and old age in the Seattle Longitudinal Study.* Unpublished doctoral dissertation, Pennsylvania State University, University Park.

Gruber-Baldini, A. L. (1991b, November). *The prevalence of chronic disease from HMO records across age and time.* Paper presented at the annual meeting of the Gerontological Society of America, San Francisco.

Gruber-Baldini, A. L., & Schaie, K. W. (1990, November). *The impact of disease upon cognitive ability functioning in the elderly.* Paper presented at the annual meeting of the Gerontological Society of America, Boston.

Gruber-Baldini, A. L., Schaie, K. W., & Willis, S. L. (1995). Similarity in married couples: A longitudinal study of mental abilities and flexibility-rigidity. *Journal of Personality and Social Psychology: Personality Processes and Individual Differences, 69,* 191–203.

Gruber-Baldini, A. L., Willis, S. L., & Schaie, K. W. (1989, November). *Health and rigidity predictors of cognitive change and training gain.* Paper presented at the annual meeting of the Gerontological Society of America, Minneapolis, MN.

Guilford, J. P. (1967). *The nature of human intelligence.* New York: McGraw-Hill.

Hall, G. S. (1922). *Senescence, the last half of life.* New York: Appleton.

Hareven, T. K. (1982). Family history at the crossroads. *Journal of Family History, 12,* ix–xxiii.

Havighurst, R. J., Neugarten, B. L., & Tobin, S. S. (1968). Disengagement and patterns of aging. In B. L. Neugarten (Ed.), *Middle age and aging* (pp. 161–177). Chicago: University of Chicago Press.

Hertzog, C. (1985). Application of confirmatory factor analysis to the study of intelligence. In D. K. Detterman (Ed.), *Current topics in human intelligence* (pp. 59–97). Norwood, NJ: Ablex.

Hertzog, C. (1989). The influence of cognitive slowing on age differences in intelligence. *Developmental Psychology, 25,* 636–651.

Hertzog, C., & Schaie, K. W. (1986). Stability and change in adult intelligence: 1. Analysis of longitudinal covariance structures. *Psychology and Aging, 1,* 159–171.

Hertzog, C., & Schaie, K. W. (1988). Stability and change in adult intelligence: 2. Simultaneous analysis of longitudinal means and covariance structures. *Psychology and Aging, 3,* 122–130.

Hertzog, C., Schaie, K. W., & Gribbin, K. (1978). Cardiovascular disease and changes in intellectual functioning from middle to old age. *Journal of Gerontology, 33,* 872–883.

Ho, H. Z., Foch, T. T., & Plomin, R. (1980). Developmental stability of the relative influence of genes and environment on specific cognitive abilities in childhood. *Developmental Psychology, 16,* 340–346.

Hollingsworth, H. L. (1927). *Mental growth and decline: A survey of developmental psychology.* New York: Appleton.

Holzman, T. G., Pellegrino, J. W., & Glaser, R. (1982). Cognitive dimensions of numerical rule induction. *Journal of Educational Psychology, 74,* 360–373.

Horn, J. L. (1970). Organization of data on life-span development of human abilities. In

L. R. Goulet & P. B. Baltes (Eds.), *Life-span developmental psychology: Research and theory* (pp. 434–466). New York: Academic Press.

Horn, J. L. (1982). The theory of fluid and crystallized intelligence in relation to concepts of cognitive psychology and aging in adulthood. In F. I. M. Craik and S. Trehub (Eds.), *Aging and cognitive processes* (pp. 237–278). New York: Plenum.

Horn, J. L. (1991). Comments on issues in factorial invariance. In L. M. Collins & J. L. Horn (Eds.), *Best methods for the analysis of change* (pp. 114–125). Washington, DC: American Psychological Association.

Horn, J. L., & McArdle, J. J. (1980). Perspectives on mathematical- statistical model building (MASMOB) in research on aging. In L. F. Poon (Ed.), *Aging in the 1980s* (pp. 503–541). Washington, DC: American Psychological Association.

Horn, J. L., & McArdle, J. J. (1992). A practical and theoretical guide to measurement invariance in aging research. *Experimental Aging Research, 18*, 117–144.

Horn, J. L., McArdle, J. J., & Mason, R. (1983). When is invariance not invariant? A practical scientist's look at the ethereal concept of factor invariance. *Southern Psychologist, 1*, 179–188.

Horst, P. (1956a). Simplified computations for the multiple group method of factor analysis. *Educational and Psychological Measurement, 16*, 101–109.

Horst, P. (1956b). A simplified method for rotating a centroid factor matrix to a simple structure hypothesis. *Journal of Experimental Education, 24*, 251–258.

Horst, P., & Schaie, K. W. (1956). The multiple group method of factor analysis and rotation to a simple structure hypothesis. *Journal of Experimental Education, 24*, 231–237.

Hultsch, D. F., Hertzog, C., Dixon, R. A., & Small, B. J. (1998). *Memory change in the aged*. New York: Cambridge University Press.

Hurtado, A. V., & Greenlick, M. R. (1971). Disease classification system for the analysis of medical care utilization. *Health Services Research, 6*, 235–250.

Idler, E. L., & Kasl, S. (1991). Health perceptions and survival: Do global evaluations of health status really predict mortality? *Journals of Gerontology: Social Sciences, 46*, S55–S65.

Isaacs, B., & Kennis, A. T. (1973). The set test as aid to the detection of dementia in old people. *British Journal of Psychiatry, 123*, 467–470.

Jarvik, L. F., Blum, J. E., & Varma, A. O. (1971). Genetic components and intellectual functioning during senescence: A 20-year study of aging twins. *Behavior Genetics, 2*, 159–171.

Jarvik, L. F., Kallman, F. J., & Falek, A. (1962). Intellectual changes in aged twins. *Journal of Gerontology, 17*, 289–294.

Jarvik, L. F., Kallman, F. J., Falek, A., & Kleber, M. M. (1957). Changing intellectual functions in senescent twins. *Acta Genetica et Statistica Medica, 7*, 421–430.

Johansson, B., & Berg, S. (1989). The robustness of the terminal decline phenomenon: Longitudinal data from the digit-span memory test. *Journal of Gerontology, 44*, P184–P186.

Jones, H. E., & Conrad, H. S. (1933). The growth and decline of intelligence: A study of a homogeneous group between the ages of ten and sixty. *Genetic Psychology Monographs, 13*, 223–298.

Jöreskog, K. G. (1971). Simultaneous factor analysis in several populations. *Psychometrika, 36*, 409–426.

Joreskog, K. G., & Sörbom, D. (1977). Statistical models and methods for analysis of longitudinal data. In D. J. Aigner & A. S. Goldberger (Eds.), *Latent variables in socioeconomic models* (pp. 285–325). Amsterdam: North Holland.

Jöreskog, K. G., & Sörbom, D. (1980). *Simultaneous analysis of longitudinal data from several cohorts* (Research Report No. 80–5). Uppsala, Sweden: University of Uppsala.

Jöreskog, K. G., & Sörbom, D. (1988). *LISREL VII—Analysis of linear structural equations systems by maximum likelihood methods.* Chicago: International Educational Services.

Jöreskog, K. G., & Sörbom, D. (1993). *LISREL 8: User's reference guide.* Chicago: Scientific Software.

Kail, R., Pellegrino, J., & Carter, P. (1980). Developmental changes in mental rotation. *Journal of Experimental Child Psychology, 39,* 102–116.

Kallman, F. J., Feingold, L., & Bondy, E. (1951). Comparative adaptational, social, and psychometric data on the life histories of senescent twin pairs. *American Journal of Human Genetics, 3,* 65–73.

Kallman, F. J., & Sander, G. (1948). Twin studies on aging and longevity. *Journal of Heredity, 39,* 349–357.

Kallman, F. J., & Sander, G. (1949). Twin studies on senescence. *American Journal of Psychiatry, 106,* 29–36.

Kamin, L. J. (1974). *The science and politics of IQ.* Hillsdale, NJ: Erlbaum.

Kaplan, E., Goodglass, H., & Weintraub, S. (1984). *The Boston Naming Test.* Philadelphia: Lee and Febinger.

Kaufman, A. S., Kaufman, J. L., McLean, J. E., & Reynolds, C. R. (1991). Is the pattern of intellectual growth and decline across the adult life span different for men and women? *Journal of Clinical Psychology, 47,* 801–820.

Kausler, D. H. (1982). *Experimental psychology and human aging.* New York: Wiley.

Kennet, J., Revell, A. J., & Schaie, K. W. (1999, November). *Early psychometric indicators of possible dementia in later life: Apo E genotypes and cognitive performance among middle-aged and older community-dwelling adults.* Poster presented at the annual meeting of the Gerontological Society of America, San Francisco.

Kennet, J., & Schaie, K. W. (1998, November). *Apolipoprotein E allele combinations, plasma lipid profiles.* Paper presented at the annual meeting of the Gerontological Society of America, Philadelphia.

Kenny, D. A. (1975). Cross-lagged panel correlation: A test for spuriousness. *Psychological Bulletin, 82,* 887–903.

Kenny, D. A. (1979). *Correlation and causality.* New York: Wiley.

Kertzer, D., & Schaie, K. W. (Eds.). (1989). *Age structuring in comparative perspective.* Hillsdale, NJ: Erlbaum.

Kiyak, H. A., Teri, L., & Borson, S. (1994). Physical and functional health assessment in normal aging and in Alzheimer's disease: Self-reports vs. family reports. *Gerontologist, 34,* 324–330.

Kleemeier, R. (1962). Intellectual changes in the senium. In *Proceedings of the Social Statistics Section of the American Statistical Society* (pp. 290–295). Washington, DC: American Statistical Society.

Kohn, M. L., Schooler, C. J., Miller, J., Miller, K. A., Schoenbach, C., & Schoenberg, R. (1983). *Work and personality: An inquiry into the impact of social stratification.* Norwood, NJ: Ablex.

Kotovsky, K., & Simon, H. (1973). Empirical tests of a theory of human acquisition of concepts for serial patterns. *Cognitive Psychology, 4,* 339–424.

Kuhlen, R. G. (1940). Social change: A neglected factor in psychological studies of the life span. *School and Society, 52,* 14–16.

Kuhlen, R. G. (1963). Age and intelligence: The significance of cultural change in longitudinal vs. cross-sectional findings. *Vita Humana, 6,* 113–124.

Lachman, J. L., Lachman, R., & Thronesbery, C. (1979). Metamemory through the adult life span. *Developmental Psychology, 15,* 543–551.

Lachman, M. E. (1983). Perceptions of intellectual aging: Antecedent or consequence of intellectual function? *Developmental Psychology, 19,* 482–498.

Lachman, M. E., & Jelalian, E. (1984). Self-efficacy and attributions for intellectual performance in young and elderly adults. *Journal of Gerontology, 39,* 577–582.

Lachman, M. E., Steinberg, E. S., & Trotter, S. W. (1987). Effects of control beliefs and attributions on memory self-assessment and performance. *Psychology and Aging, 2,* 266–271.

Lamy, P. P., Salzman, C., & Nevis-Olsesen, J. (1992). Drug prescribing patterns, risks, and compliance guidelines. In C. Salzman (Ed.), *Clinical geriatric psychopharmacology* (2nd ed., pp. 15–37). Baltimore, MD: Williams and Wilkins.

Lankes, W. (1915). Perseveration. *British Journal of Psychology, 7,* 387–419.

LaRue, A. (1992). *Aging and neuropsychological assessment: Critical issues in neuropsychology.* New York: Plenum.

Lawton, M. P., & Brody, E. M. (1969). Assessment of older people: Self-maintaining and instrumental activities of daily living. *Gerontologist, 9,* 179–185.

Ledermann, T. (2003). *Familienklima und kognitive Funktionen im Erwachsenenalter. Eine LISREL basierte Explorativuntersuchung mit Daten der Seattle Langzeitstudie* [Family environment and cognitive functioning in adults: A LISREL-based exploration of data from the Seattle Longitudinal Study]. Unpublished master's thesis, University of Fribourg, Fribourg, Switzerland.

Lerner, R. M. (1984). *On the nature of human plasticity.* New York: Cambridge University Press.

Lewin, K. (1935). *Dynamic theory of personality.* New York: McGraw-Hill.

Lindenberger, U., & Baltes, P. B. (1994). Sensory functioning and intelligence in old age. *Psychology and Aging, 9,* 339–355.

Logsdon, R. G., Gibbons, L. E., McCurry, S. M., & Teri, L. (1999). Quality of life in Alzheimer's disease: Patient and caregiver reports. *Journal of Mental Health and Aging, 5,* 21–32.

Lorenc, L., & Branthwaite, A. (1993). Are older adults less compliant with prescribed medication than younger adults? *British Journal of Clinical Psychology, 32,* 485–492.

Luchins, A. (1942). Mechanization in problem solving: The effect of Einstellung. *Psychological Monographs, 54*(6, Whole No. 248).

MacDonald, A. P., Jr. (1972). Characteristics of volunteer subjects under three recruiting methods: Pay, extra credit, and love of science. *Journal of Consulting and Clinical Psychology, 39,* 220–234.

Magnusson, D. (1998). The logic and implication of a person-oriented approach. In R. B. Cairns, L. R. Bergman, & J. Kagan (Eds.), *Methods and models for studying the individual* (pp. 33–64). Thousand Oaks, CA: Sage.

Maier, H. (1995). *Health behaviors in adults:interrelationships and correlates.* Unpublished doctoral dissertation, Pennsylvania State University, University Park.

Maier, H., & Smith, J. (1999). Psychological predictors of mortality in old age. *Journals of Gerontology: Psychological Sciences, 54B,* P44–P55.

Maitland, S. B. (1993). *Individual and lifestyle antecedents and concomitants of chronic diseases: Behavioral influences on health.* Unpublished master's thesis, Pennsylvania State University, University Park.

Maitland, S. B. (1997). *Factorial invariance and concordance of health behaviors and health status: A study of individual differences in familial context.* Unpublished doctoral dissertation, Pennsylvania State University, University Park.

Maitland, S. B., Dutta, R., Schaie, K. W., & Willis, S. L. (1992, November). *Trait invariance and cohort differences of adult personality.* Paper presented at the annual meeting of the Gerontological Society of America, Washington, DC.

Maitland, S. B., Intrieri, R. C., Schaie, K. W., & Willis, S. L. (2000). Gender differences in cognitive abilities: Invariance of covariance and latent mean structure. *Aging, Neuropsychology and Cognition, 7,* 32–53.

Maitland, S. B., O'Hanlon, A. M., & Schaie, K. W. (1990, November). *Activity patterns and dimensions across the life span.* Paper presented at the annual meeting of the Gerontological Society of America, Boston.

Maitland, S. B., & Schaie, K. W. (1991, November). *Individual and lifestyle antecedents of cardiovascular disease.* Paper presented at the annual meeting of the Gerontological Society of America, San Francisco.

Maitland, S. B., Willis, S. L., & Schaie, K. W. (1993, November). *The effect of cardiovascular disease on personality and attitudinal factors.* Paper presented at the annual meeting of the Gerontological Society of America, New Orleans, LA.

Mason, K. G., Mason, W. H., Winsborough, H. H., & Poole, W. K. (1973). Some methodological problems in cohort analyses of archival data. *American Sociological Review, 38,* 242–258.

Matarazzo, J. D. (1972). *Wechsler's measurement and appraisal of adult intelligence.* Baltimore, MD: Williams and Wilkins.

Mattis, S. (1989). *Dementia rating scale.* Odessa, FL: Psychological Assessment Resources.

Mayr, U., & Kliegl, R. (1993). Sequential and coordinative complexity: Age-based processing limitations in figural transformation. *Journal of Experimental Psychology: Learning, Memory, and Cognition, 19,* 1297–1321.

McArdle, J. J., & Anderson, E. (1990). Latent growth models for research on aging. In J. E. Birren & K. W. Schaie (Eds.), *Handbook of the psychology of aging* (3rd ed., pp. 21–44). New York: Academic Press.

McArdle, J. J., & Hamagami, F. (1991). Modeling incomplete longitudinal and cross-sectional data using latent growth structural models. In L. M. Collins & J. L. Horn (Eds.), *Best methods for the analysis of change* (pp. 276–304). Washington, DC: American Psychological Association.

McClearn, G. E., & Vogler, G. P. (2001). The genetics of behavioral aging. In J. E. Birren & K. W. Schaie (Eds.), *Handbook of the psychology of aging* (5th ed., pp. 109–131). San Diego, CA: Academic Press.

Meredith, W. (1964). Notes on factorial invariance. *Psychometrika, 29,* 177–185.

Meredith, W. (1993). Measurement invariance, factor analysis and factorial invariance. *Psychometrika, 58,* 525–543.

Mischel, W. (1973). Towards a cognitive social learning reconceptualization of personality. *Psychological Review, 80,* 252–283

Moos, R. H. (1981). *Work Environment Scale manual.* Palo Alto, CA: Consulting Psychologists Press.

Moos, R. H. (1985). Context and coping: Toward a unifying conceptual framework. *American Journal of Community Psychology, 12,* 5–25.

Moos, R. H. (1987). *The Social Climate Scales: A user's guide.* Palo Alto, CA: Consulting Psychologists Press.

Moos, R. H., & Moos, B. (1986). *Family Environment Scale manual* (2nd ed.). Palo Alto, CA: Consulting Psychologists Press.

Morrell, R. W., Park, D. C., & Poon, L. W. (1989). Quality of instructions on prescription drug labels: Effects on memory and comprehension in young and old adults. *Gerontologist, 29,* 345–354.

Morris, J. C., Edland, S., Clark, C., Galasko, C., Koss, E., Mohs, R., Van Belle, G., Fillenbaum, G., & Heyman, A. (1993). The Consortium to Establish a Registry for Alzheimer's Disease (CERAD). Part IV. Clinical and neuro-psychological assessment of Alzheimer's disease. *Neurology, 39,* 1159–1165.

Morris, J. C., Heyman, A., Mohs, R. C., Hughes, J. P., van Belle, G., Fillenbaum, G., Mellits, E. D., & Clark, C. (1989). The Consortium to Establish a Registry for Alzheimer's Disease (CERAD). Part I. Rates of cognitive change in the longitudinal assessment of probable Alzheimer's disease. *Neurology, 43,* 2457–2465.

Mulaik, S. A. (1972). *Foundations of factor analysis.* New York: McGraw-Hill.

Murstein, B. I. (1980). Mate selection in the 1970s. *Journal of Marriage and the Family, 42,* 777–792.

Muscovith, M., & Winokur, G. (1992). The neuropsychology of memory and aging. In F. I. M. Craik & T. A. Salthouse (Eds.), *Handbook of aging and cognition* (pp. 315–370). Hillsdale, NJ: Erlbaum.

Nesselroade, J. R., Baltes, P. B., & Schaie, K. W. (1972). Ontogenetic and generational components of structural and quantitative change in adult behavior. *Journal of Gerontology, 27,* 222–228.

Nesselroade, J. R., & Labouvie, E. W. (1985). Experimental design in research on aging. In J. E. Birren & K. W. Schaie (Eds.), *Handbook of the psychology of aging* (2nd ed., pp. 35–60). New York: Van Nostrand-Reinhold.

Nesselroade, J. R., Stigler, S. M., & Baltes, P. B. (1980). Regression towards the mean and the study of change. *Psychological Bulletin, 88,* 622–637.

Nguyen, H. T. (2000). *Environmental complexity factors: A study of familial similarities and differences.* Unpublished doctoral dissertation, Pennsylvania State University, University Park.

Nunnally, J. C. (1982). The study of human change: Measurement, research strategies, and methods of analysis. In B. B. Wolman (Ed.), *Handbook of developmental psychology* (pp. 133–148). Englewood Cliffs, NJ: Prentice-Hall.

O'Connell, M. B., & Johnson, J. F. (1992). Evaluation of medication knowledge in elderly patients. *Annals of Pharmacotherapy, 26,* 919–921.

O'Hanlon, A. M. (1993). *Inter-individual patterns of intellectual aging: The influence of environmental factors.* Unpublished doctoral dissertation, Pennsylvania State University, University Park.

Ory, M. C., Abeles, R. P., & Lipman, P. D. (1992). Introduction: An overview of research on aging, health, and behavior. In M. C. Ory, R. P. Abeles, & P. D. Lipman (Eds.), *Aging, health, and behavior* (pp. 1–23). Newbury Park, CA: Sage.

Owens, W. A., Jr. (1953). Age and mental abilities: A longitudinal study. *Genetic Psychology Monographs, 48,* 3–54.

Owens, W. A., Jr. (1959). Is age kinder to the initially more able? *Journal of Gerontology, 14,* 334–337.

Parasuraman, R., Greenwood, P. M., & Sunderland, T. (2002). The apolipoprotein E gene, attention, and brain function. *Neuropsychology, 16,* 254–274.

Parham, I. A., Gribbin, K., Hertzog, C., & Schaie, K. W. (1975, July). *Health status change by age and implications for adult cognitive change.* Paper presented at the 10th International Congress of Gerontology, Jerusalem.

Park, D. C., Willis, S. L., Morrow, D., Diehl, M., & Gaines, C. L. (1994). Cognitive function and medication usage in older adults. *Journal of Applied Gerontology, 13,* 39–57.

Pedersen, N. L. (1996). Gerontological behavior genetics. In J. E. Birren & K. W. Schaie (Eds.), *Handbook of the psychology of aging* (4th ed., pp. 59–77). San Diego, CA: Academic Press.

Pedersen, N. L., & Liechtenstein, P. (2000). The Swedish Twin Registry. In B. Smedby, I. Lundberg, & T. I. A. Sørensen (Eds.), *Scientific evaluation of the Swedish Twin Registry* (pp. 15–44). Stockholm: Swedish Council for Planning and Coordination of Research.

Pedersen, N. L., McClearn, G. E., Plomin, R., Nesselroade, J. R., Berg, S., & DeFore, U. (1991). The Swedish Adoption/Twin Study of Aging: An update. *Acta Geneticae Medicae et Gemellologiae, 33,* 243–250.

Pedersen, N. L., & Reynolds, C. A. (1998). Stability and change in adult personality: Genetic and environmental components. *European Journal of Personality, 12,* 365–386.

Piaget, J. (1972). Intellectual evolution from adolescence to adulthood. *Human Development, 15,* 1–12.

Plomin, R. (1983). Developmental behavior genetics. *Child Development, 54,* 253–259.

Plomin, R. (1986). *Development, genetics, and psychology.* Hillsdale, NJ: Erlbaum.

Plomin, R. (1987). The nature and nurture of cognitive abilities. In R. Sternberg (Ed.), *Advances in the psychology of human intelligence* (Vol. 4, pp. 1–33). Hillsdale, NJ: Erlbaum.

Plomin, R., & Daniels, D. (1987). Why are two children in the same family so different from each other? *Behavioral and Brain Sciences, 10,* 1–16.

Plomin, R., DeFries, J. C., & McClearn, G. E. (1980). *Behavioral genetics.* San Francisco: Freeman.

Plomin, R., & McClearn, G. E. (1990). Human behavioral genetics of aging. In J. E. Birren & K. W. Schaie (Eds.), *Handbook of the psychology of aging* (3rd ed., pp. 66–77). New York: Academic Press.

Plomin, R., Pedersen, N. L., Nesselroade, J. R., & Bergeman, C. S. (1988). Genetic influence on childhood family environment perceived retrospectively from the last half of the life span. *Developmental Psychology, 24,* 738–745.

Plomin, R., & Thompson, L. A. (1987). Life-span developmental behavior genetics. In P. B. Baltes, D. L. Featherman, & R. M. Lerner (Eds.), *Life-span development and behavior* (Vol. 8, pp. 1–31). Hillsdale, NJ: Erlbaum.

Poduslo, S. E., & Yin, X. (2001). A new locus on chromosome 19 linked with late-onset Alzheimer's disease. *Neuroreport for Rapid Communication of Neuroscience Research, 12,* 3759–3761.

Poon, L. W., Walsh-Sweeney, L., & Fozard, J. L. (1980). Memory training for the elderly. In L. W. Poon, J. L. Fozard, L. S. Cermak, D. Arenberg, & L. W. Thompson (Eds.), *New directions in memory and aging* (pp. 481–484). Hillsdale, NJ: Erlbaum.

Pressey, S. L., Janney, J. E., & Kuhlen, R. G. (1939). *Life: A psychological survey.* New York: Hayer.

Price, R. A., & Vandenberg, S. G. (1980). Spouse similarity in American and Swedish couples. *Behavior Genetics, 10,* 59–71.

Quayhagen, M. (1979). *Training spatial rotation in elderly women.* Unpublished doctoral dissertation, University of Southern California, Los Angeles.

Radloff, L. S. (1977). A self-report depression scale for research in the general population. *Applied Psychological Measurement, 3,* 385–401.

Radloff, L. S., & Teri, L. (1986). Use of the Center for Epidemiological Studies–Depression Scale with older adults. *Clinical Gerontologist, 5,* 119–137.

Reinert, G. (1970). Comparative factor analytic studies of intelligence through the human life-span. In L. R. Goulet & P. B. Baltes (Eds.), *Life-span developmental psychology: Research and theory* (pp. 468–485). New York: Academic Press.

Reitan, R. M., & Wolfson, D. (1985). *The Halstead-Reitan Neuropsychological Test Battery: Theory and clinical interpretation.* Tucson, AZ: Neuropsychology Press.

Riegel, K. F., & Riegel, R. M. (1972). Development, drop, and death. *Developmental Psychology, 6,* 306–319.

Riegel, K. F., Riegel, R. M., & Meyer, G. (1967). A study of the drop-out rates in longitudinal research on aging and the prediction of death. *Journal of Personality and Social Psychology, 4,* 342–348.

Riley, M. W. (1985). Overview and highlights of a sociological perspective. In A. B. Sørenson, F. E. Weinert, & L. R. Sherrod (Eds.), *Human development; Interdisciplinary perspectives* (pp. 153 -175). Hillsdale, NJ: Erlbaum.

Riley, M. W., Johnson, M. J., & Foner, A. (1972). *Aging and society: Vol. 3: A sociology of age stratification.* New York: Russell Sage.

Roberts, B. W., & DelVecchio, W. F. (2000). The rank-order consistency of personality traits from childhood to old age: A quantitative review of longitudinal studies. *Psychological Bulletin, 126,* 3–25.

Rodin, J., Schooler, C., & Schaie, K. W. (Eds.). (1990). *Self-directedness: Cause and effects throughout the life course.* Hillsdale, NJ: Erlbaum.

Rosen, W. G., Mohs, R. C., & Davis, K. L (1984). A new rating scale for Alzheimer's diseases. *American Journal of Psychiatry, 141,* 1356–1364.

Rosenthal, R., & Rosnow, R. L. (1975). *The volunteer subject.* New York: Wiley.

Roth, A. (2001). *Congruence types and consistency in congruence types over a fourteen-year period: Relationship with cognitive performance and rigidity-flexibility.* Unpublished master's thesis, Pennsylvania State University, University Park.

Rott, C. (1990). Intelligenzentwicklung im Alter [Development of intelligence in old age]. *Zeitschrift für Gerontologie, 23,* 252–261.

Rowe, D. C., & Plomin, R. (1981). The importance of nonshared (E1) environmental influences in behavioral development. *Developmental Psychology, 17,* 517–531.

Ryan, J. J., Paolo, A. M., & Brugardt, T. M. (1990). Test-retest stability of the WAIS-R in normal subjects 75 years and older. *Journal of Clinical Experimental Neuropsychology, 12,* 58.

Ryan, J. J., Paolo, A. M., & Brugardt, T. M. (1992). WAIS-R test-retest stability in normal persons 75 years and older. *Clinical Neuropsychologist, 6,* 3–8.

Ryder, N. B. (1965). The cohort as a concept in the study of social changes. *American Sociological Review, 30,* 843–861.

Saczynski, J. S. (2001). *Cognitive training gains in the Seattle Longitudinal Study: Individual predictors and mediators of training effects.* Unpublished doctoral dissertation, Pennsylvania State University, University Park.

Saczynski, J. S., Willis, S. L., & Schaie, K. W. (2002). Strategy use in reasoning training with older adults. *Aging, Neuropsychology and Cognition, 9,* 48–60.

Salthouse, T. A. (1982). *Adult cognition: An experimental psychology of human aging.* New York: Springer-Verlag.

Salthouse, T. A. (1985). Speed of behavior and implications for cognition. In J. E. Birren & K. W. Schaie (Eds.), *Handbook of the psychology of aging* (2nd ed., pp. 400–426). New York: Van Nostrand Reinhold.

Salthouse, T. A. (1993). Speed mediation of adult age differences in verbal tests. *Developmental Psychology, 29,* 722–738.

Salthouse, T. A., Hancock, H. E., Meinz, E. J., & Hambrick, D. Z. (1996). Interrelations of age, visual acuity, and cognitive functioning. *Journals of Gerontology: Psychological Sciences, 51B,* P317–P330.

Saunders, A. M. (2000). Apolipoprotein E and Alzheimer disease: An update on genetic and functional analyses. *Journal of Neuropathology and Experimental Neurology, 59,* 751–758.

Saunders, A. M., Strittmatter, W. J., Schmechel, D., St. George-Hyslop, P., Pericak-Vance, M. A., Joo, S. H., et al. (1993). Association of apolipoprotein E allele e4 with late-onset familial and sporadic Alzheimer's disease. *Neurology, 43,* 1467–1472.

Schaie, K. W. (1953). *Measuring behavioral rigidity: A factorial investigation of some tests of rigid behavior.* Unpublished master's thesis, University of Washington, Seattle.

Schaie, K. W. (1955). A test of behavioral rigidity. *Journal of Abnormal and Social Psychology, 51,* 604–610.

Schaie, K. W. (1958a). Differences in some personal characteristics of "rigid" and "flexible" individuals. *Journal of Clinical Psychology, 14,* 11–14.

Schaie, K. W. (1958b). Occupational level and the Primary Mental Abilities. *Journal of Educational Psychology, 40,* 299–303.

Schaie, K. W. (1958c). Rigidity-flexibility and intelligence: A cross-sectional study of the adult life-span from 20 to 70. *Psychological Monographs, 72*(9, Whole No. 462).

Schaie, K. W. (1958d). Tests of hypotheses about differences between two intercorrelation matrices. *Journal of Experimental Education, 26,* 242–245.

Schaie, K. W. (1959a). Cross-sectional methods in the study of psychological aspects of aging. *Journal of Gerontology, 14,* 208–215.

Schaie, K. W. (1959b). The effect of age on a scale of social responsibility. *Journal of Social Psychology, 50,* 221–224.

Schaie, K. W. (1960). *Manual for the Test of Behavioral Rigidity.* Palo Alto, CA: Consulting Psychologists Press.

Schaie, K. W. (1962). A field-theory approach to age changes in cognitive behavior. *Vita Humana, 5,* 129–141.

Schaie, K. W. (1963). The Color Pyramid Test: A non-verbal technique for personality assessment. *Psychological Bulletin, 60,* 530–547.

Schaie, K. W. (1965). A general model for the study of developmental problems. *Psychological Bulletin, 64,* 91–107.

Schaie, K. W. (1967). Age changes and age differences. *Gerontologist, 7,* 128–132.

Schaie, K. W. (1970). A reinterpretation of age-related changes in cognitive structure and functioning. In L. R. Goulet & P. B. Baltes (Eds.), *Life-span developmental psychology: Research and theory* (pp. 485–507). New York: Academic Press.

Schaie, K. W. (1972). Can the longitudinal method be applied to psychological studies of human development? In F. Z. Mönks, W. W. Hartup, & J. DeWitt (Eds.), *Determinants of human behavior* (pp. 3–22). New York: Academic Press.

Schaie, K. W. (1973a, August). *Cumulative health trauma and changes in adult cognitive behavior.* Paper presented at the annual meeting of the American Psychological Association, Montreal, Quebec, Canada.

Schaie, K. W. (1973b). Methodological problems in descriptive developmental research on adulthood and aging. In J. R. Nesselroade & H. W. Reese (Eds.), *Life-span developmental psychology: Methodological issues* (pp. 253–280). New York: Academic Press.

Schaie, K. W. (1974). Translations in gerontology—From lab to life: Intellectual functioning. *American Psychologist, 29,* 802–807.

Schaie, K. W. (1975). Research strategy in developmental human behavior genetics. In K. W. Schaie, E. V. Anderson, G. E. McClearn, & J. Money (Eds.), *Developmental human behavior genetics* (pp. 205–220). Lexington, MA: Heath.

Schaie, K. W. (1977). Quasi-experimental designs in the psychology of aging. In J. E. Birren & K. W. Schaie (Eds.), *Handbook of the psychology of aging* (pp. 39–58). New York: Van Nostrand Reinhold.

Schaie, K. W. (1977–1978). Toward a stage theory of adult development. *International Journal of Aging and Human Development, 8,* 129–138.

Schaie, K. W. (1978). External validity in the assessment of intellectual development in adulthood. *Journal of Gerontology, 33,* 695–701.

Schaie, K. W. (1979). The Primary Mental Abilities in adulthood: An exploration in the development of psychometric intelligence. In P. B. Baltes & O. G. Brim, Jr. (Eds.), *Life-span development and behavior* (Vol. 2, pp. 67–115). New York: Academic Press.

Schaie, K. W. (1980a). Age changes in intelligence. In R. D. Sprott (Ed.), *Age, learning ability and intelligence* (pp. 41–77). New York: Van Nostrand Reinhold.

Schaie, K. W. (1980b). Cognitive development in aging. In L. K. Obler & M. Albert (Eds.), *Language and communication in the elderly* (pp. 7–26). Lexington, MA: Heath.

Schaie, K. W. (1980c). Intelligence and problem solving. In J. E. Birren & R. B. Sloane (Eds.), *Handbook of mental health and aging* (pp. 262–280). Englewood Cliffs, NJ: Prentice-Hall.

Schaie, K. W. (1983a). The Seattle Longitudinal Study: A twenty-one-year exploration of psychometric intelligence in adulthood. In K. W. Schaie (Ed.), *Longitudinal studies of adult psychological development* (pp. 64–135). New York: Guilford.

Schaie, K. W. (1983b). What can we learn from the longitudinal study of adult psychological development. In K. W. Schaie (Ed.), *Longitudinal studies of adult psychological development* (pp. 1–19). New York: Guilford.

Schaie, K. W. (1984a). Historical time and cohort effects. In K. A. McCloskey & H. W. Reese (Eds.), *Life-span developmental psychology: Historical and generational effects* (pp. 1–15). New York: Academic Press.

Schaie, K. W. (1984b). Midlife influences upon intellectual functioning in old age. *International Journal of Behavioral Development, 7,* 463–478.

Schaie, K. W. (1985). *Manual for the Schaie-Thurstone Adult Mental Abilities Test (STAMAT).* Palo Alto, CA: Consulting Psychologists Press.

Schaie, K. W. (1986). Beyond calendar definitions of age, time and cohort: The general developmental model revisited. *Developmental Review, 6,* 252–277.

Schaie, K. W. (1987). Applications of psychometric intelligence to the prediction of everyday competence in the elderly. In C. Schooler & K. W. Schaie (Eds.), *Cognitive functioning and social structure over the life course* (pp. 50–59). Norwood, NJ: Ablex.

Schaie, K. W. (1988a). Ageism in psychological research. *American Psychologist, 43,* 179–183.

Schaie, K. W. (1988b). The delicate balance: Technology, intellectual competence, and normal aging. In G. Lesnoff-Cavaglia (Ed.), *Aging in a technological society* (Vol. 7, pp. 155–166). New York: Human Sciences Press.

Schaie, K. W. (1988c). The impact of research methodology on theory-building in the developmental sciences. In J. E. Birren & V. L. Bengtson (Eds.), *Emergent theories of aging: Psychological and social perspectives on time, self and society* (pp. 41–58). New York: Springer.

Schaie, K. W. (1988d). Internal validity threats in studies of adult cognitive development. In M. L. Howe & C. J. Brainard (Eds.), *Cognitive development in adulthood: Progress in cognitive development research* (pp. 241–272). New York: Springer-Verlag.

Schaie, K. W. (1988e). Variability in cognitive function in the elderly: Implications for social participation. In A. Woodhead, M. Bender, & R. Leonard (Ed.), *Phenotypic variation in populations: Relevance to risk assessment* (pp. 191–212). New York: Plenum.

Schaie, K. W. (1989a). The hazards of cognitive aging. *Gerontologist, 29*, 484–493.

Schaie, K. W. (1989b). Individual differences in rate of cognitive change in adulthood. In V. L. Bengtson & K. W. Schaie (Eds.), *The course of later life: Research and reflections* (pp. 68–83). New York: Springer.

Schaie, K. W. (1989c). Perceptual speed in adulthood: Cross-sectional and longitudinal studies. *Psychology and Aging, 4*, 443–453.

Schaie, K. W. (1990a). Intellectual development in adulthood. In J. E. Birren & K. W. Schaie (Eds.), *Handbook of the psychology of aging* (3rd ed., pp. 291–309). New York: Academic Press.

Schaie, K. W. (1990b). Late life potential and cohort differences in mental abilities. In M. Perlmutter (Ed.), *Late life potential* (pp. 43–62). Washington, DC: Gerontological Society of America.

Schaie, K. W. (1990c). The optimization of cognitive functioning in old age: Predictions based on cohort-sequential and longitudinal data. In P. B. Baltes & M. M. Baltes (Eds.), *Successful aging: Perspectives from the behavioral sciences* (pp. 94–117). Cambridge, UK: Cambridge University Press.

Schaie, K. W. (1992). The impact of methodological changes in gerontology. *International Journal of Aging and Human Development, 35*, 19–29.

Schaie, K. W. (1993). The Seattle Longitudinal Study: A thirty-five-year inquiry of adult intellectual development. *Zeitschrift für Gerontologie, 26*, 129–137.

Schaie, K. W. (1994a). The course of adult intellectual development. *American Psychologist, 49*, 304–313.

Schaie, K. W. (1994b). Developmental designs revisited. In S. H. Cohen & H. W. Reese (Eds.), *Life-span developmental psychology: Theoretical issues revisited* (pp. 45–64). Hillsdale, NJ: Erlbaum.

Schaie, K. W. (1995). Entwicklung im Alter: Individuelle Voraussetzungen und gesellschaftliche Konsequenzen [Development in old age? Individual assumptions and societal consequences]. In H.-U. Klose (Ed.), *USA: Alterung und Modernisierung* [Aging and modernization in the USA] (pp. 69–85). Bonn, Germany: Friedrich-Ebert Foundation.

Schaie, K. W. (1996a). Generational differences. In J. E. Birren (Ed.), *Encyclopedia of gerontology* (pp. 567–576). San Diego, CA: Academic Press.

Schaie, K. W. (1996b). *Intellectual development in adulthood: The Seattle Longitudinal Study*. New York: Cambridge University Press.

Schaie, K. W. (1996c). Intellectual functioning and aging. In J. E. Birren & K. W. Schaie (Eds.), *Handbook of the psychology of aging* (4th ed., pp. 266–287). San Diego, CA: Academic Press.

Schaie, K. W. (1996d). The natural history of a longitudinal study. In M. R. Merrens & G. G. Brannigan (Eds.), *The developmental psychologists* (pp. 232–249). New York: McGraw-Hill.

Schaie, K. W. (2000a). How does maintenance of intellectual competence contribute to quality of life and successful aging? In K. Manger (Ed.), *Jenaer Universitätsreden* [Jena University Lectures] (Vol. 9, pp. 21–40). Jena, Germany: Friedrich-Schiller-University Press.

Schaie, K. W. (2000b). The impact of longitudinal studies on understanding development from young adulthood to old age. *International Journal of Behavioral Development, 24*, 257–266.

Schaie, K. W. (2000c). Living with gerontology. In J. E. Birren & J. J. F. Schroots (Eds.), *A history of geropsychology in autobiography* (pp. 233–248). Washington, DC: American Psychological Association.

Schaie, K. W. (2000d). Longitudinal and related methodological issues in the Swedish Twin Registry. In B. Smedby, I. Lundberg, & T. I. A. Sørensen (Eds.), *Scientific evaluation of the Swedish Twin Registry* (pp. 62–74). Stockholm: Swedish Council for Planning and Coordination of Research.

Schaie, K. W., & Achenbaum, W. A. (1993). *Societal impact on aging: Historical perspectives.* New York: Springer.

Schaie, K. W., & Baltes, P. B. (1975). On sequential strategies in developmental research: Description or explanation? *Human Development, 18,* 384–390.

Schaie, K. W., Baltes, P. B., & Strother, C. R. (1964). A study of auditory sensitivity in advanced age. *Journal of Gerontology, 19,* 453–457.

Schaie, K. W., Blazer, D., & House, J. (Eds.). (1992). *Aging, health behavior and health outcomes.* Hillsdale, NJ: Erlbaum.

Schaie, K. W., & Caskie, G. I. L. (2005). Methodological issues in aging research. In D. M. Teti (Ed.), *Handbook of research methods in developmental psychology.* Cambridge, UK: Blackwell.

Schaie, K. W., Caskie, G. I. L., Revell, A. J., Willis, S. L., Kaszniak, A. W., & Teri, L. (2004). Extending neuropsychological assessments into the Primary Mental Ability space. *Aging, Neuropsychology, and Cognition, 11.*

Schaie, K. W., Chatham, L. R., & Weiss, J. M. A. (1961). The multi-professional intake assessment of older psychiatric patients. *Journal of Psychiatric Research, 1,* 92–100.

Schaie, K. W., Dutta, R., & Willis, S. L. (1991). The relationship between rigidity–flexibility and cognitive abilities in adulthood. *Psychology and Aging, 6,* 371–383.

Schaie, K. W., & Goulet, L. R. (1977). Trait theory and verbal learning processes. In R. B. Cattell & R. M. Dreger (Eds.), *Handbook of modern personality theory* (pp. 567–584). New York: Hemisphere/Halsted Press.

Schaie, K. W., & Gribbin, K. (1975). Einflüsse der aktuellen Umwelt auf die Persönlichkeitsentwicklung im Erwachsenenalter [Environmental influences on personality in adulthood]. *Zeitschrift für Entwicklungspsychologie und Pädagogische Psychologie, 7,* 233–246.

Schaie, K. W., & Heiss, R. (1964). *Color and personality.* Bern, Switzerland: Huber.

Schaie, K. W., & Hendricks, J. (Eds.). (2000). *Evolution of the aging self: Societal impacts.* New York: Springer.

Schaie, K. W., & Hertzog, C. (1982). Longitudinal methods. In B. B. Wolman (Ed.), *Handbook of developmental psychology* (pp. 91–115). Englewood Cliffs, NJ: Prentice-Hall.

Schaie, K. W., & Hertzog, C. (1983). Fourteen-year cohort-sequential studies of adult intelligence. *Developmental Psychology, 19,* 531–543.

Schaie, K. W., & Hertzog, C. (1985). Measurement in the psychology of adulthood and aging. In J. E. Birren & K. W. Schaie (Eds.), *Handbook of the psychology of aging* (2nd ed., pp. 61–92). New York: Van Nostrand Reinhold.

Schaie, K. W., & Hertzog, C. (1986). Toward a comprehensive model of adult intellectual development: Contributions of the Seattle Longitudinal Study. In R. J. Sternberg (Ed.), *Advances in human intelligence* (Vol. 3, pp. 79–118). Hillsdale, NJ: Erlbaum.

Schaie, K. W., & Hofer, S. M. (2001). Longitudinal studies in research on aging. In J. E. Birren & K. W. Schaie (Eds.), *Handbook of the psychology of aging* (5th ed., pp. 55–77). San Diego, CA: Academic Press.

Schaie, K. W., Labouvie, G. V., & Barrett, T. J. (1973). Selective attrition effects in a fourteen-year study of adult intelligence. *Journal of Gerontology, 28,* 328–334.

Schaie, K. W., Labouvie, G. V., & Buech, B. U. (1973). Generational and cohort-specific differences in adult cognitive functioning: A fourteen-year study of independent samples. *Developmental Psychology, 9,* 151–156.

Schaie, K. W., & Labouvie-Vief, G. (1974). Generational versus ontogenetic components of change in adult cognitive behavior: A fourteen-year cross-sequential study. *Developmental Psychology, 10,* 305–320.

Schaie, K. W., Leventhal, H., & Willis, S. L. (2002). *Effective health behaviors in older adults.* New York: Springer.

Schaie, K. W., Maitland, S. B., & Willis, S. L. (2000, April). *Longitudinal studies of cognitive dedifferentiation.* Paper presented at the Cognitive Aging Conference, Atlanta, GA.

Schaie, K. W., Maitland, S. B., Willis, S. L., & Intrieri, R. L. (1998). Longitudinal invariance of adult psychometric ability factor structures across seven years. *Psychology and Aging, 13,* 8–20.

Schaie, K. W., Nguyen, H. T., Willis, S. L., Dutta, R., & Yue, G. A. (2001). Environmental factors as a conceptual framework for examining cognitive performance in Chinese adults. *International Journal of Behavioral Development, 25,* 193–202.

Schaie, K. W., & O'Hanlon, A. M. (1990). The influence of social-environmental factors in the maintenance of adult intelligence. In R. Schmitz-Schertzer, A. Kruse, & E. Olbrich (Eds.), *Altern—Ein lebenslanger Prozess der sozialen Interaktion* [Aging—A lifelong process of social interaction] (pp. 55–66). Darmstadt, Germany: Steinkopf.

Schaie, K. W., & Parham, I. A. (1974). Social responsibility in adulthood: Ontogenetic and socio-cultural change. *Journal of Personality and Social Psychology, 30,* 483–492.

Schaie, K. W., & Parham, I. A. (1975). *Manual for the Test of Behavioral Rigidity.* Palo Alto, CA: Consulting Psychologists Press.

Schaie, K. W., & Parham, I. A. (1976). Stability of adult personality traits: Fact or fable? *Journal of Personality and Social Psychology, 34,* 146–158.

Schaie, K. W., & Parham, I. A. (1977). Cohort-sequential analyses of adult intellectual development. *Developmental Psychology, 12,* 649–653.

Schaie, K. W., & Pietrucha, M. (2000). *Mobility and aging.* New York: Springer.

Schaie, K. W., Plomin, R., Willis, S. L., Gruber-Baldini, A., & Dutta, R. (1992). Natural cohorts: Family similarity in adult cognition. In T. Sonderegger (Ed.), *Psychology and aging: Nebraska Symposium on Motivation, 1991* (Vol. 38, pp. 205–243). Lincoln: University of Nebraska Press.

Schaie, K. W., Plomin, R., Willis, S. L., Gruber-Baldini, A. L., Dutta, R., & Bayen, U. (1993). Family similarity in adult intellectual development. In J. J. F. Schroots (Ed.), *Aging, health and competence: The next generation of longitudinal research* (pp. 183–198). Amsterdam, Netherlands: Elsevier.

Schaie, K. W., Rommel, L. A., & Weiss, J. M. A. (1959). Judging the relative severity of psychiatric outpatient complaints. *Journal of Clinical Psychology, 15,* 380–388.

Schaie, K. W., Rosenthal, F., & Perlman, R. M. (1953). Differential deterioration of factorially "pure" mental abilities. *Journal of Gerontology, 8,* 191–196.

Schaie, K. W., & Schooler, C. E. (Eds.). (1989). *Social structure and aging: Psychological processes.* Hillsdale, NJ: Erlbaum.

Schaie, K. W., & Schooler, C. E. (Eds.). (1998). *Impact of the work place on older persons.* New York: Springer.

Schaie, K. W., & Strother, C. R. (1968a). Cognitive and personality variables in college graduates of advanced age. In G. A. Talland (Ed.), *Human behavior and aging: Recent advances in research and theory* (pp. 281–308). New York: Academic Press.

Schaie, K. W., & Strother, C. R. (1968b). The cross-sequential study of age changes in cognitive behavior. *Psychological Bulletin, 70,* 671–680.

Schaie, K. W., & Strother, C. R. (1968c). The effects of time and cohort differences on the interpretation of age changes in cognitive behavior. *Multivariate Behavioral Research, 3,* 259–294.

Schaie, K. W., & Strother, C. R. (1968d). Limits of optimal functioning in superior old adults. In S. M. Chown & K. F. Riegel (Eds.), *Interdisciplinary topics in gerontology* (pp. 132–150). Basel, Switzerland: Karger.

Schaie, K. W., & Willis, S. L. (1986a). *Adult development and aging* (2nd ed.). Boston: Little, Brown.

Schaie, K. W., & Willis, S. L. (1986b). Can intellectual decline in the elderly be reversed? *Developmental Psychology, 22,* 223–232.

Schaie, K. W., & Willis, S. L. (1991). Adult personality and psychomotor performance: Cross-sectional and longitudinal analyses. *Journals of Gerontology: Psychological Sciences, 46,* P275–P284.

Schaie, K. W., & Willis, S. L. (1993). Age difference patterns of psychometric intelligence in adulthood: Generalizability within and across ability domains. *Psychology and Aging, 8,* 44–55.

Schaie, K. W., & Willis, S. L. (1995). Perceived family environments across generations. In V. L. Bengtson, K. W. Schaie, & L. Burton (Eds.), *Societal impact on aging: Intergenerational perspectives* (pp. 174–209). New York: Springer.

Schaie, K. W., & Willis, S. L. (1999). Theories of everyday competence and aging. In V. L. Bengtson & K. W. Schaie (Eds.), *Handbook of theories of aging* (pp. 174–195). New York: Springer.

Schaie, K. W., & Willis, S. L. (2000a, August). *Cognitive abilities in new generations of elderly people.* Paper presented at the International Congress of Psychology, Stockholm, Sweden.

Schaie, K. W., & Willis, S. L. (2000b). A stage theory model of adult cognitive development revisited. In R. Rubinstein, M. Moss, & M. Kleban (Eds.), *The many dimensions of aging: Essays in honor of M. Powell Lawton* (pp. 175–193). New York: Springer.

Schaie, K. W., & Willis, S. L. (2002). *Adult development and aging* (5th ed.). Upper Saddle River, NJ: Prentice-Hall.

Schaie, K. W., Willis, S. L., & Caskie, G. I. L. (2004). The Seattle Longitudinal Study: Relation between personality and cognition. *Aging, Neuropsychology and Cognition, 11.*

Schaie, K. W., Willis, S. L., Hertzog, C., & Schulenberg, J. E. (1987). Effects of cognitive training upon primary mental ability structure. *Psychology and Aging, 2,* 233–242.

Schaie, K. W., Willis, S. L., Jay, G., & Chipuer, H. (1989). Structural invariance of cognitive abilities across the adult life span: A cross-sectional study. *Developmental Psychology, 25,* 652–662.

Schaie, K. W., Willis, S. L., & O'Hanlon, A. M. (1994). Perceived intellectual performance change over seven years. *Journals of Gerontology: Psychological Sciences, 49,* P108–P118.

Schaie, K. W., & Zuo, Y. L. (2001). Family environments and adult cognitive functioning. In R. L. Sternberg & E. Grigorenko (Eds.), *Context of intellectual development* (pp. 337–361). Hillsdale, NJ: Erlbaum.

Scheidt, R. J., & Schaie, K. W. (1978). A situational taxonomy for the elderly: Generating situational criteria. *Journal of Gerontology, 33,* 348–357.

Scheier, I., & Ferguson, G. A. (1952). Further factorial studies of tests of rigidity. *Canadian Journal of Psychology, 6,* 19–30.

Schmitz-Scherzer, R., & Thomae, H. (1983). Constancy and change of behavior in old age: Findings from the Bonn Longitudinal Study of Aging. In K. W. Schaie (Ed.), *Longitudinal studies of adult psychological development* (pp. 191–221). New York: Guilford.

Schooler, C. (1972). Social antecedents of adult psychological functioning. *American Review of Sociology, 78,* 299–322.

Schooler, C. (1987). Psychological effects of complex environments during the life span: A review and theory. In C. Schooler & K. W. Schaie (Eds.), *Cognitive functioning and social structure over the life course* (pp. 24–49). Norwood, NJ: Ablex.

Schooler, C. (1990). Psychosocial factors and effective cognitive functioning in adulthood. In J. E. Birren & K. W. Schaie (Eds.), *Handbook of the psychology of aging* (3rd ed., pp. 347–358). San Diego, CA: Academic Press.

Schooler, C., Mulatu, M. S., & Oates, G. (1999). The continuing effects of substantively complex work on the intellectual functioning of older workers. *Psychology and Aging, 14,* 483–506.

Semla, T. P., Lemke, J. H., Helling, D. K., Wallace, R. B., & Chrischilles, E. A. (1991). Perceived purpose of prescription drugs: The Iowa 65+ Rural Health Study. *DICP, the Annals of Pharmacotherapy, 25,* 410–413.

Shock, N. W., Greulick, R. C., Andres, R., Arenberg, D., Costa, P. T., Lakatta, E. G., & Tobin, J. D. (1984). *Normal human aging: The Baltimore Longitudinal Study of Aging.* Washington, DC: U.S. Government Printing Office.

Siegler, I. E. (1983). Psychological aspects of the Duke longitudinal studies. In K. W. Schaie (Ed.), *Longitudinal studies of adult psychological development* (pp. 136–190). New York: Guilford.

Siegler, I. E. (1988, August). *Developmental health psychology.* Master lecture presented as part of a series, "The Adult Years: Continuity and Change," at the annual meeting of the American Psychological Association, Washington, DC.

Simon, H., & Kotovsky, K. (1963). Human acquisition of concepts for sequential patterns. *Psychological Review, 70,* 534–546.

Sinnott, J. D. (1989). *Everyday problem solving: Theory and applications.* New York: Praeger.

Small, B. J., & Bäckman, L. (1997). Cognitive correlates of mortality: Evidence from a population sample of very old adults. *Psychology and Aging, 12,* 309–313.

Smedby, B., Lundberg, I., & Sørensen, T. I. A. (Eds.). (2000). *Scientific evaluation of the Swedish Twin Registry.* Stockholm: Swedish Council for Planning and Coordination of Research.

Smyer, M., Schaie, K. W., & Kapp, M. B. (Eds.). (1996). *Older adults' decision-making and the law.* New York: Springer.

Solon, J. A., Feeney, J. J., Jones, S. H., Rigg, R. D., & Sheps, C. G. (1967). Delineating episodes of medical care. *American Journal of Public Health, 57,* 401–408.

Solon, J. A., Rigg, R. D., Jones, S. H., Feeney, J. J., Lingner, J. W., & Sheps, C. G. (1969). Episodes of medical care: Nursing students' use of medical services. *American Journal of Public Health, 59,* 936–946.

Sörbom, D. (1975). Detection of correlated errors in longitudinal data. *British Journal of Mathematical and Statistical Psychology, 28,* 138–151.

Spreen, O., & Strauss, E. (1991). *A compendium of neuropsychological tests: Administration, norms, and commentary.* New York: Oxford University Press.

Steiger, J. H. (1990). Structural model evaluation and modification: An interval estimation approach. *Multivariate Behavioral Research, 24,* 173–180.

Sternberg, R. J. (1977). *Intelligence, information processing, and analogical reasoning: The componential analysis of human abilities.* Hillsdale, NJ: Erlbaum.

Sterns, H. L., & Sanders, R. E. (1980). Training and education in the elderly. In R. E. Turner & H. W. Reese (Eds.), *Life-span developmental psychology: Intervention* (pp. 307–330). New York: Academic Press.

Stone, V. (1980). *Structural modeling of the relations among environmental variables, health status and intelligence in adulthood.* Unpublished doctoral dissertation, University of Southern California, Los Angeles.

Strother, C. R., Schaie, K. W., & Horst, P. (1957). The relationship between advanced age and mental abilities. *Journal of Abnormal and Social Psychology, 55,* 166–170.

Sundet, J. M., Tambs, K., Magnus, P., & Berg, K. (1988). On the question of secular trends in the heritability of intelligence test scores: A study of Norwegian twins. *Intelligence, 12,* 47–59.

Swan, G. E., Carmelli, D., & LaRue, A. (1995). Performance on the digit–symbol substitution test and 5-year mortality on the Western Collaborative Group Study. *American Journal of Epidemiology, 141,* 32–40.

Terman, L. M. (1916). *The measurement of intelligence.* Boston: Houghton.

Thorndike, E. L., & Woodworth, R. S. (1901). Influence of improvement in one mental function upon the efficiency of other mental functions. *Psychological Review, 8,* 247–261, 384–395, 553–564.

Thurstone, L. L. (1938). *The primary mental abilities.* Chicago: University of Chicago Press.

Thurstone, L. L. (1947). *Multiple factor analysis.* Chicago: University of Chicago Press.

Thurstone, L. L., & Thurstone, T. G. (1949). *Examiner manual for the SRA Primary Mental Abilities Test* (Form 10–14). Chicago: Science Research Associates.

Thurstone, T. G. (1958). *Manual for the SRA Primary Mental Abilities 11–17.* Chicago: Science Research Associates.

Thurstone, T. G. (1962). *Primary mental abilities for Grades 9–12.* Chicago: Science Research Associates.

Tombaugh, T. N., & McIntyre, N. J. (1992). The MMSE: A comprehensive review. *Journal of the American Geriatric Society, 40,* 922–935.

Tucker, L. R. (1971). Relations of factor score estimates to their use. *Psychometrika, 36,* 427–436.

U.S. Department of Health and Human Services. (1992). *National Medical Expenditure Survey: Annual expenses and sources of payment for health care services.* Washington, DC: U.S. Government Printing Office.

U.S. Public Health Service. (1968). *Eighth revision of the International Classification of Diseases, adapted for use in the United States* (Public Health Service Publication No. 1693). Washington, DC: Government Printing Office.

Van Gorp, W. G., Satz, P., Kiersch, M. E., & Henry, R. (1986). Normative data on the BNT for a group of normal older adults. *Journal of Clinical Experimental Neuropsychology, 8,* 702–705.

Verhaeghen, P., & Marcoen, A. (1996). On the mechanism of plasticity in young and older adults after instruction in the Method of Loci: Evidence or an amplified model. *Psychology and Aging, 11,* 164–178.

Vickers, R. R., Conway, T. I., & Hervig, L. K. (1990). Demonstration of replicable dimensions of health behaviors. *Preventive Medicine, 19,* 377–401.

Vitaliano, P. P., Russo, J., Breen, A. R., Vitiello, M. V., & Prinz, P. N. (1986). Functional decline in the early stages of Alzheimer's disease. *Psychology of Aging, 1,* 41–46.

Wechsler, D. (1939). *The measurement of adult intelligence.* Baltimore, MD: Williams and Wilkins.

Wechsler, D. (1981). *Wechsler Adult Intelligence Scale–revised.* Cleveland, OH: Psychological Corporation.

Welsh, K. A., Butters, N., Mohs, R. C., Beekly, D., Edland, S., Fillenbaum, G., & Heyman, A. (1994). The Consortium to Establish a Registry for Alzheimer's Disease (CERAD). Part V. A normative study of the neuropsychological battery. *Neurology, 44,* 609–614.

Werner, H. (1948). *Comparative psychology of mental development.* New York: International Universities Press.

Wilkie, F., & Eisdorfer, C. (1973). Systemic disease and behavioral correlates. In L. Jarvik,

C. Eisdorfer, & J. E. Blum (Eds.), *Intellectual functioning in adults* (pp. 83–94). New York: Springer.

Willis, S. L. (1985). Towards an educational psychology of the adult learner: Cognitive and intellectual bases. In J. E. Birren & K. W. Schaie (Eds.), *Handbook of the psychology of aging* (2nd ed., pp. 818–847). New York: Van Nostrand Reinhold.

Willis, S. L. (1987). Cognitive training and everyday competence. In K. W. Schaie (Ed.), *Annual review of gerontology and geriatrics* (Vol. 7, pp. 159–188). New York: Springer.

Willis, S. L. (1989a). Cohort differences in cognitive aging: A sample case. In K. W. Schaie & C. Schooler (Eds.), *Social structure and aging: Psychological processes* (pp. 94–112). Hillsdale, NJ: Erlbaum.

Willis, S. L. (1989b). Improvement with cognitive training: Which dogs learn what tricks? In L. W. Poon, D. C. Rubin, & B. A. Wilson (Eds.), *Everyday cognition in adulthood and late life* (pp. 545–569). Cambridge: Cambridge University Press.

Willis, S. L. (1990a). Contributions of cognitive training research to understanding late life potential. In M. Perlmutter (Ed.), *Late life potential* (pp. 25–42). Washington, DC: Gerontological Society of America.

Willis, S. L. (1990b). Current issues in cognitive training research. In E. A. Lovelace (Ed.), *Aging and cognition: Mental processes, self-awareness, and interventions* (pp. 263–280). Amsterdam: Elsevier.

Willis, S. L. (1992a). Cognition and everyday competence. In K. W. Schaie (Ed.), *Annual review of gerontology and geriatrics* (Vol. 11, pp. 80–109). New York: Springer.

Willis, S. L. (1992b). *Examiner manual for the Everyday Problems Test (EPT).* Unpublished manuscript. Pennsylvania State University, University Park.

Willis, S. L. (1995). Competency and everyday problem solving in old age. In M. A. Smyer, M. Capp, & K. W. Schaie (Eds.), *Impact of the law on decision making in the elderly* (pp. 87–127). New York: Springer.

Willis, S. L. (2001). Methodological issues in behavioral intervention research with the elderly. In J. E. Birren & K. W. Schaie (Eds.), *Handbook of the psychology of aging* (5th ed., pp. 78–108). San Diego, CA: Academic Press.

Willis, S. L., & Baltes, P. B. (1981). Letter to the editor. *Journal of Gerontology, 36,* 636–638.

Willis, S. L., & Nesselroade, C. S. (1990). Long-term effects of fluid ability training in old age. *Developmental Psychology, 26,* 905–910.

Willis, S. L., & Schaie, K. W. (1983). *The Alphanumeric Rotation Test.* Unpublished manuscript, Pennsylvania State University, University Park.

Willis, S. L., & Schaie, K. W. (1986a). Practical intelligence in later adulthood. In R. J. Sternberg & R. K. Wagner (Eds.), *Practical intelligence: Origins of competence in the everyday world* (pp. 236–268). New York: Cambridge University Press.

Willis, S. L., & Schaie, K. W. (1986b). Training the elderly on the ability factors of spatial orientation and inductive reasoning. *Psychology and Aging, 1,* 239–247.

Willis, S. L., & Schaie, K. W. (1986c, August). *Training on inductive reasoning with a longitudinal sample.* Paper presented at the annual meeting of the American Psychological Association, Washington, DC.

Willis, S. L., & Schaie, K. W. (1988). Gender differences in spatial ability in old age: Longitudinal and intervention findings. *Sex Roles, 18,* 189–203.

Willis, S. L., & Schaie, K. W. (1992, November). *Maintaining and sustaining cognitive training effects in old age.* Paper presented at the annual meeting of the Gerontological Society of America, Washington, DC.

Willis, S. L., & Schaie, K. W. (1993). Everyday cognition: Taxonomic and methodological considerations. In J. M. Puckett & H. W. Reese (Eds.), *Mechanisms of everyday cognition* (pp. 33–54). Hillsdale, NJ: Erlbaum.

Willis, S. L., & Schaie, K. W. (1994a). Assessing competence in the elderly. In C. E. Fisher & R. M. Lerner (Eds.), *Applied developmental psychology* (pp. 339–372). New York: Macmillan.

Willis, S. L., & Schaie, K. W. (1994b). Cognitive training in the normal elderly. In F. Forette, Y. Christen, & F. Boller (Eds.), *Plasticité cérébrale et stimulation cognitive* [Cerebral plasticity and cognitive stimulation] (pp. 91–113). Paris: Fondation Nationale de Gérontologie.

Willis, S. L., Schaie, K. W., & Hayward, M. (1997). *Impact of social structures on decision making in the elderly.* New York: Springer.

Willis, S. L., Schaie, K. W., & Maitland, S. B. (1992, August). *Personality factors and cardiovascular disease.* Paper presented at the annual meeting of the American Psychological Association, Washington, DC.

Yerkes, R. M. (1921). Psychological examining in the United States Army. *Memoirs of the National Academy of Sciences, 15,* 1–890.

Zanjani, F. A. K. (2002). *Predicting health behavior domains using social, environmental, ability and personality determinants across young and old adults: Seattle Longitudinal Study.* Unpublished master's thesis, Pennsylvania State University, University Park.

Zarit, S. H., Pearlin, L. I., & Schaie, K. W. (Eds.). (1993). *Caregiving systems: Informal and formal helpers.* Hillsdale, NJ: Erlbaum.

Zarit, S. H., Pearlin, L. I., & Schaie, K. W. (Eds.). (2002). *Personal control in social and life course contexts.* New York: Springer.

Zelinski, E. M., Gilewski, M. J., & Schaie, K. W. (1993). Three-year longitudinal memory assessment in older adults: Little change in performance. *Psychology and Aging, 8,* 176–186.

Zieleniewski, A. M., Fulker, D. W., DeFries, J. C., & LaBuda, M. C. (1987). Multiple regression analysis of twin and sibling data. *Personality and Individual Differences, 8,* 787–791.

Zonderman, A. B, Vandenberg, S. G., Spuhler, K. P., & Fain, P. R. (1977). Assortative marriage for cognitive abilities. *Behavior Genetics, 7,* 261–271.

Author Index

Subject Index